Other Books and Series

Compilation of History of the Cherokee Indians by Emmet Starr with Combined Full Name Inde

1901-1907 Native American Census Seneca, Ea..... Ottawa, Peoria, Quapaw, and Wyandotte Indians (Under Seneca School, Indian Territory)

1932 Census of The Standing Rock Sioux Reservation with Births and Deaths 1924-1932

Kiowa, Comanche, Apache, Fort Sill Apache, Wichita, Caddo and Delaware Indians Birth and Death Rolls 1924-1932

Census of The Blackfeet, Montana, 1897- 1901 Expanded Edition

Eastern Cherokee by Blood, 1906-1910, Volumes I thru XIII

Choctaw of Mississippi Indian Census 1929-1932 with Births and Deaths 1924-1931   Volume I
Choctaw of Mississippi Indian Census 1933, 1934 & 1937, Supplemental Rolls to 1934 & 1935 with Births and Deaths 1932-1938, and Marriages 1936-1938 Volume II

Eastern Cherokee Census Cherokee, North Carolina 1930-1939 Census 1930-1931 with Births And Deaths 1924-1931 Taken By Agent L. W. Page   Volume I
Eastern Cherokee Census Cherokee, North Carolina 1930-1939 Census 1932-1933 with Births And Deaths 1930-1932 Taken By Agent R. L. Spalsbury   Volume II
Eastern Cherokee Census Cherokee, North Carolina 1930-1939 Census 1934-1937 with Births and Deaths 1925-1938 and Marriages 1936 & 1938 Taken by Agents R. L. Spalsbury And Harold W. Foght Volume III

Seminole of Florida Indian Census, 1930-1940 with Birth and Death Records, 1930-1938

Texas Cherokees 1820-1839 A Document For Litigation 1921

Starr Roll 1894 (Cherokee Payment Rolls) Districts: Canadian, Cooweescoowee, and Delaware Volume One
Starr Roll 1894 (Cherokee Payment Rolls) Districts: Flint, Going Snake, and Illinois   Volume Two
Starr Roll 1894 (Cherokee Payment Rolls) Districts: Saline, Sequoyah, and Tahlequah; Including Orphan Roll   Volume Three

Cherokee Intruder Cases Dockets of Hearings 1901-1909 Volumes I & II

Indian Wills, 1911-1921 Records of the Bureau of Indian Affairs
Books One thru Seven
Native American Wills & Probate Records 1911-1921

Other Books and Series by Jeff Bowen

Turtle Mountain Reservation Chippewa Indians 1932 Census with Births & Deaths, 1924-1932

Chickasaw By Blood Enrollment Cards 1898-1914 Volume I thru V

Cherokee Descendants East An Index to the Guion Miller Applications Volume I
Cherokee Descendants West An Index to the Guion Miller Applications Volume II (A-M)
Cherokee Descendants West An Index to the Guion Miller Applications Volume III (N-Z)

Applications for Enrollment of Seminole Newborn Freedmen, Act of 1905

Eastern Cherokee Census, Cherokee, North Carolina, 1915-1922, Taken by Agent James E. Henderson Volume I (1915-1916)
  Volume II (1917-1918)
  Volume III (1919-1920)
  Volume IV (1921-1922)

Eastern Cherokee Census, Cherokee, North Carolina, 1923-1929, Taken by Agent James E. Henderson Volume I (1923-1924)
  Volume II (1925-1926)
  Volume III (1927-1929)

Complete Delaware Roll of 1898

Applications for Enrollment of Seminole Newborn Act of 1905 Volumes I & II

North Carolina Eastern Cherokee Indian Census 1898-1899, 1904, 1906, 1909-1912, 1914   Revised and Expanded Edition

1932 Hopi and Navajo Native American Census with Birth & Death Rolls (1925-1931) Volume 1 - Hopi
1932 Hopi and Navajo Native American Census with Birth & Death Rolls (1930-1932) Volume 2 - Navajo

Western Navajo Reservation Navajo, Hopi and Paiute 1933 Census with Birth & Death Rolls 1925-1933

Cherokee Citizenship Commission Dockets 1880-1884 and 1887-1889
Volumes I thru V

Applications for Enrollment of Chickasaw Newborn Act of 1905
Volumes I thru VII
Cherokee Intermarried White 1906 Volume I thru X

Applications for Enrollment of Creek Newborn Act of 1905
Volumes I thru XIV

Other Books and Series by Jeff Bowen

Applications for Enrollment of Choctaw Newborn Act of 1905 Volumes I thru XX

Choctaw By Blood Enrollment Cards 1898-1914 Volumes I thru XX

Oglala Sioux Indians Pine Ridge Reservation 1932 Census Book I
Oglala Sioux Indians Pine Ridge Reservation Birth and Death Rolls 1924-1932 Book II

Census of the Sioux and Cheyenne Indians of Pine Ridge Agency 1896 - 1897 Book I
Census of the Sioux and Cheyenne Indians of Pine Ridge Agency 1898 - 1899 Book II

Northern Cheyenne Tongue River, Montana 1904 - 1932 Census 1904-1916 Volume I
Northern Cheyenne Tongue River, Montana 1904 - 1932 Census 1917-1926 Volume II
Northern Cheyenne Tongue River, Montana 1904 - 1932 Census 1927-1932 Volume III

Sac & Fox - Shawnee Estates 1885-1910 (Under Sac & Fox Agency) Volumes I-VIII
Sac & Fox - Shawnee Estates 1920-1924 (Under The Sac & Fox Agency, Oklahoma) & Wills 1889-1924 Volume IX
Sac & Fox - Shawnee Deaths, Cemetery, Births, & Marriage Cards (Under The Sac & Fox Agency, Oklahoma) 1853-1933 Volume X
Sac & Fox - Shawnee Marriages, Divorces, Estates Log Books Volumes 1 & 2, Log Book Births & Deaths (Under Sac & Fox Agency, Oklahoma)1846-1924 Volume XI
Sac & Fox - Shawnee Guardianships Part 1 (Under Sac & Fox Agency, Oklahoma) 1892-1909 Volume XII
Sac & Fox - Shawnee Guardianships, Part 2 (Under The Sac & Fox Agency, Oklahoma) 1902-1910 Volume XIII
Sac & Fox - Shawnee Guardianships, Part 3 (Under The Sac & Fox Agency, Oklahoma) 1906-1914 Volume XIV

Census of the Pima, Tohono O'odham (Papago), and Maricopa Indians of the Gila River, Ak Chin & Gila Bend Reservations 1932 with Birth and Death Rolls 1924-1932

Identified Mississippi Choctaw Enrollment Cards 1902-1909 Volumes I, II, III
Identified Mississippi Choctaw Enrollment Cards' Dawes Packets 1902-1909 Volumes IV, V & VI

Census of the Northern Navajo, Navajo Reservation, New Mexico, 1930 Volume I
Census of the Northern Navajo, Navajo Reservation, New Mexico, 1931 Volume II

Visit our website at **www.nativestudy.com** to learn more about these other books and series by Jeff Bowen

'Curley' Only survivor of the Custer Massacre

[Curley, the rest of his life always stated, "I did nothing special, I wasn't in the fight."]

McCracken Research Library,
Buffalo Bill Center of the West
Identifier: P.32.28

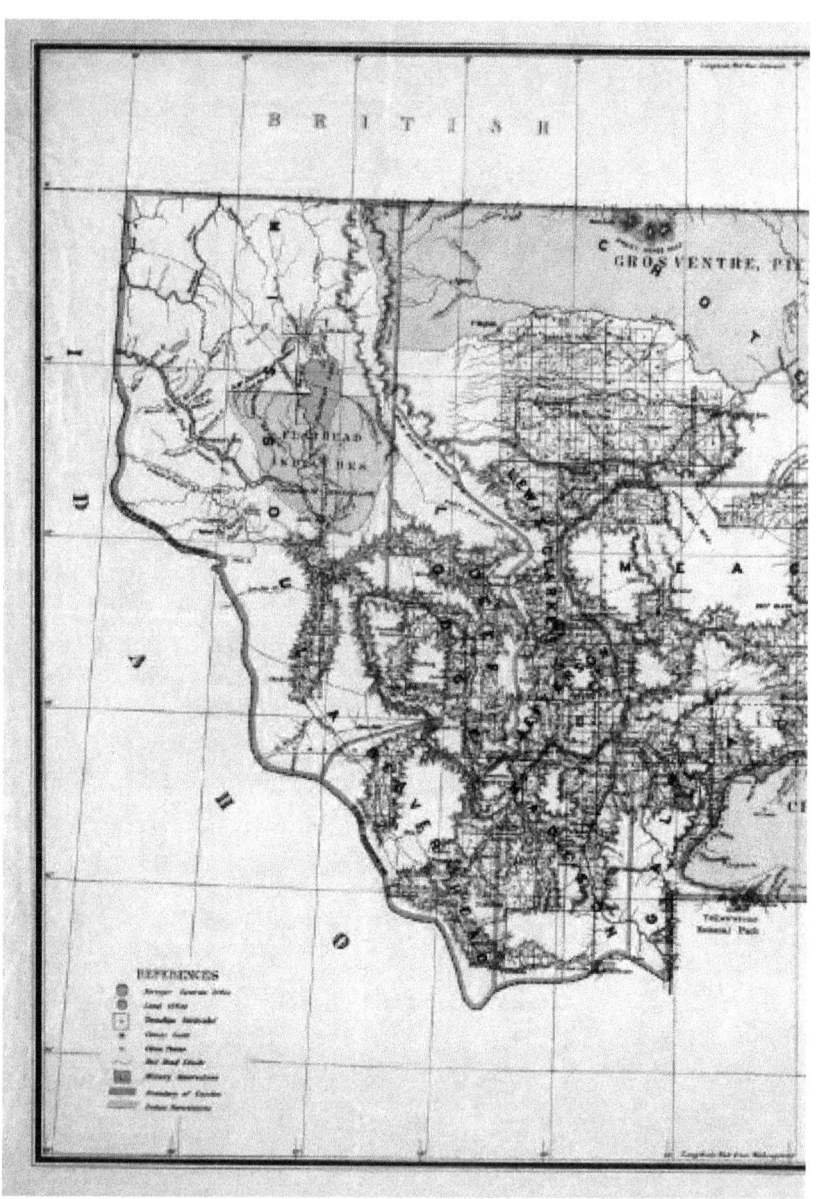

Map of
Showing Crow
C. (Charles)
Compliments of the

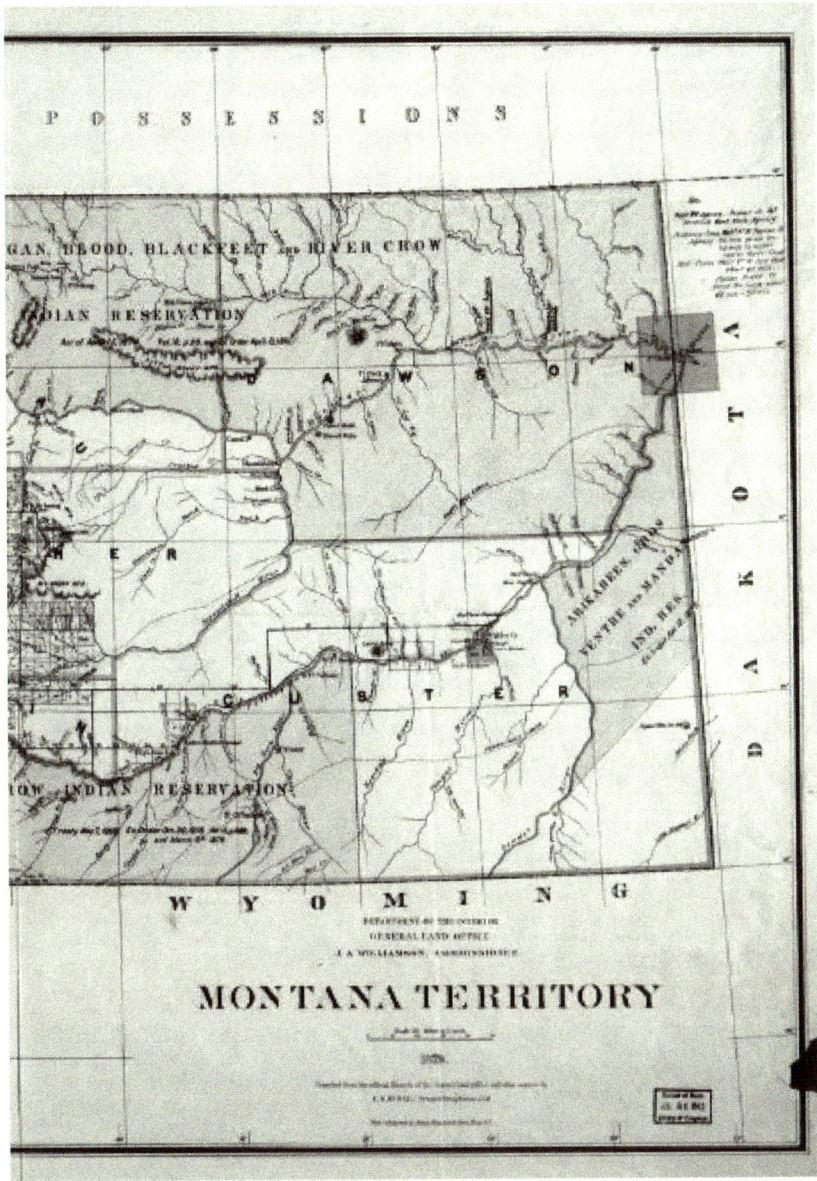

Montana Territory, 1879
Indian Reservation
Roeser
Library of Congress (G4250 1879 .R6)

CROW AGENCY MONTANA 1898 - 1905 CENSUS VOLUME I 1898 - 1901

WITH ILLUSTRATIONS

TRANSCRIBED BY
JEFF BOWEN

NATIVE STUDY
Gallipolis, Ohio
USA

Copyright © 2024
by Jeff Bowen

ALL RIGHTS RESERVED
No part of this publication may be reproduced, distributed, or transmitted in any form or by any means, without the prior written permission of the publisher.

Native Study LLC
Gallipolis, OH
www.nativestudy.com

Library of Congress Control Number: 2024914241

ISBN: 978-1-64968-170-6

Bookcover: Pencil sketch by Karl Bodmer, Newberry Library.
Quote from an *An Indian Winter* by Russell Freedman, page 17
"It was striking that all whom we had sketched had neither been wounded or killed, Maximilian noted. After that, Bodmer's portraits were pronounced "good medicine." Warriors who earlier had been reluctant to pose now insisted that the artist paint their picture."

Title Page: Holds The Enemy, Library of Congress.

All other images compliments of McCracken Research Library at the Buffalo Bill Center of the West and Library of Congress.

Made in the United States of America.

These Crow Indian Census of Montana books
are dedicated to Lord Casto (Brad).
A True Friend that never forgets you and
will never be forgotten.

Table of Contents

List of Illustrations	vi
Ratified Indian Treaty 370: Crow - Copy of Original	vii
Transcribed Miscellaneous Letters with Treaty	xxxiii
Ratified Indian Treaty 370: Crow - Transcription	xxxix
Introduction	lxv
Crow Agency Montana, 1898 Census	1
Crow Agency Montana, 1899 Census	65
Crow Agency Montana, 1900 Census	129
Crow Agency Montana, 1901 Census	193
Reference Books	255
Index	257

List of Illustrations

1.	A camp on the Little Horn River	li
2.	A 'warm' Little Crow	lii
3.	Cold day Dance Costumes	liii
4.	Elk teeth dresses	liv
5.	Little Wolf	lv
6.	'No Milk' and 'Shorty'	lvi
7.	Old time method of carrying papooses	lvii
8.	Shell on the neck	lviii
9.	Scout That Returns	lix
10.	Mother and child—Apsaroke	lx
11.	Apsaroke mother, Her Horse Kills, and child	lxi
12.	Little Iron Horse	lxii
13.	Burial of an Unknown Soldier	lxiii

[Copy of the Original Treaty]

Ratified Indian Treaty 370: Crow
Fort Laramie, Dakota Territory, May 7, 1868

Andrew Johnson,

President of the United States of America,

To all and singular to whom these presents shall come, greeting:

Whereas a Treaty was made and concluded at Fort Laramie, in the Territory of Dakota, on the seventh day of May, in the year of our Lord one thousand eight hundred and sixty-eight, by and between Lieutenant General W. T. Sherman, Brevet Major General William S. Harney, Brevet Major General Alfred H. Terry, Brevet Major General C. C. Augur, John B. Sanborn, and S. F. Tappan, Commissioners, on the part of the United States, and Che-Ra-Pee-Ish-Ka-Te, Chat-Sta-He, and other Chiefs and Headmen of the Crow tribe of Indians, on the part of said Indians, and duly authorized thereto by them, which Treaty is in the words and figures following, to wit:

Draft of a Treaty with the "Crow Indians" of Montana.

made the Seventh day of May 1868. at Fort Laramie.

Articles of a treaty made and concluded at Fort Laramie, Dakota Territory, on the seventh day of May in the year of our Lord One thousand Eight hundred and sixty eight, by and between the undersigned Commissioners on the part of the United States, and the undersigned Chiefs and headmen of, and representing, the Crow Indians; they being duly authorized to act in the premises

Article 1. From this day forward peace between the parties to this treaty shall forever continue. The Government of the United States desires peace and its honor is hereby pledged to keep it. The Indians desire peace and they hereby pledge their honor to maintain it. If bad men among the whites or among other people subject to the authority of the United States shall commit any wrong upon the person or property of the Indians, the United States will, upon proof, made to the Agent and forwarded to the Commissioner of Indian Affairs at Washington City, proceed at once to cause the offender to be arrested and punished according to the laws of the United States and also reimburse the injured person for the loss sustained;

If bad men among the Indians shall commit a wrong or depredation upon the person or property of any one, white, black or Indian, subject to the authority of the United States and at peace therewith, the Indians herein named solemnly agree that they will on proof made to their Agent and notice by him, deliver up the wrong doer to the United States, to be tried and punished according to its laws, and in case they refuse wilfully so to do, the person injured shall be reimbursed for his loss from the annuities or other moneys due or to become due to them under this or other treaties made with the United States. And the President, on advising with the Commissioner of Indian Affairs, shall prescribe such rules and regulations for ascertaining damages under the provisions of this article, as in his judgment may be proper. But no such damages shall be adjusted and paid until thoroughly examined and passed upon by the Commissioner of Indian Affairs, and no one sustaining loss while violating, or because of his violating, the provisions of this treaty or the laws of the United States shall be reimbursed therefor.

Article II   The United States agrees that the following district of Country to wit: Commencing where the 107° degree of Longitude west of Greenwich crosses the South boundary of Montana Territory, thence North along said 107th Meridian to the mid Channel of the Yellow Stone River. Thence up said mid channel of the Yellow Stone to the point where it crosses the said Southern boundary of Montana being the 45° degree of North Latitude and thence East along said parallel of Latitude to the place of beginning, shall be and the same is set apart for the absolute and undisturbed use and occupation of the Indians herein named, and for such other friendly tribes or individual Indians, as from time to time they may be willing — with the consent of the United States — to admit amongst them, and the United States now solemnly agrees that no persons, except those herein designated and authorized so to do, and except such officers, agents and employés of the government as may be authorized to enter upon Indian reservations in discharge of duties enjoined by law shall ever be permitted to pass over, settle upon or reside in the territory decribed in this article for the use of said Indians, and henceforth, they will and do hereby relinquish all title, claims or rights in and to any portion of the territory of the United States, except such as is embraced within the limits aforesaid.

Article III. The United States agrees at its own proper expense to construct on the south side of the Yellow Stone near Otter Creek, a warehouse or store room for the use of the Agent in storing goods belonging to the Indians, to cost not exceeding twenty five hundred dollars; An Agency building for the residence of the Agent, to cost not exceeding three thousand dollars; a residence for the physician to cost not more than three thousand dollars; and five other buildings, for a Carpenter, Tanner, Blacksmith, Miller and Engineer, each to cost not exceeding two thousand dollars; Also a school house or Mission building, so soon as a sufficient number of children can be induced by the Agent to attend school, which shall not cost exceeding twenty five hundred dollars

The United States agrees further to cause to be erected on said reservation, near the other buildings herein authorized, a good Steam Circular Saw Mill, with a Grist Mill and Shingle Machine attached, the same to cost not exceeding Eight thousand dollars

Weaver
July 10

Article IV. The Indians herein named agree, when the Agency house and other buildings, shall be constructed on the reservation named, they will make said reservation their permanent home, and they will make no permanent settlement elsewhere, but they shall have the right to hunt on the unoccupied lands of the United States, so long as game may be found thereon and as long as peace subsists among the Whites and Indians on the borders of the hunting districts

Article V. The United States agrees that the Agent for said Indians, shall in the future, make his home at the Agency building; that he shall reside among them, and keep an office open at all times, for the purpose of prompt and diligent enquiry into such matters of complaint by and against the Indians, as may be presented for investigation, under the provisions of their treaty stipulations, as also for the faithful discharge of other duties enjoined on him by law. In all cases of depredation on person or property, he shall cause the evidence to be taken in writing and forwarded, together with his finding, to the Commissioner of Indian Affairs, whose decision shall be binding on the parties to this treaty.

Article VI   If any individual belonging to said tribes of Indians, or legally incorporated with them, being the head of a family, shall desire to Commence farming, he shall have the privilege to select, in the presence and with the assistance of the Agent then in charge, a tract of land within said reservation, not exceeding three hundred and twenty acres in extent, which tract, when so selected, certified and recorded in the "Land Book" as herein directed, shall cease to be held in common, but the same may be occupied and held in the exclusive possession of the person selecting it, and of his family, so long as he or they may continue to cultivate it.

Any person over eighteen years of age, not being the head of a family, may in like manner, select and cause to be certified to him or her, for purposes of cultivation, a quantity of land not exceeding eighty acres in extent, and thereupon, be entitled to the exclusive possession of the same as above directed.

For each tract of land so selected, a certificate, containing a description thereof and the name of the person selecting it, with a certificate endorsed thereon, that the same has been recorded shall be delivered to the party entitled to it by the Agent, after the same shall have been recorded by him, in a book to be kept in his office, subject to inspection, which said book shall be known as the "Crow Land Book."

  The President may, at any time, order a survey of the reservation, and, when so surveyed, Congress shall provide for protecting the rights of settlers in their improvements, and may fix the character of the title held by each. The United States may pass such laws on the subject of alienation and descent of property, as between Indians and on all subjects connected with the government of the Indians on said reservations, and the internal police thereof, as may be thought proper.

Article VII. In order to insure the civilization of the tribe entering into this treaty, the necessity of education is admitted, especially by such of them as are, or may be, settled on said agricultural reservation, and they, therefore, pledge themselves to compel their children, male and female, between the ages of six and sixteen years, to attend school; and it is hereby made the duty of the Agent for said Indians, to see that this stipulation is strictly complied with; and the United States agrees that for every thirty children, between said ages, who can be induced or compelled to attend school, a house shall be provided, and a teacher, competent to teach the elementary branches of an English education, shall be furnished, who will reside among said Indians, and faithfully discharge his or her duties as a teacher. The provisions of this article to continue for twenty years.

Article VIII. When the head of a family or lodge, shall have selected lands, and received his certificate as above directed, and the Agent shall be satisfied that he intends in good faith to commence cultivating the soil for a living, he shall be entitled to receive seeds and agricultural impliments, for the first year in value one hundred dollars, and for each succeeding year he shall continue to farm for a period of three years more, he shall be entitled to receive seeds and impliments as aforesaid in value, twenty five dollars per annum

And it is further stipulated, that such persons as commence farming, shall receive instructions from the farmer herein provided for, and whenever more than one hundred persons shall enter upon the cultivation of the soil, a second blacksmith shall be provided, with such iron, steel, and other material as may be required.

Article IX. In lieu of all sums of money or other annuities provided to be paid to the Indians herein named, under any and all treaties heretofore made with them, the United States agrees to deliver at the Agency House, on the reservation herein provided for, on the first day of September of each year for thirty years, the following articles, to wit:

For each male person, over fourteen years of age, a suit of good substantial woolen clothing, consisting of coat, hat, pantaloons, flannel shirt and a pair of woolen socks.

For each female, over twelve years of age, a flannel skirt, or the goods necessary to make it; a pair of woolen hose, twelve yards of calico and twelve yards of cotton domestics.

For the boys and girls under the ages named, such flannel and cotton goods as may be needed to make each, a suit as aforesaid, together with a pair of woolen hose for each.

And, in order that the Commissioner of Indian Affairs may be able to estimate properly for the articles herein named, it shall be the duty of the Agent, each year, to forward to him a full and exact census of the Indians, on which the estimate from year to year can be based.

And, in addition to the Clothing herein named, the sum of ten dollars shall be annually appropriated for each Indian roaming and twenty dollars for each Indian engaged in agriculture for a period of ten years to be used by the Secretary of the Interior, in the purchase of such articles as, from time to time, the condition and necessities of the Indians may indicate to be proper. And if, at any time, within the ten years, it shall appear that the amount of money needed for Clothing, under this article, can be appropriated to better uses for the tribe herein named, Congress may by law, change the appropriation to other purposes, but, in no event, shall the amount of this appropriation, be withdrawn or discontinued for the period named: and the President shall, annually, detail an officer of the Army to be present and attest the delivery of all the goods, herein named, to the Indians, and he shall inspect and report on the quantity and quality of the goods and the manner of their delivery, and it is expressly stipulated that each Indian over the age of four years, who shall have removed to and settled permanently upon said reservation and complied with the stipulations of this treaty shall be entitled to receive from the United

States for the period of four years after he shall have settled upon said reservation, one pound of meat and one pound of flour per day, provided the Indians cannot furnish their own subsistence at an earlier date. And it is further stipulated that the United States will furnish and deliver to each lodge of Indians or family of persons legally incorporated with them, who shall remove to the reservation herein described and commence farming one good American Cow and one good well broken pair of American Oxen within sixty days after such lodge or family shall have so settled upon said reservation.

Article X The United States hereby agrees to furnish annually to the Indians, the Physician, Teachers, Carpenter, Miller, Engineer, Farmer and Blacksmiths as herein contemplated, and that such appropriations shall be made from time to time, on the Estimates of the Secretary of the Interior, as will be sufficient to employ such persons.

Article XI. No treaty for the cession of any portion of the reservation herein described, which may be held in common, shall be of any force or validity as against the said Indians unless executed and signed by, at least, a majority of all the adult male Indians occupying or interested in the same, and no cession by the tribe shall be understood or construed in such manner as to deprive - without his consent - any individual member of the tribe of his right to any tract of land selected by him as provided in Article VI of this treaty

Article XII. It is agreed that the sum of Five hundred dollars annually, for three years from the date when they commence to cultivate a farm, shall be expended in presents to the ten persons of said tribe who, in the judgment of the Agent, may grow the most valuable crops for the respective year

(Over)

W. T. Sherman
        Lt Genl,
        Wm S Harney
        Bvt. Maj Genl & Peace Commissioner
            Alfred H. Terry
                Bvt. Mj. Genl.
        C. C. Augur.
                Bvt. Maj Genl.
        John B. Sanborn,
        S. F. Tappan

Ashton S. H. White
        Secretary

3-31

Crows

Che-Ka-Re-Ish-Ka-Je,	his + mark	Pretty Bull (Seal)
Chat-Sta-Hee,	his + mark	Wolf Bow (Seal)
Ah-Be-Che-Se,	his + mark	Mountain Tail (Seal)
Kam-Ne-Bat-Sa,	his + mark	Black Foot (Seal)
De-Sah-ze-Cho-Se,	his + mark	White Horse (Seal)
Chin-Ita-She-Arache,	his + mark	Poor Elk (Seal)
E-Sa-Woor,	his + mark	Shot in the Jaw (Seal)
E-Sha-Chose,	his + mark	White Forehead (Seal)
——— Roo-Ita,	his + mark	Pounded Meat (Seal)
De-Ka-Ke-Up-Se,	his + mark	Bird in the Neck (Seal)
Me-Na-Che,	his + mark	The Swan (Seal)

Attest:

George B. Willis, Phonographer
John D. Howland
Alex Gardner
David Knox
Chas Freeman
Jas. C. O'Connor

And whereas, the said Treaty having been submitted to the Senate of the United States for its Constitutional action thereon, the Senate did, on the twenty-fifth day of July, one thousand eight hundred and sixty-eight, advise and consent to the ratification of the same, by a resolution in the words and figures following, to wit:

Rec 29 July
Mr Jefferson

In Executive Session,
Senate of the United States,
July 25, 1868.

Resolved, (two thirds of the Senators present concurring,) That the Senate advise and consent to the ratification of the Treaty between the United States and the Crow Indians of Montana Territory, made the seventh day of May, 1868.

Attest.
Geo. C. Gorham
Secretary.
by W. J. McDonald
Chief Clerk

Now, therefore, be it known that I, Andrew Johnson, President of the United States of America, do, in pursuance of the advice and consent of the Senate, as expressed in its resolution of the twenty-fifth of July, one thousand eight hundred and sixty-eight, accept, ratify, and confirm the said Treaty.

In testimony whereof I have hereto signed my name, and caused the seal of the United States to be affixed.

Done at the City of Washington this twelfth day of August, in the year of our Lord one thousand eight hundred and sixty-eight, and of the Independence of the United States of America the ninety-third.

Andrew Johnson

By the President:
W. Hunter.
Acting Secretary of State.

[Transcribed Miscellaneous Letters with Treaty]

Ratified Indian Treaty 370: Crow Fort Laramie, Dakota Territory, May 7, 1868

Miscellaneous Letters - August, Part II, 1868.

Rec 18. Aug.

DEPARTMENT OF THE INTERIOR.
Office of
Indian Affairs.
Washington, D. C. Aug. 18$\underline{^{th}}$ 1868.

Sir

Will you please furnish for the use of this office, six copies of each of the following named treaties, ratified at the last session of the Senate, if the same have been printed.

Pottowatomie	Feb. 27" 1867	#362
Cheyenne & Arapahoe	Oct. 28" "	#366
Kiowa Comanche & Apache	" 21" "	#365
Kiowa & Comanche	" 24" "	#364
Crows	May 7" 1868	#370
Northern Cheyenne and Arapahoes	" 10" "	#371
Navajoes	June 20" "	#372

Very respectfully
Your Obd't. Serv't.
A. C. Taylor
Commissioner

Hon Wm Hunter
Asst. Sec'y. of State.

#370.

Domestic Letters - Volume 79, page 287.

                            Department of State,
                            Washington September 3. 1868.

Hon Orville H Browning
    Secretary of the Interior.

Sir:
        I have the honor to transmit, herewith, for the use of the Department of the Interior, 250 copies of each of the following named Treaties with Indians, to wit:
    Treaty with the Crows of May 7. 1868. #370
        "   "   " Navajos of June 1. 1868. #372
        "   "   " Cheyennes & Arapahoes of October 28.1867. #366

        Be pleased to acknowledge their receipt
                I am your obedient servant
                    William H Seward

#370

xxxvi

Miscellaneous Letters - September, Part I, 1868.

RECEIVED.
SEP
5
1868

DEPARTMENT OF THE INTERIOR.

Washington, D. C, Sept: 4th 1868.

Sir,

    I have the honor to acknowledge the receipt of your letter of this date with the Indian Treaties therewith transmitted, viz:

    Treaty with Crows, of May 7. 1868. #370
       "   " Navajoes of June 1, 1868. #372
       "   " Cheyennes & Arapahoes of October 28, 1867. #366

          Very respectfully,
          Your Obt: Servant,
          W. T. Otto
          Acting Secretary.

Hon: Wm. H. Seward,
   Secretary of State.

#370.

[Transcription of the Original Treaty]

Ratified Indian Treaty 370: Crow
Fort Laramie, Dakota Territory, May 7, 1868

TREATY

BETWEEN

THE UNITED STATES OF AMERICA

AND THE

CROW TRIBE OF INDIANS.

CONCLUDED MAY 7, 1868.
RATIFICATION ADVISED JULY 25, 1868.
PROCLAIMED AUGUST 12, 1868.

ANDREW JOHNSON,

PRESIDENT OF THE UNITED STATES OF AMERICA,

TO ALL AND SINGULAR TO WHOM THESE PRESENTS SHALL COME, GREETING:

Whereas a Treaty was made and concluded at Fort Laramie, in the Territory of Dakota, on the seventh day of May, in the year of our Lord one thousand eight hundred and sixty-eight, by and between Lieutenant General W. T. Sherman, Brevet Major General William S. Harney, Brevet Major General Alfred H. Terry, Brevet Major General C. C. Augur, John B. Sanborn, and S. F. Tappan, Commissioners, on the part of the United States, and Che-Ra-Pee-Ish-Ka-Te, Chat-Sta-He, and other Chiefs and Headmen of the Crow tribe of Indians, on the part of said Indians, and duly authorized thereto by them, which Treaty is in the words and figures following, to wit:

Articles of a Treaty made and concluded at Fort Laramie, Dakota Territory, on the seventh day of May, in the year of our Lord one thousand eight hundred and sixty-eight, by and between the undersigned commissioners on the part of the United States, and the undersigned chiefs and headmen of and representing the Crow Indians, they being duly authorized to act in the premises.

ARTICLE I.

From this day forward peace between the parties to this treaty shall forever continue. The government of the United States desires peace, and its honor is hereby pledged to keep it. The Indians desire peace, and they hereby pledge their honor to maintain it. If bad men among the whites or among other people, subject to the authority of the United States, shall commit any wrong upon the person or property of the Indians, the United States will, upon proof made to the agent and forwarded to the Commissioner of Indian Affairs at Washington city, proceed at once to cause the offender to be arrested and punished according to the laws of the United States, and also reimburse the injured person for the loss sustained.

If bad men among the Indians shall commit a wrong or depredation upon the person or property of any one, white, black, or Indian, subject to the authority of the United States and at peace therewith, the Indians herein named solemnly agree that they will, on proof made to their agent and notice by him, deliver up the wrongdoer to the United States, to be tried and punished according to its laws; and in case they refuse wilfully so to do the person injured shall be reimbursed for his loss from the annuities or other moneys due or to become due to them under this or other treaties made with the United States. And the President, on advising with the Commissioner of Indian Affairs, shall prescribe such rules and regulations for ascertaining damages under the provisions of this article as in his judgment may be proper. But no such damages shall be adjusted and paid until thoroughly examined and passed upon by the Commissioner of Indian

Affairs, and no one sustaining loss while violating, or because of his violating, the provisions of this treaty or the laws of the United States shall be reimbursed therefor.

Article II.

The United States agrees that the following district of country, to wit: commencing where the 107th degree of longitude west of Greenwich crosses the south boundary of Montana Territory; thence north along said 107th meridian to the mid-channel of the Yellowstone river; thence up said mid-channel of the Yellowstone to the point where it crosses the said southern boundary of Montana, being the 45th degree of north latitude; and thence east along said parallel of latitude to the place of beginning, shall be, and the same is, set apart for the absolute and undisturbed use and occupation of the Indians herein named, and for such other friendly tribes or individual Indians as from time to time they may be willing, with the consent of the United States, to admit amongst them; and the United States now solemnly agrees that no persons, except those herein designated and authorized so to do, and except such officers, agents, and employés of the government as may be authorized to enter upon Indian reservations in discharge of duties enjoined by law, shall ever be permitted to pass over, settle upon, or reside in the territory described in this article for the use of said Indians, and henceforth they will, and do hereby, relinquish all title, claims, or rights in and to any portion of the territory of the United States, except such as is embraced within the limits aforesaid.

Article III.

The United States agrees, at its own proper expense, to construct on the south side of the Yellowstone, near Otter creek, a warehouse or storeroom for the use of the agent in storing goods belonging to the Indians, to cost not exceeding twenty-five hundred dollars; an agency building for the residence of the agent, to cost not exceeding three thousand dollars; a residence for the physician, to cost not more than three thousand dollars; and five other buildings, for a carpenter, farmer, blacksmith, miller, and engineer, each to cost not exceeding two thousand dollars; also a school-house or mission building, so soon as a sufficient number of children can be induced by the agent to attend school, which shall not cost exceeding twenty-five hundred dollars.

The United States agrees further to cause to be erected on said reservation, near the other buildings herein authorized, a good steam circular saw-mill, with a grist-mill and shingle machine attached, the same to cost not exceeding eight thousand dollars.

Article IV.

The Indians herein named agree, when the agency house and other buildings shall be constructed on the reservation named, they will make said reservation their permanent home, and they will make no permanent settlement elsewhere, but they shall have the right to hunt on the unoccupied lands of the United States so long as game may be found thereon and as long as peace subsists among the whites and Indians on the borders of the hunting districts.

Article V.

The United States agrees that the agent for said Indians shall in the future make his home at the agency building; that he shall reside among them and keep an office open at all times for the purpose of prompt and diligent inquiry into such matters of complaint, by and against the Indians, as may be presented for investigation under the provisions of their treaty stipulations, as also for the faithful discharge of other duties enjoined on him by law. In all cases of depredation on person or property, he shall cause the evidence to be taken in writing and forwarded, together with his finding, to the Commissioner of Indian Affairs, whose decision shall be binding on the parties to this treaty.

Article VI.

If any individual belonging to said tribes of Indians, or legally incorporated with them, being the head of a family, shall desire to commence farming, he shall have the privilege to select, in the presence and with the assistance of the agent then in charge, a tract of land within said reservation, not exceeding three hundred and twenty acres in extent, which tract, when so selected, certified, and recorded in the "Land Book," as herein directed, shall cease to be held in common, but the same may be occupied and held in the exclusive possession of the person selecting it, and of his family, so long as he or they may continue to cultivate it.

Any person over eighteen years of age, not being the head of a family, may in like manner select and cause to be certified to him or her, for purposes of cultivation, a quantity of land not exceeding eighty acres in extent, and thereupon be entitled to the exclusive possession of the same as above directed.

For each tract of land so selected a certificate, containing a description thereof and the name of the person selecting it, with a certificate endorsed thereon that the same has been recorded, shall be delivered to the party entitled to it by the agent, after the same shall have been recorded by him in a book to be kept in his office, subject to inspection, which said book shall be known as the "Crow Land Book."

The President may at any time order a survey of the reservation, and, when so surveyed, Congress shall provide for protecting the rights of settlers in their improvements, and may fix the character of the title held by each. The United States may pass such laws on the subject of alienation and descent of property as between Indians, and on all subjects connected with the government of the Indians on said reservations and the internal police thereof, as may be thought proper.

Article VII.

In order to insure the civilization of the tribe entering into this treaty, the necessity of education is admitted, especially by such of them as are, or may be, settled on said agricultural reservation and they therefore pledge themselves to compel their children, male and female, between the ages of six and sixteen years, to attend school; and it is hereby made the duty of the agent for said Indians to see that this stipulation is strictly complied with; and the United States agrees that for every thirty children, between said ages, who can be induced or compelled to attend school, a house shall be provided, and a teacher, competent to teach the elementary branches of an English education, shall be furnished, who will reside among said Indians, and faithfully discharge his or her duties as a teacher. The provisions of this article to continue for twenty years.

Article VIII.

When the head of a family or lodge shall have selected lands and received his certificate as above directed, and the agent shall be satisfied that he intends in good faith to commence cultivating the soil for a living, he shall be entitled to receive seeds and agricultural implements for the first year in value one hundred dollars, and for each succeeding year he shall continue to farm, for a period of three years more, he shall be entitled to receive seeds and implements as aforesaid in value twenty-five dollars per annum.

And it is further stipulated that such persons as commence farming shall receive instructions from the farmer herein provided for, and whenever more than one hundred persons shall enter upon the cultivation of the soil a second blacksmith shall be provided, with such iron, steel, and other material as may be required.

Article IX.

In lieu of all sums of money or other annuities provided to be paid to the Indians herein named, under any and all treaties heretofore made with them, the United States agrees to deliver at the agency house, on the reservation herein provided for, on the first day of September of each year for thirty years, the following articles, to wit:

For each male person, over fourteen years of age, a suit of good, substantial woolen clothing, consisting of coat, hat, pantaloons, flannel shirt, and a pair of woolen socks.

For each female, over twelve years of age, a flannel skirt, or the goods necessary to make it, a pair of woolen hose, twelve yards of calico and twelve yards of cotton domestics.

For the boys and girls under the ages named, such flannel and cotton goods as may be needed to make each a suit as aforesaid, together with a pair of woollen hose for each.

And in order that the Commissioner of Indian Affairs may be able to estimate properly for the articles herein named, it shall be the duty of the agent, each year, to forward to him a full and exact census of the Indians, on which the estimate from year to year can be based.

And, in addition to the clothing herein named, the sum of ten dollars shall be annually appropriated for each Indian roaming, and twenty dollars for each Indian engaged in agriculture, for a period of ten years, to be used by the Secretary of the Interior in the purchase of such articles as, from time to time, the condition and necessities of the Indians may indicate to be proper. And if, at any time within the ten years, it shall appear that the amount of money needed for clothing, under this article, can be appropriated to better uses for the tribe herein named, Congress may, by law, change the appropriation to other purposes; but in no event shall the amount of this appropriation be withdrawn or discontinued for the period named. And the President shall, annually, detail an officer of the army to be present and attest the delivery of all the goods herein named to the Indians, and he shall inspect and report on the quantity and quality of the goods and the manner of their delivery; and it is expressly stipulated that each Indian over the age of four years, who shall have removed to and settled permanently upon said reservation, and complied with the stipulations of this treaty, shall be entitled to receive from the United States, for the period of four years after he shall have settled upon said reservation, one pound of meat and one pound of flour per day, provided the Indians cannot furnish their own subsistence at an earlier date. And it is further stipulated, that the United States will furnish and deliver to each lodge of Indians, or family of persons legally incorporated with them, who shall remove to the reservation herein described and commence farming, one good American cow and one good, well-broken pair of American oxen, within sixty days after such lodge or family shall have so settled upon said reservation.

ARTICLE X.

The United States hereby agrees to furnish annually to the Indians the physician, teachers, carpenter, miller, engineer, farmer, and blacksmiths as herein contemplated, and that such appropriations shall be made from time to time, on the estimates of the Secretary of the Interior, as will be sufficient to employ such persons.

ARTICLE XI.

No treaty for the cession of any portion of the reservation herein described, which may be held in common, shall be of any force or validity as against the said Indians unless executed and signed by, at least, a majority of all the adult male Indians occupying or interested in the same, and no cession by the tribe shall be understood or construed in such manner as to deprive, without his consent, any individual member of the tribe of his right to any tract of land selected by him as provided in article VI of this treaty.

ARTICLE XII.

It is agreed that the sum of five hundred dollars annually, for three years from the date when they commence to cultivate a farm, shall be expended in presents to the ten persons of said tribe who, in the judgment of the agent, may grow the most valuable crops for the respective year.

W. T. SHERMAN, *Lt. Genl.*
WM. S. HARNEY,
Bvt. Majr. Gen. & Peace Commissioner.
ALFRED H. TERRY, *Bvt. M. Genl.*
C. C. AUGUR, *Bvt. Maj. Genl.*
JOHN B. SANBORN.
S. F. TAPPAN.

ASHTON S. H. WHITE, *Secretary.*

CHE-RA-PEE-ISH-KA-TE, Pretty Bull,	his x mark, [SEAL.]
CHAT-STA-HE, Wolf Bow,	his x mark, [SEAL.]
AH-BE-CHE-SE, Mountain Tail,	his x mark, [SEAL.]
KAM-NE-BUT-SA, Black Foot,	his x mark, [SEAL.]
DE-SAL-ZE-CHO-SE, White Horse,	his x mark, [SEAL.]
CHIN-KA-SHE-ARACHE, Poor Elk,	his x mark, [SEAL.]
E-SA-WOOR, Shot in the Jaw,	his x mark, [SEAL.]
E-SHA-CHOSE, White Forehead,	his x mark, [SEAL.]
—— ROO-KA, Pounded Meat,	his x mark, [SEAL.]
DE-KA-KE-UP-SE, Bird in the Neck,	his x mark, [SEAL.]
ME-NA-CHE, The Swan,	his x mark, [SEAL.]

Attest:
GEORGE B. WILLIS, *Phonographer.*
JOHN D. HOWLAND.
ALEX. GARDNER.
DAVID KNOX.
CHAS. FREEMAN.
JAS. C. O'CONNOR.

And whereas the said Treaty having been submitted to the Senate of the United States for its constitutional action thereon, the Senate did, on the twenty-fifth day of July, one thousand eight hundred and sixty-eight, advise and consent to the ratification of the same, by a resolution in the words and figures following, to wit:

IN EXECUTIVE SESSION, SENATE OF THE UNITED STATES,
July 25, 1868.

Resolved, (two-thirds of the senators present concurring,) That the Senate advise and consent to the ratification of the Treaty between the United States and the Crow Indians of Montana Territory, made the seventh day of May, 1868.

Attest: GEO. C. GORHAM,
Secretary,
By W. J. McDONALD,
Chief Clerk.

Now, therefore, be it known that I, ANDREW JOHNSON, President of the United States of America, do, in pursuance of the advice and consent of the Senate, as expressed in its resolution of the twenty-fifth of July, one thousand eight hundred and sixty-eight, accept, ratify, and confirm the said Treaty.

In testimony whereof, I have hereto signed my name, and caused the seal of the United States to be affixed.

Done at the City of Washington, this twelfth day of August, in the year of our Lord one thousand eight hundred and sixty-eight, and of the Independence of the United States of America the ninety-third.

[SEAL.]

ANDREW JOHNSON.

By the President:
W. HUNTER,
Acting Secretary of State.

MISCELLANEOUS PHOTOGRAPHS

CROW AGENCY, MONTANA

Photographer: Fred E. Miller (1868-1936)   (ca 1898)

"A camp on the Little Horn River"
Tipis and horses in camp beside Little Bighorn River.

McCracken Research Library,
Buffalo Bill Center of the West
Identifier: P.32.39

Photographer: Fred E. Miller (1868-1936)   (ca 1898)

"A 'warm' Little Crow"
Young Crow boy wearing capote made from wool blanket.

McCracken Research Library,
Buffalo Bill Center of the West
Identifier: P.32.73

Photographer: Fred E. Miller (1868-1936)   (ca 1898)

"Cold day Dance Costumes"
Five Crow men in traditional regalia.

McCracken Research Library,
Buffalo Bill Center of the West
Identifier: P.32.70

Photographer: Fred E. Miller (1868-1936)   (ca 1898)

"Elk teeth dresses"
Crow woman and daughter wearing elk tooth dresses in front of tipi.

McCracken Research Library,
Buffalo Bill Center of the West
Identifier: P.32.38

Photographer: Fred E. Miller (1868-1936)   (ca 1898)

"Little Wolf"
Little Wolf wearing non-Indian shirt with blanket around waist.

McCracken Research Library,
Buffalo Bill Center of the West
Identifier: P.32.58

Photographer: Fred E. Miller (1868-1936)   (ca 1898)

"'No Milk' and 'Shorty'"
Two Crow men wearing traditional regalia and women sitting behind them.

McCracken Research Library,
Buffalo Bill Center of the West
Identifier: P.32.66

Photographer: Fred E. Miller (1868-1936)   (ca 1898)

"Old time method of carrying papooses"
Woman wrapped in blanket holding baby in beaded cradleboard.
Buildings in background.

McCracken Research Library,
Buffalo Bill Center of the West
Identifier: P.32.93

Photographer: Fred E. Miller (1868-1936)   (ca 1898)

"Shell on the neck"
Crow man and child wearing traditional regalia. Tipis in background.

McCracken Research Library,
Buffalo Bill Center of the West
Identifier: P.32.90

Photographer: Edward S. Curtis (1868-1952)   (1908)

"Scout That Returns"
Head-and-shoulders portrait of Scout That Returns, wearing traditional clothing and beaded gauntlets.

Library of Congress
Control #2023635113

lix

Photographer: Edward S. Curtis (1868-1952) (c1908)
Mother and child--Apsaroke
Portrait of a woman holding baby in beaded cradleboard.

Library of Congress
Control #90708185

Photographer: Edward S. Curtis (1868-1952) (c1908 July 6)

Apsaroke mother, Her Horse Kills, with child secured on her back with blanket.

Library of Congress
Control #2002722302

Photographer: Richard Throssel (ca 1905)

Little Iron Horse

Indian girl facing front.

Library of Congress
Control #2002715090

Burial of an Unknown Soldier (November 11, 1921)

Photograph shows Native American Crow chief Plenty Coups with other dignitaries at the interment of the Unknown Soldier at Arlington National Cemetery, November 11, 1921.

Library of Congress
Control #2016831681

INTRODUCTION

In 1851, what is now Wyoming (Territory), an effort was about to be attempted at Fort Laramie by the U.S. leadership in the form of a general peace by treaty with numerous western tribes and naturally with the underlying motive of organizing control of their lands. While creating these borders the government wanted the tribes to feel like they had their own lands or hunting grounds but there was another plan in the works. The Native people felt the land shouldn't be owned by anyone and they knew that things would never be the same after what was about to take place, theft....

The cast of government actors about to generously offer these treaty promises or allowances to hunt on other tribal lands when needed was a deception. The Crows and their new found *'frenemies'* were about to realize another attack on their freedoms. Of course the white bureaucrats weren't thinking about or even considering the tribal cultures in their presence likely due to grave ignorance and the fact that from time immemorial these tribes had what seemed like their natural allies and enemies. Now whether friend or foe they were being consolidated and finding it was the government who was their worst enemy of all.

Still all in the name of peace, trade, and without saying it out loud, they were shouting under their breath, we just want what is yours.... Hopefully without wasting too much time on this the desire is to give you the very best short description of a gathering so huge and of what was likely over ten to twelve thousand Indians, their families, their livestock, their prairie homes and their differences in a few short sentences of what finally came to be; which won't be easy since there is so much to tell.

These people (the tribes) travelled from near and far so the all-knowing bureaucrats from Washington could just work it out here and now by just signing a paper. They'd just work it out not even caring about the lives they'd destroy as long as they achieved their nefarious motives. After reading hundreds of pages concerning this very period of time and history until now such a short and eloquent few sentences by one individual explaining the unmitigated disaster these narcissists planned out was a deception, another organized heist from the Native American community, "The treaty of 1851 was a bold attempt to bring the northern Plains' most powerful tribes into a single agreement. In many ways, it represented a phase of U.S. policy making that disappeared in the years that followed." In *The Rediscovery of America*, author Ned Blackhawk put it plainly, "By 1855, for many nations in Montana, it was abandoned altogether."[1]

The year was 1884, "The migration of the Crows out of the Rocky Mountains was not the migration of eager, landless peasants to a land of promise, but the forced retreat of landed hunters to a tiny corner of a rapidly developing federal territory. The families who travelled out of the mountains with Captain Armstrong were not coming to America, America was coming to them. It was immigration in reverse."[2]

---

[1] *The Rediscovery of America*; Pg. 307 Para. 3
[2] *Parading Through History*; Pg. 20-21 Para. 4

Though two years previous and during the close of 1882 the Crow with mixed emotions, "consisted of twenty-six loosely structured bands of fifteen to forty lodges each. While linked by clan and kin ties, these bands were units that gathered rations together, but migrated according to their own preferences and inclinations. Their leaders were largely independent from one another, even though it was clear that both the government and several ambitious chiefs were eager to establish some form of centralized leadership for the group."[3]

These Crows were watching with a hunger in their eyes and bellies while the buffalo disappeared and the game of their home the foothills of the Beartooth Mountains grew thin. Wondering day in and day out how they would feed their loved ones. These were warriors. Some were taught from as young as six years old how to become Crow wolves or scouts learning what it was to count coup how to earn the honor of a warrior, the steps to becoming a chief. The lessons of respect instilled, pressed into their very souls in becoming men and finding out they were living a calling from birth, one that was as important as breathing to live. They were taught to defend, provide, honor and be charitable.

So of course not all Crows felt that it was better to just settle along the Little Bighorn and farm on the patch of ground before them. Some Crows were afraid the bureaucrats would come up with the idea that they weren't using all of the land, so let us have the rest of it. Could it be that the Crow were having a premonition or just understood the white Europeans' form of greed. Some younger Crows felt that if they ranched and raised cattle or some form of livestock they'd need more land and be able to keep what was rightfully theirs. Others didn't want their lives to change, they wanted to hunt and find the game that provided their livelihoods for so long, they wanted tradition, culture. They didn't want to forget their past they wanted to live it. They wanted to count *"Coup"*. They lived by the coup for honor and reputation, having four general rules as to what resulted in a coup, one by commanding a horse raid on an enemy encampment, second the taking of an enemy's weapon while face to face during battle, third by touching a living adversary and finally by the taking of a tied horse or called, *"cut a horse"* from a rivals' camp. The life expectancy of the Crow Realm would soon change forever. The life of the coup would quickly disappear just two years after leaving the Stillwater Valley, in approximately twenty-four months, "The last Apsáalooke horse raid took place in 1886. No longer could social and political status be acquired through counting coup. The system that had generated chiefs and male prestige no longer existed. With the passage of time positions of tribal leadership became confused, and an entire population of men found their traditional identity in question."[4]

"In the spring of 1884, the Crows who paraded behind Captain Armstrong from the Stillwater valley to the Little Bighorn River entered a new world of record keeping as well as a new arena of experience. Unprecedented poverty and suffering lay before

---

[3] Parading Through History; Pg. 123 Para. 2
[4] The World of the Crow Indians; Pg. 33 Para. 2

them, but the ordeal to come would take place in the most intensively recorded period in Crow history."[5]

As Frederick Hoxie the author of, *Parading through History,* put it through a quote at the beginning of Chapter Five, from the Crow, Two Leggings in 1919; "Nothing happened after that. We just lived. There were no more war parties, no capturing of horses from the Piegans and the Sioux, no buffalo to hunt. There is nothing more to tell." In reading the personal interviews from both, *Plenty Coups* and *Pretty-shield Medicine Women*, they both said basically the same thing, it was over, the buffalo were gone, there is nothing left to tell.

When the government took the very words out of the Crow storytellers' mouths by turning their world upside down, by believing they were helping as they claimed the rewards, "Land". They were just suppressing a people who in their hearts were happy and took life as it came. The culture, reality, the traditions they lived and witnessed with every breath; replaced with empty bureaucratic documentation without a scent of personality only to be taken away when the storytellers themselves ceased to speak.

Some may have thought they were helping, others may never have wanted to even be there and documentation is important but the Crows as other Native peoples were larger than life. Just recording, documenting the moments and what was happening didn't frame who they were past or present. Only they knew their hearts and minds and it seems nobody was interested.

Admittedly, without these recordings or documentation we'd have no idea or even a hint of the existence as well as the span of time these legends walked among the living. But when the era of record keeping came the fragility of human life and personality slipped away from the Plains People. It became like reading an empty book with nothing on the pages.

Knowing so many Crows stood with the military during the time that Custer was running through Cheyenne, Sioux and Arapahoe camps, surrounding them along with his contemporaries. They sat in their saddles in battle form. The fog hadn't even had a chance to dissipate from the ground and the dew was still dripping with a quite force of the inevitable, because the sun hadn't risen enough yet to dry the atmosphere. You could feel the cold chill running through your bones if you happened to leave the warmth while lying peacefully under that buffalo robe. Instead they woke to the terror of cannon shot, the noise of the bugle and thunder from both pistol and rifle while just moments ago the smoke hole of every tipi admitted a slow lazy stream of a fire's thin mist. Rather than stoking the morning fire they faced death even before another day's work began. Instead family's lives were irreparably damaged forever.

Doesn't it make you curious how the Crow, the Sioux and their allies felt toward each other and what would take place later?

---

[5] Parading Through History; Pg. 126 Para. 1

One man described it best, though one man's opinion is one man's opinion. Hopefully others followed his thought pattern being he was well respected among the Crow. He was just a kid of about 18 years when he first encountered the Crow people, some thought he seemed more Crow than white. Tom LaForge a man who called himself, born an Ohio American, a scout, a guide. He married a Crow and had a Crow family. He spoke plainly in his memoir published in 1928 of the attitude from a warrior's perspective of how they felt, just what it was like, a way of life they all fully accepted from the day they were born. "I like all American Indians I ever have known. Next to the Crows, I like best the Sioux. They were wicked, but brave fighters. I used to hold our Crow tribal enmity toward them, but this feeling now is gone. I have enjoyed rehearsing with some of them the old-time struggles. I appreciate now that those deadly combats were a sportive game more than a killing because of hate."[6]

The Crow throughout their history appear to be individuals as well as independently capable. A centered people, stable. Their leadership from the early days though living in bands, even families on the prairies, taking to their own direction but when united never travelled off course in thinking of their people. It was like they carried a Constitution and Bill of Rights within each one of their hearts. Not allowing their culture and traditions to dissipate no matter who came along whether white, other tribes, government or religious institutions trying to change them. Many tried and all failed. They managed to incorporate what was useful, logical, true and helpful but they always managed to dig deep and understand who they were. They thought about their families, the generations and it seems everything else so all of the Crow could understand who they were, are and would become. Their tribal life it seems has been wrapped up from their very beginning in being generous to others though extremely wise and understanding the very difference between right and wrong. No matter who tried to tell them what path to travel it always carried them down the Crow Path only better.

From the publication, *Parading Through History, The making of the Crow Nation in America 1805-1935,* Frederick E. Hoxie explains on pages 224-225, "In his recent portrait of the Crow worldview, anthropologist, Rodney Frey argues that tribal members understand the cosmos as a giant wagon wheel in which "the spokes represent the various peoples and religions of the world, each unique unto itself." At the center is the hub, "the pervasive Maker, who is shared and touched by all." Frey contends that modern Crows see every spoke – every religious or cultural expression – to be equally connected to God. Frey illustrates this point by recalling an interview with a peyotist who displayed for him a prize peyote button which was never consumed. "This is who I pray to when someone in my family is sick or in need of something." the peyote man told Frey. When the cactus button was turned over, the visitor saw something more: "Glued to the reverse side is a picture of Jesus." On page 225, from midway to the bottom of paragraph two, is stated that the Crows, "In addition, membership in a Christian organization did not preclude participation in the Tobacco Society, a singing or hot dance group, or loyalty to the peyote ritual. At the end of a process of intense regimentation and proselytizing, the Crows seemed to have

---

[6] Memoirs of a White Crow Indian; Pg. 345 Para. 2

retained their preference for a plural approach to religious expression and to have stamped their modern existence with the values of their collective past."

It's not just the 1880's that needs to be read about in Crow history. How many times did the Crow stand up for the U.S.? It was so numerous it would be impossible to count. Yet they lost land beyond belief, "In 1825 the Crow Tribe and the United States signed a treaty of friendship. In 1851 the so-called Fort Laramie Treaty established the boundaries of the "Indian Country" for several tribes, including an area of 35,531,147 acres for the Crow Indians. This was followed by another Fort Laramie treaty in 1868, which reduced the Crow country to 8,000,400 acres.

An act of Congress in 1882 resulted in further reduction of the land, and as compensation the government was to build houses for the Crows and buy livestock for them. By this time the tribe had been settled within the boundaries of the reservation for about ten years. In 1890 more land was ceded to the government, for which the Crows received $940,000. In 1905 the last large cession was made, leaving about 2.5 million acres of land for the tribe."[7]

The Crow stood by the U.S. Army assisting as scouts, helping whenever they could, even so far as going to the Little Bighorn; they warned Custer that he needed to get out, that there were too many of their old traditional enemies (the Cheyenne, Sioux and Arapahoe) it was even said by most including his faithful scout Mitch Bouyer that he had never seen so many tipi's. Custer told the Crow that their job was to find these tribes and that they could go, but a few chose to stay with him. They died as Custer did. Custer had a habit of always riding in front of his troops, lead by example as well as being lucky clear through the Civil War, likely thinking himself invincible till that day.

You see the famous paintings, by Frederick Remington or by Cassilly Adams 1885-1888 inspired by the Crow Scout "Curly." Also the 1881 painting by John Mulvany, "Custer's Last Fight" [the Budweiser poster], famous and in almost every bar in the U.S.A. and maybe in somebody's basement. And who knows where else, showing Custer fighting on the ridge with pistol barrel in one hand and a sabre in the other to the very last. How many movies since the creation of the big screen and T.V., how many articles in magazines and newspapers? How many historians? They all debate what happened. Yet one little Crow lady by the name of Pretty-shield (in this census with her husband) being interviewed in her later years about seventy three, by a gentleman named Frank B. Linderman makes a startling statement, "My man, Goes-ahead, was with Son-of-the-morning-star when he rode down to the water of the Little Bighorn. He heard a Lakota call out to Two-bodies, who rode beside Son-of-the-morning-star, and say, 'Go back, or you will die.'

"But Son-of-the-morning-star did not go back. He went *ahead, rode into the water of the Little Bighorn, with Two-bodies* on one side of him, and his flag on the other—and he *died* there, *died in the water of the Little Bighorn,* with Two-bodies, and the blue soldier carrying his flag."

"When he fell in the water, the other blue soldiers ran back up the hill. It was now that my man, Goes-ahead, ran fast. He told me that the fighters were so many,

---

[7] From The Heart of Crow Country; Pg. 3 Para. 3-4

and so crazy, that in the thick dust and powder-smoke, anybody might easily have run away. So he, White-man-runs-him, and Hairy-moccasin, ran when they saw Son-of-the-morning-star fall into the water, with Two-bodies and the blue horse-soldier that carried his flag. My man, Goes-ahead, showed me where Son-of-the-morning-star fell into the water. [Mitch Bouyer, called Two-bodies by the Crows, was a half breed interpreter. He was killed with General Custer.]"[8]

Also mentioned in *Son of the Morningstar Custer and the Little Bighorn*, on page 304, "Dr. Marquis proposed that the general died early in the fight, whereupon Yates assumed command. Next in seniority was Captain Myles Keogh, yet he might have been killed right away, in which case Tom Custer would assume command. This sequence would explain Tom's presence. As for Lt. Smith, when E Company fell apart he might have escaped and made his way to field headquarters, which would be logical. But as Marquis himself points out, nobody knows when the general was killed."[9]

Except maybe one Crow woman and three of Custer's scouts, and a few more not saying or able to....

Yet as loyal as the Crow may have been they knew they had to out-think the others in order to survive for their generations to come. They knew who could be trusted and who couldn't. Faithful yes, but the governmental whites no matter who the Crow fought for and died the favor wasn't returned even into more modern times they still paid the full price if it wasn't their land it was their livelihoods again, their livestock by the thousands, first the buffalo next their horses. "In 1882 the Crow tribe ceded the western portion of the vast Crow Indian Reservation to the United States and moved to the eastern sector. The Indians agents' new headquarters or agency was established in the Little Bighorn Valley about thirteen miles south of what is now Hardin, Montana, in 1884. The Crow families scattered to various areas of the diminished reservation, generally under the leadership of a chief or several chiefs. The main occupation of the Crow men was the traditional raising of and caring for horses, which was all they knew and enjoyed doing. During the Spanish-American War, the conflicts of the 1890's, and World War I, the Crow horse ranchers began to farm, raising garden produce, small grains, and hay for the horses. Family herds increased rapidly. By the turn of the century, the number of horses the Crows owned was increasing rapidly, and by the end of World War I, the ranges were teeming with horses, which were becoming unmanageable and quite wild. By this time many non-Indian cattlemen and sheepmen had acquired grazing permits to large blocks of reservation land, and they were doing very well. They started complaining that wild Indian ponies were eating off their ranges, and some refused to pay their grazing fees. Before long these permittees and lessees, aided by Montana senators and congressmen, began pressuring the government to get rid of the Indian horses. About 1919 the secretary of the interior issued orders that the Crows must get rid of their horses. This was like ordering a man to kill his best friend or brother. It was also ordering a people to relinquish the traditions, customs, and values of the culture, their way of life! Naturally, no Crow could abide by the secretary's orders. The ultimatum

---

[8] Pretty-shield Medicine Woman of the Crows; Pg. 158 Para. 3-5
[9] Son of The Morning Star, [Connell]; Pg. 304 Para. 6

came about 1923, that the government would get rid of the horses. Local non-Indian cattle outfits were contracted to kill the horses on a bounty basis. The killer would be paid four dollars per animal when he produced the tip of a horse's ear. Some killers would bring in big sacks of ears. One large outfit had to import Texas gunmen to do the shooting, as local cowboys were soon disgusted with the slaughter. Of course, the Crows would not kill horses.

In a matter of three years nearly all the so-called wild mustangs were killed off. About one hundred head of the widest ones were found in the rough Rotten Grass Breaks after World War II, and the same stockman who hired the Texas gunmen hired planes and helicopters and ran the poor horses to death. In the first slaughter the government said that about forty thousand head were exterminated, but the Crows said it was many more, including many tame ranch horses, which the gunmen preyed on when it got difficult to find wild ones.

Thus by 1930 the great and proud horse people, the Absarokee, were bereft of horses. When the horse was gone, the Crow culture was severely damaged. To say the least, this was a traumatic and tragic experience for a proud horse-oriented tribe; it was worse than actual military defeat, which some Plains tribes sustained."[10]

They must have seen integrity while not understanding it, because it backfired on them like any reasonable governmental stance, they invited Plenty Coups, Crow warrior and chief to the interment of the Unknown Soldier. But he knew what he would say, Plenty Coups knew who he was as well as his people, those that invited him to Arlington that day didn't. His words reached far and worldwide that day. Below is a description from a wonderful author and researcher, this should never be forgotten.

From *Parading Through History,* by Frederick Hoxie, Pg. 344-345 Para's. 1-6 [this from a Crow study.] "The parade began sharply at 8:30 A.M. The *New York Times* reporter observed that "Washington has witnessed many notable ceremonials, but never one like this." As a military band played "Nearer My God to Thee," the silver haired president of the United States took his place behind a horse-drawn caisson carrying the remains of an unidentified soldier who had died in France three years earlier, during the final days of World War I.

President and Mrs. Harding stepped off first, followed immediately by Vice President Coolidge and his wife and Chief Justice William Howard Taft. A car carrying the crippled former president Woodrow Wilson and his wife followed close behind. In their wake marched ranks of politicians, veterans, gold star mothers, military bands and delegations from organizations as diverse as the Knights of Columbus, the American Women's League and the American Library Association. As they passed the dense crowds lining Pennsylvania Avenue, "men stood with heads uncovered in the presence of the coffin and silently followed its course as far as the eye could reach." Recalling the tearful funerals of Lincoln, Garfield and McKinley, the *Times* reporter noted that "there were tears today, but most of those who shed them were carried away by the emotion of the symbolism of patriotism which this unknown American embodied."

---

[10] From The Heart of Crow Country; Pg. 3-1 Paras. 105-107

Just before noon the procession reached its destination, Arlington National Cemetery, in the low hills west of the capital. As more than 100,000 spectators looked on, the coffin was carried to the stage of the cemetery amphitheater. Everyone was in place by 12:00 o'clock. As the hour struck, the audience stood in silence for two minutes, joined by millions of others across the country who paused in simultaneous observances. The singing of "America" brought the period of silence to a close and introduced speeches by the president and other dignitaries. They were followed by a series of international representatives (many of them in Washington for the Conference on Naval Disarmament, which would begin the next week) who presented the unknown soldier with military metals from their governments. Uniformed pallbears then carried the coffin to a nearby marble sarcophagus, placed it inside and stood at attention as a military chaplain read the funeral service.

After the chaplain had completed his prayers, Plenty Coups stepped forward. Dressed in brilliantly beaded buckskin, carrying a coups stick, and wearing an eagle-feather headdress, the seventy-two-year-old warrior's presence was a stunning match for the European generals and the officers from the Mikado's navy who stood in the front ranks of the audience in their polished boots and gold braid. The huge crowd watched in absolute silence as the Pryor leader – who had first come to Washington with Pretty Eagle and Medicine Crow more than forty years before – removed his war bonnet and laid it on the sarcophagus alongside his coup stick. Ignoring the order that he remain silent during his part of the ceremony, Plenty Coups then turned to the crowd and added his own words to those that had been pronounced earlier. Speaking in Crow, he declared, "I am glad to represent all the Indians of the United States in placing on the grave of this noble warrior this coup stick and war bonnet, every eagle feather of which represents a deed of valor by my race." He added a brief prayer: "I hope that the Great Spirit will grant that these noble warriors have not given up their lives in vain and that there will be peace to all men hereafter." As the old man completed his unauthorized address, a bugler began "taps" and a twenty-one gun salute echoed across the Potomac. His brief appearance, the *Times* reporter noted, was "one of the outstanding features of the whole remarkable ceremony."

One of the most solemn moments in our history and at Arlington of all places, like Pearl Harbor, a moment that should have been remembered in infamy, a Crow calling for peace to both white, red and all mankind…. Obviously beyond the reach of some….

In closing none of this introduction would be possible without the hard work of the researchers that loved or love Native history, they were willing to read, ask questions and consume their precious time seeking the truth. The quotes are in footnote form and they are the genius of those that loved the Crow people's culture and stories. There maybe a few more notes at the end of this missive adapted more to today, but for now a few wise words need to be shared from Plenty Coups wisdom and Frank B. Linderman's efforts. Plenty Coups medicine was the Chickadee.

"'Listen, Plenty-coups,' said a voice. 'In that tree is the lodge of the Chickadee. He is least in strength but strongest of mind among his kind. He is willing to work for wisdom. The Chickadee-person is a good listener. Nothing escapes his ears, which he has sharpened by constant use. Whenever others are talking together of their successes or failures, there you will find the Chickadee-person listening to their words. But in all his listening he tends to his own business. He never intrudes, never speaks in strange company, and yet never misses a chance to learn from others. He gains success and avoids failure by learning how others succeeded or failed, and without great trouble to himself. There is scarcely a lodge he does not visit, hardly a Person he does not know, and yet everybody likes him, because he minds his own business, or pretends to."[11]

The background for today's Crow Nation, government, education, population, events, homeland, etc. Their contribution as a whole to the history of the United States should never be forgotten and put out there for people to consume the world through.

"The Crow Indian Reservation is the homeland of the Crow Tribe. Established 1868, the reservation is located in parts of Big Horn, Yellowstone, and Treasure counties in southern Montana in the United States. The Crow Tribe has an enrolled membership of approximately 11,000, of whom 7,900 reside in the reservation. 20% speak Crow as their first language.

The reservation, the largest of the seven Indian reservations in Montana, is located in south-central Montana, bordered by Wyoming to the south and the Northern Cheyenne Indian Reservation to the east. The reservation includes the northern end of the Bighorn Mountains, Wolf Mountains, and Pryor Mountains. The Bighorn River flows north from the Montana-Wyoming state line, joining the Little Bighorn just east of Hardin. Part of the reservation boundary runs along the ridgeline separating Pryor Creek and the Yellowstone River. The city of Billings is approximately 10 miles (16 km) northwest of the reservation boundary.

It has a land area of 3,593.56 square miles (9,307.3 km^2) and a total area of 3,606.54 square miles (9,340.9 km^2), making it either the fifth or sixth-largest reservation in the country (alternating with the Standing Rock Reservation depending on whether water areas are counted). Reservation headquarters are in Crow Agency, Montana.

History
The reservation is located in old Crow country. In August 1805, fur trader Francois-Antoine Larocque camped at the Little Bighorn River and traveled through the area with a Crow group.[7]

The contemporary reservation lies at the center of the Crow Indian territory described in the 1851 Fort Laramie treaty.

Pressure from Europeans north of Yellowstone River and a Lakota (Sioux) invasion into Crow treaty guaranteed land from the east (the lead-up to Red Cloud's War) made the 1860s a trying time for the Crow. "Oglalas under Crazy Horse and Red Cloud and Hunkpapas and Minneconjous under Sitting Bull continued to follow the dwindling buffalo herds west from the Powder River, while gold seekers

---

[11] Plenty Coups Chief of the Crows; Pg. 37 Paras. 3

travelled north into the [Crow] region along the Bozeman [Trail]."Steamboats on the Missouri River brought additional prospectors into the Yellowstone area. The situation called for a new Crow treaty.

On May 7, 1868, the Crow sold around 30 million acres of their 1851 territory and agreed to live in a reservation. The border to the south was the 45th degree of north latitude, while the 107th degree of longitude west was the eastern border. Both borderlines met the Yellowstone at a point. The connection of these two points followed the course of the river and made up the last border of the 1868 reservation. It comprised about eight million acres.

Major F. D. Pease was the first civil agent at the Crow reservation, from 1870 to 1874.

Land cessions to the United States approved in 1882, 1892 and 1906 cut the western and northernmost part of the 1868 reservation.

Crow chief Plenty Coups, Robert Yellowtail and others stopped efforts to open the reservation in 1917. In a hotel room in Washington, D.C., they opened a bundle over the incense of buffalo chips from animals in the National Zoo and prayed for help. "The next day the attempted appropriation of their land was soundly defeated."

Yellowtail made headlines when he became superintendent of his own tribe's reservation in 1934, the first Indian to do so.

The reservation got its present shape after moderate land cuts in 1937 and in connection with the construction of the Bighorn Canyon Dam in the 1960s.

During the 1960s, Pauline Small became the first woman Crow reservation tribal official.

The biggest attraction in the reservation is the Little Bighorn National Monument. On June 25, 1876, combined forces from the Lakota, Northern Cheyenne, and Arapaho tribes defeated the Seventh Cavalry Regiment commanded by George Armstrong Custer. Local Crow scouts defending their reservation guided Custer.

Chief Plenty Coups (Alek-Chea-Ahoosh) State Park and Home is located near the town of Pryor. It has a small museum dedicated to Chief Plenty Coups and the Crow Tribe. The chief's two-floor lodge house and grocery store is preserved

Notable events

Since 1904, the Crow have organized the big Crow Fair, forming the "Teepee Capital of the World". By tradition, it is held the third week in August.
Crow Agency, Montana.

Crow Agency is located at 45°36′5″N 107°27′35″W (45.601383, -107.459706). Interstate 90 passes through the community, with access from Exit 509. U.S. Route 212 also passes through the town. Custer Creek runs alongside town.

History of the three locations of the "Crow Agency"

The term "Crow Agency" has been historically used since 1868 for the headquarters where the United States directed the federal interaction with the Crow tribe on its reservation. The Crow Tribe's reservations, and the tribe's relations to the

United States were defined by treaties between the Crow Tribe and the United States, and by United States statutes.

A Reservation Without An Agency (1851-1868)

The Treaty of Fort Laramie of 1851 created extensive reservation lands for the Indian tribes in Montana, Wyoming and the Dakotas at a time when the non-Indian presence in this area was limited to roving traders. A large reservation for the Crow Tribe was set out that was centered on the Big Horn Mountains and extended eastward into the Powder River basin to the banks of the Powder River. However, this treaty did not indicate agency sites for any of the tribes, including the Crows. At the time of the treaty, 1851 the Crow tribe consisted of nomadic bands whose culture was based on hunting the migratory buffalo herds, including those herds in the Powder River Country. Hunting in the Powder River area on the east side of the Big Horn Mountains brought the Crow in increasing conflict with more powerful bands of Sioux who were migrating westward. In 1863 gold was discovered in commercial quantities in the mountains of the western Montana Territory. Travelers to the gold fields left the Oregon Trail and traveled through the Powder River country, going up the east side of the Big Horns to the Yellowstone valley, and then westward. This route became known as the Bozeman Trail, and three forts were built to protect travelers. The Sioux conducted an all out war against the forts and the travelers on the Bozeman Trail called "Red Cloud's War", which finally forced the United States to agree to abandon the forts, and close the trail, and to remake the boundaries of the reservations for the Crow and Sioux in the Fort Laramie Treaty of 1868.

The First Crow Agency (1868-1874)

The Fort Laramie "Treaty with the Crows, 1868", was one of a series of treaties that recognized the encroaching presence of the Sioux tribes into the Powder River Basin, and gave them that entire area as a hunting preserve. The separate 1868 treaty with the Crow moved the center of the Crow lands to the west of the Powder River Basin, into the western portions of the Yellowstone Valley. The 1868 Treaty provided for annuities and other federal support, and stipulated that the Crow would have an agency" on the south side of the Yellowstone, near Otter Creek", close to present day Big Timber, Montana. The first Crow Agency (1869-1874) was eventually constructed about eight miles east of present-day Livingston, Montana on Mission Creek, and became known as Fort Parker. This first Crow Agency was located in the western reaches of the Yellowstone River Valley, north of the Absaroka Range of Mountains. The Crows continued a largely nomadic life style hunting on the buffalo ranges to the east, though this brought them in constant but sporadic conflict with the Sioux who dominated the Powder River area.

The Second Crow Agency (1875-1884)

In 1874 miners encroached on the western margins of Crow lands in the Absaroka Range, and the reservation was reduced in 1875. The first Crow Agency was within these ceded lands and so the Agency was relocated eastward to a new site just south of modern-day Absarokee, Montana. The second Crow Agency (1875-1884) was still located north of the Absaroka Range of Mountains but about 66 miles further east of Fort Parker in the Yellowstone Valley, on the Stillwater River which was a tributary of the Yellowstone River.

The 9-year period from 1875 to 1884 was a time of rapid transition on the plains of eastern Montana and Wyoming. In 1876 the Crows provided scouts for the United States military forces in the Great Sioux War of 1876. The defeat by the Sioux of George Armstrong Custer at the Battle of the Little Big Horn in 1876 resulted in a concerted military backlash against the Sioux, and by 1877 and 1878 the hostile bands of Sioux had either fled to Canada, or they had surrendered and were confined to reservations along the Missouri River in the Dakotas. This initially left the Crows more secure in their use of the buffalo ranges on the eastern Montana and Wyoming plains, but in 1876 and 1877 federal forts were built across this area. With hostile Indian presence essentially neutralized, hide hunters came to harvest the northern buffalo herds. By 1882 the buffalo were gone from this area. Also, in 1880 the Northern Pacific Railroad began building eastward from Bismarck, ND, and in 1882 they completed their northern transcontinental line, which passed up the Yellowstone River valley just as the last of the buffalo disappeared. Almost at once large Texas trail herds arrived in the Montana Territory to exploit the now empty open range on the vast plains of central and eastern Montana. These successive rapid changes in this 9-year period eliminated the herds of bison and reduced other wild game on which the Crow culture relied, and ended forever the Crow's nomadic way of life.

The Third Crow Agency (1884 to Present)
In 1884 these events led to the last movement of the Crow Agency to the site of its third and final location at present day Crow Agency, Montana, 60 miles SE of Billings on the Little Bighorn River. This move of over a hundred miles eastward removed the Crow people from the vicinity of the Absaroka Range of Mountains, and from the Yellowstone River valley, and placed their reservation center on the east side of the Big Horn Mountains, on the western edge of the Powder River Basin of the northern great plains.

Education
Crow Agency has an elementary school. Hardin High School serves 9th through 12th grade. Crow Agency is home to Little Big Horn College. Crow Agency, Montana 59022." [12]

The spellings of the Crow Indian names are interesting. As someone who authors and transcribes thousands of names from many different tribes you catch yourself wondering about their struggles, their lives. While reading about those lives you have a tendency to feel the neglect they received at the hands of so many. So it comes down to like Plenty Coups wanting his people to know who they were and are to this day, and understand it won't always be like this because we are our own people, not theirs, we have control over our destiny not them, be like the Chickadee....

During this work it has been noticed that the Indian spelling of some of the names from one year to another of certain individuals changed drastically. In thinking about it and going from culture to culture it leaves you seeing the habits and similarities of

---

[12] Crow Agency, Montana; Crow Indian Reservation; Wikipedia

different census takers. For the time period it could have been a person's lack of dedication or frame of mind. Maybe even their limited education or the fact that their clerical skills were lacking. Not that all were like that because thankfully in many cases they did preserve a form of record otherwise we'd have nothing today.

It was noticed from 1901 to 1902 when the Indian Agent for the Crow changed many of the Indian names recorded contained drastic spelling changes. Of course you find different spellings for an individual coming of age maybe or when they married one year or widowed the next or married a different individual or divorced. There could be a change because of something that might have affected their life to the point that it may have implied a change in their Native name giving it a different form or meaning.

You'd have to understand their lives and tribal customs to know for sure. Do we really understand after researching, we try, but in many cases over a hundred years or more the correct interpretation falls upon those that live within these pages, not us. We can only try understanding those that bravely trod those hard times. One thing we know for sure, they were honest about life while literal in naming an individual.

The materials within these volumes are transcribed from National Archive Film Records M-595; Indian Census Rolls 1885-1940; Roll 80, 1899-1905.

It is hoped that this work and study will honor the very people within and their descendants. Also that anyone that touches one of these volumes will take the time to read the important history of the Crow people; while at the same time searching out that history through some of the recommended reading.

You can find more Crow history by looking for older volumes from early historians that took the time to understand, research and in many ways become a part of that Crow history themselves. The references they used and recorded within their works are precious territory and needs to be recorded again and again so history won't repeat itself.

Jeff Bowen
Gallipolis, Ohio
NativeStudy.com

Crow Agency

Montana,

1898 Census

E. H Becker, Agent

39710 OFFICE OF Indian Affairs REC'D AUG [..] 1898

Crow Agency, Mont,
August 2, 1898

E. H. Becker
Agent

Transmitting census of
898

1 ans

DEPARTMENT OF THE INTERIOR,
UNITED STATES INDIAN SERVICE

Crow Agency, Montana, Aug. 24, 1898.

Hon. W. A. Jones,
   Commissioner of Indian Affairs,
      Washington,
         D. C.

Sir:-

   I have the honor to transmit by this mail (under separate cover) the census of the Crow tribe for the fiscal year ended June 30, 1898, as required by the Regulations, and in accordance with instructions contained in office letter "A", of June 11, 1898.

      Very respectfully,

      E. H. Becker
      U. S. Indian Agent.

CENSUS.
RECAPITULATION.

MALES..........................	963	
FEMALES........................	1040	2003
Males above 18	666	
Females above 14	802	
Males between 6 and 16	150	
Females between 6 and 16	145	
Males between 16 and 18	25	
Males under 6	133	
Females under 6	145	

BIRTHS

Males..........................	36	
Female.........................	24	60

DEATHS.

Males..........................	12	
Female	18	30
Increase in population.........		30

Census of the __Crow__ Indians of __Crow__ Agency, __Montana__ taken by __E. H. Becker__, United States Indian Agent, __June 30th__, 189__8__

Key: Number; Indian Name; English Name; Sex; Relation; Age.

1; Ahnede-ichis; Walks pretty; F; Widow; 39
2; Lagak-hishes; Howard Red Bird; M; Son; 19
3; Lagak-esash; Big Bird; M; Son; 8

4; Budesash; No Horse; M; Husband; 32
5; Oo-Lukpus; Hugs the Weasel; F; Wife; 35

6; Ook-eas; Little Antelope; F; Widow; 72

7; Nas-kowees; Bad Heart; M; Husband; 25
8; Lagaka-hishes; Red Breasted Bird; F; Wife; 22
9; Lagak-mee-da-ses; Rain Bird; F; Daughter; 4
10; Bah-wah-sone-dah-it-chice; Good Leader; F; Daughter; 1

11; Awakin-lagaks; Bird all over the Ground; M; Husband; 52
12; Mida-ichsis; Goes Well; F; Wife; 48
13; Lagak-iche; Good Bird; F; Daughter; 6

14; Ahshua-wahnaks; Crazy Head; M; Husband; 62
15; Esha-shates; Paints Pretty; F; Wife; 51
16; Esaksha-Chechedees; Hunts the Man; M; Son; 20
17; Ahwoos-makpash; Medicine Hole; F; Daughter; 16

18; Mea-daka; White Woman; M; Husband; 39
19; Oomah-sees; Sees in the Mouth; F; Wife; 32

20; Ahuk-chea-akuse; He knows his Coos; M; Husband; 38
21; Hesha-chea-makpash; Medicine White Buffalo; F; Wife; 35

22; Eescha-naks; Young Jack Rabbit; M; Husband; 51
23; Ahpit-cheis; White Crane; F; Wife; 42
24; Ahwak-amach; Sits Toward the Mountain; M; Son; 7

25; Awaksha-echete; Gros Ventre Horse; M; Husband; 56
26; Chis-sheis; Nest; F; Wife; 46
27; Ashkarooche-amach; Horn Sits Down; F; Daughter; 15

28; Ahpit-naks; Young Crane; M; Father; 58
29; Bukasa-hishes; Red Snake; F; Daughter; 10

30; ---; Andrew Wallace; M; Husband; 25
31; ---; Jennie Wallace; F; Wife; 20
32; ---; Josie Wallace; F; Daughter; 4

33; Chatis; The Wolf; M; Husband; 54
34; Cheks-doochis; Takes Five; F; Wife; 54

5

Census of the __Crow__ Indians of __Crow__ Agency, __Montana__ taken by __E. H. Becker__, United States Indian Agent, __June 30th__, 189__8__

Key: Number; Indian Name; English Name; Sex; Relation; Age.

35; Mieep-hukis; Spotted Hawk; M; Uncle; 47
36; E-step-ees; Eli Blackhawk; M; Nephew; 24
37; Chate-ela-cheis; White Bellied Wolf; M; Father; 72

38; Eche-kuis; Sweet Mouth; M; Husband; 39
39; Andicha-poois; Sore Where Whipped; F; Wife; 43

40; Wtekut-napes; Kills Close; F; Widow; 75
41; Banuka-acha-nedees; Walks Over Ice; M; Son; 20
42; Mishodechitse-lagak; Medicine Rock Bird; M; Ad Son; 8

43; Esa-keepa; Wrinkle Face; M; Husband; 42
44; Eskochea-ichis; Fights the Enemy Good; F; Wife; 45
45; Ahwotkot-dichis; Strikes same one; F; Daughter; 3

46; Eskuka-ahsees; Shows a Lance; M; Husband; 48
47; Mi-iche-doochis; Takes Pretty Things; F; Wife; 60

48; Ahma-apisch; Arm around the Neck; M; Husband; 57
49; Hederin-dichis; Strikes in a Crowd; F; Wife; 57

50; Mena-ahwotkot; One Goose; M; Husband; 56
51; Min-makpash; Medicine Water; F; Wife; 44
52; Lagak-heahsas; Bird well known; M; Son; 15
53; Ashkarooche-kahdeas; Old Horn; F; Daughter; 8
54; Beaun-dichis; Strikes plenty Women; F; Mother; 72

55; Ahka-karashsash; Dont[sic] run on top; M; Husband; 35
56; Ees-kapa; Flat Face; F; Wife; 35
57; Echete-dekash; Stays with the horse; F; Daughter; 3
---; ---; William dont[sic] run on top; M; Son; 1

58; Ekupa-cheis; Packs the Hat; M; Husband; 40
59; Ahpake-hedere-lagaks; Bird in a cloud; F; Wife; 32
60; Eesackas-ahoos; Plenty arrows; M; Son; 7

61; Miastasheda-karoos; White man runs him; M; Father; 41
62; Bechon-herepsis; Kills one with red blanket; F; Daughter; 11
63; Micha-ahcheis-botsots; Steals on camp strong; M; Son; 4

64; Meneash-koop-skuis; Sioux; M; Batchelor[sic]; 47

65; Duchkis-; Left Hand; M; Husband; 25
66; Cheis-makpash; Medicine Tail; F; Wife; 27
67; Naks-makpash; Child is Medicine; F; Daughter; 8
68; Nahkose-chedup; Bull Turtle; M; Son; 3

Census of the __Crow__ Indians of __Crow__ Agency, __Montana__ taken by __E. H. Becker__, United States Indian Agent, __June 30th__, 189__8__

Key: Number; Indian Name; English Name; Sex; Relation; Age.

69; Peritse-kahdeas; Old Crow; M; Husband 62
70; Ahoo-aroopis; Finds all; F; Wife; 38
71; Mientahtasahederimithpal; Persons in the Moon; F; Daughter; 5
72; Istuka-sa-here-dadush; Stands among the Shooters; M; Son; 4

73; Cheda-kos; Holds up; M; Husband; 40
74; Ootay-doochis; Takes a weasel; F; Wife; 18
75; Beah-kahdeas; Rock old; M; Son; 3
76; Beshay-anks; Last buffalo; M; Son; 2

77; Eskay-awotkot; One star; M; Husband; 32
78; Miastasheda-meas; White woman; F; Wife; 47
79; ---; George Washington; M; Son; 18
80; Eakpoetatska; Good sheep; F; Daughter; 3

81; Miah-hoo-ted-deas; Does lots of things; F; [Widow]; 47

82; Dutsuah-moopis; Two muskrats; F; [Widow]; 70

83; Istuka-asees; Gun shows; M; Husband; 31
84; Dakpitsa-asees; Looks at the bear; F; Wife; 26
85; Ba-orap-saskatch; Finds soon; M; Son; 3

86; Ahmatka; Long way off; F; Mother; 56
87; Mi-ich-napes; Kills pretty ones; F; Daughter; 19
88; ---; Harold rides a white horse; M; Son; 1

89; Misakohn-miches; Grandmothers knife; M; Husband; 42
90; Chisha-kahdeas; Old nest; F; Wife; 33
91; Bah-son-day; Goes ahead; F; Daughter; 16

92; Duchuis; Muskrat; F; Widow; 54

93; Esash-beeshkeda; Grey blanket; M; Husband; 41
94; Mi-iche-ose; Brings good things; F; Wife; 37
95; Etash-hishis; Red shirt; F; Daughter; 4

96; Eer-kahwash; Bird tail that rattles; M; Husband; 51
97; Kahdeish; Old; F; Wife; 52
98; Awahsha; Gros Ventre; M; Son; 9

99; Dakpitska-cheis; White bear; M; Widower; 88

100; Mahpak-hoos; Comes in a day; M; Husband; 48
101; Mahkaristish; Yearling; F; Wife; 34
102; Eisda-isischish; Loves to go after water; F; Daughter; 16

Census of the __Crow__ Indians of __Crow__ Agency, __Montana__ taken by __E. H. Becker__, United States Indian Agent, __June 30th__, 189__8__

Key: Number; Indian Name; English Name; Sex; Relation; Age.

103; Besha-chedups; Buffalo bull; M; Husband; 38
104; Meakot-kowees; Bad woman; F; Wife; 36
105; me-ichis; Pretty rock; F; Daughter; 8
106; Muna-shuis; Blue wood; M; Son; 13

107; Chatis; Wolf; M; Husband; 47
108; Midesha-doochis; Gets hold of the dead; F; Wife; 42
109; Eskoche-okepis; Shoots the enemy; M; Son; 18
110; Datsuah-doochis; Takes a sinew; F; Mother; 86

111; Dakpitska-cheis; White bear No. 2; M; Husband; 47
112; Minna-nahkuse; By the side of the water; F; Wife; 56
113; Ooet-budekeah-hele-nakuse; George White Bear; M; Son; 27
114; Besha-ekash; Russell W. Bear; M; Son; 23

115; Botsa-kowees; Bad man; M; Husband; 45
116; Bahkeed-lagaks; Black bird; F; Wife; 41

117; Ahpa-duttotoos; Cut ear; M; Husband; 46
118; Ekupa-esash; Big hat; F; Wife; 50

119; Muche-deis; Good luck; M; Husband; 40
120; Chate-heasas; Wolf well known; F; Wife; 38
121; Mea-makpash; Medicine woman; F; Daughter; 16[?]

122; Lagak-heasas; Bird well known; M; Husband; 29
123; Wahpootkamakpash; Medicine otter; F; Wife; 30

124; Echeta-kowees; Bad horse; M; Husband; 26
125; Bachos-ichis; Pretty bullrush; F; Wife; 22

126; Bahkeede-ichis; Pretty blackbird; F; Wife; 62

127; Esukis; Corner of the mouth; M; Husband; 48
128; Ismina-wisha-dochis; Takes pretty scalp; F; Wife; 49
129; Echetagash-eduse; Elk stands up; M; Son; 12

130; Ahse-desh; Shows as he goes; M; Husband; 42
131; Mi-iche-kooshdase; Goes to good things; F; Wife; 45
132; Esuktahsea-helae-nakuse; Among the hawks; F; Daughter; 15
133; Istuka-heasas; Well known arrow; M; Son; 8

134; Oeta-echeta; Iron horse; M; Husband; 24
135; Ahwoosh-akuse; Knows the sweathouse; F; Wife; 19
136; Mean-dichis; Strikes the woman; F; Daughter; 3

Census of the __Crow__ Indians of __Crow__ Agency, __Montana__ taken by __E. H. Becker__, United States Indian Agent, __June 30th__, 189**8**

Key: Number; Indian Name; English Name; Sex; Relation; Age.

137; Chate-kupis; Wolf lays down; M; Husband; 59
138; Isbedia; Kills at the door; F; Wife; 52
139; Ekuh-push; Gets down; M; Son; 19

140; Is-shu-shudish; Backbone; M; Husband; 29
141; Dutch-ka; Twin woman; F; Wife; 32
142; Mahsha-hotskish; Long feather; M; Son; 5

143; Mahsha-wots; One feather; M; Husband; 56
144; Ahta-malapes; Kills first; F; Wife; 64

145; Eche-dudees; Don't Mix; M; Husband; 26
146; Miedershase; Groans; F; Wife; 32

147; Kahdeish; Old; F; Widow; 77

148; Educhesha-heas; Plain left hand; M; Husband; 61
149; Echik-dichis; Strikes first; F; Wife; 51
150; Wutta-makpash; Medicine coyote; F; Daughter; 15

151; Lukpa-sashis; Bright wings; M; Husband; 31
152; Mah-hahchis-lukish-dish; Goes to look at the prisoners; F; Wife; 21
153; Echete-mulakis; Sings on horse; M; Son; 5
154; Echete-maks-kochetish; Horse stays all the time; F; Daughter; 3

155; Ahpewesha; Gros Ventre; M; Husband; 36
156; Ahwa-akuse; Knows the ground; F; Wife; 34
157; Eskoche-karooshes; Runs the enemy; M; Son; 5

158; Budeesh; Horse; M; Father; 41
159; ---; Mary Last Bull; F; Daughter; 1

160; Isba-ichis; Pretty louse; F; Mother; 52
161; Eisda-karooshes; Loves to run; M; Son; 17

162; Minkuus; Onion; F; Mother; 66
163; Mideras-ichis; Does good things; M; Ad Son; 15

164; Nooptah-dichis; Strikes twice; F; Widow; 82

165; Chapes; Whinners; M; Husband; 41
166; Echete-sheedes-ahkinda; Rides a yellow horse; F; Wife; 38
167; Me-makpash-ehas; The other medicine rock; F; Dau; 11

168; Ahkbahdit-napes; Kills picking berries; F; Widow; 63

Census of the __Crow__ Indians of __Crow__ Agency, __Montana__ taken by __E. H. Becker__, United States Indian Agent, __June 30th__, 1898

Key: Number; Indian Name; English Name; Sex; Relation; Age.

169; Ahaukap-meas; Flathead woman; M; Husband; 42
170; Momonots-heahsas; Well known writing; F; Wife; 31
171; Ismahka-wisha; Got a hoop; F; Daughter; 15
172; ---; Lizzie Flathead Woman; F; Daughter; 5
173; ---; Geo. Flathead Woman; M; Son; 1

174; Is-eepse-deesh; Pipe that talks; M; Husband; 31
175; Echa-shesheis; Dirty foot; F; Wife; 52
176; ---; Blanche Brown; F; Niece; 13

177; Ahta-dichis; Kills close; F; [Blank]; 54

178; Istuka-akuse; Knows the gun; M; Husband; 30
179; Esop-pontouch-cheyhaydayus; Among the sheep; F; Wife; 23
180; Bahm-batseeesash; Nobody fights them; M; Son; 4
181; Esashka-ahp-orupish; Finds things with her horse; F; Daughter; 8
182; Aka-mulukis; Sings on top; F; Daughter; 5
183; Chedup-mahkahish; Bull that raises up; M; Father; 64
184; Nash-kose; Small; F; Daughter; 21

185; Ikpam-basash; Robert Raise Up; M; Widower; 26

186; Lagak-deedes; Walking bird; M; Husband; 40
187; ee-sash-ich; Good now; F; Wife; 32

188; Esaska-huke-ahkindas; Rides a spotted horse; F; Mother; 58
189; Osus; Cant shoot him; M; Son; 17
190; Ochis-dichis; Strikes at night; F; Mother; 52
191; Dukeah-desh; Goes to war; M; Son; 30

192; Ootuh-chedups; Bull weasel; M; Husband; 27
193; Esa-kepa; Crooked face; F; Wife; 23
194; Istuka-makpash; Medicine arrow; M; Son; 7
195; Peesh-ah-deus; Rides behind; F; Daughter; 3

196; Chedup-kochetish; Bull all the time; M; [Widower]; 67

197; Malapa; The root; M; Widower; 61

198; Bedupa-bukata-dase; Beaver that passes; F; [Widow]; 36
199; Ahkinda-heahsas; Rides a horse well known; F; Daughter; 10
200; ---; Florence Beaver that passes; F; Daughter; 1

201; Minnahpesh; Swamp flag; F; Widow; 52

Census of the __Crow__ Indians of __Crow__ Agency, __Montana__ taken by __E. H. Becker__, United States Indian Agent, __June 30th__, 189__8__

Key: Number; Indian Name; English Name; Sex; Relation; Age.

202; Echeta-hukish; Spotted horse; M; Husband; 49
203; Is-epse-makpash-ichis; Pretty medicine pipe; F; Wife; 40
204; E-rooptay-chis; By herself; F; Daughter; 10
205; Istuka-ahoos; Plenty arrows; M; Son; 8
206; Opes; Smokes; M; Son; 26
207; Budeesh; Horse; F; Wife; 29

208; Booah-ahseesh; Shows a fish; M; Husband; 52
209; Mahhake-nahks; Shell child; F; Wife; 46
210; Oota-wahtadish; Weasel goes a long way; M; Son; [29]

211; Bishka-kahps; Flat Dog; M; Husband; 54
212; Meah-chedups; Woman bull; F; Wife; 50

213; Otse-muchachis; Chief at night; M; Widower; 62
214; be-du-toch-eas; Little moon; F; Daughter; 3

215; Dahpitsa-eahkotish; Little bear; M; Father; 62
216; Mahma-nudeis; Does things hard; M; Son; 21

217; Ope-edupish; Fat tobacco; M; Husband; 73
218; Dakup-makpash; Medicine calf; F; Wife; 70
219; Mahpookta-botsots; Strong otter; M; Son; 12

220; Ahpaka-hedera-dakpitsch; Bear in a cloud; M; Husband; 41
221; Miooetshede-esash; Big lark; F; Wife; 46
222; Esakakasha-manakis; Blake White Bear; M; Son; 15

223; Eep-shedish; Yellow tail; M; Husband; 36
224; ---; Mrs. S. C. Davis; F; Wife; 32
225; Mei-rauk-shay; Summer; M; Son; 10
226; Alack-chee-ichis; Has good coos; M; Son; 6

227; Nah-kaps; Flat back; M; Husband; 52
228; Ahpa-doochis; Takes together; F; Wife; 56
229; Ahsha-hedere-malapes; Kills in camp; F; Niece; 23

230; Ishda-daka; Grey eyes; F; Widow; 62

231; Chedup-akookish; Dummy bull; M; Father; 62
232; Mitet-duspis; Passes everything; M; Son; 24

233; Eem-botsesh; Blood man; M; Husband; 40
234; Ahwaka-meas; Woman on top of the ground; F; Wife; 28
235; Ikpahne-ich; Pretty medicine; F; Daughter; 6

Census of the __Crow__ Indians of __Crow__ Agency, __Montana__ taken by __E. H. Becker__, United States Indian Agent, __June 30th__, 189__8__

Key: Number; Indian Name; English Name; Sex; Relation; Age.

236; Dakpitska-ahway-roopeas; Bear goes to the other ground; M; Husband; 29
237; Kookoomish; Kittie Medicine Tail; F; Wife; 19

238; Dayka-ahspittesh; Black eagle; M; Husband; 32
239; Esa-kepa; Crooked face; F; Wife; 25
240; Iswahka-miotchedish; Lucky hoop; M; Son; 12
241; Dakpitska-ahn-duish; Bear that raises his paw; M; Son; 2
242; ---; Irene mountain; F; Sister; 15

243; Cheetaka-eahkoskat; Little prairie chicken; M; Husband; 50
244; Ahsha-ekash; Looks at the lodge; F; Wife; 52

245; Mahkawas; The bread; M; Husband; 37
246; Mekas-besas; Stoops to charge; F; Wife; 38
247; Esukcha-meas; Sparrow hawk woman; F; Mother; 78

248; Biskka-kahdeas; Old dog; M; Husband; 66
249; Me-heahsas; Well known rock; F; Wife; 55
250; Aska-wuts; Harry old dog; M; Ad son; 11

251; Eak-kin-hish-sis; Red in the chin; F; ---; 23

252; Eskochea-basash; Charges the enemy; F; Mother; 61
253; Suah-oowich; Thunder iron; M; Son; 22

254; Ahpit-kahdeas; Old crane; M; Husband; 32
255; ---; Ella Farwell; F; Wife; 28
256; ---; Mary Crane; F; Daughter; 7

257; Peah-noops; Two stinks; M; Husband; 33
258; Mea-sheedes; Yellow woman; F; Wife; 33
259; Bahshotse-basash; Rock that runs; M; Son; 9
260; Echeete-lagak; Horse bird; M; Ad son; 10

261; Besha-naks; Buffalo calf; F; Mother; 63
262; Booah-lagak; Fish bird; M; Son; 37
263; It-tah-um-bit-dosh; Pretty near fell; M; Son; 23

264; Ahpit-dakpitska; Bear crane; M; Husband; 59
265; Ische-itse; Pretty hair; F; Wife; 47
266; Dakpitska-naks; Bear child; M; Son; 11
267; Daykoosh-naks; Young eagle; M; Son; 4
268; ---; George Bear Crane; M; Son; 2

269; Isminua-wish-napes; Kills with a scalp; F; Widow; 60

Census of the __Crow__ Indians of __Crow__ Agency, __Montana__ taken by __E. H. Becker__, United States Indian Agent, __June 30th__, 189__8__

Key: Number; Indian Name; English Name; Sex; Relation; Age.

270; Botsa-nahme-napes; Kills three men; F; Mother; 46
271; Minnepahk-ichis; Ben Long Ear; M; Son; 20
272; Ahwokochedush-hela-ahmach; Sits among the cedars; F; Daughter; 15
273; Ahpay-sheedes; Yellow leaves; M; Son; 8
274; Noopta-cheis; Herbert Long Ear; M; Son; 24

275; Chedup-ehas; The other bull; M; Husband; 34
276; Ah-kish-koos; Gives to the sun; F; Wife; 22
277; Daykoosh-mahks; Eagle above; M; Son; 8

278; Ikpahne-ehas; The other medicine; M; Husband; 29
279; Ahwooch-deedis; Walks to the hole; F; Wife; 22
280; Makpash-heahsas; Shoots plain medicine; F; Daughter; 5

281; Iche-kahnetsesh; Bear claw; M; Husband; 38
282; Utsewaks-ahoos; Begs plenty; F; Wife; 32
283; Makpash-ope-ahoos; Medicine rock above; M; Son; 12
284; Peda-kosh; Brings ten times; F; Daughter; 3

285; Etashda-cheis; White shirt; M; Husband; 68
286; Dich-heahsas; Strikes well known; F; Wife; 64
287; Esaska-eko-cheesh; Horse turns around; M; Son; 29
288; ukcheesa-malapesh; Kills over beyond the other; F; Daughter; 27

289; Besheesh; Shavings; M; Husband; 56
290; Hooche-sash; Wind; F; Wife; 51

291; ---; Albert Anderson; M; Husband; 29
292; ---; Sarah Anderson; F; Wife; 23
293; ---; Fannie Anderson; F; Daughter; 5
294; ---; Helen Anderson; F; Daughter; 1

295; Echetegashes; The elk; M; Husband; 48
296; Ashu-makotesash; Big head high up; F; Wife; 42
297; Meneash-koopskuis-chedish; Hunts the Sioux; F; Daughter; 4

298; Poputa-naks; Frank Bethune; M; Batchelor[sic]; 24

299; Hoksah-napis; Comes and kills; F; Mother; 52
300; Ash-itse; Pretty river; F; Daughter; 8
301; Nas-chas; The other heart; M; Son; 24

302; Ahmbatseda-ahoos; Looks much; F; Widow; 68

303; Esash-chedup; Blanket bull; M; Husband; 30
304; Unda-ichis; Goes pretty; F; Wife; 29

Census of the __Crow__ Indians of __Crow__ Agency, __Montana__ taken by __E. H. Becker__, United States Indian Agent, __June 30th__, 189__8__

Key: Number; Indian Name; English Name; Sex; Relation; Age.

305; Botsa-miesash; Big man; M; Husband; 34
306; Minneah-pesh; Swamp flag; F; Wife; 38
307; Istuka-ahseesh; Shows his gun Michael B Man; M; Son; 11

308; Noopa-malapes; Kills twice; F; [Widow]; 62

309; Ahpa-esash; Big nose; M; Husband; 53
310; Mi-iche-doochis; Takes good things; F; Wife; 46
311; Bahsatsie-basonda; Steals on camp ahead; F; Daughter; 10

312; Nahsa-tays; Humpback; M; Husband; 50
313; Heles-beasash; Runs among them; F; Wife; 46

314; Ookah-sheis; Dust; M; ---; 30

315; Masheda-kotish; Julia Bad Boy; F; Mother; 20
316; Ahsay-chulees; Sings in camp; M; Son; 5
317; ---; Wesley Bad Boy; M; Son; 1

318; Misk-sheis; Talks everything; M; Husband; 48
319; Botsa-wot-napes; Kills one man; F; Wife; 41
320; Echete-cheis-ahkudis; Rides a white bellied horse; F; Daughter; 12

321; Karooshis-ehas; Dont run; M; Husband; 32
322; Andutsedush-heahsas; Slides down well known; F; Wife; 37
323; Minnahpesh-shoos; Plenty swamp flags; F; Daughter; 14
324; Chustak-ahkindis; Rides a greyhorse; M; Son; 10
325; ---; Mary Dont[sic] Run; F; Daughter; 1
326; Bekashes; The Bannock; F; Mother; 72

327; Eespe-ekash; Looks at the lion; F; Widow; 64

328; Chate-cheakaps; Young wolf; F; Widow; 53

329; Chedup-dashes; Bull tongue; M; Husband; 57
330; Echete-ahkin-doochis; Catches on the horses; F; Wife; 43
331; Eke-kahdish; Homer Bull Tongue; M; Son; 20
332; Echete-akahps; Thomas Jefferson; M; Son; 28

333; Helekas-ash; Along the hillside; M; Husband; 51
334; Ah-shay-dane-dee-chise; Strikes in camp; F; Wife; 40
335; Isminats-ich; Old shield; M; Son; 14
336; Bah-put-tah-way-chice; Sits to the otter; F; Daughter; 4

337; Eepse-mahka-kala-napes; Kills the one with med. pipe; F; Widow; 69

Census of the __Crow__ Indians of __Crow__ Agency, __Montana__ taken by __E. H. Becker__, United States Indian Agent, __June 30th__, 189__8__

Key: Number; Indian Name; English Name; Sex; Relation; Age.

338; Oouka-manakish; Crazy sister-in-law; M; Husband; 70
339; Makuka-ich; Carries good; F; Wife; 55
340; Esuklasa-eps-cheis; White tailed hawk; F; Daughter; 19
341; Chedups-echete; Hard heart; F; Daughter; 6

342; Basuk-ose; Goes ahead; M; Husband; 48
343; Isminats-ich; Pretty shield; F; Wife; 42
344; Ichis; Good; M; Son; 15
345; Meah-kots; Small woman; F; Daughter; 5

346; Meshodechitse; Medicine shell; F; Widow; 44

347; Botseah-bedas; Pine fire; F; Widow; 25

348; Echete-mulukis; Horse that sings; F; Mother; 31
349; Istuka-mahks; High arrow; M; Son; 5

350; Hoop-itsahkahoh; Top of the moccasin; M; Father; 24
351; Etash-shooachat; Blue shirt; M; Son; 4
352; Beka-haredich; Among the grass; F; Mother; 51

353; Ahm-botsots-heahsas; Strong well known; M; Husband; 34
354; Ahshay-hedra-dichis; Strikes in camp; F; Wife; 20
355; ---; Jane Well Known; F; Daughter; 1

356; Kahkootsa; Drunkard; M; Husband; 42
357; Bah-dahe-dane-bahdakish; Sings in the woods; F; Wife; 41
358; Mea-nakose-nahks; Young turtle woman; F; Daughter; 5
359; Oo-muttish; Iron; F; Sister; 60

360; Chate-hishes; Red wolf; M; Husband; 27
361; Besha-ekash; Comes to see the buffalo; F; Wife; 20
362; ---; Laura red wolf; F; Daughter; 1

363; Halup-eahkots; Small waist; M; Husband; 62
364; Ikpanne-maks; Medicine high up; F; Wife; 53

365; Ahwakooda-kahdish; Old all the time; M; Husband; 34
366; Istuka-makula; Shows a child; F; Wife; 30
367; Arachuka-noak; Works on the farm; M; Son; 8
368; Botsaytse; Chief; M; Son; 7
---; ---; Susie Old all the Time; F; Daughter; 1

369; Eakook-sheedees; Yellow coyote; F; Mother; 70
370; Meshak-naks; Young duck; F; Ad Dau.; 15

Census of the __Crow__ Indians of __Crow__ Agency, __Montana__ taken by __E. H. Becker__, United States Indian Agent, __June 30th__, 189__8__

Key: Number; Indian Name; English Name; Sex; Relation; Age.

371; Edukush; The meat; M; Husband; 42
372; Dudish; The back; F; Wife; 45
373; Besha-mulukis; Buffalo that sings; F; Daughter; 7
374; Nakose-nahks; Young turtle; F; Daughter; 3

375; Chate-nak-shedees; Young yellow wolf; M; Husband; 43
376; Doochis-heahsas; Takes well known; F; Wife; 43

377; Eahwookose; Inside the mouth; M; Husband; 39
378; Esutsehoom-meas; Sage woman; F; Wife; 32
379; Ahshmtse-makpash; The song is medicine; F; Daughter; 7

380; ---; Michael O'Brien; M; Orphan; 17

381; Dakpitska-kahdeas; Old bear; M; Husband; 44
382; Makupa-seesh; Hail shows; F; Wife; 37
383; Lagaka-akuse; Bird that shows; M; Son; 16
384; Ika-ahoos; Lots of stars; M; Son; 13
385; Ahshuah-dichis; Strikes inside the house; F; Dauthetr[sic]; 8
386; Eeskotchitsa-maluk-ichis; Strawberry sings pretty; F; Daughter; 6
387; Bus-suck-kose; Goes ahead; M; Son; 2

388; Dakpitska-hotskish; Long bear; M; Husband; 50
389; Eahkooka-asadish; Fox goes out; F; Wife; 50
390; Meshodechitse-lagaks; Medicine shell bird; M; Son; 17
391; Eshpeahisha-kahdeish; Horace Long Bear; M; Son; 24

392; Dotsuish; Muskrat; F; Widow; 78

393; Wahpookta-hotskish; Long otter; M; Husband; 58
394; Botseish; Pine; F; Wife; 60
395; Ahwot-saya; Ground cedar; F; Daughter; 11

396; Aritsumbitsa-kahdeish; Falls down old; M; Husband; 26
397; Isminats-makpash; Medicine shield; F; Wife; 26
398; Mea-hotchkis; Tall woman; F; Daughter; 8
399; Eikos-hishes; Red feather around his arm; M; Son; 4
400; Minnettseesh; The moon; M; Brother; 27

401; Poputa-heahsas; Plain owl; M; Husband; 38
402; Mea-shpittish; Black woman; F; Wife; 36

403; Isekoshe-noopis; Two whistles; M; Batchelor[sic]; 40
404; Isdots-ichis; Good to prisoners; F; Mother; 85

Census of the __Crow__ Indians of __Crow__ Agency, __Montana__ taken by __E. H. Becker__, United States Indian Agent, __June 30th__, 189__8__

Key: Number; Indian Name; English Name; Sex; Relation; Age.

405; Kee-osh; He says; M; Husband; 38
406; Bedupa-ekoshees; Beaver that stretches; F; Wife; 50
407; ---; Bravo; M; Son; 9

408; Ishtopish; Eyes open; F; Widow; 61

409; Dahkopoos; Cuts a hole in it; M; Husband; 33
410; Mea-daka; Grey woman; F; Wife; 38

411; Eep-kahdeas; Old tail; M; Husband; 41
412; Mi-iche-okepis; Shoots pretty things; F; Wife; 19

413; Askindes; Holds on; M; Husband; 61
414; Ahwa-akinakuse; Stands on top of the ground; F; Wife; 52
415; Oota-hotchkish; Long weasel; F; Sister; 48

416; Wahpookta-ahkaps; Otter comes out of the water; F; Widow; 64

419; Mahsheandachee; Dreamer; M; Husband; 52
420; Istuka-doochis; Takes a gun; F; Wife; 50
421; Daka-ichis-amach; Eagle sits down; M; Son; 15

422; Botsa-mahnahs; Paints her forehead; M; Husband; 48
423; Eskochea-biorup; Finds his enemy; F; Wife; 50
424; Puk-iees; Holds it in the mouth; M; Son; 17
425; Isshotse-mau-det; Horses goes in front; M; Son; 5
426; Shenokshe-mulukis; Sings on top; F; Daughter; 15
427; Usmiha-koosh-basash; Charges on the enemy; F; Mother; 72

428; Mune-skoop-doochis; Takes a crooked stick; F; Widow; 82

429; Umbich-esash; Don't fall down; M; Husband; 42
430; Esash-beduppa; Beaver robe; F; Wife; 48

431; Kahnista; Small; M; Husband; 33
432; Eshippish-day-ichis; Goes to mud pretty; F; Wife; 28
433; Beeop-huche-naks; Young hawk; M; Son; 2

434; Minekashe-ahoos; Plenty butterfly; M; Husband; 45
435; Esasku-noops; Two horses; F; Wife; 46
436; Minetotse-ish-ekash; Looks at the sun; F; Daughter; 19

437; Nak-paka-ish; Child in the mouth; M; Husband; 54
438; Kahdeas; Old; F; Wife; 52
439; Ahcheke-ichis; The spy; M; Son; 19
440; Eskoche-doochis; Joe Child in the Mouth; M; Son; 22

Census of the __Crow__ Indians of __Crow__ Agency, __Montana__ taken by __E. H. Becker__, United States Indian Agent, __June 30th__, 189__8__

Key: Number; Indian Name; English Name; Sex; Relation; Age.

441; Esa-kahnishta; Little face; M; Husband; 77
442; Noop-dichis; Strikes twice; F; Wife; 86

443; Petakus; Ten; F; ---; 20

444; Mahshooooshshesh[sic]; Red Plume; M; Husband; 68
445; Peritse-asees; Crow that shows; F; Wife; 51

446; Munask-malapes; Kills by the woods; F; Widow; 58

447; Booah-hishes; Red fish; M; Husband; 48
448; Mishodeschitse-dichis; Strikes the medicine rock; F; Wife; 44
449; Bahkeda-basash; Blackbird in front; M; Brother; 56

450; Mahkesh; Gives away; M; Husband; 40
451; Biorup-heahsas; Finds things well known; F; Wife; 26

452; Ahsha-heletam-basash; Charges through camp; M; Husband; 57
453; Oomutish; Iron; F; Wife; 51
454; Ich-kahdeas; Makes himself old; M; Son; 21
455; Besha-amach; Sits on the buffalo; F; Daughter; 23

456; Besha-chedup; Buffalo bull; M; Father; 31
457; Dakpitska-ahsuse; James Carpenter; M; Son; 16

458; Ushmiha-chedish; Enemy hunter; M; Husband; 66
459; Kotseish; Shakes; F; Wife; 56

460; Shebah-shadish; Among the fog; M; Husband; 39
461; Echete-akuse; Horse on the other side; F; Wife; 27
462; Makpash-ekash; Likes her medicine; M; Son; 10
463; Maeshoditchitse-heahsas; Well known shell; F; Daughter; 5
464; Ook-sheedis; Yellow deer; M; Son; 4

465; Ahwahkuan-dakpitske; Bear in the middle; M; Husband; 40
466; Echeta-achis; Knows a horse; F; Wife; 34
467; Awoosha-kakish; Addie; F; Daughter; 21
468; Kowees; Ruth; F; Daughter; 11

469; Dakpitska-botsots; Strong bear; M; Batchelor[sic]; 26

470; Chedup-shespitta; Black bull; M; Father; 52
471; ---; Dexter; M; Son; 20

472; Bedupa-okeah-duis; Beaver that slides; M; Husband; 61
473; Ducth-ka; Twin woman; F; Wife; 63

Census of the __Crow__ Indians of __Crow__ Agency, __Montana__ taken by __E. H. Becker__, United States Indian Agent, __June 30th__, 189__8__

Key: Number; Indian Name; English Name; Sex; Relation; Age.

474; Chate-ewotsodish; Busy wolf; M; Husband; 62
475; Minmahpesh; Swamp flag; F; Wife; 37

476; Shegak-kahpa; Flat boy; M; Batchelor[sic]; 38

477; Unmeathe; Bank; M; Husband; 33
478; Mahsha-ich-meas; Pretty feather woman; F; Wife; 29

479; Lagak-cheah-noops; Two white birds; M; Husband; 47
480; Ahpeahne-makpash; Medicine porcupine; F; Wife; 46
481; Besha-maks; Buffalo high; M; Son; 18
482; Besha-naks-noops; Among the buffalo; F; Daughter; 8
483; Etash-daka; Eagle shirt; M; Son; 4

484; Ahwoshose; Gros Ventre; F; Widow; 72

---; ~~Asla-kudish; Slings his arm; M; Husband; --~~
485; Bahsuk-naks; Turtle child; F; Widow; 63

486; Oota-hukish; Spotted weasel; F; [Widow]; 33
487; Botseah-heahsas; Fights well known; M; Ad Son; 19

488; Maudut-kudesh; Pounded meat; M; Husband; 56
489; Mahsha-undichis; Strikes feathers; F; Wife; 54

490; Mahsha-kudesh; Holds the feather; M; Husband; 48
491; Dakoshes; Eagle; F; Wife; 54
492; Besha-hishes; Throws off on the horse; M; Son; 15

493; Ahwahwun-lagaks; Bird in the ground; M; Husband; 30
494; Napes-ekash; Looks at the one that kills; F; Wife; 35
495; Minduksa-ekuroos; Runs toward the fort; M; Son; 6

496; Wutta-eahkoots; Little wolf; M; Widower; 64
497; Esdkoche-ahoos-dich; Strikes plenty enemies; F; Sister; 58
498; Dukedea-akuse; Knows the war; M; Son; 20

499; Asulktuah-basash; Runs between them; M; Husband; 25
500; Ahwoosh-heahsas; Sweathouse well known; F; Wife; 18

501; Dotska-; The twins; M; Husband; 34
502; Ikpahne-makpash; Medicine porcupine; F; Wife; 56
503; Ekupa-ich; Pretty hat; F; Mother; 78

504; Chedupa-seesh; Bull that shows; M; Hub; 28
505; Echete; Horse; F; Wife; 27

Census of the __Crow__ Indians of __Crow__ Agency, __Montana__ taken by __E. H. Becker__, United States Indian Agent, __June 30th__, 189__8__

Key: Number; Indian Name; English Name; Sex; Relation; Age.

506; Eskoche-aseesh; Spies the enemy; M; Son; 4

507; Chate-dakpitska; Bear wolf; M; Widower; 58

508; Ahmako-istisha-naks; Young swallow; M; Husband; 34
509; Oote-ewandies; Plays with the weasel; F; Wife; 20

510; Issama-malapes; Kills on her own ground; F; Mother; 58
511; Daka-makpash; Medicine eagle; M; Son; 19

512; Oowuta-ahpies; Iron necklace; F; Widow; 82

513; Nashada-esash; Charges strong; M; Husband; 57
514; Itshades; Kills in the track; F; Wife; 56
515; Bishka-botsots; Charles Strong; M; Son; 13
516; ---; Mary Charges Strong; F; Daughter; 8
517; Lagak-naks; Bird child; F; Ad Dau.; 17

518; Chate-nakish; Leads a wolf; M; Husband; 48
519; Naksha-undichis; Strikes first; F; Wife; 52
520; Mahsha-hishes-heahsas; Well known red feather; F; Gr. Daughter; 6

521; Ahmuapes; The kicker; M; Husband; 57
522; Arleunda-aches; Knows the road; F; Wife; 58

523; Eseah-koosh; Covers his face; M; Widower; 48
524; Esha-hishes-shedees; Yellow red paint; F; Daughter; 3

525; Chadupa-eda-ekash; Bull goes hunting; M; Husband; 71
526; Daka-wahtis; One buffalo calf; F; Wife; 57

527; E-o-dish; Full mouth; M; Husband; 42
528; Bedupa-ehas; The other beaver; F; Wife; 46
529; Bea-e-hosh; The other woman; F; Daughter; 13

530; Ahsho-malapes; Kills behind camp; F; Widow; 60

531; Ahshuputsuah-dooich; Gets one horn; M; Husband; 42
532; Isminats-budwasich; Shield at the door; F; Wife; 33
533; Ischesa-hela-amach; Sits toward the nest; F; Daughter; 11
~~534; Botsa-cheakoosh-napes; Kills five men; F; Daughter; 2~~

534; Dakpitska-ahoos; Plenty bears; M; Widower; 58
535; Is-os-kay-bah-chate-chis; Alexander Upshaw; M; Nephew; 22

536; Ooet-budeka-dooch; Takes a gun; M; Husband; 35

Census of the __Crow__ Indians of __Crow__ Agency, __Montana__ taken by __E. H. Becker__, United States Indian Agent, __June 30th__, 189__8__

Key: Number; Indian Name; English Name; Sex; Relation; Age.

537; Botsuah-tush; Sweet grass; F; Wife; 43

538; Shegak-amach; Bad boy; M; Husband; 31
539; Eka-ahpka-amach; Sits with a star; F; Wife; 21
540; ---; David bad boy; M; Son; 1

541; Eshash-heahsas; Plain face; F; Widow; 56

542; Isoeet-botseeh; Smart iron; M; Widower; 27

543; Epeahkot-esash; Big magpie; M; Father; 49
544; Lagak-beepish; Snow bird; M; Son; 9

545; Mahedish; Does anything; M; Husband; 38
546; Ahwaku-cheduah-neaks; Young ground cedar; F; Wife; 44
547; Echete-doochis; Takes a Pinto horse; F; Daughter; 7

548; Shegak-doochis; Boy that grabs; M; Husband; 53
549; Mekeaespe-doochis; Takes hold of the cloth; F; Wife; 57

550; Ahsha-okepish; Shoots the lodge; M; Husband; 52
551; Ikpahne-ekash; Looks at the medicine; F; Wife; 44

552; Ahrocheis; Stops; M; Husband; 30
553; Esasha-ich; Paints her face pretty; F; Wife; 28
554; Opish-ekash; Looks at the tobacco; M; Son; 11
555; Noopta-malapes; Kills twice; F; Daughter; 6
556; Istuka-mulukis; Sings to the arrow; M; Son; 4

557; Ahlud-esuhsh; Big shoulder blade; M; Husband; 46
558; Beshay-herasus; Well known buffalo; F; Wife; 35
559; Arap-apushay-dichesay; Bullets dont[sic] strike him; M; Son; 5

560; Bah-kaht-konsees; Bad baby; M; Brother; 62

561; Chedup-ah-kde-duse; Stands over a bull; M; Husband; 26
562; Ah-bah-de-itchis; Pretty medicine; F; Wife; 22
563; She-cack-bah-epash; Medicine boy; M; Son; 5

564; Chedup-quasah-dataish; Bull in sight; M; Husband; 28
565; Ahdo-chea-beas; Woman where she stops; F; Wife; 34
566; Ah-bah-keas-sash; Cloud shows plain; M; Son; 14
567; Ah-dean-day-ah-chetis; Follows the track; F; Daughter; 9

568; It-shoc-daytay; No shin bone; M; Husband; 44
569; Mahkeede-speedis; Yellow blackbird; F; Wife; 44

Census of the __Crow__ Indians of __Crow__ Agency, __Montana__ taken by __E. H. Becker__, United States Indian Agent, __June 30th__, 1898

Key: Number; Indian Name; English Name; Sex; Relation; Age.

570; Cheedup etahsich; Henry Shin Bone; M; Son; 20
571; Bah-cup-pah-deedish; Lizard that walks; F; Daughter; 11
572; Nahmis; Three; F; Mother; 72

573; Ahshkay-shopis; Four balls; M; Husband; 56
574; Meshodechitse-nishes; Red rock; F; Wife; 54
575; Kahdeeasas; Not old; M; Son; 8
576; Chayt-aputs; Wolf that looks back; M; Son; 22

577; Ahkabos; Froze; M; Husband; 35
578; Mahpay-e-kahsh; Sees in a day; F; Wife; 32
579; Espeah-kis-she-kah-deas; Old bobcat; M; Son; 5
---; Hay-day-de-qu-pish; Gets down among them; M; Son; 1

580; Mahray-keir-ahplis; Shell on the neck; M; Husband; 35
581; Ise-meneas; His door; F; Wife; 38
582; Cheedup-ay-koos; Bull that knows; M; Son; 13

583; Minnay-e-koos-chis; Comes out of the water; F; Widow; 64

584; Ahoo-ahk-ichis; Pretty on top; M; Husband; 34
585; Itshooaprsich; Pretty back of the neck; F; Wife; 33
586; Mah-hahk-ichis; Plenty shells; M; Son; 8
587; Bee-dup-che-sus; Beaver tail; F; Daughter; 4

588; Butsay-tse-dichis; Strikes the chief; F; Widow; 60

589; Meshodelhitse-wahkpahs; Medicine shell; F; Widow; 58

590; Chees-wahkpahs; Medicine tail; M; Husband; 40
591; Itshe-wahkpahs; She is medicine; F; Wife; 37

592; Cheedeer-esahs; Not afraid; M; Husband; 40
593; Noopis; Two; F; Wife; 48
594; Bah-put-chee-keep-beas; Ant woman; F; Daughter; 9
595; Bee-day-ock-key-day-itchis; Good shell; M; Son; 5

596; Escheeta-nevsaus; Knows his horse; M; Husband; 38
597; Mekahshay-hishis; Fat snake; F; Wife; 48

598; Ahpit-sheedis; Yellow crane; M; Husband; 54
599; Uk-pa-had-dee 'is[sic]; Does things together; F; Wife; 42

600; Push-ah-kos; Cut; M; [Widower]; 42
601; Ahta-huk-is-dichis; Strikes the painted arm; F; Mother; 82

Census of the __Crow__ Indians of __Crow__ Agency, __Montana__ taken by __E. H. Becker__, United States Indian Agent, __June 30th__, 189**8**

Key: Number; Indian Name; English Name; Sex; Relation; Age.

602; Wahkpahs-ne-ahoos; Plenty medicine; F; [Widow]; 42
603; Bedupdayts; No revenge; F; Daughter; 10

604; Napk-ahwot-nee 'as[sic]; One child woman; F; Widow; 54

605; Ahke-mah-kaweish; Hoop on the forehead; M; Husband; 50
606; Ahshay-whoo's-aychis; Knows the whole camp; F; Wife; 57
607; Mussick-awats; One turtle; M; Son; 8
608; Medesha-dooch; Takes the dead; F; Mother; 70

609; Ikpah-ahoos; Plenty wing; M; Husband; 48
610; Ismant-heahsas; Plain shield; F; Wife; 48

611; Aka-dundish; Stands on top; M; Husband; 26
612; Eukupae-wishdish; Strikes the hat; F; Wife; 20
613; Iagak-heahsas; Big bird; M; Son; 6

614; Ay-kuse; Knows; M; Husband; 25
615; Echick-heas; Gets there first; F; Wife; 21
616; ---; Sarah Knows; F; Daughter; 3
617; Edwea; Dummy; F; Mother; 52

618; Mumasen dichis[sic]; Strikes by the side of the water; F; Mother; 82
619; Menacheis; White goose; M; Son; 47

620; Almashus; The fog; M; Husband; 70
621; Makula-woof-dichis; Takes two guns; F; Wife; 60
622; ---; Frank Shively; M; Son; 26

623; Minooisa-kahdius; Old alligator; M; Husband; 54
624; Chut-naepis; Kills on the lookout; F; Wife; 59

625; ---; Tom Laforge; M; Husband; 33
626; Meeahkadius; Old woman; F; Wife; 32

627; Koasha; Runner; M; Husband; 46
628; Icheat-ekash; Looks at tobacco; F; Wife; 46
629; Bee-shay-ahk-ah-wah-chis; Sits on the buffalo; F; Daughter; 9

630; Dachpitsay-beedahs; Fire bear; M; Husband; 49
631; Natsaundooch; Takes plenty prisoners; F; Wife; 46
632; Itsup-eduse; The tail stands up; M; Son; 20
633; Be-ah-hush-kay; Long woman; F; Ad Dau.; 12

634; Ekeeka-dase; Goes together; M; Husband; 31
635; Makapo-ich; Pretty hail; F; Wife; 29

Census of the __Crow__ Indians of __Crow__ Agency, __Montana__ taken by __E. H. Becker__, United States Indian Agent, __June 30th__, 189**8**

Key: Number; Indian Name; English Name; Sex; Relation; Age.

636; Oatah-ich; Jane goes together; F; Daughter; 8
637; ---; Wesley Goes Together; M; Son; 2
638; Uksempash; Strikes the painted face; F; Mother; 74

639; Cheas-kuch-kish; Spotted tail; M; Husband; 48
640; Cotah-shee-dish; Yellow all over; F; Wife; 38
641; Etoshday-bah-pash; Medicine dress; F; Daughter; 16
642; Echeen-bah-pash; Medicine horse; F; Daughter; 5

643; Bit-quash; Onion; M; Husband; 43
644; Bershea-bah-pash; Medicine buffalo cow; F; Wife; 37
645; Ahwahka-wah-kess-sas; Plain mountain; F; Daughter; 7
646; Undahshay-day-bahhah-chis; Charges strong; M; Son; 4

647; Ah-chook-coode-day-dush; Strikes and strikes again; F; Widow; 39

648; Duck-bit-chay-beas; Bear woman; F; Mother; 52
649; Bee-bush-sas; Rock ahead; F; Daughter; 13

650; ---; Josh Buffalo; M; Husband; 36
651; Ah-kean-bah-dahcheakeassos; Ties a knot on top of her head; F; Wife; 28

652; Kadeas; Old; F; Widow; 48
653; Beehayday-dahwahchis; Sits among the rocks; M; Son; 10
654; ---; James Hill; M; Son; 24

655; ---; Richard Wallace; M; Husband; 32
656; Bash-it-chis; Pretty feather; F; Wife; 30
657; ---; Susie Wallace; F; Daughter; 4

658; Ah-cook-bee-dash; Hears Fire; M; Husband; 34
659; ---; Mary Bompard; F; Wife; 37

660; Ah-puch-kay; Long neck; M; Husband; 30
661; Ush-cosh-ut-tah-dup-pace; Kills close to camp; F; Wife; 38

662; ---; Louis Bompard; M; Husband; 33
663; ---; Lois Bompard; F; Wife; 29
664; ---; Peter Bompard; M; Son; 8
665; ---; Rosa Bompard; F; Daughter; 3

666; ---; Rosa Peters; F; Mother; 26
667; ---; Arthur Peters; M; Son; 9
668; ---; Elsie Peters; F; Daughter; 7
669; ---; Alfred Peters; M; Son; 5
670; ---; George Peters; M; Son; 3

Census of the __Crow__ Indians of __Crow__ Agency, __Montana__ taken by __E. H. Becker__, United States Indian Agent, __June 30th__, 189__8__

Key: Number; Indian Name; English Name; Sex; Relation; Age.

671; ---; Joseph Martinez; M; Brother; 26

672; Chate-dock-coo-chis; Young Hairy Wolf; M; Husband; 53
673; Ahdahche-waycooitchis; Comes from war pretty; F; Wife; 49
674; Up-pay-huck-kay; Long nose; M; Son; 19
675; Bah-cup-ysay-keas-sos; Striped snake well known; F; Daughter; 10

676; Dah-sea-hash; The other heart; F; Widow; 53
677; Bea-at-tah-itchis; Pretty coyote; M; Son; 23

678; Benn-da-chis; Strikes the water; F; Widow; 71
679; Dah-pittosh; Grasshopper; M; Son; 21

680; Bee-dane-dah-coos; Stops by the water; F; Widow; 28
681; Bea-ah-ha; Plenty woman; F; Daughter; 7

682; Chee-dup-chees; Grey Bull; M; Husband; 60
683; Bah-duck-cah-peas; Going about; F; Wife; 58
684; Bish-push; Alder; M; Son; 17
685; Bea-itchis; Pretty rock; F; Daughter; 8
686; Duck-bea-cheacock-indas; Rides a white hipped horse; M; Son; 21

687; Bah-chea-keas-sos; Fights well known; M; Husband; 35
688; Bah-aye-chaise; Knows everything; F; Wife; 34
689; Cheah-key-sos; Sage hen; M; Son; 13
690; Esoskah-cheeseday kaybah chach chis; Grey horse chief; M; Son; 2

691; Beedayitch-shedayopitche; Smokes; M; Husband; 70
692; Bah-pittay-dov-pus; Two otters; F; Wife; 69
693; Ush-hay-dosh-days; Goes to camp; M: Ad Son; 16

694; Echee-duch-days; Goes to the horses; M; Husband; 33
695; Dock-op-pah-dee-chis; Strikes mother and child; F; Wife; 24
696; Bah-euch-euis; Striped snake; F; Daughter; 3

697; Ah-dah-sea-ut-hoos; Shows plenty; M; Husband; 40
698; Bea-ha-wat-tosh; One woman; F; Wife; 42
699; Bah-chea-des-cha-beas; Woman herder; F; Daughetr[sic]; 4

700; Cheedup-e-hosh; The other bull; M; Husband; 30
701; Um-bah-day-es-sos; Goes farther along; F; Wife; 32
702; Dead-cosh-bah-such; High Eagle; M; son; 8
703; Uck-ea-chase; Knows; F; Mother; 68

704; Ah-wah-kah-we-sos; Big mountain; M; Husband; 41
705; Cuck-kay-dupe-dooch-chis; Takes two lances; F; Wife; 51

Census of the __Crow__ Indians of __Crow__ Agency, __Montana__ taken by __E. H. Becker__, United States Indian Agent, __June 30th__, 189__8__

Key: Number; Indian Name; English Name; Sex; Relation; Age.

706; Ish-co-chea-ha-day-dose; Runs against his enemy; M; Son; 18
707; E-chu-dah-keas-sos; Well known horse; F; Daughter; 6

708; Chea-say-itchay-bahdaykah; Pretty tail; M; Husband; 50
709; Un-dee-dich-chis; Walks pretty; F; Wife; 48

710; Bich-pus; Spaniard; M; Husband; 28
711; Bah-chick-kah-coo-deechis; Looks at one comes from war; F; Wife; 26

712; E-shoes; Back of the neck; M; Husband; 68
713; Bash-cheam-beas; White woman; F; Wife; 63

714; Bea-doo-pus; Two women; F; [Widow]; 59

715; Ah-way-e-kosh; Looks at the ground; M; Husband; 35
716; Bah-dah-kiss; Sings; F; Wife; 19

717; Dash-day-tush; No name; F; Widow; 77

718; Cah-cay-itcheas; Pretty lance; F; ---; 30

719; Op-chay-keas-sos; Voice well known; M; Husband; 50
720; Uck-bah-chay-days; Goes hunting; F; Wife; 48

721; ---; Katherine Scott; F; Mother; 26
722; ---; Paul Scott; M; Son; 7
723; ---; Emma Scott; F; Daughter; 4
724; ---; Pearl Scott; F; Daughter; 3

725; ---; Frank Shane; M; Husband; 28
726; Bah-chop-pa-dup-pas; Kills with her husband; F; Wife; 24
727; ---; Howard Shane; M; Son; 4

728; Oo-what-dah-beas; Three irons; M; Husband; 55
729; E-con-days; Old woman tooth; F; Wife; 42
730; ---; Sarah Three Irons; F; Daughter; 14
731; Dah-cheas; Drinking all the time; M; Son; 7

732; Edah-doot-chis; Takes himself; M; Husband; 32
733; Bee-dah-dosh-kain-dechis; Strikes by the side of water; F; Wife; 32
734; E-doos-sos; Cant[sic] get up; F; Mother; 62

735; She-bah-sha-dush; Fog in the morning; M; Husband; 50
736; Ease-key-pay; Crooked face child; F; Wife; 47
737; ---; John Morning; M; Son; 7
738; ---; Ruth Morning; F; Daughter; 1

Census of the __Crow__ Indians of __Crow__ Agency, __Montana__ taken by __E. H. Becker__, United States Indian Agent, __June 30th__, 189__8__

Key: Number; Indian Name; English Name; Sex; Relation; Age.

739; Pay-dutch-chee-bah-pash; Medicine crow; M; Husband; 48
740; Bah-pash; Medicine; F; Wife; 44
741; Ah-woos-dah-coos; Stays at sweathouse; M; Son; 10
742; Ah-way-chee-da-cuss; Goes pretty; M; son; 5
743; Ah-way-itchis; Good ground; M; Son; 1

744; Bee-shay-che-de-sos; Big ox; M; Husband; 63
745; Bah-dup-pay-keas-son; Kills well known; F; Wife; 61
746; Epah-dea-bah-cha-chis; Strong medicine; M; God son; 10
747; Esock-uck-bah-dah-pace; Kills with her brother; F; Sister; 58

748; ---; Wm. Elliott Towne; M; Orphan; 11
749; ---; Ida M. Towne; F; Sister; 8

750; Dosh-bah-cha-chis; Strong heart; M; Husband; 37
751; Be-dee-sheas-she-dush; Stands to the sun; F; Wife; 36

752; Duck-bit-say-pee-duck-cus; Ten bears; M; Husband; 49
753; Be-shay-ka-cheas; Buffalo that shakes; F; Wife; 38
754; E-sock-kain-dah-koos; On top of the house; M; Son; 21

755; Qua-dah-bah-chis; Sits in the middle; M Husband; 52
756; Bah-dup-pay-keas-sos; Kills well known; F; Wife; 50
757; Bee-dah-tah-shis-chay-ichis; Pretty butterfly; F; Daughter; 9

758; A-dah-shoes; Blue belly; M; Husband; 58
759; Osh-shone-bah-dup-pace; Kills in the rear of the house; F; Wife; 59

760; It-tuch-ock-in-days; Rides alone; M; Widower; 54;
761; Eche-dosh; Brings horses; F; Sister; 38
762; Eck-pah-dead-dah-cock-cush; His medicine bird; F; Daughter; 2

763; Bee-shay-dah-coos; Buffalo calf; M; Husband; 33
764; Ah-way-cook-cor-detah-heas; Goes to ground every day; F; Wife; 21
765; Bea-dah-cock-cuss; Bird woman; F; Daughter; 15
766; Epay-it-chis; Pretty tail; M; Son; 12

767; Ah-duck-che-dee-chay-itchis; Strikes his enemy pretty; M; Husband; 37
768; Es-che-key-pay; Crooked face; F; Wife; 35
769; Duck-bit-chay-haydaytahsos; Get their medicine tobacco; M; Son; 2

770; Day-chay-ah-hoos; Many prisoners; F; Widow; 35
771; Esos-kaybah-och-che-duc; Lucky horse; F; Sister; 28

772; Ah-dah-buck-ke-os; Thro s[sic] it away; M; Batchelor[sic]; 25

Census of the __Crow__ Indians of __Crow__ Agency, __Montana__ taken by __E. H. Becker__, United States Indian Agent, __June 30th__, 189__8__

Key: Number; Indian Name; English Name; Sex; Relation; Age.

773; Ea-cook-cah-cheas; White fox; M; Husband; 33
774; Bah-sho-dee-che-chay-ahhoos; Plenty medicine rock; F; Wife; 38
775; Ahway-kah-ways-bahchedis; Hunts toward the mountains; M; Son; 18
776; Dah-cock-uckpah-dah-cush; Stays with a bird; F; Daughter; 5
777; Hoo-chan-dah; Goes with the wind; F; Mother; 62

778; Dah-cock-e-wan-deas; Plays with a bird; M; Father; 42
779; Dahcock-uckbah-so-shis; Eats with a bird; M; Son; 9
780; Bah-puttah-ahway-taydas; Otter goes a long ways[sic]; M; Son; 7

781; Escock-kay-keas-sos; Well known lance; F; Widow; 71

782; Ah-dush-cos-pay; Crooked arm; M; Husband; 43
783; Ah-kok-de-chis; Catches up and strikes; F; Wife; 28
784; ---; Herbert Crooked Arm; M; Son; 9
785; Ishshane-bahduckchaydahcock; Bird ties a knot on top of his head; M; Son; 5
---; ---; James Crooked Arm; M; Son; 1

786; Bee-dup-kah-deas; Old beaver; F; Widow; 45
787; Dack-kah-shis; The eagle; F; Daughter; 17

788; Bit-choose; Wart; F; Widow; 74
789; Bee-shas-sah-hoos; Comes to the buffalo; F; Gr Dau.; 17
790; Echick-kay-sah-dish; Comes out first; F; Gr Dau.; 7

791; Chee-dup-dah-shis; Bulls tongue; M; Husband; 34
792; Bah-keam-beas; Blackbird woman; F; Wife; 28
793; Cuck-key-shean-doot-chis; Takes a yellow spotted horse; F; Daughter; 8
794; Sah-hean-bah-chais; Cree man; M; Son; 3
795; Ah-dup-pis; Stabs; F; Mother; 76

796; Bee-day-she-kosh; Looks at the water; M; Husband; 40
797; Bee-dee-dup-pase; Takes across the water; F; Wife; 38

798; Cah-kay-doot-chis; Takes a lance; F; Widow; 60

799; Bish-k-cheas; White dog; M; Husband; 44
800; Bahchay-hay-what-deechis; Strikes one man; F; Wife; 46

801; Dough-seas; Buffalo neck hair; M; Husband; 55
802; Bah-bah-dah-kosh; Nearly gone; F; Wife; 58
803; Out-tah-bah-pash; Medicine weasel; F; Gr Daughter; 16

804; Esuck-bon-tuch-chais; Mountain sheep; M; Husband; 30
805; E-cook-key-e-kosh; Looks at the fox; F; Wife; 32
806; Bah-coas; Gives things; F; Daughter; 11

Census of the __Crow__ Indians of __Crow__ Agency, __Montana__ taken by __E. H. Becker__, United States Indian Agent, __June 30th__, 189__8__

Key: Number; Indian Name; English Name; Sex; Relation; Age.

807; Dah-cock-dah-say-itchis; Good hearted bird; F; Daughter; 7
808; Che-co-key-dah-pace; Kills the young man; M; Son; 4

809; She-bish; Fat; M; Widower; 45
810; Dah-cock-dah-dah-bish; Bird flies off (Morris Schaffer); M; Son; 17

811; Edea-hay-bah-pash; Medicine breath; M; Husband; 35
812; Espea-kish-hiss; Wild cat; F; Wife; 23

813; Ah-shoos; The horn; M; Husband; 54
814; It-tuch-chis; All alone; F; Wife; 44
815; Kuck-key-con-dah-das; Goes after spotted horse; M; Son; 5

816; ---; Mrs. Wm. Blaine; F; Mother; 25
817; ---; James Blaine; M; Son; 9
818; ---; Florence Blaine; F; Daughter; 4

819; Ah-pah-seas; Shows his ear; M; [Bachelor]; 50
820; Dutch-choas; Muskrat; F; Mother; 68

821; Chay-esos; Big sheep; M; Husband; 29
822; Dock-kosh; Turtle; F; Wife; 42
823; ---; Florence Big Sheep; F; Daughter; 1

824; Dah-cup-co-dus-sos; Calf that strays; M; Husband; 39
825; Ah-wah-chis; Sits down; F; Wife; 50
826; Ahdean-dayah-waychis; Sits along the road; F; Daughter; 17

827; Dosh-bah-cha-chis; Strong heart; F; Widow; 68

828; Ahwaycah-waydanebahdahkis; Sings in the mountains; M; Husband; 26
829; Ah-wain-dah-sit-chis; Good hearted ground; F; Wife; 24
830; Bea-bah-pah-cah-weas; Bad medicine woman; F; Daughter; 7
831; Is-bah-ca-ke-ah-shees; Shows a shell; F; Daughter; 4

832; Ah-son-she-dish; Yellow head; M; Husband; 39
833; Bah-put-tah-pee-dee-chis; Strikes one with the necklace; F; Wife; 43
834; Eshe-bah-cha-shis; Mixes strong; F; Daughter; 16

835; Ah-hoe-cot-ta-dead-dish; Sun goes slow; M; Husband; 36
836; Boo-do-pah-she-dis; Yellow cedar; F; Wife; 17

837; Oo-what-kah-wish; Iron fork; M; Husband; 63
838; Bah-it-chay-doot-chis; Takes pretty things; F; Wife; 61

839; Been-dah-come-bahday-kay; Crazy Pend D'Oreille; M; Widower; 58

Census of the __Crow__ Indians of __Crow__ Agency, __Montana__ taken by __E. H. Becker__, United States Indian Agent, __June 30th__, 189**8**

Key: Number; Indian Name; English Name; Sex; Relation; Age.

840; Ock-cheas; White antelope; M; Husband; 36
841; Bah-hah-beas; Spring woman; F; Wife; 30
842; E-che-che-sosh; Big root; F; Daughter; 7
843; Ah-mah-ah-che-day-chase; Knows her luck; F; Daughter; 3

844; Bahdahkisshebahchacheas; Redwood chief; M; Widower; 49

845; ---; Mrs. F. Sucher; F; Mother; 20
846; ---; Belle Sucher; F; Daughter; 4
847; ---; Hattie Sucher; F; Daughter; 3

848; Bah-doot-che-key-pish; Takes wrinkle; M; Husband; 52
849; Dupe-tush-der-chis; Strikes both ways; F; Wife; 49
850; Chee-sos-eos; His tail shows; M; Son; 16
851; Uck-bee-che-bay-ah-hoos; Many talks with him; F; Daughter; 4

852; Shee-day; Yellow; F; Widow; 62

853; Oo-way-it-chis; Pretty paint; M; Husband; 25
854; Ahway-kawah-kain-beas; Woman on top of the mountain; F; Wife; 24
855; E-kay-sup-poas; Seven stars; F; Daughter; 10
856; Kea-sos; Plain to see; F; Daughter; 1

857; Bah-chea-keas-sos; Fights well known; M; Husband; 39
858; Is-chis-say-it-chis; Pretty nest; F; Wife; 34
859; Che-dock-cush-soo; Morning; M; Son; 14

860; Oo-what-tish; The iron; M; Husband; 39
861; Bah-show-dead-chich-itchis; Pretty medicine rock; F; Wife; 37
862; Bun-dock-cope-dah-cuss; Woodpeckers child; M; Son; 14
863; Ecup-pah-keas-sos; Gets down well known; M; Son; 12
864; Es-been-dotch-cheas; Little shield; M; Son; 7
865; Ah-duck-che-it-chis; Good coos; M; Son; 4

866; Dosh-kosh; Child; M; Husband; 37
867; Bee-dup-eas; Little beaver; F; Wife; 34
868; Bah-chay-doop-dak-pais; Kills two men; F; Mother; 70

869; ---; John Wallace; M; Husband; 39
870; Oo-tay-sah-dis; Weasel goes out; F; Wife; 46
871; ---; Carrie Wallace; F; Ad Dau.; 14

872; Oo-tay-doo-bah-kais; Cross weasel; M; Husband; 54
873; Shis-shea-bea; Hairy woman; F; Wife; 53
874; ---; Choteau; M; Son; 30

Census of the __Crow__ Indians of __Crow__ Agency, __Montana__ taken by __E. H. Becker__, United States Indian Agent, __June 30th__, 189__8__

Key: Number; Indian Name; English Name; Sex; Relation; Age.

875; Bah-kea-dah; Black bird; M; Husband; 47
876; Bah-chay-ah-kahn-dup-pace; Kills six men; F; Wife; 55

877; Ish-bern-dotch-she-dead; Yellow shield; M; Husband; 73
878; Bah-dah-kis; Sings; F; Wife; 72

879; Chate-uck-pah-dee-dish; Walks with a wolf; M; Husband; 22
880; Ko-kah-sish; Corn; F; Wife; 30
881; Echean-dock-eas; Little colt; F; Daughter; 5

882; Bee-pah-pus-sis; Round rock; M; Son; 39
883; Bah-dup-pay-keas-sos; Kills well known; F; Mother; 73
884; Hay-day-co-days; Runs in among them; M; Son; 31

885; Dupe-doot-chis; Takes two; M; Widower; 24

886; ---; Annie shows a pipe; F; Orphan; 7

887; Dakpitska-neen-dates; Bear that dont[sic] walk; M; Husband; 35
888; ---; Mrs. Wm. Hawkes; F; Wife; 32
889; ---; Lucy Hawkes; F; Daughter; 14
890; Es-chis-say-bah-posh; Medicine nest; M; Son; 2

891; Bah-chay-kah-duck-kay; Lean man; M; Widower; 83

892; Um-bah-sah-ah-hoos; Charges plenty; M; Husband; 36
893; Bah-chay-cush-bahduckkiss; Sings to man; F; Wife; 41
894; Bah-tah-day-keas-sos; Steals plain; M; Son; 13
895; Duck-cock-dah-cus; Bird; F; Daughter; 5

896; Bee-dock-cup-pis; Goose goes over the hill; M; Husband; 74
897; Um-beas-say-chu-dish; Hunts to lie down; F; Wife; 72

898; Oo-kutchis-say; Puts on antelope cap; M; Husband; 53
899; Op-put-kay; Long neck; F; Wife; 36
900; ---; Herbert Antelope Cap; M; Son; 13
901; Bay-ray-day-tuss; Proud; F; Sister; 62

902; Bah-cut-chay-itchis; Pretty striped snake; F; Widow; 49

903; Chee-say-ea-day-tuss; No hair on his tail; M; Husband; 55
904; Echean-bah-pash; Medicine horses; F; Wife; 49
905; Dah-cock-sah-hoose; Comes to the birds; F; Daughter; 19
906; Dah-cock-sah-hoos; Comes from the birds; F; Daughter; 8
907; ---; Hugh Leider; M; Son; 22

Census of the **Crow** Indians of **Crow** Agency, **Montana** taken by **E. H. Becker**, United States Indian Agent, **June 30th**, 189**8**

Key: Number; Indian Name; English Name; Sex; Relation; Age.

908; ---; Carl Leider; M; Husband; 30
909; Bahshow-deeditch-chayoppes; Medicine rock necklace; F; Wife; 16
910; ---; Agnes Leider; F; Daughter; 1

911; Ah-dup-pah-hoose; The Arapahoe; M; Husband; 49
912; A-wah-co-case; Spider; F; Wife; 36
913; Chuch-kay-esos; Big chicken; M; Son; 14
914; Ouk-be-das; Fire deer; M; Son; 9
915; Esook-cot-keh-deas; Old mouse; M; Son; 1

916; Ekup-pah-wah-chis; Sits with the stars; F; Mother; 27
917; Ekus-sah-itch-chis; Pretty snake; F; Daughter; 6

918; Bah-poe-tus; The fly; M; Husband; 68
919; Ahwayshayishdahcahkowshaybes; Gros Ventre red woman bird; F; Wife; 54

920; Isccechea-hay-dane-doctchis; Takes among the enemy No.2; M; Husband; 24
921; Uck-bah-dee-e-kosh; Looks at her medicine; F; Wife; 19
922; Bou-dooch-chis; Takes a fish; M; Son; 4

923; Chate-kah-deas; Old wolf; M; Husband; 46
924; Bosh-day-tush; No name; F; Wife; 46
925; Itch-oke-pish; Shot himself; M; Son; 6

926; E-koop-pay-bah-coosh; Hat above; F; Widow; 70
927; Bah-put-tosh; Otter; M; Son; 21
928; Ush-dosh-ka-dus; By the side of the camp; F; Sister; 88

929; Bah-dah-pah-coos; Comes from digging roots; F; Widow; 72
930; Ah-woo-kos; It s[sic] inside; M; Ad Son; 19

931; E-sess-bee-tay; Black hair; M; Husband; 49
932; Been-dah-chay-esah-hay dain-dee-chis; Strikes between the forts; F; Wife; 44
933; Bah-cup-pah-ah-hoos; Plenty hail; M; Son; 14
934; Ah-chay-it-che-poas; Jumps over; M; Son; 5
935; It-chit-chay-eas; Small medicine tobacco; F; Daughter; 3

936; Chee-dup-dah-cock-cus; Bull bird; M; Son; 26
937; Chate-bee-dish-she-days; Wolf goes to water; M; Father; 72

938; Ecupe-pay-cheas; White hat; M; Husband; 52
939; Eck-bah-dea-bah-pash; Her medicine is medicine; F; Wife; 30
940; Bea-she-pit-tas; Black rock; M; Son; 16

941; Chate-bah-pash; Medicine wolf; M; Husband; 70
942; Bee-dane-bah-dah-kiss; Sings going in; F; Wife; 60

Census of the **Crow** Indians of **Crow** Agency, **Montana** taken by **E. H. Becker**, United States Indian Agent, **June 30th**, 189**8**

Key: Number; Indian Name; English Name; Sex; Relation; Age.

943; Bim-boan-dah-pit-chase; Bear in the water; M; Husband; 28
944; She-peas; Mud; F; Wife; 23

945; Ecot-osh-heas; Shows a little; M; Husband; 34
946; Bah-dah-pay-it-chis; Kills good; F; Wife; 29
947; Uck-kosh-e-kosh; Looks at the sun; M; Son; 9
948; Bea-koc-kah-dah-biss; Rock moves along; M; Son; 4

949; Ah-peah-cos; Covers his neck; M; Husband; 59
950; is-been-dah-chay-it-chis; Pretty shield; F; Wife; 59
951; Ah-pea-chay-ah-pah-dootchis; Catches with rope on; M; Son; 2
952; Eck-bah-deas; His medicine; M; Son; 39

953; Ope-kah-deas; Old tobacco; M; Husband; 48
954; Bit-che-doot-chis; Takes a knife; F; Wife; 54
955; Dock-bit-chay-dee-dish; Bear that walks; F; Mother; 73

956; Eche-day-kah-deas; Old horse; M; Husband; 47
957; ---; Mrs. Nate Record; F; Wife; 42
958; ---; Charlie Record; M; Son; 7
959; ---; Dora Record; F; Daughter; 4
960; Bin-dotch-ut-tosh; Off shield; M; Son; 1

961; Oosh-bah-cha-chis; Strong; M; Husband; 24
962; E-say-key-pay; Wrinkle face; F; Wife; 54
963; Bah-chay-cheas; Steals on camp; M; Son; 17

964; Bah-key-day-dah-beas; Three blackbirds; F; Widow; 64

965; Up-pay-ut-tay; Sharp nose; F; Widow; 74

966; Duck-bit-chay-eck-pah-dea; Medicine bear; M; Husband; 55
967; Is-deam-day-keas-sos; Her road is plain; F; Wife; 50
968; Ah-pay-days; Goes together; F; Daughter; 9
969; Bee-cheas; Packs the rock; M; son; 10

970; Chees-she-pit-toch; Black tail; M; Husband; 45
971; Bah-day-bee-dockbahcusheas; People that shows; F; Wife; 43

972; Chate-cocush-shis; Bob tail wolf; M; Husband; 58
973; Bit-chea-bah-pash; Medicine knife; F; Wife; 56

974; Bah-tah-woas; The bell; M; Husband; 23
975; Bah-buck-but-date-chase; No medicine; F; Wife; 25
976; Duck-cock-bah-dah-cus; Crazy bird; F; Daughter; 3

Census of the __Crow__ Indians of __Crow__ Agency, __Montana__ taken by __E. H. Becker__, United States Indian Agent, __June 30th__, 1898

Key: Number; Indian Name; English Name; Sex; Relation; Age.

977; Hay-day-dee-doos; Stands among them; M; Husband; 51
978; Oat-chean-bah-dup-pace; Kills at night; F; Wife; 47
979; Esock-che-sah-keas-sos; Well known hawk; F; Daughter; 3
980; Echay-chis; His heels; M; Father; 78

981; Ah-pay-eso-chay-aeh-way-chis; Sits before a cloud; M; Husband; 48
982; Ea-cook-kah-beas; Fox woman; F; Wife; 50
983; Bob-puck-sos; Bird among the rocks; M; Son; 18
984; Echee-du-kosh-esos; Big Elk; M; Son; 7

985; Ick-kay-ah-hoos; Lots of stars; M; Husband; 40
986; Bah-son-day-ah-hoos; Goes first; F; Wife; 42

987; Bah-hay-chay-wat-tosh; Lone tree; M; Husband; 59
988; Bah-put-tuck-beaday-beas; Mink; F; Wife; 60
989; E-sah-coo-dake; Carries the arrows; M; Son; 32

990; Ish-chis-says-koos; Comes to her nest; F; Widow; 67

991; Ah-dah-sos-ea-kot-tosh; Little light; M; Husband; 46
992; Esos-kay-koo-doot-chis; Takes her horse; F; Wife; 32
993; Um-bah-coan-duck-bit-chase; Bear in the mountain; M; Son; 13
994; Ope-chu-dup-pace; Tobacco Bull; M; Son; 7
995; Chee-dup-kah-kah-dah-bis; Bull moves on; M; Son; 5
996; Ah-dah-hea-it-chis; Gets there pretty; M; Son; 4
997; Ba-chay-ha-what-dup-pace; Kills one man; F; Mother; 74

998; Es-chay-kah-deas; Old rabbit; M; Husband; 35
999; Bah-kow-say-it-chis; Pretty swamp flag; F; Wife; 30
1000; ---; Mary Old Rabbit; F; Daughter; 13
1001; Dah-kosh-bah-coos; Eagle high up; M; Son; 6

1002; Tuck-kase; Sounds of the gun; M; Husband; 27
1003; Bah-put-tay-ah-hoos; Plenty otter; F; Wife; 36
1004; Ock-kosh-de-dish; Antelope that walks; F; Daughter; 5
1005; ---; Frederick sounds the gun; M; Son; 1

1006; Boat-tay-kah-daes; Old coyote; M; Husband; 37
1007; Bah-pash; Medicine; F; Wife; 36
1008; Up-pah-sah-chers; Half white; M; Son; 16
1009; Ah-pah-kay-dainbaehdahkis; Sings in a cloud; M; Son; 12

1010; Is-be-dah-eas; Little fire; M; Husband; 48
1011; bea-it-chis-sos[sic]; Not a pretty woman; F; Wife; 46
1012; Bahputtaychee-dup-pis; Otter bull; M; Son; 23

Census of the __Crow__ Indians of __Crow__ Agency, __Montana__ taken by __E. H. Becker__, United States Indian Agent, __June 30th__, 1898

Key: Number; Indian Name; English Name; Sex; Relation; Age.

1013; Bah-pah-esos; Big Medicine; M; Husband; 42
1014; Bahduppay-chedu-chis; Strikes the one that kills; F; Wife; 42
1015; Up-pay-shu-dish; Yellow ears; F; Daughter; 15
1016; Bee-bus-sos; Rock in f ont[sic]; F; Daughter; 5

1017; Echey-she-coopy; Crooked foot; M; Husband; 80
1018; Uck-doshy-dee-dich-es; Strikes the one that charges; F; Wife; 80

1019; Bah-dah-pah-keas-sos; Digs well known; F; Widow; 68
1020; Bah-dup-kea-dupe-dootchis dup-pay; Kills one that takes two guns; F; Daughter; 36

1021; Chu-dup-pom-bish; Short bull; M; Husband; 55
1022; Oo-wat-doot-chis; Takes the iron; F; Wife; 54

1023; Ekoos-sheas; Turns around; M; Father; 34
1024; E-sos-kot-bah-deas; Working mouse; M; Son; 10

1025; Esock-cah-wah-chay-koos-say; Pretty old man; M; Husband; 52
1026; Owat-bahduck-keycon-dish; Old woman gone; F; Wife; 53
1027; Peah-key-tus; The spleen; M; Son; 17

1028; Cah-kay-bah-pash; Medicine lance; F; Widow; 54

1029; Bra-bah-chey-chis; Woman chief; M; Husband; 47
1030; Kish-sey; Big around; F; Wife; 52

1031; Deah-kah-shis; The eagle; M; Husband; 35
1032; Buss-sone-deah-ah-hoos; Goes ahead pretty; F; Wife; 33
1033; Con-hah-pagh; Medicine old woman; F; Daughter; 12

1034; Chip-pah-pos-s-shis; Ground squirrel; M; Husband; 30
1035; Bee-dick-qua-bah-dup-pace; Fools and kills the enemy; F; Wife; 33
1036; Shea-dah-chis; Fog all the time; M; Son; 7
1037; Itchit-chey-ay-ah-woos; Medicine tobacco seed; M; Son; 2

1038; Esoch-kah-dew-os; Two leggins; M; Husband; 48
1039; Is-bah-duck-chis; Ties up her bundles; F; Wife; 34
1040; Ah-dough-chea-ay-chase; Knows where she stops; F; Daughter; 16

1041; Is-ea-dea-ah-hoos; Plenty lodge poles; F; Widow; 28

1042; Ah-key-oke-bee-shey; White clay on forhead[sic]; M; Husband; 50
1043; Be-dosh; Fire; F; Wife; 40
1044; Is-been-dotch-dup-pickkish; Light shield; F; Daughter; 4
1045; Keas-sos; Plain; M; Son; 12

Census of the __Crow__ Indians of __Crow__ Agency, __Montana__ taken by __E. H. Becker__, United States Indian Agent, __June 30th__, 189__8__

Key: Number; Indian Name; English Name; Sex; Relation; Age.

1046; Ah-duck-chea-oss-ea-tuss; Shows his coos; M; Husband; 31
1047; Minne-ekoshees; Turns to the water; F; Wife; 24
1048; Oot-tay-bah-coos; Weasel high up; F; Daughter; 4

1049; Ock-pay-hiss-siss; Red wing; M; Widower; 48

1050; Duck-cock-sah-hoo-dup-pace; Kills coming to the birds; F; Mother; 58
1051; Ah-way-coe-ish-chissaydock; The swallow child; M; Son; 17

1052; Bee-ditch-key-sos; Big lake; M; Husband; 50
1053; Oo-wat-dootch-chis; Pounds the iron; F; Wife; 49
1054; Bah-show-dee-ditch-chay-sos; Big medicine rock; F; Daughter; 17
1055; Oat-tay-dock-cuss; Weasel child; M; Son; 10
1056; Chate-bick-cuss; Female wolf; F; Sister; 52

1057; E-shoe-dee-chea-ock-kin-day-dee-ditch-es; Strikes the rider of the white maned horse; F; Widow; 60

1058; Cheapcahdishtasonedonesase; Bull that shows all the time; M; Husband; 72
1059; Bah-cah-key-e-cosh; Looks at the shield; F; Wife; 30
1060; Bah-tah-wos; Plain bell; M; Son; 1

1061; Dahcock-it-chis; Good bird; M; Husband; 72
1062; Un-duck-cah-hoos; Stops at many places; F; Wife; 67

1063; Duck-bit-chay-ock-in-das; Rides a bear; M; Husband; 54
1064; Boa-it-chis; Pretty fish; F; Wife; 47
1065; Ah-dock-in-day-keas-sos; Rides well known; M; Son; 17

1066; Oo-wat-eas; Little iron; MW; Husband; 47
1067; It-chit-chea-ays; Tobacco seed; F; Wife; 44
1068; Ah-way-coe-che-daybahpash; Medicine ground cedar; F; Daughter; 21
1069; He-dah-bah-chase; Just a man; M; Son; 13

1070; Dah-cup-pis; Calf; M; Husband; 36
1071; Eas-che-kay-pay; Crooked face; F; Wife; 32

1072; Bah-che-dee-kah-deas; Old white man; M; Husband; 60
1073; Bee-shay-dee-dish; Buffalo that walks; F; Wife; 32

1074; Oke-keas-sos; Well known antelope; M; Husband; 34
1075; Uck-bah-he-dee-cose; Does anything; F; Wife; 24

1076; Che-key-pis; Crooked face No.2; M; Husband; 38
1077; Is-been-dotch-dee-chis; Takes shield once; F; Wife; 33
1078; Bah-chay-chea-a-chase; Knows to steal on camp; M; Son; 10

Census of the __Crow__ Indians of __Crow__ Agency, __Montana__ taken by __E. H. Becker__, United States Indian Agent, __June 30th__, 189**8**

Key: Number; Indian Name; English Name; Sex; Relation; Age.

1079; Bah-chay-coos-bah-duckkis; Sings to man; F; Daughter; 4

1080; Chu-dup-she-pit-tus; Black bull; M; Husband; 47
1081; Bee-day-de-cues-chis; Comes out of the water; F; Wife; 44
1082; Bah-show-dee-ditch; Medicine rock; F; daughter[sic]; 16

1083; Bim-boan-chee-dup-pis; Bull in the water; M; Husband; 59
1084; Chee-dup-eas; Young bull; F; Wife; 60

1085; Bah-it-chay-on-des-; Does many good things; M; Husband; 25
1086; Bah-put-tah-bedane-duckcoos; Otter stays in the water; F; Wife; 20
1087; Echey-day-hay-day-duss; Among the horses; F; Daughter; 3
1088; Ick-cush; Star; F; Sister; 14

1089; Ah-puss-sah-cheas; Half white; M; Husband; 59
1090; But-shay-sut-tuss; Close together; F; Wife; 50

1091; Iscoe-chehay-dane-dootchis; Takes among the enemy; M; Husband; 37
1092; Ah-shoe-hish-shis; Red hair; F; Wife; 42
1093; Pea-cah-dah-hutch; Long Piegan; M; Son; 11
1094; Bah-osh-ah-hoos; Plenty red plumes; F; Daughter; 9
1095; Dah-cock-cah-deas; Old bird; F; Mother; --

1096; Is-bin-dotch-bah-chate-chis; Shield chief; M; Husband; 31
1097; Ush-doop-tah-coe-dee; Strikes two camps; F; Wife; 30
1098; Tuck-kit-chay-ah-hoos; Shoots plenty; F; Daughter; 3

1099; Bah-ea-way-shay-dock-cuss; Young curlew; M; Husband; 46
1100; Cheas-da-ah-kay-ock-in-day-dee-chis; Rides a white horse; F; Wife; 42
1101; Shu-dish; Yellow; F; Daughter; 10
1102; Bah-sone-dace; Goes first; F; Mother; 83

1103; Who-chis-say-ah-way-chice; Sits to the wind; F; Widow; 52

1104; Dah-cock-teah-dish; The bird; M; Husband; 29
1105; Is-coe-chee-dup-pace; Kills her enemy; F; Wife; 25
1106; By-eas; Arrow point; M; Son; 5
1107; Epea-cot-a-wak-chis; Magpie sits down; M; Son; 1

1108; Ah-way-choke-kaydah-cockcus; Bird on the prairie; M; Husband; 44
1109; Be-shay-ock-kain-ahwahchis; Sits on the blanket; F; Wife; 38

1110; Chee-sock-cuss; Long tail; M; Husband; 41
1111; She-pea-day-tuss; No mud; F; Wife; 36
1112; Tick-pah-che-day-de-shis; Strikes one that pushes him; M; Son; 12
1113; Ah-we-sos; Shows big on the ground; M; Son; 8

Census of the **Crow** Indians of **Crow** Agency, **Montana** taken by **E. H. Becker**, United States Indian Agent, **June 30th**, 189**8**

Key: Number; Indian Name; English Name; Sex; Relation; Age.

1114; Hay-dain-dee-chis; Strikes among them; F; Widow; 70
1115; Chee-dup-bah-cha-ah-chis; Strong bull; M; Son; 31

1116; Bah-cup-pash; Hail; M; Husband; 31
1117; Echee-dayon-duckcoekeassos; Horses place well known; F; Wife; 32

1118; It-tuch-bah-cha-chis; Strong alone; M; Husband; 50
1119; Uck-bah-dea-ate-chase; Knows her medicine; F; Wife; 45

1120; Chate-ea-cot-tus; Little wolf; M; Husband; 74
1121; bah-dup-pay-keas-sos; Kills well known; F; Wife; 62

1122; Chee-dish; Hunts; M; Husband; 42
1123; Echee-dayhaey-dane-duckcoos; Stays with the horse; F; Wife; 38
1124; E-sop-pah-dah-tus; Has no moccasin; M; Son; 16
1125; E-sos-kay-ate-chace; Knows his horse; F; Daughter; 5

1126; Bah-dah-sure-ha-wat-tus; One blue bead; M; Husband; 50
1127; Ush-coe-sut-tah-doot-chis; Takes one close to camp; F; Wife; 48
1128; Un-dah-hea-os; Surrounds the enemy strong; M; Son; 13

1129; Duck-bit-chay-new-pew-oze; Mad at the bear; M; Husband; 36
1130; Is-eap-che-bish-ay; Got a pipe; F; Wife; 40
1131; Is-bah-it-chis; Got pretty things; F; Daughter; 11
1132; Dah-coe-tay-doot-chis; Catches the Sioux; F; Daughter; 5

1133; Sus-bah-doot-chis; Takes quick; F; Mother; 25
1134; Dah-cock-dah-cuss; Bird child; M; Son; 6
1135; Duck-bit-chay-e-sock-cuss; Bear old man; M; Son; 3

1136; Ah-she-tas; Sharp horn; M; Husband; 57
1137; Ben-cot-ish-tup-pay; Woman with eyes open; F; Wife; 57

1138; Bah-chay-bah-dah-kay; Foolish man; M; Husband; 36
1139; Hay-dane-ah-seas; Shows in a crow; F; Wife; 30
1140; ---; George Foolish man; M; Son; 1

1141; E-cuss-sah-esos; Big snake; M; Husband; 53
1142; Chedockcussakbahduppays; Kills in the morning; F; Wife; 57

1143; Bea-bah-coos; Fish high up; M; Husband; 52
1144; Chuck-ko-doot-chis; Takes five; F; Wife; 50

1145; Poe-put-tah-bah-coos; Owl above; M; Husband; 30
1146; E-che-doe-it-chis; Brings pretty horses; F; Wife; 32
1147; Ah-dah-che-e-coss; Sees the coos; F; Daughter; 10

Census of the __Crow__ Indians of __Crow__ Agency, __Montana__ taken by __E. H. Becker__, United States Indian Agent, __June 30th__, 189__8__

Key: Number; Indian Name; English Name; Sex; Relation; Age.

1148; Ume-beas; Paint woman; F; Daughter; 8

1149; Chee-dup-um-bee-chis-sos; Bull that dont[sic] fall down; M; Husband; 45
1150; Ah-see-tus; Shows; F; Wife; 32
1151; Is-been-dot-bish-eas; Got a shield; F; Mother; 70

1152; Esop-pay-shoes; Blue moccasin; M; Husband; 54
1153; Uck-ish-be-dane-de-chis; Strikes one going in the house; F; Wife; 52
1154; Chee-dup-be-day-sot; Bull near the water; M; Son; 15
1155; Boa-tah-it-chis; Pretty coyote; M; Son; 30

1156; Bah-cook-coe-tah-hoos; Comes from above; M; Husband; 32
1157; Um-bah-cone-dah-cos; Stops above; F; Wife; 35
1158; ---; Hannah comes above; F; Daughter; 1

1159; Bin-day-sop-pay-dus; River crow; M; Husband; 33
1160; Cah-pah-dias; Medicine; F; Wife; 29
1161; Chee-dup-eche-dish; Horse bull; F; Daughter; 3

1162; Es-che-kah-dish; Old rabbit woman; F; Widow; 56

1163; Cha-qua-bah-soo; Charges five times; M; Husband; 25
1164; Bea-ah-wah-chis; Woman that sits down; F; Wife; 22
1165; E-hum-dah-pace; Kills in sleep; F; Daughter; 4

[Census taker repeated the last number and then continued in sequence not noticing the mistake.]
1165; Is-coe-chea-ah-hoos; Got many enemies; M; Husband; 39
1166; Bah-put-tah-dock-cus; Young otter; F; Wife; 48
1167; Bah-key-dah-keas-sos; Plain blackbird; F; Daughter; 12

1168; Be-dup-dah-cus; Young beaver; M; Husband; 52
1169; Bak-kah-beas; Hoop woman; F; Wife; 56

1170; Umbah-owedup-ate-chace; Knows where he finds things; M; Husband; 31
1171; Qua-dus; Between; F; Wife; 32

1172; Eche-dock-in-days; Rides a horse; M; Husband; 44
1173; Ah-cam-dah-pace; Kills on top; F; Wife; 40
1174; Bah-dee-shis; Jerked meat; M; Son; 17
1175; Bah-day-key-sut-tus; Two barreled gun; M; Son; 11
1176; E-shue-eas; Feather neck; F; Daughter; 4
1177; Edock-bah-pash; Medicine form; F; Daughter; 2
1178; Is-ah-way-cone-dah-pase; Kills on her own ground; F; Mother; 72

1179; Bah-pus; Cliff; F; Widow; 46

Census of the __Crow__ Indians of __Crow__ Agency, __Montana__ taken by __E. H. Becker__, United States Indian Agent, __June 30th__, 189__8__

Key: Number; Indian Name; English Name; Sex; Relation; Age.

1180; Eche-dee-kosh-ah-way-chis; Sitting elk; M; Husband; 58
1181; Dah-cock-beas; Bird woman; F; Wife; 55

1182; Bah-che-quas; Sugar; M; Husband; 69
1183; Cuck-kay-coo-day-de-chis; Strikes the one with a lance; F; Wife; 50
1184; ---; Louise; F; Daughter; 11

1185; Dosh-shay-e-coos; Charges madly on the enemy; M; Husband; 26
1186; Um-bah-cone-hoos; Comes from above; F; Wife; 23
1187; Bick-cah-keas-sos; Well known mare; F; Daughter; 8

1188; Eche-day-itchay-ock-inday; Rides a pretty horse; M; Husband; 30
1189; Ah-woos-ah-cay-dus; On top of the sweathouse; F; Wife; 28
1190; Cah-pah-dee-it-chis; Good medicine; F; Daughter; 9
1191; Coo-bah-pay-dah-pay; Kills the same day; F; Daughter; 3

1192; Daek-it-chis; Pretty eagle; M; Husband; 53
1193; Is-been-dotch-it-chis; Pretty shield; F; Wife; 50
1194; Dack-cosh-sheedis[sic]; Yellow eagle; M; Son; 2

1195; Da-cose; Goes on; M; Husband; 57
1196; Been-dotch-us-eas; Shield that shows; F; Wife; 50

1197; Ike-cook-cus; Even; M; Husband; 27
1198; Ush-dead-it-chis; Makes a pretty lodge; F; Wife; 50

1199; Up-pah-keas-sos; Cloud well known; M; Husband; 38
1200; Con-dah-cock-cus; Old bird woman; F; Wife; 37
1201; Ush-coe-tah-cose-shis; Helps the whole camp; M; Son; 13
1202; E-dit-days; Runs against; M; Son; 5

1203; Cho-say-ick-cosh; Sees a white horse; M; Husband; 44
1204; Dosh-day-tus; No name; F; Wife; 44
1205; ---; Peter S. White Horse; M; Son; 14

1206; Duck-bit-chay-dee-dish; Bear that walks; M; Husband; 38
1207; Hock-cuss; Behind; F; Wife; 52

1208; Is-shay-dus; Hairy on top of his head; M; Husband; 52
1209; Bin-dotch-eso-chain-dus; Shield in front; F; Wife; 53

1210; Duck-cock-bea-it-chis; Pretty woman bird; F; Widow; 42
1211; E-shoe-de-chea-doot-chis; Takes horse with the white mane; [F]; Daughter; 13
1212; Bah-chay-cha-dup-pace; Kills the chief; F; Daughter; 8

1213; Duck-bit-chay-eas; Bears[sic] tooth; M; Husband; 44

Census of the __Crow__ Indians of __Crow__ Agency, __Montana__ taken by __E. H. Becker__, United States Indian Agent, __June 30th__, 189__8__

Key: Number; Indian Name; English Name; Sex; Relation; Age.

1214; Bah-chay-un-dah-pace; Kills many men; F; Wife; 42
1215; ---; Mary Bears[sic] Tooth; F; Daughter; 18
1216; Ope-bah-dah-kis; Tobacco sings; F; Ad Dau.; 5

1217; Ish-tay-ea-sos; Big eyes; M; Brother; 57

1218; Esa-pis; Shot in the face; M; Husband; 60
1219; Hoo-chis; Wind blowing; F; Wife; 54

1220; Uch-cha-key-chis; Spies on the enemy; M; Husband; 36
1221; Us-dosh-cane-doot-chis; Takes by the side of the camp; F; Wife; 40

1222; Bosh-bah-pash; Medicine feather; F; Widow; 50
1223; Edea-oke-pis; Shoots tent poles; F; Niece; 9

1224; Is-tah-waz; Eyes; M; Batchelor[sic]; 24

1225; Bah-duck-key-doot-chis; Takes a gun; M; Husband; 58
1226; Ah-way-chase; Knows the ground; F; Wife; 60

1227; Bah-owe-keas-sos; Brings well known; F; Widow; 50
1228; Bosh-doot-chis; Takes a feather; F; Daughter; 13

1229; Bah-cup-pah-e-sos; Big hail; M; Husband; 30
1230; Bah-cuch-ca-beas; Striped snake woman; F; Wife; 24
1231; beshay-ock-bah-wah-chis; Sits with a buffalo; M; Son; 5

1232; Undosh-shay-day-keas-sos; Charges well known; M; ---; 45

1233; Esop-pontah-chayhaydaydose; Among the sheep; F; Daughter; 24

1234; Ah-wah-cah-wassahwah-chis; Face toward the mountain; M; Husband; 45
1235; Peace-hay-duce; Comes behind; F; Wife; 38
1236; Oo-sha'-cane-cah-pis; Sits over a hole; F; Daughter; 9
1237; Dah-cock-shee-dish; Yellow bird; F; Daughter; 5

1238; Ah-dean-dace; The trail; F; Widow; 48
1239; Is-chie-say-be-shis; Got a nest; M; Son; 15
1240; Is-been-dotch-ah-hoos; Plenty shield; F; Daughter; 9
1241; Eche-de-she-chace; Likes the horses; F; Daughter; 8

1242; Up-pay-oakpis; Shot in the nose; M; Husband; 27
1243; Is-coe-chea-ache-chase; Knows the enemy; F; Wife; 24
1244; Ahwahcoe-ishcheshayahhoos; Plenty swallow; M; Son; 7
1245; ---; John Shot In The Nose; M; Son; 1

Census of the __Crow__ Indians of __Crow__ Agency, __Montana__ taken by __E. H. Becker__, United States Indian Agent, __June 30th__, 189__8__

Key: Number; Indian Name; English Name; Sex; Relation; Age.

1246; Been-dosh-shay-bah-pash; Medicine top; M; Widower; 32
1247; Bahkay-ahoos; Gives lots of things away; F; Daughter; 5

1248; Duck-bit-chay-che-dace; Bear gets up; M; Husband; 64
1249; Bah-put-tah-dew-pus; Two otters; F; Wife; 59

1250; It-tut-dah-cock-cus; Bird by himself; M; Batchelor[sic]; 58

1251; Chate-shay-duck-bit-chay; Mad bear wolf; M; Husband; 54
1252; Dah-hea-os; Surrounds the enemy; M; Son; 19

1253; Boop-chis; Ball; M; Husband; 34
1254; Bea-it-chay; Pretty woman; F; Wife; 30

1255; Uk-bah-dah-pay-ish-tuck-kea-doot-chis; Takes the killer of guns; M; Husband; 24
1256; Coe-what-tay-doot-chis; Takes both together; F; Wife; 24
1257; Bah-duck-kea-os-seas; Shows a gun; M; Son; 4
1258; Uk-keam-duck-chis; Ties on the foretop; F; Daughter; 8
1259; Bah-dock-key-huchkey-dooch; Takes a long gun; F; Daughter; 2

1260; Bah-duck-key-his-sis; Red gun; M; Husband; 54
1261; Bah-put-tah-cah-deas; Old otter; F; Wife; 52

1262; He-dah-wah-chace; He is a man now; M; Husband; 55
1263; Ecupe-pah-doot-chis; Takes the hat; F; Wife; 50

1264; Bah-coo-dase; Holds something; F; Widow; 87

1265; Is-tuck-kea-bah-chatechice; Gun chief; M; Husband; 51
1266; Cuck-cock-in-days; Rides a spotted horse; F; Wife; 38
1267; Be-dea-bah-pash; The door is medicine; F; Daughter; 15
1268; Ush-dosh-kay-tah-bah-sos; Runs beside the camp; M; Son; 4
1269; Bah-put-tah-beas; Woman otter; F; Mother; 77

1270; Eche-day-it-chis; Good horses; M; Husband; 33
1271; E-hum-be-shoes; More of them; F; Wife; 22
1272; Been-dah-chate-dase; Goes to the fort; F; Daughter; 3

1273; Ea-cus-sos; Snake; F; Mother; 56
1274; E-sah-duck-chis; Ties up the arrows; F; Daughter; 16

1275; Bee-dee-chay-hay-day-dus; Among the willows; F; Widow; 62

1276; E-sah-eduse-see-shis; Broken arrow; M; Husband; 38
1277; Es-tay-cheas; Grey eyes; F; Wife; 40

Census of the __Crow__ Indians of __Crow__ Agency, __Montana__ taken by __E. H. Becker__, United States Indian Agent, __June 30th__, 189__8__

Key: Number; Indian Name; English Name; Sex; Relation; Age.

1278; Ah-sah-hoos; Shows coming; F; Daughter; 4

1279; Duck-bit-tse-uppahpushcoos; Cuts the bears ears; M; Husband; 48
1280; It chis; Good; F; Wife; 45
1281; Bah-dah-kit-chice; Sings good; M; Son; 15

1282; Hay-day-dose; Right among them; M; Husband; 51
1283; E-dah-hoos; Comes herself; F; Wife; 55

1284; Kah-disc; Old woman; M; Husband; 58
1285; Day-it-chise; Goes pretty; F; Wife; 55
1286; Dah-dough-chea-day-itchice; Leads the camp pretty; F; Daughter; 11

1287; Odup-dah-pace; Finds them and kills them; M; Widower; 45
1288; Echa-dow-keas-sos; Brings horses well known; F; Daughter; 10

1289; Is-thay-dah-kish-shay; Knot between the eyes; M; Husband; 59
1290; Oo-wat-doot-chase; Takes the iron; F; Wife; 52
1291; Dock-shay-dah-beas; Three coons; F; Daughter; 15

1292; Cuck-cah-wah-chice; Sits down spotted; M; Husband; 36
1293; Bah-chay-cheas; Steals on the camp; F; Wife; 19
1294; ---; John Spotted; M; Son; 1
1295; Echee-dah-hoos; Plenty horses; M; Brother; 46

1296; Dah-cock-bah-coos; Bird above; M; Husband; 32
1297; Oo-tah-cuck-kis; Spotted weasel; F; Wife; 30
1298; Be-day-tuss; Like a fire; M; Son; 10
1299; Hoo-chice-soos; Comes against the wind; M; Son; 7
1300; Poop-kit-tah-cuck-kis; Spotted snow bird; F; Daughter; 5

1301; Chate-kah-we-sis; Skins a wolf; M; Husband; 57
1302; E-sos-kah-we-sis; Has horses; F; Wife; 50

1303; ---; Richard Cummins; M; Batchelor[sic]; 25

1304; Be-dook-sah-e-duse; Alligator stands up; M; Husband; 53
1305; Bah-put-tea-hosh; The other otter; F; Wife; 52

1306; Boat-tah-cah-dush-sis; Coyote runs; M; Husband; 38
1307; Dupe-tush-beas; Woman both ways; F; Wife; 33
1308; ---; Arnold Kosta; M; Son; 13
1309; Ah-pah-de-beas; Porcupine woman; F; Daughter; 2

1310; Ea-cus-sah-che-dup-pis; Snake bull; M; Husband; 47
1311; Oo-what-de-chise; Strikes the iron; F; Wife; 33

Census of the __Crow__ Indians of __Crow__ Agency, __Montana__ taken by __E. H. Becker__, United States Indian Agent, __June 30th__, 189__8__

Key: Number; Indian Name; English Name; Sex; Relation; Age.

1312; Bah-ow-duck-coos; Brings things always; F; Daughter; 13
1313; Boo-duke-pah-keas-sos; Plain cedar; F; Daughter; 9
1314; Che-quas; Is sweet now; M; Son; 4

1315; ---; Pius Hill; M; Orphan; 15
1316; Bea-ah-dutch-she-beas; Woman that farms; F; Sister; 9

1317; Eas-ea-coas; Covers his face; M; Husband; 41
1318; Ah-sah-date-doot-chis; Takes horses on the prairie; F; Wife; 21

1319; Bee-dish; Walking; M; Husband; 42
1320; Uck-bah-du-ick-cosh; Looks at the medicine; F; Wife; 41

1321; Eas-shee-day; Yellow face; M; Husband; 73
1322; Bea-it-chay-de-chice; Strikes the pretty woman; F; Wife; 70

1323; Ah-pit-bah-coos; Crane in the sky; M; Husband; 58
1324; Be-dup-his-shis; Red beaver; F; Wife; 63
1325; Bah-key-dah-wah-chice; Blackbird sits down; F; Daughter; 10
1326; Is-tah-dase-cheas; Big squirrel; M; Son; 13

1327; Ah-way-kah-wah-chea-days; Mountain pocket; M; Husband; 58
1328; E-chope-pice; Shoots her foot; F; Wife; 48
1329; Esos-kee-dit-bah-pash; Medicine horsewhip; M; Son; 23

1330; Ah-dah-doo-be-shay; Shot in the arm; M; Husband; 55
1331; Bea-doot-chice; Takes a woman; F; Wife; 48

1332; She-chock-ay-dus; On top of the hill; M; Husband; 59
1333; Is-bah-dah-ha-wat-ate-chice; Knows the yearling; F; Wife; 51

1334; Bosh-che-de-cot-tay; White man; M; Husband; 44
1335; Bah-cuch-cah-ah-hoos; Plenty striped snake; F; Wife; 50
1336; Eat-tosh-tay-hios-shis; Red shirt; M; Son; 21
1337; Ah-dean-day-ate-chice; Knows the road; F; Daughter; 15
1338; Dah-cock-che-deas-sos; Not afraid of a bird; M; Son; 8
1339; Dah-cock-ah-pah-hoose; Bird with plenty of wings going around; M; Son; 7
1340; Ecupe-pah-bah-put-tosh; Hat otter; F; Daughter; 1

1341; Bea-it-chay; Pretty woman; F; Widow; 40

1342; Edosh-uck-bah-dup-pace; Kills with his bro-in-law; M; Husband; 44
1343; Un-di-day-it-chice; Walks pretty; F; Wife; 42
1344; Bick-cah-hay-day-duss; Sits among the grass; F; Daughter; 15
1345; Oak-cah-sis; Antelope; F; Daughter; 13

Census of the **Crow** Indians of **Crow** Agency, **Montana** taken by **E. H. Becker**, United States Indian Agent, **June 30th**, 189**8**

Key: Number; Indian Name; English Name; Sex; Relation; Age.

1346; ---; James Buffalo; M; Husband; 24
1347; Bah-cup-pah-cheas; White hail; F; Wife; 22
1348; Is-bin-dotch-ebahick-deas; Does everything with a shield; F; Daughter; 5
1349; Cah-ditch-chea-ah-hoos; Plenty lightning; M; Son; 4

1350; Duck-bit-chay-che-sus; Bears[sic] tail; M; Husband; 58
1351; Duck-bit-chayun-dayatechase; Knows where the bear goes; F; Daughter; 24
1352; Ah-way-cah-wah-seas; Shows in the mountains; M; Son; 14

1353; Ah-pah-dee-esos; Big porcupine; M; Husband; 42
1354; Un-doc-cosh-keas-sos; Holds well known; F; Wife; 39

1355; Chee-dup-bah-chate-chice; Bull chief; M; Husband; 62
1356; Is-tuck-key-bah-chate-chice; Long gun; F; Wife; 56
1357; It-chit-che-ays; Medicine tobacco; M; Gr Son; 8

1358; Ah-shue-cheas; White horn; F; Widow; 52

1359; Isbitche-itchice-sayeacocktus; Little whetstone; M; Husband; 52
1360; E-che-dah-keas-sos; Horse well known; F; Wife; 39

1361; Che-chuk-key-sos; Big around; M; Husband; 52
1362; Cah-coa-doot-chice; Takes all the horses; F; Wife; 50
1363; Ecup-pah-ate-chice; Knows her hat; F; Mother; 74

1364; Shis-sheas; Curly; M; Husband; 48
1365; Bin-dotch-doot-chis; Takes a shield; F; Wife; 50
1366; Ah-wan-dook-cook-cos-de-tah-dah-cock-cuss; Bird another year; F; Daughter; 2

1367; Dah-cus; Balls; M; ---; 36

1368; Be-dah-dish-sos; Dont[sic] get in; F; Widow; 46
1369; Ah-pah-de-e-wan-deas; Plays with medicine; F; Daughter; 8
1370; Un-day-it-chice; Goes ahead pretty; F; Daughter; 10

1371; Ah-pit-tus; The crane; M; Husband; 42
1372; E-chee-uck-pah-dup-pace; Kills with the horses; F; Wife; 39
1373; Che-soup-pus; End of the tail; M; Son; 13
1374; Oo-shis; Hole; M; Brother; 25
1375; Esos-kah-wishes; Has horses; F; Mother; 62

1376; Oat-tay-bee-dosh; Fire weasel; M; Husband; 67
1377; Ah-dough-chea-bah-pash; Medicine where she stops; F; Wife; 62

1378; Beas; Rock; M; Widower; 36

Census of the __Crow__ Indians of __Crow__ Agency, __Montana__ taken by __E. H. Becker__. United States Indian Agent, __June 30th__, 1898

Key: Number; Indian Name; English Name; Sex; Relation; Age.

1379; Bah-show-de-chite-chase; Medicine rock; F; Daughter; 10

1380; Duck-cock-ah-shoes; Bird head; M; Husband; 40
1381; Dah-ah-sheas; Shows going; F; Wife; 34
1382; Bish-cah-duck-bit-chase; Bears dog; M; Son; 19
1383; Bah-cah-wat-tay-dace; Hoop goes a long way; M; Son; 7
1384; Oot-tah-dock-cus; Young weasel; F; Daughter; 4
1385; Is-coe-che-che-dish; Afraid of his enemy; M; Son; 13

1386; Duck-peas; Hugs; M; Husband; 52
1387; Ahwah-she-hay-danedootchice; Takes a man in a fog; F; Wife; 56
1388; Bah-duck-it-chise; Sings pretty; M; Son; 20

1389; Ah-wah-coan-de-dish; Walks in middle of the ground; M; Husband; 62
1390; Ea-cot-tus; Little; F; Wife; 53

1391; Bahshow-dechit-chaybahcoos; Medicine rock above; M; Husband; 31
1392; E-chean-dah-pace; Kills a horse; F; Wife; 30
1393; Bah-keam-boo-dish; Bull blackbird; M; Son; 8

1394; E-chean-dah-cock-cus; Bird horse; M; Husband; 24
1395; Bah-show-de-chit-chase; Medicine rock; F; Wife; 22
1396; Ea-dea-it-chice; Pretty lodge poles; F; Daughter; 5

1397; Ea-dane-deas; He does it; M; Husband; 26
1398; Bah-cook-coo-dush; She is high up; F; Wife; 30
1399; Cheach-cucs; Chicken; F; Daughter; 9
1400; Cah-paeh-dee-dock-cus; Young medicine; M; Son; 5
1401; Bah-show-dechit-chayesos; Big medicine rock; F; Mother; 50

1402; Dupe-pah-wah-dup-pace; Kills twice; F; Widow; 43
1403; Un-dah-pace; Kills plenty; F; Daughter; 13
1404; Ha-dane-dah-cock-cus; Bird among them; M; Son; 5
1405; Eat-tosh-tay-keas-sos; Plain shirt; F; Daughter; 4

1406; Up-pay-ut-tay; Sharp nose; M; Husband; 33
1407; Bah-cah-dish-tah-beas; Heifer woman; F; Div. Wife; 34
1408; Bea-bah-shay-e-sit-chace; Likes the summer; F; Daughter; 4

1409; Bin-dosh-shay-shee-dish; Yellow top; M; Batchelor[sic]; 57

1410; Bah-chay-cheas; Steals on the camp; F; Widow; 62

1411; Eak-cah-shues; Blue chin; F; Widow; 57

1412; Oo-what-tah-hoos; Plenty irons; F; Widow; 23

Census of the __Crow__ Indians of __Crow__ Agency, __Montana__ taken by __E. H. Becker__, United States Indian Agent, __June 30th__, 189__8__

Key: Number; Indian Name; English Name; Sex; Relation; Age.

1413; Eas-chay-cuck-kis; Spotted rabbit; M; Husband; 32
1414; Itch-chit-chay-bah-pash; Medicine tobacco; F; Wife; 38
1415; Oo-what-ah-shoes; Iron head; M; Son; 19
1416; Uck-bah-dea-e-wah-ick-deas; Does everything with her med.; F; Daughter; 15
1417; Oke-push; Badly shot; M; Son; 1
1418; Es-sos; Hairy; F; Mother; 64

1419; Che-dup-cho-sus; White bull; M; Husband; 70
1420; Be-dase-she-cash; Looks at the water; F; Wife; 60

1421; Bah-doo-peas; Scolds; M; Husband; 33
1422; ---; Mrs. Ben Gardiner; F; Wife; 35
1423; ---; Thomas Gardiner; M; Son; 14
1424; ---; Frank Gardiner; M; Son; 12
1425; ---; Amelia Gardiner; F; Daughter; 10

1426; Dah-cock-keas-sos; Bird well known; M; Husband; 32
1427; Bea-dosh-day-tush; Woman without a name; F; Wife; 25
1428; Ah-wah-cahn-dab-cock-cus; Mountain bird; M; Son; 1

1429; Pay-dutch-chay-ook-cusseas; Bob tailed crow; M; Husband; 52
1430; Bah-ick-cah-keas-sos; Sees well known; F; Wife; 48

1431; Eas-chee-key-pah; Crooked face; M; Husband; 58
1432; Ish-bin-dotch-bah-chate-chice; Strikes the shield first; F; Wife; 38
1433; Dah-cock-cah-doosh-sis; Bird that runs; F; Daughter; 13
1434; Doop-pah-e-che-dosh; Brings the horses; M; Son; 4

1435; Bah-ea-cah-keas-sos; Sees well known; F; Widow; 56

1436; Ah-sheas; The river; M; Husband; 68
1437; Bee-dah-dosh-cane-de-chice; Sits by the side of the water; F; Wife; 53
1438; ---; Charles Brown; M; Son; 21
1439; Ope-che-chuck-kis; Round tobacco; F; Ad Dau.; 13

1440; Uck-pah-cheas; White wings; M; Father; 62
1441; ---; Holder white wings; M; Son; 20

1442; Ecupe-pah-wish-de-chice; Strikes the one with the hat; F; Widow; 52

1443; Ah-dah-cuck-kay; Spotted arm; M; Husband; 50
1444; Ah-dow-chea-keas-sos; Whers[sic] she stops well known; F; Wife; 52
1445; Dah-pit-sah-seandahcockcus; Bird in the morning; M; Son; 19

1446; Um-bah-chea-keas-sos; Fights well known; M; Husband; 36
1447; Is-been-dotch-bah-duck-kis; Shield that sings; F; Wife; 32

47

Census of the __Crow__ Indians of __Crow__ Agency, __Montana__ taken by __E. H. Becker__, United States Indian Agent, __June 30th__, 189__8__

Key: Number; Indian Name; English Name; Sex; Relation; Age.

1448; Be-shays-de-dish; Walks to the buffalo; M; Son; 3

1449; It-chase-shay-dane-de-chase; Strikes on top of the head; M; Husband; 35
1450; Bee-shay-e-hosh; The other buffalo; F; Wife; 34
1451; Ah-wah-coo-ish-chice-say-ea-cot-tus; Little swallow; M; Son; 8

1452; Eche-dee-kosh-kah-deas; Old elk; M; Husband; 39
1453; Ook-ish-dean-day-ah-hoos; Antelope trails; F; Wife; 38
1454; E-chean-push-cush; Cuts the horse; M; Son; 8
1455; ---; Mary Old Elk; F; Daughter; 1

1456; Bah-shoes-shays; Red feather; F; [Widow]; 50
1457; Ea-dea-cah-deas; Old lodge pole; M; Son; 14

1458; Eas-pah-pus-say; Round face; M; Husband; 50
1459; Bout-tah-bah-hoos; Coyote that howls; F; Wife; 48
1460; Bah-touch-owe-duck-coos; Brings things all the time; M; Son; 16

1461; Ah-wah-cah-dace; Pukes on the ground; M; ---; 51

1462; Ah-dup-pice; Hides; M; Husband; 36
1463; Hay-day-tah-wah-sos; Goes through her enemies; F; Wife; 32
1464; Uck-bah-dea-ah-hoos; Plenty medicine; F; Daughter; 9
1465; Ook-che-dup-price; Bull deer; M; Son; 3

1466; ---; Charles Clawson; M; Batchelor[sic]; 26
1467; Echick-doot-chis; Kittie takes things first; F; Niece; 6

1468; Ah-dah-shay-chee-dish; Hunts to die; M; Husband; 60
1469; Esos-kay-it-chis; Her horse is pretty; F; Wife; 50
1470; Co-tah-dah-cock-cus; The bird everyway; M; Son; 22

1471; ---; Henry Reed; M; Batchelor[sic]; 24

1472; Archie-min-nay-tus; No milk; M; Husband; 40
1473; Ah-wane-dane-duck-coos; Stays out doors; F; Wife; 46
1474; Um-bah-dea-it-chis; His work is good; F; Daughter; 14

1475; Duck-bitchay-ucpah-dahcus; Ghost bear; M; Husband; 50
1476; Is-dotch-chea-ate-chase; Knows her prisoners; F; Wife; 45

1477; Chate-e-cah-duse; Runs the wolf; M; Husband; 66
1478; Duck-cock-beas; Bird woman; F; Wife; 52

1479; Ah-way-sheas; Fog; M; Husband; 30
1480; Is-bah-cah-bah-duck-kis; Hoop that sings; F; Wife; 24

Census of the __Crow__ Indians of __Crow__ Agency, __Montana__ taken by __E. H. Becker__, United States Indian Agent, __June 30th__, 189__8__

Key: Number; Indian Name; English Name; Sex; Relation; Age.

1481; Bah-touch-c-cook-cosh; Hears everyway; M; Husband; 42
1482; Dah-cock-ah-wah-chice; Bird sits down; F; Wife; 34
1483; Esock-chice; The hawk; M; Son; 21
1484; Un-de-chay-it-chice; Strikes pretty; M; Son; 13
1485; ---; Dorothy H. Everyway; F; Daughter; 1

1486; Ah-key-chice; The wet; M; Husband; 48
1487; Uck-sah-ey-chase; Knows her mother; F; Wife; 43
1488; Dah-say-cah-weas; Bad heart; M; Son; 15
1489; Bah-key-cush-sheas; Hoop that runs; M; Son; 12
1490; Bah-dup-peah-duc-coos; Kills right along; M; Son; 3
1491; Bah-shos; Feather; F; M-in-law; 52

1492; Ut-che-key-chis; Spies on the enemy No. 2; M; Husband; 33
1493; Bah-put-tah-bock-bus; Otter hoop; F; Wife; 22
1494; Ook-bish-cus; White tailed deer; F; Daughter; 5
1495; Oot-tah-dee-dish; Walking weasel; F; Daughter; 2

1496; Ah-way-cah-wah-sheas; Mountain that shows; M; Father; 43
1497; Is-tuck-kay-os-seas; Shows his gun; M; Son; 18
1498; Bah-put-tah-beas; Woman otter; F; Mother; 68

1499; Ish-oos; Back of the neck; M; Husband; 62
1500; Co-cosh-beas; Corn woman; F; Wife; 52
1501; Ea-cah-pish; Flat mouth; M; Son; 23

1502; Ah-wah-key-sos; Big sky; M; Husband; 42
1503; Oo-ah-wah-pash; Medicine wife; F; Wife; 32

1504; Esos-keas-sos; Blanket well known; F; Widow; 45

1505; Bit-che-doot-chis; Grabs the knife; F; Widow; 56
1506; ---; Dick Hawk; M; Son; 22

1507; Ush-ase-bah-sos; Charges on the camp; M; Hus; 62
1508; Be-shea-bah-pash; Medicine heifer; F; Wife; 58

1509; Chee-dup-chos-us; Grey bull; M; Husband; 37
1510; Ha-dane-e-cush-chice; Takes out of a crowd; F; Wife; 40
1511; Dook-ke-days; Goes to fight; F; Daughter; 4
1512; ---; Augusta grey bull; F; Daughter; 1

1513; As-says-days; Goes to the house; F; Widow; 46

1514; Chate-bah-cush-ecosh; Wolf looks up; M; ---; 38

Census of the __Crow__ Indians of __Crow__ Agency, __Montana__ taken by __E. H. Becker__, United States Indian Agent, __June 30th__, 1898

Key: Number; Indian Name; English Name; Sex; Relation; Age.

1515; Pay-dutch-chay-shee-dish; Yellow crow; M; Husband; 48
1516; Is-coe-chea-ate-chace; Knows her enemy; F; Wife; 49
1517; Ah-shoe-che-dish; Hunts the house; F; Mother; 73

1518; Duck-peace; Hugs; F; Widow; 60
1519; Eche-dock-itchay-ockindays; Rides a pretty horse; M; Son; 23

1520; Duck-bit-chay-boo-dish; Male bear; M; Husband; 26
1521; Uck-pah-deas; Works together; F; Wife; 26
1522; Ha-wan-da-bah-pash; Where he goes is medicine; F; Daughter; 11
1523; ---; Charles male bear; M; Son; 1

1524; Boa-e-hock-sos; Sings the last song; M; Husband; 33
1525; Uck-pah-dean-de-chis; Strikes plenty medicine; F; Wife; 37
1526; Ha-dane-e-cupe-pis; George Suis; M; Son; 22

1527; Ah-pit-bah-dock-cus; Crazy crane; M; Husband; 50
1528; Un-de-ditch-chis; Walks pretty; F; Wife; 48

1529; Ush-cup-cah-weas; Bad Dutchman; M; Husband; 30
1530; Boa-doo-pus; Two fish; F; Wife; 30
1531; Ome-bah-push; Medicine paint; M; Son; 1

1532; Ah-duck-chea-ah-hoos; Plenty coos; M; Husband; 50
1533; Tick-bah-dup-pace; Kills together; F; Wife; 35
1534; Kab-quah-ah-soos; Everybody knows him; M; Ad Son; 8

1535; Bea-it-chice; Pretty rock; F; Widow; 52

1536; Eas-pea-os-seas; Lion that shows; M; Husband; 50
1537; Cuck-kis; Spotted; F; Wife; 34
1538; Bondonpahhaydanedakcahcus; Bird in the cedars; M; Son; 15
1539; Ook-e-hosh; The other antelope; F; Daughter; 13
1540; Dutch-choa-dock-us; Muskrat daughter; F; Daughter; 5
1541; Dah-cock-bah-cush-days; Bird goes above; M; Son; 22
1542; Dah-he-os; Surrounded; M; Son; 2

1543; Bee-tah-was; Bell rock; M; Husband; 57
1544; Kah-wish; Bushy; F; Wife; 52
1545; Dah-cock-bah-soos; Bird high up; M; Son; 15

1546; Ecupe-pah-dah-cock-cuss; Bird hat; M; Husband; 30
1547; Is-chice-say-ah-wondabachis; Sits in her nest; F; Wife; 30
1548; Bon-don-pah-bah-coos; Cedar high up; M; Son; 12
1549; Chee-dup-be-das-dace; Bull walks to water; M; Son; 5
1550; Bah-ah-pah-dah-coos-days; Walks to growing things; F; Daughter; 3

Census of the __**Crow**__ Indians of __**Crow**__ Agency, __**Montana**__ taken by __**E. H. Becker**__, United States Indian Agent, __**June 30th**__, 189**8**

Key: Number; Indian Name; English Name; Sex; Relation; Age.

1551; Bah-put-tah-dock-cuss; Young otter; M; Husband; 60
1552; Eap-chay-ah-peas; Paipe[sic] around the neck; F; Wife; 54

1553; Bea-it-chise-sos; Not a pretty woman; F; Widow; 48

1554; Bah-dup-payishtuckkeydootchice; Takes the gun from the one that kills; M; Husband; 26
1555; Bea-cose; The woman F; Wife; 20
1556; Ah-kean-bahduckshaybah-ash; Medicine ties a knot on her head; F; Daughter; 4
1557; Ook-che-dup-pish; Bull antelope; M; Son; 3

1558; Utch-itch-ist-ton-tus; Notch; M; Husband; 36
1559; Bah-dup-pay-ate-chice; Known to kill; F; Wife; 33
1560; Dah-cock-hay-day-dus; Among the birds; M; Son; 19
1561; Eak-kay-his-shis; Red star; M; Son; 8
1562; Bish-doot-chice; Takes a blanket; F; Mother; 53

1563; Bah-put-tah-cheas; White otter; M; Husband; 57
1564; Oo-wat-tus; The iron; F; Wife; 54
1565; ---; Ben Gardiner; M; Son; 18

1566; Ish-bee-bah-pash; His rock is medicine; M; Husband; 33
1567; Bea-she-pit-tay; Black woman; F; Wife; 32

1568; E-shoe-cheas; Woodtick; M; Husband; 67
1569; Ah-cane-dah-pace; Kills across the water; F; Wife; 58

1570; Bish-cah-che-dup-pish; Bull dog; M; Husband; 39
1571; Bea-cah-weas; Bad woman; F; Wife; 42
1572; Boa-do-chis; Eats the fish; M; Son; 18

1573; Bah-duke-kea-it-chice; Good gun; M; ---; 26
1574; Uck-pah-dee-it-chice; Julia High Hawk; F; Sister; 22

1575; Kah-kay-de-chis; Strikes the lance; F; Widow; 54

1576; Duck-bit-chay-doo-puss; Two bears; M; Husband; 49
1577; Bim-boan-dee-dish; Walks in the water; F; Wfe[sic]; 47
1578; Dah-beas; Ready to fly; M; Son; 9

1579; Bah-coop-pash; Sick; M; Husband; 30
1580; Bah-chay-bah-chot-dah-pace; Kills a strong man; F; Wife; 30
1581; It-tut-bah-cheas; Fights along; M; Son; 8
1582; Ah-wah-cone-ah-way-chice; Sits on high ground; M; Son; 4

1583; Ahwaycahwaydaneduckbitchace; Bear in the mountains; M; Husband; 53

Census of the __Crow__ Indians of __Crow__ Agency, __Montana__ taken by __E. H. Becker__, United States Indian Agent, __June 30th__, 189__8__

Key: Number; Indian Name; English Name; Sex; Relation; Age.

1584; E-cupe-pah-che-shis; Puts on a hat; F; Wife; 49

1585; Ahwaycahwaydaneduckbitchace; Bear in the mountains; M; Husband; 53
1586; It-tut-doot-chice; Takes by herself; F; Wife; 50

1587; Esop-pee-e-wishes; Hairy moccasin; M; Husband; 45
1588; Bah-wah-wat-tays; Quick; F; Wife; 38
1589; Eak-ka-dah-cock-cus; Birds[sic] eggs; M; Son; 8
---; ---; Mary Hairy Moccasin; F; Daughter; 1

1590; Duck-bit-chay-bedooksahhoos; Bear comes from below; M; Husband; 58
1591; Eche-da-keas-sos; Horse well known; F; Wife; 56
1592; Bah-dup-pace-sos; Dont[sic] kill; M; Son; 7

1593; Ah-cah-pish-sis; Comes up red; M; Husband; 36
1594; Bah-put-tah-cuck-kis; Spotted otter; F; Wife; 27

1595; Che-shea-it-chice; Pretty tail; M; Husband; 44
1596; Ba-dow-e-kosh; Looks at the beads; F; Wife; 48

1597; E-sah-dut-chew-chice; Strong legs; M; Husband; 46
1598; Ah-way-uck-pah-deas; The ground is her medicine; F; Wife; 44

1599; Is-coe-che-che-dish; Hunts the enemy; M; Husband; 48
1600; Eat-tosh-da-bish-de-chice; Strikes her child; F; Wife; 56

1601; Ah-ditch-che-bah-dotchahoos; Paints herself plenty; M; Husband; 52
1602; Ah-pah-dee-it-chice; Pretty porcupine; F; Wife; 47

1603; Pah-chice; Push; M; Husband; 48
1604; Bah-chay-uck-pah-pice; Lies in bed with a man; F; Wife; 42
1605; Bah-shus-shays; Medicine dance; F; Daughter; 13

1606; Duck-bit-chay-dah-beas; Three bears; M; Husband; 38
1607; Dutch-chee-do-bah-pash; Medicine slides; F; Wife; 32
1608; Bashow-deditchchaypahsash; Medicine rock in front; F; Mother; 58

1609; Eas-shu-day; Yellow face; M; Husband; 40
1610; Bah-pee-sha-da-ah-hoos; Rides much behind; F; Wife; 33
1611; Bis-cah-she-pit-tus; Black dog; M; Son; 7

1612; Duck-bit-chay-it-chice; Pretty bear; M; Husband; 58
1613; Bah-cha-chice; Strong; F; Wife; 50

1614; Cush-some-bee-chice; Falls toward you; F; Widow; 78

Census of the __Crow__ Indians of __Crow__ Agency, __Montana__ taken by __E. H. Becker__, United States Indian Agent, __June 30th__, 189__8__

Key: Number; Indian Name; English Name; Sex; Relation; Age.

1615; Be-dup-pay-tuss; Like a beaver; F; Widow; 56
1616; Cone-dah-chice; Stays there; M; Son; 23

1617; Beday-ecupe-pahdootchice; Takes the hat; F; Widow; 60

1618; Ha-wash-tay-keas; Travels well known; M; Husband; 50
1619; Bah-it-cash; She sees it; F; Wife; 40
1620; Bak-kah-seas; Hoop that shows; M; Son; 17
1621; Ek-bah-dee-days; Medicine goes; F; Daughter; 7
1622; Is-bee-dean-bah-dup-pace; Kills in the door; F; Daughter; 11
1623; Bee-dea-it-chice; Pretty door; F; Daughter; 4

1624; E-kush-sheas; Turns back; M; Father; 40
1625; Uck-bah-dea-ush-eas; Medicine shows; F; Daughter; 9

1626; Chee-dup-keas-soo; Bull well known; M; Husband; 36
1627; Ush-ock-kay-duck-coos; Stays on top of the house; F; Wife; 30
1628; Bah-cah-key-bah-pash; Medicine shell; F; Daughter; 10
1629; Eche-dock-in-day-doot-chis; Takes the one that rides the horse; [F]; Daughter; 7
1630; Bah-eap-cap-cay-itches; Pretty hawk; F; Daughter; 4

1631; Dah-cock-beas; Bird woman; F; Widow; 46
1632; Bah-son-day-it-chis; Goes ahead pretty; F; Daughter; 16

1633; Chee-dup-chee-sus; Bulls tail; M; Husband; 23
1634; Boa-pis; Snow; F; Wife; 30

1635; Chate-dah-beas; Three wolves; M; Husband; 62
1636; Ahway-taycoe-ahway-chis; Sits down far away; F; Wife; 58

1637; Ah-dup-pis; Bull robe; M; Bachelor; 26

1638; Is-cah-ka-it-chis; Pretty lance; F; Widow; 49
1639; Is-coe-che-bah-chea-days; Goes to fight enemies; F; Widow; 80

1640; Be-shay-ah-hoos; Plenty buffalo; M; Husband; 30
1641; Duck-bit-chay-e-kos-seas; The bear turns around; F; Wife; 25
1642; It-chit-chey-ah-bah-pash; Medicine tobacco; F; Daughter; 9
1643; Bea-buckcoshsahdahcockcuss; Bird in the spring; F; Daughter; 1

1644; Ea-kock-kish-shays; Red fox; M; Bachelor; 54

1645; Duck-bit-chay-esahcoshish; Big bear; M; Husband; 57
1646; Been-de-chice; Strikes the water; F; Wife; 56

1647; Bah-put-tah-way-chate-chice; Otter chief; M; Husband; 29

53

Census of the __Crow__ Indians of __Crow__ Agency, __Montana__ taken by __E. H. Becker__, United States Indian Agent, __June 30th__, 1898

Key: Number; Indian Name; English Name; Sex; Relation; Age.

1648; Bah-she-chice; Pretty feather; F; Wife; 34

1649; Chate-ah-wah-shoes; Wolf house; M; Husband; 38
1650; Bea-cottus; Girl; F; Wife; 32

1651; Duck-bit-chay-he-dock-cuss; The bear now; M; Husband; 42
1652; Be-dup-cah-deas; Old beaver; F; Div. Wife; 30
1653; E-cush-sheas; Turns around; F; Daughter; 9

1654; Ah-pe-sah-sheedis; Yellow mule; M; Husband; 42
1655; Oot-tah-seas; Weasel that shows; F; Wife; 32
1656; Bedittah-shisshaycuckkiss; Spotted butterfly; M; Son; 11

1657; Bah-duck-key-doot-chis; Takes a gun; M; Husband; 31
1658; Bickens; Mare; F; Wife; 26
1659; ---; Susie; F; Daughter; 12
1660; Boo-dook-ah-cane-de-chis; Strikes on top of the ice; F; Daughter; 5

1661; Ick-cup-pee-dee-dah-bis; Three foretops; M; Husband; 32
1662; Cuck-key-bea; Spotted woman; F; Wife; 28
1663; Bea-huch-key; Long woman; F; Daughter; 4
1664; ---; Ruth T. Foretop; F; Daughter; 1

1665; ---; Wm. Steel Bear; M; Husband; 30
1666; ---; Esther shell on the neck; F; Wife; 23

1667; Been-dosh-kane-ah-wahchice; Sits by the water; F; [Widow]; 68

1668; Up-pay--e-wah-e-coosh[sic]; Looks with his ears; M; Husband; 33
1669; Oat-chean-bah-dup-pace; Kills at night; F; Wife; 39
1670; Ope-cah-deas; Old medicine tobacco; F; Daughter; 10
1671; Is-tuk-key-de-ditch; Strikes her gun; F; Mother; 67

1672; E-chin-doot-chice; Takes a horse; M; Husband; 29
1673; Un-dut-che-do-che-dice; Hunts to slide; F; Wife; 21
1674; Bea-bah-pash; Medicine woman; M; Son; 7
1675; Ah-shoe-ah-peas; Horn on her neck; F; Daughter; 4

1676; Pope-put-tay-ea-cot-tus; Little owl; M; Husband; 29
1677; Osh-doo-chape-ditchis; Strikes the thief in camp; F; Wife; 25
1678; Cheach-key-dock-cus; Young chicken; F; Daughter; 4

1679; E-cupe-pis; Gets down; M; Husband; 35
1680; Dah-cock-doo-pus; Two birds; F; Wife; 30
1681; Cah-dah-hay-day-duss; Bird in the rain; M; Son; 6
1682; Bah-dah-cah-deas; Old money; F; Daughter; 2

Census of the __Crow__ Indians of __Crow__ Agency, __Montana__ taken by __E. H. Becker__, United States Indian Agent, __June 30th__, 189__8__

Key: Number; Indian Name; English Name; Sex; Relation; Age.

1683; Duck-bit-chay-cah-dice; Old bear woman; F; Mother; 63

1684; Is-che-shay-ea-cot-tus; Little nest; M; Husband; 32
1685; ---; Mary Laforge; F; Wife; 25
1686; ---; Mary Little Nest; F; Daughter; 7

1687; Is-cos-chea-doe-cosh-ish; Holds the enemy; M; Husband; 30
1688; Bah-put-tah-seas; Shows the otter; F; Wife; 27
1689; Is-cah-kay-keas-sos; Plain spear; M; Son; 4
1690; ---; Robert holds the enemy; M; Son; 1

1691; ---; George Thomas; M; Bachelor; 31

1692; ---; Henry Russell; M; Husband; 29
1693; Bah-chea-cheas; Steals on camp; F; Wife; 26
1694; ---; Geo. W. Russell; M; Son; 1

1695; Ah-shoop-pahdate-cah-deas; Old horn; M; Husband; 34
1696; ---; Lucy Old Horn; F; Wife; 24
1697; ---; Fred Old Horn; M; Son; 8
1698; ---; Susie Old Horn; F; Daughter; 5

1699; Ah-day-cah-weas; Bad belly; M; Bachelor; 41

1700; Ah-day-chea-tus; White arm; M; Husband; 37
1701; Bah-cah-key-it-chice; Pretty shell; F; Wife; 33
1702; Bea-ditches; Strikes women; F; Mother; 72

1703; Bos-che-day-cah-deas; Old white man; M; Husband; 28
1704; Is-bah-hum-be-shis; Have things; F; Wife; 16

1705; Bout-tah-bah-coos-she-cosh; Coyote looks up; M; [Widower]; 71
1706; Doop-tush-ditches; Strikes both ways; F; [Mother]; 88

1707; Uck-sah-e-cos; Looks at her mother; F; Widow; 62

1708; Itche-bah-duck-shis; Plays with himself; M; Husband; 26
1709; Ah-dock-in-day-keas-sos; Horse she rides well known; F; Wife; 37
1710; ---; Charlie plays with himself; M; Son; 3

1711; Ah-way-chase; Knows the ground; M; Husband; 33
1712; ---; Perces knows the ground; F; Wife; 29
1713; ---; Lou knows the ground; F; Daughter; 2

1714; E-shue-ea-bah-pash; Medicine mane; M; Husband; 31
1715; Dah-cock-e-tuck-pos-da-tus; Bird without a cloud; F; Wife; 26

Census of the **Crow** Indians of **Crow** Agency, **Montana** taken by **E. H. Becker**, United States Indian Agent, **June 30th**, 189**8**

Key: Number; Indian Name; English Name; Sex; Relation; Age.

1716; Ush-dosh-cane-bah-dup-pace; Kills beside camp; F; Daughter; 7
1717; Uck-pah-dee-ah-seas; Shows his medicine; M; Son; 2

1718; Duckbitchay-edish-shippace; Cross bear; M; Husband; 37
1719; Is-bah-dah-hoos; Got plenty beads; F; Wife; 42
1720; Bah-pah-dish; Flower; M; Son; 12
1721; Eapchay-bahpah-dootchice; Takes the medicine pipe; F; Daughter; 3

1722; Bah-duk-keas; The gun; M; ---; 27

1723; Bah-key-de-hosh; The other blackbird; M; Husband; 29
1724; Bah-put-tah-seas; Otter that shows; F; Wife; 23
1725; Dup-pah-ecoos-seas; Turns around twice; M; Son; 8
1726; Bah-dea-ate-chice; Knows what to do; F; Daughter; 5

1727; Up-pock-cane-ditches; Strikes back of the head; F; [Widow]; 50

1728; Duck-bit-chay-cah-weas; Bad bear; M; Husband; 30
1729; Eas-cha-keep-pay; Crooked face; F; Wife; 22

1730; Iscoeche-hayday-codays; Goes among the enemy; M; Husband; 31
1731; Es-tup-poas; Shuts her eyes; F; Wife; 28
1732; Dee-cock-e-sos; Big bird; M; Son; 8
1733; Bum-bah-pash; Medicine wood; M; Son; 5

1734; ---; George Hill; M; Husband; 32
1735; ---; Mrs. George Hill; F; Wife; 22
1736; ---; Anna Hill; F; Daughter; 5
1737; ---; Mary Hill; F; Daughter; 3

1738; Chee-dup-she-chok-a-dus; Bull over the hill; M; Husband; 25
1739; Ah-pah-sut-tah-doot-chice; Takes a split ear; F; Wife; 23
1740; Dock-co-bah-pash; Medicine turtle; F; Daughter; 8

1741; Bea-dea-dush; The door; M; Husband; 27
1742; ---; Victoria Door; F; Wife; 18
1743; ---; Dora Door; F; Daughter; 2

1744; Oo-wa-shee-dish; Yellow in the mouth; M; Husband; 26
1745; Bout-tah-eas; Little coyote; F; Wife; 20
1746; Dah-cock-shee-dish; Yellow bird; F; Daughter; 4

1747; Bah-cha-cheas; Steals on the camp; M; Husband; 30
1748; Is-bah-cah-kea-ahoos; Plenty shells; F; Wife; 20

1749; Bashcheeday-shepit-tay; Light colored man; M; Husband; 26

Census of the __Crow__ Indians of __Crow__ Agency, __Montana__ taken by __E. H. Becker__, United States Indian Agent, __June 30th__, 1898

Key: Number; Indian Name; English Name; Sex; Relation; Age.

1750; Bah-ah-hoo-dup-pis; Finds plenty things; F; Wife; 25
1751; Ah-shue-ah-was-days; Horn dropped down; F; Wife; 19

1752; ---; Laura Green; F; ---; 23
1753; ---; Johnnie Shows A Pipe; M; Ad Son; 1

1754; Mah-shoe; Mint; M; Bachelor; 46

1755; Echit-che-sheas; The root; M; Bachelor; 61

1756; Ah-duk-che-bah-chate-chis; Coo Chief; M; Husband; 23
1757; Bah-cah-ca-kah-da-bish; Hoop that moves; F; Wife; 23
1758; Ope-cah-dish; Old tobacco; F; Daughter; 3
1759; ---; Florence Coo Chief; F; Daughter; 2

1760; Bash-keas-sos; Plain feather; M; Husband; 26
1761; Un-dah-coe-bah-coos; Lives high; F; Wife; 22

1762; Chee-dup-e-chee-dish; Bull horse; M; Husband; 29
1763; Shee-deak-days; Rattles going; F; Wife; 22
1764; Chas-foot-chice; Takes a roan horse; F; Daughter; 3

1765; ---; Mrs. Joe Pickett; F; Mother; 35
1766; ---; Richard A. Pickett; M; Son; 16
1767; ---; Robert A. Pickett; M; Son; 11
1768; ---; Joseph J. Pickett; M; Son; 8
1769; ---; William C. Pickett; M; Son; 5
1770; ---; Margaret Pickett; F; Daughter; 4

1771; Joseph Stewart; Joseph Stewart; M; Husband; 28
1772; Cah-coa-ays; Everything is hers; F; Wife; 25
1773; ---; Francis Stewart; M; Son; 5
1774; ---; Fannie Stewart; F; Daughter; 3
1775; ---; David Stewart; M; Brother; 24
1776; ---; Thomas Stewart; M; Brother; 26
1777; ---; Jackson Stewart; M; Brother; 21
1778; ---; William Stewart; M; Brother; 19
1779; Bah-cup-pah-e-chice; Pretty hail; F; Sister; 30

1780; ---; M. Two Belly; M; Husband; 38
1781; ---; Mrs. M. Two Belly; F; Wife; 31

1782; ---; John Wesley; M; Husband; 37
1783; ---; Jane Wesley; F; Wife; 32
1784; ---; Annie Wesley; F; Daughter; 16
1785; ---; Jennie Wesley; F; Daughter; 11

Census of the __Crow__ Indians of __Crow__ Agency, __Montana__ taken by __E. H. Becker__, United States Indian Agent, __June 30th__, 1898

Key: Number; Indian Name; English Name; Sex; Relation; Age.

1786; ---; Fannie Wesley; F; Daughter; 5

1787; ---; Mrs. James Robinson; F; Mother; 38
1788; ---; James Robinson; M; Son; 9
1789; ---; Charles Robinson; M; Son; 5
1790; ---; Ellen Robinson; F; Daughter; 4
1791; ---; Allen Robinson; M; Son; 3
1792; ---; Alice Robinson; F; Daughter; 1

1793; Mrs. G. F. Deputee; Mrs. G. F. Deputee; F; Mother; 31
1794; ---; Jennie Deputee; F; Daughter; 5
1795; ---; Flora Deputee; F; Daughter; 2
1796; ---; George Deputee; M; Son; 1

1797; ---; Mrs. Frank Gordon; F; Mother; 43
1798; ---; William Leighton; M; Son; 25

1799; ---; Mrs. B. Brave; F; Wife 33

1800; Hoo-chice; Wind; M; Husband; 34
1801; ---; Mrs. Thomas Laforge; F; Wife; 50
1802; ---; Rosa Laforge; F; Daughter; 16
1803; ---; Thomas Asa Laforge; M; Son; 14

1804; ---; John Alden; M; Husband; 30
1805; ---; Phoebe Alden; F; Wife; 19
1806; ---; Helen Alden; F; Daughter; 3

1807; ---; Mrs. J. B. Cooper; F; Mother; 58
1808; ---; Peter Cooper; M; Son; 18
1809; ---; Cynthia Cooper; F; Daughter; 13
1810; ---; Lula Cooper; F; Daughter; 10
1811; ---; Sylvester Hardy; M; Gr Son; 2

1812; ---; Martha Cooper Shenderline; F; Mother; 23
1813; ---; Joseph Shenderline; M; Son; 5
1814; ---; Edward Shenderline; M; Son; 3
1815; ---; Henry Shenderline; M; Son; 1

1816; ---; Mrs. Henry Keiser; F; Mother; 38
1817; ---; Frank Keiser; M; Son; 18
1818; ---; Myrtle Keiser; F; Daughter; 4

1819; ---; Mrs. Maggie Keiser Macer; F; Mother; 20
1820; ---; Mabel Macer; F; Daughter; 3
1821; ---; Henry Macer; M; Son; 1

Census of the __Crow__ Indians of __Crow__ Agency, __Montana__ taken by __E. H. Becker__, United States Indian Agent, __June 30th__, 1898

Key: Number; Indian Name; English Name; Sex; Relation; Age.

1822; ---; Mrs. David Yarlott; F; Mother; 50
1823; ---; Charles Yarlott; M; Son; 20
1824; ---; Frank Yarlott; M; Son; 16
1825; ---; Katie Yarlott; F; Daughter; 10

1826; ---; Mrs. John L. Smith; F; Mother; 52
1827; ---; Rosebud Farwell; M; Son; 16
1828; ---; Susan Farwell; F; Daughter; 22

1829; ---; Mrs. Al Morrison; F; Mother; 50
1830; ---; Hannah Morrison; F; Daughter; 17
1831; ---; Alvin Morrison; M; Son; 14

1832; E-say-dup-pah-choas; Points the gun in his face; M; Husband; 32
1833; ---; Mrs. Thomas Stewart; F; Wife; 39
1834; ---; Lucy Stewart; F; Daughter; 13
1835; Ah-wah-cane-cah-doos-shis; Runs over the ground; M; Son; 5

1836; ---; Mrs. R. W. Cummins; F; Mother; 48
1837; ---; Frances E?[sic] Cummins Thompson; F; Daughter; 21

1838; ---; Mrs. Thomas Kent; F; Mother; 41
1839; ---; Josephine Kent; F; Daughter; 18
1840; ---; Elizabeth Kent; F; Daughter; 16
1841; ---; Maggie Kent; F; Daughter; 11

1842; ---; Mary Kent Stevens; F; Mother; 20
1843; ---; Mary Stevens; F; Daughter; 3
1844; ---; Kent Stevens; M; Son; 2
1845; ---; Agnes Stevens; F; Daughter; 1

1846; ---; Mrs. Ella Kent Cashen; F; Mother; 22
1847; ---; Willie Cashen; M; Son; 4
1848; ---; Alice Cashen; F; Daughter; 3
1849; ---; Ella Cashen; F; Daughter; 1

1850; ---; Maggie Garrigus; F; Mother; 27
1851; ---; Mary F. Garrigus; F; Daughter; 6
1852; ---; Margaret E. Garrigus; F; Daughter; 5
1853; ---; Arthur R. Garrigus; M; Son; 3
1854; ---; Dorothy B. Gaggigus[sic]; F; Daughter; 1

1855; ---; Abbie Lande; F Mother; 24
1856; ---; Thomas A. Lande; M; Son; 3
1857; ---; Henry Dewey Lande; M; Son; 1

Census of the __Crow__ Indians of __Crow__ Agency, __Montana__ taken by __E. H. Becker__, United States Indian Agent, __June 30th__, 189__8__

Key: Number; Indian Name; English Name; Sex; Relation; Age.

1858; ---; Frederick Geisdorff; M; Bachelor; 27
1859; ---; Louisa Geisdorff; F; Sister; 23
1860; ---; Charlotte Geisdorff; F; Sister; 20

1861; ---; Mrs. George R. Davis; F; Mother; 49
1862; ---; Margaretta A. Davis; F; Daughter; 19
1863; ---; Effie N. Davis; F; Daughter; 13
1864; ---; Blaine R. Davis; M; Son; 4
1865; ---; Charles Wort Davis; M; Son; 28

1866; ---; Minnie Reed; F; Orphan; 23
1867; ---; Frances Reed; M; Brother; 20
1868; ---; Della Reed; F; Sister; 14
1869; ---; Nellie Reed; F; Sister; 12
1870; ---; Edith Reed; F; Sister; 10
1871; ---; Katie Reed; F; Sister; 8

1872; ---; Mary K. Reed; F; Orphan; 14

1873; ---; Mrs. Wm. H. White; F; Mother; 36
1874; ---; Wm. H. White; M; Son; 18
1875; ---; Mary E. White; F; Daughter; 16
1876; ---; Minnie E. White; F; Daughter; 13

1877; ---; Mrs. Thomas Shane; F; Mother; 39
1878; ---; Kittie Shane; F; Daughter; 20
1879; ---; Patrick C. Shane; M; Son; 13
1880; ---; Frank Shane; M; Son; 10
1881; ---; Josie Shane; F; Daughter; 8
1882; ---; Bessie Shane; F; Daughter; 6
1883; ---; Thomas Shane; M; Son; 4
1884; ---; Edward Shane; M; Son; 2

1885; ---; Mrs. Thomas Doyle; F; Mother; 21
1886; ---; Robert Doyle; M; Son; 1
1887; ---; Mrs. Heckenlively; F; Mother; 22
1888; ---; Guy L. Heckenlively; M; Son; 1

1889; ---; Cora Williams; F; [Orphan]; 19
1890; ---; Mattie Williams; F; Sister; 17

1891; ---; Ellen Jackson; F; Mother; 46
1892; ---; John Jackson; M; Son; 17
1893; ---; Eliza Jackson; F; Daughter; 12
1894; ---; Julia Jackson; F; Daughter; 9

Census of the __Crow__ Indians of __Crow__ Agency, __Montana__ taken by __E. H. Becker__, United States Indian Agent, __June 30th__, 189__8__

Key: Number; Indian Name; English Name; Sex; Relation; Age.

1895; ---; John Frost; M; Husband; 23
1896; ---; Is-bin-dot-bah-pash; Medicine shield; F; Wife; 18
1897; ---; Daniel L. Frost; M; Son; 1

1898; ---; Joseph Cooper; M; Husband; 26
1899; ---; Susie Cooper; F; Wife; 27
1900; ---; Theodora Cooper; F; Daughter; 6
1901; ---; Laura Cooper; F; Daughter; 5
1902; ---; Sylvania Cooper; F; Daughter; 4
1903; ---; James Cooper; M; Son; 2

1904; ---; Leartus W. Pease; M; [Bachelor]; 36

1905; ---; Levantia W. Pearson; F; Mother; 35
1906; ---; Virginia Pearson; F; Daughter; 6
1907; ---; Helen Estella Pearson; F; Daughter; 5
1908; ---; Ethel May Pearson; F; Daughter; 3

1909; ---; George W. Pease; M; Husband; 32
1910; ---; Sarah Pease; F; Wife; 31
1911; ---; David Peases[sic]; M; Son; 7
1912; ---; James Pease; M; Son; 8
1913; ---; Benjamin Peases; M; Son; 5
1914; ---; Emory Pease; M; Son; 4
1915; ---; Anson H. Pease; M; Son; 2
1916; ---; Geo. Pease; M; Son; 1

1917; ---; Mrs. Marshall; F; ---; 41

1918; Dah-cup-cah-cheas; Calf that shakes; F; ---; 48

1919; ---; Mary Townsend; F; Mother; 24
1920; ---; Mabel Magdaline Townsend; F; Daughter; 3
1921; ---; Fred A. Townsend; M; Son; 1

1922; ---; Mrs. Amy Scott; F; Mother; 20
1923; ---; George Scott; M; Son; 2
1924; ---; Elmer Scott; M; Son; 1

1925; Chate-dah-beas; Three wolves; M; [Widower]; 46

1926; Is-bah-key-cush-sheas; Hoop turns around; M; Father; 23
1927; ---; August Hoop Turns Around; M; Son; 1

1928; Chee-dup-kah-deas; Old Bull; M; Husband; 24
1929; Bah-cah-key-day-cus; Shell child; F; Wife; 19

Census of the __Crow__ Indians of __Crow__ Agency, __Montana__ taken by __E. H. Becker__, United States Indian Agent, __June 30th__, 189__8__

Key: Number; Indian Name; English Name; Sex; Relation; Age.

1930; Bah-pash; Medicine; F; Daughter; 1

1931; Ahway-tayday-cock-cuss; Bird Far Away; M; Husband; 22
1932; Bah-cah-key-pah-pash; Medicine shell; F; Div. Wife; 22
1933; A-wah-shoes; Runs into a house; F; Daughter; 3

1934; Ah-shue-cah-bay; Bush head; M; Husband; 23
1935; Cah-pah-dea-bah-ows; Medicine brings things; F; Wife; 21

1936; E-dea-hish; Breathes; M; Husband; 34
1937; Ah-woos-cah-deas; Old sweat house; F; Wife; 33

1938; ---; Martin round face; M; Husband; 25
1939; ---; Katie Dreamer; F; Wife; 22
1940; ---; Jeanette Round Face; F; Daughter; 2

1941; Tuch-chay-dah-cock-cuss; Straight bird; M; Husband; 22
1942; Is-coe-cheydoot-chis; Catches the enemy; F; Wife; 22
1943; Bah-it-chay-doot-chis; Takes pretty things; F; Daughter; 4

1944; ---; Charles Ten Bear; M; Husband; 22
1945; Cheas-day-kay-ock-in-day-ditches; Strikes riding a grey horse; F; Wife; 16
1946; ---; Frances Ten Bear; M; Son; 1

1947; Bea-sos-ecos; Looks back; M; Husband; 22
1948; Bah-o-dop-keas-sos; Finds Plain; F; Wife; 21

1949; Dah-cock-cuss; Bird; M; Husband; 22
1950; Bah-put-tah-beas; Otter woman; F; Wife; 18
1951; ---; Glenn Bird; M; Son; 2

1952; Choos-say-dah-quas; Sends part home; M; Husband; 29
1953; Oo-shay-it-chise; Pretty hole; F; Wife; 19
1954; ---; Joseph P. Home; M; Son; 2

1955; In-cup-pah-bish-de-chice; Strikes the hat; F; Mother; 39
1956; Bah-be-dish-e-sos; Broils big; M; Son; 9

1957; ---; Samuel Sumner Davis; M; Husband; 23
1958; ---; Olive Yellow Face; F; Wife; 22

1959; Bah-ea-says; Big mouth; F; Mother; 32
1960; Bee-shay-e-dews; Buffalo stands up; F; Daughter; 7
1961; Is-che-shay-esos; Big nest; F; Daughter; 2

1962; Is-oo-what-tus; Her iron; F; Mother; 25

Census of the __**Crow**__ Indians of __**Crow**__ Agency, __**Montana**__ taken by __**E. H. Becker**__, United States Indian Agent, __**June 30th**__, 189__8__

Key: Number; Indian Name; English Name; Sex; Relation; Age.

1963;   E-cosh; Looks at him; M; Son; 4

1964;   Dah-cock-ah-seas; Bird that shows; F; Widow; 50

1965;   Bah-chay-eat-che-bish-ay; Man with a beard; M; Husband; 22
1966;   Bah-oos; Brings things; F; Wife; 26
1967;   Be-shay-ah-shees; Buffalo that shows; M; Son; 11

1968;   Ecupe-pah-de-chic; Strikes the hat; F; [Widow]; 50

1969;   Be-de-he-dup-pace; Crosses the water; F; [Widow]; 58

1970;   Ba-chay-ha-wat-de-chice; Strikes one man; F; [Widow]; 53

1971;   Cha-cush; Five; F; [Widow]; 74

1972;   Bah-ay-bis-eas; Hastings[sic]; F; Mother; 33
1973;   Is-bah-cah-key-bat-pash; Her medicine shell; F; Daughter; 4
1974;   ---; Susie Spotted; F; Daughter; 1

1975;   Bah-chea-ish-it-chace; Loves to fight; M; [Bachelor]; 23

1976;   Bah-son-day-it-chice; Goes ahead pretty; M; Husband; 23
1977;   Bah-put-tah-beas; Otter woman; F; Wife; 33
1978;   ---; George Goes Ahead Pretty; M; Son; 1

1979;   ---; James Laforge; M; Husband; 21
1980;   ---; Sage Woman; F; Wife; 18
1981;   ---; William Laforge; M; Son; 3

1982;   ---; Mary Morrison Humphrey; F; Mother; 21
1983;   ---; Maud Humphrey; F; Daughter; 2

1984;   Ah-hoo-ha-e-cush-seas; Turns back plenty; M; Husband; 23
1985;   Be-shay-dane-ah-wah-chice; Sits among the rocks; F; Wife; 19

1986;   Ah-wah-cah-way-dane-chee-dup-pish; Mountain bull; M; Husband; 22
1987;   Ah-bush-it-chice; Pretty sweat house; F; Wife; 19

1988;   Co-tah-dee-dish; Weasel that walks; F; Widow; 23

1989;   Con-up-e-say; Big nose old woman; F; [Widow]; 23

1990;   Issuc-cheysah-sheedish; Yellow hawk; M; [Widower]; 41

1991;   Ecupe-pay-bee-dosh; Fire hat; M; [Widower]; 41

Census of the __Crow__ Indians of __Crow__ Agency, __Montana__ taken by __E. H. Becker__, United States Indian Agent, __June 30th__, 189__8__

Key: Number; Indian Name; English Name; Sex; Relation; Age.

1992; E-shoe-cah-dup-pace; Kills one with the big knee; F; Widow; 60

1993; Ah-quas; Covered up; M; Husband; 26
1994; Bah-pah-dit-chis; Plenty things growing; F; Wife; 21
1995; Ah-key-bee-deep-pah-cuss; Persons; F; Daughter; 4

1996; Ah-shay-day-duss; In the camp; F; [Widow]; 71

1997; Bah-dah-kut-teas; Crazy; M; Husband; 28
1998; E-kay-beas; Egg woman; F; Wife; 19

1999; Oat-cheas-du-dish; Ralph Saco; M; Husband; 21
2000; Bee-dup-dah-cuss; Young Beaver; F; Wife; 22
2001; ---; Edward Saco; M; Son; 1

2002; Echete-ichis; Pretty horse; M; Husband; 33
2003; ---; Monica Horn; F; Wife; 18

Crow Agency Montana, 1899 Census

J. E. Edwards, Agent

43368

5/9/43

Sept 5/99.

J E Edwards
U S Ind agt.

Transmits census
of the Crow Indians
for fiscal year end-
ing June 30/99

DEPARTMENT OF THE INTERIOR,
UNITED STATES INDIAN SERVICE.

Crow Agency, Montana, Sept. 5, 1899.

Hon. Commissioner of

    Indian Affairs,

        Washington, D. C.

Sir:-

    I have the honor to transmit herewith a census of the Crow tribe of Indians for the fiscal year ending June 30, 1899.

        Very respectfully,

        J. E. Edwards

        U. S. Indian Agent.

Census of the __**Crow**__ Indians of __**Crow**__ Agency __**Montana**__ taken
By __**J.E. Edwards**__, United States Indian Agent __**June 30, 1899**__

Key: Number; Indian Name; English Name; Sex; Relation; Age

1; Ahnehe-iches; Walks Pretty; F Widow; 40
2; Lagak-hishes; Howard Red Bird; M; Son; 20
3; Lagak-esash; Big Bird; M; Son; 9

4; Budesash; No Horse; M; Husband; 33
5; Oo-inkpus; Hugs the Weasel; F; Wife 36
6: ---; Gretchen No Horse; F; Daughter; 1

7; Ook-cas; Little Antelope; F; Widow; 73

8; Nas-kowees; Bad Heart; M; Husband; 26
9; Lagak-hishes; Red Breasted Bird; F; Wife; 23
10; Lagak-mes-da-ses; Rain Bird; F; Daughter; 5
11; Bah-wah-sonedah-itchis; Good Leader; F; Daughter; 3

12; Awak-in-lagaks; Bird all over Ground; M; Husband; 53
13; Mida-ichsis; Goes Well; F Wife; 49
14; Lagaks-ichis; Good Bird; F; Daughter; 8

15; Ahshua-wahnaks; Crazy Head; M; Husband; 63
16; Esha-shates; Paints Pretty; F; Wife; 52
17; Esaksha-chaschedees; Hunts the Arrow; M; Son; 21

18; Mea-daka; White Woman; M; Husband; 40
19; Ooomah-sees; See in the Mouth; F; Wife; 33

20; Ahluk-chea-akuse; He knows His Coos; M; Husband; 39
21; Besha-chea-makpash; Medicne[sic] White Buffalo; F; White; 36

22; Eescha-naks; Young Jack Rabbit; M; Husband; 52
23; Ahpit-cheis; White Crane; F; Wife; 43
24; Ahwak-amach; Sits Toward the Mountain; M; Son; 16

25; Awaksha-echete; Gros Ventre Horse; M; Husband; 57
26; Chis-sheis; Nest; F; Wife; 47
27; Ahskarooche-amach; Horse Sits Down; F; Daughter; 16

28; Ahpit-nake; Young Crane; M; Father; 59
29; Eukase-hishes; Red Snake; F; Daughter; 11

30; ---; Andrew Wallace; M; Husband; 26
31; ---; Jennie Wallace; F; Wife; 21
32; ---; Josie Wallace; F; Daughter; 5

33; Chatis; The Wolf; M; Husband; 55
34; Checks-doochis; Takes Five; F; Wife; 55

Census of the __Crow__ Indians of __Crow__ Agency __Montana__ taken
By __J.E. Edwards__, United States Indian Agent __June 30, 1899__

Key: Number; Indian Name; English Name; Sex; Relation; Age

35; E-step-aes; Eli Blackhawk; M; Son; 25
---; Chate-ela-cheis; White Bellied Wolf; M; Father; --

36; Eche-kuis; Sweet Mouth; M; Husband; 40
37; Andicha-poois; Sore Where Whipped; F; Wife; 44

38; Wtekut-napes; Kills Close; F; Widow; 76
39; Mishodechitse-lagak; Medicine Rock Bird; M; Ad. Son; 9

40; Esa-keepa; Wrinkle Face; M; Husband; 43
41; Eskochea-ichis; Fights the Enemy Good; F; Wife 46
42; Ahwotkot-dichis; Strikes Same One; F; Daughter; 4

43; Eskuka-ahsees; Shows a Lance; M; Husband; 49
44; Mi-iche-doochis; Takes Pretty Things; F; Wife; 61

45; Ahma-apische; Arm Around the Neck; M; Husband; 58
46; Hederin-dichis; Strikes in a Crowd; F; Wife; 58

47; Mena-ahwotkot; One Goose; M; Husband; 57
48; Min-makpash; Medicine Water; F; Wife; 45
49; Lagak-heahsas; Bird Well Known; M; Son; 16
50; Ashkarooches-kandeas; Old Horn; F; Daughter; 9
51; Mean-dichis; Strikes Plenty Women; F; Mother; 73

52; Ahka-karasash; Don't Run on Top; M; Husband; 36
53; Ees-kapa; Flat Face; F; Wife; 36
54; Echete-dekush; Stays with the Horse; F; Daughter; 4

55; Ekupa-cheis; Packs the Hat; M; Husband; 41
56; Ahpake-hedere-lagaks; Bird in a Cloud; F; Wife; 33
57; Eesackas-ahoos; Plenty Arrows; M; Son; 8

58; Miastacheda-karoos; White Man Runs Him; M; Husband; 42
59; Popet-itsechats; Good Owl; F; Wife; 37
60; Bechon-herepis; Kills One With Red Blanket; F; Daughter; 12
61; Micha-ahcheis-botots; Steals on Strong Camp; M; Son; 5

62; Meneash-koop-skuis; Sioux; M; Batchelr[sic]; 48

63; Duchkis; Left Hand; M; Husband; 25
64; Cheis-makpash; Medicine Tail; F; Wife; 28
65; Nakas-makpash; Child is Medicine; F; Daughter; 9
66; Nahkose-chedup; Bull Turtle; M; Son; 4
67; ---; Peter L. Hand; M; Son; 1

Census of the __Crow__ Indians of __Crow__ Agency __Montana__ taken
By __J.E. Edwards__, United States Indian Agent __June 30, 1899__

Key: Number; Indian Name; English Name; Sex; Relation; Age

68; Peritse-kandeas; Old Crow; M; Husband; 62
69; Ahoo-aroopis; Finds All; F; Wife; 39
70; Mintahsehederimitpal; Persons in the Moon; F; Daughter; 6
71; Istuka-sa-here-dadush; Stands Among The Shooters; M; Son; 5

72; Chada-kos; Holds Up; M; Husband; 41
73; Ootay-doochis; Takes a Weasel; F; Wife; 19
74; Beah-kahdeas; Rock Old; M; Son; 4
---; Beshay-ahks; Last Buffalo; M; Son; [3]

75; Eskay-ahwotkot; One Star; M; Husband; 33
76; Miastascheda-meas; White Woman; F; Wife; 48
77; ---; George Washington; M; Son; 16
78; Easpooetatsa; Good Sheep; F; Daughter; 4

79; Miah-hoo-ted-deas; Does Lots of Things; F; --[Widow]; 48

80; Dutsuah-moopis; Two Muskrats; F; --[Widow]; 71

81; Istuka-asees; Gun Shows; M; Husband; 32
82; Dakpitses-asees; Looks at the Bear; F; Wife; 27
83; Ba-orap-saskatch; Finds Soon; M; Son; 4

84; Bee-dup-pay-tus; Like a Beaver; F; Widow; 57

85; Ahmahta; Long Way Off; F; Widow; 57

86; Misakohn-miches; Grandmother's Knife; M; Husbnad[sic]; 43
87; Chisah-kahdeas; Old Nest; F; Wife; 34
88; ---; Sarah G. Knife; F; Daughter; 1

89; Duchuis; Muskrat; F; Widow; 55

90; Mi-ich-ose; Brings Good Things; F; Widow; 38
91; Etash-hishis; Red Shirt; F; Daughter; 5

92; Eer-kahwash; Bird Tail That Rattles; M; Husband; 52
93; Kahdeis; Old; F; Wife; 53

94; Dakpitska-cheis; White Bear; M; Widower; 81

95; Mahpak-hoos; Comes in a day; M; Husband; 49
96; Mahkaristish; Yearling; F; Wife; 35
97; Eisda-isischish; Loves to go after Water; F; Daughter; 11

98; Besha-chedups; Buffalo Bull #1; M; Husband; 39

Census of the __Crow__ Indians of __Crow__ Agency __Montana__ taken
By __J.E. Edwards__, United States Indian Agent __June 30, 1899__

Key: Number; Indian Name; English Name; Sex; Relation; Age

99; Meakot-kowees; Bad Woman; F; Wife; 37
100; Me-ichis; Pretty Rock; F; Daughter; 9
101; Muna-shuis; Blue Wood; M; Son; 14

102; Chatis; Wolf; M; Husband; 48
103; Midesha-doochis; Gets Hold the Dead; F; Wife; 43
104; Eskoche-okepis; Shoots the Enemy; M; Son; 19
105; Datsuah-doochis; Takes a Sinew; F; Mother; 87

106; Dakpitska-cheis; White Bear No. 2; M; Husband; 48
107; Minna-nahkuse; By the Side of the Water; F; Wife; 57
108; ---; George White Bear; M; Son; 25
109; ---; Russell W. Bear; M; Son; 23

110; Botsa-kowees; Bad Man; M; Husband; 46
111; Bahkeed-lagaks; Blackbird; F; Wife; 42

112; Ahpa-duttotoes; Cut Ear; M; Husband; 41
113; Ekupa-esash; Big Hat; F; Wife; 51

114; Duck-bea-cheacock-indas; Rides a Whitechipped Horse; M; Husband; 22
115; Mi-ich-napes; Kills Pretty Ones; F; Wife; 20
116; ---; Harold Rides a White Horse; M; Son; 2

117; Muche-dais; Good Luck; M; Husband; 41
118; Chate-hessas; Wolf Well Known; F; Wife; 39

119; Lagak-heases; Bird Well Known; Husband; 30
120; Wahpootkamakpash; Medicine Otter; F; Wife; 31

121; Echeta-kowees; Bad Horse; M; Husband; 27
122; Bachois-ichis; Pretty Bullrush; F; Wife 23

123; Bahkeede-ichis; Pretty Blackbird; F; [Widow]; 63

124; Esukis; Corner of the Mouth; M; Husband; 49
125; Iamina-wishs-doochis; Takes Pretty Scalp; F; Wife 50
126; Echeta-gash-eduse; Elk Stands Up; M; Son; 13

127; Ahse-desh; Shows as He Goes; M; Husband; 43
128; Mi-iche-kooshdess; Goes to Good Things; F; Wife; 46
129; Istuka-hcasas; Well Known Arrow; M; Son; 9

130; Opes; Smokes (Ben Spotted Horse); M; Husband; 27
131; Budeesh; Horse; F; Wife; 30

Census of the __Crow__ Indians of __Crow__ Agency __Montana__ taken
By __J.E. Edwards__, United States Indian Agent __June 30, 1899__

Key: Number; Indian Name; English Name; Sex; Relation; Age

132; Oeta-echeta; Iron Horse; M; Husbnad[sic]; 25
133; Ahwoosh-akuse; Knows the Sweat House; F; Wife; 20
134; Mean-dichis; Strikes the Woman; F; Daughter; 4

135; Chate-kupis; Wolf Lays Down; M; Husband; 60
136; Isbeda; Kills at the Door; F; Wife; 53
137; Ekuh-push; Gets Down; M; Son; 20

138; Is-shu-shudish; Backbone; M; Widower; 30
139; Mahsha-hotskish; Long Feather; Son; 6

140; Mahsha-wots; One Feather; M; Husband; 57
141; Ahta-malapes; Kills First; F; Wife; 65

142; Eche-dudees; Don't Mix; M; Husband; 27
143; Ahta-malapes; Groans; f; Wife; 33

144; Boa-ah-ta-ichis; Pretty Coyote; M; Husband; 24
145; Beedah-doshkan-dichis; Strikes by Side of Water; F; Wife; 33

146; Educhesha-heas; Plain Left Hand; M; Husband; 62
147; Echik-dichis; Strikes First; F; Wife; 52
148; Wutta-makpash; Medicine Coyote; F; Daughter; 16

149; Lukpa-sashis; Bright Wings; M; Husband; 32
150; Mah-hahchis-lukishdish; Goes to Look at Prisoners; F; Wife 22
151; Echete-mulaksis; Sings on Horse; M; Son; 6
152; Echete-maks-kochetish; Horse Stays all the Time; F; Daughter; 4

153; Ahpewsha; Gros Ventre; M; Husband; 37
154; Ahwa-akuse; Knows the Ground; F; Wife; 34
155; Eskoche-karooshes; Runs the Enemy; M; Son; 6
156; Mear-pish; Kills the Woman; F; Daughter; 1

157; Budeesh; Horse; M; Father; 42
158; ---; Mary Last Bull; F; Daughter; 2

159; Isba-ichis; Pretty Louse; F; Mother; 53
160; Eisda-karooshes; Loves to Run; M; Son; 18

161; Baruks-acha-nadees; Walks Over Ice; M; Husband; 21
162; Mea-makpash; Medicine Woman; F; Wife; 17

163; Nooptah-dichis; Strikes Twice; F; [Widow]; 83

164; Chapes; Whinners; M; Husband; 42

Census of the **Crow** Indians of **Crow** Agency **Montana** taken By **J.E. Edwards**, United States Indian Agent **June 30, 1899**

Key: Number; Indian Name; English Name; Sex; Relation; Age

165; Echete-sheedes-ahkinda; Rides a Yellow Horse; F; Wife; 39
166; Me-Makpesh-ehas; The Other Medicine Rock; F; Daughter; 12

000; 167-188 Omitted from the record for 1899.

189; Ootuh-chepups; Bull Weasel; M; Husband; 28
190; Esa-keepa; Crooked Face; F; Wife; 24
191; Istuka-makpash; Medicine Arrow; M; Son; 8
192; Peesh-ah-deus; Rides Behind; F; Daughter; 4

193; Chedup-kochetish; Bull all the time; M; [Widower]; 68

194; Malpa; The Root; M; [Widower]; 62

195; Bedupa-bukata-dase; Beaver that Passes; F; Widow; 37
196; Ahkinda-heahsas; Rides a Horse Well Known; F; Daughter; 11
197; ---; Florence Beaver Passes; F; Daughter; 2

198; Minhapesh; Swamp Flag; F; Widow; 53

199; Echete-hukish; Spotted Horse; M; Husband; 50
200; Is-espe-makpash-ichis; Pretty Medicine Pipe; F; Wife; 41
201; E-rooptay-chis; By Herself; F; Daughter; 11
202; Istuka-ahoos; Plenty Arrows; M; Son; 9
203; ---; Strikes Rider of Red Ear; M; Son; 1

204; Booah-ahseesh; Shows a Fish; M; Husband; 53
205; Mahhake-nahks; Shell Child; F; Wife; 47

206; Bishka-kahps; Flat Dog; M; Husband; 53
207; Mea-chedupa; Woman Bull; F; Wife; 51

208; Otse-muchachis; Chief at Night; M; Husband; 63
209; Uck-beeche-bay-ahhoos; Many Talks With Him; F; Wife; 25

210; Dahpitsa-eahkotish; Little Bear; M; Father; 63
211; Mahama-nudeis; Edward Little Bear; M; Son; 22

212; Ope-edupsish; Fat Tobacco; M; Husband; 74
213; Dakup-makpash; Medicine Calf; F; Wife; 71
214; Makpootka-botsots; Strong Otter; M; Son; 13

215; Ahpaka-heder-dakpitch; Bear in a Cloud; M; Husband; 42
216; Miootsheda-esash; Big Lark; F; Wife; 47
217; ---; Blake White Bear; M; Son; 16

Census of the __**Crow**__ Indians of __**Crow**__ Agency __**Montana**__ taken By __**J.E. Edwards**__, United States Indian Agent __**June 30, 1899**__

Key: Number; Indian Name; English Name; Sex; Relation; Age

218; Eep-shedish; Yellow Tail; M; Husband; 37
219; ---; Mrs. S.C. Davis; F; Wife; 33
220; Mei-rauk-shay; Summer; M; Son; 11
221; Alack-chee-ichis; Has Good Coos; M; Son; 7

222; Nah-kaps; Flat Back; M; Husband; 53
223; Ahpa-doochis; Take Together; F; Wife; 57

224; Chedup-akookish; Dummy Bull; M; Father; 63
225; Mitet-duspis; Passes Everything; M; Son; 25

226; Eem-botsesh; Blood Man; M; Husband; 41
227; Ahwaka-mees; Woman on Top of Ground; F; Wife; 29
228; Ikpahne-ich; Pretty Medicine; F; Daughter; 7
229; ---; Alberta B. Man; F; Daughter; 1

230; Dakpitska-ahway-repeas; Bear Goes to Other Ground; M; Husband; 30
231; Kookomish; Kittie Medicine Tail; F; Wife; 20
232; ---; Mary B. Ground; F; Daughter; 1

233; Dayka-ahspittesh; Black Eagle; M; Husband; 33
234; Esa-keepa; Crooked Face; F; Wife; 27
235; Iswaka-miochedish; Lucky Hoop; M; Son; 13
236; Dakpitska-ahn-duish; Bear that haises[sic] his Paw; M; Son; 3
237; ---; Irene Mountain; F; Sister; 16

238; Cheetaka-eahkoskot; Little Prairie Chicken; M; Husband; 51
239; Ahsha-ekash; Looks at the Lodge; F; Wife; 53

240; Mahkawas; The Bread; M; Husband; 38
241; Mekas-besas; Stoops to Charge; F; Wife; 39

242; Biskka-kahdeas; Old Dog; M; Husband; 67
243; Me-heahsas; Well Known Rock; F; Wife; 56
244; Aska-wuts; Harry Old Dog; M; Son; 12

245; Eak-kin-hish-sis; Red in the Chin; F; ---; 24

246; Eskochea-basash; Charges the Enemy; M; Father; 62
247; Suah-oowitch; Thundre[sic] Iron; M; Son; 23

248; Ahpit-kahdeas; Old Crane; M; Husband; 33
249; ---; Ella Farwell; F; Wife; 29
250; ---; Mary Crane; F; Daughter; 8

251; Peah-noops; Two Stinks; M; Husband; 34

Census of the __Crow__ Indians of __Crow__ Agency __Montana__ taken
By __J.E. Edwards__, United States Indian Agent __June 30, 1899__

Key: Number; Indian Name; English Name; Sex; Relation; Age

252; Oo-what-tah-hoos; Plenty Irons; F; Wife; 26

253; Booah-lagak; Fish Bird; M; [Widower]; 38
254; It-tah-um-bit-dosh; Pretty Near Fell; M; Brother; 25

255; Ahpit-dakpitska; Bear Crane; M; Husband; 60
256; Ische-itse; Pretty Hair; F; Wife; 48
257; Dakpitska-naks; Bear Child; M; Son; 12
258; Daykoosh-naks; Young Eagle; M; Son; 5
259; ---; George Bear Crane; M; Son; 3

260; Isminua-wish-napes; Kills With a Scalp; F; [Widow]; 61

261; Lagak-etashdesh; Bird Shirt; M; Husband; 59
262; Botsa-nahme-napes; Kills Three Men; F; Wife; 47
263; Minnepak-ichis; Ben Long Ear; M; Son; 21
264; Ahwokchedush-helamach; Sits Among the Cedars; F; Daughter; 16
265; Ahpay-sheedes; Yellow Leaves; M; Son; 9
266; ---; Herbert Long Ear; M; Son; 25

267; Chedup-ehas; The Other Bull; M; Husband; 35
268; Ah-kish-koss; Gives to the Sun; F; Wife; 23
269; Daykoosh-mahke; Eagle Above; M; Son; 9

270; Ikpahne-ehas; The Other Medicine; M; Husband; 30
271; Ahwooch-deedis; Walks to the Hole; F; Wife 23
272; Makpash-heahsas; Shoots Plain Medicine; F; Daughter; 6

273; Iche-kahnetsesh; Bear Claw; M; Husband; 39
274; Utsewaks-ahous; Begs Plenty; F; Wife; 33
275; Makpash-ope-ahoos; Medicine Rock Above; M; Son; 13
276; Peda-kosh; Brings Ten Times; F; Daughter; 4

277; Etashda-cheis; White Shirt; M; Husband; 69
278; Dich-heahsas; Strikes Well Known; F; Wife; 65
279; Esaska-eke-sheesh; Horse Turns Around; M; Son; 30

280; Besheesh; Shavings; M; Husband; 57
281; Hooche-sash; Wind; F; Wife; 52

282; ---; Albert Anderson; M; Husband; 30
283; ---; Sarah Anderson; F; Wife; 24
284; ---; Fannie Anderson; F; Daughter; 6

285; Echetegashes; The Elk; M; Husband; 48
286; Ashu-makotesash; Big Head High Up; F; Wife; 43

Census of the **Crow** Indians of **Crow** Agency **Montana** taken By **J.E. Edwards**, United States Indian Agent **June 30, 1899**

Key: Number; Indian Name; English Name; Sex; Relation; Age

287; Menash-kopskis-chedish; Hunts the Sioux; F; Daughter; 5

288; Poputa-naks; Frank Bethune; M; ---; 25

289; Ah-wah-cah-dace; Pukes on the Ground; M; Husband; 52
290; Hoksah-napis; Comes and Kills; F; Wife; 53
291; Asha-itse; Pretty River; F; Daughter; 9

292; Ahmbatseda-ahoos; Looks Much; F; [Widow]; 64

293; Esash-chedup; Blanket Bull; M; Husband; 31
294; Unda-ichis; Addie; F; Wife; 22
295; ---; Nettie B. Bull; F; Daughter; 1

296; Botsa-Miesash; Big Man; M; Husband; 35
297; Minnesh-pesh; Swamp Flag; F; Wife; 39
298; ---; Michael B. Man; M; Son; 12

299; Noopa-malapes; Kills Twice; F; [Widow]; 63

300; Ahpa-esash; Big Nose; M; Husband; 54
301; Mi-iche-doochis; Takes Good Things; F; Wife; 47
302; Bahsatsie-basonda; Steals on Camp Ahead; F; Daughter; 11

303; Mahshedah-kotish; Julia Bad Boy; F; Mother; 21
304; Ahsay-chulees; Sings in Camp; M; Son; 6
305; ---; Wesley Bad Boy; M; Son; 2

306; Nahsa-tays; Humpback; M; Husband; 51
307; Heles-basash; Runs Among Them; F; Wife; 47

308; Ookah-sheis; Dust; M; ---; 31

309; Misk-sheis; Talks Everything; M; Husband; 49
310; Botsa-wa-napes; Kills One Man; F; Wife; 42
311; Echete-cheis-ahkudis; Rides White Bellied Horse; F; Daughter; 13

312; Karooshis-ehas; Don't Run; M; Husband; 33
313; Andutsedush-heahsas; Slides Down Well Known; F; Wife; 38
314; Minnahpesh-ahoos; Plenty Swamp Flags; F; Daughter13
315; Chustak-ahkundis; Rides a Gray Horse; M; Son; 11
316; ---; Mary Don't Run; F; Daughter; 2
317; Bekashes; The Bannock; F; Mother; 73

318; Eespe-ekash; Looks at the Lion; F; [Widow]; 66

Census of the __Crow__ Indians of __Crow__ Agency __Montana__ taken
By __J.E. Edwards__, United States Indian Agent __June 30, 1899__

Key: Number; Indian Name; English Name; Sex; Relation; Age

319; Chate-cheakaps; Young Wolf; M; ---; 54 [Female previous years; declared male from 1899 forward.]

320; Chedup-dashes; Bull Tongue; M; Husband; 58
321; Echete-ahkin-doochis; Catches on the Horses; F; Wife; 44

322; Helekas-ash; Along the Hillside; M; Husband; 52
323; Ah-chane-deechis; Strikes in Camp; F; Wife; 41
324; Isminats-ich; Old Shield; M; Son; 15
325; Bahput-tah-way-chice; Sits to the Otter; F; Daughter; 5

326; Eepse-mahkala-napes; Kills wih[sic] Medicine Pipe; F; [Widow] 70

327; Oouka-manakish; Crazy Sister-in-law; M; Husband; 71
328; Makula-ich; Carries Good; F; Wife; 56
329; Eskulasa-epa-cheis; White Tailed Hawk; F; Daughter; 20
330; Chepups-echete; Hard Heart; F; Daughter; 7

331; Basuk-ose; Goes Ahead; M; Husband; 49
332; Isminats-ich; Pretty Shield; F; Wife; 43
333; Ichis; Good; M; Son; 16
334; Meah-kots; Small Woman; F; Daughter; 6

335; Meshodechitse; Medicine Shell; F; [Widow]; 46

336; Botseah-bedas; Pine Fire; F; ---; 26

337; Chedup-cahdish-dondase; Bull That Shows All Time; M; Husband; 34
338; Echete-mulukis; Sings; F; Wife; 32
339; Istuka-mahks; High Arrow; M; Son 6

340; Hoop-itsahkahoh; Top of the Moccasin; M; Husband; 25
341; Bah-cay-key-bah-pash; Medicine Shell; F; Wife; 23
342; ---; Runs Toward the House; F; Daughter; 4
343; Etash-shooachat; Blue Shirt; M; Son; 6

344; Ahm-botsots-heahsas; Strong Well Known; M; Husband; 35
345; Ahshay-hedra-dichis; Strikes in Camp; F; Wife; 21
346; ---; Levantia[?] S. Known; F; Daughter; 1

347; Kahkootsa; Drunkard; M; Husband; 43
348; Bahdah-dane-bahdakish; Sings in the Woods; F; Wife; 42
349; Mea-nakose-hahks; Young Turtle Woman; F; Daughter; 6

350; Chate-hishes; Red Wolf; M; Husband; 28
351; Besha-ekash; Comes to See The Buffalo; F; Wife; 21

Census of the __Crow__ Indians of __Crow__ Agency __Montana__ taken By __J.E. Edwards__, United States Indian Agent __June 30, 1899__

Key: Number; Indian Name; English Name; Sex; Relation; Age

352; ---; Laura Red Wolf; F; Daughter; 2

353; Halup-eahkots; Small Waist; M; Husband; 63
354; Ikpahn-e-naks; Medicine High Up; F; Wife; 54

355; Ahwakooda-kahdish; Old all the Time; M; Husband; 35
356; Istuka-makula; Shows a Child; F; Wife; 31
357; Arachuka-noak; Works on the Farm; M; Son; 9
358; Botsotse; Chief; M; Son; 8
359; ---; Susie Old All the Time; F; Daughter; 2

360; Eakook-sheedes; Yellow Coyote; F; Mother; 71
361; Meshak-naks; Isabel S. Knows; F; Ad. Dau. 16

362; Edukish; The Meat; M; Husband; 43
363; Dudish; The Back; F; Wife; 46
364; Beshe-mulukis; Buffalo that Sings; F; Daughter; 8
365; Nakose-nahks; Young Turtle; F; Daughter; 4

366; Chate-nak-sheedes; Young Yellow Wolf; M; Husband; 44
367; Doochis-heahsas; Takes Well Known; F; Wife; 46

368; Kahwookose; Inside the Mouth; M; ---; 40

369; ---; Michael O' Brien; M; Orphan; 18

370; Dahkpitska-kahdeas; Old Bear; M; Husband; 45
371; Makupa-Seech; Hail Shows; F; Wife; 38
372; Lagaka-akuse; Bird That Shows; M; Son; 17
373; Ika-ahoos; Lots of Stars; M; Son; 14
374; Ahshuah-dichis; Strikes Inside the House; F; Daughter; 9
375; Eskochisa-maluk-ichis; Strawberry Sings Pretty; F; Daughter; 7
376; Bus-suck-kose; Goes Ahead; M; Son; 3

377; Dakpitska-hotskish; Long Bear; M; Husband; 51
378; Eahkooka-asdish; Fox Goes Out; F; Wife; 51
379; Meshodithitse-lagaks; Medicine Shell Bird; M; Son; 18
380; Eshpeahisha-kahdeish; Horace Long Bear; M; Son; 25

381; Dotsuish; Muskrat; F; [Widow]; 79

382; Wahpootka-hotsish; Long Otter; M; Husband; 59
383; Botseish; Pine; F; Wife; 61
384; Ahwot-saya; Ground Cedar; F; Daughter; 12

385; Aritsumba-kahdeish; Falls Down Old; M; ---; 27

Census of the __Crow__ Indians of __Crow__ Agency __Montana__ taken By __J.E. Edwards__, United States Indian Agent __June 30, 1899__

Key: Number; Indian Name; English Name; Sex; Relation; Age

386; Isminats-makpash; Medicine Shield; F; Mother; 27
387; Mea-hotchkis; Tall Woman; F; Daughter; 9

388; Minnetseesh; The Moon; M; [Bachelor]; 28

389; Pohputa-heahsas; Plain Owl; M; Husband; 39
390; Mea-spittish; Black Woman; F; Wife; 37

391; Bea-it-chay; Pretty Woman; F; 31

392; Isekoshe-noopis; Two Whistles; M; [Bachelor]; 41
393; Isdots-ichis; Good to Prisoners; F; Mother; 86

394; Kee-osh; He Says; M; Husband; 39
395; Bedupa-ekoshees; Beaver that Stretches; F; Wife; 51
396; ---; Bravo; M; Son; 10

397; Ishtopish; Eyes Open; F; [Widow]; 62

398; Dahkoopis; Cuts a Hole in it; Ml Husband; 34
399; Mea-daka; Grey Woman; F; Wife; 39

400; Eep-kahdeas; Old Tail; M; Husband; 42
401; Mi-iche-okepis; Shoots Pretty Things; F; Wife; 20

402; Askindes; Holds On; M; Husband; 62
403; Ahwa-akinakuse; Stands on top of the Ground; F; Wife; 53

404; Oote-hotchkish; Long Weasel; F; ---; 49

405; Wahpotkta; Otter Comes out of Water; F; [Widow]; 65

406; Minne-koshis; Whistle Water; M; [Widower]; 39

407; Masheandache; Dreamer; M; Husband; 53
408; Istuka-doochis; Takes a Gun; F; Wife; 51
409; Daka-ichis-amach; Mortimer Dreamer; M; Son; 16

410; Botsea-Mahnahs; Paints her forehead; M; Husband; 49
411; Eskochea-biorup; Finds his enemy; F; Wife; 51
412; Puk-iees; Holds it in the mouth; M; Son; 18
413; Shenokshe-mulukis; Sings on Top; F; Daughter; 16
414; Usmiha-koosh-basash; Charges on the enemy; F; Mother; 73

415; Mune-skoop-doochis; Takes a crooked stick; F; Widow; 83

Census of the __Crow__ Indians of __Crow__ Agency __Montana__ taken
By __J.E. Edwards__, United States Indian Agent __June 30, 1899__

Key: Number; Indian Name; English Name; Sex; Relation; Age

416; Umbich-esash; Don't fall down; M; Husband; 43
417; Esash-beduppa; Beaver robe; F; Wife; 49

418; Kahnista; Small; M; Husband; 34
419; Eshippish-day-ichis; Goes to Mud Pretty; F; Wife; 29
420; Besop-huche-naks; Young hawk; M; Son; 3

421; Minekashe-ahoos; Plenty Butterfly; M; Husband; 46
422; Esaska-noops; Two horses; F; Wife; 47

423; Nak-paka-ish; Child in the mouth; M; Husband; 56
424; Kahdeas; Old; F; Wife; 53
425; Ahcheke-ichis; The Spy; M; Son; 15
426; Eskoche-doochis; Joe Child in the Mouth; M; Son; 23

427; Noop-dichis; Strikes Twice; F; Wife; 87

428; Mahshooshshesh; Red Plume; M; Husband; 69
429; Peritse-usses; Crow that shows; F; Wife; 52

430; Munask-malapes; Kills by the woods; F; [Widow]; 59

431; Booah-hishes; Red Fish; M; Husband; 49
432; Meshodischitse-dichis; Strikes the Medicine Rock; F; Wife; 45
433; Bahkeda-basash; Blackbird in Front; M; Brother; 57

434; Biorup-heahsas; Found Things Well Known; F; Widow; 27

435; Ahsha-heletam-basash; Charges Through Camp; M; Husband; 58
436; Oomutish; Iron; F; Wife; 52
437; Besha-amach; Sits on the Buffalo; F; Daughter; 24

438; Besha-chedup; Buffalo Bull; M; Father; 32
439; Dakpitska-ahsuse; James Carpenter; M; Son; 17

440; Ushmiha-chedish; Enemy Hunter; M; Husband; 67
441; Kotseish; Shakes; F; Wife; 57

442; Shebah-shadish; Among the Fog; M; Husband; 40
443; Echete-akuse; Horse on the other Side; F; Wife; 28
444; Mashoditschitse-heahsas; Well Known Shell; Daughter; 6
445; Ook-sheedis; Yellow Deer; M; Son; 5

446; Ahwahkuan-dakpitske; Bear in the Middle; M; Husband; 41
447; Echete-achis; Knows a Horse; F; Wife; 35
448; Kowees; Ruth; F; Daughter; 12

Census of the __Crow__ Indians of __Crow__ Agency __Montana__ taken
By __J.E. Edwards__, United States Indian Agent __June 30, 1899__

Key: Number; Indian Name; English Name; Sex; Relation; Age

449; Dakpitske-botsots; Strong Bear; M; Batchelor[sic]; 27

450; Chedup-shespitta; Black Bull; M; Husband; 53
451; Besha-naks; Buffalo Calf; F; Wife; 64

452; Bedupa-okeah-duis; Beaver That Slides; M; Husband; 62
453; Dutch-ka; Twin Woman; F; Wife; 64

454; Chate-ewotsodish; Busy Wolf; M; Husband; 63
455; Minmahpesh; Swamp Flag; F; Wife; 38

456; Shegak-kahpa; Flat Boy; M; Batch[sic].; 39

457; Unmeathe; Bank; M; Husband; 34
458; Mahsha-ich-meas; Pretty Feather Woman; F; Wife; 30

459; Lagak-cheah-noops; Two White Birds; M; Husband; 48
460; Ahpahne-makpash; Medicine Porcupine; F; Wife; 47
461; Besha-naks; Buffalo High; M; Son; 19
462; Besha-naks-noops; Among the Buffalo; M; Son; 14
463; Etash-daka; Eagle Shirt; M; Son; 5

464; Ahwoshose; Gros Ventre; F; Widow; 73

465; Bahsuk-naks; Turtle Child; F; Widow; 64

466; Oota-hukish; Spotted Weasel; F; Widow; 34
467; Botseah-heahsas; Fights Well Known; M; Ad. Son; 20

468; Maudut-kudesh; Pounded Meat; M; Husband; 57
469; Mahsha-undichis; Strikes Feathers; F; Wife; 55

470; Mahsha-kudesh; Holds the Feather; M; Husband; 49
471; Dakoshes; Eagle; F; Wife; 55
472; Besha-hishes; Throws off on the Horse; M; Son; 16

473; Ahwahkun-lagaks; Bird in the Ground; M; Husband; 51
474; Napes-ekash; Looks at the one that Kills; F; Wife; 36
475; Minduksa-ekuroos; Runs Toward the Fort; M; Son; 7

476; Wutta-eahkoots; Little Wolf No. 2; M; Widower; 65
477; Eskooche-ahoos-dich; Strikes Plenty Enemies; F; Sister; 59
478; Dukedea-akuse; Knows the War; M; ---; 21

479; Oo-mutish; Iron; F; Widow; 61

Census of the __Crow__ Indians of __Crow__ Agency __Montana__ taken By __J.E. Edwards__, United States Indian Agent __June 30, 1899__

Key: Number; Indian Name; English Name; Sex; Relation; Age

480; Asuk-tuah-basash; Runs Between Them; M; Husband; 26
481; Ahwoosh-heahsas; Sweathouse Well Known; F; Wife; 19
492; ---; Joseph Runs Between; M; Son; 1

483; Dotska; The Twins; M; Husband; 55
484; Ikpahne-makpash; Medicine Porcupine; F; Wife; 57
485; Ekupa-ich; Pretty Hat; F; Mother; 79

486; Chedupa-seeish; Bull that shows; M; Husband; 29
487; Echete; Horse; F; Wife; 28
488; Eskoche-aseesh; Spies the Enemy; M; Son; 5
489; ---; Ida Bull That Shows; F; Daughter; 1

490; Chate-dakpitska; Bear Wolf; M; Widower; 59

491; Ahmako-istisha-naks; Young Swallow; M; Husband; 35
492; Oote-ewandies; Plays with the Weasel; F; Wife; 21

493; Issame-malapes; Kills on her own Ground; F; Mother; 59
494; Daka-makpash; Medicine Eagle; M; Son; 20

495; Oowuta-ahpies; Iron Necklace; F; Widow; 83

496; Nahshada-esash; Charges Strong; M; Husband; 58
497; Itshades; Kills in the Track; F; Wife; 57
498; Bishka-botsots; Charles Strong; M; Son; 14
499; ---; Mary Charges Strong; F; Daughter; 9

500; Chate-nakish; Leads a Wolf; M; Husband; [49]
501; Naksha-undichis; Strikes First; F; Wife; [53]
502; Mahsha-hishes-heahsas; Well Known Red Feather; F; Gr. Dau.; 7

503; Ahmuapes; The Kicker; M; Husband; 58
504; Arleunda-aches; Knows the Road; F; Wife; 59

505; Eseah-koosh; Covers his face; M; Husband; 49
506; Uck-ish-be-dane-dechis; Strikes one going in House; F; Wife; 53
507; Cheepup-beday-sot; Bull near the Water; M; Son; 16
508; Esha-hishes-shedes; Yellow Red Paint; F; Daughter; 4

509; Chedupa-eda-ekash; Bull Goes Hunting; M; Husband; 72
510; Daka-watis; One Buffalo Calf; F; Wife; 59

511; E-o-dish; Full Mouth; M; Husband; 43
512; Bedupa-ehas; The Other Beaver; F; Wife; 47
513; Bea-e-hosh; The Other Woman; F; Daughter; 14

Census of the __Crow__ Indians of __Crow__ Agency __Montana__ taken
By __J.E. Edwards__, United States Indian Agent __June 30, 1899__

Key: Number; Indian Name; English Name; Sex; Relation; Age

514; Ahsho-malapes; Kills Behind Camp; F; Widow; 61

515; Ahshuputsuah-dooich; Gets One Horn; M; Husband; 43
516; Isminats-budwasich; Shield at the Door; F; Wife; 34
517; Ischesa-hela-amach; Sit Toward the Nest; F; Daughter; 14
518; ---; Harry Gets One Horn; M; Son; 1

519; Isos-kaybah-chatechis; Alexander Upshaw; M; Bach.; 23

520; Ooet-budeka-dooch; Takes a Gun; M; Husband; 36
521; Botsuah-tush; Sweet Grass; F; Wife; 44

522; Shegak-amach; Bad Boy; M; Husband; 32
523; Eka-ahpka-amach; Sits with a Star; F; Wife; 22
524; ---; David Bad Boy; M; Son; 2

525; Eshasha-heahsas; Plain Face; F; Widow; 57

526; Isooet-botseesh; Smart Iron; M; Widower; 28

527; Epeahkot-Esash; Big Magpie; M; Husband; 50
528; Beka-haredich; Among the Grass; F; Wife; 52
529; Lagak-beepish; Snow Bird; M; Son; 10

530; Mahedish; Does Anything; M; Husband; 39
531; Ahwaku-chedish-naks; Young Ground Cedar; F; Wife; 45
532; Echete-doochis; Takes a Pinto Horse; F; Daughter; 4

533; Shegak-doochis; Boy that Grabs; M; Husband; 54
534; Mekaspe-doochis; Takes hold of the Cloth; F; Wife; 58

535; Ahsha-ckepish; Shoots the Lodge; M; Husband; 55
536; Ikpahne-ekash; Looks at the Medicine; F; Wife; 45

537; Ahrocheis; Stops; M; Husband; 31
538; Esasha-ich; Paints her face pretty; F; Wife; 29
539; Opish-ekash; Percy Stops; M; Son; 12
540; Noopta-malapes; Kills Twice; F; Daughter; 7
541; Istuka-mulukis; Sings to the Arrow; M; Son; 3

542; Ahlud-esuhsh; Big Shoulder Blade; M; Husband; 47
543; Beshay-herasus; Well Known Buffalo; F; Wife; 36
544; Arap-apushay-dichesay; Bullets Don't Strike Him; M; Son; 6

545; Bah-kot-konsees; Bad Baby; M; [Widower]; 73

Census of the __Crow__ Indians of __Crow__ Agency __Montana__ taken
By __J.E. Edwards__, United States Indian Agent __June 30, 1899__

Key: Number; Indian Name; English Name; Sex; Relation; Age

546; Chedup-ahkade-duse; Stands over a Bull; M; Husband; 27
547; Ah-bah-de-ichis; Pretty Medicine; F; Wife; 24
548; She-cack-bah-pash; Medicine boy; M; Son; 6
549; ---; Red paint in His Medicine; M; Son; 1

550; Chedup-quasah-dataish; Bull in sight; M; Husband; 29
551; Ahdo-chea-beas; Woman where she stops; F; Wife; 35
552; Ah-bah-keas-sash; Cloud shows plain; M; Son; 15
553; Ah-dean-day-ahchetis; Follows the Track; F; Daughter; 10

554; It-shoc-daytay; No Shinbone; M; Husband; 45
555; Maheede-speedis; Yellow Blackbird; F; Wife; 45
556; Cheedup-etahsich; Henry Shinbone; M; Son; 21
557; Bah-cup-pah-deedish; Lizard that walks; F; Daughter; 12
558; Nahmis; Three; F; Mothr[sic]; 73

559; Ahshkay-shopis; Four Balls; M; Husband; 57
560; Meshoditchse-nishes; Red Rock; F; Wife; 55
561; Kahdeeasas; Not Old; M; Son; 9
562; Chate-aputs; Wolf that looks back; M; Son; 23

563; Ahkabos; Froze; M; Husband; 36
564; Mahpay-e-kahsh; Sees in a Day; F; Wife; 33
565; Espeah-kishekahdeas; Old Bobcat; M; Son; 6
566; Hay-day-de-qu-pish; Gets down among them; M; Son; 2

567; Mahray-keir-ahpis; Shell on the Neck; M; Husband; 36
568; Ise-meneas; His Door; F; Wife; 39;
569; Cheeup-ay-koos; Bull that Knows; M; Son; 14

570; Minnay-e-koos-chis; Comes out of the water; F; Widow; 65

571; Ahoo-ahk-ichis; Pretty on top; M; Husband; 35
572; Itshooaprich; Pretty back of the neck; F; Wife; 34
573; Mah-hahk-ichis; Plenty Shells; M; Son; 9
574; Bee-dup-che-sus; Beaver Tail; F; Daughter; 3

575; Butsay-tse-dichis; Strikes the Chief; F; Widow; 61

576; Chees-wahkpahs; Medicine Tail; M; Husband; 41
577; Itshe-wahkpahs; She is Medicine; F; Wife; 38

578; Chedeer-esahs; Not Afraid; M; Husband; 41
579; Noopis; Two; F; Wife; 49
580; Bah-put-cheekeep-beas; Ant Woman; F; Daughter; 10
581; Beday-ock-key-day-ichis; Good Shell; M; Son; 5

Census of the __Crow__ Indians of __Crow__ Agency __Montana__ taken
By __J.E. Edwards__, United States Indian Agent __June 30, 1899__

Key: Number; Indian Name; English Name; Sex; Relation; Age

582; ---; George Not Afraid; M; Son; 1

583; Escheeta-nevsaus; Knows His Horse; M; Husband; 39
584; Mekahshay-hishis; Fat Snake; M; Wife; 49

585; Ahpit-sheedis; Yellow Crane; M; Husband; 55
586; Ukpa-had-dee-is; Does things together; F; Wife; 43

587; Push-ah-ko; Cut; M; [Widower]; 43
588; Ahta-huk-is-dichis; Strikes the Painted Arm; F; Mother; 83

589; Wahkpahs-ne-ahoos; Plenty Medicine; F; Widow; 43

590; Napk-ahwot-nee-as; One Child Woman; F; Widow; 55

591; Ake-mah-kaweish; Hoop on the Forehead; M; Husband; 51
592; Ahshay-whoo-a-aychis; Knows the whole camp; F; Wife; 52
593; Mussick-awats; One Turtle; M; Son; 9
594; Medesha-dooch; Takes the Dead; F; Mother; 71

595; Ikpah-ahoos; Plenty Wing; M; Husband; 49
596; Ismant-heahsas; Plain Shield; F; Wife; 50

597; Lagak-heahsas; Big Bird; M; Orphan; 7

598; Ay-kuse; Knows; M; Husband; 26
599; Echick-heas; Gets there first; F; Wife; 22
600; ---; Sarah Knows; F; Daughter; 4
601; Edwea; Dummy; F; Mother; 53

602; Mumasen-dichis; Strikes by side of water; F; Mother; 83
603; Menacheis; White Goose; M; Son; 48

604; Almashus; The Fog; M; Husband; 71
605; Makula-woof-dichis; Takes Two Guns; F; Wife; 61
606; ---; Frank Shively; M; Son; 27

607; Minooksa-kahdius; Old Alligator; M; Husband; 55
608; Chut-napis; Kills on the lookout; F; Wife; 60

609; ---; Tom Laforge; M; Husband; 34
610; Meeah-kadius; Old Woman; F; Wife; 33

611; Keasha; Runner; M; Husband; 47
612; Icheat-ekash; Looks at Tobacco; F; Wife; 47
613; Beshay-ahk-ahwah-chis; Sits on the Buffalo; F; Daughter; 10

Census of the __**Crow**__ Indians of __**Crow**__ Agency __**Montana**__ taken
By __**J.E. Edwards**__, United States Indian Agent __**June 30, 1899**__

Key: Number; Indian Name; English Name; Sex; Relation; Age

614; Dachpitsay-beedahs; Fire Bear; M; Husband; 50
615; Natsaundooch; Takes plenty prisoners; F; Wife; 47
616; Itsup-eduse; Edison Fire Bear; M; Son; 21
617; Bea-huchkish; Long Woman; F; Ad. Dau. 13

618; Ekeeka-dase; Goes Together; M; Husband; 32
619; Makapo-ich; Pretty Hall; F; Wife; 30
620; Ostah-ich; Jane Goes Together; F; Daughter; 9
621; ---; Wesley Goes Together; M; Son; 3

622; Cheas-kuch-kish; Spotted Tail; M; Husband; 49
623; Cotah-shee-dish; Yellow all over; F; Wife; 39
624; Etoshday-bah-pash; Medicine Dress; F; Daughter; 17
625; Echeen-bah-pash; Medicine Horse; F; Daughter; 6

626; Bit-quash; Onion; M; Husband; 44
627; Bershea-bah-pash; Medicine Buffalo Cow; F; Wife; 39
628; Ahwaka-wah-kees-sas; Plain Mountain; F; Daughter; 8
629; Undashay-day-bahah-chis; Charges Strong; M; Son; 5

630; Up-pay-ut-tay; Sharp Nose No. 2; M; Husband; 34
631; Ah-chook-coode-daydush; Strikes and Strikes Again; F; Wife; 40

632; Duck-bit-chay-beas; Bear Woman; F; Widow; 53
633; Bee-bush-sas; Rock Ahead; F; Daughter; 14

634; ---; Josh Buffalo; M; Husband; 37
635; Ahken-bahdachek-casos; Ties Knot on top of her head; F; Wife; 29

636; Dakpitska-ahoos; Plenty Bears; M; Husband; 59
637; Kahdeas; Old; F; Wife; 49
638; Behayday-dakwahchis; Sits among the rocks; M; Son; 11

639; ---; Richard Wallace; M; Husband; 33
640; Bash-itchis; Pretty Feather; F; Wife; 31
641; ---; Susie Wallace; F; Daughter; 4

642; Ah-cook-bee-dash; Hears Fire; M; Husband; 35
643; ---; Mary Bompard; F; Wife; 38

644; Ap-puch-kay; Long Neck; M; Husband; 31
645; Ushcosh-uttah-dup-pace; Kills close to camp; F; Wife; 39
646; Bee-shay-e-duhs; Buffalo stands up; F; Daughter; 8

647; ---; Louis Bompard; M; Husband; 39
648; ---; Lois Bompard; F; Wife; 30

Census of the __Crow__ Indians of __Crow__ Agency __Montana__ taken
By __J.E. Edwards__, United States Indian Agent __June 30, 1899__

Key: Number; Indian Name; English Name; Sex; Relation; Age

649; ---; Peter Bompard; M; Son; 9
650; ---; Rosa Bompard; F; Daughter; 4

651; ---; Rosa Peters; F; Mother; 27
652; ---; Arthur Peters; M; Son; 10
653; ---; Elsie Peters; F; Daughter; 8
654; ---; George Peters; F; Son; 4

655; ---; Joseph Martinez; M; 27

656; Chate-dock-coo-chis; Young Hairy Wolf; M; Husband; 54
657; Ahdache-waycoo-itchis; Comes from war pretty; F; Wife; 50
658; Up-pay-huch-kay; Long Nose; M; Son; 17
659; Bah-cup-ysay-keas-sos; Striped snake well known; F; Daughter; 11

660; Dah-sea-hash; The other heart; F; Widow; 54
----; ~~Bea-at-tah-itchis; Pretty Coyote; M; Son; 24~~[?]

661; Been-de-chis; Strikes the water; F; Widow; 72
662; Dah-pittosh; Grasshopper; M; Son; 22

663; Awahsha; Gros Ventre; M; Husband; 30
664; Bea-dane-dah-coos; Stops by the water; F; Wife; 29
665; Bea-ah-ha; Plenty woman; F; Daughter; 8

666; Chee-dup-chees; Gray Bull; M; Husband; 61
667; Bah-duck-cah-peas; Going about; F; Wife; 59
668; Bish-push; Alder; M; Son; 18
669; Bee-itchis; Pretty Rock; F; Daughter; 9

670; Bah-aye-chaisc; Knows Everything; F; ---; 35
671; Cheah-key-sos; Sage Hen; M; Son; 14
672; Esoska-cheesday-kaybah; Grey Horse Chief; M; Son; 3

673; Bedayitch-shedayopitche; Smokes; M; Husband; 71
674; Bah-pittay-dov-pus; Two Otters; F; Wife; 70
675; Ush-hay-dosh-days; Goes to Camp; M; Ad. Son; 17

676; Eche-duch-days; Goes to the horses; M; Husband; 34
677; Dock-op-pay-dec-chis; Strikes mother and child; F; Wife; 25
678; Bah-euch-euis; Striped Snake; F; Daughter; 4

679; Ah-dah-sea-ut-hoos; Shows plenty; M; Husband; 41
680; Bea-ha-wat-tosh; One Woman; F; Wife; 43

681; Cheedup-e-hosh; The other bull; M; Husband; 31

Census of the **Crow** Indians of **Crow** Agency **Montana** taken
By **J.E. Edwards**, United States Indian Agent **June 30, 1899**

Key: Number; Indian Name; English Name; Sex; Relation; Age

682; Um-bah-day-es-sos; Goes farther along; F; Wife; 33
683; Dea-cosh-bah-cush; High Eagle; M; Son; 9
684; Uck-a-chase; Knows; F; Mother; 69

685; Ah-wah-kah-we-sos; Big Mountain; M; Husband; 42
686; Cuck-hay-dupe-doochis; Takes Two Lances; F; Wife; 52
687; Ish-co-sheahaday-dose; Runs against his enemy; M; Son; 19
688; E-chu-dah-keas-sos; Well known horse; F; Daughter; 7

689; Cheasay-itcha-baydayka; Pretty Tail; M; Husband; 51
690; Un-dee-dich-chis; Walks Pretty; F; Wife; 49

691; Bich-pus; Spaniard; M; Husband; 29
692; Bahchickah-coo-deechis; Looks at one comes frm[sic] war; F; Wife; 27

693; E-shoes; Back of the Neck; M; Husband; 69
694; Bash-eheam-beas; White Woman; F; Wife; 64

695; Bea-doo-pus; Two Women; F; [Widow]; 60

696; Ah-way-e-kosh; Looks at the Ground; M; Husband; 36
697; Bah-day-kiss; Sings; F; Wife; 20
698; ---; McKinley L. Ground; M; Son; 1

699; ---; Thomas Jefferson; M; Husband; 29
700; Lagak-naks; Bird Child; F; Wife; 18
701; ---; Lillian Jefferson; F; Daughter; 1

702; Dash-day-tush; No name; F; Widow; 78

703; E-sock-kain-dah-koos; On top of the house; M; Husband; 22
704; Minetotse-ish-ekash; Looks at the sun; F; Wife; 20
705; ---; Iowa House; F; Daughter; 1

706; Op-chay-keas-sos; Voice well known; M; Widower; 51

707; ---; Katherine Scott; F; Mother; 27
708; ---; Paul Scott; M; Son; 8
709; ---; Emma Scott; F; Daughter; 5
710; ---; Pearl Scott; F; Daughter; 4
711; ---; Frank Scott; Son; 2

712; ---; Frank Shane; M; Husband; 29
713; Bah-chop-dah-beas; Kills with her husband; F; Wife; 25
714; ---; Howard Shane; M; Son; 5
715; ---; May Shane; F; Daughter; 1 mo

Census of the __Crow__ Indians of __Crow__ Agency __Montana__ taken By __J.E. Edwards__, United States Indian Agent __June 30, 1899__

Key: Number; Indian Name; English Name; Sex; Relation; Age

716; Oo-what-dah-beas; Three irons; M; Husband; 56
717; E-con-days; Old woman tooth; F; Wife; 43
718; ---; Sarah Three Irons; F; Daughter; 14
719; Dah-cheas; Drinking all the time; M; Son; 8

720; ---; Goes Pretty; F; ---; 30

721; Edah-doot-chis; Takes himself; M; Widower; 33
722; E-doos-sos; Can't get up; F; Mother; 63

723; She-bah-sha-dush; Fog in the morning; M; Husband; 51
724; Ease-key-pay; Crooked face child; F; Wife; 48
725; ---; John Morning; M; Son; 8
726; ---; Ruth Morning; F; Daughter; 2

727; Pay-dutch-cheebah-pash; Medicine Crow; M; Husband; 49
728; Bah-pash; Medicine; F; Wife; 45
729; Ah-woos-dah-coos; Stays at Sweathouse; M; Son; 11
730; Ah-way-chee-da-cuss; Goes Pretty; M; Son; 6
731; Ah-way-itchis; Chester Medicine Crow; M; Son; 2

732; Bee-shay-che-do-sos; Big Ox; M; Widower; 64
733; Esock-uck-bahda-pace; Kills with her brother; F; Sister; 59

734; ---; Wm. Elliott Towne; M; Orphan; 12
735; ---; Ida M. Towne; F; Sister; 9

736; Dosh-bah-cha-chis; Strong Heart; M; Husband; 38
737; Be-dee-sheas-shedush; Stands to the sun; F; Wife; 37

738; Be-shay-ka-cheas; Buffalo that shakes; F; Widow; 39
739; Epah-dea-bah-cha-chis; Strong Medicine; M; Son; 11

740; Qua-dah-bah-chis; Sits in the middle; M; Husband; 53
741; Bah-dup-pay-keas-sos; Kills well known; F; Wife; 51
742; Beada-tah-shis-chay-ichis; Pretty Butterfly; F; Daughter; 10

743; A-dah-shoes; Blue Belly; M; Husband; 59
744; Osh-shone-bah-dup-pace; Kills in rear of house; F; Wife; 60

745; Eche-dosh; Brings Horses; F; Widow; 39
746; Eckpah-deadah-cock-cush; His medicine bird; F; Daughter; 3

747; Ah-way-cook-cordetahheas; Goes to ground every day; F; Widow; 22
748; Bea-dah-cock-cuss; Bird woman; F; Daughter; 16
749; Epay-itchis; Francis Tiffany; M; Son; 13

Census of the __Crow__ Indians of __Crow__ Agency __Montana__ taken
By __J.E. Edwards__, United States Indian Agent __June 30, 1899__

Key: Number; Indian Name; English Name; Sex; Relation; Age

750; Ahduck-chedechay-itchis; Strikes his enemy pretty; M; Husband; 38
751; Es-che-key-pay; Crooked face; F; Wife; 36
752; Duck-bitchay-haydatahos; Gets their medcn[sic] tobacco; M; Son; 3

753; Day-chay-ah-hoos; Many prisoners; F; Widow; 56
754; Esos-kaybah-och-che-duc; Lucky horse; F; Sister; 29

755; Ah-day-buck-ke-os; Throws it away; M; Husband; 26
756; Is-oo-what-tus; Her Iron; F; Wife; 26
757; Mea-sheedes; Yellow Woman; F; Daughter; 1

758; Ea-cook-cah-cheas; White Fox; M; Husband; 34
759; Bah-sho-deche-cha-ahoos; Plenty Medicine Rock; F; Wife; 39
760; Ahway-kahways-bahchedis; Hunts toward the mountains; M; Son; Son; 19
761; Dah-cock-uckpah-dahcus; Stays with a bird; F; Daughter; 6
762; Hoo-chan-das; Goes with the wind; F; Mother; 63

763; Dah-cock-e-wan-deas; Plays with a bird; M; Father; 43
764; Dahcock-uckbah-do-shis; Eats with a bird; M; Son; 10
765; Bah-puttah-ahway-taydas; Otter goes a long ways; M; Son; 8

766; Escock-kay-keas-sos; Well known lance; F; Widow; 72

767; Ah-dush-cos-pay; Crooked Arm; M; Husband; 44
768; Ah-kok-de-chis; Catches up and Strikes; F; Wife; 29
769; ---; Herbert Crooked Arm; M; Son; 10
770; Ishane-badukchaydacock; Bird Ties knot on top head; M; Son; 6
771; ---; James Crooked Arm; M; Son; 2

772; Bee-dup-kahdeas; Old Beaver; F; Widow; 46
773; Dack-kah-shis; The eagle; F; Daughter; 18

774; Bit-choose; Wart; F; Widow; 75
775; Bee-shas-sah-hoos; Comes to the Buffalo; F; Gr. Dau.; 18
776; Echick-kay-sah-dish; Comes out first; F; Gr. Dau.; 8

777; Cheedup-dah-shis; Bull's Tongue #2; M; Husband; 35
778; Bah-keam-beas; Blackbird Woman; F; Wife; 29
779; Cuck-key-shen-doochis; Takes yellow spotted horse; F; Daughter; 9
780; Ah-dup-pis; Stabs; F; Mother; 77

781; Bee-day-she-kosh; Looks at the water; M; Husband; 41
782; Bee-dee-dup-pase; Takes across the water; F; Wife; 39
783; Cah-kay-doot-chis; Takes a lance; F; Widow; 61

784; Bish-k-chease; White Dog; M; Husband; 45

Census of the __Crow__ Indians of __Crow__ Agency __Montana__ taken
By __J.E. Edwards__, United States Indian Agent __June 30, 1899__

Key: Number; Indian Name; English Name; Sex; Relation; Age

785; Bachayhay-what-deechis; Strikes one man; F; Wife; 47

786; Dough-seas; Buffalo neck hair; M; Husband; 56
787; Bah-bah-dah-kosh; Nearly gone; F; Wife; 59
788; Out-tah-bah-pash; Medicine Weasel; F; Gr. Dau.; 17

789; Esuck-bon-tuch-chais; Mountain Sheep; M; Husband; 31
790; E-cook-key-e-kosh; Looks at the Fox; F; Wife; 33
000; Bah-coas; Gives things; F; Daughter; 12
791; Dah-cock-day-say-itchis; Good Hearted Bird; F; Daughter; 8
792; Che-co-key-dah-pace; Kills the young man; M; Son; 5

793; She-bish; Fat; M; Widower; 46
794; Dah-cock-dah-dah-bish; Morris Schaffer; M; Son; 18

795; Edea-hay-bah-pash; Medicine breath; M; Husband; 36
796; Espea-kish-hiss; Wild Cat; F; Wife; 24

797; Ah-shoos; The Horn; M; Husband; 50
798; It-tuch-chis; All alone; F; Wife; 45
799; Kuch-key-con-dah-das; Goes after spotted horse; M; Son; 6

800; ---; Mrs. Wm. Blaine; F; Mother; 26
801; ---; James Blaine; M; Son; 11
802; ---; Florence Blaine; F; Daughter; 5

803; Ah-pah-seas; Shows his ear; M; [Bachelor]; 51
804; Dutch-choas; Muskrat; F; Mother; 69

805; Chay-esos; Big Sheep; M; Husband; 38
806; Bock-kosh; Turtle; Wife; F; 43
807; ---; Florence Big Sheep; F; Daughter; 2

808; ---; James Hill; M; [Bachelor]; 25

809; ---; Dexter; M; [Bachelor]; 24

810; Dah-cup-co-dus-sos; Calf that strays; M; Husband; 40
811; Ah-wah-chis; Sits down; F; Wife; 51
812; Ahdean-dayah-waychis; Sits along the road; F; Daughter; 18

813; Dosh-bah-cha-chis; Strong heart; F; Widow; 69

814; Ahwaycah-waydanbadakis; Sings in the Mountains; M; Husband; 27
815; Ah-wain-dah-sit-chis; Gooded-hearted ground; F; Wife; 25
816; Bea-bah-pah-cah-weas; Bad medicine woman; F; Daughter; 8

Census of the __Crow__ Indians of __Crow__ Agency __Montana__ taken
By __J.E. Edwards__, United States Indian Agent __June 30, 1899__

Key: Number; Indian Name; English Name; Sex; Relation; Age

817; Is-bah-ca-key-ah-shees; Shows a shell; F; Daughter; 5

818; Ah-son-she-dish; Yellow head; M; Husband; 40
819; Bahput-tah-peedee-chis; Strikes one with necklace; F; Wife; 44
820; Eshe-bah-cha-chis; Ruth Yellow Head; F; Daughter; 17

821; Ah-hoe-cotta-dea-dish; Sun goes slow; M; Widower; 37
822; ---; Bertha Sun Goes Slow; F; Daughter; 1

823; Oo-what-kah-wish; Iron Fork; M; Husband; 64
824; Bah-itchay-doochis; Takes Pretty Things; F; Wife; 62

825; Been-dahcom-bahdakay; Crazy Pend D'Oreille; M; Husband; 59
826; Bah-cut-chay-itchis; Pretty striped snake; F; Wife; 50

827; Ock-cheas; White antelope; M; Husband; 37
828; Bah-hah-beas; Spring Woman; F; Wife; 31
829; E-che-che-sosh; Big Root; F; Daughter; 8
830; Ah-mah-ah-che-day-chase; Knows her luck; F; Daughter; 4

831; Bahdakishebachacheas; Redwood Chief; M; Widower; 52
832; ---; Mrs. F. Sucher; F; Mother; 21
833; ---; Belle Sucher; F; Daughter; 5
834; ---; Hattie Sucher; F; Daughter; 4

835; Bah-doot-che-key-pish; Takes wrinkle; M; Husband; 53
836; Dupe-tush-der-chis; Strikes both ways; F; Wife; 50
837; Ches-sos-cos; His tail shows; M; Son; 17

838; Shee-day; Yellow; F; Widow; 73

839; Oo-way-itchis; Pretty Paint; M; Husband; 26
840; Ahway-kawah-kain-beas; Woman on top of mountain; F; Wife; 25
841; E-kay-sup-poas; Young swallow; F; Daughter; 11
842; Kea-sos; Plain to see; F; Daughter; 2

843; Bah-chea-keas-sos; Fights well known No 1; M; Husband; 40
844; Is-chis-say-it-chis; Pretty Nest; F; Wife; 35
845; Che-dock-cush-soo; Morning; M; Son; 15

846; Oo-what-tish; The Iron; M; Husband; 40
847; Bahshow-deachic-itchis; Pretty Medicine Rock; F; Wife; 38
848; Bun-dock-cope-dah-cuss; Woodpecker's child; M; Son; 15
849; Ecup-pah-keas-sos; Gets down well known; M; Son; 13
850; Es-been-dotch-cheas; Little shield; M; Son; 8

Census of the __Crow__ Indians of __Crow__ Agency __Montana__ taken By __J.E. Edwards__, United States Indian Agent __June 30, 1899__

Key: Number; Indian Name; English Name; Sex; Relation; Age

851; Ah-duck-che-itchis; Good coos; M; Son; 5

852; Dosh-kosh; Child; M; Husband; 38
853; Bee-dup-eas; Little Beaver; F; Wife; 35

854; ---; John Wallace; M; Husband; 40
855; Oo-tay-sah-dis; Weasel goes out; F; Wife; 47
856; ---; Carrie Wallace; F; Ad. Dau.; 15

857; Oo-tay-coo-bah-kais; Cross Weasel; M; Husband; 55
858; Shis-shea-bea; Hairy Woman; F; Wife; 54
859; ---; Choteau; M; Son; 31

860; Bah-kea-dah; Blackbird; M; Husband; 48
861; Bachay-ahkahn-dupace; Kills six men; F; Wife; 56

862; Ish-bern-dotch-sheda; Yellow shield; M; Husband; 74
863; Bah-dah-kis; Sings; F; Wife; 73

864; Chate-uch-pah-dee-dish; Walks with a wolf; M; Husband; 25
865; Ko-kah-sish; Corn; F; Wife; 31
866; Echean-dock-eas; Little Colt; F; Daughter; 6

867; Bee-pah-pus-sis; Round Rock; M; Son 40
868; Bah-dup-pay-keas-sos; Kills well known; F; Mother; 74
869; Hay-day-co-days; Runs in among them; M; Son; 32

870; Dupe-doot-chis; Takes Two; M; Widower; 25

871; ---; Annie Shows a Pipe; F; Orphan; 8

872; Dakpitska-neen-dates; Bear that don't walk; M; Husband; 36
873; ---; Mrs. Wm. Hawkes; F; Wife; 33
874; ---; Lucy Hawkes; F; Daughter; 15
875; Es-chis-say-bah-posh; Medicine nest; M; Son; 3

876; Bah-shay-kah-duck-kay; Lean Man; M; Widower; 44

877; Um-bah-sah-ahoos; Charges Plenty; M; Husband; 37
878; Bachay-cush-bahdukiss; Sings to Man; F; Wife; 42
879; Bah-tay-day-keas-sos; Steals Plain; M; Son; 14
880; Duck-cock-dah-cus; Bird; F; Daughter; 6
881; ---; Medicine Buffalo; M; Son; 1

882; ---; David Stewart; M; Husband; 27
883; Ekup-pah-wah-chis; Sits with the stars; F; Wife; 32

Census of the __Crow__ Indians of __Crow__ Agency __Montana__ taken By __J.E. Edwards__, United States Indian Agent __June 30, 1899__

Key: Number; Indian Name; English Name; Sex; Relation; Age

884; Ekus-sah-itch-chis; Pretty snake; F; Daughter; 7
885; ---; Richard Stewart; M; Son; 1

886; Bee-dock-cup-pis; Goose Goes over the hill; M; Husband; 75
887; Um-bees-say-chu-dish; Hunts to lie down; F; Wife; 73

888; Oo-kutchis-say; Puts on antelope cap; M; Husband; 56
889; Op-put-tay; Long Neck; F; Wife; 57
000; ---; Herbert Antelope Cap; M; Son; 14
890; Bay-ray-day-tuss; Proud; F; Sister; 63

891; Chee-say-ea-day-tuss; No hair on his tail; M; Husband; 56
892; Echean-bah-pash; Medicine horses; F; Wife; 50
893; Dah-cock-sah-hoose; Comes to the birds; F; Daughter; 18
894; Dah-cock-sah-hoos; Comes from the birds; F; Daughter; 9
895; ---; Hugh Lieder; M; Son; 23

896; ---; Carl Lieder; M; Husband; 31
897; Bashow-deedich-chayoppes; Medicine rock necklace; F; Wife; 17
898; ---; Agnes Lieder; F; Daughter; 2

899; Ah-dup-pah-hoose; The Arapahoe; M; Husband; 50
900; A-wah-co-case; Spider; F; Wife; 37
901; Chuch-kay-esos; Big Chicken; M; Son; 15
902; Ouk-be-das; Fire deer; M; Son; 10
903; Esook-cot-keh-deas; Old Mouse; M; Son; 2

904; Bah-poe-tus; The fly; M; Husband; 69
905; Awaysha-ishdahcakow-shabeas; Gros Ventre red woman bird; F; Wife; 55

906; Iscehe-haydane-doochis; Takes among the enemy #2; M; Husband; 25
907; Sus-bah-doochis; Takes quick; F; Wife; 26
908; Dah-cock-dacuss; Birdchild; M; Son; 7
909; Ducbitchay-esockcusss; Bear old man; M; Son; 4
910; Bou-doochis; Takes a fish; M; Son; 3

911; Bosh-day-tush; No Name; F; Widow; 47
912; Itch-okepish; Shot himself; M; Son; 9

913; E-koop-pay-bah-coosh; Hat above; F; Widow; 971

914; Bah-put-tosh; Otter; M; Husband; 22
915; Bah-cup-pah-e-chice; Pretty hail; F; Wife; 31

916; Ush-dosh-ka-dus; By the side of camp; F; Widow; 89

Census of the __Crow__ Indians of __Crow__ Agency __Montana__ taken By __J.E. Edwards__, United States Indian Agent __June 30, 1899__

Key: Number; Indian Name; English Name; Sex; Relation; Age

917; Bah-da-pah-coos; Comes from digging roots; Widow; 73
918; Ah-woo-coos; Sydney Wolf; M; Ad. Son; 20

919; E-sees-be-tay; Black hair; M; Husband; 50
920; Been-dah-chay-esah-hay; Strikes between the forts; F; Wife; 45
921; Bah-cup-pah-ah-hoos; Plenty hail; M; Son; 15
922; Ah-chay-itche-poas; Jumps over; M; Son; 6
923; It-chit-chay-eas; Small medicine tobacco; F; Daughter; 3
924; ---; Red Feet; M; Son; 12

925; Chate-bee-dish-she-days; Wolf goes to water; M; Father; 73
926; Cheeup-dah-cock-cus; Bull bird; M; Son; 27

927; Ecupe-pay-cheas; White hat; M; Husband; 53
928; Eck-bahdea-pah-bash; Her medicine is medicine; F; Wife; 51
929; Bes-shepittas; Black rock; M; Son; 17

930; Chate-bah-pash; Medicine wolf; M; Husband; 71
931; Ben-dane-bah-dah-cuss; Sings going in; F; Wife; 61

932; Chip-pah-pos-s-shis; Ground squirrel; M; Husband; 31
933; She-peas; Mud; F; Wife; 24

934; Ecot-osh-heas; Shows a little; M; Husband; 35
935; Bah-dah-pay-it-chis; Kills good; F; Wife; 30
936; Uck-kosh-e-cosh; Looks at the sun; M; Son; 10
937; Bea-koc-kah-dah-biss; Rock moves along; M; Son; 5

938; Ah-pesh-cos; Covers his neck; M; Husband; 60
939; Isbeen-daycha-itchis; Pretty shield; F; Wife; 60
940; Ahpaycha-apah-dootchis; Catches with rope on; M; Son; 3
941; Eck-bah-deas; His medicine; M; Son; 40

942; Ope-kah-deas; Old tobacco; M; Husband; 49
943; Bit-che-doot-chis; Takes a knife; F; Wife; 55

944; Eche-day-kah-deas; Old Horse; M; Husband; 48
945; ---; Mrs. Nate Record; F; Wife; 43
946; ---; Charlie Record; M; Son; 8
947; ---; Dora Record; F; Daughter; 5
948; Bin-dotch-ut-tosh; Off shield; M; Son; 2

949; Oosh-bah-cha-chis; Strong; M; Husband; 25
950; E-say-key-pay; Wrinkle face; F; Wife; 55
951; Bah-chay-cheas; Steals on camp; M; Son; 18

Census of the __Crow__ Indians of __Crow__ Agency __Montana__ taken
By __J.E. Edwards__, United States Indian Agent __June 30, 1899__

Key: Number; Indian Name; English Name; Sex; Relation; Age

952; Bay-kay-day-dah-beas; Three blackbirds; F; Widow; 65

953; Up-pay-ut-tay; Sharp nose No. 1; M; Widower; 73

954; Duck-bit-cha-eckpadea; Medicine bear; M; Husband; 56
955; Is-deam-day-keas-sos; Her road is plain; F; Wife; 51
956; Ah-pay-days; Goes together; F; Daughter; 10
957; Bee-cheas; Packs the rock; M; Son; 11

958; Chess-she-pit-toch; Black tail; M; Husband; 46
959; Bada-beedock-bacusheas; People that shows; F; Wife; 44

960; Chate-oocush-shis; Bob tail wolf; M; Husband; 59
961; Bit-chea-bah-pash; Medicine knife; F; Wife; 57

962; Bah-tah-woas; The bell; M; Husband; 24
963; Bah-buck-but-date-chase; No medicine; F; Wife; 26
964; Duck-cock-bah-dah-cus; Crazy bird; F; Daughter; 4

965; Hay-day-dee-doos; Stands among them; M; Husband; 52
966; Oat-chean-bah-dup-pace; Kills at night; F; Wife; 48
967; Esock-che-sah-keas-sos; Well known hawk; F; Daughter; 4

968; Ah-pay-eso-chay-awachis; Sits before a cloud; M; Husband; 49
969; Ea-cock-kah-beas; Fox woman; F; Wife; 51
970; Bob-puck-sos; Bird among the rocks; M; Son; 19
971; Echee-du-kosh-esos; Big elk; M; Son; 8

972; Ick-kay-ah-hoos; Lots of stars; M; Husband; 41
973; Bah-son-day-ah-hoos; Goes first; F; Wife; 43

974; Bah-hay-chay-wat-tosh; Lone tree; M; Husband; 60
975; Bah-puttock-beaday-beas; Mink; F; Wife; 61
976; E-sah-coo-dake; Carries the arrows; M; Son; 33

977; Ish-chis-says-koos; Comes to her nest; F; Widow; 69

978; Ah-dah-sos-ea-kot-tosh; Little light; M; Husband; 47
979; Esos-kay-koo-doot-chis; Takes her horse; F; Wife; 33
980; Umba-coan-duckbit-chase; Bear in the mountain; M; Son; 14
981; Ope-chu-dup-pace; Tobacco bull; M; Son; 8
982; Cheedup-lahka-dah-his; Bull moves on; M; Son; 6
983; Ah-dah-hes-it-chis; Gets there pretty; M; Son; 5
984; ---; Becker Little Light; M; Son; 1
985; Ba-chay-ha-what-dup-pace; Kills one man; F; Mother; 75

Census of the __Crow__ Indians of __Crow__ Agency __Montana__ taken
By __J.E. Edwards__, United States Indian Agent __June 30, 1899__

Key: Number; Indian Name; English Name; Sex; Relation; Age

986; Ea-chay-kah-deas; Old rabbit; M; Widower; 36
987; ---; Mary Old Rabit; F; Daughter; 14
988; Dah-kosh-bah-coos; Eagle high up; M; Son; 9

989; Tuch-kase; Sounds of the gun; M; Husband; 28
990; Bah-put-tay-ah-hoos; Plenty otter; F; Wife; 37
991; Ock-kosh-de-dish; Antelope that walks; F; Daughter; 6
992; ---; Frederick Sounds th(sic) Gun; M; Son; 2

993; Boat-tay-kah-deas; Old coyote; M; Husband; 38
994; Bah-pash; Medicine; F; Wife; 37
995; Up-pah-sah-chers; Half white; M; Son; 17
996; Ahpa-ka-dainbadakis; Sings in a cloud; M; Son; 13

997; Is-be-dah-eas; Little fire; M; Husband; 49
998; Bea-it-chis-sos; Not a pretty woman; F; Wife; 47
999; Bahputtaychee-dup-pis; Otter bull; M; Son; 24

1000; Bah-pah-esos; Big Medicine; M; Husband; 43
1001; Bahduppay-chedu-chis; Strikes the one that kills; F; Wife; 43
1002; Up-pay-sheedish; Yellow ears; F; Daughter; 16
1003; Bea-bus-sos; Rock in front; F; Daughter; 6

1004; Echey-she-coopy; Crooked foot; M; Husband; 81
1005; Uck-doshy-dee-dich-es; Strikes one that charges; F; Wife; 81

1006; Bah-dah-pah-keas-sos; Digs well known; F; Widow; 69
1007; Badup-keadop-doochisduppa; Kills one that takes 2 guns; Daughter; 37

1008; ---; Thomas Stewart; M; Husband; 27
1009; Ukcheese-malapesh; Kills over beyond the other; F; Wife; 28
1010 ---; Foster Stewart; M; Son; 1

1011; Che-dup-pom-bish; Short bull; M; Husband; 56
1012; Oo-wat-doohis; Takes the iron; F; Wife; 55

1013; Ekoos-sheas; Eagle turns around; M; Father; 35
1014; Esos-kot-bah-deas; Working mouse; M; Son; 11

1015; Esok-cawah-chakoos-say; Pretty old man; M; Husband; 53
1016; Owat-bahduck-keycondish; Old woman gone; F; Wife; 54
1017; Peah-key-tus; The spleen; M; Son; 18

1018; Cay-kay-bah-pash; Medicine lance; F; Widow; 55

1019; Bra-bah-chey-chis; Woman chief; M; Husband; 50

Census of the __**Crow**__ Indians of __**Crow**__ Agency __**Montana**__ taken By __**J.E. Edwards**__, United States Indian Agent __**June 30, 1899**__

Key: Number; Indian Name; English Name; Sex; Relation; Age

1020; Kish-sey; Big around; F; Wife; 53

1021; Deah-kah-sis; The eagle; M; Husband; 36
1022; Bussone-deahah-hoos; Goes ahead pretty; F; Wife; 34
1023; Con-hah-pagh; Medicine old woman; F; Daughter; 13

1024; Beedick-qua-badup-pace; Fools and kills the enemy; F; Mother; 34
1025; Shea-dah-chis; Fog all the time; M; Son; 8
1026; ---; Topsy Woodtick; F; Daughter; 1

1027; Esock-kah-dew-os; Two leggings; M; Husband; 49
1028; Is-bah-duck-chis; Ties up her bundles; F; Wife; 35
1029; Ah-dough-chea-ah-chase; Knows where she stops; F; Daughter; 17

1030; Ah-duk-che-ba-chatchis; Coo chief; M; Husband; 24
1031; Is-ea-dea-ah-hoos; Plenty lodge poles; F; Wife; 29

1032; Ah-key-oke-bee-shay; White clay on forehead; M; Husband; 51
1033; Be-dosh; Fire; F; Wife; 41
1034; Isben-doch-dup-pichish; Light shield; F; Daughter; 5
1035; Keas-sos; Plain; M; Son; 13

1036; Ah-duck-chea-oss-ea-tuss; Shows his coos; M; Husband; 32
1037; Minne-ekoshees; Turns to the water; F; Wife; 25
1038; Oot-tay-bah-coos; Weasel highup; F; Daughter; 5

1039; Ook-pay-hiss-siss; Red wing; M; Widower; 49

1040; Ducock-sahoo-dup-pace; Kills coming to the birds; F; Mother; 59
1041; Ahway-coe-ish-chisaydock; The swallow child; M; Son; 18

1042; Bee-ditch-key-sos; Big lake; M; Husband; 51
1043; Oo-wat-dootch-chis; Pounds the iron; F; Wife; 50
1044; Bashow-dee-dich-chay-sos; Big medicine rock; F; Daughter; 18
1045; Oat-tay-dock-cuss; Weasel child; M; Son; 11
1046; Chate-bick-cuss; Female wolf; F; Sister; 53

1047; E-shoe-dee-chea-ock-kin- day-dee-ditch-es; Strikes the rider of white maned horse; F; Widow; 61

1048; Bah-cay-key-e-cosh; Looks at the shield; F; Widow; 31
1049; Bah-tah-wos; Plain bell; M; Son; 2

1050; Dah-cock-it-chis; Good bird; M; Husband; 73
1051; Un-duck-cah-hoos; Stops at many places; F; Wife; 68

Census of the __Crow__ Indians of __Crow__ Agency __Montana__ taken
By __J.E. Edwards__, United States Indian Agent __June 30, 1899__

Key: Number; Indian Name; English Name; Sex; Relation; Age

1052; Duck-bitchay-ock-indas; Rides a bear; M; Husband; 55
1053; Boa-it-chis; Pretty fish; F; Wife; 48
1054; Ah-dock-inday-keas-sos; Rides well known; M; Son; 18

1055; Oo-wat-cas; Little iron; M; Husband; 48
1056; It-chit-chae-ays; Tobacco seed; F; Wife; 45
1057; He-dah-bah-chase; Just a man; M; Son; 14

1058; Dah-cup-pis; Calf; M; Husband; 37
1059; Eas-che-kay-pay; Crooked face; F; Wife; 33

1060; Bah-che-dee-kah-deas; Old white man; M; Husband; 61
1061; Bee-shay-dee-dish; Buffalo that walks; F; Wife; 33

1062; Oke-keas-sos; Well known antelope; M; Husband; 35
1063; Uck-bah-he-dee-cose; Does anything; F; Wife; 25

1064; Boa-tah-it-chis; Pretty coyote; M; Husband; 31
1065; Bah-oos; Brings things; F; Wife; 27

1066; Cheedup-shepittus; Black bull; M; Husband; 48
1067; Bee-day-de-cuss-chis; Comes out of the water; F; Wife; 45
1068; Bah-show-dee-ditch; Medicine rock; F; Daughter; 18

1069; Bim-boan-chee-duppis; Bull in the water; M; Husband; 60
1070; Che-dup-peas; Young bull; F; Wife; 61

1071; Bah-it-chay-on-deas; Does many good things; M; Husband; 26
1072; Baput-tahbedane-duckoos; Otter stays in water; F; Wife; 21
1073; Echey-day-hay-day-duss; Among the horses; F; Daughter; 4
1074; ---; Star; F; Sister; 15

1075; Ah-puss-sah-cheas; Half white; M; Husband; 60
1076; But-shay-aut-tuss; Close together; F; Wife; 51

1077; Iscochehay-dane-doochis; Take among the enemy; M; Husband; 38
1078; Ah-shoe-hish-shis; Red hair; M; Wife; 43
1079; Pea-cah-dah-hutch; Long Piegan; M; Son; 12
1080; Bah-osh-ah-hoos; Plenty red plumes; F; Daughter; 10

1081; Isbin-dochca-chate-chis; Shield chief; M; Husband; 38
1082; Esos-keas-sos; Blanket well known; F; Wife; 46

1083; Bah-ea-way-shadock-cuss; Young curlew; M; Husband; 47
1084; Cheas-kaock-inda-deechis; Rides a white horse; F; Wife; 43
1085; Shu-dish; Singing hat; F; Daughter; 11

Census of the __Crow__ Indians of __Crow__ Agency __Montana__ taken
By __J.E. Edwards__, United States Indian Agent __June 30, 1899__

Key: Number; Indian Name; English Name; Sex; Relation; Age

1086; ---; Pretty flowers; F; Daughter; 1
1087; Bah-sone-dace; Goes first; F; Mother; 84

1088; Wochis-say-ahwa-chice; Sits to the wind; F; Widow; 53

1089; Dah-cock-teah-dish; The bird; M; Husband; 30
1090; Is-coe-chee-dup-pace; Kills her enemy; F; Wife; 26
1091; By-eas; Arrow Point; M; Son; 6
1092; Epea-cot-a-wak-chis; Magpie sits down; M; Son; 2

1093; Away-choke-kayda-cockus; Bird on the prairie; M; Husband; 45
1094; Besha-ockain-awaychis; Sits on the blanket; F; Wife; 39

1095; Chee-sock-cuss; Long tail; M; Husband; 42
1096; She-pea-day-tuss; No mud; F; Wife; 37
1097; Tickpah-cheday-deshis; Strikes one that pushes him; M; Son; 13
1098; Ah-we-sos; Shows big on the ground; M; Son; 9
1099; ---; Lydia Long Tail; F; Daughter; 1

1100; Hay-dain-dec-chis; Strikes among them; F; Widow; 71
1101; Cheedup; Strong bull; M; Son; 32

1102; Bah-cup-pash; Hail; M; Husband; 32
1103; Echeedayon-duckockeasos; Horses place well known; F; Wife; 33

1104; It-tuch-bah-cha-chis; Strong alone; M; Husband; 51
1105; Uck-bah-dea-ate-chase; Knows her medicine; F; Wife; 46

1106; Chate-ea-cot-tus; Little wolf; M; Husband; 74
1107; Bah-dup-pay-keas-sos; Kills well known; F; Wife; 63

1108; Chee-dish; Hunts; M; Husband; 43
1109; Echee-dahay-daneduckoos; Stays with the horse; F; Wife; 39
1110; E-sop-pah-dah-tus; Has no moccasin; M; Son; 19
1111; E-sos-kay-ate-chace; Knows his horse; F; Daughter; 6

1112; Bah-dah-sure-ha-wattus; One blue bead; M; Husband; 51
1113; Ushoo-suttah-doo-tchis; Takes one close to camp; F; Wife; 49
1114; Un-dah-hea-sos; Surrounds the enemy strong; M; Son; 14

1115; Duckbitchay-nopew-oze; Mad at the bear; M; Husband; 37
1116; Is-eap-che-bish-ay; Got a pipe; F; Wife; 41
1117; Is-bahit-chis; Got pretty things; F; Daughter; 12
1118; Dahcoe-tay-doot-chis; Catches the Sioux; F; Daughter; 6

1119; ---; Charles Ten Bear; M; --; 23

Census of the __Crow__ Indians of __Crow__ Agency __Montana__ taken By __J.E. Edwards__, United States Indian Agent __June 30, 1899__

Key: Number; Indian Name; English Name; Sex; Relation; Age

1120; Ah-she-tas; Sharp horn; M; Husband; 58
1121; Bea-cot-ish-tup-pay; Woman with eyes open; F; Wife; 58

1122; Bah-chay-bah-day-kay; Foolish man; M; Husband; 37
1123; Hay-dane-ah-seas; Shows in a crowd; F; Wife; 31
1124; ---; George Foolish Man; M; Son; 2

1125; E-cuss-sah-esos; Big snake; M; Husband; 54
1126; Chedockcusakbadupays; Kills in the morning; F; Wife; 58

1127; Bea-bah-coos; Fish high up; M; Husbsnd[sic]; 53
1128; Chuck-ko-doot-chit; Takes five; F; Wife; 51

1129; Poe-put-tah-bah-coos; Owl above; M; Husband; 31
1130; E-che-doe-it-chis; Brings pretty horses; F; Wife; 33
1131; Ah-dah-che-e-sos; Sees the coos; F; Daughter; 11
1132; Ume-beas; Paint woman; F; Daughter; 9

1133; Cheadup-um-bee-chis-sos; Bull that don't fall down; M; Husband; 46
1134; Ah-see-tus; Shows; F; Wife; 33
1135; Is-been-dot-bish-eas; Got a shield; F; Mother; 71

1136; Esop-pay-shoes; Blue moccasin; M; Husband; 55

1137; Bah-cook-coe-tah-hoos; Comes from above; M; Husband; 33
1138; Um-bah-cone-dah-coos; Steps above; F; Wife; 36
1139; ---; Hannah Comes Above; F; Daughter; 2

1140; Bin-day-sop-pay-dus; River Crow; M; Husband; 34
1141; Cah-pah-dias; Medicine; F; Wife; 30

1142; Esutsehoom-meas; Sage woman; F; Mother; 33
1143; Ashmitee-makpash; The song is medicine; F; Daughter; 8

~~Es-che-kah-dish; Old rabbit woman; F; Widow; --~~

1144; Cha-qua-bah-soo; Charges five times; M; Husband; 27
1145; Bea-ah-wah-chis; Woman that sits down; F; Wife; 23
1146; E-hum-dah-pace; Kills in sleep; F; Daughter; 5

1147; Is-coe-chea-ahoos; Got many enemies; M; Husband; 40
1148; Bah-put-tah-dock-cus; Young otter; F; Wife; 49

1149; Be-dup-dah-cus; Young beaver; M; Husband; 53
1150; Bak-kah-beas; Hoop woman; F; Wife; 57

Census of the __Crow__ Indians of __Crow__ Agency __Montana__ taken
By __J.E. Edwards__, United States Indian Agent __June 30, 1899__

Key: Number; Indian Name; English Name; Sex; Relation; Age

1151; Umbah-owedup-ate-chase; Knows where he finds things; M; Husband; 38
1152; Qua-dus; Between; F; Wife; 33

1153; Eche-doch-in-days; Rides a horse; M; Husband; 45
1154; Ah-cam-dah-pace; Kills on top; F; Wife; 41
1155; Bah-dee-shis; Jerked meat; M; Son; 18
1156; Bah-day-key-sut-tus; Two barreled gun; M; Son 12
1157; E-shue-eas; Feather neck; F; Daughter; 5
1158; Edock-bah-pash; Medicine form; 3
1159; Is-ah-way-cone-dah-pase; Kills on her ground; F; Mother; 73

1160; Bah-pus; Cliff; F; Widow; 41

1161; Eche-dee-kosh-awaychis; Sitting elk; M; Husband; 59
1162; Dah-cock-beas; Bird woaman[sic]; F; Wife; 56

1163; Bah-che-quas; Sugar; M; Husband; 70
1164; Cuck-ca-coo-day-dechis; Strikes one with a lance; F; Wife; 51
1165; ---; Louise; F; Daughter; 12

1166; Dosh-shay-e-coos; Charges madly on the enemy; M; Husband; 27
1167; Ush-doop-tah-coe-dee; Strikes two camps; F; Wife; 31
1168; Tuck-kit-chat-ah-hoos; Shoots plenty; F; Daughter; 4

1169; Echeday-itchay-ock-inday; Rides a pretty horse; M; Husband; 31
1170; Ah-woos-ah-cay-dus; On top of the sweathouse; F; Wife; 29
1171; Cah-pah-dee-itchis; Good medicine; F; Daughter; 10
1172; Coo-bah-pay-day-pah; Kills the same day; F; Daughter; 4

1173; Daek-it-chis; Pretty eagle; M; Husband; 54
1174; Is-been-dotch-itchis; Pretty Shield; F; Wife; 51
1175; Dack-kosh-sheedis; Yellow eagle; M; Son; 3

1176; Da-cose; Goes on; M; Husband; 58
1177; Been-dotch-us-eas; Shield that shows; F; Wife; 51

1178; Ike-cook-cus; Even; M; Husband; 28
1179; Ush-dea-it-chise; Makes a pretty lodge; F; Wife; 29

1180; Up-pah-keas-sos; Cloud well known; M; Husband; 39
1181; Con-dah-cock-cus; Old bird woman; F; Wife; 38
1182; Ushcoe-tah-cose-shis; Helps the whole camp; M; Son; 14

1183; Che-say-ick-cosh; See a white horse; M; Husband; 45
1184; Dosh-day-tus; No name; F; Wife; 45
1185; ---; Peter S. White Horse; M; Son; 15

Census of the __Crow__ Indians of __Crow__ Agency __Montana__ taken By __J.E. Edwards__, United States Indian Agent __June 30, 1899__

Key: Number; Indian Name; English Name; Sex; Relation; Age

1186; Oo-shis; Hole; M; Husband; 26
1187; Ah-shue-ah-was-days; Horn dropped down; F; Wife; 20

1188; Duck-bit-chay-dee-dish; Bear that walks; M; Widower; 39

1189; Is-shay-dus; Hairy on top of his head; M; Husband; 53
1190; Bin-doch-e-so-chain-dus; Sheep in front; F; Wife; 54

1191; Duck-cock-bea-it-chis; Pretty woman bird; F; Widow; 43
1192; Esho-dechea-dootchis; Takes horse with white mane; F; Daughter; 14
1193; Bah-shay-cha-dup-pace; Kills the chief; F; Daughter; 9

1194; Duck-bit-chay-eas; Bear's tooth; M; Husband; 45
1195; Bah-chay-un-dah-pace; Kills many man; F; Wife; 43
1196; ---; Mary Bear's Tooth; F; Daughter; 19
1197; Opa-bah-dah-kis; Tobacco sings; F; Ad. Dau.; 6

1198; Ish-tay-ea-sos; Big eyes; M; --; 58

1199; Esa-pis; Shot in the face; M; Husband; 61
1200; Hoo-chis; Wind blowing; F; Wife; 55

1201; Uck-cha-key-chis; Spies on the enemy; M; Husband; 37
1202; Us-dosh-cane-doot-chis; Takes by side of camp; F; Wife; 41

1203; Bosh-bah-pash; Medicine feather; F; Widow; 51
1204; Edea-oke-pis; Shoots tent poles; F; Niece; 10

1205; Bahduck-key-dootchis; Takes a gun #1; M; Husband; 59
1206; Ah-way-chase; Knows the ground; F; Wife; 61

1207; Bah-owe-keas-sos; Brings well known; F; Widow; 51
1208; Bosh-doot-chis; Takes a feather; F; Daughter; 14

1209; Bah-cup-pah-e-sos; Big hail; M; Husband; 31
1210; Bah-cuch-ca-beas; Striped snake woman; F; Wife; 25
1211; Beshay-ook-bah-wah-chis; Sit with a buffalo; M; Son; 6

1212; Esop-ponta-chahadadose; Among the sheep; F; --; 25

1213; Awahcah-wassahwa-chis; Face toward the mountain; M; Husband; 46
1214; Peace-hay-duce; Comes behind; F; Wife; 39
1215; oo-sha-cane-ca-pis; Sits over a hole; F; Daughter; 10
1216; Dah-cock-shee-dis; Yellow bird; F; Daughter; 6

1217; Ah-dean-dace; The Trail; F; Widow; 49

Census of the __Crow__ Indians of __Crow__ Agency __Montana__ taken
By __J.E. Edwards__, United States Indian Agent __June 30, 1899__

Key: Number; Indian Name; English Name; Sex; Relation; Age

1218; Ischie-say-be-shis; Got a nest; M; Son; 16
1219; Is-been-doch-ah-hoos; Plenty Shield; F; Daughter; 14
1220; Eche-de-she-chace; Likes the horses; F; Daughter; 10

1221; Up-pay-okpis; Shot in the nose; M; Husband; 28
1222; Is-coe-ache-chea-chase; Knows the enemy; F; Wife; 25
1223; Awahoe-ischesayahoos; Plenty swallow; M; Son; 8
1224; ---; John shot in the nose; M; Son; 2

1225; Been-dosh-sha-pah-bash; Medicine top; M; Husband; 33
1226; Bah-ay-ba-eas; Has things; F; Wife; 34
1227; Isbahca-key-bot-posh; Her medicine shell; F; Daughter; 5
1228; ---; Susie Spotted; F; Daughter; 8
1229; Bahkay-ahoos; Gives lots of things away; F; Daughter; 6

1230; Duck-bit-chay-che-dace; Bear gets up; M; Husband; 65
1231; Bah-put-tah-dew-pus; Two otters; F; Wife; 60

1232; It-tut-dah-cock-cus; Bird by himself; M; Batchelor[sic]; 59

1233; Chate-sha-duck-bit-chay; Mad bear wolf; M; Husband; 55
1234; Minkuus; Onion; F; Wife; 67
1235; Mideras-ichis; Does good things; M; Ad. Son; 16
1236; Dah-hes-os; Surrounds the enemy; M; Son; 20

1237; Boop-chis; Ball; M; Husband; 35
1238; Bea-sheedes; Yellow woman; F; Wife; 34

1239; Ukbadapa-ish-tuckea-dooch; Takes the killer of guns; M; Widower; 25
1240; Bah-duck-kea-os-seas; Shows a gun; M; Son; 5
1241; Uk-keam-duck-chis; Ties on the foretop; F; Daughter; 9
1242; Badock-key-huchkey-dooch; Takes a long gun; F; Daughter; 2

1243; Bah-put-tah-cah-deas; Old otter; F; Widow; 53

1244; He-dah-wah-chace; He is a man now; M; Husband; 56
1245; Ecupe-pah-doot-chis; Takes the hat; F; Wife; 51

1246; Istuk-kea-bachata-chice; Gun chief; M; Husband; 52
1247; Cuck-cock-in-days; Rides a spotted Horse; F; Wife; 39
1248; Be-dea-bah-pash; The door is medicine; F; Daughter; 16
1249; Ushdosh-katah-bah-sos; Runs beside the camp; M; Son; 5
1250; Bah-put-tah-beas; Woman otter; F; Mother; 78

1251; Eche-day-it-chis; Good horses; M; Husband; 34
1252; E-hum-be-shoes; More of them; F; Wife; 23

Census of the __Crow__ Indians of __Crow__ Agency __Montana__ taken
By __J.E. Edwards__, United States Indian Agent __June 30, 1899__

Key: Number; Indian Name; English Name; Sex; Relation; Age

1253; Been-dah-chate-dase; Goes to the fort; F; Daughter; 5

1254; Ea-cus-sos; Snake; F; Mother; 57
1255; E-sah-duck-chis; Ties up the arrows; F; Daughter; 17

1256; Beedee-chay-hay-dus; Among willows; F; Widow; 63

1257; Esah-eduse-see-shis; Broken arrow; M; Husband; 39
1258; Es-tay-cheas; Grey eyes; F; Wife; 41

1259; Dukbitse-upah-pushcoos; Cuts the bears ears; M; Husband; 49
1260; It-chis; Good; F; Wife; 46
1261; Bah-dah-kit-chice; Sings good; M; Son; 16

1262; Hay-day-dose; Right among them; M; Husband; 52
1263; E-dah-hoos; Come herself; F; Wife; 56

1264; Kah-disc; Old woman; M; Widower; 59
1265; Dadough-cheada-itchice; Leads the camp pretty; F; Daughter; 12

1266; Odup-dah-pace; Finds and kills them; M; Widower; 46
1267; Echa-dow-keas-sos; Brings horses well known; F; Daughter; 11

1268; Ischay-dah-kish-shay; Knot between the eyes; M; Husband; 58
1269; Oo-wat-doot-chase; Takes the iron; F; Wife; 53
1270; Dock-shay-dah-beas; Three coons; F; Daughter; 16

1271; Cuck-cah-wah-chice; Sits down spotted; M; Husband; 37
1272; Bah-chay-cheas; Steals on the camp; F; Wife; 20
1273; ---; John Spotted; M; Son; 2
1274; Eches-dish-hoos; Plenty horses; M; Brother; 47

1275; Dah-cock;bah-coos; Bird above; M; Husband; 33
1276; Oo-tahcuck-kis; Spotted weasel; F; Wife; 31
1277; Be-day-tuss; Like a fire; M; Son; 11
1278; Hoo-chice-soos; Comes against the wind; M; Son; 8
1279; Poop-kit-tah-cuck-kis; Spotted snow bird; F; Daughter; 6

1280; Chate-kah-we-sis; Skins a wolf; M; Husband; 58
1281; E-sos-kah-we-sis; Has horses; F; Wife; 51

1282; ---; Richard Cummins; M; --; 26

1283; Be-dook-sah-e-duse; Alligator stands up; M; Husband; 54
1284; Bah-put-tea-hosh; The other otter; F; Wife; 53

Census of the __Crow__ Indians of __Crow__ Agency __Montana__ taken
By __J.E. Edwards__, United States Indian Agent __June 30, 1899__

Key: Number; Indian Name; English Name; Sex; Relation; Age

1285; Boat-tah-cah-dush-sis; Coyote runs; M; Husband; 39
1286; Dupe-tosh-beas; Woman both ways; F; Wife; 34
1287; ---; Arnold Kosta; M; Son; 19
1288; Ah-pah-de-beas; Porcupine woman; F; Daughter; 3

1289; Ea-cus-sah-che-dup-pis; Snake bull; M; Husband; 48
1290; Oo-what-de-chise; Strikes the iron; F; Wife; 34
1291; Bah-ow-duck-coos; Brings things always; F; Daughter; 14
1292; Boo-duke-pah-keasos; Plain cedar; F; Daughter; 10
1293; Che-quais; Is sweet now; M; Son; 4

1294; ---; Pius Hill; M; Orphan; 16
1295; Bea-ah-dutch-she-beas; Woman that farms; F; Sister; 10

1296; Eas-es-coas; Covers his face; M; Husband; 32
1297; Ahsah-date-doot-chis; Takes horses on prairie; F; Wife; 22

1298; Bee-dish; Walking; M; Husband; 44
1299; Uck-bah-du-ick-cosh; Looks at the medicine; F; Wife; 49

1300; Eas-shee-day; Yellow face; M; Husband; 74
1301; Bea-itchay-de-chice; Strikes the pretty woman; F; Wife; 71

1302; Eat-tosh-tay-his-shos; Red shirt; M; Husband; 22
1303; Ahwacoe-che-dapahpash; Medicine ground cedar; F; Wife; 22

1304; Ah-pitbah-coos; Crane in the sky; M; Husband; 59
1305; Be-dup-his-shis; Red beaver; F; Wife; 64
1306; Bah-key-dawah-chice; Blackbird sits down; F; Daughter; 11
1307; Is-tah-dase-cheas; Big squirrel; M; Son; 14

1308; Awayeah-wah-chea-days; Mountain pocket; M; Husband; 56
1309; E-chope-pice; Shoots her foot; F; Wife; 49
1310; Esos-kee-dit-bah-pash; Medicine horsewhip; M; Son; 26

1311; Ah-dah-doo-be-shay; Shot in the arm; M; Husband; 56
1312; Bea-doot-chice; Takes a woman; F; Wife; 49

1313; Shechock-ay-dus; On top of the hill; M; Husband; 60
1314; Isba-daha-wat-ate-chice; Knows the yearling; F; Wife; 52

1315; Bosh-che-de-cot-tay; White men; M; Husband; 45
1316; Bah-cuck-cah-ah-hoos; Plenty striped snake; F; Wife; 51
1317; Ah-dean-day-ate-chice; Knows the road; F; Daughter; 16
1318; Dah-cock-che-deas-sos; Not afraid of bird; M; Son; 9
1319; Dah-cock-ah-pah-hoose; Bird with plenty of wings going around; M; Son; 8

Census of the __Crow__ Indians of __Crow__ Agency __Montana__ taken By __J.E. Edwards__, United States Indian Agent __June 30, 1899__

Key: Number; Indian Name; English Name; Sex; Relation; Age

1320; Eupe-pah-bah-put-tosh; Hat otter; F; Daughter; 2

1321; Bea-it-chay; Pretty woman; F; Widow; 41

1322; Edosh-uck-bah-dup-pace; Kills with his bro-in-law; M; Husband; 45
1323; Un-di-day-it-chice; Walks pretty; F; Wife; 43
1324; Bick-cah-hay-day-duss; Sits among the grass; F; Daughter; 14
1325; Oak-cha-sis; Antelope; F; Daughter; 12

1326; ---; James Buffalo; M; Husband; 25
1327; Bah-cup-pah-cheas; White hail; F; Wife; 23
1328; Isbin-doch-ebahick-deas; Does everything with shield; F; Daughter; 6
1329; Cah-dicth-chea-ah-hoos; Plenty lighning; M; Son; 5

1330; Duck-bit-chay-che-sus; Bears tail; M; Widower; 59
1331; Duckbitchaun-dayatchase; Knows where the bear goes; F; Daughter; 15
1332; Ah-way-cah-wah-seas; Shows in the mountain; M; Son; 25

1333; Ah-pah-dee-esos; Big porcupine; M; Husband; 43
1334; Un-doo-cosh-keas-sos; Holds well known; F; Wife; 40

1335; Chee-dup-bachate-chice; Bull chief; M; Husband; 63
1336; Istuk-keybah-chate-chice; Long gun; F; Wife; 57
1337; It-chit-che-ays; Medicine tobacco; M; Gr. Son; 9

1338; Ah-shue-cheas; White horn; F; Widow; 53

1339; Isbiche-itchis-sayeacoktus; Little whetstone; M; Husband; 59
1340; Eche-dah-keas-sos; Horse well known; F; Wife; 40

1341; Cha-chuck-key-sos; Big around; M; Husband; 59
1342; Cah-coa-doot-chise; Takes all the horses; F; Wife; 51
1343; Ecup-pah-ate-chice; Knows her hat; M; Mother; 75

1344; Shis-sheas; Curly; M; Husband; 49
1345; Bin-dotch-doot-chis; Takes a shield; F; Wife; 51
1346; Awan-dookcostadacockuss; Bird another year; F; Daughter; 3

1347; Dah-cus; Balls; M; Husband; 38
1348; Petakus; Ten; F; Wife; 21

1349; Be-day-dish-sos; Don't get in; F; Widow; 47
1350; Ah-pah-de-e-wan-deas; Plays with medicine; F; Daughter; 9
1351; Un-day-it-chice; Goes ahead pretty; F; Daughter; 11

1352; Ah-pit-tus; The crane; M; Husband; 43

Census of the __Crow__ Indians of __Crow__ Agency __Montana__ taken
By __J.E. Edwards__, United States Indian Agent __June 30, 1899__

Key: Number; Indian Name; English Name; Sex; Relation; Age

1353; E-chee-uck-pahdup-pace; Kills with the horses; F; Wife; 40
1354; Che-soup-pus; End of the tail; M; Son; 14
1355; Esos-kah-wishes; Has horses; F; Mother; 73

1356; Oat-bay-bea-dosh; Fire weasel; M; Husband; 68
1357; Ah-dough-chea-bah-pash; Medicine where she stops; F; Wife; 63

1358; Beas; Rock; M; Widower; 37
1359; Bashow-de-chite-shase; Medicine rock; F; Daughter; 4
1360; ---; Standing buffalo; F; Daughter; 1

1361; Duck-cock-ah-shoes; Bird head; M; Husband; 41
1362; Dah-ah-sheas; Shows going; F; Wife; 35
1363; Bishea-duck-bit-chase; Bear's dog; M; Son; 20
1364; Bah-cah-wat-tay-dace; Hoop goes a long ways; M; Son; 8
1365; Oot-tah-dock-cus; Young weasel; F; Daughter; 5
1366: Is-coe-che-che-dish; Afraid of his enemy; M; Son; 14

1367; Duck-peas; Hugs; M; Husband; 53
1368; Awa-shehay-danedoochice; Takes a man in a fog; F; Wife; 57
1369; Bah-duck-it-chise; Sings pretty; M; Son; 21

1370; Ah-wah-coan-de-dish; Walks in middle of ground; M; Husband; 63
1371; Ea-cot-tus; Little; F; Wife; 54

1372; Basho-dechit-chabahcoos; Medicine rock above; M; Husband; 32
1373; E-cheam-dah-pace; Kills a horse; F; Wife; 31
1374; Bah-keam-boo-dish; Bull blackbird; M; Son; 9

1375; E-chean-dah-cock-cus; Bird horse; M; Husband; 25
1376; Bah-show-be-chit-chase; Medicine rock; F; Wife; 23
1377; Ea-des-it-chice; Pretty lodge poles; F; Daughter; 6

1378; Ea-dane-deas; He does it; M; Husband; 27
1379; Bah-cook-coo-dush; She is high up; F; Wife; 31
1380; Cheach-cues; Chicken; F; Daughter; 11
1381; Cah-pah-dee-dock-cus; Young medicine; M; Son; 6
1382; Bah-show-dechit-chaesos; Big medicine rock; F; Mother; 51

1383; Dupe-pah-wah-dup-pace; Kills twice; F; Widow; 44
1384; Un-dah-pace; Kill plenty; F; Daughter; 14
1385; Ha-dane-dah-cock-cus; Bird among them; M; Son; 6
1386; Eat-toch-tay-keas-sos; Plain shirt; F; Daughter; 5

1387; Bah-cah-dish-tah-beas; Heifer woman; F; Divorcee; 35
1388; Bea-bah-shay-e-sit-chace; Like the summer; F; Daughter; 5

Census of the __Crow__ Indians of __Crow__ Agency __Montana__ taken
By __J.E. Edwards__, United States Indian Agent __June 30, 1899__
Key: Number; Indian Name; English Name; Sex; Relation; Age

1389; Bin-dosh-shay-shee-dish; Yellow top; M; Batch; 58

1390; Bah-chay-cheas; Steals on the camp; F; Widow; 63

1391; Eak-cah-shues; Blue chin; F; Widow; 58

1392; Eas-chay-cuck-kis; Spotted rabbit; M; Husband; 33
1393; Itchit-chay-bah-pash; Medicine tobacco; F; Wife; 39
1394; Oo-what-ashoes; Iron head; M; Son; 20
1395; Uckbahdea-ewahickdeas; Does everything with her medc; F; Daughter; 16
1396; Oka-push; Badly shot; M; Son; 2
1397; Es-sos; Hairy; F; Mother; 65

1398; Chedup-cho-sus; White bull; M; Husband; 71
1399; Be-dase-she-cash; Looks at the water; F; Wife; 61

1400; Bah-doo-peas; Scolds; M; Husband; 34
1401; ---; Mrs. Ben Gardner(?); F; Wife; 36
1402; ---; Thomas Gardiner; M; Son; 15
1403; ---; Frank Gardner(?); M; Son; 13
1404; ---; Amelia Gardner(?); F; Daughter; 11
[Gardiner appears as correct spelling from other censuses.]

1405; Dah-cock-keah-sos; Bird well known; M; Husband; 33
1406; Bea-dosh-day-tush; Woman without a name; F; Wife; 26
1407; Awah-cahn-dob-cock-cus; Mountain bird; M; Son; 2

1408; Payduch-chay-ook-cusseas; Bob tail crow; M; Husband; 53
1409; Bah-ick-cah-keas-sos; Sees well known; F; Wife; 49

1410; Eas-chee-key-pah; Crooked face; M; Husband; 59
1411; Ishbin-doch-ba-chatechice; Strikes the shield first; F; Wife; 39
1412; Dah-cock-cah-doosh-sis; Bird that runs; F; Daughter; 14
1413; Doop-pah-e-che-dosh; Brings the horses; M; Son; 5

1414; Bah-ea-cah-keas-sos; Sees well known; F; Widow; 57

1415; Beeda-dosh-cane-dechise; Sits by side of water; F; Widow; 54
1416; ---; Charles Brown; M; Son; 22
1417; Ope-che-chuck-kis; Round tobacco; F; Ad. Dau; 14

1418; ---; Holder White Wings; M; --; 21

~~1419; Ecupe-pah-wish-de-chice; Strikes one with hat; F; Widow; 53~~
[Unclear why there's a line through entry, she's in 1900.]

110

Census of the **Crow** Indians of **Crow** Agency **Montana** taken
By **J.E. Edwards**, United States Indian Agent **June 30, 1899**

Key: Number; Indian Name; English Name; Sex; Relation; Age

1420; Ah-dah-cuck-kays; Spotted arm; M; Husband; 51
1421; Ah-dow-chea-keas-sos; Where she stops well known; F; Wife; 53
1422; Dapitsah-seandahcockcus; Bird in the morning; M; Son; 18

1423; Um-bah-chea-keas-sos; Fights well known #2; M; Husband; 37
1424; Isbeen-doch-baduck-kis; Shield that sings; F; Wife; 33
1425; Be-shaye-de-dish; Walks to the buffalo; M; Son; 4

1426; It-chase-shay-danedechase; Strikes on top of head; M; Husband; 36
1427; Bee-shay-e-hosh; The other buffalo; F; Wife; 35
1428; Awacooish-chice-sayeacotas; Little swallow; M; Son; 9

1429; Eche-dee-kosh-kahdeas; Old elk; M; Husband; 40
1430; Ookish-deanday-ah-hoos; Antelope trails; F; Wife; 39
1431; E-chean-push-cush; Cuts the horse; M; Son; 9
1432; ---; Mary Old Elk; F; Daughter; 2

1433; Bah-shoes-shays; Red feather; F; Widow; 51
1434; Es-dea-cah-deas; Old lodge pole; M; Son; 15

1435; Eas-bah-pus-say; Round face; M; Husband; 51
1436; Bout-tah-bah-hoos; Coyote that howls; F; Wife; 49
1437; Bah-touch-owe-duck-coos; Brings things all the time; M; Son; 17

1438; Nas-ehas; The other heart; M; --; 25

1439; Ah-dup-pice; Hides; M; Husband; 37
1440; Hay-day-tah-wah-sos; Goes through her enemies; F; Wife; 33
1441; Uck-bah-dea-ah-hoos; Plenty medicine; F; Daughter; 10
1442; Ook-che-dup-price; Bull deer; M; Son; 4

1443; ---; Charles Clawson; M; Batch.; 227

1444; Ah-day-shay-chee-dish; Hunts to die; M; Husband; 61
1445; Esos-kay-it-chis; Her horse is pretty; F; Wife; 51
1446; Co-tah-dah-cock-cus; The bird everyday; M; Son; 23

1447; ---; Henry Reed; M; Batch; 25

1448; Archie-min-nay-tus; No Milk; M; Husband; 41
1449; ah-wane-dane-duck-koos; Stays out doors; F; Wife; 47
1450; Um-bah-dea-it-chis; His work is good; F; Daughter; 15

1451; Duckbitch-ucpah-dahous; Ghost bear; M; Husband; 51
1452; Is-dotch-chea-ate-chase; Knows her prisoners; F; Wife; 49

Census of the __Crow__ Indians of __Crow__ Agency __Montana__ taken By __J.E. Edwards__, United States Indian Agent __June 30, 1899__

Key: Number; Indian Name; English Name; Sex; Relation; Age

1453; Chate-e-cah-duse; Runs the wolf; M; Husband; 61
1454; Duck-cock-beas: Bird woman; F; Wife; 53

1455; Ah-way-sheas; Fog; M; Husband; 31
1456; Is-bah-cah-bah-duck-kis; Hoop that sings; F; Wife; 25

1457; Bah-touch-e-cook-cosh; Hears everyway; M; Hsband[sic]; 43
1458; Dah-cock-ah-wah-chice; Bird sits down; F; Wife; 35
1459; Esock-chice; The hawk; M; Son; 22
1460; Un-de-chay-it-chice; Strikes pretty; M; Son; 14
1461; ---; Dorothy H. Everyway; F; Daughter; 2

1462; Ah-key-chice; The wet; M; Husband; 49
1463; Uck-sah-ey-chase; Knows her mother; F; Wife; 44
1464; Dah-say-cah-weas; Bad heart; M; Son; 20
1465; Bah-key-cush-sheas; Hoop that runs; M; Son; 13
1466; Bah-shos; Feather; F; M-in-law; 53

1467; Ut-che-key-chis; Spies on the enemy #2; M; Husband; 34
1468; Bah-put-tah-bock-bus; Otter hoop; F; Wife; 23
1469; Ock-bish-cus; White tailed deer; F; Daughter; 6
1470; Oot-tah-dee-dish; Walking weasel; F; Daughter; 3

1471; Ah-way-cah-wah-sheas; Mountain that shows; M; Father; 44
1472; Is-tuck-kay-os-seas; Shows his gun; M; Son; 19
1473; Bah-put-tah-beas; Woman otter; F; Mother; 69

1474; Ish-oos; Back of the neck; M; Husband; 63
1475; Co-cosh-beas; Corn woman; F; Wife; 53
1476; Ea-cah-pish; Flat mouth; M; Son; 24

1477; Ah-wah-key-sos; Big sky; M; Husband; 43
1478; Oo-ah-wah-pish; Medicine wife; F; Wife; 33

1479; Um-bah-cone-cahs; Comes from above; F; Divorcee; 24
1480; Bick-kah-keas-sos; Well known mare; F; Daughter; 7

1481; Bit-che-doot-chis; Grabs the knife; F; Widow; 51
1482; ---; Dick Hawk; M; Son; 23

1483; Ush-ase-bah-sos; Charges on the camp; M; Husband; 63
1484; Be-shea-bah-pash; Medicine heifer; F; Wife; 59

1485; Chee-dup-chos-us; Grey bull; M; Husband; 38
1486; Ha-dane-e-cush-chice; Takes out of a crowd; F; Wife; 41
1487; Dook-ke-days; Goes to fight; F; Daughter; 5

Census of the __Crow__ Indians of __Crow__ Agency __Montana__ taken By __J.E. Edwards__, United States Indian Agent __June 30, 1899__

Key: Number; Indian Name; English Name; Sex; Relation; Age

1488; ---; Augusta Grey Bull; F; Daughter; 2

1489; As-says-days; Goes to the house; F; Widow; 47

1490; Paydutch-chay-sheedish; Yellow crow; M; Husband; 49
1491; Is-coe-chea-ate-chace; Knows her enemy; F; Wife; 50
1492; Ah-shoe-che-dish; Hunts the house; F; Mother; 74

1493; Duck-peace; Hugs; F; Widow; 61
1494; Echedock-ichay-ockindays; Rides a pretty horse; M; Son; 26

1495; Duck-bit-chay-boo-dish; Male bear; M; Husband; 27
1496; Uck-pah-deas; Works together; F; Wife; 27
1497; Ha-wan-da-bah-pash; Where he goes is medicine; F; Daughter; 12

1498; ---; George Suis; M; --; 23

1499; Ah-pit-bah-dock-cus; Crazy crane; M; Husband; 51
1500; Un-de-ditch-chis; Walks pretty; F; Wife; 49

1501; Ush-cup-cah-weas; Bad Dutchman; M; Husband; 31
1502; Boa-doo-pus; Two Fish; F; Wife; 31
1503; Ome-bah-push; Medicine paint; M; Son; 2

1504; Ah-duck-chea-ah-hoos; Plenty Coos; M; Husband; 51
1505; Tick-bah-dup-pace; Kills together; F; Wife; 36
1506; Kab-quah-ah-soos; Everybody knows him; M; Ad. Son; 9

1507; Bea-it-chice; Pretty rock; F; Widow; 53

1508; Eas-pea-os-seas; Lion that shows; M; Husband; 51
1509; Cuck-kis; Spotted; F; Wife; 35
1510; Bondonpahadanedacahcus; Bird in the cedars; M; Son; 16
1511; Ook-e-hosh; The other antelope; F; Daughter; 14
1512; Dutch-choa-dock-us; Muskrat daughter; F; Daughter; 6
1513; Dah-he-os; Surrounded; M; Son; 3

1514; Bee-tah-was; Bell rock; M; Husband; 58
1515; Kah-wish; Bushy; F; Wife; 53
1516; Dah-cock-bah-coos; Bird high up; M; Son; 18

1517; Ecupe-pah-dah-cock-cuss; Bird hat; M; Husband; 31
1518; Ischic-sayawondabachis; Sits in her nest; F; Wife; 31
1519; Bon-don-pah-bah-coos; Cedar high up; M; Son; 13
1520; Chee-dup-be-das-dace; Bull walks to water; M; Son; 6
1521; Bahahpah-dah-coos-days; Walks to growing things; F; Daughter; 4

Census of the __Crow__ Indians of __Crow__ Agency __Montana__ taken
By __J.E. Edwards__, United States Indian Agent __June 30, 1899__

Key: Number; Indian Name; English Name; Sex; Relation; Age

1522; Bah-put-tah-dock-cuss; Young otter; M; Widower; 61

1523; It-tutdoot-chice; Takes by herself; F; Divorcee; 51

1524; Bea-it-chise-sos; Not a pretty woman; F; Widow; 49

1525; Baduppayish-tuckeydoochic; Takes gun from one kills; M; Husband; 27
1526; Ben-cose; The woman; F; Wife; 21
1527; Akcan-bahoukshay-bapashon; Medon [Medicine] ties a knot on her head; F; Daughter; 5
1528; Ook-che-dup-pish; Bull antelope: M; Son; 4

1529; Utch-itch-ist-ton-tus; Notch; M; Husband; 37
1530; Bah-dup-pay-ate-chice; Known to kill; F; Wife; 34
1531; Eak-kay-his-shies; Red star; M; Son; 20[?]
1532; Dah-cock-hay-day-dus; Among the birds; M; Son; 9[?]
1533; Bish-doot-chice; Takes a blanket; F; Mother; 54

1534; Bah-put-tah-cheas; White otter; M; Husband; 58
1535; Oo-wat-tus; The iron; F; Wife; 55
1536; ---; Ben Gardiner; M; Son; 19

1537; Ish-bee-bah-pash; His rock is medicine; M; Husband; 34
1538; Bea-she-pit-tay; Black woman; F; Wife; 33

1539; Ah-cane-dah-pace; Kills across the water; F; Widow; 59

1540; Bish-cay-che-dup-pish; Bull dog; M; Husband; 40
1541; Bea-cah-weas; Bad woman; F; Wife; 43
1542; Boa-do-chis; Eats the fish; M; Son; 19

1543; Bah-duke-kea-it-chice; Good gun; M; Husband; 27
1544; Bah-son-day; Goes ahead; F; Wife; 17
1545; Uck-pah-dee-it-chise; Julia High Hawk; F; Sister; 23

1546; Kah-kay-de-chis; Strikes the lance; F; Widow; 55

1547; Duck-bit-chay-doc-puss; Two bears; M; Husband; 50
1548; Bim-boan-dee-dish; Walks in the water; F; Wife; 48

1549; Bah-coop-pash; Sick; M; Husband; 37
1550; Bachay-bachot-dah-cheas; Kills a strong man; F; Wife; 31
1551; It-tut-bah-cheas; Fights alone; M; Son; 9

1552; ---; ---; --; --; --; [Blank]

Census of the __Crow__ Indians of __Crow__ Agency __Montana__ taken
By __J.E. Edwards__, United States Indian Agent __June 30, 1899__

Key: Number; Indian Name; English Name; Sex; Relation; Age

1553; Bah-op-pish; Shot in the hand; M; Husband; 56
1554; E-cupe-pah-che-shis; Puts on a hat; F; Wife; 50

1555; Away-caway-daneduckchas; Bear in the mountains; M; Widower; 54

1556; Esop-pee-e-wishes; Hairy moccasin; M; Husband; 46
1557; Bah-wah-wat-tays; Quick; F; 39
1558; Eak-ka-dah-cock-cus; Birds eggs; M; Son; 9
1559; ---; Mary Hairy Moccasin; F; Daughter; F; Daughter; 2

1558; Ducbitshay-bedook-sahoos; Bears comes from below; M; Husband; 59
1559; Eche-da-keus-sos; Horse well known; F; Wife; 57
1560; Bah-dup-pace-sos; Don't kill; M; Son; 8
[Entry numbers 1558 and 1559 repeated.]

1561; Ah-cah-pish-sis; Comes up red; M; Husband; 37
1562; Bah-put-tah-cuck-kis; Spotted otter; F; Wife; 28

1563; Che-shea-it-chise; Pretty tail; M; Husband; 45
1564; Ba-dow-e-kosh; Looks at the beads; F; Wife; 49
1565; Bahshotse-basash; Rock that runs; M; Gr. Son; 11
1566; Echeete-lagak; Horse bird; M; Gr. Son; 11

1567; E-sah-dut-chew-chice; Strong legs; M; Husband; 47
1568; Ah-way-uck-pah-deas; The ground is her medicine; F; Wife; 45

1569; Is-coe-chee-che-dish; Hunts the enemy; M; Husband; 49
1570; Eatosh-dabish-de-chice; Strikes her child; F; Wife; 51

1571; Aditch-chebah-doch-ahoos; Paints herself plenty; M; Husband; 53
1572; Ah-pah-dee-it-chice; Pretty porcupine; F; Wife; 48

1573; Pah-chice; Push; M; Husband; 49
1574; Bah-chay-uck-pah-pice; Lies in bed with a man; F; Wife; 43
1575; Bah-shus-shays; Medicine dance; F; Daughter; 14

1576; Duck-bit-chay-dah-beas; Three bears; M; Husband; 39
1577; Dutch-ke; Twin woman; F; Wife; 35
1578; Basho-dedichay-asash; Medicine rock in front; F; Mother; 59

1579; Eas-shu-day; Yellow face; M; Husband; 41
1580; Bah-pee-sha-da-ah-hoos; Rides much behind; F; Wife; 34
1581; Bis-cah-she-pit-tus; Black dog; M; Son; 10

1582; Duck-bit-chay-it-chice; Pretty bear; M; Husband; 59
1583; Bah-cha-chice; Strong; F; Wife; 51

Census of the __Crow__ Indians of __Crow__ Agency __Montana__ taken By __J.E. Edwards__, United States Indian Agent __June 30, 1899__

Key: Number; Indian Name; English Name; Sex; Relation; Age

1584; Cush-some-bee-chice; Falls toward you; F; Widow; 79

1585; Cone-dah-chice; Stays there; M; Husband; 25
1586; Dutch-chee-Do-pah-bash; Medicine slides; F; Wife; 33

1587; Beda-ecupe-padootchice; Takes a hat; F; Widow; 61

1588; Ha-wash-tay-keas; Travels well known; M; Husband; 57
1589; Bah-it-cash; She sees it; F; Wife; 41
1590; Bak-kah-seas; Hoop that shows; M; Son; 18
1591; Ek-bah-dee-days; Medicine goes; F; Daughter; 12

1592; E-kush-sheas; Turns back; M; Husband; 41
1593; Uck-pah-dean-de-chis; Strikes plenty medicine; F; Wife; 38
1594; Uck-bah-dea-ush-eas; Medicine shows; F; Daughter; 10

1595; Chee-dup-keas-sos; Bull well known; M; Husband; 37
1596; Ush-ock-kay-duck-coo; Stays on top of the house; F; Wife; 31
1597; Bahc-ay-key-bah-pash; Medicine shell; F; Daughter; 11
1598; Echdoc-inday-dootchis; Takes one that rides horses; F; Daughter; 8
1599; Bah-e-p-cap-cay-itches; Pretty hawk; F; Daughter; 3

1600; Meshodelitse-wakpahs; Medicine shell; F; Widow; 57

1601; Dah-cock-beas; Bird woman; F; Widow; 47
1602; Bah-son-day-it-chice; Goes ahead pretty; F; Daughter; 17

1603; Chee-dup-chee-sus; Bulls tail; M; Husband; 24
1604; Ah-bush-it-chice; Pretty sweathouse; F; Wife; 20

1605; Chate-dah-beas; Three wolves; M; Husband; 63
1606; Ahway-taycoe-ahway-chis; Sits down far away; F; Wife; 59

1607; Ah-dup-pice; Bull robe; M; Husband; 27
1608; Cah-cay-itcheas; Pretty lance; F; Wife; 31

1609; Is-cah-ka-it-chice; Pretty land; F; Divorcee; 50
1610; Is-coe-chee-bachea-days; Goes to fight enemies; F; Widow; 81

1611; Be-shay-ah-hoos; Plenty buffalo; M; Husband; 31
1612; Duck-bit-chay-akos-seas; The bear turns around; F; Wife; 26
1613; Itchit-chay-ah-bash-pash; Medicine tobacco; F; Daughter; 10
1614; Bea-buckcoshea-dacockcuss; Bird in the spring; F; Daughter; 2

1615; Ea-kook-kish-shays; Red fox; M; Bachelor; 55

Census of the __Crow__ Indians of __Crow__ Agency __Montana__ taken By __J.E. Edwards__, United States Indian Agent __June 30, 1899__

Key: Number; Indian Name; English Name; Sex; Relation; Age

1616; Duckbitchay-esah-coshish; Big Bear; M; Husband; 58
1617 Beende-chice; Srikes the water; F; Wife; 57

1618; Baput-tah-way-chate-chice; Otter chief; M; Husband; 30
1619; Bah-she-chice; Pretty otter; F; Wife; 35

1620; Chate-ah-wah-shoes; Wolf house; M; Husband; 39
1621; Bea-cottus; Girl; F; Wife; 33

1622; Duckbitchay-he-dock-cuss; The bear now; M; Divorced; 43
1623; E-cush-sheas; Turns around; F; Daughter; 10

1624; Ah-pe-sah-sheedis; Yellow mule; M; Husband; 43
1625; Oot-tah-seas; Weasel that shows; F; Wife; 33
1626; Beditta-shisshay-cuckiss; Spotted butterfly; M; Son; 12

1627; Bah-duck-key-doot-chis; Takes a gun #3; M; Husband; 32
1628; Bickus; Mare; F; Wife; 27
1629; ---; Susie; F; Daughter; 13
1630; Boodook-ahcane-dechis; Strikes on top of the ice; F; Daughter; 6

1631; Ick-cup-pee-dee-dah-bis; Three foretops; M; Widower; 33
1632; Ben-huch-key; Long woman; F; Daughter; 5

1633; ---; William Steal Bear; M; Husband; 31
1634; ---; Esther Shell on the Neck; F; Wife; 26

1635; Beendosh-kaneah-wachice; Sits by the water; F; Widow; 69

1636; Up-pay-e-wah-e-coosh; Looks with his ears; M; Husband; 34
1637; Oat-chean-bah-dup-pace; Kills at night; F; Wife; 40
1638; Opa-cah-deas; Old medicine tobacco; F; Daughter; 11
1639; Is-tuk-key-de-ditch; Strikes her gun; F; Mother; 69

1640; E-chin-doot-chice; Takes a horse; M; Husband; 30
1641; Un-dut-che-do-che-dice; Hunts to slide; F; Wife; 22
1642; Bea-bah-pash; Medicine woman; M; Son; 8
1643; Ah-shoe-ah-peas; Horn on her neck; F; Daughter; 5

1644; Pope-put-tay-ea-cot-tus; Little owl; M; Husband; 30
1645; Osh-doo-chape-ditchis; Strikes the thief in camp; F; Wife; 26
1646; Cheach-kay-dock-cus; Young chicken; F; Daughter; 5
1647; ---; Laura Little Owl; F; Daughter; 1

1648; E-cupe-pis; Gets down; M; Husband; 36
1649; Dah-cock-doo-pus; Two birds; F; Wife; 31

Census of the __Crow__ Indians of __Crow__ Agency __Montana__ taken By __J.E. Edwards__, United States Indian Agent __June 30, 1899__

Key: Number; Indian Name; English Name; Sex; Relation; Age

1650; Cah-dah-hay-day-duse; Bird in the rain; M; Son; 7
1651; Bah-dah-cah-deas; Old money; F; Daughter; 3
1652; Duck-bit-chay-cah-dice; Old bear woman; F; Mother; 64

1653; Ische-shay-ea-cot-tus; Little nest; M; Husband; 33
1654; ---; Mary Laforge; F; Wife; 26
1655; ---; Mary Little Nest; F; Daughter; 8

1656; Is-coe-chee-doe-cosh-ish; Holds the enemy; M; Husband; 31
1657; Bah-put-tah-seas; Shows the otter; F; Wife; 28
1658; Is-cah-kay-keas-sos; Plain spear; M; Son; 5

1659; ---; George Thomas; M; Bachelor; 32

1660; ---; Henry Russell; M; Husband; 30
1661; Bah-chea-cheas; Steals on camp; F; Wife; 27
1662; ---; Geo. W. Russell; M; Son; 2

1663; Ah-shoop-padate-cahdeas; Old horn; M; Husband; 35
1664; ---; Lucy Old Horn; F; Wife; 25
1665; ---; Fred Old Horn; M; Son; 9
1666; ---; Susie Old Horn; F; Daughter; 6

1667; Ay-day-cah-weas; Bad belly; M; Bachelor; 42

1668; Ah-day-chea-tus; White arm; M; Husband; 38
1669; Bah-cah-key-it-chice; Pretty shell; F; Wife; 34
1670; Bea-ditches; Strikes women; F; Mother; 73

1671; Bos-che-day-cah-deas; Old white man; M; Husband; 29
1672; Is-bah-hum-be-shis; Have things; F; Wife; 17

1673; Bouta-bah-coos-shecosh; Coyote looks up; M; --; [Widower]; 72
1674; Doop-tush-ditches; Strikes Both ways; F; --; [Mother]; 90

1675; Uck-sah-o-cos; Looks at her mother; F; Widow; 63
1676; Be-du-tooh-eas; Little moon; F; Gr. Dau.; 4

1677; Itche-bah-duck-shis; Plays with himself; M; Husband; 27
1678; Ah-dock-in-day-keas-sos; Horse she rides well known; F; Wife; 38
1679; ---; Charlie Plays with Himself; M; Son; 4

1680; Ah-way-chase; Knows the ground; M; Husband; 34
1681; ---; Perces knows the Ground; F; Wife; 30

1682; E-shue-ea-bah-pash; Medicine mane; M; Husband; 32

Census of the __Crow__ Indians of __Crow__ Agency __Montana__ taken
By __J.E. Edwards__, United States Indian Agent __June 30, 1899__

Key: Number; Indian Name; English Name; Sex; Relation; Age

1683; Dacock-etuck-posdatus; Bird without a cloud; F; Wife; 29
1684; Ushdosh-caneba-dup-pace; Kills beside camp; F; Daughter; 8

1685; Is-bah-dah-hoos; Got plenty beads; F; Widow; 43
1686; Bah-pah-dish; Flower; M; Son; 13
1687; Eapcha-bapah-dootchie; Takes the medicine pipe; F; Daughter; 6

1688; Bah-duk-keas; The gun; M; Husband; 28
1689; Be-dup-cah-deas; Old beaver; F; Wife; 31
1690; ---; John P. Gun; M; Son; 1

1691; ---; Charles Wort Davis; M; Bachelor; 29

1692; Bah-key-de-hosh; The other blackbird; M; Husband; 30
1693; Bah-put-tah-seas; Otter that shows; F; Wife; 24
1694; Dup-pah-ecoos-seas; Turns around twice; M; Son; 9
1695; Bah-dea-ate-chice; Knows what to do; F; Daughter; 6

1696; Up-pock-cane-ditches; Strikes back of head; F; --; [Widow]; 51

1697; Duckbitchy-cah-weas; Bad bear; M; Husband; 31
1698; Ea-che-keep-pay; Crooked face; F; Wife; 23

1699; Isooeche-hayday-codays; Goes among the enemy; M; Husband; 32
1700; Es-tup-peas; Shuts her eyes; F; Wife; 29
1701; Dee-cock-e-sos; Big bird; M; Son; 9
1702; Dum-bah-pash; Eats the wood; M; Son; 5

1703; ---; George Hill; M; Husband; 33
1704; ---; Mrs. George Hill; F; Wife; 23
1705; ---; Anna Hill; F; Daughter; 6
1706; ---; Mary Hill; F; Daughter; 4

1707; Cheedup-sho-chok-a-dus; Bull over the hill; M; Husband; 26
1708; Apah-suttah-doot-chice; Takes a split ear; F; Wife; 24
1709; Dock-co-bah-pash; Medicine turtle; F; Daughter; 6
1710; ---; Kate B. Hill; F; Daughter; 1

1711; Bea-dea-dush; The door; M; Husband; 28
1712; ---; Victoria Door; F; Wife; 19
1713; ---; Dora Door; F; Daughter; 3

1714; Oo-wa-shee-dish; Yellow in the mouth; M; Husband; 21
1715; Bout-tah-eas; Little coyote; F; Wife; 21
1716; Dack-cock-shee-dish; Yellow bird; F; Daughter; 5
0000; ---; Augusta Brass; F; Daughter; 1 [No number or in prev. Census.]

Census of the __Crow__ Indians of __Crow__ Agency __Montana__ taken
By __J.E. Edwards__, United States Indian Agent __June 30, 1899__

Key: Number; Indian Name; English Name; Sex; Relation; Age

1717; Bah-cha-cheas; Steals on the camp; M; Husband; 31
1718; Is-bah-cah-kea-shoos; Plenty shells; F; Wife; 21
1719; ---; [Echean-chea-itchis]; Pretty horse tail; F; Daughter; 1

1720; ---; Laura Green; F; --; 24

1721; Mah-soe; Mint; M; Widower; 47

1722; Bashcheedday-shepit-tay; Light colored man; M; Husband; 27
1723; Bah-cay-ca-kah-dah-bish; Hoop that moves; F; Wife; 24
1724; Ope-cah-dish; Old Tobacco; F; Daughter; 4
1725; ---; Florence Coo Chief; F; Daughter; 3

1726; Bash-keas-sos; Plain feather; M; Husband; 27
1727; Un-dah-coe-bah-coos; Lives high; F; Wife; 23
1728; ---; Josie Plain Feather; F; Daughter; 1

1729; Cheeup-e-ches-ditch; Bull horse; M; Husband; 30
1730; Shee-deak-days; Rattles going; F; Wife; 23

1731; ---; Mrs. Joe Pickett; F; Mother; 36
1732; ---; Richard A. Pickett; M; Son; 17
1733; ---; Robert A. Pickett; M; Son; 12
1734; ---; Joseph J. Pickett; M; Son; 9
1735; ---; William C. Pickett; M; Son; 6
1736; ---; Margaret Pickett; F; Daughter; 5
1737; ---; Thomas Pickett; M; Son; 1

1738; ---; Joseph Stewart; M; Husband; 29
1739; Cah-coa-ays; Everything is her; F; Wife; 26
1740; ---; Francis Stewart; M; Son; 6
1741; ---; Fannie Stewart; F; Daughter; 4

1742; ---; Jackson Stewart; M; --; 22
1743; ---; William Stewart; M; --; 20

1744; ---; M Two Belly; M; Husband; 39
1745; ---; Mrs. M. Two Belly; F; Wife; 37

1746; ---; John Wesley; M; Husband; 38
1747; ---; Jane Wesley; F; Wife; 33
1748; ---; Annie Wesley; F; Daughter; 17
1749; ---; Jennie Wesley; F; Daughter; 12
1750; ---; Fannie Wesley; F; Daughter; 6

1751; ---; Mrs. James Robinson; F; Mother; 39

Census of the __Crow__ Indians of __Crow__ Agency __Montana__ taken
By __J.E. Edwards__, United States Indian Agent __June 30, 1899__

Key: Number; Indian Name; English Name; Sex; Relation; Age

1752; ---; James Robinson; M; Son; 6
1753; ---; Charles Robinson; M; Son; 12
1754; ---; Ellen Robinson; F; Daughter; 7
1755; ---; Allen Robinson; M; Son; 4
1756; ---; Alice Robinson; F; Daughter; 2

1757; ---; Mrs. G.F. Deputee; F; Mother; 32
1758; ---; Jennie Deputee; F; Daughter; 6
1759; ---; Flora Deputee; F; Daughter; 3

1760; ---; Mrs. Frank Gordon; F; Mother; 44
1761; ---; William Leighton; M; Son; 26

1762; ---; Mrs. B. Bravo; F; --; 36

1763; Hoo-chice; Wind; M; Husband; 35
1764; ---; Mrs. Thomas Laforge; F; Wife; 51
1765; ---; Rosa Laforge; F; Daughter; 17
1766; ---; Thomas Asa Laforge; M; Son; 15

1767; ---; John Alden; M; Husband; 31
1768; ---; Phoebe Alden; F; Wife; 20
1769; ---; Richard Alden; M; Son; 1

1770; ---; Mrs. J.B. Cooper; F; Mother; 59
1771; ---; Peter Cooper; M; Son; 19
1772; ---; Cynthia Cooper; F; Daughter; 14
1773; ---; Lula Cooper; F; Daughter; 21
1774; ---; Sylvester Hardy; M; Gr. Son; 3

1775; ---; Martha Cooper Shenderline; F; Mother; 24
1776; ---; Joseph Shenderline; M; Son; 6
1777; ---; Edward Shenderline; M; Son; 4
1778; ---; Henry Shenderline; M; Son; 2

1779; ---; Mrs. Henry Keiser; F; Mother; 39
1780; ---; Frank Keiser; M; Son; 19
1781; ---; Myrtle Keiser; F; Daughter; 5

1782; ---; Mrs. Maggie Keiser Macer; F; Mother; 21
1783; ---; Mabel Macer; F; Daughter; 4
1784; ---; Henry; M; Son; 2

1785; ---; Mrs. David Yarlott; F; Mother; 51
1786; ---; Charles Yarlott; M; Son; 21
1787; ---; Frank Yarlott; M; Son; 17

Census of the __Crow__ Indians of __Crow__ Agency __Montana__ taken
By __J.E. Edwards__, United States Indian Agent __June 30, 1899__

Key: Number; Indian Name; English Name; Sex; Relation; Age

1788; ---; Katie Yarlott; F; Daughter; 11

1789; ---; Mrs. John L. Smith; F; Mother; 53
1790; ---; Rosebud Farwell; M; Son; 17
1791; ---; Susand[sic] Farwell Glenn; F; Mother; 23
1792; ---; Percival Glenn; M; Son; 1

1793; ---; Mrs. Al. Morrison; F; Mother; 51
1794; ---; Hannah Morrison; F; Daughter; 18
1795; ---; Alvin Morrison; M; Son; 16

1796; E-say-dup-pah-choas; Points the gun in his face; M; Husband; 33
1797; ---; Mrs. Thomas Stewart; F; Wife; 40
1798; ---; Lucy Stewart; F; Daughter; 14
1799; Ah-wah-caneca-dooshis; Runs over the ground; M; Son; 6

1800; ---; Mrs. R.W. Cummins; F; --; 49

1801; ---; Mrs. Thomas Kent; F; Mother; 48
1802; ---; Josephine Kent; F; Daughter; 19
1803; ---; Elizabeth Kent; F; Daughter; 17
1804; ---; Maggie Kent; F; Daughter; 12

1805; ---; Mary Kent Stevens; F; Mother; 21
1806; ---; Mary Stevens; F; Daughter; 4
1807; ---; Kent Stevens; M; Son; 3
1808; ---; Agnes Stevens; F; Daughter; 2

1809; ---; Mrs. Ella Kent Cashen; F; Mother; 23
1810; ---; Willie Cashen; M; Son; 5
1811; ---; Alice; F; Daughter; 4
1812; ---; Ella Cashen; F; Daughter; 2

1813; ---; Maggie Garrigus; F; Mother; 28
1814; ---; Mary F. Garrigus; F; Daughter; 7
1815; ---; Margaret E. Garrigus; F; Daughter; 6
1816; ---; Arthur R. Garrigus; M; Son; 4
1817; ---; Dorothy B. Garrigus; F; Daughter; 2

1818; ---; Abbie Lande; F; Mother; 25
1819; ---; Thomas A Lande; M; Son; 4
1820; ---; Henry Dewey Lande; M; Son; 1

1821; ---; Frederick Geisdorff; M; Father; 28
1822; ---; Florence Geisdorff; F; Daughter; 4
1823; ---; Francis Geisdorff; M; Son; 3

Census of the __Crow__ Indians of __Crow__ Agency __Montana__ taken By __J.E. Edwards__, United States Indian Agent __June 30, 1899__

Key: Number; Indian Name; English Name; Sex; Relation; Age

1824; ---; Frederick Geisdorff Jr.; M; Son; 2

1825; ---; Louisa Geisdorff; F; [Sister]; 24
1826; ---; Charlotte Geisdorff; F; [Sister]; 21

1827; ---; Mrs. George R. Davis; F; Mother; 50
1828; ---; Margaretta A. Davis; F; Daughter; 20
1829; ---; Effie N. Davis; F; Daughter; 14
1830; ---; Blaine R. Davis; Son; 5

1831; ---; Minnie Reed; F; Orphan; 24
1832; ---; Francis Reed; M; Brother; 21
1833; ---; Della Redd; F; Sister; 15
1834; ---; Nellie Reed; F; Sister; 13
1835; ---; Edith Reed; F; Sister; 11
1836; ---; Katie Reed; F; Sister; 9

1837; ---; Mary K. Reed; F; Orphan; 15

1838; ---; Mrs. Wm. H. White; F; Mother; 37
1839; ---; Wm. H. White; M; Son; 19
1840; ---; Mary E. White; F; Daughter; 17
1841; ---; Minnie E. White; F; Daughter; 14
1842; ---; Charles F. White; M; Son; 1

1843; ---; Mrs. Thomas Shane; F; Mother; 40
1844; ---; Kittie Shane; F; Daughter; 21
1845; ---; Patrick C. Shane; M; Son; 14
1846; ---; Frank Shane; M; Son; 11
1847; ---; Josie Shane; F; Daughter; 9
1848; ---; Bessie Shane; F; Daughter; 7
1849; ---; Thomas Shane; M; Son; 5
1850; ---; Edward Shane; M; Son; 3

1851; ---; Cora Williams; F; Orphan; 20
1852; ---; Mattie Williams; F; Sister; 18

1853; ---; Mrs. Mary Heckenlively; F; Mother; 23
1854; ---; Guy L. Heckenlively; M; Son; 2

1855; ---; Mrs. Thomas Doyle; F; Mother; 22
1856; ---; Robert Doyle; M; Son; 2
1857; ---; Frances Doyle; F; Daughter; 1

1858; ---; Ellen Jackson; F; Mother; 47
1859; ---; John Jackson; M; Son; 18

Census of the __Crow__ Indians of __Crow__ Agency __Montana__ taken
By __J.E. Edwards__, United States Indian Agent __June 30, 1899__

Key: Number; Indian Name; English Name; Sex; Relation; Age

1860; ---; Eliza Jackson; F; Daughter; 13
1861; ---; Julia Jackson; F; Daughter; 10

1862; ---; John Frost; M; Husband; 26
1863; Is-bon-dot-bah-pash; Medicine shield; F; Wife; 19
1864; ---; Daniel L. Frost; M; Son; 2

1865; ---; Joseph Cooper; F; Husband; 27
1866; ---; Susie Cooper; F; Wife; 28
1867; ---; Theodore Cooper; M; Son; 7 [Female in 1898 and 1900.]
1868; ---; Laura Cooper; F; Daughter; 6
1869; ---; Sylvania Cooper; F; Daughter; 5
1870; ---; James Cooper; M; Son; 3
1871; ---; Joseph Cooper Jr.; M; Son; 1

1872; ---; Levantia W. Pearson; F; Mother; 36
1873; ---; Virginia Pearson; F; Daughter; 7
1874; ---; Helen Estella Pearson; F; Daughter; 6
1875; ---; Ethel May Pearson; F; Daughter; 4

1876; ---; George Pease; M; Husband; 33
1877; ---; Sarah Pease; F; Wife; 32
1878; ---; David Pease; M; Son; 8
1879; ---; James Pease; M; Son; 9
1880; ---; Benjamin Pease; M; Son; 6
1881; ---; Emory; M; Son; 5
1882; ---; Anson H. Pease; M; Son; 3
1883; ---; George Pease; M; Son; 2

1884; ---; Mrs. Marshall; F; --; 42

1885; ---; Mary Townsend; F; Mother; 25
1886; ---; Mabel M. Townsend; F; Mother[sic]; 4
1887; ---; Fred A. Townsend; M; Son; 2

1888; ---; Mrs. Amy Scott; F; Mother; 21
1889; ---; George Scott; M; Son; 3
1890; ---; Elmer Scott; M; Son; 2

1891; Chate-dah-beas; Three Wolves; M; [Widower]; 47

1892; Is-bah-key-cush-sheas; Hoop turns around; M; Widower; 24
1893; ---; August Hoop Turns Around; M; Son; 2

1894; Cheedup-kah-deas; Old Bull; M; Husband; 25
1895; Bah-cah-key-day-cus; Shell child; F; Wife; 20

Census of the __Crow__ Indians of __Crow__ Agency __Montana__ taken By __J.E. Edwards__, United States Indian Agent __June 30, 1899__

Key: Number; Indian Name; English Name; Sex; Relation; Age

1896; Bach-pash; Medicine; F; Daughter; 2

1897; Ahway-tayday-cock-cuss; Bird far away; M; --; 23

1898; Ah-shue-cah-bay; Bush head; M; Husband; 24
1899; Boa-pis; Snow; F; Wife; 31

1900; E-dea-hish; Breathes; M; Husband; 35
1901; Ah-woos-cah-deas; Old sweathouse; F; Wife; 34

1902; ---; Martin Round Face; M; Husband; 26
1903; ---; Katie Dreamer; F; Wife; 23

1904; Tuch-chay-dah-cock-cuss; Straight Bird; M; Widower; 23
1905; Bah-it-chay-doot-chis; Takes pretty things; F; Daughter; 5

1906; Cheas-dakaock-inda-dichis; Strikes riding grey horse; F; Divorcee; 17
1907; ---; Frances Ten Bear; M; Son; 2

1908; Bea-sos-ecos; Looks back; M; Husband; 23
1909; Bah-o-dop-keas-sos; Finds plain; F; Wife; 22

1910; Bah-put-the-beas; Otter woman; F; Widow; 19
1911; ---; Glenn Bird; M; Son; 3

1912; Choos-say-dah-quas; Sends part home; M; Husband; 30
1913; Oo-shay-it-chise; Pretty hole; F; Wife; 20
1914; ---; Mary Part Home; F; Daughter; 1

1915; Incuppah-bish-chedice; Strikes the hat; F; Mother; 40
1916; Ba-be-dish-e-sos; Broils big; M; Son; 10

1917; ---; Samuel S. Davis; M; Widower; 24

1918; ---; Frances E.C. Thompson; F; --; 22

1919; Osus; Can't shoot him; M; Husband; 18
1920; Ahsha-hedere-malapes; Kills in camp; F; Wife; 24

1921; Dah-cock-ah-seas; Bird that shows; F; Widow; 51

1922; Bachay-eat-che-bish-ay; Man with a beard; M; Divorced; 23

1923; Ecupe-pah-de-chice; Strikes the hat; F; Widow; 51

1924; Be-de-ha-dup-pace; Crosses the water; F; Widow; 59

Census of the __Crow__ Indians of __Crow__ Agency __Montana__ taken
By __J.E. Edwards__, United States Indian Agent __June 30, 1899__

Key: Number; Indian Name; English Name; Sex; Relation; Age

1925; Ba-chay-ha-wat-de-chice; Strikes one man; F; Widow; 54

1926; Cha-cush; Five; F; Widow; 75

1927; Bah-chea-ish-it-chise; Loves to fight; M; --; 24

1928; Bah-son-day-it-chice; Goes ahead pretty; M; Husband; 24
1929; Bah-put-tah-beas; Otter woman; F; Wife; 34
1930; ---; George Goes ahead Pretty; M; Son; 2

1931; ---; James Laforge; M; Husband; 22
1932; ---; Sage woman; F; Wife; 19
1933; ---; William Laforge; M; Son; 4
1934; ---; Francis Laforge; M; Son; 2

1935; ---; Mary M. Humphrey; F; Mother; 22
1936; ---; Maud Humphrey; F; Daughter; 3

1937; Ah-hoo-ha-e-cush-seas; Turns back plenty; M; Husband; 24
1938; Be-shay-dana-awachice; Sits among to rocks; F; Wife; 20
1939; ---; High Nest; M; Son; 1

1940; Awayca-dane-cheeup-ish; Mountain bull; M; Divorced; 23

1941; Boa-e-hock-sos; Sings the last song; M; Husband; 34
1942; Oo-tah-dea-dish; Weasel that walks; F; Wife; 24

1943; Con-up-e-say; Big nose old woman; F; Widow; 82

1944; Isuc-cheydah-sheedish; Yellow hawk; M; Widower; 42

1945; Ecupe-pay-bee-dish; Fire hat; M; Widower; 42

1946; Ah-quas; Covered up; M; Husband; 27
1947; Bah-pah-dit-chis; Plenty things growing; F; Wife; 22
1948; Akey-bee-deep-pah-cuss; Persons; F; Daughter; 5

1949; Ah-shay-day-duss; In the camp; F; Widow; 72

1950; Bah-dah-kut-teas; Crazy; M; Widower; 29

1951; Oat-chees-du-dish; Ralph Saco; M; Husband; 22
1952; Bee-dup-dah-cuss; Young Beaver; F; Wife; 23

1953; Echete-ichis; Pretty horse; M; Husband; 34
1954; ---; Monica Horn; F; Wife; 19

Census of the __Crow__ Indians of __Crow__ Agency __Montana__ taken By __J.E. Edwards__, United States Indian Agent __June 30, 1899__

Key: Number; Indian Name; English Name; Sex; Relation; Age

1955; ---; Charles M; Phelps; M; Father; 27
1956; ---; Frank Phelps; M; Son; 5
1957; ---; Fred Phelps; M; Son; 4
1958; ---; Emma Phelps; F; Daughter; 2

CENSUS

RECAPITULATION.

Males…………………………943

Females…………………..........1040……1958

Males above 18………………633

Females above 14……………750

Males between 6 and 16……….150

Females between 6 and 16…...163

Males between 16 and 18………..23

Males under 6………………...111

Females under 6……………...127

BIRTHS

Males…………………………..21
Females………………………..27……...48

DEATHS

Males…………………………..44
Females………………………..38……...82

Decrease in Population…………………34.

127

Crow Agency Montana, 1900 Census

J. E. Edwards, Indian Agent

37396

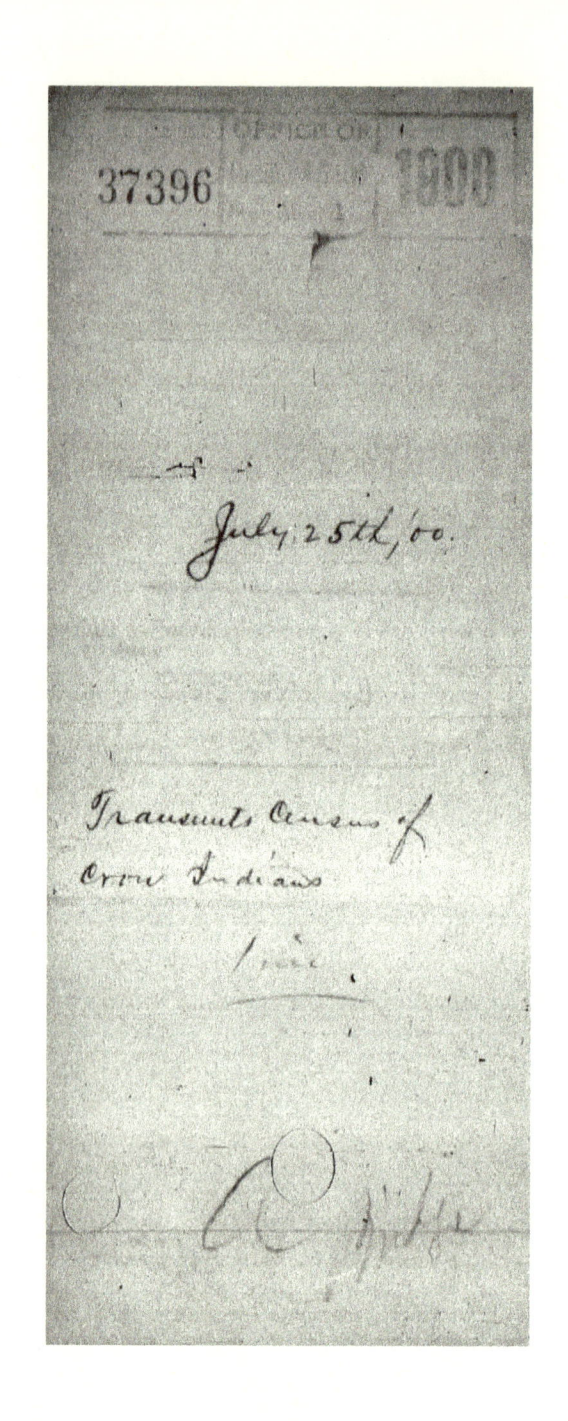

July 25th, '00.

Transmits Census of
Crow Indians
1900

Department of the Interior,
U. S. INDIAN SERVICE.

July 25th, 1900

Hon Commissioner
——— of Indian Affairs.
Washington DC

Sir

Enclosed herewith please find Census of Coos Indians as per instructions contained in circular "A" of July 11th 1900

Very respfly
P. E. Edwards
for U S Ind agt

131

RECAPITULATION.

Males 18 years old and above...................645
Males over 16 and under 18....................15
Females 14 years and above....................735
Childred 6 to 16..............................367
Children under 6..............................212
                                             1974
Less Females 14 to 16 listed twice............33
                        Total.................1941

Census of the __Crow__ Indians of __Crow__ Agency __Montana__ taken By __J.E. Edwards__, United States Indian Agent __June 30, 1900__

Key: Number; Indian Name; English Name; Sex; Relation; Age

1; Ahnehe-ichis; Walks Pretty; F Widow; 41
2; Lagak-esash; Big Bird; M; Son; 10
3; Lagak-hishes; Howard Red Bird; M; Son; 21

4; Budesesh; No Horse; M; Husband; 34
5; Oo-inkpus; Hugs the Weasel; F; Wife; 37
6; ---; Gretchen No Horse; F; Daughter; 2

7; Ook-cas; Little Antelope; F; Widow; 74

8; Nas-kowees; Bad Heart; M; Husband; 27
9; Lagaka-hishes; Red Breasted Bird; F; Wife; 24
10; Lagak-mee-da-ses; Rain Bird; F; Daughter; 6
11; Bah-wah-sonedah-itchis; Good Leader; F; Daughter; 4

12; Awak-in-lagaks; Bird All Over the Ground; M; Husband; 54
13; Mida-itches; Goes Well; F; Wife; 50
14; Lagak-itches; Good Bird; F; Daughter; 8

15; Ahshua-wahnaks; Crazy Head; M; Husband; 64
16; Esha-shates; Paints Pretty; F; Wife; 53
17; Esaksha-chaschedees; Hunts the Arrow; M; Son; 22

18; Mea-daka; White Woman; M; Husband; 41
19; Oomah-sees; Sees in the Mouth; F; Wife; 34

20; Ahluk-chea-akuse; He Knows His Coos; M; Husband; 40
21; Besha-chea-makpash; Medicine White Buffalo; F; Wife; 37

22; Eascha-naks; Young Jack Rabbit; M; Husband; 53
23; Ahpit-cheis; White Crane; F; Wife; 44
24; Ahwak-amach; Sits Toward the Mountain; M; Son; 17

25; Awaksha-echete; Gros Ventre Horse; M; Husband; 58
26; Chis-sheis; Nest; F; Wife; 48
27; Ahakarooche-amach; Horse sits down; F; Daughter; 17

28; Ahpit-nake; Young Crane; F; Widow; 60
29; Eukase-hishes; Red Snake; F; Daughter; 12

30; ---; Andrew Wallace; M; Husband; 27
31; ---; Jennie Wallace; F; Wife; 22
32; ---; Josie Wallace; F; Daughter; 6

33; Chatis; The Wolf; M; Husband; 56
34; Checks-doochis; Takes Five; F; Wife; 56

Census of the __Crow__ Indians of __Crow__ Agency __Montana__ taken By __J.E. Edwards__, United States Indian Agent __June 30, 1900__

Key: Number; Indian Name; English Name; Sex; Relation; Age

35; E-step-ees; Eli Blackhawk; M; Batchelor[sic]; 26

36; Eche-kuis; Sweet Mouth; M; Husband; 41
37; Andiche-poois; Sore Where Whipped; F; Wife; 45
38; Lagak-beepish; Snowbird; M; [Ad.] son; 10

39; Wtekut-napes; Kills Close; F; Widow; 77
40; Mishodechitse-lagak; Medicine Rock Bird; M; Ad Son; 10

41; Esa-keepa; Wrinkle Face; M; Husband; 44
42; Eskochea-ichis; Fights the Enemy Good; F; Wife; 47
43; Ahwotkot-dichis; Strikes Same One; F; Daughter; 5

44; Eskuka-ahshees; Shows a Lance; M; Husband; 50
45; Mi-iche-doochis; Takes Pretty Things; F; Wife; 62

46; Ahma-apische; Arm Around the Neck; M; Husband; 59
47; Hederin-dichis; Strikes in a Crowd; F; Wife; 59

48; Menarahwetket; One Goose; M; Husband; 58
49; Min-makpash; Medicine Water; F; Wife; 46
50; Lagk-heahsas; Bird Well Known; M; Son; 17
51; Ashkarooches-kahdeas; Old Horn; F; Daughter; 10
52; Mean-dichis; Strikes Plenty Women; F; Mother; 74

53; Ees-kapa; Flat Face; F; Widow; 37

54; Ekupa-cheis; Packs the Hat; M; Husband; 42
55; Ahpake-hedere-lagaks; Bird in a Cloud; F; Wife; 34
56; Eesackas-ahoos; Plenty Arrows; M; Son; 9

57; Miastacheda-karoos; White Man Runs Him; M; Husband; 43
58; Popet-itsechats; Good Owl; F; Wife; 38
59; Micha-ahcheis-botsots; Steals on Camp Strong; M; Son; 7

60; Meneas-koop-skuis; Sioux; M; batchelor[sic]; 49

61; Duchkis; Left Hand; M; Husband; 26
62; Cheis-makpash; Medicine Tail; F; Wife; 29
63; Nakas-makpash; Child is Medicine; F; Daughter; 10
64; Nahkose-cheedup; Bull Turtle; M; Son; 5
65; ---; Peter L. Hand; M; Son; 2

66; Peritise-kahdeas; Old Crow; M; Husband; 63
67; Ahoo-aroopis; Finds All; F; Wife; 40
68; Mintahsehederimitpal; Persons in the Moon; F; Daughter; 7

Census of the __Crow__ Indians of __Crow__ Agency __Montana__ taken
By __J.E. Edwards__, United States Indian Agent __June 30, 1900__

Key: Number; Indian Name; English Name; Sex; Relation; Age

69; Istuka-sa-here-dadush; Stands Among the Shooters; M; Son; 6
70; Botseah-botsats; Strong Fighter; M; Son; 1

71; Cheda-kos; Holds Up; M; Widower; 42
72; Beah-kahdeas; Rock Old; M; Son; 5

73; Eskay-ahwotkot; One Star; M; Husband; 34
74; Miastacheda-meas; White Woman; F; Wife; 49
75; ---; George Washington; M; Son; 17
76; Ekpetatska; Good Sheep; F; Daughter; 5

77; Miah-hoo-ted-deas; Does Lot of Things; F; Widow; 49

78; Dutsuah-noopis; Two Muskrats; F; Widow; 72

79; Istuka-asees; Gun Shows; M; Husband; 33
80; Dakpitses-ahsees; Looks at the Bear; F; Wife; 28
81; Ba-orap-saskatch; Finds Soon; M; Son; 5

82; Bee-dup-pay-tus; Like a Beaver; F; Widow; 58

83; Ahmatka; Long way off; F; Widow; 58

84; Misakohn-miches; Grandmother's Knife; M; Husband; 44
85; Chisah-kahdeas; Old Nest; F; Wife; 35
86; ---; Sarah G. Knife; [F]; [Daughter]; [1?]

87; Duchuis; Muskrat; F; Widow; 56
88; Mi-iche-ose; Brings Good Things; F; Widow; 39
89; Etash-hishes; Red Shirt; F; Daughter; 6

90; Oet-budekesh-hele-nakuse; George White Bear; M; Batchelor[sic]; 26

91; Eer-kahwash; Bird Tail That Rattles; M; Husband; 53
92; Kahdeas; Old; F; Wife; 53

93; Dakpitska-cheis; White Bear #1; M; Widower; 82

94; Mahpak-hoos; Comes in a Day; M; Husband; 50
95; Mahkaristish; Yearling; F; Wife; 36
96; ---; Celia Comes in a Day; F; Daughter; 1

97; Besha-cheedups; Buffalo Bull; M; Husband; 40
98; Meakot-kowees; Bad Woman; F; Wife; 38
99; Mea-ichis; Pretty Rock; F; Daughter; 10
100; Muna-shuis; Blue Wood; M; Son; 15

Census of the __Crow__ Indians of __Crow__ Agency __Montana__ taken
By __J.E. Edwards__, United States Indian Agent __June 30, 1900__

Key: Number; Indian Name; English Name; Sex; Relation; Age

101; Chatis; Wolf; M; Husband; 49
102; Midesha-doochis; Gets Hold of the Dead; F; Wife; 44
103; Eskoche-okepis; Shoot the Enemy; M; Son; 20
104; Dotsuah-doochis; Takes a Sinew; F; Mother; 88

105; Dakpitska-cheis; White Bear #2; M; Husband; 49
106; Minna-nahkuse; By the Side of the Water; F; Wife; 58
107; Besha-ekash; Russel W. Bear; M; Son; 24

108; Botsa-kowees; Bad Man; M; Husband; 47
109; Bahkeed-lagaks; Blackbird; F; Wife; 43

110; Ahpa-duttotoes; Cut Ear; M; Husband; 48
111; Ekupa-esash; Big Hat; F; Wife; 52

112; Duckbea-cheacock-indas; Rides White Hipped Horse; M; Husband; 23
113; Mi-ich-napes; Kills Pretty Ones; F; Wife; 21
114; ---; Harold Rides White Horse; M; Son; 3

115; Muche-deis; Good Luck; M; Husband; 42
116; Chate-heahsas; Wolf Well Known; F; Wife; 40
117; ---; Matthew G. Luck; M; Son; 1

118; Lagak-heshsas; Bird Well Known; M; Husband; 31
119; Wahpootkamakpash; Medicine Otter; F; Wife; 32

120; Echeta-kowees; Bad Horse; M; Husband; 28
121; Bachos-itchis; Pretty Bullrush; F; Wife; 24
122; ---; Jennie B. Horse; F; Daughter; 1

123; Bahkeede-itchis; Pretty Blackbird; F; Widow; 64

124; Esukis; Corner of the Mouth; M; Husband; 50
125; Iamina-wisha-doochis; Takes Pretty Scalp; F; Wife; 51
126; Echeta-gash-eduse; Elk Stands Up; M; Son; 14

127; Ahse-desh; Shows as He Goes; M; Husband; 44
128; Mi-iche-kooshdase; Goes to Good Things; F; Wife; 47
129; Istuka-heahsas; Well Known Arrow; M; Son; 10

130; Opes; Ben Spotted Horse; M; Husband; 28
131; Budeesh; Horse; F; Wife; 31
132; Bechon-herepsis; Kills One With Red Blankt[sic]; F; Daughter; 13

133; Oeta-echeta; Iron Horse; M; Husband; 26
134; Ahwoosh-akuse; Knows the Sweat House; F; Wife; 21

Census of the __Crow__ Indians of __Crow__ Agency __Montana__ taken
By __J.E. Edwards__, United States Indian Agent __June 30, 1900__

Key: Number; Indian Name; English Name; Sex; Relation; Age

135; Mean-ditches; Strikes the Woman; F; Daughter; 5

136; Chate-kupis; Wolf Lays Down; M; Husband; 61
137; Isheda; Kills at the Door; F; Wife; 54
138; Ekuh-push; Gets Down Often; M; Son; 21

139; Is-shu-shudish; Backbone; M; Widower; 31
140; Mahaha-hotskish; Long Feather; M; Son; 7

141; Mahsha-wots; One Feather; M; Husband; 58
142; Ahta-malapes; Kills First; F; Wife; 66

143; Eche-dudees; Don't Mix; M; Husband; 28
144; Misdershase; Groans; F; Wife; 34

145; Boa-at-tah-itchis; Pretty Coyote; M; Husband; 25
146; Beedah-dosh-kain-dichis; Strikes By Side of Water; F; Wife; 34

147; Educhesa-heas; Plain Left Hand; M; Husband; 63
148; Echik-dichis; Strikes First; F; Wife; 53
149; Wutta-makpash; Medicine Coyote; F; Daughter; 17

150; Lukpa-sashis; Bright Wings; M; Husband; 33
151; Mahahchis-lukish-dish; Goes to Look at Prisoners; F; Wife; 23
152; Echete-mulakis; Sings on Horse; M; Son; 7
153; Echete-maks-kochetish; Horse Stays all the Time; F; Daughter; 4

154; Ahpewesha; Gros Ventre; M; Husband; 38
155; Ahwa-akuse; Knows the Ground; F; Wife; 36
156; Bea-napes; Kills the Woman; F; Daughter; 1
157; Eskoche-karooshes; Runs the Enemy; M; Son; 7

158; Budeesh; Horse; M; Father; 43
159; Dakpitsa-ah-reandadish; Bear on the Trail; F; Daughter; 3
160; ---; Charlie Horse; M; Son; 1

161; Isba-itchis; Pretty Louse; F; Mother; 54
162; Eisda-karooshes; Loves to Run; M; Son; 19

163; Barucka-acha-nadees; Walks Over Ice; M; Husband; 22
164; Mea-makpash; Medicine Woman; F; Wife; 18

165; Nooptah-ditchis; Strikes Twice; F; Widow; 84

166; Chapes; Whinners; M; Husband; 43
167; Echete-sheedes-ahkinda; Rides a Yellow Horse; F; Wife; 40

Census of the __Crow__ Indians of __Crow__ Agency __Montana__ taken
By __J.E. Edwards__, United States Indian Agent __June 30, 1900__

Key: Number; Indian Name; English Name; Sex; Relation; Age

168; Me-makpash-ehas; The Other Medicine Rock; F; Daughter; 13
169; Ahkbahdit-napes; Kills Picking Berries; F; Widow; 65

170; Ahsukap-meas; Flathead Woman; M; Husband; 44
171; Mononots-heahsas; Well Known Writing; F; Wife; 33
172; Ismahka-wisha: Got a Hoop; F; Daughter; 17
173; ---; Lizzie Flathead Woman; F; Daughter; 7

174; Is-eepse-deesh; Pipe That Talks; M; Husband; 33
175; Echa-sheishis; Dirty Foot; F; Wife; 55
176; ---; Blanche Brown; F; Niece; 14

177; Ahta-ditchis; Big Woman; F; Widow; 56

178; Istuka-akuse; Knows the Gun; M; Husband; 32
179; Esop-pontuch-chehaydayus; Among the Sheep; F; Wife; 25
180; Bahm-batseer-esash; Nobody Fights Them; M; Son; 6
181; Esashka-ahp-orupish; Finds Things With Her Horse; F; Daughter; 10
182; Aka-malukis; Sings on Top; F; Daughter; 7
183; Echeta-cosh; Brings His Horses; M; Son; 1

184; Chedup-mahkahish; Bull That Raises Up; M; Widower; 66
185; Nash-kosh; Small; F; Daughter; 23

186; Ikpam-basash; Robert Raiseup; M; Husband; 28
187; Shee-deak-days; Rattles Going; F; Wife; 24

188; Lagak-deedes; Walking Bird; M; Husband; 42
189; Ee-sash-ich; Good Now; F; Wife; 34

190; Esaska-huka-ahkindas; Rides a Spotted Horse; F; Widow; 60

191; Ochis-dichis; Strikes at Night; F; Widow; 54
192; Dukeah-desh; Goes to War; M; Son; 32

193; Ootuh-chedups; Bull Weasel; M; Husband; 29
194; Esa-keepa; Crooked Face; F; Wife; 25
195; Istuka-makpash; Medicine Arrow; M; Son; 9

196; Chedup-kochetish; Bull All the Time; M; Widower; 69

197; Malapa; The Root; M; Widower; 63

198; Bedupa-bukata-dase; Beaver That Passes; F; Mother; 38
199; ---; Florence Beaver That Passes; F; Daughter; 3

Census of the __Crow__ Indians of __Crow__ Agency __Montana__ taken
By __J.E. Edwards__, United States Indian Agent __June 30, 1900__

Key: Number; Indian Name; English Name; Sex; Relation; Age

200; Minnahpesh; Swamp Flag; F; Widow; 54

201; Echeta-hukish; Spotted Horse; M; Husband; 51
202; Is-epse-makpash-ichis; Pretty Medicine Pipe; F; Wife; 42
203; E-rooptay-cheis; By Herself; F; Daughter; 12
204; Istuka-ahoos; Plenty Arrows; M; Son; 10
205; Aka-pish-akan-dichis; Strikes Rider of Red Ear; M; Son; 1

206; Booah-ahseesh; Shows a Fish; M; Husband; 54
207; Mahake-nahke; Shell Child; F; Wife; 48

208; Bishka-kahps; Flat Dog; M; Husband; 56
209; Mea-chedups; Woman Bull; F; Wife; 52

210; Otse-muchachis; Chief at Night; M; Husband; 64
211; Usk-beeche-bay-ahoos; Many Talks With Him; F; Wife; 26

212; Dakpitsa-eahkotish; Little Bear; M; Widower; 64

213; Ope-edupish; Fat Tobacco; M; Husband; 75
214; Dakup-makpash; Medicine Calf; F; Wife; 72
215; Mahpookta-botsots; Strong Otter; M; Son; 14

216; Ahpaka-hedere-dakpitsch; Bear in a Cloud; M; Husband; 43
217; Miooetsheda-esash; Big Lark; F; Wife; 48
218; Esakakasha-manakis; Blake White Bear; M; Son; 17

219; Eep-shedish; Yellow Tail; M; Husband; 38
220; ---; Mrs. S.C. Davis; F; Wife; 34
221; Mei-rauk-shay; Summer; M; Son; 12
222; Alack-chee-ichis; Has Good Coos; M; Son; 8

223; Nah-kaps; Flat Back; M; Husband; 54
224; Ahpa-doochis; Takes Together; F; Wife; 58

225; Chate-bah-cush-ecosh; Wolf Looks Up; M; Husband; 40
226; Oote-hotchkish; Long Weasel; F; Wife; 50

227; Cheedup-akookish; Dummy Bull; M; Widower; 65

228; Eem-botsesh; Blood Man; M; Husband; 42
229; Ahwaka-meas; Woman on Top of Ground; F; Wife; 30
230; Ikpahne-ich; Pretty Medicine; F; Daughter; 6
231; ---; Alberta Blood Man; F; Daughter; 1

232; Dakpitsa-ahway-repeas; Bear Goes to Other Ground; M; Husband; 31

Census of the __Crow__ Indians of __Crow__ Agency __Montana__ taken By __J.E. Edwards__, United States Indian Agent __June 30, 1900__

Key: Number; Indian Name; English Name; Sex; Relation; Age

233; Kookomish; Kittie Medicine Tail; F; Wife; 21
234; ---; Mary B. Ground; F; Daughter; 1

235; Dayka-ahspittech; Black Eagle; M; Husband; 34
236; Esa-keepa; Crooked Face; F; Wife; 28
237; Iswahka-miotchedish; Lucky Hoop; M; Son; 14
238; Dakpitska-ahn-duish; Bear that Raises His Paw; M; Son; 4
239; ---; Irene Mountain; F; Sister; 17

240; Cheetaka-cahkoskat; Little Prairie Chicken; M; Husband; 52
241; Ahsha-ekash; Looks at the Lodge; F; Wife; 54

242; Mahkawas; The Bread; M; Husband; 39
243; Mekas-besas; Stoops to Charge; F; Wife; 40

244; Biskka-kahdeas; Old Dog; M; Husband; 68
245; Me-heahsas; Well Known Rock; F; Wife; 57
246; Aska-wuts; Harry Old Dog; M; Son; 13

247; Eak-kin-hish-sis; Red in the Chin; F; --; 25

248; Eskochea-basah; Charges the Enemy; M; Widower; 63

249; Ahpit-kahdeas; Old Crane; M; Husband; 34
250; ---; Ella Farwell; F; Wife; 30
251; ---; Mary Crane; F; Daughter; 9
252; ---; Maud Crane; F; Daughter; 1

253; Peah-noops; Two Stinks; M; Husband; 35
254; Oo-wat-tah-hoos; Plenty Irons; F; Wife; 27
255; Opus-kittush; Long Medicine Tobacco; M; Son; 1

256; Booah-lagak; Fish Bird; M; Widower; 39

257; Ahpit-dakpitska; Bear Crane; M; Husband; 61
258; Ische-itse; Pretty Hair; F; Wife; 49
259; Dakpitske-nake; Bear Child; M; Son; 13
260; Daykoosh-naks; Young Eagle; M; Son; 6
261; ---; George Bear Crane; M; Son; 4

262; Lagak-etashdesh; Bird Shirt; M; Husband; 60
263; Botsa-nahme-napes; Kills Three Men; F; Wife; 48
264; Ahpay-sheedes; Yellow Leaves; M; Son; 10

265; Cheedup-ehas; The Other Bull; M; Husband; 36
266; Ah-kish-koos; Gives to the Sun; F; Wife; 24

Census of the __Crow__ Indians of __Crow__ Agency __Montana__ taken
By __J.E. Edwards__, United States Indian Agent __June 30, 1900__

Key: Number; Indian Name; English Name; Sex; Relation; Age

267; Daykoosh-mahks; Eagle Above; M; Son; 10

268; Ikpahne-chas; The Other Medicine; M; Husband; 31
269; Ahwooch-deedis; Walks to the Hole; F; Wife; 24
270; Makpash-heahsas; Shoots Plain Medicine; F; Daughter; 7

271; Itche-kahnetsesh; Bear Claw; M; Husband; 40
272; Utsewaks-ahoos; Begs Plenty; F; Wife; 34
273; Makpash-ope-ahoos; Medicine Rock Above; M; Son; 14
274; Peda-kosh; Brings Ten Times; F; Daughter; 5

275; Etashda-cheis; White Shirt; M; Husband; 70
276; Dich-heahsas; Strikes Well Known; F; Wife; 66
277; Esaska-eko-sheeish; Horse Turns Around; M; Son; 31

278; Besheesh; Shavings; M; Husband; 58
279; Hooche-sash; Wind; F; Wife; 53

280; ---; Albert Anderson; M; Husband; 31
281; ---; Sarah Anderson; F; Wife; 25
282; ---; Fannie Anderson; F; Daughter; 7

283; Echetegashes; The Elk; M; Husband; 49[?]
284; Ashu-makotesash; Big Head High Up; F; Wife; 44
285; Meneas-kooskuis-chedish; Hunts the Sioux; F; Daughter; 6

286; Poputa-naks; Frank Bethune; M; Husband; 26
287; Dack-kah-shis; The Eagle; F; Wife; 19

288; Ah-wah-cah-dace; Pukes on the Ground; M; Husband; 53
289; Hoksah-napis; Comes and Kills; F; Wife; 54
290; Ash-itse; Pretty River; F; Daughter; 10

291; Ahmbatseda-ahoos; Looks Much; F; Widow; 65

292; Esash-chedup; Blanket Bull; M; Husband; 32
293; Unda-itchis; Addie; F; Wife; 23
294; ---; Nettie B. Bull; F; Daughter; 1

295; Botsa-Miesash; Big Man; M; Husband; 36
296; Minnesh-pesh; Swamp Flag; F; Wife; 40
297; ---; Michael B. Man; M; Son; 13

298; Noopa-malapes; Kills Twice; F; Widow; 64

299; Ahpa-esash; Big Nose; M; Husband; 55

Census of the __Crow__ Indians of __Crow__ Agency __Montana__ taken
By __J.E. Edwards__, United States Indian Agent __June 30, 1900__

Key: Number; Indian Name; English Name; Sex; Relation; Age

300; Mi-iche-doochis; Takes Good Things; F; Wife; 48
301; Bahsatsie-basonda; Steals on Camp Ahead; F; Daughter; 12

302; ---; George Suis; M; Husband; 24
303; Mahshedah-kotish; Julia Bad Boy; F; Wife; 22
304; Ahsay-chulees; Sings in Camp; M; Son; 7
305; ---; Wesley Bad Boy; M; Son; 3

306; Nahsa-tays; Hump Back; M; Husband; 52
307; Heles-sheis; Runs Among Them; F; Wife; 48

308; Ookah-sheis; Dust; M; --; 32

309; Misk-sheiss; Talks Everything; M; Husband; 50
310; Botsa-wa-napes; Kills One Man; F; Wife; 43
311; Ah-shoe-ah-peas; Horn on Her Neck; F; Ad. Daughter; 6

312; Karooshis-eaahas; Don't Run; M; Husband; 34
313; Andutsedush-heahsas; Slides Down Well Known; F; Wife; 39
314; Minnapesh-ahoos; Plenty Swamp Flag; F; Daughter; 16
315; Chustah-ahkundis; Rides a Grey Horse; M; Son; 12
316; ---; Mary Don't Run; F; Daughter; 3
317; Bekashes; The Bannock; F; Mother; 74

318; Eespe-ekash; Looks at the Lion; F; Widow; 66

319; Chate-cheakaps; Young Wolf; M; [Widower]; 55

320; Chedup-dashes; Bull Tongue; M; Husband; 59
321; Echete-ahkin-doochis; Catches on the Horses; F; Wife; 45

322; Helekas-ash; Along the Hillside; M; Husband; 53
323; Ah-chane-deechis; Strikes in Camp; F; Wife; 42
324; Isminats-ich; Old Shield; M; Son; 16
325; Bahput-tah-way-chice; Sits to the Otter; F; Daughter; 6

326; Eepse-mahka-kala-napes; Kills One With Medcn Pipe; F; Widow; 71

327; Oouka-manakish; Crazy Sister-in-Law; M; Husband; 72
328; Makula-itch; Carries Good; F; Wife; 57
329; Chedups-echete; Hard Heart; F; Daughter; 8

330; Basuk-ose; Goes Ahead; M; Husband; 50
331; Isminats-itch; Pretty Shield; F; Wife; 44
332; Ichis; Good; M; Son; 17
333; Meah-kots; Small Woman; F; Daughter; 7

Census of the __Crow__ Indians of __Crow__ Agency __Montana__ taken By __J.E. Edwards__, United States Indian Agent __June 30, 1900__

Key: Number; Indian Name; English Name; Sex; Relation; Age

334; Meshodechitse; Medicine Shell; F; Widow; 46

335; Is-tuck-kay-os-seas; Shows His Gun; M; Husband; 20
336; Botseah-bedas; Pine Fire; F; Wife; 27

337; Chedup-cadish-dondase; Bull That Shows All Time; M; Husband; 35
338; Echete-mulukis; Sings; F; Wife; 33
339; Istuka-mahks; High Arrow; M; Son; 7

340; Hoop-itsahkahoh; Top of the Moccasin; M; Husband; 26
341; Bah-cay-key-bah-peash; Medicine Shell; F; Wife; 24
342; Ash-bedadish; Runs Into a House; F; Daughter; 5
343; Etash-shooachat; Blue Shirt; M; Son; 6

344; Ahm-botsots-heahsas; Strong Well Known; M; Husband; 36
345; Ahshay-hedra-dichis; Strikes in Camp; F; Wife; 22
346; ---; Viola S. Known; F; Daughter; 1

347; Kahkootsa; Drunkard; M; Husband; 44
348; Bahdahe-dane-bahdakish; Sings in the Woods; F; Wife; 43
349; Mea-nakose-nahks; Young Turtle Woman; F; Daughter; 7

350; Chate-hishes; Red Wolf; M; Husband; 29
351; Besha-ekash; Comes to See the Buffalo; F; Wife; 22
352; ---; Laura Red Wolf; F; Daughter; 3

353; Halup-eahkots; Small Waist; M; Husband; 64
354; Ikpahne-maks; Medicine High Up; F; Wife; 55

355; Ahwakoods-kahdeish; Old all the Time; M; Husband; 36
356; Istuka-makula; Shows a Child; F; Wife; 32
357; Arachuka-noak; Work on the Farm; M; Son; 10
358; Botsaytse; Chief; M; Son; 9
359; Botsu-tush-botsash; Runs to the Men; M; Son; 1

360; Eakook-sheedish; Yellow Coyote; F; Widow; 72

361; Edukush; The Meat; M; Husband; 44
362; Dudish; The Back; F; Wife; 47
363; Besha-mulukis; Buffalo That Sings; F; Daughter; 9
364; Nakose-nahks; Young Turtle; F; Daughter; 5

365; Chate-nak-sheedes; Young Yellow Wolf; M; Husband; 45
366; Doochis-heahsas; Takes Well Known; F; Wife; 47

367; Eahwookose; Inside the Mouth; M; Husband; 41

Census of the __Crow__ Indians of __Crow__ Agency __Montana__ taken By __J.E. Edwards__, United States Indian Agent __June 30, 1900__

Key: Number; Indian Name; English Name; Sex; Relation; Age

368; Wahkpas-ne-ahoos; Plenty Medicine; F; Wife; 44

369; ---; Michael O'Brien; M; Orphan; 19

370; Dahkpitsa-kahdeas; Old Bear; M; Husband; 46
371; Makupa-seesh; Hail Shows; F; Wife; 39
372; Lagaka-akuse; Bird That Shows; M; Son; 18
373; Ika-ahoos; Lots of Stars; M; Son; 15
374; Ahshuah-dichis; Strikes Inside the House; F; Daughter; 10
375; Eskochitsa-maluk-ichis; Strawberry Sings Pretty; F; Daughter; 8
376; Bus-sock-kose; Goes Ahead; M; Son; 4

377; Dakpitska-hotskisk; Long Bear; M; Husband; 52
378; Eahkooka-asadish; Fox Goes Out; F; Wife; 52
379; Meshodichitse-lagaks; Medicine Shell Bird; M; Son; 19
380; Eshpeahisha-kahdeish; Horace Long Bear; M; Son; 26

381; Dotsuish; Muskrat; F; Widow; 80

382; Wahpookta-hotskish; Long Otter; F; Husband; 60
383; Botseish; Pine; F; Wife; 62
384; Ahwot-saya; Ground Cedar; F; Daughter; 13

385; Aritsumbitsa-kahdeish; Falls Down Old; M; Husband; 28
386; Ah-dock-inday-keas-sos; Horse She Rides Well Known; F; Wife; 39
387; ---; Charlie Plays With Himself; Son; 5
388; Bota-hotsondish; Goes Ahead Everything; M; Son; 1

389; Minnetotseesh; The Moon; M; Batchelor[sic]; 29

390; Poputa-heahsas; Plain Owl; M; Husband; 40
391; Badup-kedupe-doochisdupay; Kills One Takes Two Guns; F; Wife; 38

392; Co-tah-dah-cock-cus; The Bird Everyway; M; Husband; 24
393; Mea-itchis; Pretty Woman; F; Wife; 32

394; Isekoshe-noopis; Two Whistles; M; Batchelor[sic]; 42
395; Isdots-ichis; Good to Prisoners; F; Mother; 87

396; Kee-osh; He Says; M; Husband; 40
397; Bedupa-ekoshees; Beaver that Stretches; F; Wife; 52
398; ---; Bravo; M; Son; 11
399; Cheedup-ahtsay-basash; Runs Over a Bull; M; Son; 1

400; Ishtopish; Eyes Open; F; Widow; 63

Census of the **Crow** Indians of **Crow** Agency **Montana** taken By **J.E. Edwards**, United States Indian Agent **June 30, 1900**

Key: Number; Indian Name; English Name; Sex; Relation; Age

401; Dahkoopis; Cuts a Hole In It; M; Husband; 35
402; Mea-daka; Grey Woman; F; Wife; 40

403; Eep-kahdeas; Old Tail; M; Husband; 43
404; Mi-iche-okepis; Shoots Pretty Things; F; Wife; 21

405; Askindes; Holds On; M; Husband; 63
406; Ahwa-akinakuse; Stands on Top of Ground; F; Wife; 54

407; Wahpotkta; Otter Comes Out of Water; F; Widow; 66

408; Minne-koshis; Whistle Water; M; Widower; 40

409; Masheandache; Dreamer; M; Husband; 54
410; Istuka-doochis; Take a Gun; F; Wife; 52
411; Daka-ichis-amach; Mortimer Dreamer; M; Son; 17

412; Botsea-mahnahs; Paints Her Forehead; M; Husband; 50
413; Eskocheabiorup; Finds His Enemy; F; Wife; 52
414; ---; Eva Forehead; F; Daughter; 1
415; Puk-iees; Holds It in the Mouth; M; Son; 19
416; Usmiha-koosh-basash; Charges on the Enemy; F; Mother; 74

417; Mune-skoop-doochis; Takes a Crooked Stick; F; Widow; 84

418; Umbich-esash; Don't Fall Down; M; Husband; 44
419; Esash-beduppa; Beaver Robe; F; Wife; 50

420; Kahnista; Small; M; Husband; 35
421; Eshippish-day-ichis; Goes to Mud Pretty; F; Wife; 30
422; Beeop-huche-naks; Young Hawk; M; Son; 4

423; Minekashe-ahoos; Plenty Butterfly; M; Husband; 47
424; Esaska-noops; Two Horses; F; Wife; 48

425; Nak-paka-ish; Child in the Mouth; M; Husband; 56
426; Kahdeas; Old; F; Wife; 54
427; Aheheke-ichis; The Spy; M; Son; 16
428; Eskoche-doochis; Joe Child in the Mouth; M; Son; 24

429; Noop-dichis; Strikes Twice; F; Widow; 88

430; Minnepahkichis; Ben Long Ear; M; Husband; 22
431; Up-pay-sheedish; Yellow Ears; F; Wife; 17

432; Mahshooshshesh; Red Plume; M; Husband; 70

Census of the __Crow__ Indians of __Crow__ Agency __Montana__ taken By __J.E. Edwards__, United States Indian Agent __June 30, 1900__

Key: Number; Indian Name; English Name; Sex; Relation; Age

433; Peritseusses; Crow That Shows; F; Wife; 53

434; Munash-malapes; Kills by the Woods; F; Widow; 60

435; Booah-hishes; Red Fish; M; Husband; 50
436; Mishodischitse-dichis; Strikes the Medicine Rock; F; Wife; 46

437; Bahkeda-basash; Blackbird in Front; M; Batchelor[sic]; 58

438; Ahsha-heletam-basash; Charges Through Camp; M; Husband; 59
439; Oomutish; Iron; F; Wife; 53

440; Besha-cheeup; Buffalo Bull; M; Widower; 33

441; Dakpitsa-ahsuse; James Carpenter; M; --; 20

442; Ushmiha-chedish; Enemy Hunter; M; Husband; 68
443; Kotseish; Shakes; F; Wife; 58

444; Shebah-sheedish; Among the Fog; M; Husband; 41
445; Echete-akuse; Horse on the Other Side; F; Wife; 29
446; Mashoditsche-heahsas; Well Known Shell; F; Daughter; 7
447; Ook-sheedish; Yellow Deer; M; Son; 6
448; ---; Jewel Among the Fog; F; Daughter; 1

449; Ahwahkuan-dakpitsa; Bear in the Middle; M; Husband; 42
450; Echeta-achis; Knows a Horse; F; Wife; 36
451; Kowees; Ruth; F; Daughter; 13

452; Dakpitsa-botsots; Strong Bear; M; Batchelor[sic]; 28

453; Cheeup-shespitta; Black Bull; M; Husband; 54
454; Besha-naks; Buffalo Calf; F; Wife; 65

455; Bedupa-okeah-duis; Beaver That Slides; M; Husband; 63
456; Dutch-ka; Twin Woman; F; Wife; 65

457; Chate-ewotsodish; Busy Wolf; M; Husband; 64
458; Minmakpash; Swamp Flag; F; Wife; 39

459; Shegak-kahpa; Flat Boy; M; Batchelor[sic]; 40

460; Unmeathe; Bank; M; Husband; 35
461; Mahsha-ich-meas; Pretty Feather Woman; F; Wife; 31
462; ---; Howard Shane; M; Ad Son; 6

Census of the __Crow__ Indians of __Crow__ Agency __Montana__ taken
By __J.E. Edwards__, United States Indian Agent __June 30, 1900__

Key: Number; Indian Name; English Name; Sex; Relation; Age

463; Lagak-cheah-noops; Two White Birds; M; Husband; 49
464; Ahpahne-makpash; Medicine Porcupine; F; Wife; 48
465; Besha-naks-noops; Among the Buffalo; F; Daughter; 15
466; Etash-dake; Eagle Shirt; M; Son; 6
467; Besha-nake; Buffalo High; M; Son; 20

468; Bahsuk-naks; Turtle Child; F; Widow; 65

469; Mahma-nudeis; Edward Little Bear; M; Husband; 23
470; Oota-hukish; Spotted Weasel; F; Wife; 35

471; Botseah-heahsas; Fights Well Known; M; Batchelor[sic]; 21

472; Maudut-kudesh; Pounded Meat; M; Husband; 58
473; Mahsha-undichis; Strikes Feathers; F; Wife; 56

474; Mahsha-kudesh; Holds the Feather; M; Husband; 50
475; Dakoshes; Eagle; F; Wife; 56
476; Besha-hishes; Throws Off on the Horse; M; Son; 17
477; ---; Amanda Holds the Feather; F; Daughter; 1

478; Ahwahkun-lagaks; Bird in the Ground; M; Husband; 52
479; Napes-ekash; Looks at One that Kills; F; Wife; 37
480; Mindukse-ekuroos; Runs Toward the Fort; M; Son; 8

481; Wutta-eahkoots; Little Wolf #2; M; Widower; 66
482; Eskoochs-ahoos-dich; Strikes Plenty Enemies; F; Sister; 60
483; Dukedea-akuse; Knows the War; M; Son; 22

484; Oomutish; Iron; F; Widow; 62

485; Asuktuah-basash; Runs Between Them; M; Husband; 27
486; Ahwoosh-heahsas; Sweathouse Well Known; F; Wife; 20
487; ---; Robert Runs Between Them; M; Son; 1

488; Dotske; The Twins; M; Husband; 56
489; Ikpahne-makpash; Medicine Porcupine; F; Wife; 58
490; Ekupa-ich; Pretty Hat; F; Mother; 71

491; Chedupa-seesh; Bull That Shows; M; Husband; 30
492; Echete; Horse; F; Wife; 29
493; Eskoche-aseesh; Spies the Enemy; M; Son; 6
494; ---; Ida Bull That Shows; F; Daughter; 1

495; Chate-dakpitsa; Bear Wolf; M; Husband; 60
496; Meshoditse-wakpahs; Medicine Shell; F; Wife; 46

Census of the __Crow__ Indians of __Crow__ Agency __Montana__ taken By __J.E. Edwards__, United States Indian Agent __June 30, 1900__

Key: Number; Indian Name; English Name; Sex; Relation; Age

497; Ahmako-istisha-naks; Young Swallow; M; Husband; 36
498; Oote-ewandies; Plays with the Weasel; F; Wife; 22

499; Issama-malapes; Kills on Her Own Ground; F; Widow; 60
500; Daka-makpash; Medicine Eagle; M; Son; 21

501; Oomuta-ahpies; Iron Necklace; F; Widow; 84

502; Washada-esash; Charges Strong; M; Husband; 59
503; Itshades; Kills in the Track; F; Wife; 58
504; Bishka-botsots; Charles Strong; M; Son; 15
505; ---; Mary Charges Strong; F; Daughter; 10

506; Chate-nakish; Leads a Wolf; M; Husband; 50
507; Naksha-undichis; Strikes First; F; Wife; 54
508; Mahsha-hishes-heahsas; Well Known Red Feather; F; Gr Dau; 8

509; Ahmuapes; The Kicker; M; Husband; 59
510; Arleunda-aches; Knows the Road; F; Wife; 60

511; Eseeah-koosh; Covers His Face; M; Husband; 50
512; Uck-ish-be-dane-dichis; Strikes One Going In House; F; Wife; 54
513; Cheedup-be-day-sot; Bull Near the Water; M; Son; 17

514; Cheedupa-ede-ekech; Bull Goes Hunting; M; Husband; 73
515; Daka-wahtis; One Buffalo Calf; F; Wife; 60

516; E-o-dish; Full Mouth; M; Husband; 44
517; Bedupa-chas; The Other Beaver; F; Wife; 48
518; Bea-e-hosh; The Other Woman; F; Daughter; 15

519; Ahshuputsuah-dooich; Get One Horn; M; Husband; 44
520; Isminats-budwasich; Shield at the Door; F; Wife; 35
521; Ischesa-hela-amach; Sits Toward the Nest; M; Son; 13
522; ---; Harry Get One Horn; M; Son; 1

523; Isoskay-bachate-chis; Alexander Upshaw; M; --; 24

524; Ooet-budeka-dooch; Takes a Gun #2; M; Husband; 37
525; Botsuah-tush; Sweet Grass; F; Wife; 45

526; Shegak-amach; Bad Boy; M; Husband; 33
527; Eka-ahpka-amach; Sits With a Star; F; Wife; 23
528; ---; David Bad Boy; M; Son; 3

529; Eshasha-heahsas; Plain Face; F; Widow; 58

Census of the __Crow__ Indians of __Crow__ Agency __Montana__ taken
By __J.E. Edwards__, United States Indian Agent __June 30, 1900__

Key: Number; Indian Name; English Name; Sex; Relation; Age

530; Isooet-botsesh; Smart Iron; M; Husband; 29
531; ---; Mary Townsend; F; Wife; 26
532; ---; Mabel M. Townsend; F; Daughter; 5
533; ---; Fred A. Townsend; M; Son; 3

534; Epeahkot-esash; Big Magpie; M; Husband; 51
535; Beka-haredich; Among the Grass; F; Wife; 53

536; Mahedish; Does Anything; M; Husband; 40
537; Ahwaku-cheduah-naks; Young Ground Cedar; F; Wife; 46

538; Shegak-doochis; Boy That Grabs; M; Husband; 55
539; Mekaspe-doochis; Takes Hold of the Cloth; F; Wife; 59

540; Ahsha-okepish; Shoots the Lodge; M; Husband; 54
541; Ikpahne-ekash; Looks at the Medicine; F; Wife; 46

542; Ahrocheis; Stops; M; Husband; 32
543; Esasha-ich; Paints Her Face Pretty; F; Wife;30
544; Opish-ekash; Looks at the Tobacco; M; Son; 13
545; Istuka-mulukis; Sings to the Arrow; F; Daughter; 6
546; ---; Paul C. Stops; M; Son; 1

547; Ahlud-esush; Big Shoulder Blade; M; Husband; 48
548; Beshay-herasus; Well Known; Buffalo; F; Wife; 37
549; Arap-apushay-dichesay; Bullets Don't Strike Him; M; Son; 7

550; Bah-kaht-konsees; Bad Baby; M; Widower; 64

551; Cheeup-ahkade-duse; Stands Over a Bull; M; Husband; 28
552; Ah-bay-da-itchis; Pretty Medicine; F; Wife; 24
553; She-cack-bah-pash; Medicine Boy; M; Son; 7

554; Cheeup-quasah-datsish; Bull In Sight; M; Husband; 30
555; Ahdo-chea-beas; Woman Whers[sic] She Stops; F; Wife; 36
556; Ah-bah-keas-sash; Cloud Shows Plain; M; Son; 16
557; Ahdean-day-ah-chatis; Follows the Track; F; Daughter; 11

558; It-schoc-daytah; No Shinbone; M; Husband; 46
559; Mahkeeda-sheedish; Yellow Blackbird; F; Wife; 46
560; Bah-cup-pay-deedish; Lizard That Walks; F; Daughter; 13
561; Cheedup-etahsich; Henry Shinbone; M; Son; 22
562; Nalmis; Three; F; Mother; 74

563; Ahshkay-shopis; Four Balls; M; Husband; 58
564; Meshoditsche-hishes; Red Rock; F; Wife; 56

Census of the __Crow__ Indians of __Crow__ Agency __Montana__ taken
By __J.E. Edwards__, United States Indian Agent __June 30, 1900__

Key: Number; Indian Name; English Name; Sex; Relation; Age

565; Kahdeeasas; Not Old; M; Son; 10
566; Chayt-aputs; Wolf That Looks Back; M; Son; 24

567; Ahkabos; Froze; M; Husband; 37
568; Mahpay-e-kash; Sees in a Day; F; Wife; 34
569; Espeah-kishe-kahdeas; Old Bobcat; M; Son; 7
570; Hayday-de-qu-pish; Gets Down Among Them; M; Son; 3

571; Mahray-keir-ahplis; Shell on the Neck; M; Husband; 37
572; Ise-meneas; His Door; F; Wife; 40
573; Cheedup-ay-koos; Bull That Knows; M; Son; 15

574; Minnay-e-koos-chis; Comes Out of the Water; F; Widow; 66

575; Ahoo-ahk-ichis; Pretty On Top; M; Husband; 36
576; Itshooaprsich; Pretty Back of the Neck; F; Wife; 35
577; Mah-hahk-ichis; Plenty Shells; M; Son; 10

578; Chees-wahkpahs; Medicine Tail; M; Husband; 42
579; Itshe-wahkpahs; She is Medicine; F; Wife; 39

580; Cheedeer-esahs; Not Afraid; M; Husband; 42
581; Noopis; Two; F; Wife; 50
582; Bahput-chee-keep-beas; Ant Woman; F; Daughter; 11
583; ---; George Not Afraid; M; Son; 2

584; Escheeta-nevsaus; Knows His Horse; M; Husband; 40
585; Mekahshay-hishis; Fat Snake; F; Wife; 50

586; Ahpit-sheedis; Yellow Crane; M; Husband; 56
587; Uk-pa-had-dee-is; Does Things Together; F; Wife; 44

588; Push-ah-kos; Cut; M; Widower; 44

589; Napk-ahwot-nee-as; One Child Woman; F; Widow; 56

590; Ahke-mah-kaweish; Hoop on the Forehead; M; Husband; 52
591; Ahshay-whoo-a-aychis; Knows the Whole Camp; F; Wife; 53
592; Mussick-awats; One Turtle; M; Son; 10
593; Medesha-dooch; Takes the Dead; F; Mother; 72

594; Ikpay-ahoos; Plenty Wing; M; Husband; 50
595; Ismant-heahsas; Plain Shield; F; Wife; 51
596; Lagak-heahsas; Big Bird; M; Gr Son; 8

597; Ay-kuse; Knows; M; Husband; 27

Census of the __**Crow**__ Indians of __**Crow**__ Agency __**Montana**__ taken
By __**J.E. Edwards**__, United States Indian Agent __**June 30, 1900**__

Key: Number; Indian Name; English Name; Sex; Relation; Age

598; Echick-heas; Gets There First; F; Wife; 23
599; ---; Sarah Knows; F; Daughter; 5
600; Edwea; Dummy; F; Mother; 54

601; Mumasen-dichis; Strikes by Side of Water; F; Widow; 84
602; Menacheis; White Goose; M; Son; 49

603; Almashus; The Fog; M; Husband; 72
604; Makula-woof-dichis; Takes Two Guns; F; Wife; 62
605; ---; Frank Shively; M; Son; 28

606; Minooksha-kahdeas; Old Alligator; M; Husband; 56
607; Chut-napis; Kills on the Lookout; F; Wife; 61

608; ---; Tom Laforge; M; Husband; 35
609; Mea-kahdeas; Old Woman; F; Wife; 34

610; Keasha; Runner; M; Husband; 48
611; Icheat-ekash; Looks at the Tobacco; F; Wife; 48
612; Beeshay-ahkah-wahchis; Sits on the Buffalo; F; Daughter; 11

613; Dakpitsa-beeadas; Firs[sic] Bear; M; Widower; 51
614; Bea-hutchkish; Long Woman; F; Ad Dau; 14

615; Ekeeka-dase; Goes Together; M; Husband; 33
616; Makapo-ich; Pretty Hail; F; Wife; 31
617; Oatah-ich; Jane Goes Together; F; Daughter; 10
618; ---; Wesley Goes Together; M; Son; 4

619; Cheas-kuch-kish; Spotted Tail; M; Husband; 50
620; Ootah-sheedish; Yellow All Over; F; Wife; 40
621; Etoshday-bachpash; Medicine Dress; F; Daughter; 18
622; Echeen-bachpash; Medicine Horse; F; Daughter; 7

623; Bit-quash; Onion; M; Husband; 45
624; Bershea-bachpash; Medicine Buffalo Cow; F; Wife; 39
625; Ahwaka-wahkees-sas; Plain Mountain; F; Daughter; 9
626; Undasha-day-bahah-chis; Charges Strong; M; Son; 6

627; Up-pay-ut-tay; Sharp Nose #2; M; Husband; 35
628; Ahchook-coode-dadush; Strikes and Strikes Again; F; Wife; 41

629; Duck-bit-chay-beas; Bear Woman; F; Widow; 54
630; Bee-bush-sas; Rock Ahead; F; Daughter; 15

631; ---; Josh Buffalo; M; Husband; 38

Census of the __Crow__ Indians of __Crow__ Agency __Montana__ taken
By __J.E. Edwards__, United States Indian Agent __June 30, 1900__

Key: Number; Indian Name; English Name; Sex; Relation; Age

632; Akean-badachek-easos; Ties Knot On Top of Head; F; Wife; 30

633; Dakpitsa-ahoos; Plenty Bears; M; Husband; 60
634; Kahdeas; Old; F; Wife; 50
635; Beehaycay-dahwahchis; Sits Among the Rocks; M; Son; 12

636; ---; Richard Wallace; M; Husband; 34
637; Bash-itchis; Pretty Feather; F; Wife; 32
638; ---; Susie Wallace; F; Daughter; 5

639; Ah-cock-bee-dash; Hears Fire; M; Husband; 36
640; ---; Mary Bompard; F; Wife; 39

641; Ah-puck-kay; Long Neck; M; Husband; 32
642; Ushcoch-uttah-dup-pace; Kills Close to Camp; F; Wife; 40
643; Bes-shay-e-duhs; Buffalo Stands Up; F; Daughter; 9

644; ---; Louis Bompard; M; Husband; 40
645; ---; Lois Bompard; F; Wife; 31
646; ---; Peter Bompard; M; Son; 10
647; ---; Rosa Bompard; F; Daughter; 5

648; ---; Rosa Peters; F; Mother; 28
649; ---; Arthur Peters; M; Son; 11
650; ---; Elsie Peters; F; Daughter; 9
651; ---; George Peters; M; Son; 5

652; ---; Joseph Martinez; M; Widower; 27

653; Chate-dock-coo-chis; Young Hairy Wolf; M; Husband; 55
654; Ahdache-waycoo-itchis; Comes From War Pretty; F; Wife; 51
655; Up-pay-huck-kay; Long Nose; M; Son; 18
656; Bah-cup-say-keas-sos; Floy Hairy Wolf; F; Daughter; 12

657; Dah-sea-hash; The Other Heart; F; Widow; 55

658; Bean-da-ichis; Strikes the Water; F; Widow; 73
659; Dah-pittosh; Grasshopper; M; Son; 23

660; Ahwahahs; Gros Ventre; M; Husband; 31
661; Bea-dane-dah-coos; Stops by the Water; F; Wife; 30
662; Bea-ahoos; Plenty Woman; F; Daughter; 9

663; Chea-dup-chees; Grey Bull; M; Husband; 62
664; Bah-duck-cah-peas; Going About; F; Wife; 60
665; Bee-itchis; Pretty Rock; F; Daughter; 10

Census of the __Crow__ Indians of __Crow__ Agency __Montana__ taken
By __J.E. Edwards__, United States Indian Agent __June 30, 1900__

Key: Number; Indian Name; English Name; Sex; Relation; Age

666; Bish-push; Alder; M; Son; 19

667; Bah-aye-chaise; Knows Everything; F; --; 36
668; Chea-key-sos; Sage Hen; M; Son; 15
669; Esoska-cheseday-kabachachis; Grey Horse Chief; M; Son; 4
670; ---; Anson Knows Everything; M; Son; 1

671; Bah-pittay-dov-pus; Two Otters; F; Widow; 71
672; Ush-hay-dosh-days; Goes to Camp; M; Son; 18

673; Echeo-duch-days; Goes to the Horses; M; Husband; 35
674; Dock-op-pah-dee-chis; Strikes Mother and Child; F; Wife; 26
675; Bah-euch-euis; Striped Snake; F; Daughter; 5

676; Ah-dah-sea-ut-hoos; Shows Plenty; M; Husband; 42
677; Bea-ha-wat-tosh; One Woman; F; Wife; 44

678; Um-bah-day-es-sos; Goes Farther Along; F; Widow; 34
679; Dea-cosh-bah-cush; High Eagle; M; Son; 10
680; Uck-a-chase; Knows; F; Mother; 70

681; Ah-wah-kah-we-sos; Big Mountain; M; Husband; 43
682; Cuckay-dups-doochis; Takes Two Lances; F; Wife; 53
683; Ish-co-che-hayda-dose; Runs Against His Enemy; M; Son; 20

684; Chesay-itche-badakah; Pretty Tail; M; Husband; 52
685; Un-dee-dichis; Walks Pretty; F; Wife; 50
686; ---; Lucy Stewart; F; Ad Dau; 15

687; Bich-pus; Spaniard; M; Husband; 30
688; Bachick-kah-coo-deechis; Looks at One Comes frm[sic] war; F; Wife; 28

689; Baam-cheem-beas; White Woman; F; Widow; 65

690; Bea-noopus; Two Women; F; Widow; 61

691; Ah-way-e-kosh; Looks at the Ground; M; Husband; 37
692; Bah-dah-kiss; Horse That Sings; F; Wife; 21
693; ---; McKinley L. Ground; M; Son; 2

694; ---; Thomas Jefferson; M; Husband; 30
695; Lagak-naks; Bird Child; F; Wife; 19
696; ---; Lillian Jefferson; F; Daughter; 1

697; Bash-day-tush; No Name; F; Widow; 79

Census of the __Crow__ Indians of __Crow__ Agency __Montana__ taken
By __J.E. Edwards__, United States Indian Agent __June 30, 1900__

Key: Number; Indian Name; English Name; Sex; Relation; Age

698; Esock-kan-dahkoos; On Top of the House; M; Husband; 23
699; Minnetotse-ish-ekash; Looks at the Sun; F; Wife; 21
700; ---; Iowa House; F; Daughter; 2

701; Up-chay-keas-sos; Voice Well Known; M; Widower; 52

702; ---; Katherine Scott; F; Mother; 28
703; ---; Paul Scott; M; Son; 9
704; ---; Emma Scott; F; Daughter; 6
705; ---; Pearl Scott; F; Daughter; 5
706; ---; Frank Scott; M; Son; 1

707; ---; Frank Shane; M; Husband; 30
708; Bah-chop-dah-beam; Kills With Her Husband; F; Wife; 26
709; ---; May Shane; F; Daughter; 1

710; Oomuta-nahbeas; Three Irons; M; Widower; 57
711; Dah-cheas; Drinking all the Time; M; Son; 9

712; Da-pit-say-seandacockcus; Bird in the Morning; M; Husband; 21
713; Unda-ichis; Goes Pretty; F; Wife; 31

714; Edah-dootchis; Takes Himself; M; --[Widower]; 34
715; E-doos-sos; Can't Get Up; F; Mother; 64

716; She-bah-sha-dush; Fog in the Morning; M; Husband; 52
717; Ease-key-pay; Crooked Face Child; F; Wife; 49
718; ---; John Morning; M; Son; 9
719; ---; Ruth Morning; F; Daughter; 3

720; Payduch-chee-bachpash; Medicine Crow; M; Husband; 50
721; Bachpash; Medicine; F; Wife; 46
722; Ah-woos-dah-cuss; Young Badger; M; Son; 12
723; Ah-way-chee-da-cuss; Goes Pretty; M; Son; 7
724; An-way-itchise; Chester Medicine Crow; M; Son; 3

725; Bee-shay-che-de-sos; Big Ox; M; Widower; 65
726; Esoc-uck-bahdah-pace; Kills With Her Brother; F; Sister; 60

727; ---; Wm. Elliott Towne; M; Orphan; 13
728; ---; Ida M. Towne; F; Sister; 10

729; Dosh-bah-cha-chis; Strong Heart; M; Husband; 39
730; Be-dee-sheas-she-dush; Stands to the Sun; F; Wife; 38

731; Be-shay-ka-hase; Buffalo That Shakes; F; Widow; 40

Census of the __Crow__ Indians of __Crow__ Agency __Montana__ taken By __J.E. Edwards__, United States Indian Agent __June 30, 1900__

Key: Number; Indian Name; English Name; Sex; Relation; Age

732; Epah-deabah-cha-chis; Strong Medicine; M; Son; 12

733; Qua-dah-bah-chis; Sits in the Middle; M; Husband; 54
734; Bahdup-pay-keas-sos; Kills Well Known; F; Wife; 52
735; Bedah-tashis-chay-ichis; Pretty Butterfly; F; Daughter; 11

736; A-dah-shoes; Blue Belly; M; Husband; 60
737; Osh-shone-badup-pace; Kills in Rear of House; F; Wife; 61

738; Eche-dosh; Brings Horses; F; Mother; 40
739; Eckpah-dea-dacock-cush; His Medicine Bird; F; Daughter; 4

740; Ahduck-cheedee-chay-ichis; Strikes His Enemy Pretty; M; Husband; 39
741; Es-che-kay-pay; Crooked Face; F; Wife; 37
742; Duckbitchay-hada-tahsos; Gets Their Medicine Tobacco; M; Son; 4

743; Day-chay-ahoos; Many Prisoners; F; Widow; 57
744; Esos-kaybah-och-che-due; Lucky Horse; F; Sister; 30

745; Cah-day-buck-kesos; Throws It Away; M; Husband; 27
746; Is-oo-what-tus; Her Iron; F; Wife; 27
747; Mes-sheadish; Yellow Woman; F; Daughter; 2

748; Ea-cook-cah-cheas; White Fox; M; Husband; 35
749; Bashheede-cheeha-ahoos; Plenty Medicine Rock; F; Wife; 40
750; Atseke-ichis; Good Watch; F; Daughter; 1
751; Ahwayka-ways-bachedis; Hunts Toward the Mountains; M; Son; 20
752; Dahcock-uckpa-doshis; Eats With a Bird; --; --; --
752; Dahcock-uckpa-do-shis; Eats With a Bird; M; Orphan; 11
753; Bahputtah-ahway-taydas; Otter Goes a Long Way; M; Brother; 9

754; Escock-kay-keas-sos; Well Known Lance; F; Widow; 73

755; Ah-dush-cos-pay; Crooked Arm; M; Husband; 45
756; Ah-kok-de-chis; Catches Up and Strikes; F; Wife; 30
757; ---; Herbert Crooked Arm; M; Son; 11
758; Ishane-baduck-chadacuck; Bird Ties Knot on Top Head; M; Son; 7
759; ---; James Crooked Arm; M; Son; 3

760; Bee-dup-kah-deas; Old Beaver; F; Widow; 47

761; Echick-kay-sah-dish; Comes Out First; F; Orphan; 9
762; Bee-shas-sah-hoos; Comes to the Buffalo; F; Sister; 19

763; Cheeup-dah-sis; Bull Tongue #2; M; Husband; 36
764; Bah-keam-beas; Blackbird Woman; F; Wife; 30

Census of the __Crow__ Indians of __Crow__ Agency __Montana__ taken
By __J.E. Edwards__, United States Indian Agent __June 30, 1900__

Key: Number; Indian Name; English Name; Sex; Relation; Age

765; Cuckey-shean-doochis; Takes Yellow Spotted Horse; F; Daughter; 10
766; Ah-dup-pis; Stabs; F; Mother; 78

767; Bee-day-she-kosh; Looks at the Water; M; Husband; 42
768; Bee-dee-dup-pace; Takes Across the Water; F; Wife; 40
769; ---; Francis Tiffany; M; Ad Son; 14

770; Cah-kay-doot-chis; Takes a Lance; F; Widow; 62

771; Bish-ka-cheas; White Dog; M; Husband; 46
772; Bachay-hay-what-deechis; Strikes One Man; F; Wife; 48

773; Dough-seas; Buffalo Neck Hair; M; Husband; 57
774; Bah-bah-dah-kosh; Nearly Gone; F; Wife; 60

775; Esuck-bon-tuch-chais; Mountain Sheep; M; Husband; 32
776; E-cook-key-e-kesh; Looks at the Fox; F; Wife; 34
777; Bacock-dahsay-itchis; Good Hearted Bird; F; Daughter; 9
778; Che-co-key-dah-pace; Kills the Young Man; M; Son; 6
779; Echeta-sheis-shash; Shows the Horse; M; Son; 1

780; Dahcock-dah-dah-bish; Morris Shaffer; M; Husband; 19
781; ---; Annie Wesley; F; Wife; 18

782; Edea-hay-bah-pash; Medicine Breath; M; Widower; 37

783; Ah-shoos; The Horn; M; Husband; 56
784; It-tuch-chis; All Alone; F; Wife; 46
785; Kuch-key-con-dah-eas; Goes After Spotted Horse; M; Son; 7

786; ---; Mrs. William Blaine; F; Mother; 27
787; ---; James Blaine; M; Son; 11
788; ---; Florence Blaine; F; Daughter; 6

789; Ah-pas-seas; Shows His Ear; M; Batchelor[sic]; 52
790; Dutch-choas; Muskrat; F; Mother; 70

791; Chay-esos; Big Sheep; M; Husband; 31
792; Dock-kosh; Turtle; F; Wife; 44
793; ---; Florence Big Sheep; F; Daughter; 3

794; ---; James Hill; M; Batchelor[sic]; 26

795; ---; Dexter; M; Husband; 25
796; Echete-cheis-ahkundis; Rides a White-Bellied Horse; F; Wife; 14

Census of the __Crow__ Indians of __Crow__ Agency __Montana__ taken By __J.E. Edwards__, United States Indian Agent __June 30, 1900__

Key: Number; Indian Name; English Name; Sex; Relation; Age

797; Ah-wah-chis; Sits Down; F; Widow; 52
798; Ahdean-dauah-waychis; Sits Along the Road; F; Daughter; 19

799; Dosh-bah-cha-chis; Strong Heart; F; Widow; 70

800; Awaycah-wadane-badakis; Sings in the Mountains; M; Husband; 28
801; Ah-wain-dah-it-chis; Good Hearted Ground; F; Wife; 26
802; Bea-bachpash-cah-weas; Bad Medicine Woman; F; Daughter; 9
803; Isbah-ca-key-ah-shees; Shows a Shell; F; Daughter; 6

804; Ah-shon-sheedish; Yellow Head; M; Husband; 41
805; Bah-put-tah-pee-deechis; Strikes One With Necklace; F; Wife; 45
806; Eshe-bah-cha-chis; Ruth Yellow Head; F; Daughter; 18

807; Ah-hoe-cot-ta-dea-dish; Sun Goes Slow; M; Widower; 38

808; Oo-what-kah-wish; Iron Fork; M; Husband; 65
809; Bah-itchay-doot-chis; Takes Pretty Things; F; Wife; 63

810; Bean-dahcome-baday-kay; Crazy Pen d'Oreille; M; Husband; 60
811; Bah-cut-chay-itchis; Pretty Striped Snake; F; Wife; 51

812; Ock-cheas; White Antelope; M; Husband; 38
813; Bah-hah-beas; Spring Woman; F; Wife; 32
814; E-che-che-sosh; Big Root; F; Daughter; 9
815; Ah-may-ahche-day-chase; Knows Her Luck; F; Daughter; 5

816; Badakis-shebacha-cheas; Redwood Chief; M; Widower; 51

817; ---; Mrs. F. Sucher; F; Mother; 22
818; ---; Belle Sucher; F; Daughter; 6
819; ---; Hattie Sucher; F; Daughter; 5

820; Bah-doot-che-key-pish; Takes Wrinkle; M; Husband; 54
821; Dupe-tush-der-chis; Strikes Both Ways; F; Wife; 51
822; Chee-sos-cos; Elmer Takes Wrinkle; M; Son; 18

823; Shee-day; Yellow; F; Widow; 64

824; Oo-way-it-chis; Pretty Paint; M; Husband; 27
825; Ahway-kawah-kain-beas; Woman on Top of Mountain; F; Wife; 26
826; E-kay-sup-peas; Seven Stars; F; Daughter; 12

827; Bah-chea-keas-sos; Fights Well Known #1; M; Husband; 41
828; Is-chis-say-it-chis; Pretty Nest; F; Wife; 36

Census of the __Crow__ Indians of __Crow__ Agency __Montana__ taken By __J.E. Edwards__, United States Indian Agent __June 30, 1900__

Key: Number; Indian Name; English Name; Sex; Relation; Age

829; Oo-what-tish; The Iron; M; Husband; 41
830; Bashow-dea-chic-itchis; Pretty Medicine Rock; F; Wife; 39
831; Bun-dock-cope-dah-cuss; Woodpecker's Child; M; Son; 16
832; Ecup-pah-keas-sos; Gets Down Well Known; M; Son; 14
833; Es-been-dotch-cheas; Little Shield; M; Son; 9
834; Ah-duchh-che-itchis; Good Coos; M; Son; 6

835; Dosh-kosh; Child; M; Husband; 39
836; Bee-dup-eas; Little Beaver; F; Wife; 36

837; ---; John Wallace; M; Husband; 41
838; Oo-tay-sah-dis; Weasel Goes Out; F; Wife; 48
839; ---; Carrie Wallace; F; Ad Dau; 16
840; E-chu-dah-keas-sos; Well Known Horse; F; Ad Dau; 8

841; Oo-tay-doo-bah-kais; Cross Weasel; M; Widower; 56

842; Ekup-pah-wah-chis; Choteau; M; Son; 32 [In checking no Indian name 1897-1898. Listed as Snapping Dog in 1901 with same Indian name #822.]

843; Bah-kea-dah; Blackbird; M; Husband; 49
844; Bachay-ahkahn-dupace; Kills Six Men; F; Wife; 57

845; Ish-bern-dotch-sheda; Yellow Shield; M; Husband; 75
846; Bah-dah-kis; Sings; F; Wife; 74

847; Chate-uck-pah-deedish; Walks With a Wolf; M; Widower; 24
848; Ecbean-dock-sass; Little Colt; F; Daughter; 7

849; Bee-pah-pus-sis; Round Rock; M; Son; 41
850; Bah-dup-pey-keasesos; Kills Well Known; F; Mother; 75
851; Hay-day-ach-days; Runs in Among Them; M; Son; 33

852; Dupe-doot-chis; Takes Two; M; Husband; 26
853; Ah-dough-chea-ah-chase; Knows Where She Stops; F; Wife; 18

854; ---; Annie Shows a Pipe; F; Orphan; 9

855; Dapitska-neen-dates; Bear That Don't Walk; M; Husband; 37
856; ---; Mrs. Wm. Hawks; F; Wife; 34
857; Ah-dup-pah-hoose; Lucy Hawks; F; Daughter; 16
858; Es-chis-say-bah-posh; Medicine Nest; M; Son; 4

859; Bah-shay-kah-duck-kay; Lean Man; M; Widower; 45

860; Um-bah-sah-ahoos; Charges Plenty; M; Husband; 38

Census of the __Crow__ Indians of __Crow__ Agency __Montana__ taken
By __J.E. Edwards__, United States Indian Agent __June 30, 1900__

Key: Number; Indian Name; English Name; Sex; Relation; Age

861; Bachay-cush-bahdukiss; Sings to Man; F; Wife; 43
862; Bah-tay-day-keas-sos; Steals Plain; M Son; 15
863; Duck-cock-dahcuss; Bird; F; Daughter; 7
864; Bashay-bachpash; Medicine Buffalo; M; Son; 1

865; ---; David Stewart; M; Husband; 26
866; Ekup-pah-wah-chis; Sits With the Stars; F; Wife; 32
867; Ekus-sah-itchis; Pretty Snake; F; Daughter; 8

868; Bee-dock-cup-pis; Goose Goes Over the Hill; M; Husband; 76
869; Um-beas-say-chu-dish; Hunts to Lie Down; F; Wife; 74

870; Oo-kutchis-say; Puts on Antelope Cap; M; Husband; 57
871; Op-put-tay; Long Neck; F; Wife; 58
872; ---; Herbert Antelope Cap; M; Son; 15
873; Bay-ray-day-tuss; Proud; F; Sister; 64

874; Mitot-duspis; Passes Everything; M; Husband; 26
875; Besha-amach; Sits on the Buffalo; F; Wife; 25 [26?]
876; Isbach-ichis; Good Hoops; M; Son; 1

877; Chee-say-ca-say-tuss; No Hair on His Tail; M; Husband; 57
878; Echean-bachpash; Medicine Horses; F; Wife; 51
879; Dah-cock-sah-hoos; Comes From the Birds; F; Daughter; 10
880; Dah-cock-sah-hoose; Comes to the Birds; F; Daughter; 19
881; ---; Hugh Leider; M; Son; 24

882; Daeka-kahdeas; Carl Leider; M; Husband; 32
883; Bashow-deedich-chayoppes; Medicine Rock Necklace; F; Wife; 18
884; ---; Agnes Leider; F; Daughter; 3

885; Ah-dup-pah-hoose; The Arapahoe; M; Husband; 51
886; A-way-co-case; Spider; F; Wife; 38
887; Chuch-kay-esos; Big Chicken; M; Son; 16
888; Ouk-be-das; Fire Deer; M; Son; 11

889; Bah-poh-tus; The Fly; M; Husband; 70
890; Awasha-ishdacako-shabea; Gros Ventre Red Wom[an] Bird; Wife; 56

891; Iscehe-haydane-doochis; Takes Among Enemy #2; M; Husband; 26
892; Sus-bah-doochis; Takes Quick; F; Wife; 27
893; Dah-cook-dacass; Bird Child; M; Son; 8
894; Dachpitsay-esock-cuss; Bear Old Man; M; Son; 5
895; ---; --; M; Son; 1

896; Bosh-day-tush; No Name; F; Widow; 48

Census of the __Crow__ Indians of __Crow__ Agency __Montana__ taken
By __J.E. Edwards__, United States Indian Agent __June 30, 1900__

Key: Number; Indian Name; English Name; Sex; Relation; Age

897; Itch-okepish; Shot Himself; M; Son; 8

898; E-koop-pay-bah-coosh; Hat Above; F; Widow; 72
899; Ush-dosh-ka-dus; By the Side of the Camp; F; Mother; 90

900; Bah-put-tosh; Otter; M; Husband; 23
901; Bah-cup-pah-e-chice; Pretty Hail; F; Wife; 32
902; Bah-dah-pah-coos; Comes From Digging Roots; Widow; 74

903; E-sees-be-tay; Black Hair; M; Husband; 51
904; Been-day-chay-esah-ay; Strikes Between the Forts; F; Wife; 46
905; Bah-cup-pah-ahoos; Plenty Hail; M; Son; 16
906; Ah-chay-itsche-peas; Jumps Over; M; Son; 7
907; It-chit-chey-eas; Small Medicine Tobacco; F; Daughter; 4
908; Echay-hishes; Red Feet; M; Son; 13

909; Chate-bee-dish-she-days; Wolf Goes to Water; M; Widower; 74
910; Cheedup-dah-cock-cus; Bull Bird; M; Son; 28

911; Ecupe-pay-cheas; White Hat; M; Husband; 54
912; Eck-bah-dea-bachpash; Her Medicine is Medicine; F; Wife; 52
913; Bea-shepittas; Black Rock; M; Son; 18

914; Chate-bachpash; Medicine Wolf; M; Husband; 72
915; Bee-dane-bah-dah-kiss; Sings Going In; F; Wife; 62

916; Chip-pah-pos-shis; Ground Squirrel; M; Widower; 32

917; Ecot-osh-heas; Shows a Little; M; Husband; 36
918; Bah-dah-pay-itchis; Kills Good; F; Wife; 31
919; Uck-kosh-e-kosh; Looks at the Sun; M; Son; 11
920; Bes-koo-kah-dah-biss; Rock Moves Along; M; Son; 6
921; Achpahnea-achpedaish; Walks With Medicine; M; Son; 1

922; Ah-peeh-cos; Covers His Neck; M; Husband; 61
923; Isbeen-dah-chay-itchis; Pretty Shield; F; Wife; 61
924; Ahpeachay-apah-doochis; Catches With Rope On; M; Son; 4
925; Eck-bah-deas; His Medicine; M; Son; 41

926; Ope-kahdeas; Old Tobacco; M; Husband; 50
927; Bit-che-doot-chis; Takes a Knife; F; Wife; 56

928; Eche-day-kahdeas; Old Horse; M; Husband; 49
929; Mea-kowees; Mrs. Nate Record; F; Wife; 44
930; Itsuitsa-ichis; Charlie Record; M; Son; 9
931; ---; Dora Record; F; Daughter; 6

Census of the __Crow__ Indians of __Crow__ Agency __Montana__ taken
By __J.E. Edwards__, United States Indian Agent __June 30, 1900__

Key: Number; Indian Name; English Name; Sex; Relation; Age

932; Bin-dotch-ut-tosh; Off Shield; M; Son; 3

933; Oosh-bah-chasis; Strong; M; Husband; 26
934; E-say-kep-pah; Wrinkle Face; F; Wife; 56
935; Bah-chay-cheas; Steals on Camp; M; Son; 19

936; Bah-key-day-nahbeas; Three Blackbird; F; Widow; 66

937; Bah-key-us-tay; Sharp Nose #1; M; Widower; 76

938; Dackbitsay-eck-pah-dea; Medicine Bear; M; Husband; 57
939; Is-deam-day-keas-sos; Her Road Is Plain; F; Wife; 52
940; Ah-pay-days; Goes Together; F; Daughter; 11
941; Bea-cheas; Packs the Rock; M; Son; 12

942; Chees-shepittich; Black Tail; M; Husband; 47
943; Baday-bedock-bacusheas; People That Shows; F; Wife; 45

944; Chate-oocush-shis; Bob Tail Wolf; M; Husband; 60
945; Bit-chea-bachpash; Medicine Knife; F; Wife; 58

946; Bah-tah-weas; The Bell; M; Husband; 25
947; Bah-buck-but-date-chase; No Medicine; F; Wife; 27
948; Duck-cock-bah-dah-cus; Crazy Bird; F; Daughter; 5

949; Hay-day-dee-doos; Stands Among Them; M; Husband; 53
950; Oat-chean-bah-dup-pace; Kills at Night; F; Wife; 49
951; Esuck-che-sah-keas-sos; Well Known Hawk; F; Daughter; 5

952; Ahpay-eso-chay-away-chis; Sits Before a Cloud; M; Husband; 50
953; Ea-cock-kah-beas; Fox Woman; F; Wife; 52
954; Echee-du-kosh-esos; Big Elk; M; Son; 9
955; Bob-puck-sos; Bird Among the Rocks; M; Son; 20

956; Ick-kay-ah-hoos; Lots of Stars; M; Husband; 42
957; Bah-son-day-ah-hoos; Goes First; F; Wife; 44

958; Bah-hay-chay-wat-tosh; Lone Tree; H; Husband; 61
959; Bah-put-tuck-beeday-beas; Mink; F; Wife; 62
960; E-sah-coo-dake; Carries the Arrows; M; Son; 34

961; Ish-chis-says-koos; Comes to Her Nest; F; Widow; 70

962; Ah-dah-sos-ea-kot-tosh; Little Light; M; Husband; 48
963; Esos-kay-koo-doot-chis; Takes Her Horse; F; Wife; 34
964; Umba-coan-duc-bitchase; Bear in the Mountain; M; Son; 15

161

Census of the __Crow__ Indians of __Crow__ Agency __Montana__ taken
By __J.E. Edwards__, United States Indian Agent __June 30, 1900__

Key: Number; Indian Name; English Name; Sex; Relation; Age

965; Ope-che-dup-pace; Tobacco Bull; M; Son; 9
966; Cheedup-kah-kah-dah-bis; Bull Moves On; M; Son; 7
967; Ah-dah-hes-itchis; Gets There Pretty; M; Son; 6
968; ---; Becker Little Light; M; Son; 2
969; Ba-chay-ha-what-dup-pace; Kills One Man; F; Mother; 76

970; Es-chay-kah-deas; Old Rabbit; M; Husband; 37
971; Ah-shoe-hishis; Red Hair; F; Wife; 44
972; ---; Mary Old Rabbit; F; Daughter; 15
973; Dah-kosh-bah-coos; Eagle High Up; M; Son; 10

974; Tuck-kase; Sounds of the Gun; M; Husband; 29
975; Bah-put-tay-ahoos; Plenty Otter; F; Wife; 38
976; Ock-kosh-de-dish; Antelope That Walks; F; Daughter; 7
977; ---; Frederick Sounds the Gun; M; Son; 3

978; Boat-tay-kadeas; Old Coyote; M; Husband; 39
979; Bachpash; Medicine; F; Wife; 38
980; Up-pah-sah-chers; Half White; M; Son; 18
981; Ahpay-kay-dainba-dahkis; Sings in a Cloud; M; Son; 14

982; Is-be-dah-eas; Little Firs[sic]; M; Husband; 50
983; Bea-itchis-sos; Not a Pretty Woman; F; Wife; 48
984; Bahputtay-cheedup-is; Otter Bull; M; Son; 25

985; Bachpash-esos; Big Medicine; M; Husband; 44
986; Bahduppay-chedu-chis; Strikes the One That Kills; F; Wife; 44
987; Bea-bus-sos; Rock in Front; F; Daughter; 7
988; ---; Edward Big Medicine; M; Son; 1

989; Echey-she-coopy; Crooked Foot; M; Husband; 82
990; Uck-dosh-dee-dichis; Strikes One That Charges; F; Wife; 82

991; Bah-dah-pah-keas-sos; Digs Well Known; F; Widow; 70

992; ---; Thomas Stewart; M; Husband; 28
993; Uckcheese-malapesh; Kills Over Beyond Other; F; Wife; 29
994; ---; Foster Stewart; M; Son; 1

995; Cheedup-pom-bish; Short Bull; M; Husband; 57
996; Oo-wat-doot-chis; Takes the Iron; F; Wife; 56

997; Ekoos-sheas; Eagle Turns Around; M; Widower; 36
998; E-sos-kot-bah-deas; Working Mouse; M; Son; 12

999; Esoc-cah-wah-chakoos-say; Pretty Old Man; M; Husband; 54

Census of the **Crow** Indians of **Crow** Agency **Montana** taken
By **J.E. Edwards**, United States Indian Agent **June 30, 1900**

Key: Number; Indian Name; English Name; Sex; Relation; Age

1000; Owat-baduck-key-condish; Old Woman Gone; F; Wife; 55
1001; Peah-key-tus; The Spleen; M; Son; 19

1002; Cah-kay-bachpash; Medicine Lance; F; Widow; 56

1003; Bra-bah-chey-chis; Woman Chief; M; Husband; 51
1004; Kish-sey; Big Around; F; Wife; 54

1005; Deah-kah-chis; The Eagle; M; Husband; 37
1006; Buss-sone-deah-ahoos; Goes Ahead Pretty; F; Wife; 35
1007; Con-Hah-pagh; Medicine Old Woman; F; Daughter; 14

1008; Beedick-qua-bah-dup-pace; Fools and Kills the Enemy; F; Mother; 35
1009; Shea-dah-chis; Fog All the Time; M; Son; 9
1010; Itchis-chey-ay-ah-woos; Medicine Tobacco Seed; M; Son; 2

1011; Esoch-kah-dew-os; Two Leggins; M; Husband; 50
1012; Is-bah-duck-chis; Ties Up Her Bundles; F; Wife; 36

1013; Ah-duck-che-ba-chatchis; Coo Chief; M; Husband; 25
1014; Is-ea-de-ahoos; Plenty Lodge Poles; F; Wife; 30

1015; Ah-key-oka-bee-shay; White Clay on Forehead; M; Husband; 52
1016; Be-dosh; Fire; F; Wife; 42
1017; Isben-doch-dup-pichis; Light Shield; F; Daughter; 6
1018; Keas-sos; Plain; M; Son; 14

1019; Ah-duck-chea-oss-ea-tuss; Shows His Coos; M; Husband; 33
1020; Minne-ekoshees; Turns to the Water; F; Wife; 26
1021; Oot-tay-bah-coos; Weasel High Up; F; Daughter; 6
1022; Mea-dichis; Strikes a Woman; F; Daughter; 1

1023; Ock-pay-hishis; Red Wing; M; Widower; 50

1024; Ducock-seh-hoo-dup-pace; Kills Coming to the Birds; F; Mother; 60
1025; Away-coe-ish-chisadock; The Swallow Child; M; Son; 19

1026; Bee-ditch-key-sos; Big Lake; M; Husband; 52
1027; Oo-what-dootchis; Pounds the Iron; F; Wife; 51
1028; Oat-tay-dock-kuss; Weasel Child; M; Son; 12
1029; Chate-bick-cuss; Female Wolf; F; Sister; 54

1030; E-shoe-dee-chea-ock-kin-day-dee-ditch-es; Strikes the Rider of the white maned Horse; F; Widow; 62

1031; Bah-cah-key-e-cosh; Looks to the Shield; F; Mother; 32

Census of the __Crow__ Indians of __Crow__ Agency __Montana__ taken
By __J.E. Edwards__, United States Indian Agent __June 30, 1900__

Key: Number; Indian Name; English Name; Sex; Relation; Age

1032; Bah-tah-wos; Plain Bell; M; Son; 3

1033; Dahcock-itchis; Goes Bird; M; Husband; 74
1034; Un-duck-cah-hoos; Stops at Many Places; F; Wife; 69

1035; Dachpitsa-ock-in-das; Rides a Bear; M; Husband; 56
1036; Boa-itchis; Pretty Fish; F; Wife; 49
1037; Ahdock-in-day-keasos; Rides Well Known; M; Son; 19

1038; Oo-wat-cas; Little Iron; M; Husband; 49
1039; It-chit-chea-ays; Tobacco Seed; F; Wife; 46
1040; He-dah-bah-chase; Just a Man; M; Son; 15

1041; Dah-cup-pis; Calf; M; Husband; 38
1042; Eas-sche-kay-pay; Crooked Face; F; Wife; 34
1043; Noopta-malapes; Kills Twice; F; Ad Dau; 8

1044; Bah-chee-dee-kahdeas; Old White Man #1; M; Husband; 62
1045; Bee-shay-dee-dish; Buffalo That Walks; F; Wife; 34

1046; Oke-keas-sos; Well Known Antelope; M; Husband; 36
1047; Uck-bah-he-dee-cose; Does Anything; F; Wife; 26

1048; Boa-tah-itchis; Pretty Coyote; M; Husband; 32
1049; Bah-cos; Brings Things; F; Wife; 28

1050; Bee-day-da-cuss-chis; Comes Out of the Water; F; Widow; 46
1051; Bah-show-dee-ditch; Medicine Rock; F; Daughter; 19

1052; Bim-boan-chee-dup-pis; Bull in the Water; M; Husband; 61
1053; Chee-dup-eas; Young Bull; F; Wife; 62

1054; Bah-it-chay-on-des; Does Many Good Things; M; Husband; 27
1055; Baputta-bedane-duckcoos; Otter Stays in the Water; F; Wife; 22
1056; Echey-dah-hay-day-cuss; Among the Horses; F; Daughter; 5
1057; ---; Annie D.M.G. Things; F; Daughter; 1
1058; ---; Star; F; Sister; 16

1059; Ah-puss-sah-cheas; Half White; M; Husband; 61
1060; But-shay-sut-tuss; Close Together; F; Wife; 52

1061; Iscoche-hadane-doochis; Takes Among the Enemy; M; Husband; 27
1062; Mea-suppittish; Black Woman; F; Wife; 38
1063; Pea-cah-dah-hutch; Long Piegan; M; Son; 13
1064; Hah-osh-ahoos; Plenty Red Plumes; F; Daughter; 11

Census of the __Crow__ Indians of __Crow__ Agency __Montana__ taken By __J.E. Edwards__, United States Indian Agent __June 30, 1900__

Key: Number; Indian Name; English Name; Sex; Relation; Age

1065; Isbindotch-bah-chate; Shield Chief; M; Husband; 39
1066; Esos-kean-sos; Blanket Well Known; F; Wife; 47

1067; Bah-es-way-shadock-cuss; Young Curlew; M; Husband; 48
1068; Cheasdacock-indechis; Rides a White Horse; F; Wife; 44
1069; Shu-dish; Singing Hat; F; Daughter; 12

1070; Bah-sone-dace; Goes First; F; Widow; 85

1071; Whochis-say-away-chice; Sits to the Wind; F; Widow; 54

1072; Dah-cock-teah-dish; The Bird; M; Husband; 31
1073; Is-coe-chee-dup-pace; Kills Her Enemy; F; Wife; 27
1074; By-eas; Arrow Point; M; Son; 7
1075; Epea-cot-a-wak-chis; Magpie Sits Down; Son; 3

1076; Away-choke-kadah-cockus; Bird on the Prairie; M; Husband; 46
1077; Beshay-ockain-awachis; Sits on the Blanket; F; Wife; 40
1078; ---; Stephen B. Prairie; M; Ad Son; 1

1079; Chee-sock-cuss; Long Tail; M; Husband; 43
1080; She-pea-day-tuss; No Mud; F; Wife; 38
1081; Tick-pah-che-day-de-shis; Strikes One That Pushes Him; M; Son; 14
1082; Ah-we-sos; Shows Big on the Ground; M; Son; 10
1083; ---; Lydia Long Tail; F; Daughter; 1

1084; Hay-dain-dee-chis; Strikes Among Them; F; Widow; 72
1085; Cheedup-bah-cha-ahchis; Strong Bull; M; Son; 33

1086; Bah-cup-pash; Hail; M; Husband; 33
1087; Echeedayon-duccekasses; Horses Place Well Known; F; Wife; 34

1088; It-tuch-bah-cha-chis; Strong Alone; M; Husband; 52
1089; Uck-bah-dea-ate-chase; Knows Her Medicine; F; Wife; 47

1090; Bah-dup-pay-keas-sos; Kills Well Known; F; Widow; 64

1091; Chee-dish; Hunts; M; Husband; 44
1092; Echee-dahay-dane-duckoos; Stays With the Horse; F; Wife; 40
1093; E-sop-pah-dah-tus; Has No Moccasin; M; Son; 18
1094; E-soa-kay-ate-chace; Knows His Horse; F; Daughter; 7

1095; Bah-dah-sure-ha-wattus; One Blue Bead; M; Husband; 52
1096; Ush-coe-sut-tah-doochis; Takes One Close to Camp; F; Wife; 50
1097; Un-dah-heahsos; Surrounds the Enemy Strong; M; Son; 15

Census of the __Crow__ Indians of __Crow__ Agency __Montana__ taken By __J.E. Edwards__, United States Indian Agent __June 30, 1900__

Key: Number; Indian Name; English Name; Sex; Relation; Age

1098; Duck-bit-chay-nowpu-oze; Mad at the Bear; M; Husband; 38
1099; Is-eap-che-bish-ay; Got a Pipe; F; Wife; 42
1100; Is-bah-it-chis; Got Pretty Things; F; Daughter; 13
1101; Dah-coe-tay-dootchis; Catches the Sioux; F; Daughter; 7

1102; ---; Charles Ten Bear; M; Husband; 24
1103; ---; Mary Bear's Tooth; F; Wife; 20

1104; Ah-she-tas; Sharp Horn; M; Husband; 59
1105; Bea-cot-ish-tup-pay; Woman With Eyes Open; F; Wife; 59

1106; Bah-chay-bah-day-kah; Foolish Man; M; Husband; 38
1107; Hay-dane-ah-seas; Shows In a Crowd; F; Wife; 32
1108; ---; George Foolish Man; M; Son; 3

1109; E-cuss-sos-esos; Big Snake; M; Husband; 55
1110; Chedoc-cuss-bahduppas; Kills In the Morning; F; Wife; 49

1111; Boa-bah-cos; Fish High Up; M; Husband; 54
1112; Chuch-ko-dootchis; Takes Five; F; Wife; 52

1113; Bee-put-tah-bah-coos; Owl Above; M; Husband; 32
1114; E-che-doe-it-chis; Brings Pretty Horses; F; Wife; 34
1115; Ah-dah-che-e-coss; Sees the Coos; F; Daughter; 12
1116; Ume-beas; Paint Woman; F; Daughter; 10

1117; Chee-dup-um-be-chisos; Bull That Don't Fall Down; M; Husband; 47
1118; Ah-see-tus; Shows; F; Wife; 34
1119; Is-been-dot-bish-eas; Got a Shield; F; Mother; 72

1120; Esop-pay-shoes; Blue Moccasin; M; --[Widower]; 56

1121; Bah-cock-coe-tah-hoos; Comes From Above; M; Husband; 34
1122; Um-bah-cone-dah-coos; Stops Above; F; Wife; 37
1123; ---; Hannah Comes Above; F; Daughter; 3

1124; Bin-day-sop-pay-dus; River Crow; M; Husband; 35
1125; Bah-pah-deas; Medicine; F; Wife; 31

1126; Echedock-ichay-ockindays; Rides a Pretty Horse #2; M; Husband; 27
1127; Esutsehoom-meas; Sage Woman; F; Wife; 34
1128; Ashmitse-makpash; The Song is Medicine; F; Daughter; 9

1129; Cha-qua-bah-aco; Charges Five Times; M; Husband; 28
1130; Bea-ah-wah-chis; Woman That Sits Down; F; Wife; 24
1131; E-hum-dah-pace; Kills in Sleep; F; Daughter; 6

Census of the __Crow__ Indians of __Crow__ Agency __Montana__ taken
By __J.E. Edwards__, United States Indian Agent __June 30, 1900__

Key: Number; Indian Name; English Name; Sex; Relation; Age

1132; Is-co-chee-ahoos; Got Many Enemies; M; Husband; 41
1133; Bah-put-tah-dock-cus; Young Otter; F; Wife; 50

1134; Bee-dup-dah-cus; Young Beaver; M; Husband; 54
1135; Bah-kah-beas; Hoop Woman; F; Wife; 58

1136; Umbah-owedup-ate-chace; Knows Where He Finds Things; M; Husband; 39
1137; Qua-dus; Between; F; Wife; 34

1138; Eche-dock-in-days; Rides a Horse; M; Husband; 46
1139; Ah-cam-dah-pace; Kills On Top; F; Wife; 42
1140; Bah-day-key-sut-tus; Two-Barrelled Gun; M; Son; 13
1141; E-shua-eas; Feather Neck; F; Daughter; 6
1142; Edock-bah-pah; Medicine Form; F; Daughter; 4
1143; Bah-dee-shis; Jerked Meat; M; Son; 19

1144; Bah-pus; Cliff; F; Widow; 48

1145; Echa-duck-kosh-awaychis; Sitting Elk; M; Husband; 60
1146; Dah-cock-beas; Bird Woman; F; Wide; 57

1147; Cuck-ca-coo-day-deechis; Strikes One With a Lance; F; Widow; 52
1148; ---; Louise; F; Daughter; 13

1149; Dosh-shay-e-coos; Charges Madly on Enemy; M; Husband; 28
1150; Ush-doop-tah-coe-dee; Strikes Two Camps; F; Wife; 32
1151; Tuck-kit-chay-ahoos; Shoots Plenty; F; Daughter; 5

1152; Echeday-itchay-ockinday; Rides a Pretty Horse; M; Husband; 32
1153; Ah-woos-ah-cay-dus; On Top of the Sweathouse; F; Wife; 30
1154; Cah-puh-dus-itchis; Good Medicine; F; Daughter; 11
1155; Coo-bah-pay-day-pah; Kills the Same Day; F; Daughter; 5
1156; ---; Carson Rides Pretty Horse; M; Son; 1

1157; Daek-itchis; Pretty Eagle; M; Husband; 55
1158; Is-been-dutch-chis; Pretty Shield; F; Wife; 52
1159; Deak-kosh-sheedish; Yellow Eagle; M; Son; 4

1160; Da-cose; Goes On; M; Husband; 59
1161; Been-dotch-us-eas; Shield That Shows; F; Wife; 52

1162; Ike-cook-cus; Even; M; Husband; 29
1163; Ush-dea-itchis; Makes a Pretty Lodge; F; Wife; 30

1164; Up-pah-keas-sos; Cloud Well Known; M; Husband; 40
1165; Con-dah-cock-cus; Old Bird Woman; F; Wife; 39

Census of the __Crow__ Indians of __Crow__ Agency __Montana__ taken
By __J.E. Edwards__, United States Indian Agent __June 30, 1900__

Key: Number; Indian Name; English Name; Sex; Relation; Age

1166; Ush-coe-tah-cose-shis; Helps the Whole Camp; M; Son; 15
1167; ---; Ben Cloud Well Known; M; Son; 1

1168; Cho-say-ick-cosh; Sees a White Horse; M; Husband; 46
1169; Dosh-day-tuss; No Name; F; Wife; 46
1170; ---; Peter S. White Horse; M; Son; 16

1171; Oo-shis; Hole; M; Husband; 27
1172; Ah-shus-ah-was-days; Horn Dropped Down; F; Wife; 21

1173; Dackbitsay-des-dish; Bear That Walks; M; Widower; 40

1174; Is-shay-dus; Hairy On Top of His Head; M; Husband; 54
1175; Bin-doch-eso-chain-dus; Sheep in Front; F; Wife; 55

1176; Duck-cock-bea-itchis; Pretty Woman Bird; F; Widow; 44
1177; Esho-dochea-dootchis; Takes Horse With White Mane; F; Daughter; 15
1178; Bah-shay-cha-dup-pace; Kills The Chief; F; Daughter; 10

1179; Duckbitchay-eas; Bear's Tooth; M; Husband; 46
1180; Bah-chay-un-dah-pace; Kills Many Men; F; Wife; 44
1181; Ope-bah-dah-kis; Tobacco Sings; F; Ad Dau; 7

1182; Ish-tay-easos; Big Eyes; M; Widower; 59

1183; Esa-pis; Shot in the Face; M; Husband; 62
1184; Hoo-chis; Wind Blowing; F; Wife; 56

1185; Uck-cha-key-chis; Spies on the Enemy; M; Husband; 38
1186; Us-dosh-cane-dootchis; Takes By Side of the Camp; F; Wife; 42

1187; Backpash-pash; Medicine Feather; F; Widow; 52
1188; Edeke-oke-pus; Shoots Tent Poles; F; Niece; 11

1189; Baduck-key-dootchis; Takes a Gun #1; M; Husband; 60
1190; Ah-way-chase; Knows the Ground; F; Wife; 62

1191; Bah-owe-keas-sos; Brings Well Known; F; Widow; 52
1192; Bosh-dootchis; Takes a Feather; F; Daughter; 15

1193; Bah-cup-pah-e-sos; Big Hail; M; Husband; 32
1194; Bah-cuch-ca-beas; Striped Snake Woman; F; Wife; 26
1195; Beshay-oek-bahwaychis; Sits With a Buffalo; M; Son; 7

1196; Esop-ponta-chahada-dose; Among the Sheep; F; ---; 26

Census of the __Crow__ Indians of __Crow__ Agency __Montana__ taken
By __J.E. Edwards__, United States Indian Agent __June 30, 1900__

Key: Number; Indian Name; English Name; Sex; Relation; Age

1197; Ahwah-cah-wassahwah-chis; Face Toward the Mountain; M; Husband; 47
1198; Peace-hay-duce; Comes Behind; F; Wife; 40
1199; Oo-sha-cane-cah-pis; Sits Over a Hole; F; Daughter; 11
1200; Dah-cock-shee-dish; Yellow Bird; F; Daughter; 7

1201; Ah-dean-dace; The Trail; F; Widow; 50
1202; Is-chie-say-be-shis; Got a Nest; M; Son; 17
1203; Is-been-dotch-ah-hoos; Plenty Shield; F; 15
1204; Eche-de-she-chace; Likes the Horses; F; Daughter; 11

1205; Up-pay-oakpis; Shot in the Nose; M; Husband; 29
1206; Is-coe-chea-ache-chase; Knows the Enemy; F; Wife; 26
1207; Ahwacce-ischeshay-ahoos; Plenty Swallow; M; Son; 9
1208; ---; John Shot in the Nose; Son; 3

1209; Been-dosh-shay-bachpash; Medicine Top; M; Husband; 34
1210; Bah-ay-ba-sas; Has Things; F; Wife; 35
1211; Isbahca-kay-bot-posh; Her Medicine Shell; F; Daughter; 6
1212; ---; Susie Spotted; F; Daughter; 9
1213; Bahkay-ahoos; Gives Lots of Things Away; F; Daughter; 7

1214; Duckbitchay-che-dace; Bear Gets Up; M; Husband; 66
1215; Bah-put-tah-dew-pus; Two Otters; F; Wife; 61

1216; It-tut-dahcock-cus; Bird By Himself; F; Widower; 60

1217; Chate-shaduckbitchay; Mad Bear Wolf; M; Husband; 56
1218; Minkuus ; Onion; F; Wife; 68
1219; Mideras-ichis; Does Good Things; M; Son; 17
1220; Dah-hea-os; Surrounds the Enemy; M; Son; 21

1221; Boop-chis; Ball; M; Husband; 36
1222; Bea-sheedes; Yellow Woman; F; Wife; 35

1223; Ukbadapa-ishtukea-doochis; Takes the Killer of Guns; M; Husband; 26
1224; Coe-what-tay-doochis; Takes Both Together; F; Wife; 26
1225; Uk-keam-duck-chis; Ties on the Foretop; F; Daughter; 10
1226; Bah-dock-key-huchkeydooch; Takes a Long Gun; F; Daughter; 3

1227; Bah-put-tah-cahdeas; Old Otter; F; Widow; 54

1228; He-dah-wah-chace; He is a Man Now; M; Husband; 57
1229; Ecupe-pah-doocthis; Takes the Hat; F; Wife; 52

1230; Istuckea-bah-chate-chice; Gun Chief; M; Husband; 53
1231; Cuck-cock-in-days; Rides a Spotted Horse; F; Wife; 40

Census of the __**Crow**__ Indians of __**Crow**__ Agency __**Montana**__ taken By __**J.E. Edwards**__, United States Indian Agent __**June 30, 1900**__

Key: Number; Indian Name; English Name; Sex; Relation; Age

1232; Ushdosh-katabah-sos; Runs Beside the Camp; M; Son; 6

1233; Echeta-ichis; Good Horses; M; Husband; 35
1234; E-hum-be-shoes; More of Them; F; Wife; 24
1235; Been-dah-chate-dase; Goes to the Fort; F; Daughter; 6

1236; Ea-cus-sos; Snake; F; Widow; 58
1237; E-sah-duck-chis; Ties Up the Arrows; F; Daughter; 18

1238; Beedee-chay-hay-day-dus; Among the Willows; Widow; 64

1239; E-sah-eduse-see-shis; Broken Arrow; M; Widower; 40

1240; Duckbitchay-uppa-pushcoos; Cuts the Bears Ears; M; Husband; 50
1241; It-chis; Good; F; Wife; 47
1242; Bah-dah-kit-chice; Sings Good; M; Son; 17

1243; Hay-day-dose; Right Among Them; M; Husband; 53
1244; E-Dah-hoos; Comes Herself; F; Wife; 57

1245; Kahdeas; Old Woman; M; Widower; 60
1246; Dadough-cheada-itchice; Leads the Camp Pretty; F; Daughter; 13

1247; Odup-dah-pace; Finds Them and Kills Them; M; Widower; 47
1248; Echa-dow-keas-sos; Brings Horses Well Known; F; Daughter; 12

1249; Is-chay-dah-kish-shay; Knot Between the Eyes; M; Husband; 59
1250; Oo-wat-doot-chase; Takes the Iron; F; Wife; 54
1251; Dock-shay-dah-beas; Three Coons; F; Daughter; 17

1252; Cuck-cah-wah-chice; Sits Down Spotted; M; Husband; 38
1253; Bah-chay-cheas; Steals on the Camp; F; Wife; 21
1254; ---; John Spotted; M; Son; 3

1255; Echee-dah-hoos; Plenty Horses; M; Widower; 48

1256; Dah-cock-bah-coos; Bird Above; M; Husband; 34
1257; Oo-tah-cuck-kis; Spotted Weasel; F; Wife; 32
1258; Be-day-tuss; Like a Fire; M; Son; 12
1259; Hoo-chice-sos; Comes Against the Wind; M; Son; 9
1260; Poop-kit-tah-cuck-kis; Spotted Snow Bird; F; Daughter; 7

1261; Chate-kah-we-sis; Skins a Wolf; M; Husband; 59
1262; E-sos-kah-we-sis; Has Horses; F; Wife; 52

1263; ---; Richard Cummins; M; Husband; 27

Census of the __**Crow**__ Indians of __**Crow**__ Agency __**Montana**__ taken By __**J.E. Edwards**__, United States Indian Agent __**June 30, 1900**__

Key: Number; Indian Name; English Name; Sex; Relation; Age

1264; Bashow-deeditch-chaysos; Big Medicine Rock; F; Wife; 19

1265; Oo-what-ah-shoes; Iron Head; M; Husband; 21
1266; Bah-ow-duck-coos; Brings Things Always; F; Wife; 15

1267; Be-dook-sah-e-duse; Alligator Stands Up; M; Husband; 55
1268; Bah-put-tea-hosh; The Other Otter; F; Wife; 54
1269; Boat-tah-cah-dush-sis; Coyote Runs; M; Widower; 40
1270; Ah-pah-de-deas; Porcupine Woman; F; Daughter; 4
1271; ---; Arnold Kosta; M; Son; 20

1272; Ea-cus-sah-che-dup-pis; Snake Bull; M; Husband; 49
1273; Oo-what-de-chise; Strikes the Iron; F; Wife; 35
1274; Boo-duke-pah-keasos; Plain Cedar; F; Daughter; 11
1275; Che-quas; Is Sweet Now; M; Son; 6
1276; ---; Matie Snake Bull; F; Daughter; 1

1277; ---; Pius Hill; M; Orphan; 17
1278; Bea-ahdutch-shebeas; Woman That Farms; F; Sister; 11

1279; Eas-ea-coas; Covers His Face; M; Husband; 33
1280; Ah-sah-date-dootchis; Takes Horses on Prairie; F; Wife; 23

1281; Bee-dish; Walking; M; Husband; 44
1282; Uck-bah-du-ick-cosh; Looks at the Medicine; F; Wife; 49

1283; Eas-shee-day; Yellow Face; M; Widower; 75
~~1284; Bea-itchay-de-chice; Strikes the Pretty Woman; F; Wife; 72~~

1284; Kat-toah-tay-hishes; Red Shirt; M; Husband; 23
1285; Ahwacos-che-dapachbash; Medicine Ground Cedar; F; Wife; 23

1286; Ah-pit-bah-coos; Crane in the Sky; M; Husband; 60
1287; Be-dup-hishis; Red Beaver; F; Wife; 65
1288; Bahkey-dah-wah-chice; Blackbird Sits Down; F; Daughter; 12
1289; Is-tah-dase-cheas; Big Squirrel; M; Son; 15

1290; Ah-way-kah-wah-chedays; Mountain Pocket; M; Husband; 57
1291; E-chope-pice; Shoots Her Foot; F; Wife; 50
1292; Esos-kee-dit-bachpash; Medicine Horsewhip; M; Son; 27

1293; Ah-dah-doo-be-shay; Shot in the Arm; M; Husband; 57
1294; Bea-dootchice; Takes a Woman; F; Wife; 50

1295; She-chock-ay-dus; On Top of the Hill; M; Husband; 61
1296; Isbada-ha-wat-atechice; Knows the Yearling; F; Wife; 53

Census of the __Crow__ Indians of __Crow__ Agency __Montana__ taken
By __J.E. Edwards__, United States Indian Agent __June 30, 1900__

Key: Number; Indian Name; English Name; Sex; Relation; Age

1297; Bosh-che-de-cot-tay; White Man; M; Husband; 46
1298; Bah-ouch-cah-ahoos; Plenty Striped Snake; F; Wife; 52
1299; Ah-dean-day-ate-chice; Knows the Road; F; Daughter; 17
1300; Dah-cock-che-deas-sos; Not Afraid of a Bird; M; Son; 10
1301; Dah-cock-ah-pah-ahoos; Bird With Plenty of Wings Going Around; F; Daughter; 9
1302; Ecupe-pah-bah-puc-tosh; Hat Otter; F; Daughter; 3

1303; Bea-it-chay; Pretty Woman; F; Widow; 42

1304; Edosh-uck-bah-dup-pace; Kills With His Bro-in-law; M; Husband; 46
1305; Un-di-day-it-chice; Walks Pretty; F; Wife; 44
1306; Oak-cah-sis; Antelope; F; Daughter; 15

1307; ---; James Buffalo; M; Husband; 26
1308; Bah-cup-pah-cheas; White Hail; F; Wife; 24
1309; Isbindotch-abahic-deas; Does Everything With Shield; F; Daughter; 7
1310; Cah-ditch-chea-ahoos; Plenty Lightning; F; Daughter; 6

1311; Duckbitchay-che-sus; Bear's Tail; M; Widower; 60
1312; Duckbitchay-undatechas; Knows Where the Bear Goes; F; Daughter; 16
1313; Ah-way-cah-wah-seas; Shows in the Mountains; M; Son; 26

1314; Ah-pah-dee-esos; Big Porcupine; M; Husband; 44
1315; Un-doo-cosh-keas-sos; Holds Well Known; F; Wife; 41

1316; Cheedup-bah-chate-chice; Bull Chief; M; Husband; 64
1317; Istuckey-bah-chate-chice; Long Gun; F; Wife; 58
1318; Itchit-che-ays; Medicine Tobacco; M; Gr Son; 10

1319; Ah-shue-cheas; White Horn; F; Widow; 54

1320; Isbitch-itchis-saeacocktus; Little Whetstone; M; Husband; 60
1321; E-che-dah-keas-sos; Horse Well Known; F; Wife; 41

1322; Che-chuck-key-sis; Big Around; M; Husband; 60
1323; Cah-eoa-doot-chice; Takes All the Horses; F; Wife; 52
1324; Ecup-pah-ate-chice; Knows Her Hat; F; Mother; 76

1325; Shis-sheas; Curly; M; Husband; 50
1326; Bin-dotch-dootchis; Takes a Shield; F; Wife; 52
1327; Awandook-cookus-detacocus; Bird Another Year; F; Daughter; 4

1328; Dah-cus; Balls; M; Husband; 38
1329; Petakus; Ten; F; Wife; 22

Census of the __**Crow**__ Indians of __**Crow**__ Agency __**Montana**__ taken
By __**J.E. Edwards**__, United States Indian Agent __**June 30, 1900**__

Key: Number; Indian Name; English Name; Sex; Relation; Age

1330; Be-day-dish-sos; Don't Get In; F; Widow; 48
1331; Ah-pah-de-e-wan-deas; Plays With Medicine; F; Daughter; 10
1332; Un-day-it-chice; Goes Ahead Pretty; F; Daughter; 12

1333; Ah-pit-tus; The Crane; M; Husband; 44
1334; Echee-uck-pah-duppace; Kills With the Horses; F; Wife; 41
1335; Che-soup-pus; End of the Tail; M; Son; 15
1336; ---; Luella Crane; F; Daughter; 1

1337; Oat-say-bee-dosh; Fire Weasel; M; Husband; 69
1338; Ah-dough-chea-bah-pash; Medicine Where She Stops; F; Wife; 64

1339; Beas; Rock; M; Father; 38
1340; Bashow-de-chite-chase; Medicine Rock; F; Daughter; 12

1341; Duck-cock-ah-shoes; Bird Head; M; Husband; 42
1342; Dah-ah-sheas; Shows Going; F; Wife; 36
1343; Baheah-wat-tay-dace; Hoop Goes a Long Way; M; Son; 9
1344; Is-coe-che-che-dish; Afraid of His Enemy; M; Son; 15
1345; Bisheah-duckbitchay; Bears Dog; M; Son; 21

1346; Duck-peas; Hugs #2; M; Husband; 54
1347; Awahshe-hay-danedoochis; Takes a Man in a Fog; F; Wife; 58
1348; Bah-duck-it-chise; Sings Pretty; M; Son; 22

1349; Ah-wah-coan-de-dish; Walks In Middle of Ground; M; Husband; 64
1350; Ea-cot-tus; Little; F; Wife; 55

1351; Bashow-dechit-chabacoos; Medicine Rock Above; M; Husband; 33
1352; E-cheam-dah-pace; Kills a Horse; F; Wife; 32
1353; Bah-keam-boo-dish; Bull Blackbird; M; Son; 10
1354; ---; Josh Medicine Rock Above; M; Son; 1

1355; E-chean-dah-cock-cus; Bird Horse; M; Husband; 26
1356; Bah-show-de-chit-chase; Medicine Rock; F; Wife; 24
1357; Ea-dea-it-chise; Pretty Lodge Poles; F; Daughter; 7

1358; Ea-dane-deas; He Does It; M; Husband; 28
1359; Bah-cock-coo-dush; She Is High Up; F; Wife; 32
1360; Cheach-cues; Chicken; F; Daughter; 11
1361; Cah-pah-dee-dock-cus; Young Medicine; M; Son; 7
1362; Bashow-deechit-chayesos; Big Medicine Rock; F; Mother; 52

1363; Dupe-pah-wah-dup-pace; Kills Twice; F; Widow; 45
1364; Un-dah-pace; Kills Plenty; F; Daughter; 15
1365; Ea-dane-dah-cock-cus; Bird Among Them; M; Son; 7

173

Census of the __Crow__ Indians of __Crow__ Agency __Montana__ taken By __J.E. Edwards__, United States Indian Agent __June 30, 1900__

Key: Number; Indian Name; English Name; Sex; Relation; Age

1366; Eat-tosh-tay-keasos; Plain Shirt; F; Daughter; 6

1367; Bah-cah-dish-tah-beas; Heifer Woman; F; Mother; 36
1368; Bea-bashay-e-sit-chace; Likes the Summer; F; Daughter; 6

1369; Bin-dosh-shay-sheedish; Yellow Top; M; Husband; 59
1370; Esos-kah-wishes; Has Horses; F; Wife; 64

1371; Bah-chay-cheas; Steals on the Camp; F; Widow; 64

1372; Eah-cah-shues; Blue Chin; F; Widow; 59

1373; Eas-chay-cuck-kis; Spotted Rabbit; M; Husband; 34
1374; Itchit-chay-bachpash; Medicine Tobacco; F; Wife; 40
1375; Uckbah-deas-ewahick-deas; Does Ev'yth'g with her Med; F; Daughter; 17
1376; Oke-push; Badly Shot; M; Son; 3
1377; Ea-sos; Hairy; F; Mother; 66

1378; Be-dase-she-cash; Looks at the Water; F; Widow; 62

1379; Bah-doo-peas; Scolds; M; Husband; 35
1380; ---; Mrs. Ben Gardiner; F; Wife; 37
1381; ---; Thomas Gardiner; M; Son; 16
1382; ---; Frank Gardiner; M; Son; 14
1383; ---; Amelia Gardiner; F; Daughter; 12

1384; Dah-cock-keah-sos; Bird Well Known; M; Husband; 34
1385; Bea-dosh-tay-tush; Woman Without a Name; F; Wife; 27
1386; Ahwahcan-dah-cock-cus; Mountain Bird; M; Son; 3

1387; Bah-ea-cah-keas-sos; Sees Well Known; F; Widow; 50

1388; Eas-chee-key-pah; Crooked Face; H; Husband; 60
1389; Isbin-Doch-bachatechic; Strikes the Shield First; F; Wife; 40
1390; Dah-cock-cah-doosh-sis; Bird That Runs; F; Daughter; 15
1391; Doop-pah-e-che-dosh; Brings Two Horses; M; Son; 6

1392; Bah-ich-cah-keas-sos; Sees Well Known; F; Widow; 58

1393; Beeda-dosh-cane-dechis; Sits By Side of Water; F; Widow; 55
1394; Ope-che-chuck-kis; Round Tobacco; F; Ad Dau; 15
1395; ---; Charles Brown; M; Son; 23

1396; ---; Holder White Wings; M; Batchelor[sic]; 22

1397; Ecupe-pah-wish-de-chice; Strikes the One With Hat; F; Widow; 54

174

Census of the __Crow__ Indians of __Crow__ Agency __Montana__ taken
By __J.E. Edwards__, United States Indian Agent __June 30, 1900__

Key: Number; Indian Name; English Name; Sex; Relation; Age

1398; Ah-dah-cuck-kay; Spotted Arm; M; Husband; 52
1399; Ah-dow-chea-keas-sos; Where She Stops Well Known; F; Wife; 54

1400; Um-bah-chea-keas-sos; Fights Well Known #2; M; Husband; 38
1401; Isbeen-dotchpa-duckiss; Shield That Sings; F; Wife; 34

1402; Itchis-shaydane-dechase; Strikes On Top Of Head; M; Husband; 37
1403; Be-shay-e-hosh; The Other Buffalo; F; Wife; 36
1404; Awacco-ish-chicay-eacott; Little Swallow; M; Son; 10
1405; Ah-pe-hosh; The Other Leaf; F; Daughter; 1

1406; Eche-dae-kosh-kahdeas; Old Elk; M; Husband; 41
1407; Ookish-dean-day-ah-hoos; Antelope Trails; F; Wife; 40
1408; E-cheam-push-cush; Cuts the Horse; M; Son; 10
1409; ---; Mary Old Elk; F; Daughter; 3

1410; Bah-shoes-shays; Red Feather; F; Widow; 52
1411; Ea-dea-cah-dees; Old Lodge Pole; M; Son; 16

1412; Eas-pah-pus-say; Round Face; M; Husband; 52
1413; Bout-tah-bah-hoos; Coyote That Howls; F; Wife; 50
1414; Bah-touch-owe-duck-coos; Brings Things all the time; M; Son; 18

1415; Nas-ehas; The Other Heart; M; Batchelor[sic]; 26

1416; Ah-dup-pice; Hides; M; Husband; 38
1417; Hay-day-tah-wah-sos; Goes Through Her Enemies; F; Wife; 34
1418; Uck-bah-dea-ah-hoos; Plenty Medicine; F; Daughter; 11
1419; Ock-che-dup-pice; Bull Deer; M; Son; 5
1420; Ate-shedahcock; Lives Everywhere; M; Son; 1

1421; ---; Charles Clawson; M; Batchelor[sic]; 28

1422; Ah-day-shay-chee-dish; Hunts to Die; M; Husband; 62
1423; Esos-kay-it-chis; Her Horse Is Pretty; F; Wife; 52

1424; ---; Henry Reed; M; Husband; 26
1425; Ahwaycook-cordetah-heas; Goes to Ground Every Day; F; Wife; 23

1426; Archie-minnay-tus; No Milk; M; Husband; 42
1427; Ah-wane-dane-duck-koos; Stays Out Doors; F; Wife; 48
1428; Um-bah-dea-itchis; His Work Is Good; F; Daughter; 16

1429; Duckbitchay-ucpah-dacus; Ghost Bear; M; Husband; 52
1430; Is-dotch-chea-ate-chase; Knows Her Prisoners; F; Wife; 50

Census of the __Crow__ Indians of __Crow__ Agency __Montana__ taken By __J.E. Edwards__, United States Indian Agent __June 30, 1900__

Key: Number; Indian Name; English Name; Sex; Relation; Age

1431; Chate-e-cah-duse; Runs the Wolf; M; Widower; 62

1432; Ah-way-sheas; Fog; M; Husband; 32
1433; Isbahcah-bah-duckiss; Hoop That Sings; F; Wife; 26

1434; Bah-touch-e-cook-cosh; Hears Everyway; M; Husband; 44
1435; Dahcock-ah-wah-chice; Bird Sits Down; F; Wife; 36
1436; Un-de-chay-itchice; Strikes Pretty; M; Son; 15
1437; Esock-chice; The Hawk; M; Son; 23

1438; Ah-key-chice; The Wet; M; Husband; 50
1439; Uck-sah-ey-chase; Knows Her Mother; F; Wife; 45
1440; Bah-key-cush-sheas; Hoop That Runs; M; Son; 14
1441; Dah-say-cah-wees; Bad Heart: M; Son; 21
1442; Bah-shoes; Feather; F; M-in-law; 54

1443; Ut-che-key-chis; Spies on the Enemy #2; M; Husband; 35
1444; Bahput-tah-bock-bus; Otter Hoop; F; Wife; 24
1445; Ook-bish-cus; White Tailed Deer; F; Daughter; 7
1446; Oot-tah-dee-dish; Walking Weasel; F; Daughter; 4

1447; Ah-way-cah-wah-sheas; Mountain ThatShows; F; Widow; 45
1448; Bah-put-tah-beas; Woman Otter; F; Mother; 70

1449; Ish-cos; Back of the Neck; M; Husband; 64
1450; Co-cosh-beas; Corn Woman; F; Wife; 54
1451; Ea-cah-pish; Flat Mouth; M; Son; 25

1452; Ah-wah-key-sos; Big Sky; M; Husband; 44
1453; Oo-ah-wah-pash; Medicine Wife; F; Wife; 34

1454; Um-bah-cone-cahs; Comes From Above; F; --;[Divorcee]; 25
1455; Bick-kah-keas-sos; Well Known Mare; F; Daughter; 8
1456; ---; Fannie C. Above; F; Daughter; 1

1457; Bit-che-doot-chis; Grabs the Knife; F; Widow; 58
1458; ---; Dick Hawk; M; Son; 24

1459; Ush-ase-bah-sos; Charges on the Camp; M; Husband; 64
1460; Be-shea-bachpash; Medicine Heifer; F; Wife; 60

1461; Chee-dup-chos-us; Grey Bull; M; Husband; 39
1462; Ha-dane-e-cush-chice; Takes Out of a Crowd; F; Wife; 42
1463; Dock-ke-days; Goes to Fight; F; Daughter; 6
1464; ---; Augusta Grey Bull; F; Daughter; 3

Census of the __Crow__ Indians of __Crow__ Agency __Montana__ taken By __J.E. Edwards__, United States Indian Agent __June 30, 1900__

Key: Number; Indian Name; English Name; Sex; Relation; Age

1465; As-says-das; Goes to the House; F; Widow; 48

1466; Padutch-chay-sheedish; Yellow Crow; M; Husband; 50
1467; Is-coe-chea-ate-chace; Knows Her Enemy; F; Wife; 51
1468; Ah-shoe-che-dish; Hunts the House; F; Mother; 75

1469; Duck-pace; Hugs; F; Widow; 62

1470; Duckbitchay-boo-dish; Male Bear; M; Widower; 28
1471; Ha-wan-da-bachpash; Where He Goes Is Medicine; F; Daughter; 13

1472; Ah-pit-bah-dock-cus; Crazy Crane; M; Husband; 52
1473; Un-dee-ditch-chis; Walks Pretty; F; Wife; 50

1474; Ush-cup-cah-weas; Bad Dutchman; M; Husband; 32
1475; Boa-doo-pus; Two Fish; F; Wife; 32
1476; Ome-bachpash; Medicine Paint; M; Son; 3

1477; Ah-duck-chea-ahoos; Plenty Coos; M; Husband; 52
1478; Tick-bah-dup-pace; Kills Together; F; Wife; 37
1479; Kah-quah-ah-soos; Everybody Knows Him; M; Ad Son; 10

1480; Bea-it-chice; Pretty Rock; F; Widow; 54

1481; Eas-pea-os-seas; Lion That Shows; M; Husband; 52
1482; Cuck-kis; Spotted; F; Wife; 36
1483; Bondonpaha-dane-dacacus; Bird In the Cedars; M; Son; 17
1484; Ock-e-hosh; The Other Antelope; F; Daughter; 15
1485; Dutch-choa-dock-cus; Muskrat Daughter; F; Daughter; 7
1486; Dah-he-os; Surrounded; M; Son; 4

1487; Bee-tah-was; Bell Rock; M; Husband; 59
1488; Kah-wish; Bushy; F; Wife; 54
1489; Dahcock-bah-soos; Bird High Up; M; Son; 19

1490; Ecupe-pahda-cock-cuss; Bird Hat; M; Husband; 32
1491; Ischis-sayah-wondabachis; Sits In Her Nest; F; Wife; 32
1492; Bon-don-pah-bah-coos; Cedar High Up; M; Son; 14
1493; Cheeup-be-das-dace; Bull Walks to Water; M; Son; 7
1494; Bah-apah-dahcoos-days; Walks to Growing Things; F; Daughter; 5

1495; Bah-put-tah-dock-cuss; Young Otter; M; Widower; 62

1496; It-tut-doot-chice; Takes By Herself; F; Widow; 52

1497; Bea-it-chise-sos; Not a Pretty Woman; F; Widow; 50

Census of the __Crow__ Indians of __Crow__ Agency __Montana__ taken By __J.E. Edwards__, United States Indian Agent __June 30, 1900__

Key: Number; Indian Name; English Name; Sex; Relation; Age

1498; Badupayish-tuckey-dootchis; Takes Gun From 1 That Kill; M; Husband; 28
1499; Bea-cose; The Woman; F; Wife; 22
1500; Akean-badicksha-bapashon; Mden[Medicine] Ties Knot On Her Head; F; Daughter; 6
1501; Ock-che-dup-pish; Bull Antelope; M; Son; 5

1502; Utch-itch-ist-ton-tus; Notch; M; Husband; 38
1503; Bahduppay-ate-chice; Known to Kill; F; Wife; 35
1504; Dahcock-hay-day-dus; Among the Birds; M; Son; 10
1505; Eak-kay-hishes; Red Star; M; Son; 21
1506; Bish-doot-chise; Takes a Blanket; F; Mother; 55

1507; Bah-put-tah-cheas; White Otter; M; Husband; 59
1508; Oo-wat-tus; The Iron; F; Wife; 56
1509; ---; Ben Gardiner; M; Son; 20

1510; Ish-bee-bachpash; His Rock Is Medicine; M; Husband; 35
1511; Mea-she-pit-tay; Black Woman; F; Wife; 34

1512; Ah-cane-dah-pace; Kills Across the Water; F; Widow; 60

1513; Bish-cah-cheduppish; Bull Dog; M; Husband; 41
1514; Bea-cowees; Bad woman; F; Wife; 44
1515; Boa-do-chis; Rats the Fish; M; Son; 20

1516; Bah-son-day; Goes Ahead; F; Widow; 18
1517; Uck-pah-dee-itchice; Julia High Hawk; F; S-in-law; 24

1518; Kah-kay-de-chis; Strikes the Lance; F; Widow; 56

1519; Duckbitshaydoo-pus; Two Bears; M; Husband; 51
1520; Bim-bean-dee-dish; Walks In the Water; F; Wife; 49

1521; Bah-coop-pash; Sick; M; Husband; 32
1522; Bachay-bahchot-dahpace; Kills a Strong Man; F; Wife; 32
1523; It-tut-bah-cheas; Fights Alone; M; Son; 10
1524; Ahway-cone-away-chice; Sits on High Ground; M; Son; 6

1525; Bah-op-pish; Shot In the Hand; M; Husband; 57
1526; Ecupe-pah-che-shis; Puts On a Hat; F; Wife; 51

1527; Away-caway-dane-duckpitsa; Bear In the Mountains; M; Widower; 55

1528; Esop-pee-e-wishes; Hairy Moccasin; M; Husband; 47
1529; Bah-wah-wat-tays; Takes Quick; F; Wife; 40
1530; Eak-ka-dah-cock-us; Bird's Eggs; M; Son; 10

Census of the __Crow__ Indians of __Crow__ Agency __Montana__ taken
By __J.E. Edwards__, United States Indian Agent __June 30, 1900__

Key: Number; Indian Name; English Name; Sex; Relation; Age

1531; ---; Mary Hairy Moccasin; F; Daughter; 3

1532; Dackpitsay-cha-bedock-sahoos; Bear Comes From Below; M; Widower; 60
1533; Bah-dup-pace-sos; Don't Kill; M; Son; 9

1534; Ah-cah-pish-sis; Comes Up Red; M; Husband; 38
1535; Bah-put-tah-cuck-kis; Spotted Otter; F; Wife; 29

1536; Chea-shea-itchice; Pretty Tail; M; Husband; 46
1537; Ba-dow-e-kosh; Looks at the Beads; F; Wife; 50
1538; Bashotshe-basosh; Rock That Runs; M; Gr Son; 12

1539; E-sah-dut-chew-chice; Strong Legs; M; Husband; 48
1540; Ah-way-uck-bachdeas; The Ground Is Her Medicine; F; Wife; 46

1541; Is-coa-chee-che-dish; Hunts the Enemy; M; Husband; 50
1542; Eatosh-dabish-de-chice; Strikes Her Child; F; Wife; 52

1543; Aditch-chebah-dochahoos; Paints Herself Plenty; M; Husband; 54
1544; Ah-pah-dee-it-chice; Pretty Porcupine; F; Wife; 49

1545; Pah-chice; Push; M; Husband; 50
1546; Bah-chay-uck-pah-pice; Lies In Bed With a Man; F; Wife; 44

1547; Duckbitshay-dah-beas; Three Bears; M; Husband; 40
1548; Dutch-ke; Twin Woman; F; Wife; 34
1549; Basho-dedich-chapasash; Medicine Rock In Front; F; Mother; 60

1550; Eas-shu-day; Yellow Face #2; M; Husband; 42
1551; Bah-pee-shada-ahoos; Rides Much Behind; F; Wife; 35
1552; Bis-cah-she-pit-tus; Black Dog; M; Son; 11
1553; ---; Dora Yellow Face; F; Daughter; 1

1554; Dachpitsay-it-chice; Pretty Bear; M; Husband; 60
1555; Bah-cah-chice; Strong; F; Wife; 52

1556; Cush-some-bee-chice; Falls Toward You; F; Widow; 80

1557; Cone-dah-chice; Stays There; M; Husband; 25
1558; Dutch-chee-do-pah-bash; Medicine Slides; F; Wife; 34

1559; Beda-ecupe-padootchice; Takes the Hat; F; Widow; 62

1560; Ha-wash-tay-keas; Travels Well Known; M; Husband; 58
1561; Bah-it-cash; She Sees It; F; Wife; 42
1562; Ek-bah-dee-days; Medicine Goes; F; Daughter; 13

Census of the __Crow__ Indians of __Crow__ Agency __Montana__ taken
By __J.E. Edwards__, United States Indian Agent __June 30, 1900__

Key: Number; Indian Name; English Name; Sex; Relation; Age

1563; Bak-kah-seas; Hoop That Shows; M; Son; 19

1564; E-kush-sheas; Turns Back; M; Husband; 42
1565; Uck-pah-dean-de-chice; Strikes Plenty Medicine; F; Wife; 39
1566; Uck-bah-dea-ush-eas; Medicine Shows; F; Daughter; 11

1567; Cheedup-keasos; Bull Well Known; M; Husband; 38
1568; Uch-ock-kay-duck-coos; Stays On Top of the House; F; Wife; 32
1569; Bah-cay-key-bachpash; Medicine Shell; F; Daughter; 12

1570; Itsup-educe; Edison Fire Bear; M; Husband; 22
1571; Bea-dah-cock-cus; Bird Woman; F; Wife; 17

1572; Dah-cock-beas; Bird Woman; F; Widow; 48
1573; Bah-son-day-it-chis; Goes Ahead Pretty; F; Daughter; 18

1574; Cheedup-chee-sus; Bull's Tail; M; Husband; 25
1575; Ah-bush-it-chice; Pretty Sweathouse; F; Wife; 21
1576; ---; Iva Bull's Tail; F; Daughter; 1

1577; Chate-dah-beas; Three Wolves; M; Husband; 64
1578; Ahway-taycoe-ahway-chis; Sits Down Far Away; F; Wife; 60

1579; Ah-dup-pice; Bull Robe; M; Husband; 28
1580; Cah-cay-itchice; Pretty Lance; F; Wife; 32

1581; Ischeka-it-chice; Pretty Land; F; Mother; 51
1582; ---; Campbell Pretty Land; M; Son; 1

1583; Iscoeche-ba-chea-days; Goes to Fight Enemies; F; Widow; 82

1584; Be-shay-ah-hoos; Plenty Buffalo; M; Husband; 32
1585; Dachbitsay-e-kos-seas; The Bear Turns Around; F; Wife; 27
1586; Itchit-chey-ah-bachpash; Medicine Tobacco; F; Daughter; 11
1587; Be-buckcoshsadacock-cus; Bird in the Spring; F; Daughter; 3

1588; Ea-cook-kish-shays; Red Fox; M; Widower; 56

1589; Duckbitsay-esah-cocish; Big Bear; M; Widower; 59

1590; Bahputtay-wa-chate-chice; Otter Chief; M; Husband; 31
1591; Bah-she-chice; Pretty Feather; F; Wife; 36

1592; Chate-ah-wah-shoes; Wolf House; M; Husband; 40
1593; Bea-cottus; Girl; F; Wife; 34

Census of the __Crow__ Indians of __Crow__ Agency __Montana__ taken By __J.E. Edwards__, United States Indian Agent __June 30, 1900__

Key: Number; Indian Name; English Name; Sex; Relation; Age

1594; Dachbitsay-he-dock-cus; The Bear Now; M; Father; 44
1595; E-cosh-sheas; Turns Around; F; Daughter; 11

1596; Ah-pe-sah-sheedish; Yellow Mule; M; Husband; 44
1597; Oct-tah-seas; Weasel That Shows; F; Wife; 34
1598; Beditta-shishay-cuckiss; Spotted Butterfly; M; Son; 13

1599; Bah-duck-key-dootchis; Takes a Gun #3; M; Husband; 33
1600; Bickus; Mare; F; Wife; 28
1601; ---; Susie; F; Daughter; 14
1602; Boodock-ahcane-deechis; Strikes On Top of Ice; F; Daughter; 7

1603; Ick-cup-pee-dee-dah-bish; Three Foretops; M; Widower; 34
1604; Bea-huch-key; Long Woman; F; Daughter; 6

1605; ---; William Steal Bear; M; Husband; 32
1606; ---; Esther Shell On The Neck; F; Wife; 25
1607; Beday-ock-ke-day-ichis; Good Shell; M; Ad Son; 7

1608; Beendosh-kanesh-wachice; Sits By the Water; F; Widow; 70

1609; Up-pay-e-wah-wah-e-cosh; Looks With His Ears; M; Husband; 35
1610; Oat-chean-bah-dup-pace; Kills at Night; F; Wife; 41
1611; Ope-cha-deas; Old Medicine Tobacco; F; Daughter; 12
1612; Is-tuk-key-de-ditch; Strikes Her Gun; F; Mother; 70

1613; E-chin-doot-chice; Takes a Horse; M; Husband; 31
1614; Un-dut-che-do-che-dice; Hunts to Slide; F; Wife; 23
1615; Bea-bachpash; Medicine Woman; M; Son; 9
1616; ---; Jessie T. Horse; F; Daughter; 1

1617; Pope-put-tay-ea-cottus; Little Owl; M; Husband; 31
1618; Osh-doo-chape-ditchis; Strikes the Thief in Camp; F; Wife; 27
1619; Cheach-key-dock-cus; Young Chicken; F; Daughter; 6
1620; ---; Laura Little Owl; F; Daughter; 2

1621; E-cupe-pis; Gets Down; M; Husband; 37
1622; Dah-cock-doo-pus; Two Birds; F; Wife; 32
1623; Cah-dah-hay-day-duse; Bird In the Rain; M; Son; 8
1624; Bah-dah-cah-deas; Old Money; F; Daughter; 4
1625; Duckbitshay-cah-dice; Old Bear Woman; F; Mother; 65

1626; Ische-ahay-ea-cot-tus; Little Nest; M; Husband; 34
1627; ---; Mary Laforge; F; Wife; 27
1628; ---; Mary Little Nest; F; Daughter; 9

181

Census of the __Crow__ Indians of __Crow__ Agency __Montana__ taken By __J.E. Edwards__, United States Indian Agent __June 30, 1900__

Key: Number; Indian Name; English Name; Sex; Relation; Age

1629; Is-coe-chea-docosh-ish; Holds the Enemy; M; Husband; 32
1630; Bah-put-tah-seas; Shows the Otter; F; Wife; 29
1631; Is-cah-kay-keas-sos; Plain Spear; M; Son; 6
1632; Bacombatshay-bachpash; Medicine Lark; M; Son; 1

1633; ---; George Thomas; M; Widower; 33

1634; ---; Henry Russell; M; Husband; 31
1635; Bah-chea-sheas; Steals on Camp; F; Wife; 28
1636; ---; Geo. W. Russell; M; Son; 3

1637; Ah-shoop-padate-cahdeas; Old Horn; M; Husband; 36
1638; ---; Lucy Old Horn; F; Wife; 26
1639; ---; Susie Old Horn; F; Daughter; 7
1640; ---; Fred Old Horn; M; Son; 10
1641; ---; Clarence Old Horn; M; Son; 1

1642; Ay-day-cah-weas; Bad Belly; M; Batchelor[sic]; 43

1643; Ah-day-chea-tus; White Arm; M; Husband; 39
1644; Bah-cah-key-it-chice; Pretty Shell; F; Wife; 35
1645; Bea-ditches; Strikes Women; F; Mother; 74

1646; Bos-che-day-cah-deas; Old White Man #2; M; Husband; 30
1647; Is-bah-hum-be-shis; Have Things; F; Wife; 18

1648; Bouta-bah-coos-shecosh; Coyote Looks Up; M; Widower; 73
1649; Doop-tush-ditches; Strikes Both Ways; F; Mother; 90

1650; Uck-sah-e-cos; Looks at Her Mother; F; Widow; 64
1651; Be-coo-took-eas; Little Moon; F; Gr Dau; 5

1652; Itche-bah-duck-shis; Plays With Himself; M; Husband; 28
1653; Isminats-makpash; Medicine; Shield; F; Wife; 28
1654; Mea-hotchkis; Tall Woman; F; Daughter; 10
1655; Dachbitsay-bishea; Dog Bear; M; Son; 1

1656; Ah-way-chase; Knows the Ground; M; Husband; 35
1657; ---; Perces Knows the Ground; F; Wife; 31

1658; E-shue-es-bachpash; Medicine Mane; M; Husband; 33
1659; Dacock-etuck-posdatus; Bird Without a Cloud; F; Wife; 28
1660; Ushdosh-caneba-duppace; Kills Beside Camp; F; Daughter; 9
1661; ---; Cora Medicine Mane; F; Daughter; 1

1662; Is-bah-dah-hoos; Got Plenty Beads; F; Widow; 44

Census of the __Crow__ Indians of __Crow__ Agency __Montana__ taken By __J.E. Edwards__, United States Indian Agent __June 30, 1900__

Key: Number; Indian Name; English Name; Sex; Relation; Age

1663; Bah-pah-dish; Flower; M; Son; 14
1664; Eapcha-bapah-dootchis; Takes the Medicine Pipe; F; Daughter; 7

1665; Bah-duk-keas; The Gun; M; Husband; 29
1666; Be-dup-cah-deas; Old Beaver; F; Wife; 32
1667; ---; John P. Gun; M; Son; 2

1668; ---; Charles Wort Davis; M; Batchelor[sic]; 30

1669; Bah-key-de-hosh; The Other Blackbird; M; Husband; 31
1670; Bah-put-tah-seas; Otter That Shows; F; Wife; 25
1671; Dup-pah-ecos-seas; Turns Around Twice; M; Son; 10
1672; Bah-dea-ate-chice; Knows What To Do; F; Daughter; 7

1673; Up-poch-cane-dichis; Strikes Back of the Head; F; Widow; 52

1674; Dachbitsa-cowees; Bad Bear; M; Husband; 32
1675; Eas-che-keep-pay; Crooked Face; F; Wife; 24

1676; Iscoeche-hay-day-codays; Goes Among the Enemy; M; Husband; 33
1677; Es-tup-peas; Shuts Her Eyes; F; Wife; 30
1678; Dee-cock-e-sos; Big Bird; M; Son; 10
1679; Dum-bachpash; Eats the Wood; M; Son; 6
1680; ---; Amos Goes Among the Enemy; M; Son; 1

1681; ---; George Hill; M; Husband; 34
1682; ---; Mrs. George Hill; F; Wife; 24
1683; ---; Anna Hill; F; Daughter; 7
1684; ---; Mary Hill; F; Daughter; 5

1685; Cheedup-sho-chok-a-dus; Bull Over the Hill; M; Husband; 27
1686; Apah-suttah-doochice; Takes a Split Ear; F; Wife; 25
1687; Dach-co-bachpash; Medicine Turtle; F; Daughter; 7

1688; Bea-dea-dush; The Door; M; Husband; 29
1689; ---; Victoria Door; F; Wife; 20
1690; ---; Dora Door; F; Daugher[sic]; 4

1691; Oo-wa-sheedish; Yellow In the Mouth; M; Husband; 28
1692; Bout-tah-eas; Little Coyote; F; Wife; 22
1693; Dach-cock-sheedish; Yellow Bird; F; Daughter; 6

1694; Bah-cha-cheas; Steals on the Camp; M; Husband; 32
1695; Is-bah-cah-kea-ahoos; Plenty Shells; F; Wife; 22
1696; Echean-chea-itchis; Pretty Horse Tail; F; Daughter; 1

Census of the **Crow** Indians of **Crow** Agency **Montana** taken
By **J.E. Edwards**, United States Indian Agent **June 30, 1900**

Key: Number; Indian Name; English Name; Sex; Relation; Age

1697; ---; Laura Green; F; --[Married White]; 25

1698; Mah-soe; Mint; M; Widower; 48

1699; Bascheeda-schepittay; Light Colored Man; M; Husband; 28
1700; Bah-cay-ca-cah-dah-bish; Hoop That Moves; F; Wife; 25
1701; Ope-cah-deas; Old Tobacco; F; Daughter; 5
1702; ---; Florence Coo Chief; F; Daughter; 4

1703; Bash-keas-sos; Plain Feather; M; Husband; 28
1704; Un-dah-coe-bah-coos; Live High; F; Wife; 24

1705; Cheeup-e-ches-ditch; Bull Horse; M; Father; 31
1706; Echete-doochis; Takes a Pinto Horse; F; Daughter; 5

1707; ---; Mrs. Joe Pickett; F; Mother; F; 37
1708; ---; Robert A. Pickett; M; Son; 13
1709; ---; Joseph J. Pickett; M; Son; 10
1710; ---; William C. Pickett; M; Son; 7
1711; ---; Margaret Pickett; F; Daughter; 6

1712; ---; Joseph Stewart; M; Husband; 30
1713; Cah-coa-ays; Everything is Here; F; Wife; 27
1714; ---; Francis Stewart; M; Son; 7
1715; ---; Fannie Stewart; F; Daughter; 5

1716; ---; William Stewart; M; Batchelor[sic]; 21

1717; ---; M. Two Belly; M; Husband; 40
1718; ---; Mrs; M. Two Belly; F; Wife; 38
1719; Ahkinda-heahsos; Rides a Horse Well Known; F; Ad Dau; 12

1720; ---; John Wesley; M; Husband; 39
1721; ---; Jane Wesley; F; Wife; 34
1722; ---; Jennie Wesley; F; Daughter; 13
1723; ---; Fannie Wesley; F; Daughter; 7

1724; ---; Mrs. James Robinson; F; Mother; 40
1725; ---; James Robinson; M; Son; 7
1726; ---; Charles Robinson; M; Son; 13
1727; ---; Ellen Robinson; F; Daughter; 8
1728; ---; Allen Robinson; M; Son; 5
1729; ---; Alice Robinson; F; Daughter; 3

1730; ---; Mrs. G.F. Deputee; F; Mother; 33
1731; ---; Jennie Deputee; F; Daughter; 7

Census of the __Crow__ Indians of __Crow__ Agency __**Montana**__ taken By __**J.E. Edwards**__, United States Indian Agent __**June 30, 1900**__

Key: Number; Indian Name; English Name; Sex; Relation; Age

1732; ---; Flora Deputee; F; Daughter; 5

1733; ---; Mrs. Frank Gordon; F; --[Married White]; 45

1734; ---; Mrs. B. Bravo; F; --[Married White]; 57

1735; Hoo-chice; Wind; M; Husband; 36
1736; ---; Mrs. Thos. Laforge; F; Wife; 52
1737; ---; Rosa Laforge; F; Daughter; 18
1738; ---; Thomas Asa Laforge; M; Son; 16

1739; ---; John Alden; M; Husband; 32
1740; ---; Phoebe Alden; F; Wife; 21

1741; ---; Mrs. J.B. Cooper; F; Mother; 60
1742; ---; Cynthia Cooper; F; Daughter; 15
1743; ---; Sylvester Hardy; M; Gr Son; 4
1744; ---; Peter Cooper; M; Son; 20
1745; ---; Lule[sic] Cooper; F; Daughter; 22

1746; ---; Martha C. Shenderli[sic]; F; Mother; 25
1747; ---; Josepg[sic] Shenderlin[sic]; M; Son; 7
1748; ---; Edward Shenderlin; M; Son; 5
1749; ---; Henry Shenderlin; M; Son; 3
1750; ---; Rachel Shenderlin; F; Daughter; 1

1751; ---; Mrs. Henry Keiser; F; Mother; 40
1752; ---; Myrtle Keiser; F; Daughter; 6
1753; ---; Frank Keiser; M; Son; 20

1754; ---; Mrs. Maggie K. Macer; F; Mother; 22
1755; ---; Mabel Macer; F; Daughter; 5
1756; ---; Henry Macer; M; Son; 3
1757; ---; Edward Macer; M; Son; 1

1758; ---; Mrs. David Yarlott; F; Mother; 52
1759; ---; Frabk[sic] Yarlott; M; Son; 18
1760; ---; Katie Yarlott; F; Daughter; 12
1761; ---; Charles Yarlott; M; Son; 22

1762; ---; Mrs. John L. Smith; F; Mother; 54
1763; ---; Rosebud Farwell; M; Son; 18

1764; ---; Susan Farwell Glenn; F; Mother; 24
1765; ---; Percival Glenn; M; Son; [1]

Census of the __Crow__ Indians of __Crow__ Agency __Montana__ taken
By __J.E. Edwards__, United States Indian Agent __June 30, 1900__

Key: Number; Indian Name; English Name; Sex; Relation; Age

1766; ---; Mrs. Al. Morrison; F; Mother; 52
1768; ---; Hannah Morrison; F; Daughter; 19
1767; ---; Alvin Morrison; M; Son; 17

1769; E-say-dup-pah-choas; Points the Gun In His Face; M; Husband; 34
1770; ---; Mrs. Thomas Stewart; F; Wife; 41
1771; Ah-wah-caneca-dooshis; Runs Over the Ground; M; Son; 7

1772; ---; Mrs. R.W. Cummins; F; -- [Married White]; 50

1773; ---; Mrs. Thomas Kent; F; Mother; 49
1774; ---; Elizabeth Kent; F; Daughter; 18
1775; ---; Maggie Kent; F; Daughter; 13
1776; ---; Josephine Kent; F; Daughter; 20

1777; ---; Mary K. Stevens; F; Mother; 22
1778; ---; Mary Stevens; F; Daughter; 5
1779; ---; Kent Stevens; M; Son; 4
1780; ---; Agnes Stevens; F; Daughter; 3

1781; ---; Mrs. Ella K. Cashen; F; Mother; 24
1782; ---; Willie Cashen; M; Son; 6
1783; ---; Alice Cashen; F; Daughter; 5
1784; ---; Ella Cashen; F; Daughter; 3
1785; ---; Cecelia Cashen; F; Daughter; 1

1786; ---; Maggie Garrigus; F; Mother; 29
1787; ---; Mary F. Garrigus; F; Daughter; 8
1788; ---; Margaret E. Garrigus; F; Daughter; 7
1789; ---; Arthur R. Garrigus; M; Son; 6
1790; ---; Dorothy B. Garrigus; F; Daughter; 3

1791; ---; Abbie Lande; F; Mother; 26
1792; ---; Thomas A. Lande; M; Son; 5
1793; ---; Henry D. Lande; M; Son; 2

1794; ---; Frederick Geisdorff; M; Father; 29
1795; ---; Florence Geisdorff; F; Daughter; 5
1796; ---; Francis Geisdorff; M; Son; 4
1797; ---; Frederick Geisdorff Jr.; M; Son; 3
1798; ---; Louisa Geisdorff; F; Sister; 25
1799; ---; Charlotte Geisdorff; F; Sister; 22

1800; ---; Margaret A. Davis-Howe; F; Mother; 21
1801; ---; Robert S. Howe; M; Son; 1
1802; ---; Blaine R. Davis; M; Brother; 6

Census of the __Crow__ Indians of __Crow__ Agency __Montana__ taken
By __J.E. Edwards__, United States Indian Agent __June 30, 1900__

Key: Number; Indian Name; English Name; Sex; Relation; Age

1803; ---; Effie N. Davis; F; Sister; 15

1804; ---; Minnie Reed; F; Orphan; 25
1805; ---; Francis Reed; M; Brother; 22
1806; ---; Della Reed; F; Sister; 16
1807; ---; Nellie Reed; F; Sister; 14
1808; ---; Edith Reed; F; Sister; 12
1809; ---; Katie Reed; F; Sister; 10

1810; ---; Mary K. Reed; F; Orphan; 16

1811; ---; Mrs. Wm. H. White; F; Mother; 38
1812; ---; Mary E. White; F; Daughter; 18
1813; ---; Minnie E. White; F; Daughter; 15
1814; ---; Charles F. White; M; Son; 2
1815; ---; Wm. H. White; M; Son; 20

1816; ---; Mrs. Thomas Shane; F; Mother; 41
1817; ---; Patrick C. Shane; M; Son; 15
1818; ---; Frank Shane; M; Son; 12
1819; ---; Josie Shane; F; Daughter; 10
1820; ---; Bessie Shane; F; Daughter; 8
1821; ---; Thomas Shane; M; Son; 6
1822; ---; Edward Shane; M; Son; 4
1823; ---; Kittie Shane; F; Daughter; 22

1824; ---; Cora Williams; F; Orphan; 21
1825; ---; Mattie Williams; F; Sister; 19

1826; ---; Mrs. Mary Heckenlively; F; Mother; 24
1827; ---; Guy L. Heckenlively; M; Son; 3
1828; ---; Howard C. Heckenlively; M; Son; 1

1829; ---; Mrs. Thos. Doyle; F; Mother; 23
1830; ---; Robert Doyle; M; Son; 3
1831; ---; Frances Doyle; F; Daughter; 2

1832; ---; Ellen Jackson; F; Mother; 48
1833; ---; Eliza Jackson; F; Daughter; 14
1834; ---; Julia Jackson; F; Daughter; 11
1835; ---; John Jackson; M; Son; 19

1836; ---; John Frost; M; Husband; 27
1837; Is-bon-dot-bachpash; Medicine Shield; F; Wife; 20
1838; ---; Daniel L. Frost; M; Son; 3

1839; ---; Joseph Cooper; M; Husband; 28

Census of the __Crow__ Indians of __Crow__ Agency __Montana__ taken
By __J.E. Edwards__, United States Indian Agent __June 30, 1900__

Key: Number; Indian Name; English Name; Sex; Relation; Age

1840; ---; Susie Cooper; F; Wife; 29
1841; ---; Theodora Cooper; F; Daughter; 8
1842; ---; Laura Cooper; F; Daughter; 7
1843; ---; Sylvania Cooper; F; Daughter; 6
1844; ---; James Cooper; M; Son; 4
1845; ---; Joseph Cooper Jr.; M; Son; 2

1846; Ah-woo-coos; Sydney Wolf; M; Husband; 21
1847; Ahwokchedush-delemach; Edith Long Ear; F; Wife; 17

1848; ---; Levantia W. Pearson; F; Mother; 37
1849; ---; Virginia Pearson; F; Daughter; 8
1850; ---; Helen E. Pearson; F; Daughter; 7
1851; ---; Ethel M. Pearson; F; Daughter; 5

1852; ---; George W. Pease; M; Husband; 34
1853; ---; Sarah Pease; F; Wife; 33
1854; ---; David Pease; M; Son; 8
1855; ---; James Pease; M; Son; 10
1856; ---; Benjamin Pease; M; Son; 7
1857; ---; Emory Pease; M; Son; 6
1858; ---; Anson H. Pease; M; Son; 4
1859; ---; George Pease; M; Son; 3
1860; ---; Oliver Pease; M; Son; 1

1861; ---; Mrs. Marshall; F; [Married White]; 43

1862; ---; Mrs. Amy Scott; F; Mother; 22
1863; ---; George Scott; M; Son; 4
1864; ---; Elmer Scott; M; Son; 3

1865; Chate-dah-beas; Three Wolves; M; Widower; 48

1866; Is-bah-key-cush-sheas; Hoop Turns Around; M; Father; 25
1867; ---; August Hoop Turns Around; M; Son; 3
1868; ---; Caroline Hoop Turns Around; F; Daughter; 1

1869; Cheedup-kahdeas; Old Bull; M; Husband; 26
1870; Bah-cah-key-day-cus; Shell Child; F; Wife; 21
1871; Bachpash; Medicine; F; Daughter; 3

1872; Ahway-taday-cock-cus; Bird Far Away; M; [Bachelor]; 24

1873; Ah-shue-cay-bay; Bush Head; M; Husband; 25
1874; Boa-pis; Snow; F; Wife; 32

Census of the __Crow__ Indians of __Crow__ Agency __Montana__ taken
By __J.E. Edwards__, United States Indian Agent __June 30, 1900__

Key: Number; Indian Name; English Name; Sex; Relation; Age

1875; Ah-woos-cahdeas; Old Sweathouse; F; Widow; 35

1876; ---; Martin Round Face; M; Husband; 27
1877; ---; Katie Dreamer; F; Wife; 24

1878; Tuch-chay-dah-cockus; Strianght[sic] Bird; M; Widower; 24
1879; Bah-itchay-dootchis; Takes Pretty Things; F; Daughter; 6

1880; Chea-dacock-inda-dichus; Strikes Riding Grey Horse; F; Divorced; 18
1881; ---; Frances Ten Bear; M; Son; 3

1882; Bea-sos-coos; Looks Back; M; Husband; 24
1883; Bah-o-dop-keas-sos; Finds Plain; F; Wife; 23

1884; Bah-put-tah-beas; Otter Woman; F; Widow; 20
1885; ---; Glenn Bird; M; Son; 4

1886; Choos-say-dah-quas; Sends Part Home; M; Husband; 31
1887; Oo-shay-it-chise; Pretty Hole; F; Wife; 21

1888; Incuppah-bish-chedice; Strikes the Hat; F; Mother; 41
1889; Ba-be-dish-e-sos; Strikes Big; M; Son; 11

1890; ---; Samuel S. Davis; M; Widower; 25

1891; Osus; Can't Shoot Him; M; Husband; 19
1892; Ahsha-hedere-malapes; Kills In Camp; Wife; 25
1893; Ahshashe-duschice; Turns Round the Camp; M; Son; 1

1894; Dah-cock-ah-seas; Bird That Shows; F; Widow; 52

1895; Bachay-eatche-bish-ay; Man With a Beard; M; --[Divorced]; 24

1896; Ecupe-pah-de-chice; Strikes the Hat; F; Widow; 52

1897; Be-de-ha-dup-pace; Crosses the Water; F; Widow; 60

1898; Bachay-ha-wat-dechice; Strikes One Man; F; Widow; 55

1899; Suah-cowutish; Thunder Iron; M; Husband; 24
1900; Ahke-mulukish; Sings On Top; F; Wife; 17

1901; Cha-cush; Five; F; Widow; 76

1902; Bah-shus-shays; Medicine Dance; F; Widow; 15

Census of the **Crow** Indians of **Crow** Agency **Montana** taken
By **J.E. Edwards**, United States Indian Agent **June 30, 1900**

Key: Number; Indian Name; English Name; Sex; Relation; Age

1903; Bah-choa-ish-itchice; Loves to Fight; M; Batchelor[sic]; 25

1904; Bah-son-day-itchice; Goes Ahead Pretty; M; Husband; 25
1905; Bah-put-tah-beas; Otter Woman; F; Wife; 35

1906; ---; James Laforge; M; Husband; 23
1907; ---; Sage Woman; F; Wife; 20
1908; ---; William Laforge; M; Son; 5
1909; ---; Francis Laforge; M; Son; 3

1910; ---; Mary M. Humphrey; F; Mother; 23
1911; ---; Maud Humphrey; F; Daughter; 4
1912; ---; Lillie Humphrey; F; Daughter; 1

1913; Ah-hoo-ha-e-cuch-seas; Turns Back Plenty; M; Husband; 25
1914; Beshay-dane-awachice; Sits Among the Rocks; F; Wife; 21
1915; ---; High Nest; M; Son; 2

1916; Awaca-dane-cheedup-ish; Mountain Bull; M; --[Divorced]; 24

1917; Boa-e-hock-sos; Sings the Last Song; M; Widower; 35

1918; Con-up-e-say; Big Nose Old Woman; F; Widow; 83

1919; Isuc-cheyday-sheedish; Yellow Hawk; M; Widower; 43

1920; Ecupe-pay-bee-dish; Fire Hat; M; Widower; 43

1921; ---; Jackson Stewart; M; Husband; 23
1922; Eskulusa-epa-cheis; White Tailed Hawk; F; Wife; 21

1923; Ah-quas; Covered Up; M; Husband; 28
1924; Bah-pah-dit-chice; Plenty Things Growing; F; Wife; 23

1925; ---; Richard Pickett; M; Father; 18
1926; ---; Thomas Pickett; M; Son; 2

1927; Bah-dah-kut-teas; Crazy; M; Widower; 30

1928; Oat-chees-du-dish; Ralph Saco; M; Husband; 23
1929; Bee-dop-dah-cuss; Young Beaver; F; Wife; 24
1930; ---; Minnie Saco; F; Daughter; 1

1931; Echete-itchice; Pretty Horse; M; Husband; 35
1932; ---; Monica Horn; F; Wife; 20

Census of the __**Crow**__ Indians of __**Crow**__ Agency __**Montana**__ taken By __**J.E. Edwards**__, United States Indian Agent __**June 30, 1900**__

Key: Number; Indian Name; English Name; Sex; Relation; Age

1933; ---; Charles M. Phelps; M; Father; 28
1934; ---; Frank Phelps; M; Son; 6
1935; ---; Fred Phelps; M; Son; 5
1936; ---; Emma Phelps; F; Daughter; 3
1937; ---; Bud Phelps; M; Son; 1

1938; ---; Mrs. Rosa Milliken; F; Mother; 38
1939; ---; John Wesley Milliken; M; Son; 17
1940; ---; Claude Milliken; M; Son; 21
1941; ---; Leroy Milliken; M; Son; 19

Crow Agency Montana, 1901 Census

J. E. Edwards, Indian Agent

48004 — OFFICE OF Indian Affairs Rec SEP 11 1901

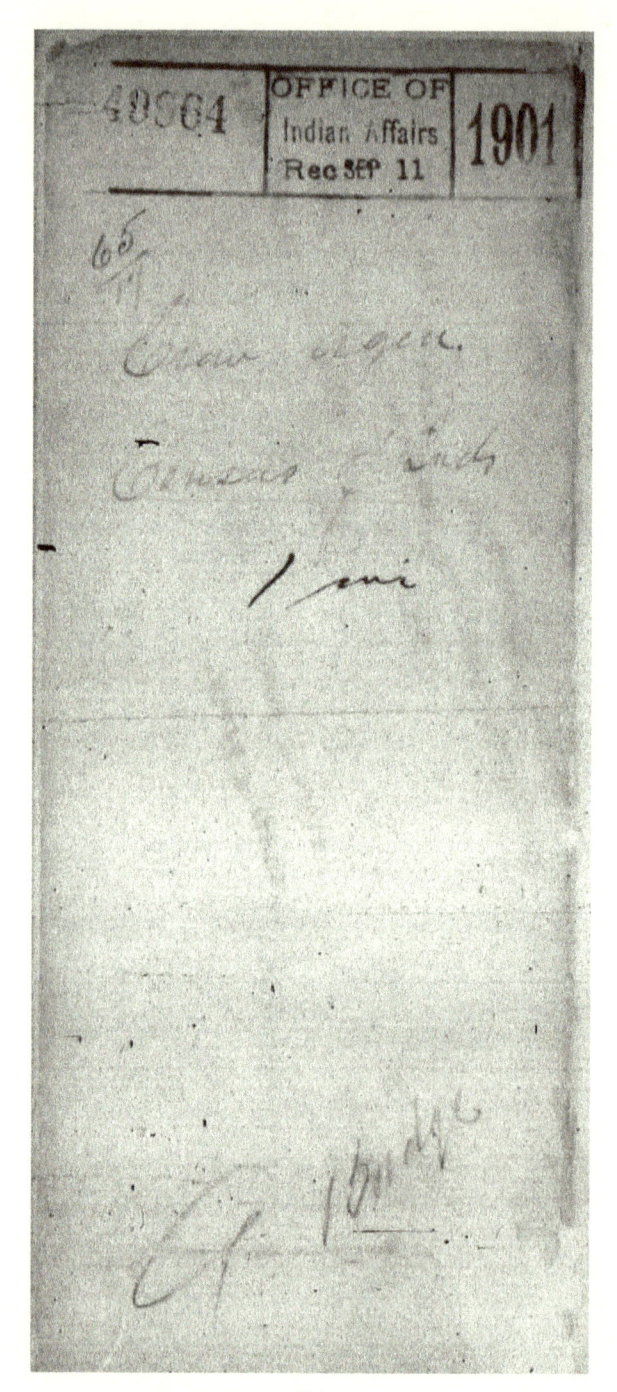

65/11

Crow Agency.

Census of Inds

1 encl

DEPARTMENT OF THE INTERIOR,
UNITED STATES INDIAN SERVICE,

Crow Agency, Montana, September 7th, 1901.

Hon. Commissioner Indian Affairs,
          Washington, D, C,

Sir:

I have the honor to transmit herewith a census of the Crow tribe of Indians for the fiscal year 1901, ending June 30th, 1901,

Very respectfully,

U. S. Indian Agent.

CENSUS 1901, CROW
RECAPITULATION SHEET.

Males 18 and above............640
Males 16 and 17............. 28
Males 6 to 16................155
Males under 6................116.................1939

Females 14 and above......... 724
Females 6 to 16..............187
Females under 6.............. 80.......991
Less Females 14 and 15 listed twice..... 19..........972......1911

Births:------Male......30
            Female....24.....54

Deaths:------Male......44
            Female....40.....84

Decrease in population..........30

Children 6 to 16..................342
Children under 6..................196

CENSUS OF THE CROW TRIBE OF INDIANS MADE AT THE CLOSE OF THE FISCAL YEAR 1901 AT CROW AGENCY, MONTANA, BY J. E. EDWARDS, UNITED STATES INDIAN AGENT,

Census of the __Crow__ Indians of __Crow__ Agency __Montana__ taken
By __J.E. Edwards__, United States Indian Agent __June 30, 1901__

Key: Number; Indian Name; English Name; Sex; Relation; Age

1; Ahnehe-ichis; Walks Pretty; F Widow; 42
2; Lagak-esash; Big Bird; M; Son; 11

3; Budesesh; No Horse; M; Husband; 35
4; Oo-inkpus; Hugs the Weasel; F; Wife; 38
5; ---; Gretchen No Horse; F; Daughter; 3

6; Ook-eas; Little Antelope; F; Widow; 74

7; Nas-kowees; Bad Heart; M; Husband; 28
8; Lagak-hishis; Red Breasted Bird; F; Wife; 25
9; Lagak-mee-da-ses; Rain Bird; F; Daughter; 7
10; Bah-wah-sone-dah-ichis; Good Leader; F; Daughter; 5
11; ---; Fred Bad Heart; M; Son; 1

12; Awak-in-lagaks; Bird All Over the Ground; M; Husband; 55
13; Mida-itches; Goes Well; F; Wife; 51
14; Lagak-iches; Good Bird; F; Daughter; 9

15; Ahshua-wahnaks; Crazy Head; M; Husband; 65
16; Esha-shates; Paints Pretty; F; Wife; 54

17; Mea-daka; White Woman; M; Husband; 42
18; Oomah-sees; Sees in the Mouth; F; Wife; 35

19; Ahluk-cheaakuse; He Knows His Coos; M; Husband; 41
20; Besha-chea-makpash; Medicine White Buffalo; F; Wife; 38

21; Eascha-naks; Young Jack Rabbit; M; Husband; 54
22; Ahpit-cheas; White Crane; F; Wife; 45
23; Ahwak-amach; Sits Toward the Mountain; M; Son; 18

24; Awaksha-echete; Gros Ventre Horse; M; Husband; 59
25; Chis-sheis; Nest; F; Wife; 49

26; Ahpit-nake; Young Crane; F; Widow; 61
27; Eukase-hishes; Red Snake; F; Daughter; 13

28; ---; Andrew Wallace; M; Husband; 28
29; ---; Jennie Wallace; F; Wife; 23
30; ---; Josie Wallace; F; Daughter; 7
31; ---; Harry Wallace; M; Son; 1

32; Checks-doochis; Takes Five; F; Widow; 57

33; E-step-ees; Eli Blackhawk; M; Batchelor[sic]; 27

Census of the __Crow__ Indians of __Crow__ Agency __Montana__ taken
By __J.E. Edwards__, United States Indian Agent __June 30, 1901__

Key: Number; Indian Name; English Name; Sex; Relation; Age

34; Eche-kuis; Sweet Mouth; M; Husband; 42
35; Andiche-poois; Sore Where Whipped; F; Wife; 46
36; Lagak-beepish; Snowbird; M; Ad son; 11

37; Wtekut-napes; Kills Close; F; Widow; 78
38; Mishodechitse-lagak; Medicine Rock Bird; M; Ad. Son; 11

39; Esa-keepa; Wrinkle Face; M; Husband; 45
40; Eskochea-ichis; Fights the Enemy Good; F; Wife; 48
41; Ahwotkot-dichis; Strikes Same One; F; Daughter; 6

42; Eskuka-ahshees; Shows a Lance; M; Husband; 51
43; Mi-iche-doochis; Takes Pretty Things; F; Wife; 63

44; Ahma-apische; Arm Around the Neck; M; Husband; 60
45; Hederin-dichis; Strikes in a Crowd; F; Wife; 60

46; Menar-ahwetkot; One Goose; M; Husband; 59
47; Min-makpash; Medicine Water; F; Wife; 47
48; Lagak-heahsas; Bird Well Known; M; Son; 18
49; Ashkaroochis-kahdeas; Old Horn; F; Daughter; 11
50; Mean-dichis; Strikes Plenty Women; F; Mother; 75

51; Esa-keepa; Flat Face; F; Widow; 38

52; Ekupa-cheis; Packs the Hat; M; Husband; 43
53; Ahpake-hedere-Lagaks; Bird in a Cloud; F; Wife; 35
54; Eesackas-ahoos; Plenty Arrows; M; Son; 10

55; Miastasheeda-karoos; White Man Runs Him; K; Husband; 43
56; Popet-itsecahts; Good Owl; F; Wife; 39
57; Micha-ahcheis-botsots; Steals on Camp Strong; M; Son; 7
58; Bechon-herepsis; Kills One With Red Blanket; F; Daughter; 14

59; Meneas-koop-shuis; Sioux; M; Batchelor[sic]; 50

60; Duchkis; Left Hand; M; Husband; 27
61; Cheis-makpash; Medicine Tail; F; Wife; 30
62; Nakas-makpash; Child is Medicine; F; Daughter; 11
63; Nahkose-cheedup; Bull Turtle; M; Son; 6
64; ---; Peter L. Hand; M; Son; 3

65; Peritisa-kahdeas; Old Crow; M; Husband; 64
66; Ahoo-aroopis; Finds All; F; Wife; 41
67; Mintahsehederemitpal; Persons in the Moon; F; Daughter; 8
68; Istuka-sa-here-dadush; Stands Among the Shooters; M; Son; 7

Census of the __Crow__ Indians of __Crow__ Agency __Montana__ taken
By __J.E. Edwards__, United States Indian Agent __June 30, 1901__

Key: Number; Indian Name; English Name; Sex; Relation; Age

69; Botseah-botsots; Strong Fighter; M; Son; 2

70; Cheda-kos; Holds Up; M; Widower; 43
71; Beah-kahdeas; Rock Old; M; Son; 6

72; Eskay-ahwotkot; One Star; M; Husband; 35
73; Miastacheeda-meas; White Woman; F; Wife; 50
74; ---; George Washington Hogan; M; Son; 18
75; Ekpetatska; Good Sheep; F; Daughter; 6

76; Istuka-asees; Gun Shows; M; Husband; 34
77; Dakpitses-ahsees; Looks at the Bear; F; Wife; 29
78; Ba-orap-saskatch; Finds Soon; M; Son; 6

79; Bee-dup-pay-tus; Like a Beaver; F; Widow; 59

80; Ahmatka; Long Way Off; F; Widow; 59

81; Misakohn-michis; Grandmother's Knife; M; Husband; 45
82; Chisah-kahdeas; Old Nest; F; Wife; 36
83; ---; Sarah G. Knife; [F]; [Daughter]; 2

84; Duchuis; Muskrat; F; Widow; 57

85; Esa-keepa; Crooked Face; F; Mother; 26
86; Istuka-makpash; Medicine Arrow; M; Son; 10

87; Oet-budekesh-helenakuse; George White Bear; M; Batch; 27

88; Eer-kahwash; Bird Tail That Rattles; M; Husband; 54
89; Kahdeas; Old; F; Wife; 54

90; Mahpak-hoos; Comes in a Day; M; Husband; 51
91; Mahkaristish; Yearling; F; Wife; 37
92; ---; Celia Comes in a Day; F; Daughter; 2

93; Besha-cheedups; Buffalo Bull #1; M; Husband; 41
94; Meakot-kowees; Bad Woman; F; Wife; 39
95; Mea-ichis; Pretty Rock; F; Daughter; 11
96; Muna-shuis; Blue Wood; M; Son; 16

97; Chatis; Wolf; M; Husband; 50
98; Midesha-doochis; Gets Hold of the Dead; F; Wife; 45
99; Eskoche-okepis; Shoot the Enemy; M; Son; 21
100; Dotsuah-doochis; Takes a Sinew; F; Mother; 89

Census of the **Crow** Indians of **Crow** Agency **Montana** taken By **J.E. Edwards**, United States Indian Agent **June 30, 1901**

Key: Number; Indian Name; English Name; Sex; Relation; Age

101; Dakpitsa-cheis; White Bear #2; M; Husband; 50
102; Minna-nahkuse; By the Side of the Water; F; Wife; 59
103; Besha-ekash; Russell W. Bear; M; Son; 25

104; Botsa-kowees; Bad Man; M; Husband; 48
105; Bahkeed-lagaks; Blackbird; F; Wife; 44

106; Ahpa-duttotoes; Cut Ear; M; Husband; 49
107; Ekupa-esash; Big Hat; F; Wife; 53

108; Duckbea-cheacock-indas; Rides White Hipped Horse; M; Husband; 24
109; Mi-ich-napes; Kills Pretty Ones; F; Wife; 22
110; ---; Harold Rides White Horse; M; Son; 4

111; Muche-deis; Good Luck; M; Husband; 43
112; Chate-heahsas; Wolf Well Known; F; Wife; 41
113; ---; Matthew G. Luck; M; Son; 2

114; Lagak-heshsas; Bird Well Known; M; Husband; 32
115; Wahpootkamakpash; Medicine Otter; F; Wife; 33

116; Echeta-kowees; Bad Horse; M; Husband; 29
117; Bachos-itchis; Pretty Bullrush; F; Wife; 25
118; ---; Jennie B. Horse; F; Daughter; 2

119; Esukis; Corner of the Mouth; M; Husband; 51
120; Ismina-wisha-doochis; Takes Pretty Scalp; F; Wife; 52
121; Echeta-gash-eduse; Elk Stands Up; M; Son; 15

122; Ahse-desh; Shows as He Goes; M; Husband; 45
123; Mi-iche-kooshdase; Goes to Good Things; F; Wife; 48

124; Opes; Ben Spotted Horse; M; Husband; 29
125; Budeesh; Horse; F; Wife; 32

126; Oeta-echeta; Iron Horse; M; Husband; 27
127; Ahwoosh-akuse; Knows the Sweathouse; F; Wife; 22
128; Mean-ditchis; Strikes the Woman; F; Daughter; 6

129; Chate-kupis; Wolf Lays Down; M; Husband; 62
130; Isheda; Kills at the Door; F; Wife; 55
131; Ekuh-push; Gets Down Often; M; Son; 22

132; Bah-aye-chaise; Knows Everything; F; Widow; 37
133; Chea-kay-sos; Sage Hen; M; Son; 16
134; Mahaha-hotchkish; Long Feather; M; Son; 8

Census of the __Crow__ Indians of __Crow__ Agency __Montana__ taken
By __J.E. Edwards__, United States Indian Agent __June 30, 1901__

Key: Number; Indian Name; English Name; Sex; Relation; Age

135; ---; Anson Knows Everything; M; Son; 1

136; Mahsha-wots; One Feather; M; Husband; 59
137; Ahta-malapes; Kills First; F; Wife; 67

138; Eche-dudees; Don't Mix; M; Husband; 29
139; Misdershase; Groans; F; Wife; 35

140; Boa-ayy-tah-itchis; Pretty Coyote; M; Husband; 26
141; Beedah-dosh-kain-dichis; Strikes by Side of Water; F; Wife; 35
142; Ah-ruck-chea-heahsas; Plain Coos; F; Daughter; 1

143; Educhesa-heas; Plain Left Hand; M; Husband; 64
144; Echik-dichis; Strikes First; F; Wife; 54

145; Lukpa-sashis; Bright Wings; M; Husband; 34
146; Mahahchis-lukish-dish; Goes to Look at Prisoners; F; Wife; 24
147; Echete-mulakis; Sings on Horse; M; Son; 8
148; Echete-maks-kochetish; Horse Stays all the Time; F; Daugh.; 5

149; Ahpewesha; Gros Ventre; M; Husband; 39
150; Ahwa-akuse; Knows the Ground; F; Wife; 37
151; Escoche-karooshes; Runs the Enemy; M; Son; 8

152; Budeesh; Horse; M; Father; 44
153; Dakpitsa-a-reandadish; Bear on the Trail; F; Daugh.; 4
154; ---; Charlie Horse; M; Son; 2

155; Isba-itchis; Pretty Louse; F; Mother; 55
156; Eisda-karooshes; Loves to Run; M; Son; 20

157; Barucka-acha-nadees; Walks Over Ice; M; Husband; 23
158; Mea-makpash; Medicine Woman; F; Wife; 19

159; Nooptah-ditchis; Strikes Twice; F; Widow; 85

160; Chapes; Whinners; M; Husband; 44
161; Echete-sheedes-ahkinda; Rides a Yellow Horse; F; Wife; 41
162; Me-makpash-ehos; The Other Medicine Rock; F; Daugh.; 14

163; Ahkbahdit-napes; Kills Picking Berries; F; Widow; 66

164; Ahsukap-meas; Flathead Woman; M; Husband; 45
165; Mononots-heahsas; Well Known Writing; F; Wife; 34
176; ---; Lizzie Flathead Woman; F; Daughter; 8
177; Meacahcha-ahoos; Plenty Ducks; M; Son; 1

Census of the __Crow__ Indians of __Crow__ Agency __Montana__ taken
By __J.E. Edwards__, United States Indian Agent __June 30, 1901__
Key: Number; Indian Name; English Name; Sex; Relation; Age

168; Is-eepse-deesh; pipe[sic] That Talks; M; Husband; 34
169; Echa-sheishis; Dirty Foot; F; Wife; 56
170; ---; Blanche Brown; F; Niece; 15

171; Ahta-ditchis; Big Woman; F; Widow; 57

172; Istuka-akuse; Knows the Gun; M; Husband; 33
173; Esop-pontuch-chehadaydus; Among the Shepp[sic]; F; Wife; 26
174; Bahm-batseer-esash; Nobody Fights Them; m; Son; 7
175; Esasahka-ahp-orupish; Finds Things With Her Horse; F; Daug.; 11
176; Aka-malukis; Sings on Top; F; Daugh.; 8
177; Echeta-cosh; Brings His Horses; M; Son; 2

178; Nosh-kosh; Small; F; Maiden; 24

179; Ikpam-basash; Robert Raiseup; M; Husband; 29
180; Shee-deak-days; Rattles Going; F; Wife; 25

181; Lagak-deedes; Walking Bird; M; Husband; 43
182; Ee-sach-ich; Good Now; F; Wife; 35

183; Esaska-huka-ahkindas; Rides a Spotted Horse; F; Widow; 61

184; Ochis-dichis; Strikes at Night; F; Widow; 55
185; Dukeah-desh; Goes to War; M; Son; 33

186; Ootuh-chedups; Bull Weasel; M; Husband; 30
187; Uckbah-deas-ewahic-deas; Does Ev'th'g With Her Med; F; Wife; 18

188; Cheedup-kochetish; Bull All the Time; M; Widower; 70

189; Malapa; The Root; M; Widower; 64

190; Bedupa-bukata-dase; Beaver That Passes; F; Mother; 39
191; ---; Florence Beaver Passes; F; Daugh.; 4

192; Mannahpesh; Swamp Flag; F; Widow; 55

193; Echeta-hukish; Spotted Horse; M; Husband; 52
194; Is-eepse-makpash-ichis; Pretty Medicine Pipe; F; Wife; 43
195; E-rooptay-cheis; By Herself; F; Daugh; 13
196; Istuka-ahoos; Plenty Arrows; M; Son; 11
197; Aka-pish-akan-dichis; Strikes Rider of Red Ear; M; Son; 2

198; Booah-ahseesh; Shows a Fish; M; Husband; 55
199; Mahake-nahke; Shell Child; F; Wife; 49

Census of the __Crow__ Indians of __Crow__ Agency __Montana__ taken
By __J.E. Edwards__, United States Indian Agent __June 30, 1901__

Key: Number; Indian Name; English Name; Sex; Relation; Age

200; Bishka-kahps; Flat Dog; M; Husband; 57
201; Mea-cheedups; Woman Bull; F; Wife; 53

202; Otse-muchachis; Chief at Night; M; Husband; 51[? Previous year age 64 other times like 1902 age 41, different years different ages. Gets younger.]
203; Usk-beeche-bay-ahoos; Many Talks With Him; F; Wife; 27

204; Dakpitsa-eahkoshkat; Little Bear; M; Widower; 65

205; Ope-edupish; Fat Tobacco; M; Husband; 76
206; Dakup-makpash; Medicine Calf; F; Wife; 73
207; Mahpootka-botsots; Strong Otter; M; Son; 15

208; Ahpaka-hedere-dakpitsch; Bear in a Cloud; M; Husband; 44
209; Miooetsheda-esash; Big Lark; F; Wife; 49
210; Esakakasha-manakis; Blake White Bear; M; Son; 18
211; Aska-wuts; Harry Old Dog; M; Son; 14

212; Eep-sheedis; Yellow Tail; M; Husband; 39
213; ---; Mrs. S.C. Davis; F; Wife; 35
214; Mei-rauk-shay; Summer; M; Son; 13
215; Alack-chee-ichis; Has Good Coos; M; Son; 9

216; Nah-kaps; Flat Back; M; Husband; 55
217; Ahpa-doochis; Takes Together; F; Wife; 59

218; Chate-bah-cush-ecosh; Wolf Looks Up; M; Husband; 41
219; Oote-hotchkish; Long Weasel; F; Wife; 51

220; Cheedup-akookish; Dummy Bull; M; Widower; 65

221; Eem-botsesh; Blood Man; M; Husband; 43
222; Ahwaka-meas; Woman on Top of Ground; F; Wife; 31
223; Ikpahne-ich; Pretty Medicine; F; Daugh.; 7
224; ---; Alberta Blood Man; F; Daugh.; 1

225; Dakpitsa-ahway-repeas; Bear Goes to Other Ground; M; Divorced; 32

226; Kookomish; Kittie Medicine Tail; F; Divorced; 22
227; ---; Mary B. Ground; F; Daugh.; 2

228; Dayka-ahspittech; Black Eagle; M; Husband; 35
229; Esa-keepa; Crooked Face; F; Wife; 29
230; Iswahka-miotchedish; Lucky Hoop; M; Son; 15
231; Dakpitska-ahn-duish; Bear that Raises His Paw; M; Son; 5

Census of the __Crow__ Indians of __Crow__ Agency __Montana__ taken
By __J.E. Edwards__, United States Indian Agent __June 30, 1901__

Key: Number; Indian Name; English Name; Sex; Relation; Age

232; Cheetaka-cahkoskat; Little Prairie Chicken; M; Husband; 53
233; Ahsha-ekash; Looks at the Lodge; F; Wife; 55

234; Mahkawas; The Bread; M; Husband; 40
235; Mekas-beasas; Stoops to Charge; F; Wife; 41

236; Bishka-kahdeas; Old Dog; M; Husband; 69
237; Mea-heahsas; Well Known Rock; F; Wife; 58

238; Lagak-hishis; Howard Red Bird; M; Widower; 22
239; Bahn-dush-tsay-heahsas; Plain Bead Work; F; Daugh.; 1

240; Eskochea-basah; Charges the Enemy; M; Widower; 64

241; Ahpit-kahdeas; Old Crane; M; Husband; 35
242; ---; Ella Farwell; F; Wife; 31
243; ---; Mary Crane; F; Daugh.; 10
244; ---; Maud Crane; F; Daugh.; 2

245; Peah-noops; Two Stinks; M; Husband; 36
246; Oowattah-ahoos; Plenty Irons; F; Wife; 28
247; Opus-kittush; Long Medicine Tobacco; M; Son; 2

248; Booah-lagak; Fish Bird; M; Widower; 40

249; Ahpit-dakpitska; Bear Crane; M; Husband; 62
250; Ische-itse; Pretty Hair; F; Wife; 50
251; Dakpitske-nake; Bear Child; M; Son; 14
252; Daykoosh-naks; Young Eagle; M; Son; 7
253; ---; George Bear Crane; M; Son; 5

254; Lagak-etashdesh; Bird Shirt; M; Husband; 61
255; Botsa-nahme-napes; Kills Three Men; F; Wife; 49
256; Ahpay-sheedes; Yellow Leaves; M; Son; 11

257; Cheedup-ehas; The Other Bull; M; Widower; 37
258; Daykoosh-mahks; Eagle Above; M; Son; 11

259; Ikpahne-chas; The Other Medicine; M; Husband; 32
260; Ahwooch-deedis; Walks to the Hole; F; Wife; 25
261; Makpash-heahsas; Shoots Plain Medicine; F; Daugh.; 8
262; Ache-lagaks; Bird Everyway; M; Son; 1

263; Itche-kahnetsesh; Bear Claw; M; Husband; 41
264; Utsewaks-ahoos; Begs Plenty; F; Wife; 35
265; Makpash-ope-ahoos; Medicine Rock Above; M; Son; 15

Census of the __Crow__ Indians of __Crow__ Agency __Montana__ taken
By __J.E. Edwards__, United States Indian Agent __June 30, 1901__

Key: Number; Indian Name; English Name; Sex; Relation; Age

266; Peda-kosh; Brings Ten Times; F; Daugh.; 6

267; Etashda-cheis; White Shirt; M; Husband; 71
268; Dich-heahsas; Strikes Well Known; F; Wife; 67
269; Esaska-eko-sheeish; Horse Turns Around; M; Son; 32

270; Besheesh; Shavings; M; Husband; 59
271; Hooche-sash; Wind; F; Wife; 54

272; ---; Albert Anderson; M; Husband; 32
273; ---; Sarah Anderson; F; Wife; 26
274; ---; Fannie Anderson; F; Daugh.; 8
275; ---; Rosa Anderson; F; Daugh.; 1

276; Echetegashes; The Elk; M; Husband; 51[?]
277; Ashu-makotesash; Big Head High Up; F; Wife; 45
278; Meneas-kooskuis-chedish; Hunts the Sioux; F; Daughter; 7

279; Poputa-naks; Frank Bethune; M; Husband; 27
280; Ah-dean-day-ate-chice; Knows the Road; F; Wife; 18

281; Ah-wah-cah-dace; Pukes on the Ground; M; Husband; 54
282; Hoksah-napis; Comes and Kills; F; Wife; 55
283; Ash-itse; Pretty River; F; Daugh.; 11

284; Esaska-schascheedes; Hunts the Arrow; M; Husband; 23
285; Wutta-makpash; Medicine Coyote; F; Wife; 18
286; ---; Joseph Hunts the Arrow; M; Son; 1

287; Esash-chedup; Blanket Bull; M; Husband; 33
288; Unda-itchis; Addie; F; Wife; 24
289; ---; Stanton B. Bull; M; Son; 2

290; Botsa-miesah; Big Man; M; Husband; 37
291; Minnesh-pesh; Swamp Flag; F; Wife; 41
292; ---; Michael B. Man; M; Son; 14

293; Noopa-malapes; Kills Twice; F; Widow; 65

294; Ahpa-esash; Big Nose; M; Husband; 56
295; Mi-iche-doochis; Takes Good Things; F; Wife; 49
296; Bahsatsie-basonda; Steals on Camp Ahead; F; Daugh.; 13

297; ---; George Suis; M; Husband; 25
298; Mahsheda-kotish; Julia Bad Boy; F; Wife; 23
299; Ahsay-chulees; Sings in Camp; M; Son; 8

Census of the __Crow__ Indians of __Crow__ Agency __Montana__ taken By __J.E. Edwards__, United States Indian Agent __June 30, 1901__

Key: Number; Indian Name; English Name; Sex; Relation; Age

300; ---; Wesley Bad Boy; M; Son; 4

301; Nahsah-tays; Hump Back; M; Husband; 53
302; Heles-sheis; Runs Among Them; F; Wife; 49

303; Oookah-sheis; Dust; M; Married Cheyenne; 33

304; Misk-sheiss; Talks Everything; M; Husband; 51
305; Botsa-wa-napes; Kills One Man; F; Wife; 44
306; Ah-shoe-ah-peas; Horn on Her Neck; F; Ad Dau; 7

307; Karooshis-eahas; Don't Run; M; Husband; 35
308; Andutsedush-heahsas; Slides Down Well Known; F; Wife; 40
309; Minnapesh-ahoos; Plenty Swamp Flag; F; Daugh.; 17
310; Chustah-ahkundis; Rides a Grey Horse; M; Son; 13
311; ---; Mary Don't Run; F; Daugh.; 4
312; Bekashes; The Bannock; F; Mother; 75

313; Eespe-ekash; Looks at the Lion; F; Widow; 67

314; Chate-cheakaps; Young Wolf; M; Widower; 56

315; Chedup-dashes; Bull Tongue; M; Husband; 60
316; Echete-ahkin-doochis; Catches on the Horses; F; Wife; 46

317; Helekas-ash; Along the Hillside; M; Divorced; 54
318; Isminats-ich; Old Shield; M; Son; 17

319; Eepse-mahka-kala-napes; Kills One With Medcn Pipe; F; Widow; 72

320; Oouka-manakish; Crazy Sister-in-Law; M; Husband; 73
321; Makula-ich; Carries Good; F; Wife; 58
322; Cheedups-echete; Hard Heart; F; Daugh.; 9

323; Basuk-ose; Goes Ahead; M; Husband; 51
324; Isminats-ich; Pretty Shield; F; Wife; 45
325; Ichis; Good; M; Son; 18
326; Meah-kots; Small Woman; F; Daugh.; 8

327; Meshodechitse; Medicine Shell; F; Widow; 47

328; Is-tuck-kay-os-seas; Shows His Gun; M; Divorced; 21

329; Chedup-cadish-dondase; Bull That Shows All Time; M; Husband; 36
330; Echete-mulukis; Sings; F; Wife; 34
331; Istuka-mahks; High Arrow; M; Son; 8

Census of the __Crow__ Indians of __Crow__ Agency __Montana__ taken By __J.E. Edwards__, United States Indian Agent __June 30, 1901__

Key: Number; Indian Name; English Name; Sex; Relation; Age

332; Hoop-itsahkahoh; Top of the Moccasin; M; Husband; 27
333; Bah-cay-key-bah-peash; Medicine Shell; F; Wife; 25
334; Etash-shooachat; Blue Shirt; M; Son; 7
335; ---; William Moccasin; M; Son; 1

336; Ahm-botsots-heahsas; Strong Well Known; M; Husband; 37
337; Ahshay-hedra-dichis; Strikes in Camp; F; Wife; 23
338; ---; Viola S. Known; F; Daugh.; 2

339; Kahkootsa; Drunkard; M; Husband; 45
340; Bahdahe-dane-bahdakish; Sings in the Woods; F; Wife; 44
341; Mea-nakose-nahks; Young Turtle Woman; F; Daugh.; 8

342; Chate-hishes; Red Wolf; M; Husband; 30
343; Besha-ekash; Comes to See the Buffalo; F; Wife; 23
344; ---; Laura Red Wolf; F; Daughter; 4

345; Ikpahne-naks; Medicine High Up; F; Widow; 56

346; Ahwakooda-kahdish; Old all the Time; M; Husband; 37
347; Istuka-makula; Shows a Child; F; Wife; 33
348; Arachuaka-noak; Work on the Farm; M; Son; 11
349; Botsaytse; Chief; M; Son; 10
350; Botsu-tush-botsash; Runs to the Men; M; Son; 2

351; Eakkook-sheedish; Yellow Coyote; F; Widow; 73

352; Edukish; The Meat; M; Husband; 45
353; Dudish; The Back; F; Wife; 48
354; Besha-mulukis; Buffalo That Sings; F; Daughter; 10
355; Nakose-nahks; Young Turtle; F; Daughter; 6

356; Chate-nak-sheedes; Young Yellow Wolf; M; Husband; 45
357; Doochis-heahsas; Takes Well Known; F; Wife; 48

358; Eahwookose; Inside the Mouth; M; Husband; 42
359; Makpash-ne-ahoos; Plenty Medicine; F; Wife; 45

360; Dahkpitsa-kahdeas; Old Bear; M; Husband; 47
361; Makupa-seesh; Hail Shows; F; Wife; 40
362; Ika-ahoos; Lots of Stars; M; Son; 16
363; Ahshua-dichis; Strikes Inside the House; F; Daughter; 11
364; Eskochitsa-maluk-ichis; Strawberry Sings Pretty; F; Daughter; 9
365; Bus-sock-kose; Goes Ahead; M; Son; 5
366; Lagaka-akuse; Bird That Shows; M; Son; 19

Census of the __Crow__ Indians of __Crow__ Agency __Montana__ taken By __J.E. Edwards__, United States Indian Agent __June 30, 1901__

Key: Number; Indian Name; English Name; Sex; Relation; Age

367; Eahkooka-asadish; Fox Goes Out; F; Widow; 53
368; Meshoditshe-lagak; Medicine Shell Bird; M; Son; 20
369; Eshpeahshea-kahdeish; Horace Long Bear; M; Son; 27

370; Dotsuish; Muskrat; F; Widow; 81

378; Minnetotseesh; The Moon; M; Batchelor[sic]; 30

379; Poputa-heahsas; Plain Owl; M; Husband; 41
380; Badup-kedup-duchis-dupay; Kills One Takes Two Guns; F; Wife; 39

381; Co-tah-dah-cock-cus; Swallow Bird; M; Husband; 25
382; Mea-itchis; Pretty Woman; F; Wife; 33

383; Isokoshe-noopis; Two Whistles; M; Widower; 43
384; Isdots-itchis; Good to Prisoners; F; Mother; 88

385; Kee-osh; He Says; M; Husband; 41
386; Bedupa-ekoshees; Beaver that Stretches; F; Wife; 53
387; ---; Bravo; M; Son; 12

388; Ishtopish; Eyes Open; F; Widow; 64

389; Dahkoopis; Cuts a Hole In It; M; Husband; 36
390; Mea-daka; Grey Woman; F; Wife; 41

391; Eep-kahdeas; Old Tail; M; Husband; 44
392; Mi-iche-okepis; Shoots Pretty Things; F; Wife; 22

393; Askindes; Holds On; M; Husband; 64
394; Ahwa-akinakuse; Stands on Top of Ground; F; Wife; 55

395; Wahpotkta; Otter Comes Out of Water; F; Widow; 67

396; Minne-koshis; Whistle Water; M; Widower; 41

397; Masheandache; Dreamer; M; Husband; 55
398; Istuka-doochis; Take a Gun; F; Wife; 53
399; Daka-ichis-amach; Mortimer Dreamer; M; Son; 18

400; Botsea-mahnahs; Paints Her Forehead; M; Husband; 51
401; Eskocheabiorup; Finds His Enemy; F; Wife; 53
402; ---; Eva Forehead; F; Daughter; 2
403; Puk-iees; Holds It in the Mouth; M; Son; 20

404; Mune-skoop-doochis; Takes a Crooked Stick; F; Widow; 85

Census of the __Crow__ Indians of __Crow__ Agency __Montana__ taken
By __J.E. Edwards__, United States Indian Agent __June 30, 1901__

Key: Number; Indian Name; English Name; Sex; Relation; Age

405; Umbich-esash; Don't Fall Down; M; Husband; 45
406; Esash-beduppa; Beaver Robe; F; Wife; 51

407; Kahnista; Small; M; Husband; 36
408; Eshippish-day-ichis; Goes to Mud Pretty; F; Wife; 31
409; Beeop-huche-naks; Young Hawk; M; Son; 5

423; Minnekashe-ahoos; Plenty Butterfly; M; Husband; 48
424; Esaka-noops; Two Horses; F; Wife; 49

412; Nak-paka-ish; Child in the Mouth; M; Husband; 57
413; Kahdeas; Old; F; Wife; 55
414; Ahcheke-ichis; The Spy; M; Son; 17
415; Eskoche-doochis; Joe Child in the Mouth; M; Son; 25

416; Noop-dichis; Strikes Twice; F; Widow; 89

417; Minnepahkichis; Ben Long Ear; M; Husband; 23
418; Up-pay-sheedish; Yellow Ears; F; Wife; 18
419; ---; Estella L. Ear; F; Daughter; 1

420; Peritseusses; Crow That Shows; F; Wife; 54
421; Esoskachesdakabachais; Grey Horse Chief; M; Ad Son; 5

422; Munash-malapes; Kills by the Woods; F; Widow; 61

423; Booah-hishes; Red Fish; M; Husband; 51
424; Mishoditsche-dichis; Strikes the Medicine Rock; F; Wife; 47
425; Bahkeda-basash; Blackbird in Front; M; Brother; 59

426; Ahsha-heletam-basash; Charges Through Camp; M; Husband; 60
427; Oomutish; Iron; F; Wife; 54

428; Besha-Cheeup; Buffalo Bull #2; M; Widower; 34

429; Ushmiha-chedish; Enemy Hunter; M; Husband; 69
430; Kotseish; Shakes; F; Wife; 59

431; Shebah-sheedish; Among the Fog; M; Husband; 42
432; Echeta-akuse; Horse on the Other Side; F; Wife; 30
433; Meshoritshe-heahsas; Well Known Shell; F; Daughter; 8
434; Ooka-sheedish; Yellow Deer; M; Son; 7
435; ---; Jewel Among the Fog; F; Daughter; 2

436; Ahwahkuan-dakpitsa; Bear in the Middle; M; Husband; 43
437; Echeta-achis; Knows a Horse; F; Wife; 37

Census of the __Crow__ Indians of __Crow__ Agency __Montana__ taken
By __J.E. Edwards__, United States Indian Agent __June 30, 1901__

Key: Number; Indian Name; English Name; Sex; Relation; Age

438; ---; [Kowees]; Ruth; F; Daughter; 14

438; Cheeduppa-shespitta; Black Bull; M; Husband; 55
440; Besha-naks; Buffalo Calf; F; Wife; 66

441; Bedupa-okeah-duis; Beaver That Slides; M; Husband; 64
442; Dutch-ka; Twin Woman; F; Wife; 66

443; Chate-ewotsodish; Busy Wolf; M; Husband; 65
444; Minnakpash; Swamp Flag; F; Wife; 40

445; Shegak-kahpa; Flat Boy; M; Husband; 41
446; Bah-che-chice; Pretty Feather; F; Wife; 37

447; Unmeathe; Bank; M; Husband; 36
448; Mahsha-ich-meas; Pretty Feather Woman; F; Wife; 32
449; ---; Howard Shane; M; Ad Son; 7

450; Lagak-cheah-noops; Two White Birds; M; Husband; 50
451; Ahkpahne-makpash; Medicine Porcupine; F; Wife; 49
452; Besha-naks-noops; Among the Buffalo; M; Son; 16 [Daughter in 1900.]
453; Etasch-daeka; Eagle Shirt; M; Son; 7

454; Bahsuk-naks; Turtle Child; F; Widow; 66

455; Mahma-nudeis; Edward Little Bear; M; Husband; 24
456; Oota-hukish; Spotted Weasel; F; Wife; 36

457; Maudut-kudesh; Pounded Meat; M; Husband; 59
458; Mahsha-undichis; Strikes Feathers; F; Wife; 57

459; Mahsha-kudesh; Holds the Feather; M; Husband; 51
460; Dakoshes; Eagle; F; Wife; 57
461; Besha-hishis; Throws Off on the Horse; M; Son; 18

462; Ahwahkun-lagaks; Bird in the Ground; M; Husband; 53
463; Napes-ekash; Looks at One that Kills; F; Wife; 38
464; Mindukse-ekuroos; Runs Toward the Fort; M; Son; 9

465; Wutta-eahkoots; Little Wolf #2; M; Widower; 66
466; Eskoochea-ahoos-dich; Strikes Plenty Enemies; F; Sister; 61
467; Dukedea-akuse; Knows the War; M; Son; 23

468; Oomutish; Iron; F; Widow; 63

469; Asuktuah-basash; Runs Between Them; M; Husband; 28

Census of the __Crow__ Indians of __Crow__ Agency __Montana__ taken
By __J.E. Edwards__, United States Indian Agent __June 30, 1901__

Key: Number; Indian Name; English Name; Sex; Relation; Age

470; Ahwoosh-heahsas; Sweathouse Well Known; F; Wife; 21
471; ---; Robert Runs Between Them; M; Son; 2

472; Dotske; The Twins; M; Husband; 57
473; Ikpahne-makpash; Medicine Porcupine; F; Wife; 59
474; Ekupa-ie; Pretty Hat; F; Mother; 72

475; Chedupa-seesh; Bull That Shows; M; Husband; 31
476; Echete; Horse; F; Wife; 30
477; Eskoche-aseesh; Spies the Enemy; M; Son; 7
478; ---; Ida Bull That Shows; F; Daughter; 2

479; Meshoditsche-wakpahs; Medicine Shell; F; Widow; 47

480; Ahmako-istisha-naks; Young Swallow; M; Husband; 37
481; Oote-ewandies; Plays with the Weasel; F; Wife; 23
482; Ech-keas-boatush; Egg Inside the Bird; M; Son; 1

483; Issama-malapes; Kills on Her Own Ground; F; Widow; 61
484; Daeka-makpash; Medicine Eagle; M; Son; 22

485; Oomuta-ahpies; Iron Necklace; F; Widow; 85

486; Washada-esash; Charges Strong; M; Husband; 60
487; Itshades; Kills in the Track; F; Wife; 59
488; Bishka-botsots; Charles Strong; M; Son; 16
489; ---; Mary Charges Strong; F; Daughter; 11

490; Chate-nakish; Leads a Wolf; M; Husband; 51
491; Naksha-undichis; Strikes First; F; Wife; 55
492; Masha-hishes-heahsas; Well Known Red Feather; F; Gr Dau; 9
493; Eskochea-ichis; Pretty Enemy; M; Son; 1

494; Ahmuapes; The Kicker; M; Husband; 60
495; Arleunda-aches; Knows the Road; F; Wife; 61

496; Eseeah-koosh; Covers His Face; M; Husband; 51
497; Uckish-bedane-dichis; Strikes One Going In House; F; Wife; 55
498; Cheedup-be-day-sot; Bull Near the Water; M; Son; 18

499; Cheedupa-ede-ekech; Bull Goes Hunting; M; Husband; 74
500; Daka-wahtis; One Buffalo Calf; F; Wife; 60

501; E-o-dish; Full Mouth; M; Husband; 45
502; Bedupa-ehas; The Other Beaver; F; Wife; 49
503; Bea-ehos; The Other Woman; F; Daughter; 16

Census of the __Crow__ Indians of __Crow__ Agency __Montana__ taken
By __J.E. Edwards__, United States Indian Agent __June 30, 1901__

Key: Number; Indian Name; English Name; Sex; Relation; Age

504; Ahshuputsuah-dooich; Get One Horn; M; Husband; 45
505; Isminats-budwasich; Shield at the Door; F; Wife; 36
506; Ischesa-hela-amach; Sits Toward the Nest; M; Son; 14

507; Isoskay-bachate-chis; Alexander Upshaw; M; Married White W; 25

508; Ooat-budeka-dooch; Takes a Gun #2; M; Husband; 38
509; Botsuah-tush; Sweet Grass; F; Wife; 46

510; Shegack-amach; Bad Boy; M; Husband; 34
511; Eka-ahpka-amach; Sits With a Star; F; Wife; 24
512; ---; David Bad Boy; M; Son; 4

513; Eshasha-heahsas; Plain Face; F; Widow; 59

514; Isooet-botsesh; Smart Iron; M; Husband; 30
515; ---; Mary Townsend; F; Wife; 27
516; ---; Mabel M. Townsend; F; Daughter; 6
517; ---; Fred A. Townsend; M; Son; 4

518; Epeahkot-esash; Big Magpie; M; Husband; 52
519; Beka-haredich; Among the Grass; F; Wife; 54

520; Mahedish; Does Anything; M; Husband; 41
521; Ahwaku-cheduah-naks; Young Ground Cedar; F; Wife; 47

522; Shagak-doochis; Boy That Grabs; M; Husband; 57[?]
523; Mekaspe-doochis; Takes Hold of the Cloth; F; Wife; 60

524; Ahsha-okepish; Shoots the Lodge; M; Husband; 55
525; Ikpahne-ekash; Looks at the Medicine; F; Wife; 47

526; Ahrocheis; Stops; M; Husband; 33
527; Esasha-ich; Paints Her Face Pretty; F; Wife; 31
528; Opish-ekash; Percy Stops; M; Son; 14
529; Istuka-mulukis; Sings to the Arrow; F; Daughter; 7
530; ---; Paul C. Stops; M; Son; 2

531; Ahlud-esush; Big Shoulder Blade; M; Husband; 49
532; Beshay-heahsus; Well Known; Buffalo; F; Wife; 38
533; Arap-apushay-dichesay; Bullets Don't Strike Him; M; Son; 8

534; Bah-kaht-konsees; Bad Baby; M; Widower; 65

535; Cheeup-ahkade-duse; Stands Over a Bull; M; Husband; 29
536; Ah-bay-da-itchis; Pretty Medicine; F; Wife; 25

Census of the __Crow__ Indians of __Crow__ Agency __Montana__ taken
By __J.E. Edwards__, United States Indian Agent __June 30, 1901__

Key: Number; Indian Name; English Name; Sex; Relation; Age

537; She-cack-bah-pash; Medicine Boy; M; Son; 8
538; Bapash-to-ba-deedish; Otter Walks to Water; F; Daughter; 1

539; Cheeup-quasah-datsish; Bull In Sight; M; Husband; 31
540; Bosh-dootchis; Takes a Feather; F; Wife; 16

541; It-schoc-daytah; No Shinbone; M; Husband; 47
542; Mahkeeda-sheedish; Yellow Blackbird; F; Wife; 47
543; Bah-cup-pay-deedish; Lizard That Walks; F; Daughter; 14
544; Cheedup-etahsich; Henry Shinbone; M; Son; 23
545; Nahmis; Three; F; Mother; 75

546; Ahshkay-shopis; Four Balls; M; Husband; 59
547; Meshoditsche-hishes; Red Rock; F; Wife; 57
548; Kahdeasas; Not Old; M; Son; 11

549; Ahkabosh; Froze; M; Husband; 38
550; Mahpay-e-kash; Sees in a Day; F; Wife; 35
551; Espeah-kishe-kahdeas; Old Bobcat; M; Son; 8
552; Hayday-de-qu-pish; Gets Down Among Them; M; Son; 4

553; Mahray-keir-ahplis; Shell on the Neck; M; Husband; 38
554; Ise-meneas; His Door; F; Wife; 41
555; Cheedup-ay-koos; Bull That Knows; M; Son; 16

556; Minnay-e-koos-chis; Comes Out of the Water; F; Widow; 67

557; Ahoo-ahk-ichis; Pretty On Top; M; Husband; 37
558; Itshooaprsich; Pretty Back of the Neck; F; Wife; 36
559; Mah-hahk-ichis; Plenty Shells; M; Son; 11

560; Ahdo-chea-beas; Woman Where She Stops; F; Divorced; 37
561; Ah-bah-keas-sash; Cloud Shows Plain; M; Son; 17
562; Ahdean-day-ah-chatis; Follows the Track; F; Daughter; 12

563; Chees-makpash; Medicine Tail; M; Husband; 43
564; Itshe-mahkpash; She is Medicine; F; Wife; 40

565; Cheedeer-esahs; Not Afraid; M; Husband; 43
566; Noopis; Two; F; Wife; 51
567; Bahput-chee-keep-beas; Ant Woman; F; Daughter; 12
568; ---; George Not Afraid; M; Son; 3

569; Escheeta-nevsaus; Knows His Horse; M; Husband; 41
570; Mekayshay-hishis; Fat Snake; F; Wife; 51

Census of the __Crow__ Indians of __Crow__ Agency __Montana__ taken
By __J.E. Edwards__, United States Indian Agent __June 30, 1901__

Key: Number; Indian Name; English Name; Sex; Relation; Age

571; Ahpiet-sheedis; Yellow Crane; M; Husband; 57
572; Uk-pa-had-dee-is; Does Things Together; F; Wife; 45

573; Push-ah-kos; Cut; M; Widower; 45

574; Dakpitsa-ahshuse; James Carpenter; M; --; 21
575; Ismahka-wisha: Got a Hoop; F; Wife; 18

576; Napk-ahwot-nee-as; One Child Woman; F; Widow; 57

577; Ahke-mah-kaweish; Hoop on the Forehead; M; Husband; 53
578; Ahshay-whoo-a-aychis; Knows the Whole Camp; F; Wife; 54
579; Mussick-awats; One Turtle; M; Son; 11
580; Medesha-dooch; Takes the Dead; F; Mother; 73

581; Ikpay-ahoos; Plenty Wing; M; Husband; 51
582; Ismanat-heahsas; Plain Shield; F; Wife; 52
583; Lagak-heahsas; Big Bird; M; Gr Son; 9

584; Bah-dee-shis; Jerked Meat; M; Husband; 20
585; Botseah-bedas; Pine Fire; F; Wife; 28

586; Ay-kuse; Knows; M; Husband; 28
587; Echick-heas; Gets There First; F; Wife; 24
588; ---; Sarah Knows; F; Daughter; 6
589; Edwea; Dummy; F; Mother; 55

590; Mumasen-dichis; Strikes by Side of Water; F; Widow; 85
591; Menacheis; White Goose; M; Son; 50

592; Almasus; The Fog; M; Husband; 73
593; Makula-wood-dichis; Takes Two Guns; F; Wife; 63

594; Minooksha-kahdeas; Old Alligator; M; Husband; 57
595; Chut-napis; Kills on the Lookout; F; Wife; 62

596; ---; Tom Laforge; M; Husband; 36
597; Mea-kahdeas; Old Woman; F; Wife; 35

598; Keasha; Runner; M; Husband; 49
599; Icheat-ekash; Looks at the Tobacco; F; Wife; 49
600; Beeshay-ahkak-wahchis; Sits on the Buffalo; F; Daughter; 12

601; Dakpitsa-beeadas; Fire Bear; M; Widower; 52
602; Bea-hutchkis; Long Woman; F; Ad Dau; 15

Census of the __Crow__ Indians of __Crow__ Agency __Montana__ taken By __J.E. Edwards__, United States Indian Agent __June 30, 1901__

Key: Number; Indian Name; English Name; Sex; Relation; Age

603; Ekeeka-dase; Goes Together; M; Husband; 34
604; Makapo-ich; Pretty Hail; F; Wife; 32
605; Oatah-ich; Jane Goes Together; F; Daughter; 11
606; ---; Wesley Goes Together; M; Son; 5

607; Cheas-kuch-kish; Spotted Tail; M; Husband; 51
608; Ootah-sheedish; Yellow All Over; F; Wife; 41
609; Etoshday-bachpash; Medicine Dress; F; Daughter; 19
610; Echeen-bachpash; Medicine Horse; F; Daughter; 8

611; Bit-quash; Onion; M; Husband; 46
612; Bershea-bachpash; Medicine Buffalo Cow; F; Wife; 40
613; Ahwaka-wahkees-sas; Plain Mountain; F; Daughter; 10
614; Undasha-day-bahah-chis; Charges Strong; M; Son; 7

615; Up-pay-ut-tay; Sharp Nose #2; M; Husband; 36
616; Ahchook-coode-dadush; Strikes and Strikes Again; F; Wife; 42

617; Dachpitsa-beas; Bear Woman; F; Widow; 55
618; Bee-bush-sas; Rock Ahead; F; Daughter; 16

619; ---; Josh Buffalo; M; Husband; 39
620; Akean-badacheck-easos; Ties Knot on Top of Head; F; Wife; 31
621; ---; Meadow Lark Stays; F; Daughter; 1

622; Dakpitsa-ahoos; Plenty Bears; M; Husband; 61
623; Kahdeas; Old; F; Wife; 51

624; ---; Richard Wallace; M; Husband; 35
625; Bash-ichis; Pretty Feather; F; Wife; 33
626; ---; Susie Wallace; F; Daughter; 6

627; Ah-cock-bee-dash; Hears Fire; M; Husband; 37
628; ---; Mary Bompard; F; Wife; 40

629; Ah-puck-kay; Long Neck; M; Husband; 33
630; Ushcock-uttah-dup-pace; Kills Close to Camp; F; Wife; 41
631; Bes-shay-e-duhs; Buffalo Stands Up; F; Daughter; 10

632; ---; Louis Bompard; M; Husband; 41
633; ---; Lois Bompard; F; Wife; 32
634; ---; Peter Bompard; M; Son; 11
635; ---; Rosa Bompard; F; Daughter; 6

636; ---; Rosa Peters; F; Mother; 29
637; ---; Arthur Peters; M; Son; 12

Census of the __Crow__ Indians of __Crow__ Agency __Montana__ taken
By __J.E. Edwards__, United States Indian Agent __June 30, 1901__

Key: Number; Indian Name; English Name; Sex; Relation; Age

638; ---; Elsie Peters; F; Daughter; 10
639; ---; George Peters; M; Son; 6
640; ---; Alice Peters; F; Daughter; 1

641; ---; Joseph Martinez; M; Widower; 28

642; Chate-dock-coo-chis; Young Hairy Wolf; M; Husband; 56
643; Ahdache-waycoo-itchis; Comes From War Pretty; F; Wife; 52
644; Bah-cup-say-keas-sos; Floy Hairy Wolf; F; Daughter; 13
645; Up-pay-huch-kay; Long Nose; M; Son; 19

646; Dah-sea-hash; The Other Heart; F; Widow; 56

647; Bean-da-ichis; Strikes the Water; F; Widow; 74
648; Dah-pittosh; Grasshopper; M; Son; 24

649; Ahwahahs; Gros Ventre; M; Husband; 32
650; Bea-dane-dah-coos; Stops by the Water; F; Wife; 31
651; Bea-ahoos; Plenty Woman; F; Daughter; 10

652; Chea-dup-cheeis; Grey Bull; M; Husband; 63
653; Bah-duck-cah-peas; Going About; F; Wife; 61
654; Bee-itchis; Pretty Rock; F; Daughter; 11
655; Bish-push; Cut #2; M; Son; 20

656; Bah-pittay-dov-pus; Two Otters; F; Widow; 72
657; Ush-hay-dosh-days; Goes to Camp; M; Son; 19

658; Echeo-duch-days; Goes to the Horses; M; Husband; 36
659; Bah-euch-euis; Striped Snake; F; Daughter; 6

660; Ah-dah-sea-ahoos; Shows Plenty; M; Husband; 43
661; Bea-ha-wat-tosh; One Woman; F; Wife; 45

662; Um-bah-day-es-sos; Goes Farther Along; F; Widow; 35
663; Uck-a-chase; Knows; F; Mother; 71
664; Dea-cosh-bah-cush; High Eagle; M; Son; 11

665; Ah-wah-kah-we-sos; Big Mountain; M; Husband; 44
666; Cuckay-dups-doochis; Takes Two Lances; F; Wife; 54
667; Ish-co-che-hayda-dose; Runs Against His Enemy; M; Son; 21

668; Chesay-itche-badakah; Pretty Tail; M; Husband; 53
669; Un-dee-dichis; Walks Pretty; F; Wife; 51
670; ---; Lucy Stewart; F; Ad Dau; 16

Census of the __Crow__ Indians of __Crow__ Agency __Montana__ taken
By __J.E. Edwards__, United States Indian Agent __June 30, 1901__

Key: Number; Indian Name; English Name; Sex; Relation; Age

671; Bich-pus; Spaniard; M; Husband; 31
672; Bachic-kahcoo-deechis; Looks at One Comes From War; F; Wife; 29

673; Baam-cheem-beas; White Woman; F; Widow; 66

674; Bea-noopus; Two Women; F; Widow; 62

675; Ah-way-e-kosh; Looks at the Ground; M; Husband; 38
676; Bah-dah-kiss; Horse That Sings; F; Wife; 22
677; ---; McKinley L. Ground; M; Son; 3

678; ---; Thomas Jefferson; M; Husband; 31
679; Lagak-naks; Bird Child; F; Wife; 20
680; ---; Lillian Jefferson; F; Daughter; 2

681; Bash-day-tush; No Name; F; Widow; 80

682; Esock-kan-dahkos; On Top of the House; M; Husband; 24
683; Minnetotse-ish-ekash; Looks at the Sun; F; Wife; 22
684; ---; Iowa House; M; Son; 3 [Daughter in 1900.]
685; ---; Florida House; F; Daughter; 1

686; Up-chay-keas-sos; Voice Well Known; M; Widower; 53

687; ---; Katherine Scott; F; Mother; 29
688; ---; Paul Scott; M; Son; 10
689; ---; Emma Scott; F; Daughter; 7
690; ---; Pearl Scott; F; Daughter; 6
691; ---; Frank Scott; M; Son; 1

692; ---; Frank Shane; M; Husband; 31
693; Bah-chop-dah-beam; Kills With Her Husband; F; Wife; 27

694; Oomuta-nahbeas; Three Irons; M; Widower; 58
695; Dah-cheas; Drinking all the Time; M; Son; 10

696; Dapitsay-seandacocus; Bird in the Morning; M; Husband; 22
697; Unda-ichis; Goes Pretty; F; Wife; 32

698; Eday-dootchis; Takes Himself; M; Husband; 35
699; Dack-kah-shis; The Eagle; F; Wife; 20
700; E-doos-sos; Can't Get Up; F; Mother; 65

701; She-bah-sha-dush; Fog in the Morning; M; Husband; 53
702; Easa-key-pay-naks; Crooked Face Child; F; Wife; 50
703; ---; John Morning; M; Son; 10

Census of the __Crow__ Indians of __Crow__ Agency __Montana__ taken
By __J.E. Edwards__, United States Indian Agent __June 30, 1901__

Key: Number; Indian Name; English Name; Sex; Relation; Age

704; ---; Ruth Morning; F; Daughter; 4

705; Payduch-chee-bachpash; Medicine Crow; M; Husband; 51
706; Bachpash; Medicine; F; Wife; 47
707; Ah-woos-dah-cuss; Young Badger; M; Son; 13
708; Ah-way-chee-da-cuss; Goes Pretty; M; Son; 8
709; Ah-way-itchise; Chester Medicine Crow; M; Son; 3

710; Bee-shay-che-de-esos; Big Ox; M; Widower; 66
711; Esoc-uck-bahdah-pace; Kills With Her Brother; F; Sister; 61

712; ---; Wm. Elliott Towne; M; Orphan; 14
713; ---; Ida M. Towne; F; Sister; 11

714; Dosh-bah-cha-chis; Strong Heart; M; Husband; 40
715; Be-dee-sheas-she-dush; Stands to the Sun; F; Wife; 39

716; Qua-dah-bah-chis; Sits in the Middle; M; Husband; 55
717; Bahdup-pay-heahsos; Kills Well Known; F; Wife; 53
718; Bedah-tashis-chay-ichis; Pretty Butterfly; F; Daughter; 12

719; A-dah-shoes; Blue Belly; M; Husband; 61
720; Osh-shone-badup-pace; Kills in rear of House; F; Wife; 62

721; Eche-dosh; Brings Horses; F; Mother; 41
722; Eckpah-dea-dacock-cush; His Medicine Bird; F; Daughter; 5
723; Dacock-uckbah-do-shis; Eats with a Bird; M; Ad son; 12
724; Bahputtah-ahway-taydas; Otter goes a long ways; M; Ad son; 10

725; Ahduckchee-chay-ichis; Strikes His Enemy Pretty; M; Husband; 40
726; Es-che-kay-pay; Crooked Face; F; Wife; 38
727; Dackpitsay-hada-tahsos; Gets Their Medicine Tobacco; M; Son; 5

728; Day-chay-ahoos; Many Prisoners; F; Widow; 58

729; Cah-dah-buck-kesos; Throws It Away; M; Husband; 28
730; Is-oo-what-tus; Her Iron; F; Wife; 28

731; Ea-cook-cah-cheas; White Fox; M; Husband; 36
732; Basheede-checa-ahoos; Plenty Medicine Rock; F; Wife; 41
733; Dah-cock-uckpah-dahcus; Stays with a Bird; F; Daughter; 8

734; Ahwayka-ways-bachedis; David Dawes; M; Husband; 21
735; ---; Mary Bear's Tooth; F; Wife; 21

736; Escock-kay-keas-sos; Well Known Lance; F; Widow; 74

Census of the __Crow__ Indians of __Crow__ Agency __Montana__ taken
By __J.E. Edwards__, United States Indian Agent __June 30, 1901__

Key: Number; Indian Name; English Name; Sex; Relation; Age

737; Ah-dush-cos-pay; Crooked Arm; M; Husband; 46
738; Ah-kok-de-chis; Catches up and Strikes; F; Wife; 31
739; ---; Herbert Crooked Arm; M; Son; 12
740; Ishane-baduck-chadacock; Bird Ties Knot Top Head; M; Son; 18[?]
[7 years in 1900.]
741; ---; James Crooked Arm; M; Son; 4

742; Bee-dup-kah-deas; Old Beaver; F; Widow; 48

743; Bee-shas-sah-hoos; Comes to the Buffalo; F; Maiden; 20

744; Cheeup-dah-sis; Bull Tongue #2; M; Husband; 37
745; Bah-keam-beas; Blackbird Woman; F; Wife; 31
746; Cuckey-shean-doochis; Takes Yellow Spotted Horse; F; Daughter; 11
747; Ah-dup-pis; Stabs; F; Mother; 79

748; Bee-day-she-kosh; Looks at the Water; M; Husband; 43
749; Bee-dee-dup-pace; Takes Across the Water; F; Wife; 41
750; ---; Francis Tiffany; M; Ad son; 15

751; Cah-kay-doot-chis; Takes a Lance; F; Widow; 63

752; Bish-ka-cheis; White Dog; M; Husband; 47
753; Bachay-hay-what-deechis; Strikes One Man; F; Wife; 49

754; Dough-seas; Buffalo Neck Hair; M; Husband; 58
755; Bah-bah-dah-cosh; Nearly Gone; F; Wife; 60

756; Esuck-bon-tuch-chais; Mountain Sheep; M; Husband; 33
757; E-cook-key-e-kosh; Looks at the Fox; F; Wife; 35
758; Bacock-dahsay-itchis; Good Hearted Bird; F; Daughter; 10
759; Che-co-key-dah-pace; Kills the Young Man; M; Son; 7

760; Dahcock-dah-dah-bish; Morris Shaffer; M; Husband; 20
761; ---; Annie Wesley; F; Wife; 19

762; Edea-hay-bah-pash; Medicine Breath; M; Widower; 38

763; Ah-shoos; The Horn; M; Husband; 57
764; It-tuch-chis; All Alone; F; Wife; 47
765; Kuck-key-con-dah-das; Goes After Spotted Horse; M; Son; 8

766; ---; Mrs. William Blaine; F; Mother; 28
767; ---; James Blaine; M; Son; 12
768; ---; Florence Blaine; F; Daughter; 7

Census of the __Crow__ Indians of __Crow__ Agency __Montana__ taken By __J.E. Edwards__, United States Indian Agent __June 30, 1901__

Key: Number; Indian Name; English Name; Sex; Relation; Age

769; Ah-pas-seas; Shows His Ear; M; Widower; 53
770; Dutch-choas; Muskrat; F; Mother; 71

771; Chay-esos; Big Sheep; M; Husband; 32
772; Dock-kosh; Turtle; F; Wife; 45
773; ---; Florence Big Sheep; F; Daughter; 4

774; ---; James Hill; M; Batchelor[sic]; 27

775; ---; Dexter; M; Husband; 26
776; Echete-cheis-ahkundis; Rides a White Bellied Horse; F; Wife; 15

777; Ah-wah-chis; Sits Down; F; Widow; 53
778; Ahdean-dauah-waychis; Sits Along the Road; F; Daughter; 20

779; Dosh-bah-cha-chis; Strong Heart; F; Widow; 71

780; Awaycah-wadane-badakis; Sings in the Mountains; M; Husband; 29
781; Esos-Kaybah-och-che-duc; Lucky Horse; F; Wife; 31

782; Sh-chon-sheedish; Yellow Head; M; Husband; 42
783; Bahput-tah-pee-deechis; Strikes One With Necklace; F; Wife; 46
784; Eshe-bah-cha-chis; Ruth Yellow Head; F; Daughter; 16

785; Ah-hoc-cot-dea-dish; Sun Goes Slow; M; Husband; 39
786; Oak-cah-sis; Antelope; F; Wife; 16
787; Ahwaycaway-dedawah; Sits on the Mountain; M; Son; 1

788; Oo-what-kah-wish; Iron Fork; M; Husband; 66
789; Bah-itchay-doot-chis; Takes Pretty Things; F; Wife; 64

790; Bean-dahcome-baday-kay; Crazy Pen d'Oreille; M; Husband; 61
791; Bah-cut-chay-itchis; Pretty Striped Snake; F; Wife; 52

792; Ock-cheis; White Antelope; M; Husband; 39
793; Bah-hah-beas; Spring Woman; F; Wife; 33
794; E-che-che-sosh; Big Root; F; Daughter; 10
795; Ah-may-ahche-day-chase; Knows Her Luck; F; Daughter; 6

796; Badakis-shebacha-cheis; Redwood Chief; M; Widower; 52

797; ---; Mrs. F. Sucher; F; Mother; 23
798; ---; Belle Sucher; F; Daughter; 7
799; ---; Hattie Sucher; F; Daughter; 6

800; Bah-doot-cha-key-pish; Takes Wrinkle; M; Husband; 55

Census of the __Crow__ Indians of __Crow__ Agency __Montana__ taken By __J.E. Edwards__, United States Indian Agent __June 30, 1901__

Key: Number; Indian Name; English Name; Sex; Relation; Age

801; Dupe-tush-der-chis; Strikes Both Ways; F; Wife; 52
802; Chee-sos-cos; Elmer Takes Wrinkle; M; Son; 19

803; Shee-day; Yellow; F; Widow; 65

804; Oo-way-it-chis; Pretty Paint; M; Husband; 28
805; Ahway-kawah-kain-beas; Woman on Top of Mountain; F; Wife; 27
806; E-kay-sup-peas; Seven Stars; F; Daughter; 13
807; Echick-kay-sah-dish; Comes Out First; F; Ad Dau.; 10

808; Bah-chea-keas-sos; Fights Well Known #1; M; Husband; 42
809; Is-chis-say-it-chis; Pretty Nest; F; Wife; 37

810; Oo-What-tish; The Iron; M; Husband; 42
811; Bashow-dea-chic-itchis; Pretty Medicine Rock; F; Wife; 40
812; Bun-dock-cope-dah-cuss; Woodpecker's Child; M; Son; 17
813; Ecup-pah-keas-sos; Gets Down Well Known; M; Son; 15
814; Es-been-dotch-cheas; Little Shield; M; Son; 10
815; Ah-duch-che-itchis; Good Coos; M; Son; 7

816; Dosh-kosh; Child; M; Husband; 40
817; Bee-dup-eas; Little Beaver; F; Wife; 37

818; ---; John Wallace; M; Husband; 42
819; Oo-tay-sah-dis; Weasel Goes Out; F; Wife; 49
820; E-chu-dah-keas-sos; Well Known Horse; F; Ad Dau.; 9

821; Oo-tay-doo-bah-kais; Cross Weasel; M; Widower; 57
822; Ekup-pah-wah-chis; Snapping Dog; M; Son; 33 [Choteau in 1900.]

823; Bah-kea-dah; Blackbird; M; Husband; 50
824; Bachay-ahkahn-dupace; Kills Six Men; F; Wife; 58

825; Ish-bern-dotch-sheda; Yellow Shield; M; Husband; 76
826; Bah-dah-kis; Sings; F; Wife; 75

827; Chate-uck-pah-deedish; Walks With a Wolf; M; Widower; 25
828; Ecbean-dock-sass; Little Colt; F; Daughter; 8

829; Bee-pah-pus-sis; Round Rock; M; Son; 42
830; Bah-dup-pay-keasos; Kills Well Known; F; Mother; 76
831; Hay-day-ach-days; Runs in Among Them; M; Son; 34

832; Dupe-doot-chis; Takes Two; M; Husband; 27
833; Ah-dough-chea-ah-chase; Knows Where She Stops; F; Wife; 19

Census of the __Crow__ Indians of __Crow__ Agency __Montana__ taken
By __J.E. Edwards__, United States Indian Agent __June 30, 1901__

Key: Number; Indian Name; English Name; Sex; Relation; Age

834; Dapitska-neen-dates; Bear That Don't Walk; M; Husband; 38
835; ---; Mrs. Wm. Hawks; F; Wife; 35
836; Ah-dup-pah-hoose; Lucy Hawks; F; Daughter; 17
837; Es-chis-say-bah-pash; Medicine Nest; M; Son; 5
838; ---; Annie Shows a Pipe; F; Daughter; 10

839; Bah-shay-kah-duck-kay; Lean Man; M; Widower; 46

840; Um-bah-sah-ahoos; Charges Plenty; M; Husband; 39
841; Bachay-cush-bahdukiss; Sings to Man; F; Wife; 44
842; Bah-tay-day-keas-sos; Steals Plain; M Son; 16
843; Duck-cock-dahcuss; Bird; F; Daughter; 8
844; Bashay-bachpash; Medicine Buffalo; M; Son; 2

845; ---; David Stewart; M; Husband; 27
846; Ekup-pah-wah-chis; Sits With the Stars; F; Wife; 33
847; Ekus-sah-itchis; Pretty Snake; F; Daughter; 9

848; Bee-dock-cup-pis; Goose Goes Over the Hill; M; Husband; 77
849; Um-beas-say-chu-dish; Hunts to Lie Down; F; Wife; 75

850; Oo-kutchis-say; Puts on Antelope Cap; M; Husband; 58
851; Op-put-tay; Long Neck; F; Wife; 59
852; ---; Herbert Antelope Cap; M; Son; 16
853; Bay-ray-day-tuss; Proud; F; Sister; 65

854; Mitot-duspis; Passes Everything; M; Husband; 27
855; Besha-amach; Sits on the Buffalo; F; Wife; 27

856; Echean-bachpash; Medicine Horses; F; Widow; 52
857; Dah-coock-sah-hoos; Comes From the Birds; M; Son; 11 [In 1900 a daughter.]
858; ---; Hugh Leider; M; Son; 25

859; Daeka-kahdeas; Carl Leider; M; Husband; 33
860; Basho-deedich-chayoppes; Medicine Rock Necklace; F; Wife; 19
861; ---; Agnes Leider; F; Daughter; 4
862; ---; Carl Leider, Jr.; M; Son; 1

863; Ah-dup-pah-hoose; The Arapahoe; M; Husband; 52
864; A-way-co-case; Spider; F; Wife; 39
865; Chuch-kay-esos; Big Chicken; M; Son; 17
866; Ouka-be-das; Fire Deer; M; Son; 12

867; Bah-put-tus; The Fly; M; Husband; 71
868; Awasha-ishdaco-shabea; Gros Ventre Red Wom[an] Bird; Wife; 57

Census of the __Crow__ Indians of __Crow__ Agency __Montana__ taken
By __J.E. Edwards__, United States Indian Agent __June 30, 1901__

Key: Number; Indian Name; English Name; Sex; Relation; Age

869; Iscehe-haydane-doochis; Takes Among Enemy #2; M; Husband; 27
870; Sus-bah-doochis; Takes Quick; F; Wife; 28
871; Dah-cook-dacass; Bird Child; M; Son; 9
872; Dackpitsa-esock-cuss; Bear Old Man; M; Son; 6

873; Bosh-day-tush; No Name; F; Widow; 49
874; Itch-okepish; Shot Himself; M; Son; 9

875; E-kupa-pay-bah-coosh; Hat Above; F; Widow; 73

876; Bah-put-tosh; Otter; M; Husband; 24
877; Bah-cup-pah-e-chice; Pretty Hail; F; Wife; 33

878; E-sees-be-tay; Black Hair; M; Husband; 52
879; Been-day-chay-esa-hay; Strikes Between the Forts; F; Wife; 47
880; Bah-cup-pah-ahoos; Plenty Hail; M; Son; 17
881; Ah-chay-itsche-peas; Jumps Over; M; Son; 8
882; It-chit-chey-eas; Small Medicine Tobacco; F; Daughter; 5
883; Echay-hishes; Red Feet; M; Son; 14

884; Chate-bee-dish-she-days; Wolf Goes to Water; M; Widower; 75

885; Cheedup-dah-cock-cus; Bull Bird; M; Divorced; 29

886; Un-day-it-chice; Goes Ahead Pretty; F; Divorced; 18

887; Ecupe-pay-cheis; White Hat; M; Husband; 55
888; Eck-bah-dea-bachpash; Her Medicine is Medicine; F; Wife; 53
889; Bea-shepittas; Black Rock; M; Son; 19

890; Chate-bachpash; Medicine Wolf; M; Husband; 73
891; Bee-dane-bah-dah-kiss; Sings Going In; F; Wife; 63

892; Chip-pah-pos-shis; Ground Squirrel; M; Husband; 33
893; Ah-way-cah-wah-sheas; Mountain That Shows; F; Wife; 46

894; Ecot-osh-heas; Shows a Little; M; Husband; 37
895; Bah-dah-pay-itchis; Kills Good; F; Wife; 32
896; Uck-kosh-e-kosh; Looks at the Sun; M; Son; 12
897; Bes-koo-kah-dah-biss; Iron Wings; M; Son; 5 [Name, Rock Moves Along age 6 in 1900.]
898; Achpanea-achpedaish; Walks With Medicine; M; Son; 2

899; Ah-peeh-cos; Covers His Neck; M; Husband; 62
900; Isbeen-dah-chay-itchis; Pretty Shield; F; Wife; 62
901; Ahpeachay-apah-doochis; Catches With Rope On; M; Son; 5

Census of the __Crow__ Indians of __Crow__ Agency __Montana__ taken
By __J.E. Edwards__, United States Indian Agent __June 30, 1901__

Key: Number; Indian Name; English Name; Sex; Relation; Age

902; Ope-kahdeas; Old Tobacco; M; Husband; 51
903; Bit-che-doot-chis; Takes a Knife; F; Wife; 57

904; Eche-day-kahdeas; Old Horse; M; Husband; 50
905; Mea-kowees; Mrs. Nate Record; F; Wife; 45
906; Itsuitsa-ichis; Charlie Record; M; Son; 10
907; ---; Dora Record; F; Daughter; 7
908; Bin-dotch-ut-tosh; Off Shield; M; Son; 4

909; Oosh-bah-chasis; Strong; M; Divorced; 27

910; E-say-kep-pa; Wrinkle Face; F; Divorced; 57
911; Bah-chay-cheas; Steals on Camp; M; Son; 20

912; Bah-key-us-tay; Sharp Nose #1; M; Widower; 77

913; Dackpitsay-eck-pah-dea; Medicine Bear; M; Husband; 58
914; Is-deam-day-keas-sos; Her Road Is Plain; F; Wife; 53
915; Ah-pay-days; Goes Together; F; Daughter; 12
916; Bea-cheas; Packs the Rock; M; Son; 13

917; Chees-shepittich; Black Tail; M; Husband; 48
918; Baday-bedok-bacusheas; People That Shows; F; Wife; 46

919; Chate-oocush-shis; Bob Tail Wolf; M; Husband; 61
920; Bit-chea-bachpash; Medicine Knife; F; Wife; 59

921; Bah-tah-weas; The Bell; M; Husband; 26
922; Bah-buck-but-date-chase; No Medicine; F; Wife; 28
923; Duck-cock-bah-dah-cuss; Crazy Bird; F; Daughter; 6
924; Money-kahdish; Begs for Money; F; Daughter; 1

925; Hay-day-dee-doos; Stands Among Them; M; Husband; 54
926; Oat-cheam-bah-dup-pace; Kills at Night; F; Wife; 50
927; Esuck-che-sah-keas-sos; Well Known Hawk; F; Daughter; 6

928; Ahpay-eso-chay-away-chis; Sits Before a Cloud; M; Husband; 51
929; Ea-cock-kah-beas; Fox Woman; F; Wife; 53
930; Echee-du-kish-esos; Big Elk; M; Son; 10
931; Bob-puck-sos; Bird Among the Rocks; M; Son; 21

932; Ick-kay-ah-hoos; Lots of Stars; M; Husband; 43
933; Bah-son-day-ah-hoos; Goes First; F; Wife; 45

934; Bah-hay-chay-wat-tosh; Lone Tree; H; Husband; 62
935; Bah-put-tuck-beeday-beas; Mink; F; Wife; 63

Census of the **Crow** Indians of **Crow** Agency **Montana** taken
By **J.E. Edwards**, United States Indian Agent **June 30, 1901**

Key: Number; Indian Name; English Name; Sex; Relation; Age

936; E-sah-coo-dake; Carries the Arrows; M; Son; 35

937; Ish-chis-says-koos; Comes to Her Nest; F; Widow; 71

938; Ah-dah-sos-ea-kot-tosh; Little Light; M; Husband; 49
939; Esos-kay-koo-doot-chis; Takes Her Horse; F; Wife; 35
940; Umba-coan-duc-bitchase; Bear in the Mountain; M; Son; 16
941; Ope-cheedup-pace; Tobacco Bull; M; Son; 10
942; Cheedup-kah-kah-dah-bis; Bull Moves On; M; Son; 8
943; Ah-dah-hes-itchis; Gets There Pretty; M; Son; 7
944; ---; Becker Little Light; M; Son; 3
945; Ba-chay-ha-what-duppace; Kills One Man; F; Mother; 77

946; Es-chay-kah-deas; Old Rabbit; M; Husband; 38
947; Ah-shoe-hishes; Red Hair; F; Wife; 45
948; ---; Mary Old Rabbit; F; Daughter; 16
949; Dah-kosh-bah-coos; Eagle High Up; M; Son; 11
950; Bah-osh-ahoos; Plenty Red Plumes; F; Daughter; 12

951; Tuck-kase; Sounds of the Gun; M; Husband; 30
952; Bah-put-tay-ahoos; Plenty Otter; F; Wife; 39
953; Ock-kosh-de-dish; Antelope That Walks; F; Daughter; 8
954; ---; Frederick Sounds the Gun; M; Son; 4

955; Boat-tay-kadeas; Old Coyote; M; Husband; 40
956; Bachpash; Medicine; F; Wife; 39
957; Ahpay-kay-dainba-dahkis; Sings in a Cloud; M; Son; 15
958; Up-pah-sah-chers; Half White; M; Son; 19

959; Is-be-dah-eas; Little Fire; M; Husband; 51
960; Bea-itchis-sos; Not a Pretty Woman; F; Wife; 49
961; Bahputta-cheedup-pis; Otter Bull; M; Son; 26

962; Bachpash-esos; Big Medicine; M; Husband; 45
963; Bahduppay-chedu-chis; Strikes One That Kills; F; Wife; 45
964; Bea-bus-sos; Rock in Front; F; Daughter; 8
965; ---; Edward Big Medicine; M; Son; 2

966; Uck-dosh-dee-dichis; Strikes One That Charges; F; Widow; 83

967; Bah-dah-pah-keas-sos; Digs Well Known; F; Widow; 71

968; ---; Thomas Stewart; M; Husband; 29
969; Uckcheese-malapesh; Kills Over Beyond Other; F; Wife; 30

970; Cheedup-pom-bish; Short Bull; M; Husband; 58

Census of the __Crow__ Indians of __Crow__ Agency __Montana__ taken
By __J.E. Edwards__, United States Indian Agent __June 30, 1901__

Key: Number; Indian Name; English Name; Sex; Relation; Age

971; Oo-wat-doot-chice; Takes the Iron; F; Wife; 57

972; Ekoos-sheas; Eagle Turns Around; M; Husband; 37
973; Bah-owe-keas-sos; Brings Well Known; F; Wife; 53
974; E-sos-kot-bah-deas; Working Mouse; M; Son; 13

975; Esoc-cah-wah-chakoos-say; Pretty Old Man; M; Husband; 55
976; Owat-baduck-key-condish; Old Woman Gone; F; Wife; 56
977; Peah-key-tus; The Spleen; M; Son; 20

978; Cah-kay-bachpash; Medicine Lance; F; Widow; 57

979; Bea-bah-chey-chis; Woman Chief; M; Husband; 52
980; Kish-sey; Big Around; F; Wife; 55
981; Shea-dah-chis; Fog All the Time; M; Gr Son; 10

982; Daekahshis; The Eagle; M; Husband; 38
983; Buss-sone-deah-ahoos; Goes Ahead Pretty; F; Wife; 36
984; Con-bachpash; Medicine Old Woman; F; Daughter; 15

985; Esoch-kah-de-rooch; Two Leggins; M; Husband; 51
986; Is-bah-duck-chics; Ties Up Her Bundles; F; Wife; 37

987; Ah-duck-che-bachatchis; Coo Chief; M; Divorced; 26
988; Is-ea-de-ahoos; Plenty Lodge Poles; F; Divorced; 31

989; Ah-key-ca-bee-shay; White Clay on Forehead; M; Husband; 53
990; Be-dosh; Fire; F; Wife; 43
991; Isben-doch-dup-pichis; Light Shield; F; Daughter; 7
992; Keas-sos; Plain; M; Son; 15

993; Ahduckchea-oss-ea-tuss; Shows His Coos; M; Husband; 34
994; Minne-ekoshees; Turns to the Water; F; Wife; 27

995; Ock-pay-hishis; Red Wing; M; Husband; 51
996; Ah-chane-deechis; Strikes in Camp; F; Wife; 43
997; Bahput-tah-way-chice; Sits to the Otter; F; Daughter; 7

998; Ducock-seh-hoo-duppace; Kills Coming to the Birds; F; Mother; 61
999; Away-coe-ish-chisadock; The Swallow Child; M; Son; 20

1000; Bee-ditch-key-sos; Big Lake; M; Husband; 53
1001; Oowhat-dootchis; Pounds the Iron; F; Wife; 52
1002; Oat-tay-dock-kuss; Weasel Child; M; Son; 13
1003; Chate-bick-cuss; Female Wolf; F; Sister; 55

Census of the __Crow__ Indians of __Crow__ Agency __Montana__ taken
By __J.E. Edwards__, United States Indian Agent __June 30, 1901__
Key: Number; Indian Name; English Name; Sex; Relation; Age

1004; E-shoe-dee-chea-ock-kin-day-dee-ditch-es; Strikes the Rider of the White Maned Horse; F; Widow; 63

1005; Ea-cah-pish; Flat Mouth; M; Husband; 26
1006; Bah-cah-key-e-cosh; Looks to the Shield; F; Wife; 33
1007; Bah-tah-wos; Plain Bell; M; Son; 4

1008; Un-duck-cah-hoos; Stops at Many Places; F; Widow; 70

1009; Dachpitsa-ock-in-dus; Rides a Bear; M; Husband; 57
1010; Boa-itchis; Pretty Fish; F; Wife; 50
1011; Ahdock-in-day-keasos; Rides Well Known; M; Son; 20

1012; Oo-wat-eas; Little Iron; M; Husband; 50
1013; It-chit-chea-ays; Tobacco Seed; F; Wife; 47
1014; He-dah-bah-chase; Just a Man; M; Son; 16

1015; Dah-cup-pis; Calf; M; Husband; 39
1016; Eas-seh-keapa; Crooked Face; F; Wife; 35
1017; Noopta-malapes; Kills Twice; F; Ad Dau; 9

1018; Bah-chee-dee-kahdeas; Old White Man #1; M; Husband; 63
1019; Bee-shay-dee-dish; Buffalo That Walks; F; Wife; 35

1020; Oke-keas-sos; Well Known Antelope; M; Husband; 37
1021; Uck-bah-he-dee-co-se; Does Anything; F; Wife; 27

1022; Boa-tah-itchice; Pretty Coyote; M; Husband; 33
1023; Bah-cos; Brings Things; F; Wife; 29

1024; Bee-day-da-cuss-chis; Comes Out of the Water; F; Widow; 47
1025; Bah-show-dee-ditch; Medicine Rock; F; Daughter; 20

1026; Bim-boan-cheeduppis; Bull in the Water; M; Husband; 62
1027; Cheedup-eas; Young Bull; F; Wife; 63

1028; Bah-it-chay-on-des; Does Many Good Things; M; Husband; 28
1029; Baputta-bedane-duckcoos; Otter Stays in the Water; F; Wife; 23
1030; Echey-dah-hay-day-cuss; Among the Horses; F; Daughter; 6
1031; ---; Annie D.M.G. Things; F; Daughter; 2
1032; ---; Star; F; Sister; 17

1033; Ah-puss-sah-cheas; Half White; M; Husband; 62
1034; But-shay-sut-tuss; Close Together; F; Wife; 53

1035; Iscoche-hadane-doochis; Takes Among the Enemy; M; Husband; ~~28~~ 39

227

Census of the __Crow__ Indians of __Crow__ Agency __Montana__ taken
By __J.E. Edwards__, United States Indian Agent __June 30, 1901__

Key: Number; Indian Name; English Name; Sex; Relation; Age

1036; Mea-schpittash; Black Woman; F; Wife; 39
1037; Pea-cah-dah-hutch; Long Piegan; M; Son; 14

1038; Isbindotch-bah-chate; Shield Chief; M; Husband; 40
1039; Esos-kean-sos; Blanket Well Known; F; Wife; 48

1040; Bah-os-way-shadock-cuss; Young Curlew; M; Husband; 49
1041; Cheasdacock-indechis; Rides a White Horse; F; Wife; 45
1042; Shu-dish; Singing Hat; F; Daughter; 13

1043; Whochis-say-away-chice; Sits to the Wind; F; Widow; 55

1044; Dah-cock-teah-dish; The Bird; M; Husband; 32
1045; Is-coe-chee-dup-pace; Kills Her Enemy; F; Wife; 28
1046; By-eas; Arrow Point; M; Son; 8

1047; Away-choke-kadah-cockus; Bird on the Prairie; M; Husband; 47
1048; Beshay-ockain-awachis; Sits on the Blanket; F; Wife; 41
1049; Asha-bachpash-shekuish; Medicine Sweet Camp; F; Daughter; 1

1050; Chee-sock-cuss; Long Tail; M; Husband; 44
1051; She-pay-day-tuss; No Mud; F; Wife; 39
1052; Tick-pah-cheday-de-shis; Strikes One That Pushes Him; M; Son; 15
1053; Ah-we-sos; Shows Big on the Ground; M; Son; 11
1054; ---; Lydia Long Tail; F; Daughter; 2

1055; Hay-dain-dee-chis; Strikes Among Them; F; Widow; 73
1056; Cheedup-bah-cha-ahchis; Strong Bull; M; Son; 34

1057; Bah-cup-pash; Hail; M; Husband; 34
1058; Echeedayon-duccekasses; Horses Place Well Known; F; Wife; 35

1059; It-tuch-bah-cha-chis; Strong Alone; M; Husband; 53
1060; Uck-bah-dea-ate-chase; Knows Her Medicine; F; Wife; 48

1061; Chee-dish; Hunts; M; Husband; 45
1062; Echee-dahay-dane-duckoos; Stays With the Horse; F; Wife; 41
1063; E-soa-kay-ate-chace; Knows His Horse; F; Daughter; 8
1064; E-sop-pah-day-tus; Has No Moccasin; M; Son; 19

1065; Bah-dah-sure-ha-wattus; One Blue Bead; M; Husband; 53
1066; Ush-coe-sut-tah-doochis; Takes One Close to Camp; F; Wife; 51
1067; Un-dah-heahsos; Surrounds the Enemy Strong; M; Son; 16

1068; Dackpitsa-newpu-oze; Mad at the Bear; M; Husband; 39
1069; Is-eap-che-bish-ay; Got a Pipe; F; Wife; 43

Census of the __Crow__ Indians of __Crow__ Agency __Montana__ taken By __J.E. Edwards__, United States Indian Agent __June 30, 1901__

Key: Number; Indian Name; English Name; Sex; Relation; Age

1070; Is-bah-it-chise; Got Pretty Things; F; Daughter; 14
1071; Dah-ece-tay-dootchis; Catches the Sioux; F; Daughter; 8

1072; ---; Charles Ten Bear; M; Divorced; 25

1073; Ah-she-tas; Sharp Horn; M; Husband; 60
1074; Bea-cot-ish-tup-pay; Woman With Eyes Open; F; Wife; 70? [60]

1075; Bah-chay-bah-day-kah; Foolish Man; M; Husband; 39
1076; Hay-dane-ah-seas; Shows In a Crowd; F; Wife; 33
1077; ---; George Foolish Man; M; Son; 4

1078; E-cuss-sos-esos; Big Snake; M; Husband; 56
1079; Chadoc-cuss-bahduppas; Kills In the Morning; F; Wife; 50

1080; Boa-bah-cos; Fish High Up; M; Husband; 55
1081; Chuch-ko-dootchis; Takes Five; F; Wife; 53

1082; Bee-put-tah-bah-coos; Owl Above; M; Husband; 33
1083; E-che-doe-it-chis; Brings Pretty Horses; F; Wife; 35
1084; Ah-dah-che-e-coss; Sees the Coos; F; Daughter; 13
1085; Ume-beas; Paint Woman; F; Daughter; 11

1086; Chee-dup-um-be-chisos; Bull That Don't Fall Down; M; Husband; 48
1087; Ah-see-tus; Shows; F; Wife; 35
1088; Is-been-dot-bish-eas; Got a Shield; F; Mother; 73

1089; Esop-pay-shoes; Blue Moccasin; M; Widower; 57

1090; Bah-cock-coe-tah-hoos; Comes From Above; M; Husband; 35
1091; Um-bah-cone-dah-coos; Stops Above; F; Wife; 38
1092; ---; Hannah Comes Above; F; Daughter; 4

1093; Bin-day-sop-pay-dus; River Crow; M; Divorced; 36

1094; Echeedock-ichay-ockindays; Rides a Pretty Horse #2; M; Husband; 28
1095; Esutseom-meas; Sage Woman; F; Wife; 35
1096; Ash-itse-makpash; The Song is Medicine; F; Daughter; 10

1097; Cha-qua-bah-sco; Charges Five Times; M; Husband; 28
1098; Bea-ah-wah-chis; Woman That Sits Down; F; Wife; 25
1099; E-hum-dah-pace; Kills in Sleep; F; Daughter; 7

1100; Is-coe-chea-ah-hoos; Got Many Enemies; M; Husband; 42
1101; Bah-put-tah-dock-cus; Young Otter; F; Wife; 51

Census of the __Crow__ Indians of __Crow__ Agency __Montana__ taken
By __J.E. Edwards__, United States Indian Agent __June 30, 1901__

Key: Number; Indian Name; English Name; Sex; Relation; Age

1102; Be-dup-dah-cus; Young Beaver; M; Husband; 55
1103; Bak-kah-beas; Hoop Woman; F; Wife; 59

1104; Umbah-owedup-ate-chace; Knows Where He Finds Things; M; Husband; 40
1105; Qua-dus; Between; F; Wife; 35

1106; Eche-dock-in-days; Rides a Horse; M; Husband; 47
1107; Ah-cam-dah-pace; Kills On Top; F; Wife; 43
1108; Bah-day-key-sut-tus; Two-Barrelled Gun; M; Son; 14
1109; E-shue-eas; Feather Neck; F; Daughter; 7
1110; ---; Ernest R. Horse; M; Son; 1

1111; Bah-pus; Cliff; F; Widow; 49

1112; Echede-kosh-ahway-itchis; Sitting Elk; M; Husband; 61
1113; Dah-cock-beas; Bird Woman; F; Wife; 58

1114; Duck-kay-coo-day-de-chis; Strikes One With a Lance; F; Widow; 53
1115; ---; Louise; F; Daughter; 14

1116; Dosh-shay-e-coos; Charges Madly on the Enemy; M; Husband; 29
1117; Ush-doop-tah-coe-dee; Strikes Two Camps; F; Wife; 33
1118; Tuck-kit-chay-ah-hoos; Shoots Plenty; F; Daughter; 6

1119; Echeday-itchay-ock; Rides a Pretty Horse; M; Husband; 33
1120; Ah-woos-ah-cay-dus; On Top of the Sweathouse; F; Wife; 31
1121; Ach-pah-dea-itchise; Good Medicine; F; Daughter; 12
1122; Coo-bah-pay-day-bah; Kills the Same Day; F; Daughter; 6
1123; ---; Carson Rides Pretty Horse; M; Son; 1

1124; Daeka-itchis; Pretty Eagle; M; Husband; 56
1125; Is-been-dotch-itchis; Pretty Shield; F; Wife; 53
1126; Daeka-sheedis; Yellow Eagle; M; Son; 5

1127; Da-cose; Goes On; M; Husband; 60
1128; Been-dotch-us-eas; Shield That Shows; F; Wife; 53
1129; Bechaykay-dahwachis; Sits Among the Rocks; M; Ad Son; 13

1130; Ike-cook-cus; Even; M; Husband; 30
1131; Ush-dea-itchis; Makes a Pretty Lodge; F; Wife; 31

1132; Up-pah-keas-sos; Cloud Well Known; M; Husband; 41
1133; Con-dah-cock-cus; Old Bird Woman; F; Wife; 40
1134; Ushcoe-tah-cose-shis; Helps the Whole Camp; M; Son; 16
1135; ---; Ben Cloud Well Known; M; Son; 2

Census of the __Crow__ Indians of __Crow__ Agency __Montana__ taken
By __J.E. Edwards__, United States Indian Agent __June 30, 1901__

Key: Number; Indian Name; English Name; Sex; Relation; Age

1136; Cho-say-ick-cosh; Sees a White Horse; M; Husband; 47
1137; Dosh-day-tuss; No Name; F; Wife; 47
1138; ---; Peter S. White Horse; M; Son; 17

1139; Oo-shis; Hole; M; Divorced; 28

1140; Dackpitsa-chey-deedish; Bear That Walks; M; Husband; 41
1141; Beedic-quabah-dup-pace; Fools and Kills the Enemy; F; Wife; 36
1142; ---; Strikes Enemy on Prairie; M; Son; 1

1143; Is-shay-dus; Hairy On Top of His Head; M; Husband; 55
1144; Bin-doch-e-so-chain-dus; Sheep in Front; F; Wife; 56

1145; Duck-cock-bea-itchis; Pretty Woman Bird; F; Mother; 45
1146; Esho-dechea-doochis; Takes Horse With Wh[ite] Mane; F; Daughter; 16
1147; Bah-shay-cha-dup-pace; Kills the Chief; F; Daughter; 11

1148; Bah-chay-un-dah-pace; Kills Many Men; F; Widow; 45
1149; Ope-bah-dah-kis; Tobacco Sings; F; Ad Dau.; 8

1150; Ish-tay-ea-sos; Big Eyes; M; Batchelor[sic]; 60

1151; Hoo-chis; Wind Blowing; F; Widow; 57

1152; Uck-cha-key-chis; Spies on the Enemy; M; Husband; 39
1153; ---; Mrs. Henry Keiser; F; Wife; 41

1154; Us-dosh-cane-dootchis; Takes By Side of Camp; F; Divorced; 43

1155; Backpash-pash; Medicine Feather; F; Widow; 53
1156; Edeka-oke-pus; Shoots Tent Poles; F; Niece; 12

1157; Baduck-key-dootchis; Takes a Gun #1; M; Husband; 61
1158; Ah-way-chise; Knows the Ground; F; Wife; 63

1159; Bah-cup-pah-e-sos; Big Hail; M; Husband; 33
1160; Bah-cuck-ca-beas; Striped Snake Woman; F; Wife; 27
1161; Beshay-cok-bahwaychis; Sits With a Buffalo; M; Son; 8

1162; Ah-way-cah-wah-seas; Shows in the Mountain; M; Husband; 27
1163; Esop-ponta-chahada-dose; Among the Sheep; F; Wife; 27

1164; Awaycah-wassahwa-chis; Face Toward the Mountain; M; Husband; 48
1165; Peace-hay-duce; Comes Behind; F; Wife; 41
1166; Oo-sha-cane-ca-pis; Sits Over a Hole; F; Daughter; 11
1167; Dah-cock-shee-dis; Yellow Bird; F; Daughter; 8

Census of the __Crow__ Indians of __Crow__ Agency __Montana__ taken By __J.E. Edwards__, United States Indian Agent __June 30, 1901__

Key: Number; Indian Name; English Name; Sex; Relation; Age

1168; Ah-dean-dace; The Trail; F; Widow; 51
1169; Is-chie-say-be-shis; Got a Nest; M; Son; 18
1170; Is-been-doch-ah-hoos; Plenty Shield; F; Daughter; 16
1171; Eche-de-she-chase; Likes the Horses; F; Daughter; 11

1172; Up-pay-okpis; Shot in the Nose; M; Husband; 30
1173; Osh-doo-chape-ditchis; Strikes the Thief in Camp; F; Wife; 28
1174; Cheach-key-dock-cus; Young Chicken; F; Daughter; 7
1175; ---; Laura Little Owl; F; Daughter; 3

1176; Been-dosh-shay-bachpash; Medicine Top; M; Husband; 35
1177; Ah-shus-ah-was-days; Horn Dropped Down; F; Wife; 22
1178; Bahkay ahoos; Gives Lots of Things Away; F; Daughter; 8

1179; Bah-ay-ba-sos; Has Things; F; Divorced; 36
1180; Isbahca-kay-bot-posh; Her Medicine Shell; F; Daughter; 7
1181; ---; Susie Spotted; F; Daughter; 10

1182; Dackpitsa-che-dace; Bear Gets Up; M; Husband; 67
1183; Bah-put-tah-dew-pus; Two Otters; F; Wife; 62

1184; It-tut-dah-cock-cus; Bird By Himself; F; Widower; 61

1185; Chate-sha-dachpitsa; Mad Bear Wolf; M; Widower; 57
1186; Mideras-ichis; Does Good Things; M; AD Son; 17
1187; Dah-hes-os; Surrounds the Enemy; M; Son; 22

1188; Boop-chis; Ball; M; Husband; 37
1189; Bea-sheedis; Yellow Woman; F; Wife; 36

1190; Ukbadapa-ishtukea-dooch; Takes Gun From One That Kls; M; Husband; 26
1191; Coa-wat-tay-doochis; Takes Both Together; F; Wife; 27
1192; Uk-keam-duck-chis; Ties on the Fortop; F; Daughter; 11

1193; Bah-put-tah-cahdeas; Old Otter; F; Widow; 55

1194; He-dah-wah-chace; He is a Man Now; M; Husband; 58
1195; Ecupe-pah-dootchis; Takes the Hat; F; Wife; 53

1196; Istuckea-bah-chate-chice; Gun Chief; M; Husband; 54
1197; Cuck-cock-in-days; Rides a Spotted Horse; F; Wife; 41
1198; Ushdosh-katabah-sos; Runs Beside the Camp; M; Son; 7

1199; Echete-itchis; Good Horses; M; Husband; 36
1200; E-hum-be-shoes; More of Them; F; Wife; 25
1201; Been-dah-chate-dase; Goes to the Fort; F; Daughter; 7

Census of the __Crow__ Indians of __Crow__ Agency __Montana__ taken
By __J.E. Edwards__, United States Indian Agent __June 30, 1901__

Key: Number; Indian Name; English Name; Sex; Relation; Age

1202; Ea-cus-sos; Snake; F; Widow; 59
1203; E-sah-duck-chis; Ties Up the Arrows; F; Daughter; 19

1204; Beedee-chay-hay-day-dus; Among the Willows; Widow; 65

1205; Dackpitsa-uppa-pushcoos; Cuts the Bear's Ears; M; Husband; 51
1206; It-chis; Good; F; Wife; 48
1207; Bah-dah-kit-chice; Sings Good; M; Son; 18

1208; Hay-day-dose; Right Among Them; M; Husband; 54
1209; E-dah-hoos; Comes Herself; F; Wife; 58

1210; Dadough-cheada-itchice; Leads the Camp Pretty; F; Orphan; 14

1211; Odup-dah-pace; Finds Them and Kills Them; M; Widower; 48
1212; Echa-dow-keas-sos; Brings Horses Well Known; F; Daughter; 13

1213; Is-chay-dah-kish-shay; Knot Between the Eyes; M; Husband; 60
1214; Oo-what-doot-chace; Takes the Iron; F; Wife; 55
1215; Dock-shay-dah-beas; Katie H. Adams [Three Coons]; F; Daughter; 18

1216; Cuck-cah-wah-chice; Sits Down Spotted; M; Husband; 39
1217; Bah-chay-cheas; Steals on the Camp; F; Wife; 22
1218; ---; John Spotted; M; Son; 4

1219; Echee-dah-ahhoos; Plenty Horses; M; Widower; 49

1220; Dah-cock-bah-coos; Bird Above; M; Husband; 35
1221; Oo-tah-cuck-kis; Spotted Weasel; F; Wife; 33
1222; Be-day-tuss; Like a Fire; M; Son; 13
1223; Hoo-chice-cos; Comes Against the Wind; M; Son; 10
1224; Poop-kit-tah-cuck-kis; Spotted Snowbird; F; Daughter; 8

1225; Chate-kah-we-sis; Skins a Wolf; M; Husband; 60
1226; E-sos-kah-we-sis; Has Horses; F; Wife; 53

1227; ---; Richard Cummins; M; Divorced; 28

1228; Oo-what-ah-shoes; Iron Head; M; Husband; 22
1229; Bah-ow-duck-coos; Brings Things Always; F; Wife; 16

1230; Be-dook-sah-e-duse; Alligator Stands Up; M; Husband; 56
1231; Bah-put-tah-hosh; The Other Otter; F; Wife; 54

1232; Boat-tah-cah-dush-sis; Coyote Runs; M; Husband; 41
1233; Be-shay-ka-hase; Buffalo That Shakes; F; Widow; 41

Census of the __Crow__ Indians of __Crow__ Agency __Montana__ taken
By __J.E. Edwards__, United States Indian Agent __June 30, 1901__

Key: Number; Indian Name; English Name; Sex; Relation; Age

1234; Epah-deabah-cha-chis; Strong Medicine; M; Son; 13
1235; Ah-pah-de-deas; Porcupine Woman; F; Daughter; 5

1236; Ea-cus-sah-cheduppis; Snake Bull; M; Husband; 50
1237; Oo-what-de-chise; Strikes the Iron; F; Wife; 36
1238; Boo-duke-pah-keasos; Plain Cedar; F; Daughter; 12
1239; Che-quas; Is Sweet Now; M; Son; 7
1240; ---; Matie Snake Bull; F; Daughter; 1

1241; ---; Pius Hill; M; Orphan; 18
1242; Bea-ahdutch-shebeas; Woman That Farms; F; Sister; 12

1243; Eas-ea-coas; Covers His Face; M; Divorced; 34

1244; Bee-dish; Walking; M; Husband; 45
1245; Uck-bah-du-ick-cosh; Looks at the Medicine; F; Wife; 50
1246; Ba-be-dish-e-sos; Broils Big; M; Ad son; 12

1247; ---; Arnold Kosta; M; Husband; 21
1248; Ah-wain-dah-it-chis; Good Hearted Ground; F; Wife; 27
1249; Bea-bachpash-cah-weas; Bad Medicine Woman; F; Daughter; 10
1250; Isbah-ca-key-ah-shees; Shows a Shell; F; Daughter; 7

1251; Kat-toah-tay-hishes; Red Shirt; M; Husband; 24
1252; ---; Carrie Wallace; F; Wife; 17

1253; Be-dup-hishes; Red Beaver; F; Divorced; 66
1254; Bahkay-dah-way-chice; Blackbird Sits Down; F; Daughter; 13
1255; Is-tah-dase-cheas; Big Squirrel; M; Son; 16

1256; Ah-way-kah-way-chedays; Mountian Pocket; M; Husband; 58
1257; E-chope-pice; Shoots Her Foot; F; Wife; 51
1258; Esos-kee-dit-bachpash; Medicine Horsewhip; M; Son; 28

1259; Ah-dah-doo-be-shay; Shot in the Arm; M; Husband; 58
1260; Bea-dootchis; Takes a Woman; F; Wife; 51

1261; She-chock-ay-dus; On Top of the Hill; M; Husband; 62
1262; Isbada-ha-wat-atechice; Knows the Yearling; F; Wife; 54

1263; Bosh-che-de-cot-tay; White Man; M; Husband; 47
1264; Bah-ouch-cah-ahoos; Plenty Striped Snake; F; Wife; 53
1265; Dah-cock-che-deas-sos; Not Afraid of a Bird; M; Son; 11
1266; Dah-cock-ah-pah-ahoos; Bird With Plenty of Wings Going Around; F; Daughter; 10
1267; Ecupe-pah-bah-puc-tosh; Hat Otter; F; Daughter; 4

Census of the __Crow__ Indians of __Crow__ Agency __Montana__ taken
By __J.E. Edwards__, United States Indian Agent __June 30, 1901__

Key: Number; Indian Name; English Name; Sex; Relation; Age

1268; Bea-itchay; Not a Pretty Woman; F; Widow; 43

1269; Edush-uck-bah-dup-pace; Kills With His Bro-in-law; M; Husband; 47
1270; Un-di-day-it-chice; Walks Pretty; F; Wife; 45

1271; ---; James Buffalo; M; Husband; 27
1272; Bah-cup-pah-cheas; White Hail; F; Wife; 25
1273; Cah-ditch-chea-ahoos; Plenty Lightning; F; Daughter; 7

1274; Dachpitsay-che-sus; Bear's Tail; M; Widower; 61
1275; Dackpitsay-undatechas; Knows Where the Bear Goes; F; Daughter; 17

1276; Ah-pah-dee-esos; Big Porcupine; M; Husband; 45
1277; Un-doo-cosh-keas-sos; Holds Well Known; F; Wife; 42

1278; Cheedup-bah-chate-chice; Bull Chief; M; Husband; 65
1279; Istuckey-bah-chate-chice; Long Gun; F; Wife; 59
1280; Itchit-che-ays; Medicine Tobacco; M; Gr Son; 11

1281; Ah-shue-cheas; White Horn; F; Widow; 55

1282; Isbitch-ichis-secocktus; Little Whetstone; M; Husband; 61
1283; E-che-dah-keas-sos; Horse Well Known; F; Wife; 42

1284; Che-chuck-key-sis; Big Around; M; Husband; 61
1285; Cah-coa-doot-chice; Takes All the Horses; F; Wife; 53
1286; Isbindotch-abahic-deas; Does Ev'y'g With a Shield; F; Ad Dau; 8
1287; Ecup-pah-ate-chice; Knows Her Hat; F; Mother; 77

1288; Shis-sheas; Curly; M; Husband; 51
1289; Bin-dotch-dootchis; Takes a Shield; F; Wife; 53
1290; Awandook-cookus-detacus; Bird Another Year; F; Daughter; 5

1291; Dah-cus; Balls; M; Widower; 39

1292; Be-day-dish-sos; Don't Get In; F; Widow; 49
1293; Ah-pah-de-e-wan-deas; Plays With Medicine; F; Daughter; 11

1294; Ah-pit-tus; The Crane; M; Husband; 45
1295; Echee-uck-pah-duppace; Kills With the Horses; F; Wife; 42
1296; Cha-soup-pus; End of the Tail; M; Son; 16

1297; Oatsaybee-dosh; Fire Weasel; M; Husband; 70
1298; Ah-douch-chea-pashpash; Medicine Where She Stops; F; Wife; 65

1299; Beas; Rock; M; Father; 39

Census of the __Crow__ Indians of __Crow__ Agency __Montana__ taken
By __J.E. Edwards__, United States Indian Agent __June 30, 1901__

Key: Number; Indian Name; English Name; Sex; Relation; Age

1300; Bashow-da-chite-chase; Medicine Rock; F; Daughter; 13

1301; Duck-cock-ah-shoes; Bird Head; M; Husband; 43
1302; Dah-ah-sheas; Shows Going; F; Wife; 37
1303; Is-coe-che-che-dish; Afraid of His Enemy; M; Son; 16
1304; Oo-what-bea-kahdeas; Old Weasel Woman; F; Daughter; 1
1305; Bishka-dackpitsa; Bear's Dog; M; Son; 22

1306; Duck-peas; Hugs #2; M; Husband; 55
1307; Awayshe-hay-danedoochis; Takes a Man in a Fog; F; Wife; 59
1308; Bah-duck-it-chise; Sings Pretty; M; Son; 23

1309; Ah-wah-coan-de-dish; Walks In Middle of Ground; M; Husband; 65
1310; Ea-cot-tus; Little; F; Wife; 56

1311; Bashow-dechit-chabacoos; Medicine Rock Above; M; Husband; 34
1312; E-cheam-dah-pace; Kills a Horse; F; Wife; 33
1313; Bah-keam-boo-dish; Bull Blackbird; M; Son; 11

1314; E-chean-dah-cock-cus; Bird Horse; M; Husband; 27
1315; Bah-show-de-chit-chase; Medicine Rock; F; Wife; 25
1316; Ea-dea-it-chise; Pretty Lodge Poles; F; Daughter; 8

1317; Ea-dane-deas; He Does It; M; Husband; 29
1318; Bah-cock-coo-dush; She Is High Up; F; Wife; 33
1319; Cheach-cuce; Chicken; F; Daughter; 12
1320; Cah-pah-dee-dock-cus; Young Medicine; M; Son; 8
1321; ---; Harry Alligator; M; Son; 1
1322; Eah-show-dechit-chaesos; Big Medicine Rock; F; Mother; 52

1323; Esah-eduse-see-shis; Broken Arrow; M; Husband; 41
1324; Dupe-pah-wah-dup-pace; Kills Twice; F; Widow; 41? [45]
1325; Un-dah-pace; Kills Plenty; F; Daughter; 16
1326; Ha-dane-dah-cock-cus; Bird Among Them; M; Son; 8
1327; Eat-toch-tay-keas-sos; Plain Shirt; F; Daughter; 7
1328; ---; Takes Things on Top House; F; Daughter; 1

1329; Bah-cah-dish-tah-beas; Heifer Woman; F; Widow; 37
1330; Bin-dosh-shay-shee-dish; Yellow Top; M; Divorced; 60

1331; Esos-kah-wishes; Has Horses; F; Divorced; 65

1332; Bah-chay-cheas; Steals on the Camp; F; Widow; 65

1333; Eak-cah-shues; Blue Chin; F; Widow; 60

Census of the __Crow__ Indians of __Crow__ Agency __Montana__ taken By __J.E. Edwards__, United States Indian Agent __June 30, 1901__

Key: Number; Indian Name; English Name; Sex; Relation; Age

1334; Eas-hay-cuck-kis; Spotted Rabbit; M; Husband; 35
1335; Itchit-chay-bachpash; Medicine Tobacco; F; Wife; 41
1336; Oke-push; Badly Shot; M; Son; 4
1337; Ea-sos; Hairy; F; Mother; 67

1338; Be-dase-che-cash; Looks at the Water; F; Widow; 63

1339; Bah-doo-peas; Scolds; M; Husband; 36
1340; ---; Mrs. Ben Gardiner; F; Wife; 38
1341; ---; Thomas Gardiner; M; Son; 17
1342; ---; Frank Gardiner; M; Son; 15
1343; ---; Amelia Gardiner; F; Daughter; 13

1344; Dah-cock-keas-sos; Bird Well Known; M; Husband; 35
1345; Bea-dosh-day-tush; Woman Without a Name; F; Wife; 28
1346; Away-cahn-dob-cock-cus; Mountain Bird; M; Son; 4

1347; Bah-ick-cah-keas-sos; Sees Well Known; F; Widow; 51

1348; Isbindoch-bachatechice; Strikes the Shield First; F; Widow; 41
1349; Dah-cock-cah-doosh-sis; Bird That Runs; F; Daughter; 16
1350; Doop-pah-c-che-dosh; Brings Two Horses; M; Son; 7

1351; Bah-ich-cah-keas-sos; Sees Well Known; F; Widow; 59
1352; Oot-tay-bah-coes; Weasel High Up; F; Ad Dau; 7

1353; Ope-che-chuck-kis; Round Tobacco; F; Orphan; 16

1354; ---; Charles Brown; M; Batchelor[sic]; 24

1355; ---; Holder White Wings; M; Batchelor[sic]; 23

1356; Ecupe-pah-wish-de-chice; Strikes One With the Hat; F; Widow; 55

1357; Ah-dah-cuck-kay; Spotted Arm; M; Husband; 53
1358; Ah-dow-hea-keas-sos; Where She Stops Well Known; F; Wife; 55

1359; Um-bah-chea-keas-sos; Fights Well Known #2; M; Husband; 39
1360; Isbeen-dotchpa-duckiss; Shield That Sings; F; Wife; 35

1361; Itchis-shaydane-dechase; Strikes On Top Of Head; M; Husband; 38
1362; Be-shay-e-has; The Other Buffalo; F; Wife; 37
1363; Awacco-ish-hicay-eacott; Little Swallow; M; Son; 11
1364; Ah-pe-hosh; The Other Leaf; F; Daughter; 2

1365; Eche-dee-kosh-kahdeas; Old Elk; M; Husband; 42

Census of the __Crow__ Indians of __Crow__ Agency __Montana__ taken
By __J.E. Edwards__, United States Indian Agent __June 30, 1901__

Key: Number; Indian Name; English Name; Sex; Relation; Age

1366; Ookish-dean-day-ah-hoos; Antelope Trails; F; Wife; 41
1367; Echeam-push-cush; Cuts the Horse; M; Son; 11
1368; ---; Mary Old Elk; F; Daughter; 4

1369; Bah-shoes-shays; Red Feather; F; Widow; 53
1370; Ea-dea-cah-deas; Old Lodge Pole; M; Son; 17

1371; Boat-tah-bah-hoos; Coyote That Howls; F; Widow; 51
1372; Bah-touch-owe-duck-coos; Brings Things all the time; M; Son; 19

1373; Nas-ehas; The Other Heart; M; Batchelor[sic]; 27

1374; Ah-dup-pice; Hides; M; Husband; 39
1375; Hay-day-tah-wah-sos; Goes Through Her Enemies; F; Wife; 35
1376; Uck-bah-dea-ah-hoos; Plenty Medicine; F; Daughter; 12
1377; Ock-che-dup-pice; Bull Deer; M; Son; 6
1378; Ate-shedacock; Lives Everywhere; M; Son; 2

1379; ---; Charles Clawson; M; Batchelor[sic]; 29

1380; Ah-day-shay-chee-dish; Hunts to Die; M; Husband; 63
1381; Esos-kay-it-chis; Her Horse Is Pretty; F; Wife; 53

1382; ---; Henry Reed; M; Divorced; 27

1383; Archie-minnay-tus; No Milk; M; Husband; 43
1384; Ah-wane-dane-duck-koos; Stays Out Doors; F; Wife; 49

1385; Dackpitsa-ucpah-dacus; Ghost Bear; M; Husband; 53
1386; Is-dotch-che-ate-chase; Knows Her Prisoners; 51

1387; Ah-way-sheas; Fog; M; Husband; 33
1388; Isbahcah-bah-duckiss; Hoop That Sings; F; Wife; 27

1389; Bah-touch-e-cook-cah; Hears Everyway; M; Husband; 45
1390; Dahcock-ah-way-chice; Bird Sits Down; F; Wife; 37
1391; Un-de-chay-itchis; Strikes Pretty; M; Son; 16
1392; Ahrikinda-aet-chase; Knows What She Rides; F; Daughter; 1
1393; Esock-chice; The Hawk; M; Son; 24

1394; Ah-key-chice; The Wet; M; Husband; 51
1395; Uck-sah-ay-chase; Knows Her Mother; F; Wife; 46
1396; Bah-key-cush-sheas; Hoop That Runs; M; Son; 15
1397; Dah-say-cah-wees; Bad Heart: M; Son; 22
1398; Bah-shoes; Feather; F; M-in-law; 55

Census of the __Crow__ Indians of __Crow__ Agency __Montana__ taken
By __J.E. Edwards__, United States Indian Agent __June 30, 1901__

Key: Number; Indian Name; English Name; Sex; Relation; Age

1399; Ut-che-key-chis; Spies on the Enemy #2; M; Husband; 36
1400; Bahput-tah-bock-bus; Otter Hoop; F; Wife; 22 ? [23years in 1899.]
1401; Ook-bish-cus; White Tailed Deer; F; Daughter; 8
1402; Oot-tah-dee-dish; Walking Weasel; F; Daughter; 5

1403; Bah-put-tah-beas; Woman Otter; F; Widow; 71

1404; Ish-cos; Back of the Neck; M; Husband; 65
1405; Co-cosh-beas; Corn Woman; F; Wife; 55

1406; Ah-wah-key-sos; Big Sky; M; Husband; 45
1407; Oo-ah-wah-pash; Medicine Wife; F; Wife; 35

1408; Bah-chea-ish-itchice; Loves to Fight; M; Husband; 26
1409; Um-bah-cone-cahs; Comes From Above; F; Wife; 26
1410; Bick-kah-keas-sos; Well Known Mare; F; Daughter; 9
1411; ---; Fannie C. Above; F; Daughter; 1

1412; Bit-che-doot-chis; Grabs the Knife; F; Widow; 59

1413; ---; Dick Hawk; M; Husband; 25
1414; Ah-sah-date-dootchis; Takes Horses on Prairie; F; Wife; 24

1415; Ush-ase-bah-sos; Charges on the Camp; M; Husband; 65
1416; Be-shea-bachpash; Medicine Heifer; F; Wife; 61

1417; Chee-dup-chos-us; Grey Bull; M; Husband; 40
1418; Ha-dane-e-cush-chice; Takes Out of a Crowd; F; Wife; 43
1419; Dock-ke-days; Goes to Fight; F; Daughter; 7
1420; ---; Augusta Grey Bull; F; Daughter; 4

1421; Padutch-chay-sheedish; Yellow Crow; M; Husband; 51
1422; Is-coe-chea-ate-chace; Knows Her Enemy; F; Wife; 52
1423; Ah-shoe-che-dish; Hunts the House; F; Mother; 76

1424; Duck-pace; Hugs; F; Widow; 63

1425; Dackpitsay-boo-dish; Male Bear; M; Husband; 29
1426; Um-bah-dea-itchis; His Work Is Good; F; Wife; 17
1427; Ha-wan-da-bachpash; Where He Goes Is Medicine; F; Ad Dau; 14

1428; Ah-pit-bah-dock-cus; Crazy Crane; M; Husband; 53
1429; Un-dee-ditch-chis; Walks Pretty; F; Wife; 51

1430; Ush-cup-cah-weas; Bad Dutchman; M; Husband; 33
1431; Boa-doo-pus; Two Fish; F; Wife; 33

Census of the __Crow__ Indians of __Crow__ Agency __Montana__ taken By __J.E. Edwards__, United States Indian Agent __June 30, 1901__

Key: Number; Indian Name; English Name; Sex; Relation; Age

1432; Ome-bachpash; Medicine Paint; M; Son; 4

1433; Ah-ruck-chea-ahoos; Plenty Coos; M; Husband; 53
1434; Tick-bah-dup-pace; Kills Together; F; Wife; 38
1435; Kah-quah-ah-soos; Everybody Knows Him; M; Son-ad; 11

1436; Bea-it-chice; Pretty Rock; F; Widow; 55
1437; Uck-bah-dea-ush-eas; Medicine Shows; F; Ad Dau; 12

1428; Eas-pea-os-seas; Lion That Shows; M; Husband; 53
1439; Cuck-pis; Spotted; F; Wife; 37
1440; Bondonpaha-dane-dacacus; Bird In the Cedars; M; Son; 18
1441; Ock-e-hosh; The Other Antelope; F; Daughter; 16
1442; Dutch-choa-dock-cus; Muskrat Daughter; F; Daughter; 8
1443; Dah-he-os; Surrounded; M; Son; 5

1444; Bee-tah-was; Bell Rock; M; Husband; 60
1445; Kah-wish; Bushy; F; Wife; 55
1446; Dahcock-bah-soos; Bird High Up; M; Son; 20

1447; Ecupe-pahda-cock-cuss; Bird Hat; M; Husband; 33
1448; Ischis-sayah-wondabachis; Sits In Her Nest; F; Wife; 33
1449; Bon-don-pah-bah-coos; Cedar High Up; M; Son; 15
1450; Cheeup-be-das-dace; Bull Walks to Water; M; Son; 8
1451; Bah-apah-dahcoos-days; Walks to Growing Things; F; Daughter; 6
1452; Botsa-botsots; Strong Man; M; Son; 1

1453; Bah-put-tah-dock-cuss; Young Otter; M; Widower; 63

1454; It-tut-doot-chice; Takes By Herself; F; Widow; 53

1455; Badupayish-tukey-dootchis; Takes Gun From 1 That Kills; M; Husband; 29
1456; Bea-cose; The Woman; F; Wife; 23
1457; Akean-badiksha-bapashon; Mden[Medicine] Ties Knot On Her Head; F; Daughter; 7
1458; Ock-che-dup-pish; Bull Antelope; M; Son; 6

1459; Utch-itch-ist-ton-tus; Notch; M; Husband; 39
1460; Bahduppay-ate-chice; Known to Kill; F; Wife; 36
1461; Dahcock-hay-day-dus; Among the Birds; M; Son; 11
1462; Eak-kay-hishes; Red Star; M; Son; 22
1463; Bish-doot-chise; Takes a Blanket; F; Mother; 56

1464; Oo-wat-tus; The Iron; F; Widow; 57
1465; ---; Ben Gardiner; M; Son; 21

Census of the __Crow__ Indians of __Crow__ Agency __Montana__ taken
By __J.E. Edwards__, United States Indian Agent __June 30, 1901__

Key: Number; Indian Name; English Name; Sex; Relation; Age

1466; Ish-bee-bachpash; His Rock Is Medicine; M; Husband; 36
1467; Mea-shepittay; Black Woman; F; Wife; 35

1468; Ah-cane-dah-pace; Kills Across the Water; F; Widow; 61

1469; Bea-cowees; Bad woman; F; Widow; 45

1470; Bah-son-day; Goes Ahead; F; Widow; 19
1471; Uck-pah-dee-itchice; Julia High Hawk; F; S-in-law; 25

1472; Kah-key-de-chis; Strikes the Lance; F; Widow; 57

1473; Dackpitsa-doopus; Two Bears; M; Husband; 52
1474; Bim-bean-dee-dish; Walks In the Water; F; Wife; 50

1475; Bah-coop-pah; Sick; M; Husband; 33
1476; Bachay-bahchot-dahpace; Kills a Strong Man; F; Wife; 33
1477; It-tut-bah-heas; Fights Alone; M; Son; 11
1478; Ahway-cone-away-chice; Sits on High Ground; M; Son; 7

1479; Bah-op-pish; Shot In the Hand; M; Husband; 58
1480; Ecupe-pah-che-shis; Puts on a Hat; F; Wife; 52

1481; Away-caway-dane-dackpitsa; Bear In the Mountains; M; Widower; 56

1482; Esop-pee-e-wishes; Hairy Moccasin; M; Husband; 48
1483; Bah-wah-wat-tays; [Takes] Quick; F; Wife; 41
1484; Eak-ka-dah-cock-us; Bird's Eggs; M; Son; 11
1485; ---; Mary Hairy Moccasin; F; Daughter; 4

1486; Dakpitsa-chabeddok-sahoo; Bear Comes From Below; M; Widower Husband; 61
1487; Bah-dup-pace-sos; Don't Kill; M; Son; 10

1488; Ah-cah-pish-sis; Comes Up Red; M; Husband; 39
1489; Bah-put-tah-cuck-kis; Spotted Otter; F; Wife; 30

1490; Chea-shea-itchice; Pretty Tail; M; Husband; 47
1491; Ba-dow-e-kosh; Looks at the Beads; F; Wife; 51
1492; Bashotshe-basosh; Rock That Runs; M; Gr Son; 13

1493; Is-coa-chee-che-dish; Hunts the Enemy; M; Husband; 51
1494; Eatosh-dabish-de-chice; Strikes Her Child; F; Wife; 53

1495; Aditch-chebah-dochahoos; Paints Herself Plenty; M; Husband; 55
1496; Ah-pah-dee-it-chice; Pretty Porcupine; F; Wife; 50

Census of the __Crow__ Indians of __Crow__ Agency __Montana__ taken By __J.E. Edwards__, United States Indian Agent __June 30, 1901__

Key: Number; Indian Name; English Name; Sex; Relation; Age

1497; Pah-chice; Push; M; Husband; 51
1498; Bah-chay-uck-pah-pice; Lies In Bed With a Man; F; Wife; 45

1499; Dackpitsay-dah-beas; Three Bears; M; Divorced; 41

1500; Dutch-ke; Twin Woman; F; Divorced; 35
1501; Basho-dedich-chapasash; Medicine Rock In Front; F; Mother; 61

1502; Eas-shu-day; Yellow Face #2; M; Husband; 43
1503; Bah-pee-shada-ahoos; Rides Much Behind; F; Wife; 36
1504; Bis-cah-she-pit-tus; Black Dog; M; Son; 12
1505; ---; Dora Yellow Face; F; Daughter; 2

1506; Dackpitsa-it-chice; Pretty Bear; M; Husband; 61
1507; Bah-cah-chice; Strong; F; Wife; 53

1508; Cush-some-bee-chice; Falls Toward You; F; Widow; 81

1509; Cone-dah-chice; Stays There; M; Husband; 26
1510; Dutch-chee-do-pah-bash; Medicine Slides; F; Wife; 35

1511; Beda-ecupe-padootchice; Takes the Hat; F; Widow; 63

1512; Ha-wash-tay-keas; Travels Well Known; M; Husband; 59
1513; Bah-it-cash; She Sees It; F; Wife; 43
1514; Ak-bah-dee-days; Medicine Goes; F; Daughter; 14
1515; Bak-kah-seas; Hoop That Shows; M; Son; 20

1516; E-kush-sheas; Turns Back; M; Husband; 43
1517; Uck-pah-dean-de-chice; Strikes Plenty Medicine; F; Wife; 40

1518; Cheedup-keasos; Bull Well Known; M; Husband; 39
1519; Uch-ock-kay-duck-coos; Stays On Top of House; F; Wife; 33
1520; Bah-cay-key-bachpash; Medicine Shell; F; Daughter; 13
1521; Echdoc-inday-dootchis; Takes One That Rides Horse; F; Daughter; 9
1522; Lagek-tee-cha-ditch; Bird Gets Up; M; Son; 1

1523; Itsup-educe; Edison Fire Bear; M; Husband; 23
1524; Bea-dah-cock-cus; Bird Woman; F; Wife; 18

1525; Dah-cock-beas; Bird Woman; F; Widow; 49

1526; Cheedup-chee-sus; Bull's Tail; M; Husband; 26
1527; Ah-bush-it-chice; Pretty Sweathouse; F; Wife; 22
1528; ---; Iva Bull's Tail; F; Daughter; 2

Census of the __Crow__ Indians of __Crow__ Agency __Montana__ taken
By __J.E. Edwards__, United States Indian Agent __June 30, 1901__

Key: Number; Indian Name; English Name; Sex; Relation; Age

1529; Chate-dah-beas; Three Wolves; M; Husband; 65
1530; Ahway-taycoe-ahway-chis; Sits Down Far Away; F; Wife; 61

1531; Ah-dup-pice; Bull Robe; M; Husband; 29
1532; Cah-cay-itchice; Pretty Land [Lance 1899-1900.]; F; Wife; 33

1533; Ischeka-it-chice; Pretty Lance [Land 1899-1900.]; F; Mother; 52
1534; ---; Campbell Pretty Lance [Land in 1900.]; M; Son; 2

1535; Iscoeche-a-bachea-days; Goes to Fight Enemies; F; Widow; 83

1536; Be-shay-ah-hoos; Plenty Buffalo; M; Husband; 33
1537; Dachpitsa-e-sos-seas; The Bear Turns Around; F; Wife; 28
1538; Itchit-chey-ah-bachpash; Medicine Tobacco; F; Daughter; 12
1539; Be-duckoshsadacock; Bird in the Spring; F; Daughter; 4
1540; Ope-hayday-muluchis; Sings Among the Tobacco; M; Son; 1

1541; Ea-cook-kish-shays; Red Fox; M; Widower; 57

1542; Dackpitsa-esah-cocish; Big Bear; M; Widower; 60

1543; Bahputtay-wachate-chice; Otter Chief; M; Husband; 32
1544; Miah-hoo-ted-deas; Does Lot of Things; F; Wife; 50

1545; Chate-ah-wah-shoes; Wolf House; M; Husband; 41
1546; Bea-cottus; Girl; F; Wife; 35

1547; Dachpitsa-he-dock-cus; The Bear Now; M; Widower; 45
1548; E-cosh-sheas; Turns Around; F; Daughter; 12

1549; Ah-pe-sah-sheedish; Yellow Mule; M; Husband; 45
1550; Oct-tah-seas; Weasel That Shows; F; Wife; 35
1551; Beditta-shishay-cuckiss; Spotted Butterfly; M; Son; 14

1552; Bah-duck-key-dootchis; Takes a Gun #3; M; Husband; 34
1553; Bickus; Mare; F; Wife; 29
1554; ---; Susie; F; Daughter; 15
1555; Boodock-ahcane-deechis; Strikes On Top of Ice; F; Daughter; 8

1556; Ick-cup-pee-dee-dah-bish; Three Foretops; M; Husband; 35
1557; Mi-iche-ose; Brings Good Things; F; Wife; 40
1558; Etash-hishes; Red Shirt; F; Daughter; 7
1559; Bea-huckey; Long Woman; F; Daughter; 7

1560; ---; William Steal Bear; M; Husband; 33
1561; ---; Esther Shell On The Neck; F; Wife; 26

Census of the __Crow__ Indians of __Crow__ Agency __Montana__ taken
By __J.E. Edwards__, United States Indian Agent __June 30, 1901__

Key: Number; Indian Name; English Name; Sex; Relation; Age

1562; Beday-ock-ke-day-ichis; Good Shell; M; Ad Son; 8

1563; Beendosh-kanesh-wachice; Sits By the Water; F; Widow; 71

1564; Up-pay-e-wah-wah-e-cosh; Looks With His Ears; M; Husband; 36
1565; Oat-chean-bah-dup-pace; Kills at Night; F; Wife; 42
1566; Ope-cha-deas; Old Medicine Tobacco; F; Daughter; 13

1567; Is-tuk-key-de-ditch; Strikes Her Gun; F; Widow; 71

1568; E-chin-doot-chice; Takes a Horse; M; Husband; 32
1569; Undut-che-do-che-dice; Hunts to Slide; F; Wife; 24
1570; Bea-bachpash; Medicine Woman; M; Son; 10
1571; ---; Jessie T. Horses[sic]; F; Daughter; 2

1572; Pope-put-tay-oa-cottus; Little Owl; M; Husband; 32
1573; Is-coe-chea-ache-chase; Knows the Enemy; F; Wife; 27
1574; Ahwacce-ischesay-ahoos; Plenty Swallow; M; Son; 10
1575; ---; John Shot in the Nose; M; Son; 4

1576; E-cupe-pis; Gets Down; M; Husband; 38
1577; Dah-cock-doo-pus; Two Birds; F; Wife; 33
1578; Cah-dah-hay-day-duse; Bird In the Rain; M; Son; 9
1579; Bah-dah-cah-deas; Old Money; F; Daughter; 6

1580; Dackpitsa-cah-dice; Old Bear Woman; F; Gr Mo; 66
1581; ---; Thomas Gets Down; M; Gr Son; 1

1582; Ische-ahay-ea-cot-tus; Little Nest; M; Husband; 35
1583; ---; Mary Laforge; F; Wife; 28
1584; ---; Mary Little Nest; F; Daughter; 10

1585; Is-coe-chea-docosh-ish; Holds the Enemy; M; Husband; 33
1586; Bah-put-tah-seas; Shows the Otter; F; Wife; 30
1587; Is-cah-kay-keas-sos; Plain Spear; M; Son; 7
1588; Bacombatshay-bachpash; Medicine Lark; M; Son; 2

1589; ---; George Thomas; M; Widower; 34

1590; ---; Henry Russell; M; Husband; 32
1591; Bah-chea-sheas; Steals on Camp; F; Wf; 29
1592; ---; Geo. W. Russell; M; Son; 4

1593; Ah-shoop-padate-cahdeas; Old Horn; M; Husband; 37
1594; ---; Lucy Old Horn; F; Wife; 27
1595; ---; Fred Old Horn; M; Son; 11

Census of the __Crow__ Indians of __Crow__ Agency __Montana__ taken
By __J.E. Edwards__, United States Indian Agent __June 30, 1901__

Key: Number; Indian Name; English Name; Sex; Relation; Age

1596; ---; Susie Old Horn; F; Daughter; 8
1597; ---; Clarence Old Horn; M; Son; 2

1598; Ay-day-cah-weas; Bad Belly; M; Batchelor[sic]; 44

1599; Ah-day-chea-tus; White Arm; M; Husband; 40
1600; Bah-cah-key-it-chice; Pretty Shell; F; Wife; 36
1601; Bea-ditches; Strikes Woman; F; Mother; 75

1602; Bos-che-day-cah-deas; Old White Man #2; M; Husband; 31
1603; Is-bah-hum-be-shis; Have Things; F; Wife; 19

1604; Bouta-bah-coos-shecosh; Coyote Looks Up; M; Widower; 74
1605; Doop-tush-ditches; Strikes Both Ways; F; Mother; 90

1606; Uck-sah-e-cos; Looks at Her Mother; F; Wiodw[sic]; 65
1607; Be-coo-took-eas; Little Moon; F; Gr Dau; 6

1608; Itche-bah-duck-shis; Plays With Himself; M; Husband; 29
1609; Isminats-makpash; Medicine Shield; F; Wife; 29
1610; MEa-hotchkis; Tall Woman; F; Daughter; 11
1611; Dackpitsa-bishea; Dog Bear; M; Son; 2

1612; Ah-way-chase; Knows the Ground; M; Husband; 36
1613; ---; Perses Knows the Ground; F; Wife; 32

1614; E-shue-es-bachpash; Medicine Mane; M; Husband; 34
1615; Dacock-etuck-posdatus; Bird Without a Cloud; F; Wife; 29
1616; Ushdosh-caneba-duppace; Kills Beside Camp; F; Daughter; 10

1617; Is-bah-dah-hoos; Got Plenty Beads; F; Widow; 45
1618; Bah-pah-dish; Flower; M; Son; 15
1619; EApcha-bapah-dootchis; Takes the Medicine Pipe; F; Daughter; 8

1620; Bah-duk-keas; The Gun; M; Husband; 30
1621; Be-dup-cah-deas; Old Beaver; F; Wife; 33
1622; ---; John T. Gun; M; Son; 3

1623; ---; Charles Wort Davis; M; Batchelor[sic]; 31

1624; Bah-key-de-hosh; The Other Blackbird; M; Husband; 32
1625; Bah-put-tah-seas; Otter That Shows; F; Wife; 26
1626; Dup-pah-ecos-seas; Turns Around Twice; M; Son; 11
1627; Bah-dea-ate-chice; Knows What To Do; F; Daughter; 8

1628; Up-poch-cane-dichis; Strikes Back of the Head; F; Widow; 53

Census of the __Crow__ Indians of __Crow__ Agency __Montana__ taken By __J.E. Edwards__, United States Indian Agent __June 30, 1901__

Key: Number; Indian Name; English Name; Sex; Relation; Age

1629; Dackpitsa-cowees; Bad Bear; M; Husband; 33
1630; Eas-che-keep-pay; Crooked Face; F; Wife; 25

1631; Iscoche-hayday-codays; Goes Among the Enemy; M; Husband; 34
1632; Es-tup-peas; Shuts Her Eyes; F; Wife; 31
1633; Dee-cock-e-sos; Big Bird; M; Son; 11
1634; Dum-bachpash; Eats the Wood; M; Son; 7
1635; ---; Amos Goes Among the Enemy; M; Son; 2

1636; ---; George Hill; M; Husband; 35
1637; ---; Mrs. George Hill; F; Wife; 25
1638; ---; Anna Hill; F; Daughter; 8
1639; ---; Mary Hill; F; Daughter; 6
1640; ---; Amanda Hill; F; Daughter; 1

1641; Cheedup-sho-chok-a-dus; Bull Over the Hill; M; Husband; 28
1642; Apah-suttah-doochice; Takes a Split Ear; F; Wife; 26
1643; DAch-co-bachpash; Medicine Turtle; F; Daughter; 8

1644; Bea-dea-dush; The Door; M; Husband; 30
1645; ---; Victoria Door; F; Wife; 21
1646; ---; Dora Door; F; Daughter; 5

1647; Oo-wa-sheedish; Yellow In the Mouth; M; Husband; 29
1648; BOut-tah-eas; Little Coyote; F; Wife; 23
1649; Dach-cock-sheedish; Yellow Bird; F; Daughter; 7
1650; ---; (No name reported); F; Daughter; 1

1651; ---; Laura Green; F; Married White; 26

1652; Mah-soe; Mint; M; Widower; 49

1653; Bascheeda-schepittay; Light Colored Man; M; Husband; 29
1654; Bahcay-cacah-dah-bish; Hoop That Moves; F; Wife; 26
1655; Ope-cah-deas; Old Tobacco; F; Daughter; 6
1656; ---; Florence Coo Chief; F; Daughter; 5
1657; ---; Fire Squirrel; M; Son; 1

1658; Bash-keas-sos; Plain Feather; M; Husband; 29
1659; Un-dah-coe-bah-coos; Lives High; F; Wife; 25

1660; Cheeup-e-ches-ditch; Bull Horse; M; Father; 32
1661; Echete-dootchis; Takes a Pinto Horse; F; Daughter; 6

1662; ---; Mrs. Joe Pickett; F; Mother; F; 38
1663; ---; Robert A. Pickett; M; Son; 14

Census of the __Crow__ Indians of __Crow__ Agency __Montana__ taken
By __J.E. Edwards__, United States Indian Agent __June 30, 1901__

Key: Number; Indian Name; English Name; Sex; Relation; Age

1664; ---; Joseph J. Pickett; M; Son; 11
1665; ---; William C. Pickett; M; Son; 8
1666; ---; Margaret Pickett; F; Daughter; 7

1667; ---; Joseph Stewart; M; Husband; 31
1668; Cah-coa-ays; Everything is Here; F; Wife; 28
1669; ---; Francis Stewart; M; Son; 8
1670; ---; Fannie Stewart; F; Daughter; 6
1671; ---; Robert Stewart; M; Son; 1

1672; ---; William Stewart; M; Batchelor[sic]; 22

1673; ---; M. Two Belly; M; Husband; 41
1674; ---; Mrs; M. Two Belly; F; Wife; 39
1675; Ahkinda-heahsos; Rides a Horse Well Known; F; Ad Dau; 13

1676; ---; John Wesley; M; Husband; 40
1677; ---; Jane Wesley; F; Wife; 35
1678; ---; Jennie Wesley; F; Daughter; 14
1679; ---; Fannie Wesley; F; Daughter; 8
1680; ---; Inez Wesley; F; Daughter; 1

1681; ---; Mrs. James Robinson; F; Mother; 41
1682; ---; James Robinson; M; Son; 8
1683; ---; Charles Robinson; M; Son; 14
1684; ---; Ellen Robinson; F; Daughter; 9
1685; ---; Allen Robinson; M; Son; 6
1686; ---; Alice Robinson; F; Daughter; 4

1687; ---; Mrs. G.F. Deputee; F; Mother; 34
1688; ---; Jennie Deputee; F; Daughter; 8
1689; ---; Flora Deputee; F; Daughter; 6

1690; ---; Mrs. Frank Gordon; F; Married White; 46

1691; ---; Mrs. B. Bravo; F; Married White; 58

1692; Hoo-chice; Wind; M; Husband; 37
1693; ---; Mrs. Thos. Laforge; F; Wife; 53
1694; ---; Thomas Asa Laforge; M; Son; 17
1695; ---; Rosa Laforge; F; Daughter; 19

1696; ---; John Alden; M; Husband; 33
1697; ---; Phoebe Alden; F; Wife; 22
1698; ---; Alvin Alden; M; Son; 1

Census of the __Crow__ Indians of __Crow__ Agency __Montana__ taken By __J.E. Edwards__, United States Indian Agent __June 30, 1901__

Key: Number; Indian Name; English Name; Sex; Relation; Age

1699; ---; Mrs. J.B. Cooper; F; Mother; 61
1700; ---; Cynthia Cooper; F; Daughter; 16
1701; ---; Sylvester Hardy; M; Gr Son; 5
1702; ---; Peter Cooper; M; Son; 21
1703; ---; Lulu Cooper; F; Daughter; 23

1704; ---; Martha C. Schenderline [?]; F; Mother; 26
1705; ---; Joseph Schenderline; M; Son; 8
1706; ---; Edward Schenderline; M; Son; 6
1707; ---; Henry Schenderline; M; Son; 4
1708; ---; Rachel Schenderline; F; Daughter; 2

1709; ---; Myrtle Keiser; F; --; 7
1710; ---; Frank Keiser; M; --; 21

1711; ---; Mrs. Maggie K. Macer; F; Mother; 23
1712; ---; Mabel Macer; F; Daughter; 6
1713; ---; Henry Macer; M; Son; 4
1714; ---; Edwards[sic] Macer; M; Son; 2

1715; ---; Mrs. David Yarlott; F; Mother; 53
1716; ---; Katie Yarlott; F; Daughter; 13
1717; ---; Frank Yarlott; M; Son; 19
1718; ---; Charles Yarlott; M; Son; 23

1719; ---; Rosebud Farwell; M; Married Cherokee; 19

1720; ---; Susan Farwell-Glenn; F; Mother; 25
1721; ---; Percival Glenn; M; Son; 2
1722; ---; Louisa Pearl Glenn; F; Daughter; 6m

1723; ---; Mrs. Al. Morrison; F; Mother; 53
1724; ---; Alvin Morrison; M; Son; 18
1725; ---; Hannah Morrison; F; Daughter; 20

1726; E-say-dup-pah-choas; points the Gun In His Face; M; Husband; 35
1727; ---; Mrs. Thomas Stewart; F; Wife; 42
1728; Ah-wah-caneca-dooshis; Runs Over the Ground; M; Son; 8

1729; ---; Mrs. R.W. Cummins; F; Married White; 51

1730; ---; Mrs. Thomas Kent; F; Mother; 49
1731; ---; Maggie Kent; F; Daughter; 14
1732; ---; Elizabeth Kent; F; Daughter; 19
1733; ---; Josephine Kent-Williams; F; Daughter; 21

Census of the __Crow__ Indians of __Crow__ Agency __Montana__ taken
By __J.E. Edwards__, United States Indian Agent __June 30, 1901__

Key: Number; Indian Name; English Name; Sex; Relation; Age

1734; ---; Mary K. Stevens; F; Mother; 23
1735; ---; Clarence L. Stevens; M; Son; 6
1736; ---; Kent Stevens; M; Son; 5
1737; ---; Agnes Stevens; F; Daughter; 4
1738; ---; John T. Stevens; M; Son; 1

1739; ---; Mrs. Ella K. Cashen; F; Mother; 25
1740; ---; Willie Cashen; M; Son; 7
1741; ---; Alice Cashen; F; Daughter; 6
1742; ---; Ella Cashen; F; Daughter; 4
1743; ---; Cecelia Cashen; F; Daughter; 2

1744; ---; Maggie Garrigus; F; Mother; 30
1745; ---; Mary F. Garrigus; F; Daughter; 9
1746; ---; Margaret E. Garrigus; F; Daughter; 8
1747; ---; Arthur R. Garrigus; M; Son; 6
1748; ---; Dorothy B. Garrigus; F; Daughter; 4

1749; ---; Abbie Lande; F; Mother; 27
1750; ---; Henry D. Lande; M; Son; 3
1751; ---; George A. Lande; M; Son; 1

1752; ---; Frederick Geisdorff; M; Father; 30
1753; ---; Florence Geisdorff; F; Daughter; 6
1754; ---; Francis Geisdorff; M; Son; 5
1755; ---; Frederick Geisdorff Jr.; M; Son; 4
1756; ---; Louisa Geisdorff; F; Sister; 26
1757; ---; Charlotte Geisdorff; F; Sister; 23

1758; ---; Margaret A. Davis-Howe; F; Mother; 22
1759; ---; Robert S. Howe; M; Son; 2
1760; ---; Blaine R. Davis; M; Brother; 7
1761; ---; Effie N. Davis; F; Sister; 16

1762; ---; Minnie Reed; F; Orphan; 26
1763; ---; Francis Reed; M; Brother; 23
1764; ---; Della Reed; F; Sister; 17
1765; ---; Nellie Reed; F; Sister; 15
1766; ---; Edith Reed; F; Sister; 13
1767; ---; Katie Reed; F; Sister; 11

1768; ---; Mary K. Reed; F; Orphan; 17

1769; ---; Mrs. Wm. H. White; F; Mother; 39
1770; ---; Minnie E. White; F; Daughter; 16
1771; ---; Charles F. White; M; Son; 3

Census of the __Crow__ Indians of __Crow__ Agency __Montana__ taken By __J.E. Edwards__, United States Indian Agent __June 30, 1901__

Key: Number; Indian Name; English Name; Sex; Relation; Age

1772; ---; Ada M. White; F; Daughter; 1
1773; ---; Mary E. White; F; Daughter; 19
1774; ---; Wm. H. White; M; Son; 21

1775; ---; Mrs. Thomas Shane; F; Mother; 42
1776; ---; Patrick C. Shane; M; Son; 16
1777; ---; Frank Shane; M; Son; 13
1778; ---; Josie Shane; F; Daughter; 11
1779; ---; Bessie Shane; F; Daughter; 9
1780; ---; Thomas Shane; M; Son; M; 7
1781; ---; Edward Shane; M; Son; 5
1782; ---; Kittie Shane; F; Daughter; 23

1783; ---; Cora Williams [Schroeder]; F; Mother; 22
1784; ---; ---[Elmer E. Schroeder]; M; Son; 1

1785; ---; Mattie Williams; F; --; 20

1786; ---; Mrs. Mary Heckenlively; F; Mother; 25
1787; ---; Guy L. Heckenlively; M; Son; 4
1788; ---; Howard C. Heckenlively; M; Son; 2

1789; ---; Mrs. Thosmas Doyle; F; Mother; 24
1790; ---; Robert Doyle; M; Son; 4
1791; ---; Frances Doyle; F; Daughter; 3
1792; ---; John Doyle; M; Son; 1

1793; ---; Ellen Jackson; F; Mother; 49
1794; ---; Eliza Jackson; F; Daughter; 15
1795; ---; Julia Jackson; F; Daughter; 12
1796; ---; John Jackson; M; Son; 20

1797; ---; John Frost; M; Husband; 28
1798; Is-bon-dot-bachpash; Medicine Shield; F; Wife; 21
1799; ---; Daniel L. Frost; M; Son; 4

1800; ---; Joseph Cooper; M; Husband; 29
1801; ---; Susie Cooper; F; Wife; 30
1802; ---; Theodore Cooper; F; Son; 9 [While seeking a full search for this child's sex and age it was found that within different census periods this child was a Dau., age 5 in 1897; Dau., age 6 in 1898; a Son age 7 in 1899; Dau., age 8 in 1900; Son age 9 in 1901; Son age 10 in 1902; Son age 11 in 1903. Anything found in other records will be recorded without note.]
1803; ---; Laura Cooper; F; Daughter; 8
1804; ---; Sylvania Cooper; F; Daughter; 7
1805; ---; James Cooper; M; Son; 5

Census of the __Crow__ Indians of __Crow__ Agency __Montana__ taken By __J.E. Edwards__, United States Indian Agent __June 30, 1901__

Key: Number; Indian Name; English Name; Sex; Relation; Age

1806; ---; Joseph Cooper Jr.; M; Son; 3

1807; Ah-woo-coos; Sydney Wolf; M; Husband; 22
1808; Ahwokchedus-helemach; Edith Long Ear; F; Wife; 18

1809; ---; Levantia W. Pearson; F; Mother; 38
1810; ---; Virginia Pearson; F; Daughter; 9
1811; ---; Helen E. Pearson; F; Daughter; 8
1812; ---; Ethel M. Pearson; F; Daughter; 6

1813; ---; George W. Pease; M; Husband; 35
1814; ---; Sarah Pease; F; Wife; 9[sic]; [34]
1815; ---; David Pease; M; Son; 9
1816; ---; James Pease; M; Son; 11
1817; ---; Benjamin Pease; M; Son; 8
1818; ---; Emory Pease; M; Son; 7
1819; ---; Anson H. Pease; M; Son; 5
1820; ---; George Pease; M; Son; 4
1821; ---; Oliver Pease; M; Son; 1

1822; ---; Mrs. Marshall; F; Married White; 44

1823; ---; Mrs. Amy Scott; F; Mother; 23
1824; ---; George Scott; M; Son; 5
1825; ---; Elmer Scott; M; Son; 4
1826; ---; Irene Scott; F; Daughter; 1 m
1827; ---; June Scott; F; Daughter; 1 m

1828; CHate-dah-beas; Three Wolves; M; Widower; 49

1829; Is-bah-key-cush-sheas; Hoop Turns Around; M; Married Cheyenne; 26
1830; ---; August Hoop Turns Around; M; Son; 4

1831; Cheedup-kahdeas; Old Bull; M; Husband; 27
1832; Bah-ah-key-day-cus; Shell Child; F; Wife; 22
1833; Bachpash; Medicine; F; Daughter; 4
1834; ---; Kills With Her Horse; F; Daughter; 5m

1835; Ahway-taday-coock-cus; Bird Far Away; M; Batchelor[sic]; 25

1836; Ah-shue-cay-bah; Bush Head; M; Husband; 26
1837; Boa-pis; Snow; F; Wife; 33

1838; Chayte-aputs; Wolf That Looks back; M; Husband; 25
1839; Ah-woos-cahdeas; Old Sweathouse; F; Widow; 36

Census of the __Crow__ Indians of __Crow__ Agency __Montana__ taken By __J.E. Edwards__, United States Indian Agent __June 30, 1901__

Key: Number; Indian Name; English Name; Sex; Relation; Age

1840; ---; Martin Round Face; M; Husband; 28
1841; ---; Katie Dreamer; F; Wife; 25

1842; Tuch-chay-dah-cockus; Straight Bird; M; Husband; 25
1843; Dah-cock-sah-hoos; Comes to the Birds; F; Wife; 20

1844; Chea-dacock-inda-dichis; Strikes Riding Grey Horse; F; Divorced; 19
1845; ---; Frances Ten Bear; M; Son; 4

1846; Bea-sos-coos; Looks Back; M; Husband; 25
1847; Bah-o-dop-keas-sos; Finds Plain; F; Wife; 24

1848; Bah-put-tah-beas; Otter Woman; F; Widow; 21
1849; ---; Glenn Bird; M; Son; 5

1850; Choos-say-dah-quas; Sends Part Home; M; Widower; 33

1851; Ah-pit-bah-coos; Crane in the Sky; M; Husband; 61
1852; Incuppah-bish-chedice; Strikes the Hat; F; Mother; 42
1863; ---; Stephen B. Prairie; M; Son; 2

1854; ---; Samuel S. Davis; M; Batchelor[sic]; 26

1855; ---; Frank Shively; M; Batchelor; 29

1856; Osue; Can't Shoot Him; M; Husband; 20
1857; Ahakarooche-amach; Horse sits down; F; Wife; 18
1858; Ahshashe-duschice; Turns Round the Camp; M; Son; 2

1859; Dah-cock-ah-seas; Bird That Shows; F; Widow; 53

1860; Bachay-eatche-bish-ay; Man With a Beard; M; Husband; 25
1861; Is-bah-cah-kea-ahoos; Plenty Shells; F; Wife; 23

1862; Ecupe-pah-de-chice; Strikes the Hat; F; Widow; 53

1863; Be-de-ha-dup-pace; Crosses the Water; F; Widow; 61

1864; Bachay-ha-what-dechice; Strikes One Man; F; Widow; 56

1865; Suah-cowutish; Thunder Iron; M; Widower; 25

1866: Cha-cush; Five; F; Widow; 77

1867; Esock-chice; The Hawk; M; Husband; 24 [Also #1393.]
1868; Bah-shus-shays; Medicine Dance; F; Wife; 16

Census of the __Crow__ Indians of __Crow__ Agency __Montana__ taken By __J.E. Edwards__, United States Indian Agent __June 30, 1901__

Key: Number; Indian Name; English Name; Sex; Relation; Age

1869; Bah-son-day-itchice; Goes Ahead Pretty; M; Husband; 26
1870; Bah-put-tah-beas; Otter Woman; F; Wife; 36

1871; ---; James Laforge; M; Husband; 24
1872; ---; Sage Woman; F; Wife; 21
1873; ---; William Laforge; M; Son; 6
1874; ---; Francis Laforge; M; Son; 4

1875; ---; Mary M. Humphrey; F; Mother; 24
1876; ---; Maud Humphrey; F; Daughter; 5
1877; ---; Lillie Humphrey; F; Daughter; 2

1878; Ah-hoo-ha-e-cush-cuss; Turns Back Plenty; M; Husband; 26
1879; Beshay-dane-awachice; Sits Among the Rocks; F; Wife; 22
1880; ---; High Nest; M; Son; 3

1881; Awaca-dane-cheedup-ish; Mountain Bull; M; Husband; 25
1882; Ahwaycook-cordetah-heas; Goes to Ground Every Day; F; Wife; 24

1883; Boa-e-hock-sos; Sings the Last Song; M; Husband; 36
1884; As-says-das; Goes to the House; F; Wife; 49

1885; Con-up-e-say; Big Nose Old Woman; F; Widow; 84

1886; Isuc-cheyday-sheedish; Yellow Hawk; M; Widower; 44

1887; ---; Jackson Stewart; M; Husband; 24
1888; Eskulusa-epa-cheis; White Tailed Hawk; F; Wife; 22
1889; ---; ---; F; Dau; 4 m

1890; Ah-quas; Covered Up; M; Husband; 29
1891; Bah-pah-dit-chice; Plenty Things Growing; F; Wife; 24

1892; ---; Richard Pickett; M; Father; 19
1893; ---; Thomas Pickett; M; Son; 3
1894; ---; Lizzie Pickett; F; Daugh; 1 m

1895; Bah-dah-kut-teas; Crazy; M; Husband; 31
1896; Bashow-deeditch-chaysos; Big Medicine Rock; F; Wife; 20
1897; ---; Sits With the Coyote; M; Son; 7 m

1898; Oat-chees-du-dish; Walks At Night; M; Husband; 24 [Ralph Saco in 1900.]
1899; Bee-dop-dah-cuss; Young Beaver; F; Wife; 25
1900; ---; Minnie Saco; F; Daughter; 2

1901; Echete-itchice; Pretty Horse; M; Husband; 36

Census of the __Crow__ Indians of __Crow__ Agency __Montana__ taken
By __J.E. Edwards__, United States Indian Agent __June 30, 1901__

Key: Number; Indian Name; English Name; Sex; Relation; Age

1902; ---; Monica Horn; F; Wife; 21

1903; ---; Charles M. Phelps; M; Father; 28
1904; ---; Frank Phelps; M; Son; 7
1905; ---; Fred Phelps; M; Son; 6
1906; ---; Emma Phelps; F; Daughter; 4
1907; ---; Bud Phelps; M; Son; 2

1908; ---; Mrs. Rosa Milliken; F; Mother; 39
1909; ---; John Wesley Milliken; M; Son; 18
1910; ---; Claude Milliken; M; Son; 22
1911; ---; Leroy Milliken; M; Son; 20

Research Books

Blackhawk, Ned, New Haven and London, 2023, *The Rediscovery of America,* Yale University Press Books

Frey, Rodney, Norman, Oklahoma, 1987, *The World of the Crow Indians*, University of Oklahoma Press

Hoxie, Frederick E., New York, New York, 1995, *Parading Through History,* Cambridge University Press

Laforge, Thomas H., Lincoln, 1928, *Memoirs of a White Crow Indian (As told by Thomas B. Marquis),* The Century Co. (University of Nebraska Press) (First Bison Books Printing 1974)

Linderman, Frank B., Lincoln and London, 1930, *Plenty-coups: Chief of the Crows,* University of Nebraska Press (First Nebraska Paperback Printing 1962)

Linderman, Frank B., New York, 1932, *Pretty-shield: Medicine Woman of the Crows,* Harper Collins Books (First Harper Perennial Paperback Published 2021)

Lowie, Robert H., New York, 1919, *The Tobacco Society of the Crow Indians*, The American Museum of Natural History

Medicine Crow, Joseph, Lincoln and London, 1992, *From The Heart Of The Crow Country: The Crow Indians' Own Stories*, University of Nebraska Press (First Bison Books Printing 2000)

Connell, Evan S., New York, New York, 1984, *Son of the Morning Star Custer and the Little Big Horn*, Harper & Row, Publishers, Inc. (parallel reading)

Index

P257(No name reported) 246
[Echean-chea-itchis] 120
[Kowees] 210
[Lance 1899-1900] 243
[Land 1899-1900] 243
[Land in 1900] 243
[Schroeder], [Elmer E.] 250
[Takes] Quick 241
[Three Coons] 233

Ache-lagaks 204
Ach-pah-dea-itchise 230
Achpahnea-achpedaish 160
Achpanea-achpedaish 223
A-dah-shoes 27,90,155,218
Adams, Katie H. 233
Addie 18,77,141,205
Aditch-chebah-doch-ahoos 115
Aditch-chebah-dochahoos 179,241
Afraid of His Enemy 173,236
Afraid of his enemy 46,109
Ahakarooche-amach 133,252
Ahaukap-meas 10
Ah-bah-de-ichis 85
Ah-bah-de-itchis 21
Ah-bah-keas-sash 21,85,149,213
Ah-bay-da-itchis 149,212
Ah-bush-it-chice 63,116,180,242
Ah-cah-pish-sis 52,115,179,241
Ah-cam-dah-pace 39,103,167,230
Ah-cane-dah-pace 51,114,178,241
Ah-chane-deechis 78,142,226
Ah-chay-it-che-poas 32
Ah-chay-itche-poas 96
Ah-chay-itsche-peas 160,223
Ahcheke-ichis 17,81,209
Ahchook-coode-dadush 151,215
Ah-chook-coode-day-dush 24
Ah-chook-coode-daydush 87
Ah-cock-bee-dash 152,215
Ah-cook-bee-dash 24,87
Ahdache-waycoo-itchis..... 88,152,216
Ah-dah-buck-ke-os 27
Ah-dah-che-e-coss 38,166,229
Ah-dah-che-e-sos 102
Ahdahche-waycooitchis 25
Ah-dah-cuck-kay 47,175,237
Ah-dah-cuck-kays 111

Ah-dah-doo-be-shay .. 44,107,171,234
Ah-dah-hea-it-chis 34
Ah-dah-hes-it-chis 97
Ah-dah-hes-itchis 162,225
Ah-dah-sea-ahoos 216
Ah-dah-sea-ut-hoos 25,88,153
Ah-dah-shay-chee-dish 48
Ah-dah-sos-ea-kot-tosh 34,97,161,
 225
Ah-day-buck-ke-os 91
Ah-day-cah-weas 55
Ah-day-chea-tus 55,118,182,245
Ah-day-shay-chee-dish ... 111,175,238
Ah-dean-dace 41,104,169,232
Ahdean-dauah-waychis 157,220
Ahdean-day-ah-chatis 149,213
Ah-dean-day-ah-chetis 21
Ah-dean-day-ahchetis 85
Ahdean-dayah-waychis 29,92
Ah-dean-day-ate-chice 44,107,172,
 205
Ah-ditch-che-bah-dotchahoos 52
Ahdo-chea-beas 21,85,149,213
Ahdock-in-day-keasos 164,227
Ah-dock-in-day-keas-sos 36,55,118
Ah-dock-inday-keas-sos 100,144
Ah-douch-chea-pashpash 235
Ah-dough-chea-ah-chase .. 99,158,221
Ah-dough-chea-ay-chase 35
Ah-dough-chea-bah-pash.. 45,109,173
Ah-dow-chea-keas-sos 47,111,175
Ah-dow-hea-keas-sos 237
Ah-duch-che-itchis 221
Ah-duchh-che-itchis 158
Ah-duck-chea-ah-hoos 50,113
Ah-duck-chea-ahoos 177
Ah-duck-chea-oss-ea-tuss ... 36,99,163
Ahduckchea-oss-ea-tuss 226
Ah-duck-che-ba-chatchis 163
Ah-duck-che-bachatchis 226
Ahduck-chedechay-itchis 91
Ah-duck-che-dee-chay-itchis 27
Ahduckchee-chay-ichis 218
Ahduck-cheedee-chay-ichis 155
Ah-duck-che-it-chis 30
Ah-duck-che-itchis 94
Ah-duk-che-ba-chatchis 99
Ah-duk-che-bah-chate-chis 57

Index

Ah-dup-pah-hoose......32,95,158–159, ...222
Ah-dup-pice ....48,111,116,175, ...180,238,243
Ah-dup-pis 28,53,91,156,219
Ah-dush-cos-pay 28,91,155,219
Aheheke-ichis 145
Ah-hoc-cot-dea-dish.....................220
Ah-hoe-cot-ta-dead-dish 29
Ah-hoe-cot-ta-dea-dish 157
Ah-hoe-cotta-dea-dish.................... 93
Ah-hoo-ha-e-cuch-seas 190
Ah-hoo-ha-e-cush-cuss 253
Ah-hoo-ha-e-cush-seas.............63,126
Ahkabos 22,85,150
Ahkabosh 213
Ahka-karasash................................. 70
Ahka-karashsash 6
Ahkbahdit-napes 9,138,201
Ah-kean-bah-dahcheakeassos 24
Ah-kean-bahduckshaybah-ash 51
Ahke-mah-kaweish 23,150,214
Ahke-mulukish..............................189
Ahken-bahdachek-casos................. 87
Ah-key-bee-deep-pah-cuss............. 64
Ah-key-ca-bee-shay 226
Ah-key-chice.............49,112,176,238
Ah-key-oka-bee-shay 163
Ah-key-oke-bee-shay 99
Ah-key-oke-bee-shey 35
Ahkinda-heahsas........................10,74
Ahkinda-heahsos....................184,247
Ah-kish-koos 13,140
Ah-kish-koss 76
Ah-kok-de-chis 28,91,155,219
Ahkpahne-makpash.......................210
Ahlud-esuhsh 21,84
Ahlud-esush 149,212
Ahluk-chea-akuse....................69,133
Ahluk-cheaakuse............................197
Ahma-apisch 6
Ahma-apische 70,134,198
Ah-mah-ah-che-day-chase 30,93
Ahmahta.. 71
Ahmako-istisha-naks....20,83,148,211
Ahmatka................................7,135,199
Ah-may-ahche-day-chase.......157,220
Ahmbatseda-ahoos 13,77,141

Ahm-botsots-heahsas... 15,78,143,207
Ahmuapes.................... 20,83,148,211
Ahnede-ichis...................................... 5
Ahnehe-iches 69
Ahnehe-ichis................................. 133
    Walks Pretty 197
Ahoo-ahk-ichis 22,85,150,213
Ahoo-aroopis 7,71,134,198
Ahpa-doochis............... 11,75,139,203
Ahpa-duttotoes 72,136,200
Ahpa-duttotoos 8
Ahpa-esash 14,77,141,205
Ah-pah-de-beas....................... 43,107
Ah-pah-de-deas..................... 171,234
Ah-pah-dee-esos 45,108,172,235
Ah-pah-dee-it-chice ... 52,115,179,241
Ah-pah-de-e-wan-deas..... 45,108,173, ...235
Ah-pah-kay-dainbaehdahkis 34
Ahpahne-makpash 82,147
Ah-pah-seas 29,92
Ah-pah-sut-tah-doot-chice.............. 56
Ahpa-ka-dainbadakis 98
Ahpaka-hedera-dakpitsch 11
Ahpaka-heder-dakpitch................... 74
Ahpaka-hedere-dakpitsch 139,203
Ahpake-hedere-Lagaks 198
Ahpake-hedere-lagaks 6,70,134
Ah-pas-seas 156,220
Ahpaycha-apah-dootchis 96
Ah-pay-days 33,97,161,224
Ah-pay-eso-chay-aeh-way-chis 34
Ah-pay-eso-chay-awachis............... 97
Ahpay-eso-chay-away-chis.... 161,224
Ahpay-kay-dainba-dahkis....... 162,225
Ahpay-sheedes............. 13,76,140,204
Ah-pea-chay-ah-pah-dootchis......... 33
Ahpeachay-apah-doochis........ 160,223
Ah-peah-cos.................................... 33
Ahpeahne-makpash 19
Ah-peeh-cos............................. 160,223
Ah-pe-hosh 175,237
Ah-pe-sah-sheedis 54,117
Ah-pe-sah-sheedish 181,243
Ah-pesh-cos.................................... 96
Ahpewesha 9,137,201
Ahpewsha 73
Ahpiet-sheedis 214

Index

Ah-pit-bah-coos 44,171,252
Ah-pitbah-coos 107
Ah-pit-bah-dock-cus .. 50,113,177,239
Ahpit-cheas 197
Ahpit-cheis 5,69,133
Ahpit-dakpitska 12,76,140,204
Ahpit-kahdeas 12,75,140,204
Ahpit-nake 69,133,197
Ahpit-naks.. 5
Ahpit-sheedis 22,86,150
Ah-pit-tus 45,108,173,235
Ah-puch-kay 24
Ah-puck-kay 152,215
Ah-puss-sah-cheas 37,100,164,227
Ah-quas 64,126,190,253
Ahrikinda-aet-chase 238
Ahrocheis 21,84,149,212
Ah-ruck-chea-ahoos 240
Ah-ruck-chea-heahsas 201
Ah-sah-date-doot-chis 44
Ah-sah-date-dootchis 171,239
Ahsah-date-doot-chis 107
Ah-sah-hoos 43
Ahsay-chulees 14,77,142,205
Ahse-desh..................... 8,72,136,200
Ah-see-tus 39,102,166,229
Ahsha-ckepish................................ 84
Ahsha-ekash 12,75,140,204
Ahsha-hedere-malapes 11,125,189
Ahsha-heletam-basash . 18,81,146,209
Ahsha-okepish..................... 21,149,212
Ahshashe-duschice................. 189,252
Ah-shay-dane-dee-chise 14
Ah-shay-day-duss 64,126
Ahshay-hedra-dichis 15,78,143,207
Ahshay-whoo-a-aychis......86,150,214
Ahshay-whoo's-aychis 23
Ah-sheas....................................... 47
Ah-she-tas 38,102,166,229
Ahshkay-shopis............. 22,85,149,213
Ahshmtse-makpash 16
Ah-shoe-ah-peas 54,117,142,206
Ah-shoe-che-dish 50,113,177,239
Ah-shoe-hishes 225
Ah-shoe-hishis 162
Ah-shoe-hish-shis 37,100
Ahsho-malapes...........................20,84
Ah-shon-sheedish..........................157

Ah-shoop-padate-cahdeas..... 118,182,
.... 244
Ah-shoop-pahdate-cah-deas 55
Ah-shoos.................... 29,92,156,219
Ahshua-dichis..............................207
Ahshuah-dichis.................. 16,79,144
Ahshua-wahnaks............. 5,69,133,197
Ah-shue-ah-was-days 57,104
Ah-shue-cah-bay..................... 62,125
Ah-shue-cay-bah.......................... 251
Ah-shue-cay-bay.......................... 188
Ah-shue-cheas 45,108,172,235
Ahshuputsuah-dooich .. 20,84,148,212
Ah-shus-ah-was-days............. 168,232
Ahskarooche-amach 69
Ah-son-she-dish........................ 29,93
Ahsukap-meas 138,201
Ahta-dichis 10
Ahta-ditchis 138,202
Ahta-huk-is-dichis 22,86
Ahta-malapes................. 9,73,137,201
Ahuk-chea-akuse 5
Ahwa-akinakuse 17,80,145,208
Ahwa-akuse 9,73,137,201
Ahwacce-ischesay-ahoos............. 244
Ahwacce-ischeshay-ahoos............ 169
Ahwacoe-che-dapahpash 107
Ahwacos-che-dapachbash............. 171
Ahwahahs 152,216
Ah-wah-cah-dace......... 48,77,141,205
Ah-wah-cahn-dab-cock-cus........... 47
Ah-wah-cah-wassahwah-chis 41
Ahwah-cah-wassahwah-chis......... 169
Ah-wah-cah-way-dane-chee-dup-pish
.... 63
Ahwahcan-dah-cock-cus............... 174
Ah-wah-caneca-dooshis.. 122,186,248
Ah-wah-cane-cah-doos-shis 59
Ah-wah-chis 29,92,157,220
Ah-wah-coan-de-dish 46,109,173,
.... 236
Ahwahcoe-ishcheshayahhoos 41
Ah-wah-cone-ah-way-chice............ 51
Ah-wah-coo-ish-chice-say-ea-cot-tus.
.... 48
Ah-wah-kah-we-sos..... 25,89,153,216
Ahwahka-wah-kess-sas 24
Ah-wah-key-sos......... 49,112,176,239

Index

Ahwahkuan-dakpitsa............. 146,209
Ahwahkuan-dakpitske................ 18,81
Ahwahkun-lagaks.............. 82,147,210
Ahwah-she-hay-danedootchice...... 46
Ahwahwun-lagaks......................... 19
Ah-wain-dah-it-chis 157,234
Ah-wain-dah-sit-chis..................... 29
Ahwak-amach 5,69,133,197
Ahwaka-meas.................... 11,139,203
Ahwaka-mees............................... 75
Ahwaka-wah-kees-sas................... 87
Ahwaka-wahkees-sas 151,215
Ahwakooda-kahdish............ 15,79,207
Ahwakoods-kahdeish 143
Ahwaku-chedish-naks.................... 84
Ahwaku-cheduah-naks........... 149,212
Ahwaku-cheduah-neaks 21
Ah-wan-dook-cook-cos-de-tah-dah-cock
 -cuss... 45
Ah-wane-dane-duck-coos 48
Ah-wane-dane-duck-koos 175,238
ah-wane-dane-duck-koos 111
Ah-way-cah-wah-seas 45,108,172,
.... 231
Ah-way-cah-wah-sheas 49,112,176,
.... 223
Ahwaycah-waydanbadakis............. 92
Ahwaycah-waydanebahdahkis........ 29
Ahwaycahwaydaneduckbitchace........
.... 51–52
Ahwaycaway-dedawah 220
Ah-way-chase 41,55,104,118,168,
.... 182,245
Ah-way-chee-da-cuss...27,90,154,218
Ah-way-chise 231
Ah-way-choke-kaydah-cockcus 37
Ah-way-coe-che-daybahpash 36
Ahway-coe-ish-chisaydock 99
Ah-way-coe-ish-chissaydock 36
Ahway-cone-away-chice........ 178,241
Ah-way-cook-cor-detah-heas 27
Ah-way-cook-cordetahheas............ 90
Ahwaycook-cordetah-heas..... 175,253
Ah-way-e-kosh............. 26,89,153,217
Ah-way-itchis................................27,90
Ah-way-itchise 218
Ah-way-kah-wah-chea-days 44
Ah-way-kah-wah-chedays............. 171

Ah-way-kah-way-chedays 234
Ahway-kah-ways-bahchedis........... 28
Ahway-kahways-bahchedis 91
Ahway-kawah-kain-beas ... 30,93,157,
.... 221
Ahwayka-ways-bachedis 155,218
Ahwayshayishdahcahkowshaybes.. 32
Ah-way-sheas 48,112,176,238
Ahway-taday-cock-cus 188
Ahway-taday-coock-cus 251
Ahway-taycoe-ahway-chis
.... 53,116,180,243
Ahway-tayday-cock-cuss......... 62,125
Ah-way-uck-bachdeas 179
Ah-way-uck-pah-deas............. 52,115
Ah-we-sos................. 37,101,165,228
Ahwokchedush-delemach............. 188
Ahwokchedus-helemach................ 251
Ahwokchedush-helamach............... 76
Ahwokochedush-hela-ahmach........ 13
Ahwooch-deedis 13,76,141,204
Ah-woo-coos 96,188,251
Ah-woo-kos 32
Ah-woos-ah-cay-dus.. 40,103,167,230
Ah-woos-cah-deas 62,125
Ah-woos-cahdeas 189,251
Ah-woos-dah-coos.....................27,90
Ah-woos-dah-cuss 154,218
Ahwoosh-akuse 8,73,136,200
Ahwoosh-heahsas 19,83,147,211
Ahwoos-makpash 5
Ahwoshose 19,82
Ahwotkot-dichis 6,70,134,198
Ahwot-saya........................ 16,79,144
Aka-dundish 23
Aka-malukis 138,202
Aka-mulukis 10
Aka-pish-akan-dichis............. 139,202
Ak-bah-dee-days.......................... 242
Akcan-bahoukshay-bapashon 114
Akean-badacheck-easos................ 215
Akean-badachek-easos 152
Akean-badicksha-bapashon 178
Akean-badiksha-bapashon 240
Ake-mah-kaweish........................... 86
Akey-bee-deep-pah-cuss............... 126
Alack-chee-ichis 11,75,139,203
Alden

Index

Alvin 247
   Helen 58
   John 58,121,185,247
   Phoebe 58,121,185,247
   Richard 121
Alder 25,88,153
Alice 122
All Alone 156,219
All alone 29,92
Alligator, Harry 236
Alligator Stands Up 171,233
Alligator stands up 43,106
Almashus 23,86,151
Almasus 214
Along the Hillside 78,142,206
Along the hillside 14
Among the Birds 178,240
Among the birds 51,114
Among the Buffalo 82,147,210
Among the buffalo 19
Among the Fog 81,146,209
   Jewel 146,209
Among the fog 18
Among the Grass 84,149,212
Among the grass 15
Among the hawks 8
Among the Horses 164,227
Among the horses 37,100
Among the Sheep 138,168,231
Among the sheep 10,41,104
Among the Shepp[sic] 202
Among the Willows 170,233
Among the willows 42
Among willows 106
Anderson
   Albert 13,76,141,205
   Fannie 13,76,141,205
   Helen 13
   Rosa 205
   Sarah 13,76,141,205
Andicha-poois 6,70
Andiche-poois 134,198
Andutsedush-heahsas ... 14,77,142,206
Ant Woman 85,150,213
Ant woman 22
Antelope 44,108,172,220
Antelope Cap, Herbert .31,95,159,222
Antelope That Walks 162,225

Antelope that walks 34,98
Antelope Trails 175,238
Antelope trails 48,111
An-way-itchise 154
Apah-suttah-doochice 183,246
Apah-suttah-doot-chice 119
Ap-puch-kay 87
Arachuaka-noak 207
Arachuka-noak 15,79,143
Arap-apushay-dichesay 21,84,149,
.... 212
Archie-min-nay-tus 48,111
Archie-minnay-tus 175,238
Aritsumba-kahdeish 79
Aritsumbitsa-kahdeish 16,144
Arleunda-aches 20,83,148,211
Arm Around the Neck 70,134,198
Arm around the Neck 6
Arrow Point 101,165,228
Arrow point 37
Asha-bachpash-shekuish 228
Asha-itse 77
Ash-bedadish 143
Ash-itse 13,141,205
Ash-itse-makpash 229
Ashkarooche-amach 5
Ashkarooche-kahdeas 6
Ashkarooches-kahdeas 134
Ashkarooches-kandeas 70
Ashkaroochis-kahdeas 198
Ashmitee-makpash 102
Ashmitse-makpash 166
Ashu-makotesash 13,76,141,205
Aska-wuts 12,75,140,203
Askindes 17,80,145,208
~~Asla-kudish~~ 19
As-says-das 177,253
As-says-days 49,113
Asuk-tuah-basash 83
Asuktuah-basash 147,210
Asulktuah-basash 19
Ate-shedacock 238
Ate-shedahcock 175
Atseke-ichis 155
Augusta 113
Awaca-dane-cheedup-ish 190,253
Awacco-ish-chicay-eacott 175
Awacco-ish-hicay-eacott 237

Index

Awacooish-chice-sayeacotas 111
Awah-cahn-dob-cock-cus 110
Awahcah-wassahwa-chis 104
A-wah-co-case 32,95
Awahoe-ischesayahoos 105
Awahsha 7,88
Awahshe-hay-danedoochis 173
A-wah-shoes 62
Awak-in-lagaks 69,133,197
Awakin-lagaks 5
Awaksha-echete 5,69,133,197
Awandook-cookus-detacocus 172
Awandook-cookus-detacus 235
Awan-dookcostadacockuss 108
Awasha-ishdacako-shabea 159
Awasha-ishdaco-shabea 222
Awa-shehay-danedoochice 109
Awayca-dane-cheeup-ish 126
Away-cahn-dob-cock-cus 237
Awaycah-wadane-badakis 157,220
Awaycah-wassahwa-chis 231
Away-caway-dane-dackpitsa 241
Away-caway-daneduckchas 115
Away-caway-dane-duckpitsa 178
Away-choke-kadah-cockus 165,228
Away-choke-kayda-cockus 101
A-way-co-case 159
Away-coe-ish-chisadock 163,226
Awayeah-wah-chea-days 107
Awaysha-ishdahcakow-shabeas 95
Awayshe-hay-danedoochis 236
Awoosha-kakish 18
Ay-day-cah-weas 118,182,245
Ay-kuse 23,86,150,214

B Man, Michael 14
B. Bull
   Nettie 77,141
   Stanton 205
B. Ground, Mary 75,140,203
B. Hill, Kate 119
B. Horse, Jennie 136,200
B. Man
   Alberta 75
   Michael 141,205
   Micheal 77
B. Prairie, Stephen 165
Baam-cheem-beas 153,217

Ba-be-dish-e-sos 125,189,234
Bachay-ahkahn-dupace 94,158,221
Bachay-bachot-dah-cheas 114
Bachay-bahchot-dahpace 178,241
Bachay-cush-bahdukiss 94,159,222
Bachay-eat-che-bish-ay 125
Bachay-eatche-bish-ay 189,252
Ba-chay-ha-wat-de-chice 63,126
Bachay-ha-wat-dechice 189
Bachay-ha-what-dechice 252
Ba-chay-ha-what-dup-pace . 34,97,162
Ba-chay-ha-what-duppace 225
Bachay-hay-what-deechis 156,219
Bachayhay-what-deechis 92
Bachic-kahcoo-deechis 217
Bachick-kah-coo-deechis 153
Bachois-ichis 72
Bachos-ichis 8
Bachos-itchis 136,200
Bach-pash 125
Bachpash ... 154,162,188,218,225,251
Bachpash-esos 162,225
Back of the Neck 89,176,239
Back of the neck 26,49,112
Backbone 9,73,137
Backpash-pash 168,231
Bacock-dahsay-itchis 156,219
Bacombatshay-bachpash 182,244
Bad Baby 84,149,212
Bad baby 21
Bad Bear 183,246
Bad bear 56,119
Bad Belly 182,245
Bad belly 55,118
Bad Boy 84,148,212
   David 84,148,212
   Julia 14,77,142,205
   Wesley 14,77,142,206
Bad boy 21
bad boy, David 21
Bad Dutchman 50,113,177,239
Bad Heart 5,69,133,176,197,238
   Fred 197
Bad heart 49,112
Bad Horse 72,136,200
Bad horse 8
Bad Man 72,136,200
Bad man 8

Index

Bad Medicine Woman 157,234
Bad medicine woman 29,92
Bad Woman 72,135,199
Bad woman 8,51,114,178,241
Bada-beedock-bacusheas 97
Badakis-shebacha-cheas 157
Badakis-shebacha-cheis 220
Baday-bedock-bacusheas 161
Baday-bedok-bacusheas 224
Badly Shot 174,237
Badly shot 47,110
Badock-key-huchkey-dooch 105
Ba-dow-e-kosh 52,115,179,241
Baduck-key-dootchis 168,231
Badupayish-tuckey-dootchis 178
Badupayish-tukey-dootchis 240
Badup-keadop-doochisduppa 98
Badup-kedup-duchis-dupay 208
Badup-kedupe-doochisdupay 144
Baduppayish-tuckeydoochic 114
Bah-ah-hoo-dup-pis 57
Bah-ah-key-day-cus 251
Bah-ah-pah-dah-coos-days 50
Bahahpah-dah-coos-days 113
Bah-apah-dahcoos-days 177,240
Bah-ay-ba-eas 105
Bah-ay-ba-sas 169
Bah-ay-ba-sos 232
Bah-ay-bis-eas 63
Bah-aye-chaisc 88
Bah-aye-chaise 25,153,200
Bah-bah-dah-cosh 219
Bah-bah-dah-kosh 28,92,156
Bah-be-dish-e-sos 62
Bah-buck-but-date-chase 33,97,161,
 224
Bah-cah-ca-kah-da-bish 57
Bah-cah-chice 179,242
Bah-cah-dish-tah-beas 46,109,174,
 236
Bah-cah-key-bah-pash 53
Bah-cah-key-day-cus 61,124,188
Bah-cah-key-e-cosh 36,163,227
Bah-cah-key-it-chice .. 55,118,182,245
Bah-cah-key-pah-pash 62
Bah-cah-wat-tay-dace 109
Bah-cay-ca-cah-dah-bish 184
Bahcay-cacah-dah-bish 246

Bah-cay-ca-kah-dah-bish 120
Bah-cay-key-bachpash 180,242
Bah-cay-key-bah-pash 78
Bahc-ay-key-bah-pash 116
Bah-cay-key-bah-peash 143,207
Bah-cay-key-e-cosh 99
Bah-cha-cheas 56,120,183
Bah-cha-chice 52,115
Bah-chay-ah-kahn-dup-pace 31
Bah-chay-bah-chot-dah-pace 51
Bah-chay-bah-dah-kay 38
Bah-chay-bah-day-kah 166,229
Bah-chay-bah-day-kay 102
Bah-chay-cha-dup-pace 40
Bah-chay-chea-a-chase 36
Bah-chay-cheas 33,43,46,96,106,
 110,161,170,174,224,233,236
Bah-chay-coos-bah-duckkis 37
Bah-chay-cush-bahduckkiss 31
Bah-chay-doop-dak-pais 30
Bah-chay-eat-che-bish-ay 63
Bahchay-hay-what-deechis 28
Bah-chay-kah-duck-kay 31
Bah-chay-uck-pah-pice 52,115,179,
 242
Bah-chay-un-dah-pace 41,104,168,
 231
Bah-chea-cheas 55,118
Bah-chea-des-cha-beas 25
Bah-chea-ish-it-chace 63
Bah-chea-ish-itchice 239
Bah-chea-ish-it-chise 126
Bah-chea-keas-sos .. 25,30,93,157,221
Bah-chea-sheas 182,244
Bah-che-chice 210
Bah-che-dee-kah-deas 36,100
Bah-chee-dee-kahdeas 164,227
Bah-che-quas 40,103
Bahchickah-coo-deechis 89
Bah-chick-kah-coo-deechis 26
Bah-choa-ish-itchice 190
Bah-chop-dah-beam 154,217
Bah-chop-dah-beas 89
Bah-chop-pa-dup-pas 26
Bah-coas 28
~~Bah-coas~~ 92
Bah-cock-coe-tah-hoos 166,229
Bah-cock-coo-dush 173,236

263

Index

Bah-coo-dase................................... 42
Bah-cook-coe-tah-hoos 39,102
Bah-cook-coo-dush 46,109
Bah-coop-pah..............................241
Bah-coop-pash 51,114,178
Bah-cos 164,227
Bah-cuch-ca-beas..............41,104,168
Bah-cuch-cah-ah-hoos.................... 44
Bah-cuck-ca-beas..........................231
Bah-cuck-cah-ah-hoos...................107
Bah-cup-pah-ah-hoos 32,96
Bah-cup-pah-ahoos 160,223
Bah-cup-pah-cheas.....45,108,172,235
Bah-cup-pah-deedish 22,85
Bah-cup-pah-e-chice 57,95,160,223
Bah-cup-pah-e-sos 41,104,168,231
Bah-cup-pash 38,101,165,228
Bah-cup-pay-deedish 149,213
Bah-cup-say-keas-sos.............152,216
Bah-cup-ysay-keas-sos...............25,88
Bah-cut-chay-itchis 31,93,157,220
Bah-dah-cah-deas........54,118,181,244
Bahdah-dane-bahdakish 78
Bah-dahe-dane-bahdakish 15
Bahdahe-dane-bahdakish 143,207
Bah-dah-kis...................31,94,158,221
Bah-dah-kiss 26,153,217
Bahdahkisshebahchacheas 30
Bah-dah-kit-chice........43,106,170,233
Bah-dah-kut-teas 64,126,190,253
Bah-dah-pah-coos 32,160
Bah-dah-pah-keas-sos ..35,98,162,225
Bah-dah-pay-it-chis 33,96
Bah-dah-pay-itchis 160,223
Bah-dah-sure-ha-wat-tus 38
Bah-dah-sure-ha-wattus ..101,165,228
Bahdakishebachacheas................... 93
Bah-da-pah-coos 96
Bah-day-bee-dockbahcusheas 33
Bah-day-key-sut-tus ...39,103,167,230
Bah-day-kiss 89
Bah-dea-ate-chice........56,119,183,245
Bah-dee-shis................39,103,167,214
Bah-dock-key-huchkey-dooch 42
Bah-dock-key-huchkeydooch.........169
Bah-doo-peas 47,110,174,237
Bah-doot-cha-key-pish..................220
Bah-doot-che-key-pish........30,93,157

Bah-duck-cah-peas 25,88,152,216
Bah-duck-it-chise 46,109,173,236
Bah-duck-kea-os-seas.............. 42,105
Bah-duck-key-doot-chis 41,54,117
Bah-duck-key-dootchis.......... 181,243
Bahduck-key-dootchis 104
Bah-duck-key-his-sis 42
Bah-duke-kea-it-chice 51,114
Bah-duk-keas............ 56,119,183,245
Bah-dup-kea-dupe-dootchis dup-pay..
.... 35
Bah-dup-pace-sos 52,115,179,241
Bah-dup-pay-ate-chice............. 51,114
Bahduppay-ate-chice 178,240
Bahduppay-chedu-chis 35,98,162,
.... 225
Bahdup-pay-heahsos.................... 218
Bah-dup-payishtuckkeydootchice... 51
Bah-dup-pay-keasos 221
Bah-dup-pay-keas-son 27
Bah-dup-pay-keas-sos 27,31,90,
.... 94,101,165
Bahdup-pay-keas-sos 155
bah-dup-pay-keas-sos 38
Bah-dup-peah-duc-coos 49
Bah-dup-pey-keasesos 158
Bah-ea-cah-keas-sos 47,110,174
Baheah-wat-tay-dace 173
Bah-eap-cap-cay-itches 53
Bah-ea-says 62
Bah-ea-way-shadock-cuss 100
Bah-ea-way-shay-dock-cuss 37
Bah-e-p-cap-cay-itches 116
Bah-es-way-shadock-cuss............. 165
Bah-euch-euis.............. 25,88,153,216
Bah-hah-beas 30,93,157,220
Bah-hay-chay-wat-tosh...... 34,97,161,
.... 224
Bah-ich-cah-keas-sos............. 174,237
Bah-ick-cah-keas-sos......... 47,110,237
Bah-it-cash................. 53,116,179,242
Bah-itchay-doochis........................ 93
Bah-it-chay-doot-chis 29,62,125
Bah-itchay-doot-chis 157,220
Bah-itchay-dootchis..................... 189
Bah-it-chay-on-deas.................... 100
Bah-it-chay-on-des 164,227
Bah-it-chay-on-des- 37

264

Index

Bah-kah-beas 167
Bah-kaht-konsees 21,149,212
Bahkay ahoos 232
Bahkay-ahoos 42,105,169
Bahkay-dah-way-chice 234
Bah-kea-dah 31,94,158,221
Bah-keam-beas 28,91,155,219
Bah-keam-boo-dish 46,109,173,236
Bahkeda-basash 18,81,146,209
Bahkeede-ichis 8,72
Bahkeede-itchis 136
Bahkeed-lagaks 8,72,136,200
Bah-key-cush-sheas ... 49,112,176,238
Bah-key-dah-keas-sos 39
Bah-key-dah-wah-chice 44
Bahkey-dah-wah-chice 171
Bah-key-dawah-chice 107
Bah-key-day-dah-beas 33
Bah-key-day-nahbeas 161
Bah-key-de-hosh 56,119,183,245
Bah-key-us-tay 161,224
Bah-kot-konsees 84
Bah-kow-say-it-chis 34
Bahm-batseeesash 10
Bahm-batseer-esash 138,202
Bahn-dush-tsay-heahsas 204
Bah-o-dop-keas-sos 62,125,189,252
Bah-oos 63,100
Bah-op-pish 115,178,241
Bah-osh-ah-hoos 37,100
Bah-osh-ahoos 225
Bah-os-way-shadock-cuss 228
Bah-ouch-cah-ahoos 172,234
Bah-ow-duck-coos 44,107,171,233
Bah-owe-keas-sos 41,104,168,226
Bah-pah-deas 166
Bah-pah-dish 56,119,183,245
Bah-pah-dit-chice 190,253
Bah-pah-dit-chis 64,126
Bah-pah-esos 35,98
Bah-pash 27,34,62,90,98
Bah-pee-sha-da-ah-hoos 52,115
Bah-pee-shada-ahoos 179,242
Bah-pittay-dov-pus 25,88,153,216
Bah-poe-tus 32,95
Bah-poh-tus 159
Bah-pus 39,103,167,230
Bah-put-chee-keep-beas 22

Bahput-chee-keep-beas 150,213
Bah-put-cheekeep-beeas 85
Bahputta-cheedup-pis 225
Bah-puttah-ahway-taydas 28,91
Bahputtah-ahway-taydas 155,218
Bah-put-tah-beas 42,49,62–63,105,
 .112,126,176,189–190,239,252–253
Bah-put-tah-bedane-duckcoos 37
Bah-put-tah-bock-bus 49,112
Bahput-tah-bock-bus 176,239
Bah-put-tah-cah-deas 42,105
Bah-put-tah-cahdeas 169,232
Bah-put-tah-cheas 51,114,178
Bah-put-tah-cuck-kis . 52,115,179,241
Bah-put-tah-dew-pus 42,105,169,
.... 232
Bah-put-tah-dock-cus 39,102,167,
.... 229
Bah-put-tah-dock-cuss 50,114,177,
.... 240
Bah-put-tah-hosh 233
Bah-put-tah-pee-dee-chis 29
Bah-put-tah-pee-deechis 157
Bahput-tah-pee-deechis 220
Bah-put-tah-peedee-chis 93
Bah-put-tah-seas 55–56,118–119,
.... 182–183,244–245
Bah-put-tah-way-chate-chice 53
Bah-put-tah-way-chice 14
Bahput-tah-way-chice 78,142,226
Bah-put-tay-ah-hoos 34,98
Bah-put-tay-ahoos 162,225
Bahputtay-cheedup-is 162
Bahputtaychee-dup-pis 34,98
Bahputtay-wa-chate-chice 180
Bahputtay-wachate-chice 243
Bah-put-tea-hosh 43,106,171
Bah-put-the-beas 125
Bah-puttock-beaday-beas 97
Bah-put-tosh 32,95,160,223
Bah-put-tuck-beaday-beas 34
Bah-put-tuck-beeday-beas 161,224
Bah-put-tus 222
Bahsatsie-basonda 14,77,142,205
Bah-shay-cha-dup-pace .. 104,168,231
Bah-shay-kah-duck-kay 94,158,222
Bah-she-chice 54,117,180
Bah-sho-deche-cha-ahoos 91

Index

Bah-sho-dee-che-chay-ahhoos 28
Bah-shoes 176,238
Bah-shoes-shays 48,111,175,238
Bah-shos 49,112
Bahshotse-basash 12,115
Bah-show-be-chit-chase 109
Bahshow-deachic-itchis 93
Bah-show-dead-chich-itchis 30
Bah-show-dechit-chaesos 109
Bah-show-de-chit-chase 46,173,236
Bahshow-dechit-chaybahcoos 46
Bah-show-dechit-chayesos 46
Bah-show-de-chite-chase 46
Bah-show-dee-ditch ... 37,100,164,227
Bahshow-deeditch-chayoppes 32
Bah-show-dee-ditch-chay-sos 36
Bah-shus-shays 52,115,189,252
Bah-son-day 7,114,178,241
Bah-son-day-ah-hoos ... 34,97,161,224
Bah-son-day-it-chice 63,116,126
Bah-son-day-itchice 190,253
Bah-son-day-it-chis 53,180
Bah-sone-dace 37,101,165
Bahsuk-naks 19,82,147,210
Bah-tah-day-keas-sos 31
Bah-tah-weas 161,224
Bah-tah-woas 33,97
Bah-tah-wos 36,99,164,227
Bah-tay-day-keas-sos 94,159,222
Bah-touch-c-cook-cosh 49
Bah-touch-e-cook-cah 238
Bah-touch-e-cook-cosh 112,176
Bah-touch-owe-duck-coos
  48,111,175,238
Bah-wah-sone-dah-ichis 197
Bah-wah-sone-dah-it-chice 5
Bah-wah-sonedah-itchis 69,133
Bah-wah-wat-tays 52,115,178,241
Bak-kah-beas 39,102,230
Bak-kah-seas 53,116,180,242
Ball 42,105,169,232
Balls 45,108,172,235
Bank 19,82,146,210
Banuka-acha-nadees 6
Ba-orap-saskatch 71,135,199
Bapash-to-ba-deedish 213
Baputta-bedane-duckcoos 164,227
Baput-tahbedane-duckoos 100

Baput-tah-way-chate-chice 117
Barucka-acha-nadees 137,201
Baruks-acha-nadees 73
Bascheeda-schepittay 184,246
Bashay-bachpash 159,222
Bash-cheam-beas 26
Bashcheeday-shepit-tay 56
Bashcheedday-shepit-tay 120
Bash-day-tush 153,217
Basheede-checa-ahoos 218
Bash-eheam-beas 89
Bashheede-cheeha-ahoos 155
Bash-ichis 215
Bash-it-chis 24
Bash-itchis 87,152
Bash-keas-sos 57,120,184,246
Basho-dechit-chabahcoos 109
Basho-dedichay-asash 115
Basho-dedich-chapasash 179,242
Basho-deedich-chayoppes 222
Bashotshe-basosh 179,241
Bashow-da-chite-chase 236
Bashow-dea-chic-itchis 158,221
Bashow-dechit-chabacoos 173,236
Bashow-de-chite-chase 173
Bashow-de-chite-shase 109
Bashow-deeditchchaypahsash 52
Bashow-deechit-chayesos 173
Bashow-deedich-chayoppes 95,159
Bashow-dee-dich-chay-sos 99
Bashow-deeditch-chaysos 171,253
Basuk-ose 15,78,142,206
Bay-kay-day-dah-beas 97
Bay-ray-day-tuss 31,95,159,222
Bea-ah-dutch-she-beas 44,107
Bea-ahdutch-shebeas 171,234
Bea-ah-ha 25,88
Bea-ahoos 152,216
Bea-ah-wah-chis 39,102,166,229
Bea-at-tah-itchis 25
~~Bea-at-tah-itchis~~ 88
Bea-bachpash 181,244
Bea-bachpash-cah-weas 157,234
Bea-bah-chey-chis 226
Bea-bah-coos 38,102
Bea-bah-pah-cah-weas 29,92
Bea-bah-pash 54,117
Bea-bah-shay-e-sit-chace 46,109

Index

Bea-bashay-e-sit-chace 174
Bea-buckcoshea-dacockcuss 116
Bea-buckcoshsahdahcockcuss........ 53
Bea-bus-sos 98,162,225
Bea-cah-weas 51,114
Bea-cheas 161,224
Bea-cose 51,178,240
Bea-cot-ish-tup-pay 102,166,229
Bea-cottus 54,117,180,243
Bea-cowees 178,241
Bea-dah-cock-cus 180,242
Bea-dah-cock-cuss 27,90
Bea-dane-dah-coos...........88,152,216
Beada-tah-shis-chay-ichis 90
Bea-dea-dush................56,119,183,246
Bea-ditches................55,118,182,245
Bea-doo-pus 26,89
Bea-doot-chice 44,107
Bea-dootchice 171
Bea-dootchis 234
Bea-dosh-day-tush 47,110,237
Bea-dosh-tay-tush 174
Bea-ehos.......................................211
Bea-e-hosh 20,83,148
Bea-ha-wat-tosh 25,88,153,216
Be-ah-hush-kay 23
Beah-kahdeas 7,71,135,199
Bea-huch-key 54,181
Bea-huchkish 87
Bea-huckey 243
Bea-hutchkis 214
Bea-hutchkish 151
Bea-it-chay 42,44,80,108,172
Bea-itchay 235
Bea-it-chay-de-chice 44
Bea-itchay-de-chice 107
~~Bea-itchay-de-chice~~ 171
Bea-it-chice 50,113,177,240
Bea-itchis 25
Bea-it-chise-sos................51,114,177
Bea-it-chis-sos............................... 98
Bea-itchis-sos..........................162,225
bea-it-chis-sos[sic] 34
Bea-koc-kah-dah-biss................33,96
Bea-napes 137
Bean-dahcome-baday-kay.......157,220
Bean-da-ichis 152,216
Bea-noopus 153,217

Bear Child......................... 76,140,204
Bear child 12
Bear Claw 76,141,204
Bear claw 13
Bear Comes From Below....... 179,241
Bear comes from below 52
Bear Crane....................... 76,140,204
George 12,76,140,204
Bear crane..................................... 12
Bear Gets Up 169,232
Bear gets up............................ 42,105
Bear Goes to Other Ground 75,139,
.... 203
Bear goes to the other ground 12
Bear in a Cloud................. 74,139,203
Bear in a cloud............................... 11
Bear in the Middle 81,146,209
Bear in the middle 18
Bear in the Mountain 161,225
Bear in the mountain...................34,97
Bear In the Mountains 178,241
Bear in the mountains 51–52,115
Bear in the water............................ 33
Bear Old Man 159,223
Bear old man 38,95
Bear on the Trail 137,201
Bear That Don't Walk 158,222
Bear that don't walk 94
Bear that dont[sic] walk................... 31
Bear that haises[sic] his Paw 75
Bear that Raises His Paw 140,203
Bear that raises his paw 12
Bear That Walks 168,231
Bear that walks 33,40,104
Bear Wolf 83,147
Bear wolf.. 20
Bear Woman................. 87,151,215
Bear woman................................... 24
Bear's dog................................... 109
Bear's Tail 172,235
Bear's Tooth 168
Mary 104,166,218
Bear's tooth 104
Bears comes from below 115
Bears Dog................................... 173
Bears dog...................................... 46
Bears tail..................................... 108
Bears[sic] tail.................................. 45

Index

Bears[sic] Tooth, Mary 41
Bears[sic] tooth 40
Beas 45,109,173,235
Bea-sheedes 105,169
Bea-sheedis 232
Bea-she-pit-tas 32
Bea-shepittas 160,223
Bea-she-pit-tay 51,114
Bea-sos-coos 189,252
Bea-sos-ecos 62,125
Beaun-dichis 6
Beaver Passes, Florence 74,202
Beaver Robe 145,209
Beaver robe 17,81
Beaver Tail 85
Beaver tail 22
Beaver That Passes 138,202
    Florence 138
Beaver that Passes 74
Beaver that passes 10
    Florence 10
Beaver That Slides 82,146,210
Beaver that slides 18
Beaver that Stretches 80,144,208
Beaver that stretches 17
Be-buckcoshsadacock-cus 180
Bechaykay-dahwachis 230
Bechon-herepis 70
Bechon-herepsis 6,136,198
Becker, E. H. 1–3,5–64
Be-coo-took-eas 182,245
Beda-ecupe-padootchice . 116,179,242
Be-dah-dish-sos 45
Bedah-tashis-chay-ichis 155,218
Be-dase-che-cash 237
Be-dase-she-cash 47,110,174
Be-day-dish-sos 108,173,235
Beday-ecupe-pahdootchice 53
Bedayitch-shedayopitche 88
Beday-ock-ke-day-ichis 181,244
Beday-ock-key-day-ichis 85
Be-day-tuss 43,106,170,233
Be-dea-bah-pash 42,105
Be-dee-sheas-she-dush 27,154,218
Be-dee-sheas-shedush 90
Be-de-ha-dup-pace 125,189,252
Be-de-he-dup-pace 63
Bedittah-shisshaycuckkiss 54

Beditta-shishay-cuckiss 181,243
Beditta-shisshay-cuckiss 117
Be-dook-sah-e-duse ... 43,106,171,233
Be-dosh 35,99,163,226
Be-duckoshsadacock 243
Bedupa-bukata-dase 10,74,138,202
Bedupa-chas 148
Bedupa-ehas 20,83,211
Bedupa-ekoshees 17,80,144,208
Bedupa-okeah-duis 18,82,146,210
Be-dup-cah-deas 54,119,183,245
Be-dup-dah-cus 39,102,230
Bedupdayts 23
Be-dup-hishes 234
Be-dup-hishis 171
Be-dup-his-shis 44,107
Be-dup-pay-tuss 53
be-du-toch-eas 11
Be-du-tooh-eas 118
Bee-bush-sas 24,87,151,215
Bee-bus-sos 35
Bee-cheas 33,97
Beeda-dosh-cane-dechis 174
Beeda-dosh-cane-dechise 110
Bee-dah-dosh-cane-de-chice 47
Bee-dah-dosh-kain-dechis 26
Beedah-dosh-kain-dichis 137,201
Beedah-doshkan-dichis 73
Bee-dah-tah-shis-chay-ichis 27
Bee-dane-bah-dah-kiss 32,160,223
Bee-dane-dah-coos 25
Bee-day-da-cuss-chis 164,227
Bee-day-de-cues-chis 37
Bee-day-de-cuss-chis 100
Beedayitch-shedayopitche 25
Bee-day-ock-key-day-itchis 22
Bee-day-she-kosh 28,91,156,219
Bee-dea-it-chice 53
Bee-dee-chay-hay-day-dus 42
Beedee-chay-hay-day-dus 170,233
Beedee-chay-hay-dus 106
Bee-dee-dup-pace 156,219
Bee-dee-dup-pase 28,91
Beedick-qua-badup-pace 99
Bee-dick-qua-bah-dup-pace 35
Beedick-qua-bah-dup-pace 163
Beedic-quabah-dup-pace 231
Bee-dish 44,107,171,234

Index

Bee-ditch-key-sos.........36,99,163,226
Bee-dock-cup-pis 31,95,159,222
Bee-dop-dah-cuss...................190,253
Bee-dup-che-sus.........................22,85
Bee-dup-dah-cus 167
Bee-dup-dah-cuss....................64,126
Bee-dup-eas 30,94,158,221
Bee-dup-kah-deas..............28,155,219
Bee-dup-kahdeas............................ 91
Bee-dup-pay-tus................71,135,199
Beehaycay-dahwahchis..................152
Beehayday-dahwahchis.................. 24
Bee-itchis 88,152,216
Been-dah-chate-dase ..42,106,170,232
Been-dah-chay-esah-hay 96
Been-dah-chay-esah-hay dain-dee-chis
.... 32
Been-dahcom-bahdakay.................. 93
Been-dah-come-bahday-kay........... 29
Been-day-chay-esa-hay 223
Been-day-chay-esah-ay 160
Been-de-chice 53
Beende-chice..................................117
Been-de-chis 88
Beendosh-kaneah-wachice 117
Been-dosh-kane-ah-wahchice 54
Beendosh-kanesh-wachice 181,244
Been-dosh-sha-pah-bash 105
Been-dosh-shay-bachpash......169,232
Been-dosh-shay-bah-pash 42
Been-dotch-us-eas......40,103,167,230
Beeop-huche-naks............17,145,209
Bee-pah-pus-sis............31,94,158,221
Bee-put-tah-bah-coos 166,229
Bee-shas-sah-hoos..........28,91,155,219
Bee-shay-ahk-ah-wah-chis............. 23
Beeshay-ahkah-wahchis.................151
Beeshay-ahkak-wahchis.................214
Bee-shay-che-de-esos....................218
Bee-shay-che-de-sos 27,154
Bee-shay-che-do-sos 90
Bee-shay-dah-coos 27
Bee-shay-dee-dish.......36,100,164,227
Bee-shay-e-dews 62
Bee-shay-e-duhs............................. 87
Bee-shay-e-hosh.....................48,111
Bee-tah-was 50,113,177,240
Begs for Money..............................224

Begs Plenty........................ 76,141,204
Begs plenty 13
Behayday-dakwahchis 87
Behind 40
Beka-haredich............. 15,84,149,212
Bekashes..................... 14,77,142,206
Bell Rock 177,240
Bell rock 50,113
Ben-cose 114
Ben-cot-ish-tup-pay 38
Ben-dane-bah-dah-cuss 96
Ben-huch-key 117
Benn-da-chis................................... 25
Bershea-bachpash 151,215
Bershea-bah-pash 24,87
Besha-amach 18,81,159,222
Besha-chea-makpash 69,133,197
Besha-chedup............................. 18,81
Besha-chedups........................... 8,71
Besha-cheedups 135,199
Besha-Cheeup................................209
Besha-cheeup................................146
Besha-ekash 8,15,78,136,143,200,
....207
Besha-hishes.................... 19,82,147
Besha-hishis.................................. 210
Besha-maks 19
Besha-mulukis 16,143,207
Besha-nake 147
Besha-naks................ 12,82,146,210
Besha-naks-noops......... 19,82,147,210
Besha-ockain-awaychis 101
Be-shay-ah-hoos 53,116,180,243
Beshay-ahk-ahwah-chis.................. 86
Beshay-ahks.................................... 71
Be-shay-ah-shees 63
Beshay-anks......................................7
Beshay-cok-bahwaychis 231
Be-shay-dana-awachice 126
Be-shay-dane-ah-wah-chice 63
Beshay-dane-awachice 190,253
Be-shaye-de-dish 111
Be-shay-e-has 237
Be-shay-e-hosh 175
Beshay-heahsus.............................212
Beshay-herasus................. 21,84,149
Be-shay-ka-cheas..................... 27,90
Be-shay-ka-hase 154,233

Index

Beshay-ockain-awachis 165,228
beshay-ock-bah-wah-chis 41
Be-shay-ock-kain-ahwahchis 37
Beshay-oek-bahwaychis 168
Beshay-ook-bah-wah-chis 104
Be-shays-de-dish 48
Be-shea-bachpash 176,239
Be-shea-bah-pash 49,112
Besheesh 13,76,141,205
Beshe-mulukis 79
Bes-koo-kah-dah-biss 160,223
Besop-huche-naks 81
Bes-shay-e-duhs 152,215
Bes-shepittas 96
Bethune, Frank 13,77,141,205
Between 39,103,167,230
Bich-pus 26,89,153,217
Bick-cah-hay-day-duss 44,108
Bick-cah-keas-sos 40
Bickens 54
Bick-kah-keas-sos 112,176,239
Bickus 117,181,243
Big Around 163,172,226,235
Big around 35,45,99,108
Big Bear 117,180,243
Big bear 53
Big Bird 5,69,86,133,150,183,
.... 197,214,246
Big bird 23,56,119
Big Chicken 95,159,222
Big chicken 32
Big Elk 34,161,224
Big elk 97
Big Eyes 168,231
Big eyes 41,104
Big Hail 168,231
Big hail 41,104
Big Hat 72,136,200
Big hat 8
Big Head High Up 76,141,205
Big head high up 13
Big Lake 163,226
Big lake 36,99
Big Lark 74,139,203
Big lark 11
Big Magpie 84,149,212
Big magpie 21
Big Man 77,141,205

Big man 14
Big Medicine 35,98,162,225
    Edward 162,225
Big Medicine Rock.. 171,173,236,253
Big medicine rock 36,46,99,109
Big Mountain 89,153,216
Big mountain 25
Big mouth 62
Big nest 62
Big Nose 77,141,205
Big nose 14
Big Nose Old Woman 190,253
Big nose old woman 63,126
Big Ox 90,154,218
Big ox 27
Big Porcupine 172,235
Big porcupine 45,108
Big Root 93,157,220
Big root 30
Big Sheep 92,156,220
    Florence 29
~~Big Sheep, Florence~~ 92
Big Sheep, Florence 156,220
Big sheep 29
Big Shoulder Blade 84,149,212
Big shoulder blade 21
Big Sky 176,239
Big sky 49,112
Big Snake 166,229
Big snake 38,102
Big Squirrel 171,234
Big squirrel 44,107
Big Woman 138,202
Bim-bean-dee-dish 178,241
Bim-boan-chee-dup-pis 37,164
Bim-boan-chee-duppis 100
Bim-boan-cheeduppis 227
Bim-boan-dah-pit-chase 33
Bim-boan-dee-dish 51,114
Bin-day-sop-pay-dus . 39,102,166,229
Bin-doch-e-so-chain-dus 104,231
Bin-doch-eso-chain-dus 168
Bin-dosh-shay-shee-dish... 46,110,236
Bin-dosh-shay-sheedish 174
Bin-dotch-doot-chis 45,108
Bin-dotch-dootchis 172,235
Bin-dotch-eso-chain-dus 40
Bin-dotch-ut-tosh 33,96,161,224

Index

Biorup-heahsas 18,81
Bird 31,62,94,159,222
    Glenn 62,125,189
Bird Above 170,233
Bird above 43,106
Bird all over Ground 69
Bird All Over the Ground 133,197
Bird all over the Ground 5
Bird Among the Rocks 161,224
Bird among the rocks 34,97
Bird Among Them 173,236
Bird among them 46,109
Bird Another Year 172,235
Bird another year 45,108
Bird By Himself 169,232
Bird by himself 42,105
Bird Child 89,153,159,217,223
Bird child 20,38
Bird Everyway 204
Bird Far Away 62,188,251
Bird far away 125
Bird flies off 29
Bird Gets Up 242
Bird goes above 50
Bird Hat 177,240
Bird hat 50,113
Bird Head 173,236
Bird head 46,109
Bird High Up 177,240
Bird high up 50,113
Bird Horse 173,236
Bird horse 46,109
Bird in a Cloud 70,134,198
Bird in a cloud 6
Bird In the Cedars 177,240
Bird in the cedars 50,113
Bird in the Ground 82,147,210
Bird in the ground 19
Bird in the Morning 154,217
Bird in the morning 47,111
Bird In the Rain 181,244
Bird in the rain 54,118
Bird in the Spring 180,243
Bird in the spring 53,116
Bird on the Prairie 165,228
Bird on the prairie 37,101
Bird Shirt 76,140,204
Bird Sits Down 176,238

Bird sits down 49,112
Bird Tail That Rattles 71,135,199
Bird tail that rattles 7
Bird That Runs 174,237
Bird that runs 47,110
Bird That Shows . 79,144,189,207,252
Bird that shows 16,63,125
Bird ties a knot on top of his head .. 28
Bird Ties Knot on Top Head 155
Bird Ties knot on top head 91
Bird Ties Knot Top Head 219
Bird Well Known 70,72,134,136,
    174,198,200,237
Bird well known 6,8,110
Bird With Plenty of Wings Going
    Around 172,234
Bird with plenty of wings going around
    44,107
Bird Without a Cloud 182,245
Bird without a cloud 55,119
Bird woaman[sic] 103
Bird Woman 167,180,230,242
Bird woman .. 27,40,48,53,90,112,116
Bird, Glenn 252
Bird's Eggs 178,241
Birdchild 95
Birds eggs 115
Birds[sic] eggs 52
Bis-cah-she-pit-tus 52,115,179,242
Bish-cah-che-dup-pish 51
Bish-cah-cheduppish 178
Bish-cah-duck-bit-chase 46
Bish-cay-che-dup-pish 114
Bish-doot-chice 51,114
Bish-doot-chise 178,240
Bishea-duck-bit-chase 109
Bisheah-duckbitchay 173
Bishka-botsots 20,83,148,211
Bish-ka-cheas 156
Bish-ka-cheis 219
Bishka-dackpitsa 236
Bishka-kahdeas 204
Bishka-kahps 11,74,139,203
Bish-k-cheas 28
Bish-k-chease 91
Bish-push 25,88,153,216
Biskka-kahdeas 12,75,140
Bit-chea-bachpash 161,224

Index

Bit-chea-bah-pash 33,97
Bit-che-doot-chis............33,49,96,112,
..................................160,176,224,239
Bit-choose 28,91
Bit-quash 24,87,151,215
Black bird...8,31
Black Bull 82,146,210
Black bull 18,37,100
Black Dog 179,242
Black dog 52,115
Black Eagle 75,140,203
Black eagle.. 12
Black Hair 160,223
Black hair 32,96
Black Rock 160,223
Black rock 32,96
Black Tail 161,224
Black tail 33,97
Black Woman.......80,164,178,228,241
Black woman 16,51,114
Blackbird 72,94,136,158,200,221
Blackbird in Front.............81,146,209
Blackbird in front 18
Blackbird Sits Down 171,234
Blackbird sits down..................44,107
Blackbird Woman 91,155,219
Blackbird woman 28
Blackhawk, Eli...............6,70,134,197
Blaine
    Florence 29,92,156,219
    James........................29,92,156,219
    Mrs. William......................156,219
    Mrs. Wm. 29,92
Blanket Bull 77,141,205
Blanket bull 13
Blanket Well Known...............165,228
Blanket well known 49,100
Blood Man 75,139,203
    Alberta 139,203
Blood man 11
Blue Belly 90,155,218
Blue belly 27
Blue Chin 174,236
Blue chin 46,110
Blue Moccasin 166,229
Blue moccasin 39,102
Blue Shirt 78,143,207
Blue shirt 15

Blue Wood.................... 72,135,199
Blue wood.. 8
Boa-ah-ta-ichis 73
Boa-at-tah-itchis 137
Boa-ayy-tah-itchis 201
Boa-bah-cos................... 166,229
Boa-do-chis 51,114,178
Boa-doo-pus 50,113,177,239
Boa-e-hock-sos 50,126,190,253
Boa-it-chis 36,100
Boa-itchis............................... 164,227
Boa-pis 53,125,188,251
Boa-tah-itchice 227
Boa-tah-it-chis 39,100
Boa-tah-itchis 164
Boat-tah-bah-hoos 238
Boat-tah-cah-dush-sis 43,107,171,
.... 233
Boat-tay-kadeas 162,225
Boat-tay-kah-daes...................... 34
Boat-tay-kah-deas...................... 98
Bob tail crow 110
Bob Tail Wolf...................... 161,224
Bob tail wolf................................ 33,97
Bob tailed crow............................. 47
Bob-puck-sos............... 34,97,161,224
Bock-kosh.. 92
Bompard
    Lois....................... 24,87,152,215
    Louis..................... 24,87,152,215
    Mary 24,87,152,215
    Peter....................... 24,88,152,215
    Rosa....................... 24,88,152,215
Bondonpaha-dane-dacacus 177,240
Bondonpahadanedacahcus............ 113
Bon-don-pah-bah-coos 50,113,177,
.... 240
Bondonpahhaydanedakcahcus........ 50
Booah-ahseesh............ 11,74,139,202
Booah-hishes 18,81,146,209
Booah-lagak.............. 12,76,140,204
Boodock-ahcane-deechis 181,243
Boo-dook-ah-cane-de-chis........... 54
Boodook-ahcane-dechis.............. 117
Boo-do-pah-she-dis 29
Boo-duke-pah-keasos 107,171,234
Boo-duke-pah-keas-sos 44
Boop-chis.................. 42,105,169,232

Index

Bos-che-day-cah-deas 55,118,182,
....245
Bosh-bah-pash 41,104
Bosh-che-de-cot-tay ... 44,107,172,234
Bosh-day-tush 32,95,159,223
Bosh-doot-chis 41,104
Bosh-dootchis 168,213
Bota-hotsondish 144
Botsa-botsots 240
Botsa-cheakoosh-napes 20
Botsa-kowees 8,72,136,200
Botsa-mahnahs 17
Botsa-miesah 205
Botsa-Miesash 141
Botsa-Miesash 77
Botsa-miesash 14
Botsa-nahme-napes 13,76,140,204
Botsa-wa-napes 77,142,206
Botsa-wot-napes 14
Botsaytse 15,143,207
Botseah-bedas 15,78,143,214
Botseah-botsats 135
Botseah-botsots 199
Botseah-heahsas 19,82,147
Botsea-Mahnahs 80
Botsea-mahnahs 145,208
Botseish 16,79,144
Botsotse 79
Botsuah-tush 21,84,148,212
Botsu-tush-botsash 143,207
Bou-dooch-chis 32
Bou-doochis 95
Bouta-bah-coos-shecosh . 118,182,245
Bout-tah-bah-coos-she-cosh 55
Bout-tah-bah-hoos 48,111,175
BOut-tah-eas 246
Bout-tah-eas 56,119,183
Boy That Grabs 149,212
Boy that Grabs 84
Boy that grabs 21
Bra-bah-chey-chis 35,98,163
Brass, Augusta 119
Brave, Mrs. B. 58
Bravo 17,80,144,208
    Mrs. B. 121,185,247
Breathes 62,125
Bright Wings 73,137,201
Bright wings 9

Brings Good Things 71,135,243
Brings good things 7
Brings His Horses 138,202
Brings Horses 90,155,218
Brings horses 27
Brings Horses Well Known ... 170,233
Brings horses well known 43,106
Brings Pretty Horses 166,229
Brings pretty horses 38,102
Brings Ten Times 76,141,205
Brings ten times 13
Brings the horses 47,110
Brings Things 164,227
Brings things 63,100
Brings Things all the time 175,238
Brings things all the time 48,111
Brings Things Always 171,233
Brings things always 44,107
Brings Two Horses 174,237
Brings Well Known 168,226
Brings well known 41,104
Broils Big 234
Broils big 62,125
Broken Arrow 170,236
Broken arrow 42,106
Brown
    Blanche 10,138,202
    Charles 47,110,174,237
Budeesh 9,11,72–73,136–137,
.... 200–201
Budesash 5,69
Budesesh 133,197
Buffalo
    James 45,108,172,235
    Josh 24,87,151,215
Buffalo Bull 81,135,146
Buffalo bull 8,18
Buffalo Bull #1 71,199
Buffalo Bull #2 209
Buffalo Calf 82,146,210
Buffalo calf 12,27
Buffalo High 82,147
Buffalo high 19
Buffalo Neck Hair 156,219
Buffalo neck hair 28,92
Buffalo Stands Up 152,215
Buffalo stands up 62,87
Buffalo That Shakes 154,233

273

Index

Buffalo that shakes 27,90
Buffalo that shows 63
Buffalo That Sings 143,207
Buffalo that Sings 79
Buffalo that sings 16
Buffalo That Walks 164,227
Buffalo that walks 36,100
Bukasa-hishes 5
Bull All the Time 138,202
Bull all the time 10,74
Bull Antelope 178,240
Bull antelope 51,114
Bull Bird 160,223
Bull bird 32,96
Bull Blackbird 173,236
Bull blackbird 46,109
Bull Chief 172,235
Bull chief 45,108
Bull Deer 175,238
Bull deer 48,111
Bull Dog 178
Bull dog 51,114
Bull Goes Hunting 83,148,211
Bull goes hunting 20
Bull Horse 184,246
Bull horse 57,120
Bull In Sight 149,213
Bull in sight 21,85
Bull in the Water 164,227
Bull in the water 37,100
Bull Moves On 162,225
Bull moves on 34,97
Bull Near the Water 148,211
Bull near the Water 83
Bull near the water 39
Bull Over the Hill 183,246
Bull over the hill 56,119
Bull Robe 180
Bull robe 53,116
Bull That Don't Fall Down 166,229
Bull that don't fall down 102
Bull that dont[sic] fall down 39
Bull That Knows 150,213
Bull that Knows 85
Bull that knows 22
Bull That Raises Up 138
Bull that raises up 10
Bull That Shows 147,211

Ida 83,147,211
Bull that shows 19,83
Bull that shows all the time 36
Bull That Shows All Time 78,143,
.... 206
Bull Tongue 78,142,206
Homer 14
Bull tongue 14
Bull Tongue #2 155,219
Bull Turtle 6,70,134,198
Bull Walks to Water 177,240
Bull walks to water 50,113
Bull Weasel 74,138,202
Bull weasel 10
Bull Well Known 180,242
Bull well known 53,116
Bull's Tail 180,242
Iva 180,242
Bull's Tongue #2 91
Bullets Don't Strike Him .. 84,149,212
Bullets dont[sic] strike him 21
Bulls tail 53,116
Bulls tongue 28
Bum-bah-pash 56
Bun-dock-cope-dah-cuss ... 30,93,158,
.... 221
Bush Head 188,251
Bush head 62,125
Bushy 50,113,177,240
Bus-sock-kose 144,207
Bussone-deahah-hoos 99
Buss-sone-deah-ah-hoos 35
Buss-sone-deah-ahoos 163,226
Bus-suck-kose 16,79
Busy Wolf 82,146,210
Busy wolf 19
Butsay-tse-dichis 22,85
But-shay-aut-tuss 100
But-shay-sut-tuss 37,164,227
By Herself 74,139,202
By herself 11
By the side of camp 95
By the Side of the Camp 160
By the side of the camp 32
By the Side of the Water ... 72,136,200
By the side of the water 8
By-eas 37,101,165,228

274

Index

C. Above, Fannie 176,239
Cah-cay-itcheas 26,116
Cah-cay-itchice 180,243
Cah-coa-ays 57,120,184,247
Cah-coa-doot-chice 45,235
Cah-coa-doot-chise 108
Cah-dah-buck-kesos 218
Cah-dah-hay-day-duse 118,181,244
Cah-dah-hay-day-duss 54
Cah-day-buck-kesos 155
Cah-dicth-chea-ah-hoos 108
Cah-ditch-chea-ah-hoos 45
Cah-ditch-chea-ahoos 172,235
Cah-eoa-doot-chice 172
Cah-kay-bachpash 163,226
Cah-kay-bah-pash 35
Cah-kay-doot-chis 28,91,156,219
Cah-paeh-dee-dock-cus 46
Cah-pah-dea-bah-ows 62
Cah-pah-dee-dock-cus..... 109,173,236
Cah-pah-dee-it-chis 40
Cah-pah-dee-itchis 103
Cah-pah-dias 39,102
Cah-puh-dus-itchis 167
Calf 36,164,227
Calf that shakes 61
Calf that strays 29,92
Can't Get Up 154,217
Can't get up 90
Can't Shoot Him 189,252
Can't shoot him 125
Cant shoot him 10
Cant[sic] get up 26
Carpenter, James 18,81,146,214
Carries Good 78,142,206
Carries good 15
Carries the Arrows 161,225
Carries the arrows 34,97
Cashen
    Alice 59,186,249
    Cecelia 186,249
    Ella 59,122,186,249
    Mrs. Ella K. 186,249
    Mrs. Ella Kent 59,122
    Willie 59,122,186,249
Catches on the Horses 78,142,206
Catches on the horses 14
Catches the enemy 62

Catches the Sioux 38,101,166,229
Catches Up and Strikes 155
Catches up and Strikes 91,219
Catches up and strikes 28
Catches With Rope On 160,223
Catches with rope on 33,96
Cay-kay-bah-pash 98
Cedar High Up 177,240
Cedar high up 50,113
Cha-chuck-key-sos 108
Cha-cush 63,126,189,252
Chada-kos 71
Chadoc-cuss-bahduppas 229
Chadupa-eda-ekash 20
Chapes 9,73,137,201
Cha-qua-bah-aco 166
Cha-qua-bah-sco 229
Cha-qua-bah-soo 39,102
Charges Five Times 166,229
Charges five times 39,102
Charges Madly on Enemy 167
Charges Madly on the Enemy 230
Charges madly on the enemy ... 40,103
Charges on the Camp 176,239
Charges on the camp 49,112
Charges on the Enemy 145
Charges on the enemy 17,80
Charges Plenty 94,158,222
Charges plenty 31
Charges Strong 83,87,148,151,211,
.... 215
    Mary 20,83,148,211
Charges strong 20,24
Charges the Enemy 75,140,204
Charges the enemy 12
Charges Through Camp.... 81,146,209
Charges through camp 18
Charges well known 41
Chas-foot-chice 57
Cha-soup-pus 235
Chate-ah-wah-shoes... 54,117,180,243
Chate-aputs 85
Chate-bachpash 160,223
Chate-bah-cush-ecosh 49,139,203
Chate-bah-pash 32,96
Chate-bee-dish-she-days.... 32,96,160,
.... 223
Chate-bick-cuss 36,99,163,226

275

Index

Chate-cheakaps 14,78,142,206
Chate-cocush-shis 33
Chate-dah-beas............ 53,61,116,124,
.... 180,188,243
CHate-dah-beas............................251
Chate-dakpitsa..............................147
Chate-dakpitska.........................20,83
Chate-dock-coo-chis 25,88,152,216
Chate-ea-cot-tus 38,101
Chate-e-cah-duse...............48,112,176
Chate-ela-cheis............................6,70
Chate-ewotsodish 19,82,146,210
Chate-heahsas 136,200
Chate-heasas 8
Chate-hessas.................................. 72
Chate-hishes..................15,78,143,207
Chate-kah-deas............................... 32
Chate-kah-we-sis......... 43,106,170,233
Chate-kupis 9,73,137,200
Chate-nakish 20,83,148,211
Chate-nak-shedees 16
Chate-nak-sheedes 79,143,207
Chate-oocush-shis 97,161,224
Chate-sha-dachpitsa 232
Chate-sha-duck-bit-chay 105
Chate-shaduckbitchay 169
Chate-shay-duck-bit-chay 42
Chate-uch-pah-dee-dish 94
Chate-uck-pah-dee-dish 31
Chate-uck-pah-deedish...........158,221
Chatis 5,8,69,72,133,136,199
Chay-esos....................29,92,156,220
Chayt-aputs 22,150
Chayte-aputs 251
Cheach-cuce.................................236
Cheach-cucs 46
Cheach-cues..........................109,173
Cheach-kay-dock-cus....................117
Cheach-key-dock-cus.........54,181,232
Chea-dacock-inda-dichis...............252
Chea-dacock-inda-dichus...............189
Chea-dup-cheeis............................216
Chea-dup-chees............................152
Cheadup-um-bee-chis-sos 102
Cheah-key-sos...........................25,88
Chea-kay-sos...............................200
Chea-key-sos...............................153
Cheapcahdishtasonedonesase......... 36

Cheasay-itcha-baydayka................ 89
Chea-say-itchay-bahdaykah............ 26
Cheas-da-ah-kay-ock-in-day-dee-chis
.... 37
Cheasdacock-indechis 165,228
Cheas-dakaock-inda-dichis........... 125
Cheas-day-kay-ock-in-day-ditches . 62
Chea-shea-itchice 179,241
Cheas-kaock-inda-deechis 100
Cheas-kuch-kish 24,87,151,215
Che-chuck-key-sis 172,235
Che-chuk-key-sos 45
Checks-doochis................. 69,133,197
Che-co-key-dah-pace... 29,92,156,219
Cheda-kos........................... 7,135,199
Chedeer-esahs................................ 85
Chedoc-cuss-bahduppas 166
Chedockcusakbadupays................ 102
Che-dock-cush-soo 30,93
Chedockcussakbahduppays 38
Chedupa-eda-ekash....................... 83
Chedup-ahkade-duse 85
Chedup-ah-kde-duse
    Chedup-ah-kde-duse 21
Chedup-akookish....................... 11,75
Chedupa-seeish.............................. 83
Chedupa-seesh............... 19,147,211
Chedup-cadish-dondase......... 143,206
Chedup-cahdish-dondase................ 78
Che-dup-cho-sus........................... 47
Chedup-cho-sus 110
Chedup-dashes............. 14,78,142,206
Chedup-ehas 13,76
Chedup-kochetish 10,74,138
Chedup-mahkahish 10,138
Che-dup-peas................................ 100
Che-dup-pom-bish........................ 98
Chedup-quasah-dataish............. 21,85
Chedups-echete..................... 15,142
Chedup-shespitta 18,82
Cheedeer-esahs.................. 22,150,213
Chee-dish................. 38,101,165,228
Cheedup.. 101
Cheedup etahsich............................22
Cheedupa-ede-ekech............... 148,211
Cheedup-ahtsay-basash 144
Cheedup-akookish 139,203
Cheedup-ay-koos.............. 22,150,213

Index

Chee-dup-bachate-chice 108
Chee-dup-bah-cha-ah-chis 38
Cheedup-bah-cha-ahchis 165,228
Chee-dup-bah-chate-chice..............45
Cheedup-bah-chate-chice 172,235
Chee-dup-be-das-dace..............50,113
Chee-dup-be-day-sot 39
Cheedup-be-day-sot 148,211
Chee-dup-chees..........................25,88
Chee-dup-chee-sus 53,116
Cheedup-chee-sus 180,242
Chee-dup-chos-us........49,112,176,239
Chee-dup-dah-cock-cus...................32
Cheedup-dah-cock-cus 160,223
Chee-dup-dah-shis 28
Cheedup-dah-shis............................91
Chee-dup-eas............................37,164
Cheedup-eas....................................227
Chee-dup-eche-dish 39
Chee-dup-e-chee-dish 57
Cheedup-ehas...........................140,204
Cheedup-e-hosh 25,88
Cheedup-etahsich...............85,149,213
Chee-dup-kah-deas..........................61
Cheedup-kah-deas 124
Cheedup-kahdeas 188,251
Chee-dup-kah-kah-dah-bis 34
Cheedup-kah-kah-dah-bis 162,225
Cheedup-keasos 180,242
Chee-dup-keas-soo 53
Chee-dup-keas-sos 116
Cheedup-kochetish.........................202
Cheedup-lahka-dah-his 97
Cheeduppa-shespitta 210
Cheedup-pom-bish 162,225
Cheedups-echete 206
Chee-dup-she-chok-a-dus 56
Cheedup-shepittus.........................100
Cheedup-sho-chok-a-dus........119,183,
.... 246
Chee-dup-um-be-chisos 166,229
Chee-dup-um-bee-chis-sos 39
Cheepup-beday-sot..........................83
Chee-say-ca-say-tuss......................159
Chee-say-ea-day-tuss 31,95
Chees-makpash 213
Chee-sock-cuss 37,101,165,228
Chee-sos-cos 157,221

Chee-sos-eos....................................30
Chees-shepittich 161,224
Chees-she-pit-toch 33
Chees-wahkpahs 22,85,150
Cheetaka-cahkoskat 140,204
Cheetaka-eahkoskat 12
Cheetaka-eahkoskot 75
Cheeup-ahkade-duse...............149,212
Cheeup-ay-koos 85
Cheeup-be-das-dace................177,240
Cheeup-dah-cock-cus 96
Cheeup-dah-sis 155,219
Cheeup-e-ches-ditch 120,184,246
Cheeup-quasah-datsish 149,213
Cheeup-shespitta............................146
Cheis-makpash 6,70,134,198
Che-key-pis 36
Cheks-doochis 5
Chepups-echete................................78
Che-quais 107
Che-quas 44,171,234
Che-say-ick-cosh 103
Chesay-itche-badakah............153,216
Che-shea-it-chice 52
Che-shea-it-chise 115
Che-soup-pus.....................45,109,173
Ches-sos-cos 93
Chess-she-pit-toch 97
Chicken......................46,109,173,236
Chief................................15,79,143,207
Chief at Night 74,139,203
Chief at night..................................11
Child 30,94,158,221
Child in the Mouth.................145,209
    Joe 17,81,145,209
Child in the mouth 17,81
Child is Medicine 6,70,134,198
Chip-pah-pos-shis 160,223
Chip-pah-pos-s-shis 35,96
Chisah-kahdeas.......................71,135,199
Chisha-kahdeas 7
Chis-sheis 5,69,133,197
Choos-say-dah-quas... 62,125,189,252
Cho-say-ick-cosh 40,168,231
Choteau....................30,94,158,221
Chuch-kay-esos 32,95,159,222
Chuch-ko-dootchis 166,229
Chuck-ko-doot-chis 38

Index

Chuck-ko-doot-chit 102
Chu-dup-pom-bish 35
Chu-dup-she-pit-tus 37
Chustah-ahkundis 142,206
Chustak-ahkindis 14
Chustak-ahkundis 77
Chut-naepis 23
Chut-napis 86,151,214
Clawson, Charles 48,111,175,238
Cliff 39,103,167,230
Close Together 164,227
Close together 37,100
Cloud Shows Plain 149,213
Cloud shows plain 21,85
Cloud Well Known 167,230
    Ben 168,230
Cloud well known 40,103
Coa-wat-tay-doochis 232
Co-cosh-beas 49,112,176,239
Coe-what-tay-doochis 169
Coe-what-tay-doot-chis 42
Come herself 106
Comes Above, Hannah 102,166,229
comes above, Hannah 39
Comes Against the Wind 170,233
Comes against the wind 43,106
Comes and Kills 77,141,205
Comes and kills 13
Comes Behind 169,231
Comes behind 41,104
Comes From Above 166,176,229,
    239
Comes from above 39–40,102,112
Comes From Digging Roots 160
Comes from digging roots 32,96
Comes From the Birds 159,222
Comes from the birds 31,95
Comes From War Pretty 152,216
Comes from war pretty 25,88
Comes Herself 170,233
Comes herself 43
Comes in a Day 135,199
    Celia 135,199
Comes in a day 7,71
Comes Out First 155,221
Comes out first 28,91
Comes Out of the Water 150,164,
    213,227

Comes out of the water .. 22,37,85,100
Comes to Her Nest 161,225
Comes to her nest 34,97
Comes to See The Buffalo 78
Comes to See the Buffalo 143,207
Comes to see the buffalo 15
Comes to the Birds 159,252
Comes to the birds 31,95
Comes to the Buffalo 91,155,219
Comes to the buffalo 28
Comes Up Red 179,241
Comes up red 52,115
Con-bachpash 226
Con-dah-cock-cus 40,103,167,230
Cone-dah-chice 53,116,179,242
Con-Hah-pagh 163
Con-hah-pagh 35,99
Con-up-e-say 63,126,190,253
Coo Chief 57,163,226
    Florence 57,120,184,246
Coo chief 99
Coo-bah-pay-dah-pay 40
Coo-bah-pay-day-bah 230
Coo-bah-pay-day-pah 103,167
Cooper
    Cynthia 58,121,185,248
    James 61,124,188
    Joseph 61,124,187
    Joseph, Jr. 124,188
    Laura 61,124,188
    Lula 58,121
    Lule[sic] 185
    Lulu 248
    Mrs. J. B. 58
    Mrs. J.B. 121,185,248
    Peter 58,121,185,248
    Susie 61,124,188
    Sylvania 61,124,188
    Theodora 61,188
    Theodore 124
    James 250
    Joseph 250
    Joseph, Jr. 251
    Laura 250
    Susie 250
    Sylvania 250
    Theodore 250
Corn 31,94

Index

Corn Woman 176,239
Corn woman 49,112
Corner of the Mouth 72,136,200
Corner of the mouth 8
Co-tah-dah-cock-cus .. 48,111,144,208
Co-tah-dee-dish 63
Cotah-shee-dish 24,87
Covered Up 190
Covered up 64,126
Covers His Face 148,171,211,234
Covers his face 20,44,83,107
Covers His Neck 160,223
Covers his neck 33,96
Coyote Looks Up 182,245
Coyote looks up 55,118
Coyote Runs 171,233
Coyote runs 43,107
Coyote That Howls 175,238
Coyote that howls 48,111
Crane
    Luella 173
    Mary 12,75,140,204
    Maud 140,204
Crane in the Sky 171,252
Crane in the sky 44,107
Crazy 64,126,190
Crazy Bird 161,224
Crazy bird 33,97
Crazy Crane 177,239
Crazy crane 50,113
Crazy Head 5,69,133,197
Crazy Sister-in-Law 142,206
Crazy Sister-in-law 78
Crazy sister-in-law 15
Crazy 253
Cree man 28
Crooked Arm 91,155,219
    Herbert 28,91,155,219
    James 28,91,155,219
Crooked arm 28
Crooked Face 74–75,138,140,155,
... 164,174,183,199,203,218,227,246
Crooked face 10,12,27,36,47,56,
.................................91,100,110,119
Crooked Face Child 154,217
Crooked face child 26,90
Crooked face No.2 36
Crooked Foot 162

Crooked foot 35,98
Cross bear 56
Cross Weasel 94,158,221
Cross weasel 30
Crosses the Water 189
Crosses the water 63,125
Crosses the Water 252
Crow That Shows 146,209
Crow that shows 18,81
Cuckay-dups-doochis 153,216
Cuck-ca-coo-day-dechis 103
Cuck-ca-coo-day-deechis 167
Cuck-cah-wah-chice .. 43,106,170,233
Cuck-cock-in-days 42,105,169,232
Cuckey-shean-doochis 156,219
Cuck-hay-dupe-doochis 89
Cuck-kay-coo-day-de-chis 40
Cuck-kay-dupe-dooch-chis 25
Cuck-key-bea 54
Cuck-key-shean-doot-chis 28
Cuck-key-shen-doochis 91
Cuck-kis 50,113,177
Cuck-pis 240
Cummins
    Mrs. R. W. 59
    Mrs. R.W. 122,186,248
    Richard 43,106,170,233
Curly 45,108,172,235
Cush-some-bee-chice 52,116,179,
....242
Cut 22,86,150,214
Cut Ear 72,136,200
Cut ear 8
Cuts a Hole In It 145,208
Cuts a Hole in it 80
Cuts a hole in it 17
Cuts the Bear's Ears 233
Cuts the Bears Ears 170
Cuts the bears ears 43,106
Cuts the Horse 175,238
Cuts the horse 48,111

D.M.G. Things, Annie 164,227
D'Oreille, Crazy Pen 93
d'Oreille, Crazy Pen 157,220
Dachbitsa-cowees 183
Dachbitsay-bishea 182
Dachbitsay-e-kos-seas 180

Index

Dachbitsay-he-dock-cus 181
DAch-co-bachpash 246
Dach-co-bachpash 183
Dach-cock-sheedish 183,246
Dachpitsa-beas 215
Dachpitsa-e-sos-seas 243
Dachpitsa-he-dock-cus 243
Dachpitsa-ock-in-das 164
Dachpitsa-ock-in-dus 227
Dachpitsay-beedahs 23,87
Dachpitsay-che-sus 235
Dachpitsay-esock-cuss 159
Dachpitsay-it-chice 179
Dackbitsay-des-dish 168
Dackbitsay-eck-pah-dea 161
Dack-cock-shee-dish 119
Dack-cosh-sheedis[sic] 40
Dack-kah-shis 28,91,141,217
Dack-kosh-sheedis 103
Dackpitsa-bishea 245
Dackpitsa-cah-dice 244
Dackpitsa-che-dace 232
Dackpitsa-chey-deedish 231
Dackpitsa-cowees 246
Dackpitsa-doopus 241
Dackpitsa-esah-cocish 243
Dackpitsa-esock-cuss 223
Dackpitsa-it-chice 242
Dackpitsa-newpu-oze 228
Dackpitsa-ucpah-dacus 238
Dackpitsa-uppa-pushcoos 233
Dackpitsay-boo-dish 239
Dackpitsay-cha-bedock-sahoos 179
Dackpitsay-dah-beas 242
Dackpitsay-eck-pah-dea 224
Dackpitsay-hada-tahsos 218
Dackpitsay-undatechas 235
Dacock-etuck-posdatus ... 119,182,245
Dacock-uckbah-do-shis 218
Da-cose 40,103,167,230
Dadough-cheada-itchice .. 106,170,233
Daekahshis 226
Daeka-itchis 230
Daeka-kahdeas 159,222
Daeka-makpash 211
Daeka-sheedis 230
Daek-it-chis 40,103
Daek-itchis 167

Dah-ah-sheas 46,109,173,236
Dah-beas 51
Dah-cheas 26,90,154,217
Dah-cock-ah-pah-ahoos 172,234
Dah-cock-ah-pah-hoose 44,107
Dah-cock-ah-seas 63,125,189,252
Dah-cock-ah-wah-chice 49,112
Dahcock-ah-wah-chice 176
Dahcock-ah-way-chice 238
Dah-cock-bah-coos 43,113,170,233
Dah-cockbah-coos 106
Dah-cock-bah-cush-days 50
Dah-cock-bah-soos 50
Dahcock-bah-soos 177,240
Dah-cock-beas 40,53,103,116,
 167,180,230,242
Dah-cock-cah-deas 37
Dah-cock-cah-doosh-sis .. 47,110,174,
 237
Dah-cock-che-deas-sos 44,107,172,
 234
Dah-cock-cuss 62
Dah-cock-dacuss 95
Dah-cock-dah-cuss 38
Dah-cock-dah-dah-bish 29
Dahcock-dah-dah-bish 156,219
Dah-cock-dah-say-itchis 29
Dah-cock-day-say-itchis 92
Dah-cock-doo-pus 54,117,181,244
Dah-cock-e-tuck-pos-da-tus 55
Dah-cock-e-wan-deas 28,91
Dah-cock-hay-day-dus 51,114
Dahcock-hay-day-dus 178,240
Dah-cock-it-chis 99
Dahcock-it-chis 36
Dahcock-itchis 164
Dah-cock-keah-sos 110,174
Dah-cock-keas-sos 47,237
Dah-cock-sah-hoos 31,95,159,252
Dah-cock-sah-hoose 31,95,159
Dah-cock-shee-dis 104,231
Dah-cock-shee-dish 41,56,169
Dah-cock-teah-dish 37,101,165,228
Dahcock-uckbah-do-shis 91
Dahcock-uckbah-so-shis 28
Dahcock-uckpa-do-shis 155
Dahcock-uckpa-doshis 155
Dah-cock-uckpah-dahcus 91,218

280

Index

Dah-cock-uckpah-dah-cush............ 28
Dah-coe-tay-doot-chis................... 38
Dah-coe-tay-dootchis...................166
Dahcoe-tay-doot-chis...................101
Dah-coock-sah-hoos.....................222
Dah-cook-dacass 159,223
Dah-cup-cah-cheas......................... 61
Dah-cup-co-dus-sos 29,92
Dah-cup-pis................36,100,164,227
Dah-cus......................45,108,172,235
Dah-dough-chea-day-itchice 43
Dah-ece-tay-dootchis...................229
Dah-hea-os..................................42,169
Dah-he-os..................50,113,177,240
Dah-hes-os 105,232
Dahkoopis 80,145,208
Dahkopoos 17
Dah-kosh-bah-coos 34,98,162,225
Dahkpitsa-kahdeas 144,207
Dahkpitska-kahdeas 79
Dahpitsa-eahkotish....................11,74
Dah-pit-sah-seandahcockcus 47
Dah-pittosh.................25,88,152,216
Dah-say-cah-weas 49,112
Dah-say-cah-wees 176,238
Dah-sea-hash...............25,88,152,216
Daka-ichis-amach.........17,80,145,208
Daka-makpash.....................20,83,148
Daka-wahtis 20,148,211
Daka-watis 83
Dakoshes.......................19,82,147,210
Dakpitsa-ahoos...........................152,215
Dakpitsa-ah-reandadish................137
Dakpitsa-ahshuse 214
Dakpitsa-ahsuse 146
Dakpitsa-ahway-repeas 139,203
Dakpitsa-a-reandadish.................201
Dakpitsa-beeadas 151,214
Dakpitsa-botsots............................146
Dakpitsa-chabeddok-sahoo 241
Dakpitsa-cheis................................200
Dakpitsa-eahkoshkat 203
Dakpitsa-eahkotish........................139
Dakpitsa-saskatch............................. 7
Dakpitses-ahsees 135,199
Dakpitses-asees 71
Dakpitska-ahn-duish 12,75,140,203
Dakpitska-ahoos........................20,87

Dakpitska-ahsuse 18,81
Dakpitska-ahway-repeas................ 75
Dakpitska-ahway-roopeas.............. 12
Dakpitska-botsots 18
Dakpitska-cheis .. 7–8,71–72,135–136
Dakpitska-hotskish 16,79
Dakpitska-hotskisk 144
Dakpitska-kahdeas 16
Dakpitska-naks 12,76
Dakpitska-neen-dates................. 31,94
Dakpitske-botsots 82
Dakpitske-nake 140,204
Dakup-makpash 11,74,139,203
Dapitsah-seandahcockcus............. 111
Da-pit-say-seandacockcus 154
Dapitsay-seandacocus..................217
Dapitska-neen-dates................. 158,222
Dash-day-tush............................26,89
Datsuah-doochis.........................8,72
Davis
  Blaine R...................... 60,123,186
  Charles Wort......... 60,119,183,245
  Effie N. 60,123,187
  Margaretta A...................... 60,123
  Mrs. George R. 60,123
  Mrs. S. C. 11
  Mrs. S.C...................... 75,139,203
  Samuel S...................... 125,189
  Samuel Sumner........................ 62
  Blaine R.................................. 249
  Effie N. 249
  Samuel S................................. 252
Davis-Howe, Margaret A....... 186,249
Dawes, David 218
Day-chay-ah-hoos.....................27,91
Day-chay-ahoos 155,218
Day-it-chise 43
Dayka-ahspittech 140,203
Dayka-ahspittesh 12,75
Daykoosh-mahke 76
Daykoosh-mahks 13,141,204
Daykoosh-naks 12,76,140,204
Dea-cosh-bah-cush 89,153,216
Dead-cosh-bah-such 25
Deah-kah-chis 163
Deah-kah-shis 35
Deah-kah-sis................................. 99
Deak-kosh-sheedish 167

Index

Dee-cock-e-sos 56,119,183,246
Deputee
    Flora 58,121,185,247
    George 58
    Jennie 58,121,184,247
    Mrs. G. F. 58
    Mrs. G.F. 121,184,247
Dexter 18,92,156,220
Dich-heahsas 13,76,141,205
Digs Well Known 162,225
Digs well known 35,98
Dirty Foot 138,202
Dirty foot 10
Dock-bit-chay-dee-dish 33
Dock-co-bah-pash 56,119
Dock-ke-days 176,239
Dock-kosh 29,156,220
Dock-op-pah-dee-chis 25,153
Dock-op-pay-dec-chis 88
Dock-shay-dah-beas ... 43,106,170,233
Does Anything 84,149,164,212,227
Does anything 21,36,100
Does Ev'y'g With a Shield 235
Does Ev'yth'g with her Med 174
Does everything with a shield 45
Does everything with her med. 47
Does everything with her medc 110
Does Everything With Shield 172
Does everything with shield 108
Does Ev'th'g With Her Med 202
Does Good Things 169,232
Does good things 9,105
Does Lot of Things 135,243
Does Lots of Things 71
Does lots of things 7
Does Many Good Things 164,227
Does many good things 37,100
Does things hard 11
Does Things Together 150,214
Does things together 22,86
Dog Bear 182,245
Don't Fall Down 145,209
Don't fall down 81
Don't Get In 173,235
Don't get in 108
Don't Kill 179,241
Don't kill 115
Don't Mix 73,137,201

Don't Run 77,142,206
    Mary 77,142,206
Don't Run on Top 70
Don't fall down 17
Don't Mix 9
Dont run 14
Dont[sic] get in 45
Dont[sic] kill 52
Dont[sic] Run, Mary 14
Dont[sic] run on top 6
dont[sic] run on top, William 6
Doochis-heahsas 16,79,143,207
Dook-ke-days 49,112
Doop-pah-c-che-dosh 237
Doop-pah-e-che-dosh 47,110,174
Doop-tush-ditches 55,118,182,245
Door
    Dora 56,119,183,246
    Victoria 56,119,183,246
D'Oreill, Crazy Pend 29
Dosh-bah-cha-chis ... 27,29,90,92,154,
.... 157,218,220
Dosh-day-tus 40,103
Dosh-day-tuss 168,231
Dosh-kosh 30,94,158,221
Dosh-shay-e-coos 40,103,167,230
Dotska 83
Dotska- 19
Dotske 147,211
Dotsuah-doochis 136,199
Dotsuish 16,79,144,208
Dough-seas 28,92,156,219
Doyle
    Frances 123,187
    Mrs. Thomas 60,123
    Mrs. Thos. 187
    Robert 60,123,187
    Frances 250
    John 250
    Mrs. Thosmas 250
    Robert 250
Dreamer 17,80,145,208
    Katie 62,125,189
    Mortimer 80,145,208
    Katie 252
Drinking all the Time 154,217
Drinking all the time 26,90
Drunkard 15,78,143,207

Index

Ducbitchay-esockcusss 95
Ducbitshay-bedook-sahoos 115
Duchkis 70,134,198
Duchkis- 6
Duchuis 7,71,135,199
Duck-bea-cheacock-indas 25,72
Duckbea-cheacock-indas 136,200
Duck-bit-cha-eckpadea 97
Duckbitchaun-dayatchase 108
Duck-bit-chay-akos-seas 116
Duck-bit-chay-beas 24,87,151
Duck-bit-chay-bedooksahhoos 52
Duck-bit-chay-boo-dish 50,113
Duckbitchay-boo-dish 177
Duck-bit-chay-cah-dice 55,118
Duck-bit-chay-cah-weas 56
Duck-bit-chay-che-dace 42,105
Duckbitchay-che-dace 169
Duck-bit-chay-che-sus 45,108
Duckbitchay-che-sus 172
Duck-bit-chay-dah-beas 52,115
Duck-bit-chay-dee-dish 40,104
Duck-bit-chay-doc-puss 114
Duck-bit-chay-doo-puss 51
Duck-bit-chay-eas 40,104
Duckbitchay-eas 168
Duck-bit-chay-eck-pah-dea 33
Duckbitchay-edish-shippace 56
Duck-bit-chay-e-kos-seas 53
Duck-bit-chay-esahcoshish 53
Duckbitchay-esah-coshish 117
Duck-bit-chay-e-sock-cuss 38
Duckbitchay-hada-tahsos 155
Duck-bitchay-haydatahos 91
Duck-bit-chay-haydaytahsos 27
Duck-bit-chay-he-dock-cuss 54
Duckbitchay-he-dock-cuss 117
Duck-bit-chay-it-chice 52,115
Duck-bit-chay-new-pew-oze 38
Duckbitchay-nopew-oze 101
Duck-bit-chay-nowpu-oze 166
Duck-bit-chay-ock-in-das 36
Duck-bitchay-ock-indas 100
Duckbitchay-ucpah-dacus 175
Duck-bitchay-ucpah-dahcus 48
Duckbitchay-undatechas 172
Duck-bit-chayun-dayatechase 45
Duckbitchay-uppa-pushcoos 170

Duckbitch-ucpah-dahous 111
Duckbitchy-cah-weas 119
Duckbitsay-esah-cocish 180
Duck-bit-say-pee-duck-cus 27
Duckbitshay-cah-dice 181
Duckbitshay-dah-beas 179
Duckbitshaydoo-pus 178
Duck-bit-tse-uppahpushcoos 43
Duck-cock-ah-shoes .. 46,109,173,236
Duck-cock-bah-dah-cus 33,97,161
Duck-cock-bah-dah-cuss 224
Duck-cock-bea-it-chis 40,104
Duck-cock-bea-itchis 168,231
Duck-cock-beas 48,112
Duck-cock-dah-cus 31,94
Duck-cock-dahcuss 159,222
Duck-cock-sah-hoo-dup-pace 36
Duck-kay-coo-day-de-chis 230
Duck-pace 177,239
Duck-peace 50,113
Duck-peas 46,109,173,236
Ducock-sahoo-dup-pace 99
Ducock-seh-hoo-dup-pace 163
Ducock-seh-hoo-duppace 226
Ducth-ka 18
Dudish 16,79,143,207
Dukbitse-upah-pushcoos 106
Dukeah-desh 10,138,202
Dukedea-akuse 19,82,147,210
Dum-bachpash 183,246
Dum-bah-pash 119
Dummy 23,86,151,214
Dummy Bull 75,139,203
Dummy bull 11
Dupe-doot-chis 31,94,158,221
Dupe-pah-wah-dup-pace .. 46,109,173,
 236
Dupe-tosh-beas 107
Dupe-tush-beas 43
Dupe-tush-der-chis 30,93,157,221
Dup-pah-ecoos-seas 56,119
Dup-pah-ecos-seas 183,245
Dust 14,77,142,206
Dutch-chee-do-bah-pash 52
Dutch-chee-Do-pah-bash 116
Dutch-chee-do-pah-bash 179,242
Dutch-choa-dock-cus 177,240
Dutch-choa-dock-us 50,113

Index

Dutch-choas 29,92,156,220
Dutch-ka........................9,82,146,210
Dutch-ke.........................115,179,242
Dutsuah-moopis 7,71
Dutsuah-noopis 135

Ea-cah-pish 49,112,176,227
Ea-cah-pish Flat Mouth................227
Ea-chay-kah-deas..........................98
Ea-che-keep-pay 119
Ea-cock-kah-beas..............97,161,224
Ea-cook-cah-cheas 28,91,155,218
Ea-cook-kah-beas.......................... 34
Ea-cook-kish-shays 180,243
Ea-cot-tus 46,109,173,236
Ea-cus-sah-che-dup-pis 43,107,171
Ea-cus-sah-cheduppis....................234
Ea-cus-sos 42,106,170,233
Ea-dane-dah-cock-cus 173
Ea-dane-deas..............46,109,173,236
Ea-dea-cah-deas 48,238
Ea-dea-cah-dees 175
Ea-dea-it-chice 46
Ea-dea-it-chise 173,236
Ea-des-it-chice 109
Eagle 19,82,147,210
Eagle Above.....................76,141,204
Eagle above.................................... 13
Eagle High Up........................162,225
Eagle high up 34,98
Eagle Shirt.......................82,147,210
Eagle shirt 19
Eagle sits down 17
Eagle Turns Around...............162,226
Eagle turns around 98
Eah-cah-shues 174
Eahkooka-asadish............16,144,208
Eahkooka-asdish 79
Eah-show-dechit-chaesos..............236
Eahwookose 16,143,207
Eak-cah-shues 46,110,236
Eak-ka-dah-cock-cus.................52,115
Eak-ka-dah-cock-us 178,241
Eak-kay-hishes 178
Eak-kay-his-shies 114
Eak-kay-his-shis 51
Eak-kin-hish-sis 12,75,140
Eakkook-sheedish 207

Ea-kock-kish-shays........................53
Ea-kook-kish-shays 116
Eakook-sheedees 15
Eakook-sheedes 79
Eakook-sheedish..........................143
Eakpoetatska.................................. 7
Eapcha-bapah-dootchie................119
EApcha-bapah-dootchis............... 245
Eapcha-bapah-dootchis................183
Eap-chay-ah-peas 51
Eapchay-bahpah-dootchice............ 56
Easa-key-pay-naks........................217
Eas-bah-pus-say............................111
Eas-cha-keep-pay 56
Eascha-naks......................... 133,197
Eas-chay-cuck-kis.............. 47,110,174
Eas-chee-key-pah 47,110,174
Eas-che-kay-pay 36,100
Eas-che-keep-pay 183,246
Eas-ea-coas....................... 44,171,234
Ease-key-pay 26,90,154
Eas-es-coas 107
Eas-hay-cuck-kis 237
Ea-sos 174,237
Eas-pah-pus-say........................48,175
Eas-pea-os-seas.......... 50,113,177,240
Easpooetatsa................................. 71
Eas-sche-kay-pay........................ 164
Eas-seh-keapa.............................227
Eas-shee-day 44,107,171
Eas-shu-day 52,115,179,242
Eatosh-dabish-de-chice... 115,179,241
Eats the fish 51,114
Eats the Wood....................... 183,246
Eats the wood 119
Eats With a Bird 155
Eats with a Bird 218
Eats with a bird 28,91
Eat-toch-tay-keas-sos.......... 109,236
Eat-tosh-da-bish-de-chice 52
Eat-tosh-tay-hios-shis 44
Eat-tosh-tay-his-shos 107
Eat-tosh-tay-keasos.................... 174
Eat-tosh-tay-keas-sos.................... 46
Ecbean-dock-sass 158,221
Echa-dow-keas-sos 43,106,170,233
Echa-duck-kosh-awaychis........... 167
Echa-sheishis........................ 138,202

Index

Echa-shesheis 10
Echay-chis 34
Echay-hishes 160,223
Echdoc-inday-dootchis 116,242
E-cheam-dah-pace 109,173,236
E-cheam-push-cush 175
Echeam-push-cush 238
Echean-bachpash 159,222
Echean-bah-pash 31,95
Echean-chea-itchis 183
E-chean-dah-cock-cus 46,109,173,
 236
E-chean-dah-pace 46
Echean-dock-eas 31,94
E-chean-push-cush 48,111
E-che-che-sosh 30,93,157,220
Eche-dae-kosh-kahdeas 175
E-che-dah-keas-sos 45,172,235
Eche-dah-keas-sos 108
Eche-da-keas-sos 52
Eche-da-keus-sos 115
Echeday-itchay-ock 230
Eche-day-itchay-ock-inday 40
Echeday-itchay-ock-inday 103
Echeday-itchay-ockinday 167
Eche-day-it-chis 42,105
Eche-day-kah-deas 33,96
Eche-day-kahdeas 160,224
Eche-dee-kosh-ah-way-chis 40
Eche-dee-kosh-awaychis 103
Eche-dee-kosh-kah-deas 48
Eche-dee-kosh-kahdeas 111,237
Echede-kosh-ahway-itchis 230
Eche-de-she-chace 41,105,169
Eche-de-she-chase 232
Eche-doch-in-days 103
Echedock-ichay-ockindays 113,166
Eche-dock-in-day-doot-chis 53
Eche-dock-in-days 39,167,230
Eche-dock-itchay-ockindays 50
E-che-doe-it-chis 38,102,166,229
Eche-dosh 27,90,155,218
Eche-duch-days 88
Eche-dudees 9,73,137,201
Echee-dah-ahhoos 233
Echee-dahay-dane-duckoos 165,228
Echee-dahay-daneduckoos 101
Echee-dah-hoos 43,170

Echee-dayhaey-dane-duckcoos 38
Echeedayon-duccekasses 165,228
Echee-dayon-duckcoekeassos 38
Echeedayon-duckockeasos 101
Echeedock-ichay-ockindays 229
Echee-duch-days 25
Echee-du-kish-esos 224
Echee-du-kosh-esos 34,97,161
Echeen-bachpash 151,215
Echeen-bah-pash...................... 24,87
Echeete-lagak 12,115
E-chee-uck-pah-dup-pace 45
E-chee-uck-pahdup-pace 109
Echee-uck-pah-duppace 173,235
Eche-kuis 6,70,134,198
Echeo-duch-days 153,216
Eches-dish-hoos 106
Echeta-achis 18,146,209
Echeta-akuse 209
Echeta-cosh 138,202
Echeta-gash-eduse 72,136,200
Echetagash-eduse 8
Echeta-hukish 11,139,202
Echeta-ichis 170
Echeta-kowees 8,72,136,200
Echeta-sheis-shash 156
Echete 19,83,147,211
Echete-achis 81
Echete-ahkin-doochis .. 14,78,142,206
Echete-akahps 14
Echete-akuse 18,81,146
Echete-cheis-ahkudis 14,77
Echete-cheis-ahkundis 156,220
Echete-dekash.................................. 6
Echete-dekush................................ 70
Echete-doochis 21,84,184
Echete-dootchis 246
Echetegashes 13,76,141,205
Echete-hukish 74
Echete-ichis 64,126
Echete-itchice 190,253
Echete-itchis 232
Echete-maks-kochetish.. 9,73,137,201
Echete-mulakis 9,137,201
Echete-mulaksis 73
Echete-mulukis 15,78,143,206
Echete-sheedes-ahkinda. 9,74,137,201
Echey-dah-hay-day-cuss 164,227

285

Index

Echey-day-hay-day-duss 37,100
Echey-she-coopy 35,98,162
Echick-doot-chis 48
Echick-heas 23,86,151,214
Echick-kay-sah-dish 28,91,155,221
Echik-dichis 9,73,137,201
E-chin-doot-chice 54,117,181,244
Echit-che-sheas 57
Ech-keas-boatush 211
E-chope-pice 44,107,171,234
E-chu-dah-keas-sos 26,89,158,221
Eck-bah-dea-bachpash 160,223
Eck-bah-dea-bah-pash 32
Eck-bahdea-pah-bash 96
Eck-bah-deas 33,96,160
Eckpah-dea-dacock-cush 155,218
Eckpah-deadah-cock-cush 90
Eck-pah-dead-dah-cock-cush 27
E-con-days 26,90
E-cook-key-e-kesh 156
E-cook-key-e-kosh 28,92,219
E-cosh 63
E-cosh-sheas 181,243
Ecot-osh-heas 33,96,160,223
Ecupe-pah-bah-puc-tosh 172,234
Ecupe-pah-bah-put-tosh 44
E-cupe-pah-che-shis 52,115
Ecupe-pah-che-shis 178,241
Ecupe-pahda-cock-cuss 177,240
Ecupe-pah-dah-cock-cuss 50,113
Ecupe-pah-de-chic 63
Ecupe-pah-de-chice 125,189,252
Ecupe-pah-doocthis 169
Ecupe-pah-doot-chis 42,105
Ecupe-pah-dootchis 232
Ecupe-pah-wish-de-chice 47
~~Ecupe-pah-wish-de-chice~~ 110
Ecupe-pah-wish-de-chice 174,237
Ecupe-pay-bee-dish 126,190
Ecupe-pay-bee-dosh 63
Ecupe-pay-cheas 32,96,160
Ecupe-pay-cheis 223
E-cupe-pis 54,117,181,244
Ecup-pah-ate-chice 45,108,172,235
Ecup-pah-keas-sos 30,93,158,221
E-cush-sheas 54,117
E-cuss-sah-esos 38,102
E-cuss-sos-esos 166,229

Edah-doot-chis 26,90
Edah-dootchis 154
E-Dah-hoos 170
E-dah-hoos 43,106,233
Eday-dootchis 217
Edea-hay-bah-pash 29,92,156,219
E-dea-hish 62,125
Edea-oke-pis 41,104
Edeka-oke-pus 231
Edeke-oke-pus 168
E-dit-days 40
Edock-bah-pah 167
Edock-bah-pash 39,103
E-doos-sos 26,90,154,217
Edosh-uck-bah-dup-pace .. 44,108,172
Educhesa-heas 137,201
Educhesha-heas 9,73
Edukish 79,207
Edukush 16,143
Edush-uck-bah-dup-pace 235
Edwards, J. E. 64–66,69–127,129,
.... 131,133–191,193,196–254
Edwea 23,86,151,214
Eem-botsesh 11,75,139,203
Eep-kahdeas 17,80,145,208
Eepse-mahka-kala-napes .. 14,142,206
Eepse-mahkala-napes 78
Eep-shedish 11,75,139
Eep-sheedis 203
Eer-kahwash 7,71,135,199
Ee-sach-ich 202
Eesackas-ahoos 6,70,134,198
Ee-sash-ich 138
ee-sash-ich 10
Eescha-naks 5,69
Ees-kapa 6,70,134
Eeskotchitsa-maluk-ichis 16
Eespe-ekash 14,77,142,206
Egg Inside the Bird 211
Egg woman 64
E-hum-be-shoes 42,105,170,232
E-hum-dah-pace 39,102,166,229
Eikos-hishes 16
Eisda-isischish 7,71
Eisda-karooshes 9,73,137,201
Eka-ahpka-amach 21,84,148,212
E-kay-beas 64
E-kay-sup-peas 157,221

Index

E-kay-sup-poas 30,93
Ek-bah-dee-days 53,116,179
Ekeeka-dase 23,87,151,215
Eke-kahdish 14
E-koop-pay-bah-coosh 32,95,160
Ekoos-sheas 35,98,162,226
Ekpetatska 135,199
Ekuh-push 9,73,137,200
Ekupa-cheis 6,70,134,198
Ekupa-esash 8,72,136,200
Ekupa-ich 19,83,147
Ekupa-ie 211
E-kupa-pay-bah-coosh 223
Ekup-pah-wah-chis 32,94,158–159,
 221–222
E-kush-sheas 53,116,180,242
Ekus-sah-itch-chis 32,95
Ekus-sah-itchis 159,222
Elk Stands Up 72,136,200
Elk stands up 8
End of the Tail 173,235
End of the tail 45,109
Enemy Hunter 81,146,209
Enemy hunter 18
E-o-dish 20,83,148,211
Epah-dea-bah-cha-chis 27,90
Epah-deabah-cha-chis 155,234
Epay-it-chis 27
Epay-itchis 90
Epea-cot-a-wak-chis 37,101,165
Epeahkot-Esash 84
Epeahkot-esash 21,149,212
E-rooptay-cheis 139,202
E-rooptay-chis 11,74
E-sah-coo-dake 34,97,161,225
E-sah-duck-chis 42,106,170,233
E-sah-dut-chew-chice 52,115,179
E-sah-eduse-see-shis 42,170
Esah-eduse-see-shis 106,236
Esa-kahnishta 18
Esakakasha-manakis 11,139,203
Esaka-noops 209
Esa-keepa 6,70,74–75,134,138,
 140,198–199,203
Esa-kepa 10,12
Esaksha-chaschedees 69,133
Esaksha-Chechedees 5
Esa-pis 41,104,168

Esasahka-ahp-orupish 202
Esasha-ich 21,84,149,212
Esash-beduppa 17,81,145,209
Esash-beeshkeda 7
Esash-chedup 13,77,141,205
Esashka-ahp-orupish 10,138
Esaska-eke-sheesh 76
Esaska-eko-cheesh 13
Esaska-eko-sheeish 141,205
Esaska-huka-ahkindas 138,202
Esaska-huke-ahkindas 10
Esaska-noops 81,145
Esaska-schascheedes 205
Esasku-noops 17
E-say-dup-pah-choas . 59,122,186,248
E-say-kep-pa 224
E-say-kep-pah 161
E-say-key-pay 33,96
Es-been-dotch-cheas 30,93,158,221
Es-chay-kah-deas 34,162,225
Escheeta-nevsaus 22,86,150,213
Es-che-kah-dish 39
Es-che-kah-dish 102
Es-che-kay-pay 155,218
Es-che-key-pay 27,91
Es-chis-say-bah-pash 222
Es-chis-say-bah-posh 31,94,158
Escoche-karooshes 201
Escock-kay-keas-sos 28,91,155,218
Es-dea-cah-deas 111
Esdkoche-ahoos-dich 19
Eseah-koosh 20,83
Eseeah-koosh 148,211
E-sees-be-tay 96,160,223
E-sess-bee-tay 32
Esha-hishes-shedees 20
Esha-hishes-shedes 83
Eshasha-heahsas 84,148,212
Esha-shates 5,69,133,197
Eshash-heahsas 21
Eshe-bah-cha-chis 93,157,220
Eshe-bah-cha-shis 29
Eshippish-day-ichis 17,81,145,209
Esho-dechea-doochis 231
Esho-dechea-dootchis 104
Esho-dochea-dootchis 168
E-shoe-cah-dup-pace 64
E-shoe-cheas 51

Index

E-shoe-de-chea-doot-chis............... 40
E-shoe-dee-chea-ock-kin-day-dee-ditch-es 99
E-shoe-dee-chea-ock-kin-day-dee-ditch-es 36,163,226
E-shoes...26,89
Eshpeahisha-kahdeish 16,79,144
Eshpeahshea-kahdeish 208
E-shua-eas......................................167
E-shue-ea-bah-pash..................55,118
E-shue-eas........................39,103,230
E-shue-es-bachpash................182,245
Eskay-ahwotkot..................71,135,199
Eskay-awotkot................................. 7
Eskochea-basah......................140,204
Eskochea-basash 12,75
Eskochea-biorup 17,80
Eskocheabiorup.......................145,208
Eskochea-ichis 6,70,134,198,211
Eskoche-aseesh 20,83,147,211
Eskoche-doochis 17,81,145,209
Eskoche-karooshes..................9,73,137
Eskoche-okepis 8,72,136,199
Eskochisa-maluk-ichis 79
Eskochitsa-maluk-ichis 144,207
Eskoochea-ahoos-dich 210
Eskooche-ahoos-dich 82
Eskoochs-ahoos-dich 147
Eskuka-ahsees 6,70
Eskuka-ahshees......................134,198
Eskulasa-epa-cheis........................ 78
Eskulusa-epa-cheis................190,253
E-soa-kay-ate-chace................165,228
Esoc-cah-wah-chakoos-say 162,226
Esoch-kah-de-rooch 226
Esoch-kah-dew-os.....................35,163
Esock-cah-wah-chay-koos-say 35
Esock-che-sah-keas-sos..............34,97
Esock-chice 49,112,176,238,252
Esock-kah-dew-os 99
E-sock-kain-dah-koos 27,89
Esock-kan-dahkoos 154
Esock-kan-dahkos 217
Esock-uck-bah-dah-pace 27
Esock-uck-bahda-pace 90
Esoc-uck-bahdah-pace 154,218
Esok-cawah-chakoos-say 98
Esook-cot-keh-deas..................32,95

E-sop-pah-dah-tus.............38,101,165
E-sop-pah-day-tus.........................228
Esop-pay-shoes...........39,102,166,229
Esop-pee-e-wishes.....52,115,178,241
Esop-ponta-chahada-dose......168,231
Esop-ponta-chahadadose 104
Esop-pontah-chayhaydaydose 41
Esop-pontouch-cheyhaydayus 10
Esop-pontuch-chehadaydus 202
Esop-pontuch-chehaydayus 138
Esoska-cheesday-kaybah 88
Esoskachesdakabachais 209
Esoska-cheseday-kabachachis 153
Esoskah-cheeseday kaybah chach chis
....25
E-sos-kah-we-sis.........43,106,170,233
Esos-kah-wishes 45,109,174,236
E-sos-kay-ate-chace................38,101
Esos-Kaybah-och-che-duc 220
Esos-kaybah-och-che-duc..........27,91
Esos-kaybah-och-che-due.............155
Esos-kay-it-chis 48,111,175,238
Esos-kay-koo-doot-chis.....34,97,161,
....225
Esos-kean-sos 165,228
Esos-keas-sos........................ 49,100
Esos-kee-dit-bachpash 171,234
Esos-kee-dit-bah-pash 44,107
E-sos-kot-bah-deas 35,162,226
Esos-kot-bah-deas......................... 98
Espeah-kishe-kahdeas............150,213
Espeah-kishekahdeas 85
Espeah-kis-she-kah-deas................22
Espea-kish-hiss........................29,92
Es-sos 47,110
Es-tay-cheas.............................42,106
E-step-aes................................... 70
E-step-ees 6,134,197
Es-tup-peas 119,183,246
Es-tup-poas................................... 56
Esuck-bon-tuch-chais ..28,92,156,219
Esuck-che-sah-keas-sos 161,224
Esukcha-meas............................... 12
Esukis 8,72,136,200
Esuklasa-eps-cheis.......................15
Esuktahsea-helae-nakuse................. 8
Esutsehoom-meas............. 16,102,166
Esutseom-meas............................229

Index

Etasch-daeka 210
Etashda-cheis 13,76,141,205
Etash-daka 19,82
Etash-dake 147
Etash-hishes 135,243
Etash-hishis 7,71
Etash-shooachat 15,78,143,207
Etoshday-bachpash 151,215
Etoshday-bah-pash 24,87
Eukase-hishes 69,133,197
Eukupae-wishdish 23
Eupe-pah-bah-put-tosh 108
Even 40,103,167,230
Everybody Knows Him 177,240
Everybody knows him 50,113
Everything is her 120
Everything is Here 184,247
Everything is hers 57
Eyes 41
Eyes Open 80,144,208
Eyes open 17

Face Toward the Mountain 169,231
Face toward the mountain 41,104
Falls Down Old 79,144
Falls down old 16
Falls Toward You 179,242
Falls toward you 52,116
Farwell
    Ella 12,75,140,204
    Rosebud 59,122,185,248
    Susan 59
Farwell-Glenn, Susan 248
Fat 29,92
Fat Snake 86,150,213
Fat snake 22
Fat Tobacco 74,139,203
Fat tobacco 11
Feather 49,112,176,238
Feather Neck 167,230
Feather neck 39,103
Female Wolf 163,226
Female wolf 36,99
Fights Alone 178,241
Fights alone 114
Fights along 51
Fights the Enemy Good 6,70,134,
 198

Fights Well Known 82,147
Fights well known 19,25,30,47
Fights Well Known #1 157,221
Fights Well Known #2 175,237
Fights well known #2 111
Fights well known No 1 93
Finds All 71,134,198
Finds all 7
Finds and kills them 106
Finds His Enemy 145,208
Finds his enemy 17,80
Finds Plain 62,189,252
Finds plain 125
Finds plenty things 57
Finds Soon 71,135,199
Finds soon 7
Finds Them and Kills Them .. 170,233
Finds them and kills them 43
Finds things well known 18
Finds Things With Her Horse 138,
 202
Finds things with her horse 10
Fire 35,99,163,226
Fire Bear 87,214
    Edison 87,180,242
Fire bear 23
Fire Deer 159,222
Fire deer 32
Fire Hat 190
Fire hat 63,126
Fire Squirrel 246
Fire Weasel 173,235
Fire weasel 45,109
Firs[sic] Bear 151
Fish Bird 76,140,204
Fish bird 12
Fish High Up 166,229
Fish high up 38,102
Five 63,126,189,252
Flat Back 75,139,203
Flat back 11
Flat Boy 82,146,210
Flat boy 19
Flat Dog 11,74,139,203
Flat Face 6,70,134,198
Flat Mouth 176
Flat mouth 49,112
Flathead Woman 138,201

Index

Geo... 10
   Lizzie 10,138,201
Flathead woman 10
Flower 56,119,183,245
Fog 48,112,176,238
Fog All the Time 163,226
Fog all the time 35,99
Fog in the Morning 154,217
Fog in the morning 26,90
Follows the Track.............. 85,149,213
Follows the track 21
Foolish Man 166,229
   George...................... 102,166,229
Foolish man 38,102
   George....................................... 38
Fools and Kills the Enemy 163,231
Fools and kills the enemy........... 35,99
Forehead, Eva 145,208
Found Things Well Known............ 81
Four Balls...................... 85,149,213
Four balls 22
Fox Goes Out 79,144,208
Fox goes out................................. 16
Fox Woman........................... 161,224
Fox woman 34,97
Frances 125
Francis Tiffany................. 90,156,219
Frost
   Daniel L. 61,124,187
   John............................. 61,124,187
   Daniel L. 250
   John.. 250
Froze 22,85,150,213
Full Mouth 83,148,211
Full mouth...................................... 20

G. Knife, Sarah 71,135,199
G. Luck, Matthew 136,200
Gaggigus[sic], Dorothy B. 59
Gardiner
   Amelia........................ 47,174,237
   Ben..................... 51,114,178,240
   Frank.......................... 47,174,237
   Mrs. Ben 47,174,237
   Thomas 47,110,174,237
Gardner
   Amelia.................................... 110
   Frank...................................... 110

   Mrs. Ben 110
Garrigus
   Arthur R..................... 59,122,186
   Dorothy B. 122,186
   Maggie................. 59,122,186,249
   Margaret E. 59,122,186,249
   Mary F. 59,122,186,249
   Arthur R.................................. 249
   Dorothy B. 249
Geisdorff
   Charlotte..................... 60,123,186
   Florence........................... 122,186
   Francis 122,186
   Frederick.................... 60,122,186
   Frederick, Jr..................... 123,186
   Louisa......................... 60,123,186
   Charlotte................................ 249
   Florence................................. 249
   Francis 249
   Frederick................................ 249
   Frederick, Jr........................... 249
   Louisa.................................... 249
Get One Horn 148,212
   Harry 148
Get their medicine tobacco 27
Gets Down........................ 73,181,244
   Thomas................................. 244
Gets down............................ 9,54,117
Gets Down Among Them....... 150,213
Gets down among them 22,85
Gets Down Often.................. 137,200
Gets Down Well Known........ 158,221
Gets down well known 30,93
Gets Hold of the Dead 136,199
Gets hold of the dead...................... 8
Gets Hold the Dead........................72
Gets One Horn................................84
   Harry 84
Gets one horn.................................20
Gets their medcn[sic] tobacco..........91
Gets Their Medicine Tobacco 155,218
Gets There First 151,214
Gets there first 23,86
Gets There Pretty 162,225
Gets there pretty 34,97
Ghost Bear............................ 175,238
Ghost bear............................. 48,111
Girl 54,117,180,243

290

Index

Gives Lots of Things Away ...169,232
Gives lots of things away 42,105
Gives things 28
~~Gives things~~ 92
Gives to the Sun 76,140
Gives to the sun............................... 13
Glenn
    Louisa Pearl 248
    Percival 122,185,248
    Susan Farwell............................185
    Susand[sic] Farwell...................122
Goes After Spotted Horse 156,219
Goes after spotted horse.............29,92
Goes Ahead.........78–79,142,144,178,
   206–207,241
Goes ahead......................7,15–16,114
Goes Ahead Everything 144
Goes Ahead Pretty ..163,173,180,190,
   223,226,253
    George... 63
Goes ahead Pretty, George............126
Goes ahead pretty.......35,45,53,63,99,
   108,116,126
Goes Among the Enemy 183,246
    Amos...................................183,246
Goes among the enemy 56,119
Goes Bird......................................164
Goes Farther Along................153,216
Goes farther along.......................25,89
Goes First.................... 161,165,224
Goes first................34,37,97,101
Goes hunting 26
Goes On 167,230
Goes on 40,103
Goes Pretty...........90,154,217–218
Goes pretty 13,27,43
Goes Through Her Enemies ...175,238
Goes through her enemies........48,111
Goes to Camp...................88,153,216
Goes to camp................................. 25
Goes to Fight..........................176,239
Goes to fight.............................49,112
Goes to Fight Enemies 180,243
Goes to fight enemies............53,116
Goes to Good Things 72,136,200
Goes to good things................... 8
Goes to Ground Every Day 175,253
Goes to ground every day 27,90

Goes to Look at Prisoners. 73,137,201
Goes to look at the prisoners 9
Goes to Mud Pretty........... 81,145,209
Goes to mud pretty 17
Goes to the Fort 170,232
Goes to the fort 42,106
Goes to the Horses................. 153,216
Goes to the horses....................25,88
Goes to the House.................. 177,253
Goes to the house................... 49,113
Goes to War........................... 138,202
Goes to war..................................... 10
Goes Together 87,151,161,215,224
    Jane............................... 87,151,215
    Wesley 24,87,151,215
Goes together...................... 23,33,97
goes together, Jane........................ 24
Goes Well 5,69,133,197
Goes with the wind................... 28,91
Going About 152,216
Going about 25,88
Good ...15,43,78,106,142,170,206,233
Good Bird..................... 5,69,133,197
Good bird................................... 36,99
Good Coos 158,221
Good coos............................... 30,94
Good ground.................................27
Good gun 51,114
Good Hearted Bird 92,156,219
Good hearted bird 29
Good Hearted Ground 157,234
Good hearted ground 29
Good Hoops................................ 159
Good Horses....................... 170,232
Good horses............................ 42,105
Good Leader 5,69,133,197
Good Luck 72,136,200
Good luck 8
Good Medicine 167,230
Good medicine............................. 103
Good Now 138,202
Good now 10
Good Owl 70,134,198
Good Sheep 71,135,199
Good sheep.................................... 7
Good Shell............... 85,181,244
Good shell................................ 22
Good to Prisoners 80,144,208

291

Index

Good to prisoners 16
Good Watch 155
Gooded-hearted ground 92
Goose Goes Over the Hill 159,222
Goose Goes over the hill 95
Goose goes over the hill 31
Gordon, Mrs. Frank 58,121,185,247
Got a Hoop 138,214
Got a hoop 10
Got a Nest 169,232
Got a nest 41,105
Got a Pipe 166,228
Got a pipe 38,101
Got a Shield 166,229
Got a shield 39,102
Got Many Enemies 167,229
Got many enemies 39,102
Got Plenty Beads 182,245
Got plenty beads 56,119
Got Pretty Things 166,229
Got pretty things 38,101
Grabs the Knife 176,239
Grabs the knife 49,112
Grandmother's Knife 71,135,199
Grandmothers knife 7
Grasshopper 25,88,152,216
Gray Bull 88
Green, Laura 57,120,184,246
Grey blanket 7
Grey Bull 25,113,152,176,216,239
    Augusta 176,239
Grey bull 49,112
grey bull, Augusta 49
Grey eyes 11,42,106
Grey Horse Chief 88,153,209
Grey horse chief 25
Grey Woman 80,145,208
Grey woman 17
Groans 9,73,137,201
Gros Ventre 7,9,19,73,82,88,137,
    152,201,216
Gros Ventre Horse 5,69,133,197
Gros Ventre Red Wom[an] Bird .. 159,
    222
Gros Ventre red woman bird 32,95
Ground Cedar 79,144
Ground cedar 16
Ground Squirrel 160,223

Ground squirrel 35,96
Gun
    Gun 119
    John P. 183
Gun Chief 169,232
Gun chief 42,105
Gun Shows 71,135,199
Gun shows 7

H. Everyway, Dorothy 49,112
Ha-dane-dah-cock-cus 46,109,236
Ha-dane-e-cupe-pis 50
Ha-dane-e-cush-chice 49,112,176,
    239
Hah-osh-ahoos 164
Hail 38,101,165,228
Hail Shows 79,144,207
Hail shows 16
Hairy 47,110,174,237
Hairy Moccasin 178,241
    Mary 52,115,179,241
Hairy moccasin 52,115
Hairy On Top of His Head 168,231
Hairy on top of his head 40,104
Hairy Wolf, Floy 152,216
Hairy Woman 94
Hairy woman 30
Half White 162,164,225,227
Half white 34,37,98,100
Halup-eahkots 15,79,143
Hard Heart 78,142,206
Hard heart 15
Hardy, Sylvester 58,121,185,248
Has Good Coos 75,139,203
Has good coos 11
Has Horses 170,174,233,236
Has horses 43,45,106,109
Has no mocascasin 101
Has No Moccasin 165,228
Has no moccasin 38
Has Things 169,232
Has things 105
Hasthings[sic] 63
Hat Above 160,223
Hat above 32,95
Hat Otter 172,234
Hat otter 44,108
Have Things 182,245

292

Index

Have things 55,118
Ha-wan-da-bachpash 177,239
Ha-wan-da-bah-pash 50,113
Ha-wash-tay-keas 53,116,179,242
Hawk, Dick 49,112,176,239
Hawkes
    Lucy 31,94
    Mrs. Wm. 31,94
Hawks
    Lucy 158,222
    Mrs. Wm. 158,222
Hay-dain-dec-chis 101
Hay-dain-dee-chis 38,165,228
Hay-dane-ah-seas 38,102,166,229
Hay-day-ach-days 158,221
Hay-day-co-days 31,94
Hay-day-dee-doos 34,97,161,224
Hay-day-de-qu-pish 22,85
Hayday-de-qu-pish 150,213
Hay-day-dose 43,106,170,233
Hay-day-tah-wah-sos 48,111,175,
    238
He Does It 173,236
He does it 46,109
He is a Man Now 169,232
He is a man now 42,105
He Knows His Coos 133,197
He knows His Coos 69
He knows his Coos 5
He Says 80,144,208
He says 17
Hears Everyway 176,238
Hears everyway 49,112
Hears Fire 24,87,152,215
Heckenlively
    Guy L. 60,123,187
    Howard C. 187
    Mrs. 60
    Mrs. Mary 123,187
    Guy L. 250
    Howard C. 250
    Mrs. Mary 250
He-dah-bah-chase 36,100,164,227
He-dah-wah-chace 42,105,169,232
Hederin-dichis 6,70,134,198
Heifer Woman 174,236
Heifer woman 46,109
Helekas-ash 14,78,142,206

Heles-basash 77
Heles-beasash 14
Heles-sheis 142,206
Helps the Whole Camp 168,230
Helps the whole camp 40,103
Henry 121
Her Horse Is Pretty 175,238
Her horse is pretty 48,111
Her Iron 91,155,218
Her iron 62
Her Medicine is Medicine 160,223
Her medicine is medicine 32,96
Her Medicine Shell 169,232
Her medicine shell 63,105
Her Road Is Plain 161,224
Her road is plain 33,97
Hesha-chea-makpash 5
Hides 48,111,175,238
High Arrow 78,143,206
High arrow 15
High Eagle 25,89,153,216
High Hawk, Julia 51,114,178,241
High Nest 126,190,253
Hill
    Amanda 246
    Anna 56,119,183,246
    George 56,119,183,246
    James 24,92,156,220
    Mary 56,119,183,246
    Mrs. George 56,119,183,246
    Pius 44,107,171,234
His Door 85,150
His door 22
His heels 34
His Medicine 160
His medicine 33,96
His Medicine Bird 155,218
His medicine bird 27
His Rock Is Medicine 178,241
His rock is medicine 51,114
His tail shows 30
His Work Is Good 175,239
His work is good 48,111
Hock-cuss 40
Hogan, George Washington 199
Hoksah-napis 13,77,141,205
Holds It in the Mouth 145,208
Holds it in the mouth 17,80

293

Index

Holds On 80,145,208
Holds on 17
Holds something 42
Holds the Enemy 182,244
Holds the enemy 55,118
holds the enemy, Robert................. 55
Holds the Feather 82,147,210
    Amanda....................................147
Holds the feather 19
Holds Up 71,135,199
Holds up 7
Holds Well Known................. 172,235
Holds well known 45,108
Hole.................... 45,104,168,231
Hoo-chan-dah......................... 28
Hoo-chan-das 91
Hooche-sash................ 13,76,141,205
Hoo-chice.................. 58,121,185,247
Hoo-chice-cos 233
Hoo-chice-soos 43,106
Hoo-chice-sos 170
Hoo-chis..................... 41,104,168,231
Hoop Goes a Long Way 173
Hoop goes a long way 46
Hoop goes a long ways 109
Hoop on the Forehead 86,150,214
Hoop on the forehead 23
Hoop That Moves 184,246
Hoop that moves 57,120
Hoop That Runs 176,238
Hoop that runs..................... 49,112
Hoop That Shows................... 180,242
Hoop that shows..................... 53,116
Hoop That Sings 176,238
Hoop that sings 48,112
Hoop Turns Around 188,251
    August................... 61,124,188,251
    Caroline....................................188
Hoop turns around................. 61,124
Hoop Woman 167,230
Hoop woman 39,102
Hoop-itsahkahoh 15,78,143,207
Horn, Monica 64,126,190
Horn Dropped Down............ 168,232
Horn dropped down 57,104
Horn on Her Neck 142,206
Horn on her neck................... 54,117
Horn Sits Down 5

Horn, Monica............................... 254
Horse 9,11,19,72–73,83,136–137,
    147,200–201,211
    Charlie 137,201
Horse bird............................... 12,115
Horse bull 39
Horse on the Other Side.......... 146,209
Horse on the other Side 81
Horse on the other side 18
Horse She Rides Well Known 144
Horse she rides well known..... 55,118
Horse Sits Down............................ 69
Horse sits down 133,252
Horse Stays all the Time... 73,137,201
Horse stays all the time.................... 9
Horse That Sings 153,217
Horse that sings 15
Horse Turns Around 76,141,205
Horse turns around 13
Horse Well Known 172,235
Horse well known........ 45,52,108,115
Horses goes in front...................... 17
Horses Place Well Known 165,228
Horses place well known 38,101
House
    Florida 217
    Iowa........................... 89,154,217
Howe, Robert S. 186,249
Hugs 46,50,109,113,177,239
Hugs #2 173,236
Hugs the Weasel............. 5,69,133,197
Hump Back........................... 142,206
Humpback 14,77
Humphrey
    Lillie 190
    Mary M................................. 126,190
    Mary Morrison 63
    Maud 63,126,190
    Lillie 253
    Mary M..................................... 253
    Maud 253
Hunts 38,101,165,228
Hunts the Arrow 69,133,205
    Joseph................................... 205
Hunts the Enemy 179,241
Hunts the enemy 52,115
Hunts the House 177,239
Hunts the house 50,113

Index

Hunts the Man 5
Hunts the Sioux 13,77,141,205
Hunts to Die 175,238
Hunts to die 48,111
Hunts to Lie Down 159,222
Hunts to lie down 31,95
Hunts to Slide 181,244
Hunts to slide 54,117
Hunts Toward the Mountains 155
Hunts toward the mountains 28,91

Iamina-wisha-doochis 136
Iamina-wishs-doochis 72
Icheat-ekash 23,86,151,214
Iche-kahnetsesh 13,76
Ichis 15,78,142,206
Ich-kahdeas 18
Ick-cup-pee-dee-dah-bis 54,117
Ick-cup-pee-dee-dah-bish 181,243
Ick-cush 37
Ick-kay-ah-hoos 34,97,161,224
Ika-ahoos 16,79,144,207
Ike-cook-cus 40,103,167,230
Ikpah-ahoos 23,86
Ikpahne-chas 141,204
Ikpahne-ehas 13,76
Ikpahne-ekash 21,84,149,212
Ikpahne-ich 11,75,139,203
Ikpahne-makpash 19,83,147,211
Ikpahne-maks 143
Ikpahn-e-naks 79
Ikpahne-naks 207
Ikpam-basash 10,202
Ikpanne-maks 15
Ikpay-ahoos 150,214
In the camp 64,126
Incuppah-bish-chedice 125,189,252
In-cup-pah-bish-de-chice 62
Inside the Mouth 79,143,207
Inside the mouth 16
Iron.... 15,18,81–82,146–147,209–210
Iron Fork 93,157,220
Iron fork 29
Iron Head 171,233
Iron head 47,110
Iron Horse 73,136,200
Iron horse 8
Iron Necklace 83,148,211

Iron necklace 20
Iron Wings 223
Is Sweet Now 171,234
Is sweet now 44,107
Is-ah-way-cone-dah-pase 39,103
Isbach-ichis 159
Isba-daha-wat-ate-chice 107
Isbada-ha-wat-atechice 171,234
Isbahcah-bah-duckiss 176,238
Is-bah-cah-bah-duck-kis 112
Is-bah-cah-kea-ahoos 56,183,252
Is-bah-cah-kea-shoos 120
Is-bah-cah-key-bat-pash 63
Isbahca-kay-bot-posh 169,232
Is-bah-ca-ke-ah-shees 29
Is-bah-ca-key-ah-shees 93
Isbah-ca-key-ah-shees 157,234
Isbahca-key-bot-posh 105
Is-bah-dah-ha-wat-ate-chice 44
Is-bah-dah-hoos 56,119,182,245
Is-bah-duck-chics 226
Is-bah-duck-chis 35,99,163
Is-bah-hum-be-shis 55,118,182,245
Is-bah-it-chis 38,166
Is-bahit-chis 101
Is-bah-it-chise 229
Is-bah-key-cush-sheas 61,124,188,
 251
Isba-ichis 9,73
Isba-itchis 137,201
Isbeda 73
Is-be-dah-eas 34,98,162,225
Isbedia 9
Is-bee-dean-bah-dup-pace 53
Isbeen-dah-chay-itchis 160,223
is-been-dah-chay-it-chis 33
Isbeen-daycha-itchis 96
Is-been-doch-ah-hoos 105,232
Isbeen-doch-baduck-kis 111
Is-been-dot-bish-eas... 39,102,166,229
Is-been-dotch-ah-hoos 41,169
Is-been-dotch-bah-duck-kis 47
Is-been-dotch-dee-chis 36
Is-been-dotch-dup-pickkish 35
Is-been-dotch-it-chis 40
Is-been-dotch-itchis 103,230
Isbeen-dotchpa-duckiss 175,237
Is-been-dutch-chis 167

Index

Isben-doch-dup-pichis............ 163,226
Isben-doch-dup-pichish................. 99
Isbiche-itchis-sayeacoktus.............108
Isbin-Doch-bachatechic................174
Isbindoch-bachatechice.................237
Isbin-dochca-chate-chis.................100
Isbin-doch-ebahick-deas 108
Is-bin-dot-bah-pash 61
Isbindotch-abahic-deas...........172,235
Isbindotch-bah-chate...............165,228
Is-bin-dotch-bah-chate-chis............. 37
Is-bin-dotch-ebahick-deas 45
Isbitche-itchice-sayeacocktus......... 45
Isbitch-ichis-secocktus 235
Isbitch-itchis-saeacocktus 172
Is-bon-dot-bachpash...............187,250
Is-bon-dot-bah-pash 124
Is-cah-ka-it-chice 116
Is-cah-ka-it-chis 53
Is-cah-kay-keas-sos 55,118,182,244
Isccechea-hay-dane-doctchis.......... 32
Iscehe-haydane-doochis....95,159,223
Is-chay-dah-kish-shay 170,233
Ischay-dah-kish-shay 106
Ische-ahay-ea-cot-tus 181,244
Ische-itse 12,76,140,204
Ischeka-it-chice 180,243
Ischesa-hela-amach 20,84,148,212
Is-che-shay-ea-cot-tus 55
Ische-shay-ea-cot-tus 118
Is-che-shay-esos 62
Is-chice-say-ah-wondabachis 50
Ischic-sayawondabachis................113
Is-chie-say-be-shis 41,169,232
Ischie-say-be-shis..........................105
Ischis-sayah-wondabachis......177,240
Is-chis-say-it-chis 30,93,157,221
Is-coa-chee-che-dish 179,241
Is-co-chee-ahoos 167
Iscoche-hadane-doochis..........164,227
Iscochehay-dane-doochis...............100
Iscoche-hayday-codays 246
Is-coe-ache-chea-chase 105
Is-coe-chea-ache-chase 41,169,244
Is-coe-chea-ah-hoos 39,229
Is-coe-chea-ahoos..........................102
Is-coe-chea-ate-chace.50,113,177,239
Iscoeche-a-bachea-days.................243

Is-coe-chea-docosh-ish 182,244
Iscoeche-ba-chea-days.................. 180
Is-coe-che-bah-chea-days 53
Is-coe-che-che-dish..... 46,52,109,173,
.... 236
Is-coe-chee-bachea-days............... 116
Is-coe-chee-che-dish..................... 115
Is-coe-chee-doe-cosh-ish 118
Is-coe-chee-dup-pace. 37,101,165,228
Iscoe-chehay-dane-dootchis 37
Iscoeche-hay-day-codays.............. 183
Iscoeche-hayday-codays 56
Is-coe-cheydoot-chis...................... 62
Is-cos-chea-doe-cosh-ish 55
Is-deam-day-keas-sos .. 33,97,161,224
Is-dotch-chea-ate-chase 48,111,175
Is-dotch-che-ate-chase 238
Isdots-ichis......................... 16,80,144
Isdots-itchis 208
Is-ea-dea-ah-hoos 35,99
Is-ea-de-ahoos........................ 163,226
Is-eap-che-bish-ay 38,101,166,228
Is-eepse-deesh.................. 10,138,202
Is-eepse-makpash-ichis................. 202
Isekoshe-noopis 16,80,144
Ise-meneas 22,85,150,213
Is-epse-makpash-ichis 11,139
Is-espe-makpash-ichis 74
Ishane-baduck-chadacock 219
Ishane-baduck-chadacuck 155
Ishane-badukchaydacock............... 91
Ish-bee-bachpash 178,241
Ish-bee-bah-pash..................... 51,114
Ish-bern-dotch-sheda 94,158,221
Ish-bern-dotch-she-dead 31
Ishbin-doch-ba-chatechice............ 110
Ish-bin-dotch-bah-chate-chice 47
Ish-chis-says-koos 34,97,161,225
Ish-co-chea-ha-day-dose................ 26
Ish-co-che-hayda-dose 153,216
Ish-cos 176,239
Ish-co-sheahaday-dose................... 89
Ishda-daka 11
Isheda 137,200
Ish-oos 49,112
Ishshane-bahduckchaydahcock........ 28
Ish-tay-ea-sos.................... 41,104,231
Ish-tay-easos................................. 168

Index

Ishtopish 17,80,144,208
Ismahka-wisha 10,138,214
Ismanat-heahsas 214
Ismant-heahsas 23,86,150
Isminats-budwasich 20,84,148,212
Isminats-ich 14–15,78,142,206
Isminats-itch 142
Isminats-makpash 16,80,182,245
Ismina-wisha-dochis 8
Ismina-wisha-doochis 200
Isminua-wish-napes 12,76
Isoeet-botseeh 21
Isokoshe-noopis 208
Isooeche-hayday-codays 119
Isooet-botseesh 84
Isooet-botsesh 149
Is-oo-what-tus 62,91,155,218
Isoskay-bachate-chis 148,212
Is-os-kay-bah-chate-chis 20
Isos-kaybah-chatechis 84
Issama-malapes 20,148,211
Issame-malapes 83
Is-shay-dus 40,104,168,231
Isshotse-mau-det 17
Is-shu-shudish 9,73,137
Issuc-cheysah-sheedish 63
Is-tah-dase-cheas 44,107,171,234
Is-tah-waz 41
Is-thay-dah-kish-shay 43
Istuckea-bah-chate-chice 169
Istuckey-bah-chate-chice 172,235
Is-tuck-kay-os-seas 49,112,143,206
Is-tuck-kea-bah-chatechice 42
Is-tuck-key-bah-chate-chice 45
Istuka-ahoos 11,74,139,202
Istuka-ahseesh 14
Istuka-akuse 10,138,202
Istuka-asees 7,71,135,199
Istuka-doochis 17,80,145,208
Istuka-hcasas 72
Istuka-heahsas 136
Istuka-heasas 8
Istuka-mahks 15,78,143,206
Istuka-makpash 10,74,138,199
Istuka-makula 15,79,143,207
Istuka-mulukis 21,84,149,212
Istuka-sa-here-dadush 7,71,135,198
Istuk-kea-bachata-chice 105

Istuk-keybah-chate-chice 108
Is-tuk-key-de-ditch 54,117,181,244
Isuc-cheydah-sheedish 126
Isuc-cheyday-sheedish 190,253
Iswahka-miotchedish 12,140,203
It chis 43
It s[sic] inside 32
It-chase-shay-dane-de-chase 48
It-chase-shay-danedechase 111
Itch-chit-chay-bah-pash 47
Itche-bah-duck-shis ... 55,118,182,245
Itche-kahnetsesh 141,204
It-chis 106,170,233
Itchis-chey-ay-ah-woos 163
Itchis-shaydane-dechase 175,237
It-chit-chae-ays 100
Itchit-chay-ah-bash-pash 116
Itchit-chay-bachpash 174,237
Itchit-chay-bah-pash 110
It-chit-chay-eas 32,96
It-chit-chea-ays 36,164,227
It-chit-che-ays 45,108
Itchit-che-ays 172,235
Itchit-chey-ah-bachpash 180,243
It-chit-chey-ah-bah-pash 53
Itchit-chey-ay-ah-woos 35
It-chit-chey-eas 160,223
Itch-oke-pish 32
Itch-okepish 95,160,223
It-schoc-daytah 149,213
Itshades 20,83,148,211
Itshe-mahkpash 213
Itshe-wahkpahs 22,85,150
It-shoc-daytay 21,85
Itshooaprich 85
Itshooaprsich 22,150,213
Itsuitsa-ichis 160,224
Itsup-educe 180,242
Itsup-eduse 23,87
It-tah-um-bit-dosh 12,76
It-tuch-bah-cha-chis ... 38,101,165,228
It-tuch-chis 29,92,156,219
It-tuch-ock-in-days 27
It-tut-bah-cheas 51,114,178
It-tut-bah-heas 241
It-tut-dah-cock-cus 42,105,232
It-tut-dahcock-cus 169
It-tut-doot-chice 52,177,240

Index

It-tutdoot-chice 114

Jackson
   Eliza 60,124,187
   Ellen 60,123,187
   John 60,123,187
   Julia 60,124,187
   Eliza 250
   Ellen 250
   John 250
   Julia 250
Jefferson
   Lillian 89,153,217
   Thomas 14,89,153,217
Jerked Meat 167,214
Jerked meat 39,103
Jones, Hon. W. A. 3
Jumps Over 160,223
Jumps over 32,96
Just a Man 164,227
Just a man 36,100

Kab-quah-ah-soos 50,113
Kadeas 24
Kahdeas 17,81,87,135,145,152,
   170,199,209,215
Kahdeasas 213
Kahdeeasas 22,85,150
Kahdeis 71
Kahdeish 7,9
Kah-disc 43,106
Kah-kay-de-chis 51,114,178
Kah-key-de-chis 241
Kahkootsa 15,78,143,207
Kahnista 17,81,145,209
Kah-quah-ah-soos 177,240
Kah-wish 50,113,177,240
Kahwookose 79
Karooshis-eaahas 142
Karooshis-eahas 206
Karooshis-ehas 14,77
Kat-toah-tay-hishes 171,234
Keasha 86,151,214
Kea-sos 30,93
Keas-sos 35,99,163,226
Kee-osh 17,80,144,208
Keiser
   Frank 58,121,185,248

Mrs. Henry 58,121,185,231
Myrtle 58,121,185,248
Kent
   Elizabeth 59,122,186,248
   Josephine 59,122,186
   Maggie 59,122,186,248
   Mrs. Thomas 59,122,186,248
Kent-Williams, Josephine 248
Kill plenty 109
Kills a Horse 173,236
Kills a horse 46,109
Kills a Strong Man 178,241
Kills a strong man 51,114
Kills Across the Water 178,241
Kills across the water 51,114
Kills at Night 161,181,224,244
Kills at night 34,54,97,117
Kills at the Door 73,137,200
Kills at the door 9
Kills Behind Camp 84
Kills behind camp 20
Kills Beside Camp 182,245
Kills beside camp 56,119
Kills by the Woods 146,209
Kills by the woods 18,81
Kills Close 6,70,134,198
Kills close 10
Kills Close to Camp 152,215
Kills close to camp 24,87
Kills Coming to the Birds 163,226
Kills coming to the birds 36,99
Kills First 73,137,201
Kills first 9
Kills five men 20
Kills Good 160,223
Kills good 33,96
Kills Her Enemy 165,228
Kills her enemy 37,101
Kills In Camp 189
Kills in camp 11,125
Kills in Rear of House 155
Kills in rear of House 218
Kills in rear of house 90
Kills in Sleep 166,229
Kills in sleep 39,102
Kills in the door 53
Kills In the Morning 166,229
Kills in the morning 38,102

298

Index

Kills in the rear of the house 27
Kills in the Track 83,148,211
Kills in the track........................... 20
Kills many man 104
Kills Many Men 168,231
Kills many men 41
Kills on her ground 103
Kills on Her Own Ground 148,211
Kills on her own Ground................ 83
Kills on her own ground.............20,39
Kills on the Lookout 151,214
Kills on the lookout...................23,86
Kills On Top 167,230
Kills on top................................39,103
Kills One Man..... 77,142,162,206,225
Kills one man 14,34,97
Kills One Takes Two Guns 144,208
Kills one that takes 2 guns 98
Kills one that takes two guns........... 35
Kills One With Medcn Pipe ...142,206
Kills One With Red Blanket 70,198
Kills one with red blanket 6
Kills One With Red Blankt[sic] 136
Kills one with the big knee............. 64
Kills Over Beyond Other 162,225
Kills over beyond the other 13,98
Kills Picking Berries 138,201
Kills picking berries 9
Kills Plenty 173,236
Kills plenty.................................... 46
Kills Pretty Ones 72,136,200
Kills pretty ones 7
Kills right along 49
Kills Six Men 158,221
Kills six men 31,94
Kills The Chief..............................168
Kills the Chief................................231
Kills the chief............................40,104
Kills the one with med. pipe 14
Kills the Same Day 167,230
Kills the same day....................40,103
Kills the Woman 73,137
Kills the Young Man............156,219
Kills the young man 29,92
Kills Three Men 76,140,204
Kills three men 13
Kills Together 177,240
Kills together............................50,113

Kills Twice 77,84,141,164,173,
.... 205,227,236
Kills twice.................... 14,21,46,109
Kills two men 30
Kills Well Known... 155,158,165,218,
....221
Kills well known.. 27,31,38,90,94,101
Kills wih[sic] Medicine Pipe 78
Kills With a Scalp........................ 76
Kills with a scalp 12
Kills With Her Brother 154,218
Kills with her brother................27,90
Kills With Her Horse 251
Kills With Her Husband 154,217
Kills with her husband 26,89
Kills With His Bro-in-law 172,235
Kills with his bro-in-law.......... 44,108
Kills With the Horses 173,235
Kills with the horses 45,109
Kish-sey 35,99,163,226
Knot Between the Eyes.......... 170,233
Knot between the eyes............ 43,106
Known to Kill....................... 178,240
Known to kill........................... 51,114
Knows...23,25,86,89,150,153,214,216
  Sarah.................. 23,86,151,214
Knows a Horse 81,146,209
Knows a horse 18
Knows Everything 88,153,200
  Anson 153,201
Knows everything............................25
Knows Her Enemy 177,239
Knows her enemy 50,113
Knows Her Hat...................... 172,235
Knows her hat....................... 45,108
Knows Her Luck................... 157,220
Knows her luck........................ 30,93
Knows Her Medicine............. 165,228
Knows her medicine 38,101
Knows Her Mother................ 176,238
Knows her mother 49,112
Knows Her Prisoners............. 175,238
Knows her prisoners 48,111
Knows His Horse...... 86,150,165,213,
.... 228
Knows his horse 22,38,101
Knows the Enemy................. 169,244
Knows the enemy 41,105

Index

Knows the Ground 73,137,168,
.... 182,201,231,245
    Perces 182
    Perses 245
Knows the ground 9,41,55,104,118
knows the Ground, Perces 118
knows the ground
    Lou 55
    Perces 55
Knows the Gun 138,202
Knows the gun 10
Knows the Road .. 83,148,172,205,211
Knows the road 20,44,107
Knows the Sweat House 73,136
Knows the Sweathouse 200
Knows the sweathouse 8
Knows the War 82,147,210
Knows the war 19
Knows the Whole Camp 150,214
Knows the whole camp 23,86
Knows the Yearling 171,234
Knows the yearling 44,107
Knows to steal on camp 36
Knows What She Rides 238
Knows What To Do 183,245
Knows what to do 56,119
Knows Where He Finds Things ... 167,
.... 230
Knows where he finds things ... 39,103
Knows Where She Stops 158,221
Knows where she stops 35,99
Knows Where the Bear Goes 172,
.... 235
Knows where the bear goes 45,108
Koasha 23
Ko-kah-sish 31,94
Kookomish 75,140,203
Kookoomish 12
Kosta, Arnold 43,107,171,234
Kotseish 18,81,146,209
Kowees 18,81,146
Kuch-key-con-dah-das 92
Kuch-key-con-dah-eas 156
Kuck-key-con-dah-das 29,219

L. Ear, Estella 209
L. Ground, McKinley 89,153,217
L. Hand, Peter 70,134,198

Laforge
    Francis 126,190
    James 63,126,190
    Mary 55,118,181,244
    Mrs. Thomas 58,121
    Mrs. Thos. 185,247
    Rosa 58,121,185,247
    Thomas Asa 58,121,185,247
    Tom 23,86,151,214
    William 63,126,190
    Francis 253
    James 253
    William 253
Lagaka-akuse 16,79,144,207
Lagaka-hishes 5,133
Lagak-beepish 21,84,134,198
Lagak-cheah-noops 19,82,147,210
Lagak-deedes 10,138,202
Lagak-esash 5,69,133,197
Lagak-etashdesh 76,140,204
Lagak-heahsas ... 6,70,86,150,198,214
lagak-heahsas 23
Lagak-heasas 8
Lagak-heases 72
Lagak-heshsas 136,200
Lagak-hishes 5,69,133
Lagak-hishis 197,204
Lagak-iche 5
Lagak-iches 197
Lagak-itches 133
Lagak-mee-da-ses 5,133,197
Lagak-mes-da-ses 69
Lagak-naks 20,89,153,217
Lagaks-ichis 69
Lagek-tee-cha-ditch 242
Lagk-heahsas 134
Lande
    Abbie 59,122,186
    Henry D. 186
    Henry Dewey 59,122
    Thomas A 122
    Thomas A. 59,186
    Abbie 249
    George A. 249
    Henry D. 249
Last Buffalo 71
Last buffalo 7
Last Bull, Mary 9,73

Index

Leads a Wolf 83,148,211
Leads a wolf 20
Leads the Camp Pretty 170,233
Leads the camp pretty 43,106
Lean Man 94,158,222
Lean man 31
Left Hand 6,70,134,198
Leider
    Agnes 32,159,222
    Carl 32,159,222
    Carl, Jr. 222
    Hugh 31,159,222
Leighton, William 58,121
Lieder
    Agnes 95
    Carl 95
    Hugh 95
Lies In Bed With a Man 179,242
Lies in bed with a man 52,115
Light Colored Man 184,246
Light colored man 56,120
Light Shield 163,226
Light shield 35,99
Like a Beaver 71,135,199
Like a beaver 53
Like a Fire 170,233
Like a fire 43,106
Like the summer 109
Likes her medicine 18
Likes the Horses 169,232
Likes the horses 41,105
Likes the Summer 174
Likes the summer 46
Lion That Shows 177,240
Lion that shows 50,113
Little 46,109,173,236
Little Antelope 5,69,133,197
Little Bear 74,139,203
    Edward 74,147,210
Little bear 11
Little Beaver 94,158,221
Little beaver 30
Little Colt 94,158,221
Little colt 31
Little Coyote 183,246
Little coyote 56,119
Little face 18
Little Fire 225

Little fire 34,98
Little Firs[sic] 162
Little Iron 164,227
Little iron 36,100
Little Light 161,225
    Becker 97,162,225
Little light 34,97
Little Moon 182,245
Little moon 11,118
Little Nest 181,244
    Mary 55,118,181,244
Little nest 55,118
Little Owl 181,244
    Laura 117,181,232
Little owl 54,117
Little Prairie Chicken 75,140,204
Little prairie chicken 12
Little Shield 158,221
Little shield 30,93
Little Swallow 175,237
Little swallow 48,111
Little Whetstone 172,235
Little whetstone 45,108
Little wolf 19,38,101
Little Wolf #2 147,210
Little Wolf No. 2 82
Live High 184
Lives Everywhere 175,238
Lives High 246
Lives high 57,120
Lizard That Walks 149,213
Lizard that walks 22
Lone Tree 161,224
Lone tree 34,97
Long Bear 79,144
    Horace 16,79,144,208
Long bear 16
Long Ear
    Ben 13,76,145,209
    Edith 188,251
    Herbert 13,76
Long Feather 73,137,200
Long feather 9
Long Gun 172,235
Long gun 45,108
Long Medicine Tobacco 140,204
Long Neck 87,95,152,159,215,222
Long neck 24,31

Index

Long Nose..........................88,152,216
Long nose..25
Long Otter..............................79,144
Long otter..16
Long Piegan 37,100,164,228
Long Tail...............................165,228
    Lydia........................101,165,228
Long tail....................................37,101
Long Way Off..........................71,199
Long way off............................7,135
Long Weasel 80,139,203
Long weasel 17
Long Woman 87,151,181,214,243
Long woman 23,54,117
Looks at her medicine 32
Looks at Her Mother..............182,245
Looks at her mother 55,118
Looks at him 63
Looks at One Comes frm[sic] war 153
Looks at one comes frm[sic] war ...89
Looks at One Comes From War....217
Looks at one comes from war 26
Looks at One that Kills 147,210
Looks at the Beads 179,241
Looks at the beads....................52,115
Looks at the Bear 71,135,199
Looks at the Fox...................92,156,219
Looks at the fox 28
Looks at the Ground..........89,153,217
Looks at the ground........................26
Looks at the Lion 77,142,206
Looks at the lion.............................14
Looks at the Lodge............75,140,204
Looks at the lodge..........................12
Looks at the Medicine......84,149,171,
....212,234
Looks at the medicine 21,44,107
Looks at the one that Kills 82
Looks at the one that kills 19
Looks at the shield.....................36,99
Looks at the Sun........154,160,217,223
Looks at the sun 17,33,89,96
Looks at the Tobacco 149,151,214
Looks at the tobacco 21
Looks at the Water ...156,174,219,237
Looks at the water..........28,47,91,110
Looks at Tobacco 86
Looks at tobacco 23

Looks Back........................... 189,252
Looks back 62,125
Looks Much......................... 77,141
Looks much 13
Looks to the Shield................ 163,227
Looks With His Ears............. 181,244
Looks with his ears.................. 54,117
Lots of Stars........ 79,144,161,207,224
Lots of stars 16,34,97
Louise....................... 40,103,167,230
Loves to Fight....................... 190,239
Loves to fight......................... 63,126
Loves to go after Water 71
Loves to go after water 7
Loves to Run 73,137,201
Loves to run.................................... 9
Lucky Hoop..................... 75,140,203
Lucky hoop.................................... 12
Lucky Horse 155,220
Lucky horse 27,91
Lukpa-sashis................. 9,73,137,201

Macer
    Edward 185
    Edwards[sic]............................ 248
    Henry........................... 58,185,248
    Mabel................... 58,121,185,248
    Mrs. Maggie K. 185,248
    Mrs. Maggie Keiser............ 58,121
Mad at the Bear 166,228
Mad at the bear...................... 38,101
Mad Bear Wolf...................... 169,232
Mad bear wolf......................... 42,105
Magpie Sits Down 165
Magpie sits down................... 37,101
Mahaha-hotchkish 200
Mahaha-hotskish........................... 137
Mahahchis-lukish-dish........... 137,201
Mahake-nahke 139,202
Mahama-nudeis 74
Mahedish 21,84,149,212
Maheede-speedis 85
Mah-hahchis-lukish-dish 9
Mah-hahchis-lukishdish................. 73
Mah-hahk-ichis............. 22,85,150,213
Mahhake-nahks....................... 11,74
Mahkaristish 7,71,135,199
Mahkawas................. 12,75,140,204

302

Index

Mahkeeda-sheedish 149,213
Mahkeede-speedis 21
Mahkesh 18
Mahma-nudeis 11,147,210
Mahpak-hoos 7,71,135,199
Mahpay-e-kahsh 22,85
Mahpay-e-kash 150,213
Mahpookta-botsots 11,139
Mahpootka-botsots 203
Mahray-keir-ahpis 85
Mahray-keir-ahplis 22,150,213
Mahsha-hishes-heahsas 20,83,148
Mahsha-hotskish 9,73
Mahsha-ich-meas 19,82,146,210
Mahsha-kudesh 19,82,147,210
Mahsha-undichis 19,82,147,210
Mahsha-wots 9,73,137,201
Mahsheandachee 17
Mahshedah-kotish 77,142
Mahsheda-kotish 205
Mah-shoe 57
Mahshooooshshesh[sic] 18
Mahshooshshesh 81,145
Mah-soe 120,184,246
Makapo-ich 23,87,151,215
Makes a Pretty Lodge 167,230
Makes a pretty lodge 40,103
Makes himself old 18
Makpash-ekash 18
Makpash-heahsas 13,76,141,204
Makpash-ne-ahoos 207
Makpash-ope-ahoos 13,76,141,204
Makpootka-botsots 74
Makuka-ich 15
Makula-ich 78,206
Makula-itch 142
Makula-wood-dichis 214
Makula-woof-dichis 23,86,151
Makupa-Seech 79
Makupa-seesh 16,144,207
Malapa 10,138,202
Male Bear 177,239
Male bear 50,113
male bear, Charles 50
Malpa 74
Man With a Beard 189,252
Man with a beard 63,125
Mannahpesh 202

Many Prisoners 155,218
Many prisoners 27,91
Many Talks With Him 74,139,203
Many talks with him 30
Mare 54,117,181,243
Marshall, Mrs. 61,124,188,251
Martinez, Joseph 25,88,152,216
Masha-hishes-heahsas 211
Masheandache 80,145,208
Masheda-kotish 14
Mashoditsche-heahsas 146
Mashoditschitse-heahsas 81
Maudut-kudesh 19,82,147,210
Mden[Medicine] Ties Knot On Her
    Head 178,240
Meacahcha-ahoos 201
Mea-chedupa 74
Mea-chedups 139
Mea-cheedups 203
Mea-daka 5,17,69,80,133,145,197,
    208
Mea-dichis 163
Meadow Lark Stays 215
Meah-chedups 11
Mea-heahsas 204
Meah-kots 15,78,142,206
MEa-hotchkis 245
Mea-hotchkis 16,80,182
Mea-ichis 135,199
Mea-itchis 144,208
Mea-kahdeas 151,214
Meakot-kowees 8,72,135,199
Mea-kowees 160,224
Mea-makpash 8,73,137,201
Mea-nakose-hahks 78
Mea-nakose-nahks 15,143,207
Mean-dichis 8,70,73,134,198
Mean-ditches 137
Mean-ditchis 200
Mear-pish 73
Mea-schpittash 228
Mea-sheedes 12,91
Mea-she-pit-tay 178
Mea-shepittay 241
Mea-shpittish 16
Mea-spittish 80
Mea-suppittish 164
Medesha-dooch 23,86,150,214

303

Index

Medicine .... 27,34,39,62,90,98,102, ... 125,154,162,166,188,218,225
Medicine Arrow 74,138,199
Medicine arrow 10
Medicine Bear 161,224
Medicine bear 33,97
Medicine Boy 149,213
Medicine boy 21,85
Medicine Breath 156,219
Medicine breath 29,92
Medicine brings things 62
Medicine Buffalo 159,222
Medicine Buffalo Cow 87,151,215
Medicine buffalo cow 24
Medicine Calf 74,139,203
Medicine calf 11
Medicine Coyote 73,137,205
Medicine coyote 9
Medicine Crow 90,154,218
    Chester 90,154,218
Medicine crow 27
Medicine Dance 189
Medicine dance 52,115
Medicine Dance 252
Medicine Dress 87,151,215
Medicine dress 24
Medicine Eagle 83,148,211
Medicine eagle 20
Medicine Feather 168,231
Medicine feather 41,104
Medicine Form 167
Medicine form 39,103
Medicine Goes 179,242
Medicine goes 53,116
Medicine Ground Cedar 171
Medicine ground cedar 36,107
Medicine Heifer 176,239
Medicine heifer 49,112
Medicine High Up 79,143,207
Medicine high up 15
Medicine Hole 5
Medicine Horse 87,151,215
Medicine horse 24
Medicine Horses 159,222
Medicine horses 31,95
Medicine Horsewhip 171,234
Medicine horsewhip 44,107
Medicine Knife 161,224

Medicine knife 33,97
Medicine Lance 163,226
Medicine lance 35,98
Medicine Lark 182,244
Medicine Mane 182,245
    Cora 182
Medicine mane 55,118
Medicine Nest 158,222
Medicine nest 31,94
Medicine Old Woman 163,226
Medicine old woman 35,99
Medicine Otter 72,136,200
Medicine otter 8
Medicine Paint 177,240
Medicine paint 50,113
Medicine Porcupine 82–83,147,210–211
Medicine porcupine 19
Medicine Rock 164,173,227,236
Medicine rock 37,46,100,109
Medicine Rock Above ..... 76,141,173, ... 204,236
    Josh 173
Medicine rock above 13,46,109
Medicine Rock Bird 6,70,134,198
Medicine Rock In Front 179,242
Medicine rock in front 52,115
Medicine Rock Necklace 159,222
Medicine rock necklace 32,95
Medicine Shell .... 78,143,147,180, ... 206–207,211,242
Medicine shell 15,22,53,62,116
Medicine Shell Bird 79,144,208
Medicine shell bird 16
Medicine Shield .. 80,182,187,245,250
Medicine shield 16,61,124
Medicine Shows 180,240
Medicine shows 53,116
Medicine Slides 179,242
Medicine slides 52,116
Medicine Sweet Camp 228
Medicine Tail .... 6,70,85,134,150,198, ... 213
    Kittie 12,75,140,203
Medicine tail 22
Medicine ties a knot on her head 51
Medicine Tobacco .. 172,174,180,235, ... 237,243
Medicine tobacco... 45,47,53,108,110,

Index

....116
Medicine Tobacco Seed 163
Medicine tobacco seed 35
Medicine Top 169,232
Medicine top 42,105
Medicine Turtle 183,246
Medicine turtle 56,119
Medicine Water 6,70,134,198
Medicine Weasel........................... 92
Medicine weasel........................... 28
Medicine Where She Stops 173,235
Medicine where she stops 45,109
Medicine White Buffalo......5,133,197
Medicine Wife 176,239
Medicine wife 49,112
Medicine Wolf 160,223
Medicine wolf 32,96
Medicine Woman.......73,137,181,201,
....244
Medicine woman...................8,54,117
Medicine wood............................. 56
Medicine 251
Medicne[sic] White Buffalo........... 69
Medon [Medicine] ties a knot on her
  head 114
Meeah-kadius............................... 86
Meeahkadius 23
Me-heahsas 12,75,140
Me-ichis....................................... 72
me-ichis... 8
Mei-rauk-shay 11,75,139,203
Mekahshay-hishis................22,86,150
Mekas-beasas 204
Mekas-besas 12,75,140
Mekaspe-doochis 84,149,212
Mekayshay-hishis.......................213
Mekeaespe-doochis........................ 21
Me-makpash-ehas 9,138
Me-makpash-ehos 201
Me-Makpesh-ehas....................... 74
Mena-ahwotkot 6,70
Menacheis.................23,86,151,214
Menarahwetket.........................134
Menar-ahwetkot 198
Menash-kopskis-chedish 77
Meneash-koop-skuis 6,70
Meneash-koopskuis-chedish 13
Meneas-koop-shuis 198

Meneas-koop-skuis.....................134
Meneas-kooskuis-chedish...... 141,205
Meshak-naks...........................15,79
Meshodechitse 15,78,143,206
Meshodechitse-lagaks.................. 16
Meshodechitse-nishes....................22
Meshodelhitse-wahkpahs...............22
Meshodelitse-wakpahs 116
Meshodichitse-lagaks 144
Meshodischitse-dichis 81
Meshoditchse-nishes.......................85
Meshodithitse-lagaks 79
Meshoditsche-hishes.............. 149,213
Meshoditsche-wakpahs 211
Meshoditse-wakpahs 147
Meshoditshe-lagak......................208
Meshoritshe-heahsas...................209
Mes-sheadish 155
Miah-hoo-ted-deas......... 7,71,135,243
Miastacheda-karoos 70,134
Miastacheda-meas 135
Miastacheeda-meas.....................199
Miastascheda-meas.......................71
Miastasheda-karoos 6
Miastasheda-meas...........................7
Miastasheeda-karoos 198
Micha-ahcheis-botots.................... 70
Micha-ahcheis-botsots........ 6,134,198
Mida-ichsis 5,69
Mida-itches 133,197
Mideras-ichis 9,105,169,232
Midesha-doochis.............. 8,72,136,199
Miedershase 9
Mieep-hukis....................................6
Mientahtasahederimithpal.................7
Mi-iche-doochis........... 6,14,70,77,134,
....142,198,205
Mi-iche-kooshdase 8,136,200
Mi-iche-kooshdess....................... 72
Mi-iche-okepis............. 17,80,145,208
Mi-iche-ose............................. 7,135,243
Mi-ich-napes 7,72,136,200
Mi-ich-ose 71
Milliken
   Claude....................................191
   John Wesley 191
   Leroy 191
   Mrs. Rosa 191

305

Index

Claude 254
John Wesley 254
Leroy 254
Mrs. Rosa 254
Minduksa-ekuroos 19,82
Mindukse-ekuroos 147,210
Minekashe-ahoos 17,81,145
Minetotse-ish-ekash 17,89
Minhapesh 74
Mink 34,97,161,224
Minkuus 9,105,169
Minmahpesh 19,82
Min-makpash 6,70,134,198
Minmakpash 146
Minnahpesh 10,139
Minnahpesh-ahoos 77
Minnahpesh-shoos 14
Minnakpash 210
Minna-nahkuse 8,72,136,200
Minnapesh-ahoos 142,206
Minnay-e-koos-chis 22,85,150,213
Minneah-pesh 14
Minne-ekoshees 36,99,163,226
Minnekashe-ahoos 209
Minne-koshis 80,145,208
Minnepahk-ichis 13
Minnepahkichis 145,209
Minnepak-ichis 76
Minnesh-pesh 77,141,205
Minnetotseesh 144,208
Minnetotse-ish-ekash 154,217
Minnetseesh 80
Minnettseesh 16
Minooisa-kahdius 23
Minooksa-kahdius 86
Minooksha-kahdeas 151,214
Mint 57,120,184,246
Mintahsehederemitpal 198
Mintahsehederimitpal 71,134
Miooetsheda-esash 139,203
Miooetshede-esash 11
Miootsheda-esash 74
Misakohn-miches 7,71,135
Misakohn-michis 199
Misdershase 137,201
Mishodechitse-lagak 6,70,134,198
Mishodeschitse-dichis 18
Mishodischitse-dichis 146

Mishoditsche-dichis 209
Misk-sheis 14,77
Misk-sheiss 142,206
Mitet-duspis 11,75
Mitot-duspis 159,222
Mixes strong 29
Moccasin, William 207
Momonots-heahsas 10
Money-kahdish 224
Mononots-heahsas 138,201
More of Them 170,232
More of them 42,105
Morning 30,93
John 26,90,154,217
Ruth 26,90,154,218
Morrison
Alvin 59,122,186,248
Hannah 59,122,186,248
Mrs. Al 59
Mrs. Al. 122,186,248
Mountain, Irene 75,140
mountain, Irene 12
Mountain Bird 174,237
Mountain bird 47,110
Mountain Bull 190,253
Mountain bull 63,126
Mountain Pocket 171
Mountain pocket 44,107
Mountain Sheep 92,156,219
Mountain sheep 28
Mountain That Shows 176,223
Mountain that shows 49,112
Mountian Pocket 234
Muche-dais 72
Muche-deis 8,136,200
Mud 33,96
Mumasen dichis[sic] 23
Mumasen-dichis 86,151,214
Munash-malapes 146,209
Muna-shuis 8,72,135,199
Munask-malapes 18,81
Mune-skoop-doochis ... 17,80,145,208
Muskrat 7,16,29,71,79,92,135,
.... 144,156,199,208,220
Muskrat Daughter 177,240
Muskrat daughter 50,113
Mussick-awats 23,86,150,214

306

Index

Nah-kaps 11,75,139,203
Nahkose-chedup.........................6,70
Nahkose-cheedup..................134,198
Nahmis..................................22,85,213
Nahsah-tays..................................206
Nahsa-tays................................14,77,142
Nahshada-esash.............................. 83
Nakas-makpash 70,134,198
Nakose-nahks...............16,79,143,207
Nak-paka-ish.................17,81,145,209
Naksha-undichis...........20,83,148,211
Naks-makpash..................................... 6
Nalmis...149
Napes-ekash...................19,82,147,210
Napk-ahwot-nee 'as[sic]................. 23
Napk-ahwot-nee-as 86,150,214
Nas-chas..................................... 13
Nas-ehas........................111,175,238
Nashada-esash.............................. 20
Nash-kose.................................... 10
Nash-kosh.....................................138
Nas-kowees...................5,69,133,197
Natsaundooch..........................23,87
Nearly Gone...........................156,219
Nearly gone...............................28,92
Nest......................5,69,133,197
No Hair on His Tail........................159
No hair on his tail.......................31,95
No Horse 5,69,133,197
 Gretchen........................69,133,197
No Medicine.............................161,224
No medicine.............................33,97
No Milk.......................111,175,238
No milk 48
No Mud............................165,228
No mud 37,101
No Name............95,153,159,168,217,
....223,231
No name..............26,32,40,89,103
No revenge............................ 23
No shin bone 21
No Shinbone....................85,149,213
Nobody Fights Them 138,202
Nobody fights them........................ 10
Noopa-malapes 14,77,141,205
Noop-dichis...................18,81,145,209
Noopis....................22,85,150,213
Noopta-cheis............................. 13

Nooptah-dichis 9,73
Nooptah-ditchis 137,201
Noopta-malapes........... 21,84,164,227
Nosh-kosh................................... 202
Not a Pretty Woman 162,177,225,
.... 235
Not a pretty woman 34,51,98,114
Not Afraid........................ 85,150,213
 George........................ 86,150,213
Not afraid.. 22
Not Afraid of a Bird............... 172,234
Not afraid of a bird 44
Not afraid of bird 107
Not Old............................. 85,150,213
Not old... 22
Notch 51,114,178,240

O' Brien, Michael........................ 79
O'Brien, Michael........................ 144
Oak-cah-sis 44,172,220
Oak-cha-sis 108
Oatah-ich 24,151,215
Oat-bay-bea-dosh 109
Oat-cheam-bah-dup-pace............ 224
Oat-chean-bah-dup-pace....... 34,54,97,
.... 117,161,181,244
Oat-cheas-du-dish 64
Oat-chees-du-dish............ 126,190,253
Oat-say-bee-dosh 173
Oatsaybee-dosh............................ 235
Oat-tay-bee-dosh 45
Oat-tay-dock-cuss 36,99
Oat-tay-dock-kuss................. 163,226
O'Brien, Michael........................... 16
Ochis-dichis................... 10,138,202
Ock-bish-cus................................ 112
Ock-cheas 30,93,157
Ock-che-dup-pice 175,238
Ock-che-dup-pish 178,240
Ock-cheis 220
Ock-e-hosh 177,240
Ock-kosh-de-dish 34,98,162,225
Ock-pay-hishis........................ 163,226
Ock-pay-hiss-siss......................... 36
Oct-tah-seas 181,243
Odup-dah-pace 43,106,170,233
Oeta-echeta................... 8,73,136,200
Oet-budekesh-hele-nakuse........ 135

Index

Oet-budekesh-helenakuse 199
Off Shield................................161,224
Off shield 33,96
Oka-push...110
Oke-keas-sos...............36,100,164,227
Oke-push...............................47,174,237
Old 7,9,17,24,71,81,87,135,
.... 145,152,199,209,215
Old All the Time, Susie................ 79
Old all the Time 79,143,207
    Susie... 15
Old all the time................................ 15
Old Alligator.....................86,151,214
Old alligator 23
Old Bear..........................79,144,207
Old bear.. 16
Old Bear Woman 181,244
Old bear woman.....................55,118
Old Beaver 91,155,183,219,245
Old beaver............................28,54,119
Old bird 37
Old Bird Woman....................167,230
Old bird woman 40,103
Old Bobcat 85,150,213
Old bobcat... 22
Old Bull......................61,124,188,251
Old Coyote 162,225
Old coyote....................................34,98
Old Crane 75,140,204
Old crane... 12
Old Crow...........................7,71,134,198
Old Dog..............................75,140,204
    Harry 75,140,203
Old dog 12
old dog, Harry 12
Old Elk.....................................175,237
    Mary....................48,111,175,238
Old elk 48,111
Old Horn 6,70,134,182,198,244
    Clarence 182,245
    Fred 55,118,182,244
    Lucy 55,118,182,244
    Susie..........................55,118,182,245
Old horn 55,118
Old Horse........................96,160,224
Old horse.. 33
Old Lodge Pole 175,238
Old lodge pole.........................48,111

Old Medicine Tobacco 181,244
Old medicine tobacco 54,117
Old Money.............................. 181,244
Old money 54,118
Old Mouse 95
Old mouse.................................... 32
Old Nest....................... 71,135,199
Old nest 7
Old Otter............................... 169,232
Old otter................................. 42,105
Old Rabbit 162,225
    Mary 34,162,225
Old rabbit............................... 34,98
Old rabbit woman 39
~~Old rabbit woman~~ 102
Old Rabitt, Mary............................98
Old Shield............... 78,142,206
Old shield 14
Old sweat house............................ 62
Old Sweathouse 189,251
Old sweathouse............................ 125
Old Tail 80,145,208
Old tail.. 17
Old Tobacco 120,160,184,224,246
Old tobacco.......................... 33,57,96
Old Weasel Woman....................... 236
Old white man 36,55,100,118
Old White Man #1 164,227
Old White Man #2 182,245
Old wolf.. 32
Old Woman 86,151,170,214
Old woman 23,43,106
Old Woman Gone.................. 163,226
Old woman gone.......................... 35,98
Old woman tooth 26,90
Ome-bachpash 177,240
Ome-bah-push 50,113
On Top of the Hill 171,234
On top of the hill..................... 44,107
On Top of the House 154,217
On top of the house................... 27,89
On Top of the Sweathouse..... 167,230
On top of the sweathouse......... 40,103
One Blue Bead........................ 165,228
One blue bead........................... 38,101
One Buffalo Calf 83,148,211
One buffalo calf............................. 20
One Child Woman........... 86,150,214

308

Index

One child woman 23
One Feather 73,137,201
One feather 9
One Goose 6,70,134,198
One Star 71,135,199
One star 7
One Turtle 86,150,214
One turtle 23
One Woman 88,153,216
One woman 25
Onion 9,24,87,105,151,169,215
Oo-ah-wah-pash 49,176,239
Oo-ah-wah-pish 112
Ooat-budeka-dooch 212
Ooet-budeka-dooch 20,84,148
Ooet-budekeah-hele-nakuse 8
Oo-inkpus 69,133,197
Ookah-sheis 14,77,142
Ooka-sheedish 209
Ook-bish-cus 49,176,239
Ook-cas 69,133
Ook-che-dup-pish 51,114
Ook-che-dup-price 48,111
Ook-eas 5,197
Ook-e-hosh 50,113
Ook-ish-dean-day-ah-hoos 48
Ookish-dean-day-ah-hoos 175,238
Ookish-deanday-ah-hoos 111
Ook-pay-hiss-siss 99
Ook-sheedis 18,81
Ook-sheedish 146
Oo-kutchis-say 31,95,159,222
Oo-Lukpus 5
Oomah-sees 5,133,197
Oomuta-ahpies 148,211
Oomuta-nahbeas 154,217
Oo-mutish 82
Oomutish 18,81,146–147,209–210
Oo-muttish 15
Oookah-sheis 206
Ooomah-sees 69
Oo-sha'-cane-cah-pis 41
Oo-sha-cane-cah-pis 169
Oo-sha-cane-ca-pis 231
oo-sha-cane-ca-pis 104
Oo-shay-it-chise 62,125,189
Oosh-bah-cha-chis 33,96
Oosh-bah-chasis 161,224

Oo-shis 45,104,168,231
Oo-tah-cuck-kis 43,170,233
Oo-tahcuck-kis 106
Oo-tah-dea-dish 126
Oota-hotchkish 17
Ootah-sheedish 151,215
Oota-hukish 19,82,147,210
Oota-wahtadish 11
Oo-tay-coo-bah-kais 94
Oo-tay-doo-bah-kais 30,158,221
Ootay-doochis 7,71
Oo-tay-sah-dis 30,94,158,221
Oote-ewandies 20,83,148,211
Oote-hotchkish 80,139,203
Oot-tah-dee-dish 49,112,176,239
Oot-tah-dock-cus 46,109
Oot-tah-seas 54,117
Oot-tay-bah-coes 237
Oot-tay-bah-coos 36,99,163
Ootuh-chedups 10,138,202
Ootuh-chepups 74
Oouka-manakish 15,78,142,206
Oo-wa-shee-dish 56,119
Oo-wa-sheedish 183,246
Oo-wat-cas 100,164
Oo-wat-doohis 98
Oo-wat-doot-chase 43,106,170
Oo-wat-dootch-chis 36,99
Oo-wat-doot-chice 226
Oo-wat-doot-chis 35,162
Oo-wat-eas 36,227
Oowattah-ahoos 204
Oo-wat-tah-hoos 140
Oo-wat-tus 51,114,178,240
Oo-way-it-chis 30,157,221
Oo-way-itchis 93
Oo-what-ah-shoes 47,171,233
Oo-what-ashoes 110
Oo-what-bea-kahdeas 236
Oo-what-dah-beas 26,90
Oo-what-de-chise 43,107,171,234
Oo-what-doot-chace 233
Oo-what-dootchis 163
Oowhat-dootchis 226
Oo-what-kah-wish 29,93,157,220
Oo-what-tah-hoos 46,76
Oo-What-tish 221
Oo-what-tish 30,93,158

Index

Oowuta-ahpies 20,83
Opa-bah-dah-kis 104
Opa-cah-deas 117
Op-chay-keas-sos 26,89
Ope-bah-dah-kis 41,168,231
Ope-cah-deas 54,184,246
Ope-cah-dish 57,120
Ope-cha-deas 181,244
Ope-che-chuck-kis 47,110,174,237
Ope-che-dup-pace 162
Ope-cheedup-pace 225
Ope-chu-dup-pace 34,97
Ope-edupish 11,139,203
Ope-edupsish 74
Ope-hayday-muluchis 243
Ope-kah-deas 33,96
Ope-kahdeas 160,224
Opes 11,72,136,200
Opish-ekash 21,84,149,212
Op-put-kay 31
Op-put-tay 95,159,222
Opus-kittush 140,204
Osh-doo-chape-ditchis 54,117,181,
.... 232
Osh-shone-badup-pace 155,218
Osh-shone-bah-dup-pace 27,90
Ostah-ich 87
Osue 252
Osus 10,125,189
Otse-muchachis 11,74,139,203
Otter 32,95,160,223
Otter Bull 162,225
Otter bull 34,98
Otter Chief 180,243
Otter chief 53,117
Otter comes out of the water 17
Otter Comes Out of Water 145,208
Otter Comes out of Water 80
Otter Goes a Long Way 155
Otter goes a long ways 91,218
Otter goes a long ways[sic] 28
Otter Hoop 176,239
Otter hoop 49,112
Otter Stays in the Water 164,227
Otter stays in the water 37
Otter stays in water 100
Otter That Shows 183,245
Otter that shows 56,119

Otter Walks to Water 213
Otter Woman 189–190,252–253
Otter woman 62–63,125–126
Ouka-be-das 222
Ouk-be-das 32,95,159
Out-tah-bah-pash 28,92
Owat-baduck-key-condish 163,226
Owat-bahduck-keycon-dish 35
Owat-bahduck-keycondish 98
Owl Above 166,229
Owl above 38,102

P. Home, Joseph 62
Packs the Hat 6,70,134,198
Packs the Rock 161,224
Packs the rock 33,97
Padutch-chay-sheedish 177,239
Pah-chice 52,115,179,242
Paint Woman 166,229
Paint woman 39,102
Paints Her Face Pretty 149,212
Paints her face pretty 21,84
Paints Her Forehead 145,208
Paints her forehead 17,80
Paints Herself Plenty 179,241
Paints herself plenty 52,115
Paints Pretty 5,69,133,197
Paipe[sic] around the neck 51
Part Home, Mary 125
Passes Everything 75,159,222
Passes everything 11
Payduch-chee-bachpash 154,218
Pay-dutch-chay-ook-cusseas 47
Pay-dutch-chay-shee-dish 50
Paydutch-chay-sheedish 113
Pay-dutch-chee-bah-pash 27
Pay-dutch-cheebah-pash 90
Pea-cah-dah-hutch 37,100,164,228
Peace-hay-duce 41,104,169,231
Peah-key-tus 35,98,163,226
Peah-noops 12,75,140,204
Pearson
    Ethel M. 188
    Ethel May 61,124
    Helen E. 188
    Helen Estella 61,124
    Levantia W. 61,124,188
    Virginia 61,124,188

310

Index

Ethel M. 251
Helen E. 251
Levantia W. 251
Virginia 251
Pease
   Anson H. 61,124,188
   Benjamin 124,188
   David 124,188
   Emory 61,188
   Geo. 61
   George 124,188
   George W. 61,188
   James 61,124,188
   Leartus W. 61
   Oliver 188
   Sarah 61,124,188
   Anson H. 251
   Benjamin 251
   David 251
   Emory 251
   George 251
   George W. 251
   James 251
   Oliver 251
   Sarah 251
Peases[sic]
   Benjamin 61
   David 61
Peda-kosh 13,76,141,205
Peesh-ah-deus 10,74
People That Shows 161,224
People that shows 33,97
Peritisa-kahdeas 198
Peritise-kahdeas 134
Peritse-asees 18
Peritse-kahdeas 7
Peritse-kandeas 71
Peritse-usses 81
Peritseusses 146,209
Persons 64,126
Persons in the Moon 7,71,134,198
Petakus 18,108,172
Peters
   Alfred 24
   Alice 216
   Arthur 24,88,152,215
   Elsie 24,88,152,216
   George 24,88,152,216

Rosa 24,88,152,215
Phelps
   Bud 191
   Charles M 126
   Charles M. 191
   Emma 126,191
   Frank 126,191
   Fred 126,191
   Bud 254
   Charles M. 254
   Emma 254
   Frank 254
   Fred 254
Pickett
   Joseph J. 57,120,184,247
   Margaret 57,120,184,247
   Mrs. Joe 57,120,184,246
   Richard 190
   Richard A. 57,120
   Robert A. 57,120,184,246
   Thomas 120,190
   William C. 57,120,184,247
   Lizzie 253
   Richard 253
   Thomas 253
Pine 16,79,144
Pine Fire 78,143,214
Pine fire 15
Pipe That Talks 138
Pipe that talks 10
pipe That Talks 202
Plain 35,99,163,226
Plain Bead Work 204
Plain Bell 164,227
Plain bell 36,99
Plain blackbird 39
Plain Cedar 171,234
Plain cedar 44,107
Plain Coos 201
Plain Face 84,148,212
Plain face 21
Plain Feather 184,246
   Josie 120
Plain feather 57,120
Plain Left Hand 73,137,201
Plain left hand 9
Plain Mountain 87,151,215
Plain mountain 24

Index

Plain Owl 80,144,208
Plain owl 16
Plain Shield 86,150,214
Plain shield...................................... 23
Plain Shirt 174,236
Plain shirt...............................46,109
Plain Spear 182,244
Plain spear.............................55,118
Plain to see 30,93
Plays with a bird.........................28,91
Plays With Himself................182,245
    Charlie...144
Plays with Himself, Charlie 118
Plays with himself.....................55,118
plays with himself, Charlie 55
Plays With Medicine................173,235
Plays with medicine 45,108
Plays with the Weasel 83,148,211
Plays with the weasel 20
Plenty Arrows 70,74,134,139,198,
....202
Plenty arrows 6,11
Plenty Bears 87,152,215
Plenty bears 20
Plenty Buffalo 180,243
Plenty buffalo...........................53,116
Plenty Butterfly 81,145,209
Plenty butterfly............................... 17
Plenty Coos 113,177,240
Plenty coos 50
Plenty Ducks 201
Plenty Hail 160,223
Plenty hail 32,96
Plenty Horses 170,233
Plenty horses...........................43,106
Plenty Irons 76,140,204
Plenty irons 46
Plenty lighning 108
Plenty Lightning.....................172,235
Plenty lightning............................. 45
Plenty Lodge Poles................163,226
Plenty lodge poles 35,99
Plenty Medicine ..86,144,175,207,238
Plenty medicine...................23,48,111
Plenty Medicine Rock........91,155,218
Plenty medicine rock...................... 28
Plenty Otter 162,225
Plenty otter..............................34,98

Plenty Red Plumes................. 164,225
Plenty red plumes 37,100
Plenty Shells 85,150,183,213,252
Plenty shells........................22,56,120
Plenty Shield................... 105,169,232
Plenty shield 41
Plenty Striped Snake.............. 172,234
Plenty striped snake................ 44,107
Plenty Swallow...................... 169,244
Plenty swallow........................ 41,105
Plenty Swamp Flag................ 142,206
Plenty Swamp Flags 77
Plenty swamp flags......................... 14
Plenty Things Growing.......... 190,253
Plenty things growing.............. 64,126
Plenty Wing.................... 86,150,214
Plenty wing..................................... 23
Plenty Woman 152,216
Plenty woman 25,88
Poe-put-tah-bah-coos............... 38,102
Pohputa-heahsas 80
Points the Gun In His Face 186
Points the gun in his face......... 59,122
points the Gun In His Face 248
Poop-kit-tah-cuck-kis 43,106,170,
....233
Pope-put-tay-ea-cot-tus 54,117
Pope-put-tay-ea-cottus................... 181
Pope-put-tay-oa-cottus.................. 244
Popet-itsecahts............................... 198
Popet-itsechats......................... 70,134
Poputa-heahsas 16,144,208
Poputa-naks 13,77,141,205
Porcupine Woman 171,234
Porcupine woman 43,107
Pounded Meat.................. 82,147,210
Pounded meat 19
Pounds the Iron................... 163,226
Pounds the iron 36,99
Prairie, Stephen B. 252
Pretty Back of the Neck.......... 150,213
Pretty back of the neck 22,85
Pretty Bear............................. 179,242
Pretty bear..................................... 115
Pretty Blackbird...................... 72,136
Pretty blackbird 8
Pretty Bullrush............... 72,136,200
Pretty bullrush 8

Index

Pretty Butterfly..................90,155,218
Pretty butterfly 27
Pretty Coyote 73
~~Pretty Coyote~~ 88
Pretty Coyote 137,164,201,227
Pretty coyote 25,39,100
Pretty Eagle.........................167,230
Pretty eagle 40,103
Pretty Enemy.................................211
Pretty Feather......87,152,180,210,215
Pretty feather............................24,54
Pretty Feather Woman 82,146,210
Pretty feather woman 19
Pretty Fish...............................164,227
Pretty fish..............................36,100
Pretty flowers................................101
Pretty Hail 151,160,215,223
Pretty hail..........................23,57,95
Pretty Hair........................76,140,204
Pretty hair............................. 12
Pretty Hall 87
Pretty Hat 83,147,211
Pretty hat....................................... 19
Pretty hawk 53,116
Pretty Hole 189
Pretty hole..............................62,125
Pretty Horse 190,253
Pretty horse 64,126
Pretty Horse Tail 183
Pretty horse tail 120
Pretty Lance 180,243
    Campbell....................................243
Pretty lance 26,53,116
Pretty Land........................180,243
    Campbell....................................180
Pretty land..............................116
Pretty Lodge Poles 173,236
Pretty lodge poles...................46,109
Pretty Louse 73,137,201
Pretty louse 9
Pretty Medicine 75,85,139,149,203,
....212
Pretty medicine 11,21
Pretty Medicine Pipe.........74,139,202
Pretty medicine pipe........................ 11
Pretty Medicine Rock.........93,158,221
Pretty medicine rock 30
Pretty Near Fell 76

Pretty near fell 12
Pretty Nest 93,157,221
Pretty nest..30
Pretty Old Man 162,226
Pretty old man.....................35,98
Pretty On Top 150,213
Pretty on top 22,85
Pretty Paint 93,157,221
Pretty paint 30
Pretty Porcupine 179,241
Pretty porcupine.....................52,115
Pretty River...................... 77,141,205
Pretty river................................... 13
Pretty Rock
.......72,88,135,152,177,199,216,240
Pretty rock 8,25,50,113
Pretty Shell 182,245
Pretty shell 55,118
Pretty Shield 78,103,142,160,167,
.... 206,223,230
Pretty shield.....................15,33,40,96
Pretty Snake........................... 159,222
Pretty snake 32,95
Pretty Striped Snake 157,220
Pretty striped snake....................31,93
Pretty swamp flag 34
Pretty sweat house 63
Pretty Sweathouse 180,242
Pretty sweathouse 116
Pretty Tail 89,153,179,216,241
Pretty tail 26–27,52,115
Pretty Woman............ 80,144,172,208
Pretty woman..................... 42,44,108
Pretty Woman Bird................. 168,231
Pretty woman bird 40,104
Proud 31,95,159,222
Pukes on the Ground......... 77,141,205
Pukes on the ground 48
Puk-iees 17,80,145,208
Push 52,115,179,242
Push-ah-ko.. 86
Push-ah-kos 22,150,214
Puts On a Hat................................ 178
Puts on a Hat............................... 241
Puts on a hat 52,115
Puts on Antelope Cap 159,222
Puts on antelope cap 31,95

313

Index

Qua-dah-bah-chis 27,90,155,218
Qua-dus......................39,103,167,230
Quick..52,115

R. Horse, Ernest 230
Rain Bird........................5,69,133,197
Raise Up, Robert................................ 10
Raiseup, Robert.........................138,202
Rats the Fish.....................................178
Rattles Going 138,202
Rattles going 57,120
Ready to fly.. 51
Record
    Charlie.....................33,96,160,224
    Dora 33,96,160,224
    Mrs. Nate 33,96,160,224
Red Beaver................................171,234
Red beaver 44,107
Red Bird, Howard..........5,69,133,204
Red Breasted Bird 5,69,133,197
Red Feather.................................175,238
Red feather....................................48,111
Red feather around his arm 16
Red Feet 96,160,223
Red Fish 81,146,209
Red fish... 18
Red Fox......................................180,243
Red fox..53,116
Red gun... 42
Red Hair.......................................162,225
Red hair..37,100
Red in the Chin 75,140
Red in the chin 12
Red paint in His Medicine.............. 85
Red Plume................................18,81,145
Red Rock.....................................85,149,213
Red rock... 22
Red Shirt 71,135,171,234,243
Red shirt..7,44,107
Red Snake 5,69,133,197
Red Star....................................178,240
Red star 51,114
Red Wing 163,226
Red wing..36,99
Red Wolf..................................78,143,207
    Laura 79,143,207
Red wolf.. 15
red wolf, Laura 15

Redwood Chief.................. 93,157,220
Redwood chief.................................... 30
Reed
    Della 60,123,187
    Edith 60,123,187
    Frances 60
    Francis 123,187
    Henry.................. 48,111,175,238
    Katie 60,123,187
    Mary K. 60,123,187
    Minnie 60,123,187
    Nellie 60,123,187
    Della 249
    Edith 249
    Francis 249
    Katie 249
    Mary K. 249
    Minnie 249
    Nellie 249
Rides a Bear......................... 164,227
Rides a bear 36,100
Rides a Gray Horse....................... 77
Rides a Grey Horse............... 142,206
Rides a greyhorse 14
Rides a Horse....................... 167,230
Rides a horse 39,103
Rides a Horse Well Known 74,184,
.... 247
Rides a horse well known............... 10
Rides a Pretty Horse 167,230
Rides a pretty horse 40,50,103,113
Rides a Pretty Horse #2 166,229
Rides a Spotted Horse.... 138,169,202,
.... 232
Rides a spotted Horse 105
Rides a spotted horse 10,42
Rides a White Bellied Horse......... 220
Rides a white bellied horse 14
Rides a white hipped horse 25
Rides a White Horse............. 165,228
    Harold................................... 72
Rides a white horse................. 37,100
rides a white horse, Harold 7
Rides a White-Bellied Horse 156
Rides a Whitechipped Horse 72
Rides a Yellow Horse........ 74,137,201
Rides a yellow horse......................... 9
Rides alone 27

Index

Rides Behind 74
Rides behind 10
Rides Much Behind 179,242
Rides much behind 52,115
Rides Pretty Horse, Carson 167,230
Rides Well Known 164,227
Rides well known 36,100
Rides White Bellied Horse 77
Rides White Hipped Horse..... 136,200
Rides White Horse, Harold 136,200
Right Among Them 170,233
Right among them 43,106
River Crow 102,166,229
River crow 39
Robinson
    Alice 58,121,184,247
    Allen 58,121,184,247
    Charles 58,121,184,247
    Ellen 58,121,184,247
    James 58,121,184,247
    Mrs. James 58,120,184,247
Rock 45,109,173,235
Rock Ahead 87,151,215
Rock ahead 24
Rock in f ont[sic] 35
Rock in Front 162,225
Rock in front 98
Rock Moves Along 160,223
Rock moves along 33,96
Rock Old 71,135,199
Rock old 7
Rock That Runs 179,241
Rock that runs 12,115
Round Face 175
    Jeanette 62
    Martin 125,189
Round face 48,111
round face, Martin 62
Round Face, Martin 252
Round Rock 94,158,221
Round rock 31
Round Tobacco 174,237
Round tobacco 47,110
Runner 23,86,151,214
Runs against 40
Runs Against His Enemy 153,216
Runs against his enemy 26,89
Runs Among Them 77,142,206

Runs among them 14
Runs Beside the Camp 170,232
Runs beside the camp 42,105
Runs Between, Joseph 83
Runs Between Them 83,147,210
    Robert 147,211
Runs between them 19
Runs in Among Them 158,221
Runs in among them 31,94
Runs Into a House 143
Runs into a house 62
Runs Over a Bull 144
Runs Over the Ground 186,248
Runs over the ground 59,122
Runs the Enemy 73,137,201
Runs the enemy 9
Runs the Wolf 176
Runs the wolf 48,112
Runs to the Men 143,207
Runs Toward the Fort 82,147,210
Runs toward the fort 19
Runs Toward the House 78
Russell
    Geo. W. 55,118,182,244
    Henry 55,118,182,244
Ruth 18,81,146,210

S. Known
    Levantia[?] 78
    Viola 143,207
S. Knows, Isabel 79
S. White Horse, Peter 40,103,168,
    231
Saco
    Edward 64
    Minnie 190
    Ralph 64,126,190,253
    Minnie 253
Sage Hen 88,153,200
Sage hen 25
Sage Woman 63,166,190,229,253
Sage woman 16,102,126
Sah-hean-bah-chais 28
s-bah-cah-bah-duck-kis 48
Schaffer, Morris 29,92
Schenderline [?]
    Edward 248
    Henry 248

Index

Joseph 248
Martha C. 248
Rachel 248
Scolds 47,110,174,237
Scott
    Elmer 61,124,188
    Emma 26,89,154,217
    Frank 89,154,217
    George 61,124,188
    Katherine 26,89,154,217
    Mrs. Amy 61,124,188
    Paul 26,89,154,217
    Pearl 26,89,154,217
    Elmer 251
    George 251
    Irene 251
    June 251
    Mrs. Amy 251
See a white horse 103
See in the Mouth 69
Sees a White Horse 168,231
Sees a white horse 40
Sees in a Day 85,150,213
Sees in a day 22
Sees in the Mouth 5,133,197
Sees the Coos 166,229
Sees the coos 38,102
Sees Well Known 174,237
Sees well known 47,110
Sends Part Home 189,252
Sends part home 62,125
Seven Stars 157,221
Seven stars 30
Shaffer, Morris 156,219
Shagak-doochis 212
Shakes 18,81,146,209
Shane
    Bessie 60,123,187
    Edward 60,123,187
    Frank 26,60,89,123,154,187,217
    Howard 26,89,146,210
    Josie 60,123,187
    Kittie 60,123,187
    May 89,154
    Mrs. Thomas 60,123,187
    Patrick C. 60,123,187
    Thomas 60,123,187
    Bessie 250

Edward 250
Frank 250
Josie 250
Kittie 250
Mrs. Thomas 250
Patrick C. 250
Thomas 250
Sharp Horn 166,229
Sharp horn 38,102
Sharp nose 33,46
Sharp Nose #1 161,224
Sharp Nose #2 151,215
Sharp nose No. 1 97
Sharp Nose No. 2 87
Shavings 13,76,141,205
Sh-chon-sheedish 220
She Is High Up 173,236
She is high up 46,109
She is Medicine 85,150,213
She is medicine 22
She Sees It 179,242
She sees it 53,116
Shea-dah-chis 35,99,163,226
Shebah-shadish 18,81
She-bah-sha-dush 26,90,154,217
Shebah-sheedish 146,209
She-bish 29,92
She-cack-bah-epash 21
She-cack-bah-pash 85,149,213
She-chock-ay-dus 44,171,234
Shechock-ay-dus 107
Shee-day 30,93,157,221
Shee-deak-days 57,120,138,202
Sheep in Front 168,231
Sheep in front 104
Shegack-amach 212
Shegak-amach 21,84,148
Shegak-doochis 21,84,149
Shegak-kahpa 19,82,146,210
Shell Child 74,139,188,202,251
Shell child 11,61,124
Shell On The Neck, Esther 181,243
Shell on the Neck 85,150,213
    Esther 117
Shell on the neck 22
shell on the neck, Esther 54
Shenderli[sic], Martha C. 185
Shenderlin[sic]

Index

Edward 185
Henry 185
Josepg[sic] 185
Rachel 185
Shenderline
   Edward 58,121
   Henry 58,121
   Joseph 58,121
   Martha Cooper 58,121
Shenokshe-mulukis 17,80
She-pay-day-tuss 228
She-pea-day-tuss 37,101,165
She-peas 33,96
Shield at the Door 84,148,212
Shield at the door 20
Shield Chief 165,228
Shield chief 37,100
Shield in front 40
Shield That Shows 167,230
Shield that shows 40,103
Shield That Sings 175,237
Shield that sings 47,111
Shin Bone, Henry 22
Shinbone, Henry 85,149,213
Shis-shea-bea 30,94
Shis-sheas 45,108,172,235
Shively, Frank 23,86,151,252
Shoot the Enemy 136,199
Shoots Her Foot 171,234
Shoots her foot 44,107
Shoots Plain Medicine 76,141,204
Shoots plain medicine 13
Shoots Plenty 167,230
Shoots plenty 37,103
Shoots Pretty Things 80,145,208
Shoots pretty things 17
Shoots Tent Poles 168,231
Shoots tent poles 41,104
Shoots the Enemy 72
Shoots the enemy 8
Shoots the Lodge 84,149,212
Shoots the lodge 21
Short Bull 162,225
Short bull 35,98
Shot Himself 160,223
Shot himself 32,95
Shot in the Arm 171,234
Shot in the arm 44,107

Shot in the Face 168
Shot in the face 41,104
Shot In the Hand 178,241
Shot in the hand 115
Shot In The Nose, John 41
Shot in the Nose 169,232
   John 169,244
Shot in the nose 41,105
shot in the nose, John 105
Shows 39,102,166,229
Shows a Child 79,143,207
Shows a child 15
Shows a Fish 74,139,202
Shows a fish 11
Shows a gun 42,105
Shows a Lance 6,70,134,198
Shows a Little 160,223
Shows a little 33,96
Shows A Pipe, Johnnie 57
Shows a Pipe, Annie 94,158,222
shows a pipe, Annie 31
Shows a Shell 157,234
Shows a shell 29,93
Shows as He Goes 72,136,200
Shows as he goes 8
Shows Big on the Ground 165,228
Shows big on the ground 37,101
Shows coming 43
Shows Going 173,236
Shows going 46,109
Shows His Coos 163,226
Shows his coos 36,99
Shows His Ear 156,220
Shows his ear 29
Shows His Gun 143,206
Shows his gun 14,49,112
Shows his medicine 56
Shows in a crow 38
Shows In a Crowd 166,229
Shows in a crowd 102
Shows in the Mountain 231
Shows in the mountain 108
Shows in the Mountains *172*
Shows in the mountains 45
Shows Plenty 153,216
Shows plenty 25,88
Shows the Horse 156
Shows the Otter 182,244

Index

Shows the otter..........................55,118	Sits before a cloud 34,97
Shu-dish 37,100,165,228	Sits By Side of Water 174
Shuts Her Eyes......................183,246	Sits by side of water.....................110
Shuts her eyes 56,119	Sits by the side of the water...........47
Sick 51,114,178,241	Sits By the Water.................181,244
Singing Hat 165,228	Sits by the water 54,117
Singing hat 100	Sits Down 157,220
Sings ....26,31,78,89,94,143,158, ...206,221	Sits down 29,92
Sings Among the Tobacco 243	Sits Down Far Away.............180,243
Sings Going In 160,223	Sits down far away 53,116
Sings going in 32,96	Sits Down Spotted 170,233
Sings Good................................170,233	Sits down spotted.....................43,106
Sings good................................43,106	Sits In Her Nest 177,240
Sings in a Cloud.....................162,225	Sits in her nest 50,113
Sings in a cloud..........................34,98	Sits in the Middle...................155,218
Sings in Camp....................77,142,205	Sits in the middle 27,90
Sings in camp............................ 14	Sits on High Ground 178,241
Sings in the Mountains.......92,157,220	Sits on high ground........................51
Sings in the mountains 29	Sits on the Blanket.................165,228
Sings in the Woods 78,143,207	Sits on the blanket 37,101
Sings in the woods 15	Sits on the Buffalo ...... 81,86,151,159, ...214,222
Sings on Horse 73,137,201	Sits on the buffalo....................18,23
Sings on horse 9	Sits on the Mountain....................220
Sings On Top 189	Sits Over a Hole....................169,231
Sings on Top 80,138,202	Sits over a hole 41,104
Sings on top 10,17	Sits to the Otter.................78,142,226
Sings Pretty 173,236	Sits to the otter................................14
Sings pretty................................46,109	Sits to the Wind 165,228
Sings the Last Song.................190,253	Sits to the wind 37,101
Sings the last song..................50,126	Sits Toward the Mountain ... 5,69,133, ...197
Sings to Man 94,159,222	Sits Toward the Nest............148,212
Sings to man..................................31,37	Sits toward the nest........................20
Sings to the Arrow 84,149,212	Sits With a Buffalo 168,231
Sings to the arrow 21	Sits with a buffalo.........................41
Sioux 6,70,134,198	Sits With a Star 148,212
Sit Toward the Nest........................ 84	Sits with a Star............................84
Sit with a buffalo...........................104	Sits with a star 21
Sits Along the Road 157,220	Sits With the Coyote....................253
Sits along the road....................29,92	Sits With the Stars 159,222
Sits Among the Cedars................... 76	Sits with the stars....................32,94
Sits among the cedars................... 13	Sitting Elk.............................167,230
Sits among the grass................44,108	Sitting elk 40,103
Sits Among the Rocks.... 152,190,230, ...253	Skins a Wolf..........................170,233
Sits among the rocks 24,63,87	Skins a wolf...........................43,106
Sits among to rocks 126	Slides Down Well Known ...... 77,142, ...206
Sits Before a Cloud 161,224	

318

Index

Slides down well known 14
~~Slings his arm~~.................................... 19
Small 10,17,81,138,145,202,209
Small Medicine Tobacco........ 160,223
Small medicine tobacco 32,96
Small Waist................................. 79,143
Small waist.. 15
Small Woman.................... 78,142,206
Small woman 15
Smart Iron 84,149,212
Smart iron 21
Smith, Mrs. John L........... 59,122,185
Smokes............................... 11,25,72,88
Snake..................... 42,106,170,233
Snake Bull................................. 171,234
  Matie 171,234
Snake bull 43,107
Snapping Dog................................ 221
Snow 53,125,188
Snow Bird 84
Snow bird 21
Snow 251
Snowbird................................... 134,198
Sore Where Whipped 6,70,134,198
Sounds of the Gun.................. 162,225
Sounds of the gun..................... 34,98
Sounds th(sic) Gun, Frederick........ 98
Sounds the Gun, Frederick 162,225
sounds the gun, Frederick 34
Spaniard 26,89,153,217
Sparrow hawk woman.................... 12
Spider........................... 32,95,159,222
Spies on the Enemy................. 168,231
Spies on the enemy 41,104
Spies on the Enemy #2........... 176,239
Spies on the enemy #2 112
Spies on the enemy No. 2............... 49
Spies the Enemy................ 83,147,211
Spies the enemy 20
Spotted 50,113,177,240
  John................... 43,106,170,233
  Susie.................... 63,105,169,232
Spotted Arm............................ 175,237
Spotted arm............................... 47,111
Spotted Butterfly..................... 181,243
Spotted butterfly...................... 54,117
Spotted Hawk..................................... 6
Spotted Horse.................... 74,139,202

Ben 72,136,200
Spotted horse 11
Spotted Otter.......................... 179,241
Spotted otter 52,115
Spotted Rabbit 174,237
Spotted rabbit 47,110
Spotted Snow Bird........................ 170
Spotted snow bird................... 43,106
Spotted Snowbird 233
Spotted Tail 87,151,215
Spotted tail...................................... 24
Spotted Weasel ... 82,147,170,210,233
Spotted weasel.................. 19,43,106
Spotted woman 54
Spring Woman................. 93,157,220
Spring woman................................ 30
Srikes the water 117
Stabs 28,91,156,219
Standing buffalo 109
Stands Among The Shooters 71
Stands Among the Shooters... 135,198
Stands among the Shooters............... 7
Stands Among Them 161,224
Stands among them................. 34,97
Stands on top 23
Stands on Top of Ground....... 145,208
Stands on top of the Ground 80
Stands on top of the ground 17
Stands Over a Bull................. 149,212
Stands over a Bull........................... 85
Stands over a bull 21
Stands to the Sun 154,218
Stands to the sun 27,90
Star 37,100,164,227
Stays at Sweathouse....................... 90
Stays at sweathouse....................... 27
Stays On Top of House................ 242
Stays On Top of the House........... 180
Stays on top of the house 53,116
Stays Out Doors.................... 175,238
Stays out doors 48,111
Stays There............................ 179,242
Stays there 53,116
Stays with a Bird 218
Stays with a bird 28,91
Stays With the Horse 165,228
Stays with the Horse 70
Stays with the horse............. 6,38,101

319

Index

Steal Bear, William 117,181,243
Steals on Camp 161,182,224,244
Steals on camp 33,55,96,118
Steals on Camp Ahead 77,142,205
Steals on camp ahead 14
Steals on Camp Strong 134,198
Steals on camp strong 6
Steals on Strong Camp 70
Steals on the Camp.. 170,174,183,233, ...236
Steals on the camp.........43,46,56,106, ...110,120
Steals Plain............................159,222
Steals plain................................... 31
Steel Bear, Wm. 54
Steps above 102
Stevens
    Agnes 59,122,186,249
    Clarence L..................................249
    John T. 249
    Kent 59,122,186,249
    Mary.............................59,122,186
    Mary K...............................186,249
    Mary Kent..........................59,122
Stewart
    David...................57,94,159,222
    Fannie 57,120,184,247
    Foster 98,162
    Francis...................57,120,184,247
    Jackson........................57,120,190
    Joseph 57,120,184,247
    Lucy 59,122,153,216
    Mrs. Thomas 59,122,186,248
    Richard....................................... 95
    Robert 247
    Thomas 57,98,162,225
    William 57,120,184,247
    Jackson..253
Stoops to Charge...............75,140,204
Stoops to charge............................. 12
Stops 21,84,149,212
    Paul C. 149,212
    Percy 84,212
Stops Above........................166,229
Stops above 39
Stops at Many Places 164,227
Stops at many places..................36,99
Stops by the Water 152,216

Stops by the water 25,88
Straight Bird 125,252
Straight bird.................................. 62
Strawberry Sings Pretty 79,144,207
Strawberry sings pretty 16
Strianght[sic] Bird 189
Strikes a Woman.......................... 163
Strikes Among Them............. 165,228
Strikes among them 38,101
Strikes and Strikes Again.. 87,151,215
Strikes and strikes again 24
Strikes at Night...................... 138,202
Strikes at night............................... 10
Strikes back of head..................... 119
Strikes Back of the Head 183,245
Strikes back of the head................. 56
Strikes Between the Forts 160,223
Strikes between the forts............ 32,96
Strikes Big 189
Strikes Both Ways ... 157,182,221,245
Strikes Both ways 118
Strikes both ways................. 30,55,93
Strikes By Side of Water 137
Strikes by Side of Water .. 73,151,201, ...214
Strikes by side of water 86
Strikes by the side of the water 23
Strikes by the side of water............. 26
Strikes Enemy on Prairie 231
Strikes Feathers 82,147,210
Strikes feathers 19
Strikes First.... 73,83,137,148,201,211
Strikes first 9,20
Strikes Her Child 179,241
Strikes her child....................... 52,115
Strikes Her Gun 181,244
Strikes her gun......................... 54,117
Strikes His Enemy Pretty....... 155,218
Strikes his enemy pretty 27,91
Strikes in a Crowd 6,70,134,198
Strikes in Camp .... 78,142–143,207, ...226
Strikes in camp 14–15
Strikes Inside the House ... 79,144,207
Strikes inside the house 16
Strikes Mother and Child............. 153
Strikes mother and child............ 25,88
Strikes On Top Of Head 175,237

320

Index

Strikes on top of head....................111
Strikes On Top of Ice.............181,243
Strikes on top of the head............... 48
Strikes on top of the ice............54,117
Strikes One Going In House .. 148,211
Strikes one going in House 83
Strikes one going in the house........ 39
Strikes One Man 156,189,219,252
Strikes one man..............28,63,92,126
Strikes One That Charges.......162,225
Strikes one that charges.................. 98
Strikes One That Kills...................225
Strikes One That Pushes Him........165, 228
Strikes one that pushes him......37,101
Strikes One With a Lance 167,230
Strikes one with a lance.................103
~~Strikes one with hat~~........................110
Strikes One With Necklace 157,220
Strikes one with necklace............... 93
Strikes One With the Hat 237
Strikes one with the necklace.......... 29
Strikes Plenty Enemies......82,147,210
Strikes plenty enemies 19
Strikes Plenty Medicine.........180,242
Strikes plenty medicine............50,116
Strikes Plenty Women.......70,134,198
Strikes plenty Women..................... 6
Strikes Pretty.........................176,238
Strikes pretty 49,112
Strikes Rider of Red Ear ...74,139,202
Strikes riding a grey horse............... 62
Strikes Riding Grey Horse 189,252
Strikes riding grey horse 125
Strikes Same One...............70,134,198
Strikes same one 6
Strikes the Chief.............................. 85
Strikes the chief............................... 22
Strikes the Hat.........................189,252
Strikes the hat..................23,62–63,125
Strikes the Iron.......................171,234
Strikes the iron 43,107
Strikes the Lance....................178,241
Strikes the lance 51,114
Strikes the Medicine Rock 81,146, 209
Strikes the medicine rock 18
Strikes the one that charges........... 35

Strikes the One That Kills............. 162
Strikes the one that kills.............35,98
Strikes the one with a lance 40
Strikes the One With Hat............... 174
Strikes the one with the hat............. 47
Strikes the Painted Arm.................. 86
Strikes the painted arm 22
Strikes the painted face................... 24
~~Strikes the Pretty Woman~~............. 171
Strikes the pretty woman 44,107
Strikes the Rider of the White Maned Horse... 227
Strikes the Rider of the white maned Horse.. 163
Strikes the rider of the white maned horse..36
Strikes the rider of white maned horse 99
Strikes the Shield First...........174,237
Strikes the shield first 47,110
Strikes the Thief in Camp......181,232
Strikes the thief in camp 54,117
Strikes the Water 152,216
Strikes the water 25,53,88
Strikes the Woman 73,137,200
Strikes the woman 8
Strikes Twice. 73,81,137,145,201,209
Strikes twice 9,18
Strikes Two Camps................. 167,230
Strikes two camps....................37,103
Strikes Well Known..........76,141,205
Strikes well known 13
Strikes Woman 182,245
Strikes women 55,118
Striped Snake.....................88,153,216
Striped snake 25
Striped snake well known..........25,88
Striped Snake Woman 168,231
Striped snake woman...............41,104
Strong 33,52,96,115,161,179,224, 242
    Charles................... 20,83,148
    Strong 211
Strong Alone...................... 165,228
Strong alone...........................38,101
Strong Bear......................... 82,146
Strong bear 18
Strong Bull 165,228

Index

Strong bull..................................38,101
Strong Fighter 135,199
Strong Heart........90,154,157,218,220
Strong heart............................27,29,92
Strong Legs..................................179
Strong legs 52,115
Strong Man 240
Strong Medicine................90,155,234
Strong medicine 27
Strong Otter.......................74,139,203
Strong otter 11
Strong Well Known 78,143,207
Strong well known 15
Suah-cowutish......................189,252
Suah-oowich 12
Suah-oowitch 75
Sucher
    Belle.........................30,93,157,220
    Hattie........................30,93,157,220
    Mrs. F.......................30,93,157,220
Sugar...40,103
Suis, George................50,113,142,205
Summer 11,75,139,203
Sun Goes Slow.......................157,220
    Bertha... 93
Sun goes slow 29,93
Surrounded.................50,113,177,240
Surrounds the Enemy 169,232
Surrounds the enemy................42,105
Surrounds the Enemy Strong .165,228
Surrounds the enemy strong.....38,101
Sus-bah-doochis................95,159,223
Sus-bah-doot-chis.......................... 38
Susie.........................54,117,181,243
Swallow Bird 208
Swamp Flag 74,77,82,139,141,146,
   202,205,210
Swamp flag 10,14,19
Sweathouse Well Known ..83,147,211
Sweathouse well known................ 19
Sweet Grass........................84,148,212
Sweet grass 21
Sweet Mouth 6,70,134,198

T. Foretop, Ruth............................ 54
T. Gun, John...................................245
T. Horse, Jessie 181
T. Horses[sic], Jessie.....................244

Take a Gun 145,208
Take among the enemy................. 100
Take Together............................... 75
Takes a Blanket 178,240
Takes a blanket................... 51,114
Takes a Crooked Stick........... 145,208
Takes a crooked stick 17,80
Takes a Feather..................... 168,213
Takes a feather..................... 41,104
Takes a fish........................32,95
Takes a Gun 80,84
Takes a gun.............. 17,20,41,54
Takes a Gun #1 168,231
Takes a gun #1............................. 104
Takes a Gun #2..................... 148,212
Takes a Gun #3 181,243
Takes a gun #3............................. 117
Takes a hat.................................. 116
Takes a Horse 181,244
Takes a horse 54,117
Takes a Knife....................... 160,224
Takes a knife 33,96
Takes a Lance 156,219
Takes a lance 28,91
Takes a Long Gun 169
Takes a long gun 42,105
Takes a Man in a Fog 173,236
Takes a man in a fog................ 46,109
Takes a Pinto Horse.......... 84,184,246
Takes a Pinto horse.........................21
Takes a roan horse 57
Takes a Shield...................... 172,235
Takes a shield 45,108
Takes a Sinew................. 72,136,199
Takes a sinew 8
Takes a Split Ear................... 183,246
Takes a split ear 56,119
Takes a Weasel 71
Takes a weasel................................. 7
Takes a Woman 171,234
Takes a woman 44,107
Takes a yellow spotted horse 28
Takes Across the Water......... 156,219
Takes across the water............. 28,91
Takes All the Horses............. 172,235
Takes all the horses............... 45,108
Takes Among Enemy #2 159,223
Takes Among the Enemy....... 164,227

Index

Takes among the enemy 37
Takes among the enemy #2 95
Takes among the enemy No.2 32
Takes Both Together 169,232
Takes both together 42
Takes By Herself 177,240
Takes by herself 52,114
Takes By Side of Camp 231
Takes by side of camp 104
Takes By Side of the Camp 168
Takes by the side of the camp 41
Takes Five 5,69,133,166,197,229
Takes five 38,102
Takes Good Things 77,142,205
Takes good things 14
Takes Gun From 1 That Kill 178
Takes Gun From 1 That Kills 240
Takes gun from one kills 114
Takes Gun From One That Kls 232
Takes Her Horse 161,225
Takes her horse 34,97
Takes Himself 154,217
Takes himself 26,90
Takes Hold of the Cloth 149,212
Takes hold of the Cloth 84
Takes hold of the cloth 21
Takes horse with the white mane ... 40
Takes Horse With Wh[ite] Mane ..231
Takes Horse With White Mane 168
Takes horse with white mane 104
Takes Horses on Prairie 171,239
Takes horses on prairie 107
Takes horses on the prairie 44
Takes One Close to Camp 165,228
Takes one close to camp 38,101
Takes One That Rides Horse 242
Takes one that rides horses 116
Takes Out of a Crowd 176,239
Takes out of a crowd 49,112
Takes plenty prisoners 23,87
Takes Pretty Scalp 72,136,200
Takes pretty scalp 8
Takes Pretty Things 6,70,93,134,
 157,189,198,220
Takes pretty things 29,62,125
Takes Quick 159,178,223
Takes quick 38,95
Takes shield once 36

Takes the Dead 86,150,214
Takes the dead 23
Takes the gun from the one that kills..
 51
Takes the Hat 169,179,232,242
Takes the hat 42,53,105
Takes the Iron 162,170,226,233
Takes the iron 35,43,98,106
Takes the Killer of Guns 169
Takes the killer of guns 42,105
Takes the Medicine Pipe 183,245
Takes the medicine pipe 56,119
Takes the one that rides the horse ... 53
takes things first, Kittie 48
Takes Things on Top House 236
Takes Together 139,203
Takes together 11
Takes Two 94,158,221
Takes two 31
Takes Two Guns 86,151,214
Takes two guns 23
Takes Two Lances 89,153,216
Takes two lances 25
Takes Well Known 79,143,207
Takes well known 16
Takes Wrinkle 157,220
 Elmer 157,221
Takes wrinkle 30,93
Takes Yellow Spotted Horse . 156,219
Takes yellow spotted horse 91
Talks Everything 77,142,206
Talks everything 14
Tall Woman 80,182,245
Tall woman 16
Ten 18,108,172
Ten Bear 125
 Charles 62,101,166,229
 Frances 62,189,252
Ten bears 27
The Arapahoe 32,95,159,222
The Back 79,143,207
The back 16
The Bannock 14,77,142,206
The Bear Now 181,243
The bear now 54,117
The Bear Turns Around 180,243
The bear turns around 53,116
The Bell 161,224

323

Index

The bell 33,97
The Bird 165,228
The bird 37,101
The bird everyday 111
The Bird Everyway 144
The bird everyway 48
The Bread 75,140,204
The bread 12
The Crane 173,235
The crane 45,108
The Door 183,246
The door 56,119
The door is medicine 42,105
The Eagle 141,163,217,226
The eagle 28,35,91,99
The Elk 76,141,205
The elk 13
The Fly 159,222
The fly 32,95
The Fog 86,151,214
The fog 23
The Ground Is Her Medicine 179
The ground is her medicine 52,115
The Gun 183,245
The gun 56,119
The Hawk 176,238
The hawk 49,112
The Hawk 252
The Horn 92,156,219
The horn 29
The Iron 93,158,178,221,240
The iron 30,51,114
The Kicker 83,148,211
The kicker 20
The Meat 79,143,207
The meat 16
The Moon 80,144,208
The moon 16
The Other Antelope 177,240
The other antelope 50,113
The Other Beaver 83,148,211
The other beaver 20
The Other Blackbird 183,245
The other blackbird 56,119
The Other Buffalo 175,237
The other buffalo 48,111
The Other Bull 76,140,204
The other bull 13,25,88

The Other Heart 152,175,216,238
The other heart 13,25,88,111
The Other Leaf 175,237
The Other Medicine 76,141,204
The other medicine 13
The Other Medicine Rock 74,138,201
The other medicine rock 9
The Other Otter 171,233
The other otter 43,106
The Other Woman 83,148,211
The other woman 20
The river 47
The Root 74,138,202
The root 10,57
The Song is Medicine 166,229
The song is medicine 16,102
The Spleen 163,226
The spleen 35,98
The Spy 81,145,209
The spy 17
The Swallow Child 163,226
The swallow child 36,99
The tail stands up 23
The Trail 104,169,232
The trail 41
The Twins 83,147,211
The twins 19
The Wet 176,238
The wet 49,112
The Wolf 5,69,133
The Woman 178,240
The woman 51,114
Thomas, George 55,118,182,244
Thompson
    Frances E.C. 125
    Frances E?[sic] Cummins 59
Three 22,85,149,213
Three Bears 179,242
Three bears 52,115
Three Blackbird 161
Three blackbirds 33,97
Three Coons 170
Three coons 43,106
Three Foretops 181,243
Three foretops 54,117
Three Irons 154,217
    Sarah 26,90
Three irons 26,90

Index

Three Wolves 124,180,188,243,251
Three wolves 53,61,116
Thro s[sic] it away 27
Throws It Away 155,218
Throws it away 91
Throws Off on the Horse 147,210
Throws off on the Horse 82
Throws off on the horse 19
Thunder Iron 189,252
Thunder iron 12
Thundre[sic] Iron 75
Tick-bah-dup-pace 50,113,177,240
Tick-pah-che-day-de-shis 37,165
Tick-pah-cheday-de-shis 228
Tickpah-cheday-deshis 101
Ties a knot on top of her head 24
Ties Knot On Top of Head 152
Ties Knot on Top of Head 215
Ties Knot on top of her head 87
Ties on the Foretop 169
Ties on the foretop 42,105
Ties on the Fortop 232
Ties Up Her Bundles 163,226
Ties up her bundles 35,99
Ties Up the Arrows 170,233
Ties up the arrows 106
Tobacco Bull 34,162,225
Tobacco bull 97
Tobacco Seed 164,227
Tobacco seed 36,100
Tobacco Sings 168,231
Tobacco sings 41,104
Top of the Moccasin 78,143,207
Top of the moccasin 15
Towne
    Ida M. 27,90,154,218
    Wm. Elliott 27,90,154,218
Townsend
    Fred A. 61,124,149,212
    Mabel M. 124,149,212
    Mabel Magdaline 61
    Mary 61,124,149,212
Travels Well Known 179,242
Travels well known 53,116
Tuch-chay-dah-cock-cuss 62,125
Tuch-chay-dah-cockus 189,252
Tuch-kase 98
Tuck-kase 34,162,225

Tuck-kit-chay-ah-hoos 37,230
Tuck-kit-chay-ahoos 167
Turns Around 181,243
Turns around 35,54,117
Turns Around Twice 183,245
Turns around twice 56,119
Turns Back 180,242
Turns back 53,116
Turns Back Plenty 190,253
Turns back plenty 63,126
Turns Round the Camp 189,252
Turns to the Water 163,226
Turns to the water 36,99
Turtle 29,92,156,220
Turtle Child 82,147,210
Turtle child 19
Twin Woman 82,146,179,210,242
Twin woman 9,18,115
Two 22,85,150,213
Two barreled gun 39,103
Two Bears 178,241
Two bears 51,114
Two Belly
    M 120
    M. 57,184,247
    Mrs M. 184,247
    Mrs. M. 57,120
Two Birds 181,244
Two birds 54,117
Two Fish 113,177,239
Two fish 50
Two Horses 145,209
Two horses 17,81
Two leggings 99
Two Leggins 163,226
Two leggins 35
Two Muskrats 71,135
Two muskrats 7
Two Otters 88,153,169,216,232
Two otters 25,42,105
Two Stinks 75,140,204
Two stinks 12
Two Whistles 80,144,208
Two whistles 16
Two White Birds 82,147,210
Two white birds 19
Two Women 89,153,217
Two women 26

Index

Two-Barrelled Gun 167,230

Uch-cha-key-chis 41
Uch-ock-kay-duck-coos 180,242
Uck-a-chase......................89,153,216
Uck-bah-chay-days 26
Uck-bah-dea-ah-hoos 48,111,175,
....238
Uck-bah-dea-ate-chase.....38,101,165,
....228
Uck-bah-dea-e-wah-ick-deas 47
Uckbahdea-ewahickdeas 110
Uckbah-deas-ewahic-deas..............202
Uckbah-deas-ewahick-deas............174
Uck-bah-dea-ush-eas........53,116,180,
....240
Uck-bah-dee-e-kosh 32
Uck-bah-du-ick-cosh........44,107,171,
....234
Uck-bah-he-dee-co-se 227
Uck-bah-he-dee-cose 36,100,164
Uck-bee-che-bay-ah-hoos 30
Uck-beeche-bay-ahhoos................. 74
Uck-cha-key-chis 104,168,231
Uckcheese-malapesh 162,225
Uck-dosh-dee-dichis 162,225
Uck-doshy-dee-dich-es 35,98
Uck-ea-chase.................................. 25
Uck-ish-be-dane-de-chis 39
Uck-ish-be-dane-dechis.................. 83
Uck-ish-be-dane-dichis 148
Uckish-bedane-dichis.....................211
Uck-kosh-e-cosh 96
Uck-kosh-e-kosh 33,160,223
Uck-pah-cheas.................................47
Uck-pah-dean-de-chice 180,242
Uck-pah-dean-de-chis 50,116
Uck-pah-deas 50,113
Uck-pah-dee-ah-seas 56
Uck-pah-dee-it-chice 51
Uck-pah-dee-itchice 178,241
Uck-pah-dee-it-chise 114
Uck-sah-ay-chase 238
Uck-sah-e-cos 55,182,245
Uck-sah-ey-chase 49,112,176
Uck-sah-o-cos 118
Ukbadapa-ish-tuckea-dooch.........105
Ukbadapa-ishtukea-dooch............232

Ukbadapa-ishtukea-doochis.......... 169
Uk-bah-dah-pay-ish-tuck-kea-doot-chis
.... 42
ukcheesa-malapesh 13
Ukcheese-malapesh 98
Uk-keam-duck-chis ... 42,105,169,232
Uk-pa-had-dee 'is[sic].................... 22
Uk-pa-had-dee-is 150,214
Ukpa-had-dee-is 86
Uksempash 24
Umba-coan-duc-bitchase 161,225
Umba-coan-duckbit-chase 97
Um-bah-chea-keas-sos..... 47,111,175,
....237
Um-bah-coan-duck-bit-chase 34
Um-bah-cone-cahs.......... 112,176,239
Um-bah-cone-dah-coos .. 102,166,229
Um-bah-cone-dah-cos 39
Um-bah-cone-hoos 40
Um-bah-day-es-sos....... 25,89,153,216
Um-bah-dea-it-chis 48,111
Um-bah-dea-itchis 175,239
Umbah-owedup-ate-chace 39,167,
.... 230
Umbah-owedup-ate-chase 103
Um-bah-sah-ah-hoos 31
Um-bah-sah-ahoos 94,158,222
Um-beas-say-chu-dish 31,159,222
Um-bees-say-chu-dish 95
Umbich-esash 17,81,145,209
Ume-beas.................... 39,102,166,229
Un-dah-coe-bah-coos....... 57,120,184,
....246
Un-dah-heahsos 165,228
Un-dah-hea-os 38
Un-dah-hea-sos.............................. 101
Un-dah-pace 46,109,173,236
Undahshay-day-bahhah-chis........... 24
Unda-ichis 13,77,154,217
Unda-itchis 141,205
Undasha-day-bahah-chis........ 151,215
Undashay-day-bahah-chis.............. 87
Un-day-it-chice.......... 45,108,173,223
Un-de-chay-it-chice 49,112
Un-de-chay-itchice 176
Un-de-chay-itchis 238
Un-de-ditch-chis 50,113
Un-dee-dich-chis 26,89

326

Index

Un-dee-dichis 153,216
Un-dee-ditch-chis 177,239
Un-di-day-it-chice 44,108,172,235
Un-doc-cosh-keas-sos 45
Un-doo-cosh-keas-sos 108,172,235
Undosh-shay-day-keas-sos 41
Un-duck-cah-hoos 36,99,164,227
Un-dut-che-do-che-dice 54,117,181
Undut-che-do-che-dice 244
Unmeathe 19,82,146,210
Up-chay-keas-sos 154,217
Up-pah-keas-sos 40,103,167,230
Up-pah-sah-chers 34,98,162,225
Up-pay-e-wah-e-coosh 117
Up-pay--e-wah-e-coosh[sic] 54
Up-pay-e-wah-wah-e-cosh 181,244
Up-pay-huch-kay 88,216
Up-pay-huck-kay 25,152
Up-pay-oakpis 41,169
Up-pay-okpis 105,232
Up-pay-sheedish 98,145,209
Up-pay-shu-dish 35
Up-pay-ut-tay 33,46,87,97,151,215
Up-poch-cane-dichis 183,245
Up-pock-cane-ditches 56,119
Upshaw, Alexander 20,84,148,212
Us-dosh-cane-doot-chis 41,104
Us-dosh-cane-dootchis 168,231
Ush-ase-bah-sos 49,112,176,239
Ushcoch-uttah-dup-pace 152
Ushcock-uttah-dup-pace 215
Ush-coe-sut-tah-doochis 165,228
Ush-coe-sut-tah-doot-chis 38
Ush-coe-tah-cose-shis 40,168
Ushcoe-tah-cose-shis 103,230
Ush-cosh-ut-tah-dup-pace 24
Ushcosh-uttah-dup-pace 87
Ush-cup-cah-weas 50,113,177,239
Ush-dead-it-chis 40
Ush-dea-itchis 167,230
Ush-dea-it-chise 103
Ush-doop-tah-coe-dee 37,103,167,230
Ushdosh-caneba-dup-pace 119
Ushdosh-caneba-duppace 182,245
Ush-dosh-cane-bah-dup-pace 56
Ush-dosh-ka-dus 32,95,160
Ushdosh-katabah-sos 170,232
Ushdosh-katah-bah-sos 105

Ush-dosh-kay-tah-bah-sos 42
Ush-hay-dosh-days 25,88,153,216
Ushmiha-chedish 18,81,146,209
Ush-ock-kay-duck-coo 116
Ush-ock-kay-duck-coos 53
Ushoo-suttah-doo-tchis 101
Usk-beeche-bay-ahoos 139,203
Usmiha-koosh-basash 17,80,145
Ut-che-key-chis 49,112,176,239
Utch-itch-ist-ton-tus... 51,114,178,240
Utsewaks-ahoos 13,141,204
Utsewaks-ahous 76

Voice Well Known 154,217
Voice well known 26,89

W. Bear
 Russel 136
 Russell 8,72,200
Wahkpahs-ne-ahoos 23,86
Wahkpas-ne-ahoos 144
Wahpookta-ahkaps 17
Wahpookta-hotskish 16,144
Wahpootka-hotsish 79
Wahpootkamakpash 8,72,136,200
Wahpotkta 80,145,208
Walking 44,107,171,234
Walking Bird 138,202
Walking bird 10
Walking Weasel 176,239
Walking weasel 49,112
Walks At Night 253
Walks In Middle of Ground ... 173,236
Walks in middle of ground 109
Walks in middle of the ground 46
Walks In the Water 178,241
Walks in the water 51,114
Walks Over Ice 6,73,137,201
Walks Pretty 69,89,133,153,172,
 177,216,235,239
Walks pretty 5,26,44,50,108,113
Walks to Growing Things 177,240
Walks to growing things 50,113
Walks to the buffalo 48,111
Walks to the Hole 76,141,204
Walks to the hole 13
Walks With a Wolf 158,221
Walks with a wolf 31,94

Index

Walks With Medicine 160,223
Wallace
    Andrew 5,69,133,197
    Carrie 30,94,158,234
    Harry 197
    Jennie 5,69,133,197
    John 30,94,158,221
    Josie 5,69,133,197
    Richard 24,87,152,215
    Susie 24,87,152,215
Wart 28,91
Washada-esash 148,211
Washington, George 7,71,135
Weasel Child 163,226
Weasel child 36,99
Weasel goes a long way 11
Weasel Goes Out 158,221
Weasel goes out 30,94
Weasel High Up 163,237
Weasel high up 36
Weasel highup 99
Weasel That Shows 181,243
Weasel that shows 54,117
Weasel that walks 63,126
Well Known, Jane 15
Well Known Antelope 164,227
Well known antelope 36,100
Well Known Arrow 72,136
Well known arrow 8
Well Known Buffalo 84,149,212
Well known buffalo 21
Well Known Hawk 161,224
Well known hawk 34,97
Well Known Horse 158,221
Well known horse 26,89
Well Known Lance 155,218
Well known lance 28,91
Well Known Mare 176,239
Well known mare 40,112
Well Known Red Feather .. 83,148,211
Well known red feather 20
Well Known Rock 75,140,204
Well known rock 12
Well Known Shell 81,146,209
Well known shell 18
Well Known Writing 138,201
Well known writing 10
Wesley

Annie 57,120,156,219
Fannie 58,120,184,247
Inez 247
Jane 57,120,184,247
Jennie 57,120,184,247
John 57,120,184,247
Where He Goes Is Medicine .. 177,239
Where he goes is medicine 50,113
Where She Stops Well Known 175,237
Where she stops well known 111
Whers[sic] she stops well known 47
Whinners 9,73,137,201
Whistle Water 80,145,208
White
    Charles F. 123,187
    Mary E. 60,123,187
    Minnie E. 60,123,187
    Mrs. Wm. H. 60,123,187
    Wm. H. 60,123,187
White Antelope 157,220
White antelope 30,93
White Arm 182,245
White arm 55,118
White Bear 71
    Blake 11,74,139,203
    George 8,72,135,199
White bear 7
White Bear #1 135
White Bear #2 136,200
White Bear No. 2 72
White bear No. 2 8
White Bellied Wolf 6,70
White bull 47,110
White Clay on Forehead 163,226
White clay on forehead 99
White clay on forhead[sic] 35
White Crane 5,69,133,197
White Dog 91,156,219
White dog 28
White Fox 91,155,218
White fox 28
White Goose 86,151,214
White goose 23
White Hail 172,235
White hail 45,108
White Hat 160,223
White hat 32,96
White Horn 172,235

328

Index

White horn 45,108
White Man 172,234
White man....................................... 44
White Man Runs Him 70,134,198
White man runs him 6
White men......................................107
White Otter 178
White otter 51,114
White Shirt........................ 76,141,205
White shirt...................................... 13
White Tailed Deer................... 176,239
White tailed deer 49,112
White Tailed Hawk 78,190,253
White tailed hawk 15
White Wings 110
    Holder 110,174,237
White wings 47
white wings, Holder 47
White Woman 5,69,71,89,133,135,
   153,197,199,217
White woman 7,26
White
    Ada M. 250
    Charles F. 249
    Mary E. 250
    Minnie E. 249
    Mrs. Wm. H. 249
    Wm. H. 250
Who-chis-say-ah-way-chice............ 37
Whochis-say-away-chice 165,228
Wild Cat.. 92
Wild cat.. 29
Williams
    Cora 60,123,187
    Mattie 60,123,187
Williams [Schroeder], Cora 250
Williams, Mattie 250
Wind .. 13,58,76,121,141,185,205,247
Wind Blowing....................... 168,231
Wind blowing.......................... 41,104
Wochis-say-ahwa-chice 101
Wolf 8,72,136,199
    Sydney 96,188
Wolf Goes to Water 160,223
Wolf goes to water 32,96
Wolf House............................ 180,243
Wolf house............................... 54,117
Wolf Lays Down..................... 73,137,200

Wolf lays down................................ 9
Wolf Looks Up 139,203
Wolf looks up 49
Wolf That Looks Back 150
Wolf That Looks back 251
Wolf that looks back................. 22,85
Wolf Well Known 72,136,200
Wolf well known 8
Wolf, Sydney................................ 251
Woman both ways 43,107
Woman Bull 74,139,203
Woman bull 11
Woman Chief 163,226
Woman chief 35,98
Woman herder 25
Woman on Top of Ground...... 75,139,
    203
Woman on Top of Mountain . 157,221
Woman on top of mountain 93
Woman on top of the ground 11
Woman on top of the mountain 30
Woman Otter 176,239
Woman otter 42,49,105,112
Woman That Farms 171,234
Woman that farms 44,107
Woman That Sits Down 166,229
Woman that sits down 39,102
Woman Where She Stops 213
Woman where she stops 21,85
Woman Whers[sic] She Stops 149
Woman With Eyes Open 166,229
Woman with eyes open............. 38,102
Woman Without a Name 174,237
Woman without a name......... 47,110
Woodpecker's Child 158,221
Woodpecker's child 93
Woodpeckers child 30
Woodtick 51
    Topsy...99
Work on the Farm................. 143,207
Working Mouse 162,226
Working mouse 35,98
Works on the Farm 79
Works on the farm 15
Works together 50,113
Wrinkle Face ... 6,70,134,161,198,224
Wrinkle face 33,96
Wtekut-napes................. 6,70,134,198

Index

Wutta-eahkoots 19,82,147,210
Wutta-makpash 9,73,137,205

Yarlott
    Charles 59,121,185,248
    Frabk[sic] 185
    Frank 59,121,248
    Katie 59,122,185,248
    Mrs. David 59,121,185,248
Yearling 7,71,135,199
Yellow 30,37,93,157,221
Yellow All Over 151,215
Yellow all over 24,87
Yellow Bird 169,183,231,246
Yellow bird 41,56,104
Yellow Blackbird 85,149,213
Yellow blackbird 21
Yellow cedar 29
Yellow Coyote 79,143,207
Yellow coyote 15
Yellow Crane 86,150,214
Yellow crane 22
Yellow Crow 177,239
Yellow crow 50,113
Yellow Deer 81,146,209
Yellow deer 18
Yellow Eagle 167,230
Yellow eagle 40,103
Yellow Ears 145,209
Yellow ears 35,98
Yellow Face 171
    Dora 179,242
    Olive 62
Yellow face 44,52,107,115
Yellow Face #2 179,242
Yellow Hawk 190,253
Yellow hawk 63,126
Yellow Head 157,220
    Ruth 93,157,220
Yellow head 29,93
Yellow In the Mouth 183,246
Yellow in the mouth 56,119
Yellow Leaves 76,140,204
Yellow leaves 13
Yellow Mule 181,243
Yellow mule 54
Yellow Red Paint 83
Yellow red paint 20

Yellow Shield 158,221
Yellow shield 31,94
Yellow Tail 75,139,203
Yellow tail 11
Yellow Top 174,236
Yellow top 46,110
Yellow Woman 91,155,169,232
Yellow woman 12,105
Young Badger 154,218
Young Beaver 64,126,167,190,230,
.... 253
Young beaver 39,102
Young Bull 164,227
Young bull 37,100
Young Chicken 181,232
Young chicken 54,117
Young Crane 5,69,133,197
Young Curlew 165,228
Young curlew 37,100
Young duck 15
Young Eagle 76,140,204
Young eagle 12
Young Ground Cedar 84,149,212
Young ground cedar 21
Young Hairy Wolf 25,88,152,216
Young Hawk 145,209
Young hawk 17,81
Young Jack Rabbit 5,69,133,197
Young Medicine 173,236
Young medicine 46,109
Young Otter 167,177,229,240
Young otter 39,51,102,114
Young Swallow 83,148,211
Young swallow 20,93
Young Turtle 79,143,207
Young turtle 16
Young Turtle Woman 78,143,207
Young turtle woman 15
Young weasel 46,109
Young Wolf 78,142,206
Young wolf 14
Young Yellow Wolf 79,143,207
Young yellow wolf 16

330